D0803343

Greece

Greece

A Phaidon Cultural Guide

With over 450 colour illustrations
and 12 pages of maps

Phaidon

Editor: Franz N. Mehling

Contributors: Prof. Dr Evangelos Konstantinou, Dimitrios Kounavos, Leonidas Lolis, Dr Marianne Mehling, Gerhard Rebhan, Dr Helena Theophilidou, Leonidas Tromaras

Photographs: Greek Tourist Board (Athens and Frankfurt), Archiv Gunda Amberg, Farbfotolabor Hans Wittreich, Helmut Busch, Mary Galiatsatos, Werner Grabinger, Prof. Dr Evangelos Konstantinou, Dimitrios Kounavos, Maria Linhart, Dr Herbert Neumaier, Bernhard Rauscher, Wolfgang Schenk, Hans Joachim Schwerdhöfer

Maps: Huber & Oberländer, Munich

Ground-plans: Herstellung + Grafik, Lidl

Phaidon Press Limited, Littlegate House, St Ebbe's Street, Oxford OX1 1SQ

First published in English 1985
Originally published as *Knaurs Kulturführer in Farbe: Griechenland*
© Droemersche Verlagsanstalt Th. Knaur Nachf. Munich/Zurich 1982
Translation © Phaidon Press Limited 1985

British Library Cataloguing in Publication Data

Greece. — (A Phaidon cultural guide)
  1. Greece — Description and travel — 1981–
  — Guide-books
  I. Knaurs Kulturführer in Farbe:
  Griechenland. *English*
  914.95′0476   DF716

  ISBN 0-7148-2356-2

All rights reserved. No part of this publication may be reproduced, stored in a retrieval system or transmitted, in any form or by any means, electronic, mechanical, photocopying, recording or otherwise, without the prior permission of Phaidon Press.

Translated and edited by Babel Translations, London
Typeset by Electronic Village Limited, Richmond, Surrey
Printed in Spain by H. Fournier, S.A.–Vitoria

Cover illustration: The Parthenon, from the south-west
(photo: K. Kerth — ZEFA)

Preface

'Fair Greece,' wrote Byron, 'Immortal, though no more; though fallen, great.' For evidence of this immortality and greatness one need look no further than the culture of the whole Western world, which has its roots in the civilization of the Ancient Greeks.

Around 5000 BC the Cretans began to develop a new and unique culture, which reached its highest levels of sophistication with the Minoans at around 2000 and later in Mycene. This culture displays a refinement which was only ever previously evidenced in Egypt. The 'geometric' style was developed originally on the Greek mainland around 900 BC. This rapidly became more realistic and developed into classical Greek art, which flourished around the 5C BC and developed into Hellenism (c.300–100). The Greek techniques of architecture, sculpture and painting (which we can now see only in vase paintings, as almost all the frescos have been lost) have been imitated time and again, though only equalled during the period of the Renaissance; they also served as the inspiration for the baroque and classicism; romanticism and abstract art, too, have not entirely shaken off the precepts of Greek antiquity. All European art, in fact, is based on Greek principles, and it is no wonder that reverent visitors return again and again to gaze at the Acropolis and the countless archaeological sites spread over the mainland and islands.

But successive civilizations have received more from the ancient Greeks than buildings and statues: innumerable sagas and myths have given us an image of their spiritual and cultural life, and their view of the world. It is the country where Socrates, Plato and Aristotle philosophized about the origin of the world and of thought; men like Pythagoras and Euclid achieved great feats of scientific understanding. Greece was the land where theatre originated, and the first Olympic Games took place in the stadium at Olympia. Homer is the father of all forms of story-telling, and the citizens of the city state of Athens were the first to practise what we now know as democracy.

After Greece lost its territorial and cultural supremacy, first to Rome and then to Byzantium, it lost the ability to develop its own culture any further, and remained artistically and culturally subjugated until 1830. As a result, the visitor to Greece finds not only magnificent remains from classical antiquity, but also evidence of Turkish, Byzantine and Venetian civilization, the appreciation of which offers far more than a mere exercise in tourism.

This book will guide travellers towards Greece's treasures, both great and small, and help them to recognize and understand what they see.

As with the other guides in this series, the entries are arranged in alphabetical order for easy reference. There are over 450 illustrations in colour, showing ancient ruins, excavations, churches, palaces, castles, theatres, museums and art treasures, and including ground-plans of many famous buildings.

The heading to each entry gives the town in bold type and, immediately below, the district and region and a reference to the map section (pp. 290–301), giving page number and grid reference. (Since each map covers two pages and the system of grid squares runs across both pages, only even-numbered page numbers are given.)

The appendices consist of a list of minor places cross-referred to the entries in which they appear and a glossary of technical terms.

The publishers would be grateful for notification of any errors or omissions.

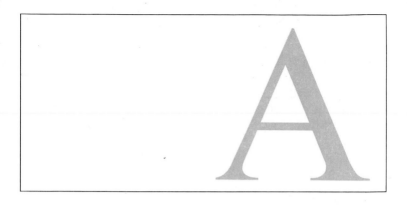

Aegina (I)/ΑΙΓΙΝΑ
Aegean Islands/Saronic Islands   p.294□H 9

The island of Aegina (33 sq. miles, 10,000 inhabitants) lies in the middle of the Saronic Gulf, and is a favourite spot for excursions and swimming for modern Athenians.

History: The island was settled by the 4th millennium BC (remains on the acropolis). The port was in existence by the 3rd millennium and trading links existed with Crete, the mainland, and the Cyclades (pottery now in the town museum). It was settled in the 2nd millennium by the Achaeans and later by the Ionians. The legendary founder-king was Aiakos, son of Zeus and Aegina, daughter of the river-god, after whom the island, formerly known as *Oinóne* ('wine island'), was named. Aiakos was made judge of the dead together with Minos and Rhadamanthys because of his rectitude. Around 950 BC Aegina was invaded by Dorians, becoming a member of the Amphictyony of Póros, and prospered greatly during the 7&6C BC trading in silver with Spain. As the most flourishing Doric trading port of the day it founded the first mint in Greece in 656 BC; its coins were decorated with tortoises.

The bronze statues cast from Aeginetan ore were famous. It reached its zenith with the construction of the temple of Aphaia in 480 BC, for which Pindar composed a festive ode. There was bitter rivalry between Aegina and the great sea-power of Athens (Piraeus) culminating in war and the Athenian victory of 458 and the conquest of Aegina in 455 BC. The fortifications were razed, the ships surrendered, and a high tribute imposed. In 431 BC the inhabitants were expelled and replaced by Athenian colonists. The island declined in importance from this time on. It was subsequently bought by Pérgamon and fell to Rome in 133 BC. In the Byzantine period it was much plundered by the Saracens, and the capital was moved inland to Palaiokhóra. From 1204–1317 it was held by the Franks and Venetians, by the Catalans until 1452, and by the Venetians up to 1715. In 1537 it was attacked and plundered by the corsair Khair-ed-Din. It became a Turkish possession 1715 – 1826 when it was finally liberated. In 1828 Capodistria made it the temporary capital of his first free Greek government, which was subsequently transferred to Návplion and later Athens.

Aegina (5,700 inhab.): The island's capital occupies the site of the ancient city of Aígina (founded *c.* 2500 BC), of which a few ruins survive.

Temple of Apollo (10 minutes walk from the harbour in the direction of Kolóna): Only one column without capital remains (6C BC). The building stood on the site of a 7C shrine (remains of a sacrificial interment and a rectangular house with three rooms). SE of the temple are the remains of the foundations of an archaic propylon; SW are traces of two small temples and a circular foundation (tomb). To the N. are the remains of a *bouleuterion*, and to the W. traces of the Hellenistic *Attaleion*. NE of the town remains of an ancient *aqueduct* (6/5C) can be seen. The *cathedral* (1806) has some fine icons. Near the harbour is the pretty chapel of *Ágios Nikolaos*. The *city museum* near the cathedral has finds from the 3rd millennium to the Roman period. There is a fine collection of figurines and pottery from the prehistoric, Mycenean, and classical periods (3500–450 BC) revealing the history of the island's settlement. Other points of interest are the collections of oil-lamps (600–500 BC), bronze objects, terracottas, remains of funerary reliefs and sculptures (fragmentary) and the fine 'Aegina Sphinx' (6C), together with fragments from the temple of Aphaia (most of the so-called 'Aeginetan' sculptures are in the Munich Glyptothek). There are also fragments from the Temple of Apollo (5C).

Environs: The church of *Agii Theodori* (also known as Omorfi Ekklisía, the 'lovely church') lies *c.* 4 km. E. of the town and was founded in 1282 (foundation inscription on the S. wall). The barrel-vaulting is decorated with frescos of New Testament scenes (nativity, crucifixion, resurrection), with the Panagía (Mother of God) on the apse. Monastery of *Ágios Nektarios* (7.5 km. W.). This was the residence of Metropolitan Nektarios (d.1920, canonized 1961), and has become a famous place of pilgrimage. Monastery of the *Panagia Chrysoleontissa* ('Mother of God of the golden lion'): This dates from the 16C, and

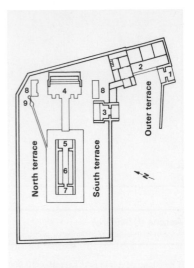

Aegina, Temple of Aphaia 1 outer propylon **2** columned hall and priests' chambers **3** inner propylon **4** sacrificial altar **5** pronaos (vestibule) **6** cella **7** opisthodomos **8** pedestals of statues **9** cistern

has defensive walls and a tower. The monastic church (enlarged in 1806) has a fine carved iconostasis with Old Testament scenes, saints and angels; icon of the Panagía ascribed to St. Luke.

Paleokhóra ('old town'): The former medieval island capital lies on a slope of the mountain (8 km. E. of Aegina). It was founded in the 9C as a refuge, several times destroyed, and finally abandoned *c.* 1800. Only a few secular buildings stand out from the *remains of the Venetian fort* (built 1654), but most of the more than 20 churches are still in a good state. Most of these are barrel-vaulted chapels built of whitewashed, undressed grey stone. They date from the 13C (pointed vaulting). The earliest are domed and shaped like a Greek cross. The iconostases are of masonry and decorated with fine frescos. *Episkopí church*

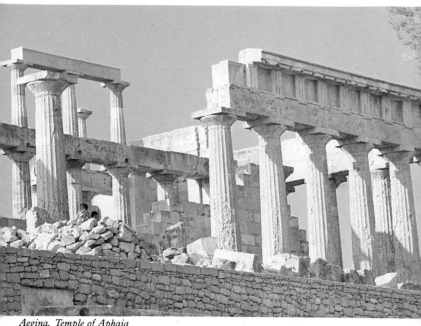

Aegina, Temple of Aphaia

(former main church of Aegina): 17C frescos. On the iconostasis is an icon of the Panagía (Mother of God) from the 16/17C. St.Dionysios of Zákynthos lived here, and his cell in the court is preserved. Other notable buildings are the *Stavros Basilica*, the chapel of *Ágios Nikolaos* (carvings), the ruined monastery of *Agia Kyriaki* (abandoned *c.* 1830), the church of *Zoodochos Pigí* ('Spring of life') with well-preserved 17C frescos, the church of *Ágios Ioannis* (Theológos), 14C with later frescos, the church of *Ágios Nikolaos*, the earliest on the site, the church of *Ágios Evthymios* with frescos in the Peloponnesian style, the church of *Ágios Georgios* with frescos of St.George and St.Dominica portrayed as a Byzantine princess, and the church of *Ágios Stefanos*. In the centre of the island rises *Mt. Profítis Ilias* (of the Prophet Elijah), 1,745 ft., visible from far around (fine views). Ruins of the foundations of an early archaic *sanctuary of Zeus* have been discovered here (now the chapel of the Prophet Elijah); there are also the remains of an altar to Zeus Panhellenios. On the N. slopes are ancient stepped terraces and the little church *Ton Angelon* ('of the Angels'). On the S. slopes are the remains of a Mycenean settlement (rectangular house foundations).

Temple of Aphaia (modern Gr.: Afea): Built of Aeginetan limestone *c.*480 BC, this still well-preserved Doric temple has a superb site on the summit of a wooded hill (10 km. E. of the town of Aegina, above the port of *Agía Marína*); there is a fine view to the E., over the Saronic Gulf. It occupies the site of an earlier temple (built *c.*570, destroyed *c.*510), also dedicated to the primitive local goddess Aphaía. A

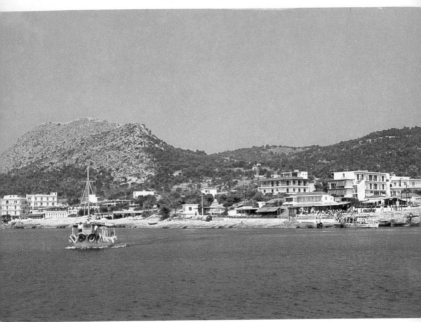

Agia Marina (Aegina), view

daughter of Zeus, Aphaia fled from King Minos and Crete in a fishing-boat to preserve her virginity, and landed at Aegina (links with Cretan culture). The Doric temple was built on a raised terrace above the earlier temple *in antis* (6C). In the buried temple the German archaeologist Adolf Furtwängler (father of the conductor Wilhelm Furtwängler) discovered in 1901 the altar and ivory statue of Aphaia and an important inscription bearing her name (6C BC). This disproved the earlier view that the temple had been dedicated to Athene. The second temple was begun *c.*500 BC, at the time of Aegina's greatest power; of the 32 columns around the cella 23 still remain or have been restored, along with part of the architrave. The *peripteros* was probably not completed until after the Battle of Salamis (480 BC). When the Aeginetans were expelled in 431 BC, the

temple was also abandoned. In *c.*480 BC the whole temple area was formed into unitary structure. It was given rectangular walls, supported to the E. and N. by terraced walls. The sanctuary was entered from the SE. Two *gateways* (the inner and outer *propylon*) enclosed the *priests' chambers* (columned hall with four columns, foundations surviving). Near the entrance were the *purification basins*. Beyond the inner door lay a *ramp*, an *altar for burnt offerings*, and the temple (45 ft. 2 in. x 94 ft. 6 in.). There were 6 columns on the shorter and 12 on the longer sides (height of columns 16 ft., distance between the columns 8ft.). Most of the columns of the *peristasis* are still standing; they are slenderer than those of other early classical Doric temples. The *cella* had a pronaos and opisthodomos, and was divided into three aisles internally. The central aisle (10 ft.)

was lined by two two-tiered rows of columns; the floor of the narrow side-aisles (35 in.) was slightly raised. The *cult-statue of Aphaia* stood against the rear wall between the last pair of columns but one, and on festivals was wheeled out of the cella (sanctum) to the altar. The foundation, cella walls, and inner and outer rows of columns are of limestone which was decorated with a fine layer of stucco painted to look like marble, which is still visible in parts. The *roof ornament* and *pediment carvings* of Parian marble are divided between the Munich Glyptothek, and the museums in Athens and Aegina. The figures were painted, using white for flesh, and the pediment background was blue. The earlier *W. pediment* was built around 510 BC, and depicted Aeginetan heroes fighting before Troy (Ajax and Teucer, grandson of Aiakos). In the centre stands the armed figure of Pallas Athena, patron-goddess of the Greeks. The E. pediment (which is the second, the earlier figures being buried), shows the capture of Troy by Telamon (father of Ajax and son of Aiakos), together with Herakles. The goddess Athena takes an active part in the fighting. The figures from the pediments were bought in 1812 by King Ludwig I of Bavaria, and are now in the Aeginetan collection in the Munich Glyptothek. The temple of Aphaia is architecturally close to other late archaic shrines, such as the temple of Ceres (Athenaion) in Poseidonia (Paestum) and the temple of Herakles in Agrigento (both *c.* 500 BC).

Agía Rúmeli/ΑΓΙΑ ΡΟΥΜΕΛΙ
Chaniá/Crete   p.298☐F 14

The village of Agía Rúmeli lies on the S. coast of the island, at the end of the gorge of Samariá, the deepest and most impressive of the gorges in Crete's limestone mountains (18 km. long, with cliffs up to 2,000 ft. high). Nearby is a Turkish *castle* which used to guard the entrance to the gorge. In ancient times the Doric city of *Tarra (Tárrha)* lay right on the coast SW of Agía Rúmeli.
The site of the temple of Apollo is today occupied by a little *church of Our Lady* (Panagia) from the 16C. Some Roman floor mosaics are still visible.

Environs: Ágios Pávlos: A footpath runs E. along the coast leading after some forty minutes walk to the small and extremely charming church of Ágios Pávlos built of undressed stone with a symmetrical ground plan, and with a few remains of 12C frescos within. **Ágios Ioánnis:** Another two hours walk eastwards leads to the lonely village of Ágios Ioánnis with its two frescoed late Byzantine churches, *Ágios Ioáannis* and the *Panagia*.

Agía Triáda/ΑΓΙΑ ΤΡΙΑΔΑ
Iráklion/Crete   p.298☐G 14

On the S. coast two km. W. from Phaistós are the ruins of a *royal villa*. Like the second palace at Phaistós it was built during the first half of the 16C BC, and was destroyed along with Phaistós, Knossós, and Mália towards the end of the 15C. The villa is not large, but very fine, and furnished with superb works of art. Around it were found various buildings, some dating from just after the villa, including the *necropolis* with its circular tombs on the hill, where the famous *limestone sarcophagus* decorated with paintings and dating from *c.*1400 BC was found, now in the Iráklion museum. The impressive representations of offerings to the dead shed much light on Minoan cult practices.

Minoan temple: The Minoan temple at the SE edge of the complex is earlier than the villa, dating probably from at least

1700 BC; superb frescos were discovered here. Most of the buildings around the villa have been excavated; they are clearly divided into N. and W. quarters, and are later than the villa. Among them are the ruins of a settlement with an agora and shops occupied between 1375 and 1100.

Ágios Nikólaos/ΑΓΙΟΣ ΝΙΚΟΛΑΟΣ
Lasithi/Crete   p.298☐I 14

Near the Lasithi plateau on the bay of Mirabello is one of the most attractive sites in Greece—Ágios Nikólaos with its pretty little harbour. The name Mirabello comes from a Genoese castle which dominated the present town in the 12C.

Church of Ágios Nikólaos: The town was first founded in 1869. Behind the Minos Beach Bungalow-Hotel is the little single-aisled church with 9C frescos, the only examples of this type preserved here, and the 11C ones, painted over the 9C

Gorge of Samariá (Agía Rúmeli)

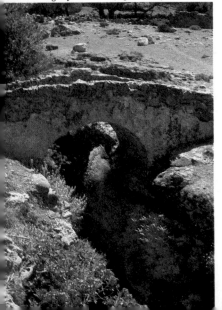

frescos later. The 9C frescos are purely ornamental and in rich colours, whilst the 11C work is figurative. The town took its name from the small old stone church with its bell tower, drum and dome.

Panagia: The later single-aisled church of Our Lady has some good 14C frescos.

Museum: The museum which lies on the Iráklion road out of town is also worth visiting, with a fine collection of Minoan finds.

Environs: Olús/Oloús/Elús/Elúnta: 12 km. to the N. of Ágios Nikólaos was the now-submerged ancient city of Olús. Foundations of the walls are still visible on the coast of the peninsula. Of the early Christian basilica only the very fine floor mosaics survive, with ornamental decoration, plants and fish. **Spinalónga:** The fishing-village of Elúnta (Minoan finds) close by is the point of departure for the boat to the impressive and well-preserved Venetian fortress of Spinalónga. **Neápolis:** 15 km. NW of Ágios Nikólaos (c. 4,000 inhab.). The ruins of two small Byzantine churches, *Sotíros Christú* and *Ágios Antónios* stand just outside the town. There is a small museum with antiquities from Elúntaa and the Hellenic site of Dréros. **Dréros:** The ruins of a Hellenic settlement dating from about 700 BC have been found 4 km. from Neápolis. The remains of two acropolises, an agora, a temple, a prytanaion, a cult-site and a necropolis have been excavated.

Agrínion/ΑΓΡΙΝΙΟΝ
Aetolia/Central Greece   p.294☐D 7

This is the agricultural centre of W. cen-

Gorge of Samariá (Agía Rúmeli) ▷

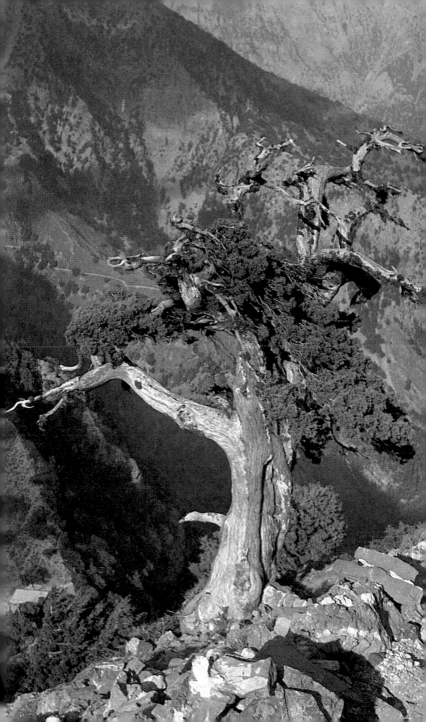

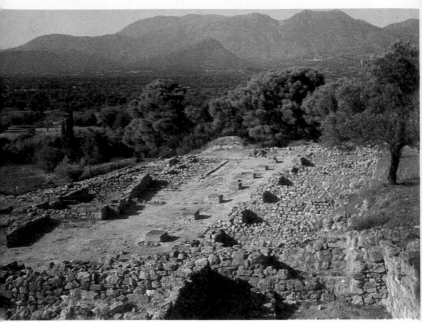

Agía Triáda, shops

tral Greece (pop. *c.* 30,000), and the commercial exchange for cotton, wheat, and tobacco. The city has few sights of interest, and was rebuilt after the earthquake of 1887. There is a small museum with finds from the environs. The ancient settlement lay some 3 km. NW of Agrínion; hardly any traces survive.

Environs: Some 12 km. NW along the Amfilokhía road are the remains of **Strátos,** the ancient capital of Akarnania. The area was already settled in the pre-Hellenic period (finds), and was fortified in the 5C BC with a well-preserved *city wall* taking in 4 hills. Following a struggle with Sparta during the 5C BC the city knew a period of prosperity during the Hellenistic age under the rule of Macedonia, after 338 BC. When Akarnania was divided up in 263 BC, Strátos lost its im-

portance. The modern village lies inside the ancient city walls, which stretched down to the River Acheloos, famed in legend for the fight of the river-god with Herakles. The impressive *Great Gate* to the S. has *projecting towers.* N. of this lie the ruins of the *agora.* The city was divided by a diagonal wall running N-S, with the *cavea* of a Macedonin *theatre* to the E. The *acropolis* lay on the highest point in the N. Beside the city wall in the W. are the remains of a *sacred enclosure* with a *temple of Zeus* (Zeus Stratios). This was a peripteral Doric temple with an Ionic peristyle around the cella, built *c.*360 BC. In the neighbourhood are the *ruined foundations* of other buildings and an *altar,* excavated by the French School after 1910. 13 km. SE of Agrínion on Lake Trikhonis is the village of **Paravóla**, with the scanty remains of an *ancient settlement,* probably

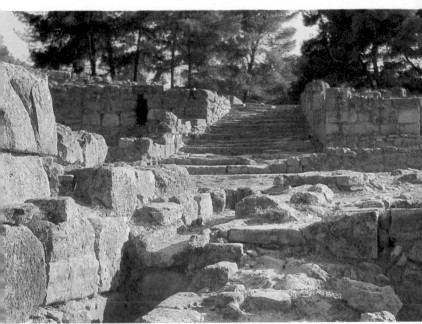

Agía Triáda, entrance steps

Agía Triáda, Royal Villa 1 portico 2 paved steps, the 'Sea Approach' 3 stairs leading to the court of the altars 4 court of the altars, the centre of the ruined villa 5 portico, which was built later in Mycenean times over the ruins of the villa 6 staircase to the upper storey 7 loggia 8 stores 9 Mycenean megaron 10 room with alabaster slabs 11 staircase 12 workroom and archive, where tablets covered with Linear A script were found 13 terrace 14 room which was formerly decorated with frescos, now housed in the Iráklion Museum, some of the most impressive works of art surviving from the early Palatial period; the most impressive fresco depicts a creeping wildcat in a thicket 15 portico 16 king's private chambers 17 living room 18 stores 19 Ágios Georgios, late Byzantine chapel with 14C frescos 20 1700 BC Minoan temple 21 probably the servants' living quarters 22 shops from the settlement of 1375–1100 BC settlement 23 open columned hall 24 settlement 25 Minoan round tomb, with a necropolis.

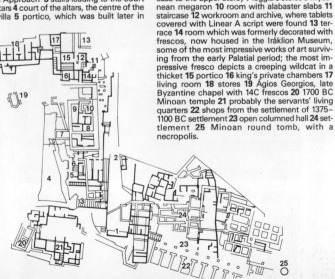

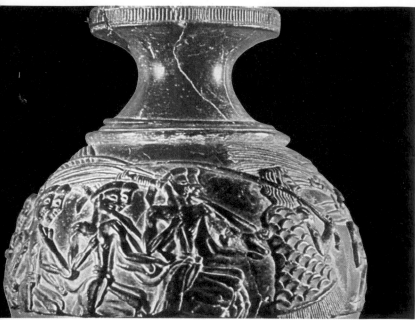

Agía Triáda, carved vase from the 16C BC (Archaeological Museum, Iráklion)

Agía Triáda, limestone sarcophagus from c. 1400 BC, Archaeological Museum, Iráklion

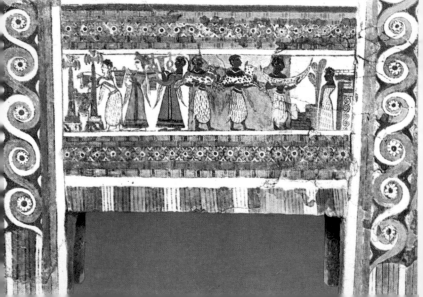

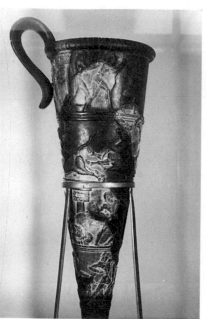

*Agía Triáda, steatite rhyton
(Archaeological Museum, Iráklion)*

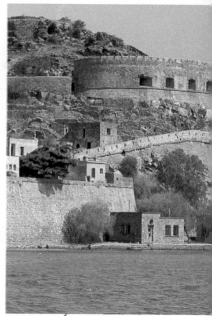

*Spinalónga (Ágios Nikólaos), Venetian
fortress*

Bukátion, with its city walls. On a hill are
the remains of some Hellenistic *defensive
walls* and a *watch-tower*.

Aígion/ΑΙΓΙΟΝ
Achaía/Peloponnese   p.294☐E 8

This charming coastal town (19,000 inhab.) lies 33 km. E. of Pátras in the
Achaean countryside. The modern commercial town occupies the site of the ancient city of *Aígion* where Agamemnon
summoned the leaders of the Achaean
League to the fight against the Trojan
enemy. At one time (373 BC) Aígion was
the capital of the Achaean League. During
the Middle Ages it was known by the name
of *Vostítsa (Vostice)* and was the seat of a
Frankish barony. On the rocky slopes of the
lower town by the sea stood the sacred
grove with its *sanctuary to Zeus* (Zeus
Homarios), the sanctuary of the Achaean
League where the annual gatherings were
held. Caves and remains of a spring survive. Of the ancient settlement there are
still some remains of walls by the harbour
and a rocky way with chambers, store-
houses, and cisterns.

Environs: In the village of **Risómylos** (4
km. E.) are a few traces of the ancient city
of *Helíke (Elíki)*, where there was a famous
sanctuary of Poseidon. The site was destroyed in the 4C BC by an earthquake,
when part sank into the sea. Some 12 km.
SW lies the delightful hill-town of **Dafné**
(with a pretty monastic church), at the foot
of Mt.Panakhaikon (6,320 ft.). S. of **Diakoftó** (some 14 km. SE) is the start of the

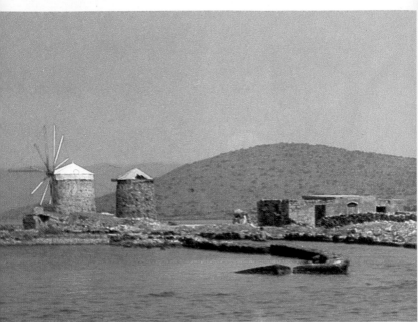

Olús (Ágios Nikólaos), isthmus

narrow, wooded *gorge of Vuraikos*, served by a rack and pinion railway (see Kalávryta). The country is superb and there are fine views.

Aitolikón/ΑΙΤΟΛΙΚΟΝ
Aetolia/Central Greece   p.294☐D 8

This picturesque town was built in the Middle Ages on a small island lying between the lagoons of Aitolikón and Mesolóngion (to the S.), and is joined to the mainland by two earth causeways. It is some 15 km. from Mesolóngion.

Environs: The area around the mouth of the river Acheloos, the longest in Greece, is interesting. The river god Acheloos has entered Greek mythology for his struggle with Herakles, when he changed into a snake and a bull. He was the eldest son of Okeanos, the ocean-god, and thus the symbol of a river. The *Echinádes* ('Hedgehog-islands') in the river-mouth have been known since antiquity; as a result of the constant silting up they have formed the present swampy, reed-covered marshland ('Little Holland'), chiefly used as winter pasture by the Sarakatzanai shepherds. Some 15 km. SW at *Trikárdo Kástro* are the interesting but overgrown ruins of the ancient port of **Oiniádai**, named after the Aetolian King Oineus. The harbour has dried up, and the remains of quays and docks are visible. In antiquity and particularly in the 5&4C BC it was courted for the sake of its strategically-situated harbour, and was captured several times. In 1901 an American team excavated the remains of a *theatre*, uncovering more than 20 rows of seats and the SE part of the or-

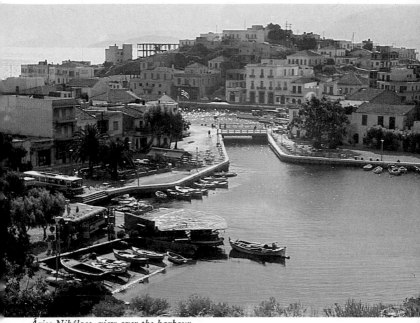

Ágios Nikólaos, view over the harbour

chestra. On the hill to the SE is the ancient *acropolis* with remains of polygonal walls from the 6C BC and a large and overgrown gateway. Near the harbour are the ruins of ancient *baths*. Parts of the 5 miles of *city walls* survive, within which are some remains of houses, temples, and cisterns. To the NE is a cave with a natural echo, the reputed home of the vampire-witch Lamía.

Akharnái/ΑΧΑΡΝΑΙ
Attica/Central Greece   p.294☐H 8

This is now part of Greater Athens (12 km. N. of the city centre), with *c.* 10,000 inhabitants. As *Akharnaí* it played an important part in Attica during the classical period as a fortified provincial deme. The comedian Aristophanes dedicated his play 'The Acharnians' to it (425 BC).

Fortifications: Remains are visible on a hill (ancient acropolis).

Mycenean Beehive Tomb (Tholos): Interesting remains of the construction, *c.* 26 ft. in diameter and height, with a Dromos (approach road) 85 ft. long.

Environs: To the N. lie the foothills of **Mount Párnis** (4, 635 ft.), the highest mountain in Attica forming the natural boundary with Boeotia to the N. Here in ancient times Zeus Ombrios was worshipped as rain-bringer, and bears and wild boars were hunted. There is a superb view over Athens and the Saronic Gulf. The mountain-top has been developed as a health resort and ski centre. Some 5 km. to the NW is the town of **Khasiá** (also called *Fyli*) on the slopes of Parnis with the interesting remains of the old Attic border

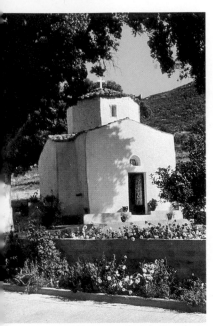

Korónia (Alalkomenaí), Agia Paraskevi

fort of *Phylé* (modern *Fylí*): the well-preserved *Fortress* dating from the 4C BC built above an earlier structure guarded the road from Attica to Boeotia (Fylí pass). The strong *Walls* are 8 ft. thick and built of squared blocks; lengths of 55 ft. survive in the E. and SE. There are also remains of four *towers* and two *gates*. To the W. and SW the wall has collapsed into the gorge. The *ancient settlement of Phylé* lay to the E. of the fortress (some ruins near the church of Agía Paraskevi). Nearby stands the attractive monastery of the **Panagía Klistón** (above the gorge) dating from the Byzantine period (13C) with later restorations. The interesting old cross-domed *church* has 18C frescos and a collection of valuable *church artifacts*. Some 5 km. to the NE at Tatói and Varybóbi on the wooded slopes of Parnis are the remains of the ancient deme (district town) of **Dekéleia**

(**Dekélia**), which played an important part in the Peloponnesian War (413 BC). Nearby is the attractive monastery of the *Kimisis Theotoku* and the former *Royal Palace of Tatoi* built by King George I with its model vineyard.

Áktion/Actium/AKTION
Akarnania/West Central Greece   p.294☐C 6

The sparse remains of the Corinthian colony of *Anaktórion (7C BC)* lie in the foothills on the Gulf of Ambrákia, opposite the modern Préveza, 61 km. W. of Amfilokhía. The foothills and city later took the name of Áktion. The place became famous after the decisive sea-battle fought in 31 BC off Actium, at which the fleet of Octavian, later the Emperor Augustus, defeated the fleet and army of Antony and Cleopatra, so ensuring that the capital of the West remained in Rome, and not in the E. in Alexandria.

Temple of Apollo Aktios (7C BC: The old temple was enlarged by Augustus in memory of the battle of Actium, and the Aktia, or Aktian Games were re-established. Foundations of the temple survive, part of them built into a small Turkish *fortification*, as do those of the ancient *harbour* to the S. of the temple. The actual 'City of Victory', *Nikópolis* (see entry) which Augustus founded lay N. of Préveza.

Environs: On the N. promontory, opposite Préveza (connected by ferry) are the remains of a Venetian **fortress.** On a hill above the ancient harbour 1 km. to the S. stands the small Byzantine church of the **Twelve Apostles** *(Dodeka Apostoli).*

Alalkomenaí/ΑΛΑΛΚΟΜΕΝΑΙ
Boeotia/Central Greece   p.294☐G 8

This ancient town is some 17 km. from

Aliartos. Here stood the famous chryselephantine statue of Athena which was later carried off to Rome.

Environs: Korónia (some 6 km. W.): This famous ancient city is now a village of some 700 inhabitants. The city was mentioned by Xenophon, Thucydides, Pausanias, and even by Homer. It was founded by the Boeotians expelled from Thessaly and led by Koronaios, a son of Athamas. In 447 BC the Athenians suffered a severe reverse here in their struggle against the Boeotians. In 171 BC Korónia was destroyed by the Romans. Of the once famous temples and altars to Athena Homonoia, where the great pan-Boeotian games ('Ta Panviotia') were held, nothing remains. E. of Korónia is the Byzantine monastery of *Agia Paraskevi*. On a hill 4 km. SW of *Mamúra* are the remains of ancient brick houses, a theatre, and the ruins of an old wall. Not far away is a Catalan castle.

Alexandrúpolis/ΑΛΕΧΑΝΔΡΟΥΠΟΛΙΣ
Évros/Thrace   p.292☐L 2/3

Alexandrúpolis (pop. 25,000, with a Turkish minority) lies on the sea and is a modern port.
It was founded in 1876 as the capital of Évros, the E. border region with Turkey. In earlier times the city was known as *Dedeagaç*. In 1920 it was renamed Alexandrúpolis in honour of the then Greek King Alexander.
There is an annual flower festival (Anthestiria) from the 1–10 June, with dances and theatrical performances. In July and August variety is provided by the wine festivals.

Environs: Outside the city are the archaeological remains of the ancient cities of Dorisko, Trajanupolis, and Amphitriti.

Mákri (15 km. W.): Nearby is an as yet unexcavated Cyclopean cave. **Mesímvria** (20 km. W.): An archaeological zone where excavations are still in progress. A few Roman buildings have been opened to the public. **Féres** (30 km. NE): Here stands the church of *Agia Sofía*, a copy in miniature of its famous namesake in Istanbul, well worth a visit. The spa waters of Féres are also famous for their therapeutic qualities in kidney disease and internal inflammations. **Didymótikhon** (94 km. NE): This is a Byzantine city with a well-preserved double wall. Inscriptions reveal that this city was built on the site of the destroyed Roman city of Plotinúpolis founded by Trajan in honour of his wife Plotina. The archaeological collection and museum of folk art are worth a visit. **Suflí** (65 km. NE): This is a smaller city with a museum of folk art, and famous for its silk industry.

Alikanú/Alikanós/Alikianú/
ΑΛΥΚΙΑΝΟΥ
Chaniá/Crete   p.298☐F 14

The village lies some 12 km. SW of Chaniá, and has a chapel of Ágios Georgios dating from 1343 with frescos by Pávlos Provatá from 1430. On the edge of the village is the 10/11C basilica of Ágios Ioannis with a nave and two aisles.

Environs: Mesklá: Some 9 km. further S. is Mesklá with its Byzantine church of the Saviour *Sotiros Christu,*—fine frescos (1303). On the S. edge of the village is a *church of the Panagia,* built over the ruins of an ancient temple of Venus, of which only the mosaic floor now survives. The temple is assumed to have belonged to the ancient city of *Rhizenía* which once occupied the site.
There are also Byzantine frescos in the other churches of the village.

Almyrós/ΑΛΜΥΡΟΣ
Magnisia/Thessaly   p.294□F 6

This little Thessalian country town (pop.
c. 6,000) lies 44 km. SW of the city of Vólos
near the Pagasitic Gulf.

Museum (on the main Platia square):
This exhibits prehistoric finds, Neolithic
idols, Mycenean vases, and stele from the
Hellenistic and Roman periods dug up at
Zarélia in the neighbourhood of Almyrós.

Environs: Amaliápolis (some 12 km. E.
on the coast): This is a small spa and sea-
bathing resort, with the scanty ruins of the
archaic settlement of *Álos* (walls and
towers) nearby. **Pteleós** (24 km. SE): Remains of the ancient port mentioned as
early as Homer, with the partially-
surviving *city walls*. Four Mycenean *tombs*
have been uncovered here. Nearby is the
village of Pteleón. In the village of **Pelasgía,** (c. 50 km. S.), which recalls the ancient name of Thessaly, are the remains of
the ancient *acropolis* of Lárissa Kremasté,

captured and destroyed by Demetrios
Poliorketes in 302 BC and by the Romans
in 171 BC. Nearby, in the village of **Rakhóna** and elsewhere are more archaic ruins
belonging to the settlement of *Alópe*, already famous in Homer's time (Iliad II,
682).

Alónnisos/ΑΛΟΝΝΗΣΟΣ
Northern Sporades/Aegean Islands
                                          p.296□H 6

This peaceful, wooded, hilly island lies E.
of Skópelos. It covers 25 sq. miles and has
a population of c. 1,500.

Alónnisos (pop. 350): The capital (also
known as *Khóra*) in the SW of the island
occupies a charming site above the port of
Patitíri, 2 km. to the E. (pop. 600), where
many of the inhabitants moved after the
earthquake of 1965. Near Patitíri are the
remains of the ancient settlement of *Ikos,*
(another ancient name for the island), at
the village of *Kokkonókastro* ('Red Castle'):
the remains of the *city walls* and *agora* are

Amaliápolis (Almyrós), panorama

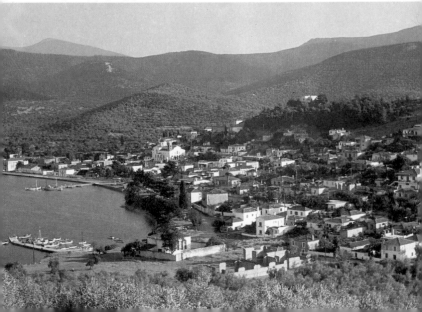

visible (marble fragments under the sea). On the islet opposite Palaeolithic finds were made in 1970; dating from 100,000 – 33,000 BC, they are among the earliest traces of man in the Aegean.

Environs: On the neighbouring island of *Kyra Panagia* to the NE (9.6 sq. miles) is the monastery of the same name, a dependency of Mt.Athos. Finds from the Neolithic period dating from around 6000 BC have also been made. E. lies the monastic island of *Pipéri* ('Pepper Island', 2.7 sq. miles) with a beautiful cross-domed church belonging to the former monastery. On the volcanic island of *Psathúra* are ancient remains, some of them underwater. The little island of *Skántzura* (3 sq. miles) to the SE has a small monastery of the *Panagia Evangelistria.*

Amfíklia/ΑΜΦΙΚΛΕΙΑ
Ftiótis/Phthiótis/Central Greece   p.294☐F 7

This little country town with a population of 3,000 lies in the valley of the Kifisos on the N. foothills of Mt.Parnassos, 49 km. SE of Lamía. In antiquity the town was famed for its *Mysteries of Dionysos*, who with Apollo was Lord of Parnassos.

Ancient fortifications: Fragments of a defensive wall survive (cemetery). The tower with ruined fortifications is of Venetian origin.

Environs: Lílaia (*c.* 5 km. W.): The remains of this ancient city with its *defensive walls* and *towers* (*c.*300 BC) are visible. Some 8 km. SE are the ancient *city fortifications* of **Tithoréa** with a superb 4C BC *acropolis* with the Parnassos masif as backdrop. Further up at about 2,625 ft. above sea-level is the interesting Byzantine *mountain monastery of Dadiú* ('Torch monastery'), also called the *Panagia Gavriotissa*. Large parts of the *cross-domed church* with

its *wall paintings* date from the restoration in 1756. It was damaged in the Greek War of Liberation in 1821 when it was a centre of resistance, and again restored in 1836–48. Some 11 km. E. of Amfíklia are the ruins of the ancient Phokian capital of **Eláteia** *(Elátia)*: Philip II of Macedon begn his victorious drive through Greece by capturing this fortified city in 399 BC. Only a few remnants of the *residential quarter* and *acropolis* survive. On the hill of *Kastro Lasu* two hours' walk to the N. is a ruined *sanctuary of Athena*, with foundations of a Doric temple, capitals and column drums. Here the acts of the Phokian Amphictyonic League were promulgated (rich epigraphical finds). There are superb views over Parnassos and down into the vale of Kifisos.

Amfilokhía/ΑΜΦΙΛΟΧΙΑ
Akarnania/Central Greece   p.294☐D 7

This little fishing-town (pop. 5,000) on the SE of the Ambrakian Gulf occupies a site like an amphitheatre on a mountain-slope, with *ruins of a fortress.* Here stood the acropolis of the ancient settlement of *Herákleia (Limnaía).* Two walls led down to the bay below. The site was rebuilt by the Byzantines, and Ali Pasha founded a village here in the 18C. The Turkish caravanserai on the shore, formerly 'Karvasarás', was named *Amfilokhía* after the ancient district.

Environs: The ruins of the ancient city of **Amphílokhoi** (also called 'Amphilokhian Argos') are some 11 km. N. along the Arta road, in the village of **Lutrón:** The city was supposedly founded by Amphilokhos, a hero from the Trojan war who came originally from Árgos in the Peloponnese, hence 'Árgos Amphilokhikón'. The city played a minor role in the 5C BC as a rival of the N. gulf city of Ambrakía (modern Árta). On the S. shore of the Gulf is

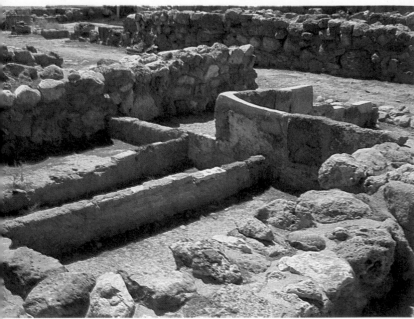

Nirú Kháni (Amnisós), Minoan villa

the port of **Vónitsa** (37 km. W.), pop. 2,
500. It is dominated by the *ruins of a
Byzantine-Venetian fortress*, built in 1479
against the Turks. The commander's
house survives, as do a chapel and the remains of a large cistern. There is a lovely
view over the Gulf from here. Below the
castle is the little basilica of the *Agii
Apostoli* with fine decorations and paintings. Further on is the *basilica of St.
Nikolaos* with unusual painted motifs of
lions with human faces. Opposite the island of Levkás (*c.* 57 km. W.) is a small
Turkish fort on a rocky promontory
guarding the straits. Nearby is the fortress
of **Santa Maura**, built by the Franks in
the 13C and later rebuilt by Venetians and
Turks. An arched aqueduct for spring
water also survives. In the middle of the
fortress is an outer harbour with mole and
lighthouse.

Ámfissa/Ámphissa/ΑΜΦΙΣΣΑ
Fokís/Phokís/Central Greece   p.294☐F 7

This attractive little country town (pop. *c.*
6,000) is the centre of the Nomos of Fokís
(Phokís). In antiquity it was the Lokrian
capital (ancient region of Lokrís). The city
came into conflict with the Delphic Amphictyonic League over the fertile 'Sacred
Plain' to the SE, now very picturesque
with its dense, age-old olive-trees. After the
3rd Sacred War (356–46 BC) King Philip
of Macedon, whose assistance had been re-
quested, destroyed the city (338 BC). After
1204 the ancient acropolis was turned into
a fortress by Frankish and later by Catalan
knights, under the name of *Salóna*.

Ruined Castle of Kástro: This dates
from the 13C, and stands on the acropolis

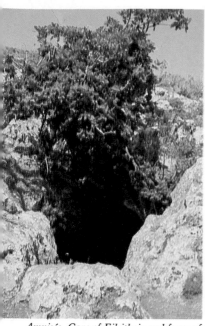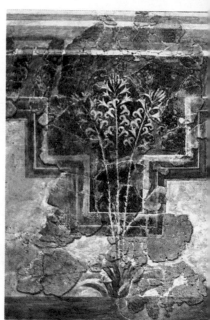

Amnisós, Cave of Eileithyia and fresco of the lilies (Arch. Museum, Iráklion)

hill, part of it above ancient *polygonal wall masonry*. Especially in the N. and W. fragments of ancient blocks can be seen in the wall. The castle had three enceintes flanked by a powerful tower. The *castle gate* is badly damaged. Behind it are a ramp and cannon-platform. The inner fortifications of the main block have a damaged free-standing *tower* or keep and two *cisterns*. To the N. is an earlier *round tower* (13C). In the S. the wall follows the lay-out of the ancient fortifications (steep cliffs).

Environs: To the W. and NW rises the great Giona massif (7,874 ft.), facing Mt.Parnassos (8,202 ft.) in the E. The road to the N. towards Brálos runs through charming countryside between the wooded uplands and over the impressive Amvlema pass (2,790 ft.). Here stood the ancient **Kytínion** (hardly any traces survive) with a 13C *fort* in the village of **Pýrgos** (11 km.

N.). There is a monument to the War of Liberation of 1821, when 180 Greeks defended the pass against 6,000 Turks. Some 33 km. further N. is the picturesque mountain village of **Gravía** at the head of a gorge. The road from Ámfissa to Lidoríkion (some 46 km. W.) passes through lovely mountain scenery, with Mt.Verdusia (7,874 ft.) in the background. On the S. slopes of the Giona massif is the town of **Malandrínon**, some 38 km. to the SW, with the ruins of the ancient city of *Phýskeis*, the ancient acropolis has walls and the ruined foundations of ancient buildings, as well as a chapel. NW of the city walls are the remains of an *exedra* with *inscriptions*. Nearby is a *ruined Byzantine church* above traces of a *temple of Zeus*. The chapel of the *Agii Apostoli* also has *traces of a temple*. N. of the site are extensive foundations (5&4C BC) of a *temple of Athena*.

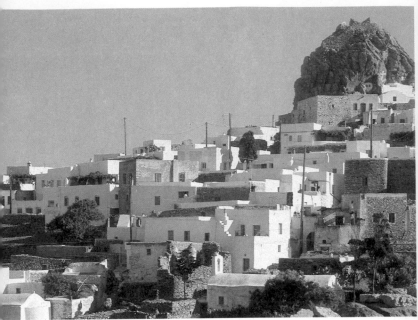

Amorgós, view

Amnisós/Amnissós/ΑΜΝΙΣΟΣ
Iráklion/Crete   p.298□H 14

7 km. E. of Iráklion on the N. coast of Crete are the ruins of ancient Amnisós. Here the *villa of the lilies*, an aristocratic villa with a terrace, shrine, reception room and light-well, was discovered. The fresco of the lilies from the villa is now in the archaeological museum in Iráklion. Amnisós was probably the Minoan port of Knossós, and was settled in the Neolithic.

Environs: Cave of Eileithyia (modern Ilíthya): At Palaiokhora the road forks, one part leading to Episkopí. Near here the cave of Eileithyia was discovered. According to tradition Eileithyia, a fertility goddess, was a daughter of Hera. Countless women came here on pilgrimage from Neolithic times up to AD 600 to pray for children in this stalactite cave, which measures 200 ft. long by 40 ft. wide by 13 ft. high. It is a cult-site of extreme antiquity and has been in existence since about 5000 BC, although at first there were only dwellings and graves here, the sanctuary coming later. In 1886 the cave, mentioned as far back as Homer (Odyssey 19, 185 ff.), and long forgotten, was rediscovered, and systematically excavated in the years following 1929. The finds are in the Iráklion museum. **Nirú Kháni:** 5 km. E. of Amnisós at Nirú Kháni are the remains of a late Minoan aristocratic villa built around 1500 BC and discovered in 1919. The foundations of several paved courts, halls, corridors, and store-rooms and a crypt shrine can be discerned fairly easily. The archaeologist Sir Arthur Evans believed that the house was the seat of a High

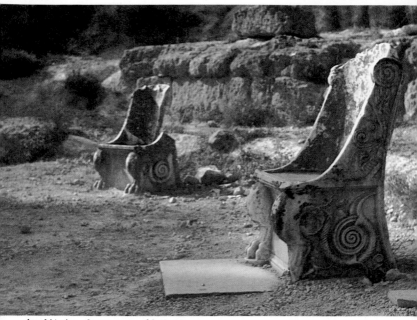

Amphiáreion, theatre, seats of honour

Priest, but the geologist Wunderlich considered that this and all the larger Minoan excavations such as Knossós, Phaistós and Mália were burial grounds connected with special cults. The modern view is that the building was a noble's villa.

Amorgós/ΑΜΟΡΓΟΣ
Aegean Islands/Cyclades   p.300□M 11

This narrow, elongated island (20 miles by 1.5–3 wide) in the SE Cyclades covers 47.5 sq. miles and has a population of some 1, 900. It is not as yet on the tourist routes.

History: The island ws already inhabited during the period of the Cycladic culture (3/2 millennia BC), and was settled by the Ionians around 1000 BC. It was of little

importance in antiquity, and was a Roman place of banishment. During the Middle Ages it belonged mostly to the Duchy of Naxos, falling later under Turkish domination (1537–1830).

Amorgós (also *Khóra*, 'Town'): The 13C capital stands in the centre of the island, 4 km. above the picturesque harbour of *Katápola* in the W. Above the town rises the ruined castle of *Apano-Kastro*, built by the Ghizzi in the 13C. The white houses have fragments of ancient reliefs built into the masonry. In the school there is a little *collection of antiquities*. In the port of Katápola are the remains of the ancient city of *Minóa*, with a gymnasion and temple of Apollo. Some ancient fragments have been incorporated into the pretty 17C church of the *Panagía Katapolianí*. Near the port *Cycladic finds* were made in the 19C (marble idols now in the National Museum in Athens).

Environs: About an hour's walk from the capital along a footpath, above the steep SE coast rises the impressive monastery of the *Panagía Khosoviótissa* with a wonder-working icon. It was founded in 1088 by the Byzantine Emperor Alexios I Komnenos. On the 2nd floor is the 11C icon chapel, with the miraculous image of Our Lady decorated with gold- and silver-work on the wall. The chapel terrace affords a superb view over the sea. Only scanty remains survive of the two ancient towns of *Aigiáli* in the NE and *Arkesíni* in the SW.

Amphiáreion/Amfiárion/
ΑΜΦΙΑΡΕΙΟΝ
Attica/Central Greece   p.296☐H 8

The excavations of the ancient oracle and spa of Amphiáreion are situated in the N. of Attica, some 49 km. N. of Athens, be-

twen the towns of Kálamos and Oropós. The name is derived from Amphiaraos, the legendary King of Argos. He was a wise seer and king who took part in the expedition of the Argonauts, and was persuaded by his wife Eriphyle (who had been bribed with a precious necklace) to take part in the bloody expedition of the Seven against Thebes. Zeus saved him from the foe by swallowing him up with his chariot in a crevasse in the earth and raising him to the rank of hero. It was believed that he had returned in a spring on the site of the Amphiáreion, to soothe and heal the sick who fasted and practised incubation here, seeking the interpretation of their dreams.

Excavation zone: In the SW in the 4C BC stood the Doric *temple of Amphiaraos*, supported in the S. by a high foundation. The *temple in antis* of which parts survive consisted of a pronaos, a cella with two rows of 5 columns, and a small entrance porch in the SW. The central area contained a *sacrificial altar* and a statue of Amphiaraos, of which the plinth and some fragments survive. In front of the temple

Andrávida, Agia Sofia

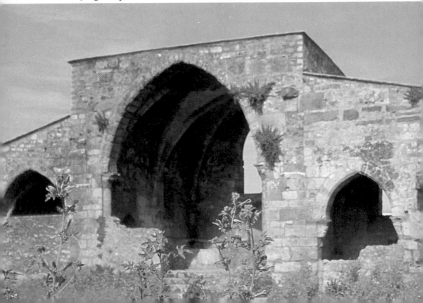

in the NE are the ruined foundations of a large *altar* in 5 sections (Zeus, Herakles and Apollo, heroes, Hestia, Aphrodite and Athena, and Pan and Nymphs). Near the altar is a *healing spring*, into which patients threw silver coins after their cure. Behind is a stepped *exedra* and a terrace with a *plinth* with countless *votive gifts*, mostly Roman. Adjoining this in the NE is an elongated *portico* (stoa) from the 4C BC measuring 360 ft. in length by 36 ft. wide, with an outer row of 44 Doric and an inner row of 17 Ionic columns. This was the room in which incubation or healing, dreaming, sleep was practised, furnished with couches (klinai) of which some marble feet survive. Interpreters expounded the meaning of the dreams. There were also trained doctors at hand, chiefly in the Roman period. In the NE are Roman *baths* supplied by an *aqueduct*. The Hellenistic *theatre* in the bckground to the NW has a fine acoustic and was the site of the musical contests held at the quadrennial festival since 332 BC. There was originally seating for 3,000 spectators; the lower stepped rows survive, as do five marble seats of honour with inscriptions. 8 Doric stage columns have been re-erected on the *skene* building, and the slits for wooden stage flats or 'pínakes' are visible, as are the remains of the *orchestra* (*c.* 40 ft. in diameter) and parodoi or entrances. On the far side of the stream are traces of a *settlement* with extensive houses, some of them peristyled, for treatment, pilgrims, and priests. In front are remains of a *klepsydra* (water-clock) with a tank and outflow pipe.

Museum: The little museum in front of the columned hall has *fragments of sculpture* and parts of the temple entablature, and *inscriptions*. Some *funerary stele*, a *statue of Amphiaraos* and the statue of a doctor (Amphilokhos) are of interest.

Environs: The remains of the ancient Attic-Boeotian city of **Oropós,** which frequently changed hands, are situated some 10 km. NW of the shrine. Only scant traces of the ancient *Polis Oropós* can be seen in the modern harbour of **Skála Oropú** (ferry to Erétria/Euboea) and in the neighbouring town of **Néa Palátia**.

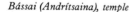
Bássai (Andrítsaina), temple

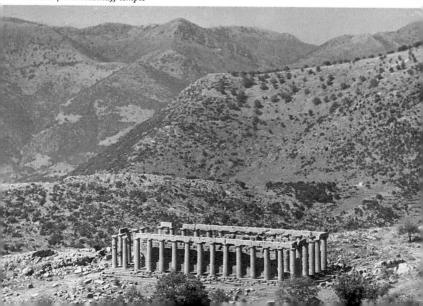

Anáfı (I)/ΑΝΑΦΗ
Cyclades/Aegean Islands   p.300☐L/M 12

The south-easternmost of the Cyclades (14.7 sq. miles, *c.* 400 inhab.) lies some 20 km. E. of Santorini. It is bare and infertile and hardly opened up to tourist traffic.

History: The island was perhaps originally a Phoenician colony, but was settled by Dorians. It played a small part as a member of the Attic naval league. Venice took it for the first time in 1207 but it reverted to Byzantine rule in 1269. From 1307 it was again subject to the Venetian rulers of Naxos until it fell to the Turks in 1537.

Anáfı (pop. 400): The little capital also known as *Khóra* ('village'), lies in the SW of the island above the port of *Ágios Nikólaos*. On the castle hill are traces of a Venetian fort (*kastro*, 14C). The town was badly damaged by the earthquake of 1957, as was neighbouring Santorini.

Environs: The ancient city of *Anáphe* (now in ruins) lay some 5 km. (2 hours walk) E. on the conical peak of *Kastelli*. The ruins contain a number of burial chambers with niches (8C BC), remnants of city walls, cisterns, and the traces of a temple dedicated to Apollo and Asklepios. An ancient marble sarcophagus with reliefs of sphinxes and Pegasos is of interest. The ancient port was in the S. at *Katalimátsa* (only 9 sparse remnants). The isthmus in the SE (some 7 km. from the capital) is the site of the remains of an ancient *shrine of Apollo* (5&4C BC); here today stands the *Zoodóchos Pigí* monastery (17C), with ancient marble building materials (e.g. lintel with inscription). Another interesting area of ruins is on the *Kálamos* peninsula (marble cliffs) to the S., where there are remains of the 14C Venetian castle and the little church of *Panagía Kalamiotissa* with a wonder-working icon.

Andravída/ΑΝΔΡΑΒΙΔΑ
Elis/Peloponnese   p.294☐D 9

This is a small town with some 3,000 inhabitants. During the Frankish period it was called *Andréville*, and was once the flourishing capital of Morea (or Achaea) under Guillaume de Villehardouin and later under Guillaume de Champlitte.

Agia Sofıa: 13C Gothic church with fine vaulting.

Andrítsaina/ΑΝΔΡΙΤΣΑΙΝΑ
Elis/Peloponnese   p.294☐E 10

The town is 64 km. SE of Pýrgos at the foot of Mt. Lykaion (pop. 1,032).

Library: This contains archaeological finds from the vicinity and documents from the Greek War of Liberation of 1821.

Environs: Bássai/Vásses (14 km. S): The temple of Apollo Epikourios stands at over 4,000 ft. above sea-level. It dates from the classical period and was the work of Iktinos, architect of the Parthenon.

According to Pausanias the temple was founded by the inhabitants of Phigalía as a thanks-offering to Apollo Epikourios for his protection against an outbreak of plague during the Peloponnesian War. The temple was discovered in 1765 by the Frenchman Bocher. Systematic investigations began in the 19C under the British. The frieze and metopes were taken to the British Museum in London in 1811. The frieze depicts the battle of Herakles against the Amazons and the Lapiths fighting the Centaurs, whilst the metopes have representations of the gods.

Temple: The limestone peripteros is Doric,

Bássai (Andrítsaina), temple ▷

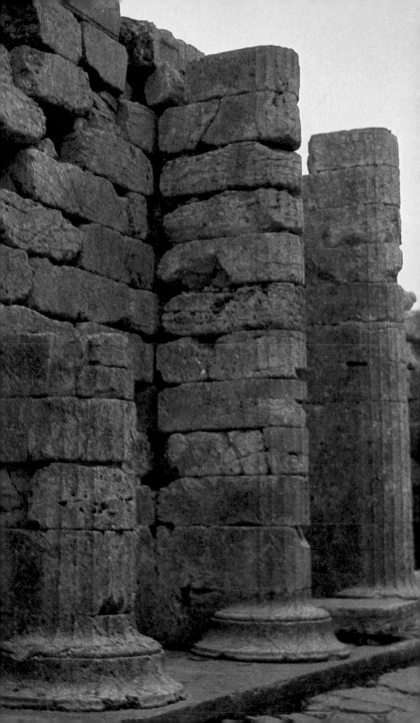

with six columns on the short side and fifteen on the long side in place of the usual thirteen, creating an elongated effect. It is oriented not to the E. but, for unknown reasons, to the N. (perhaps following the lay-out of an earlier, smaller temple).

To judge from the style of the frieze, the temple at Bássai was built after the Parthenon, which was finished in 438/7, and before 420, when the plague reached Phigalía. The cella has pronaos and opisthodomos, and another room for the cult-statue. This opened directly into the cella through a double passage formed by the diagonally placed terminal antae of the cella and a free-standing central column. Both the free-standing column and the engaged columns had Corinthian capitals, which made their first appearance in Greek architecture here, and seem to have been invented by Iktinos.

The *cult-statue* was probably a xoanon and faced E. to judge from the orientation of the floor slabs which are laid differently from those in the cella. The E. wall had a door which formed an additional source of light for the cult-image.

To the NW are remains of two small temples dedicated to Aphrodite and Artemis.

Ándros/ΑΝΔΡΟΣ
Cyclades/Aegean Islands   p.296☐K 9

The island of Andros covers some 147 sq. miles (pop. 11, 000) and is the second largest of the Cyclades after Naxos. It is separated from Euboea (Evia) by straits nearly 7 miles wide, and from the neighbouring island of Tínos by narrows ('Steno') 1300 yards across.

History: The island was settled around 1000 BC by Ionians from Euboea. Later it became a member of the Attic naval league (Athenian garrison). In the Hellenistic period it was disputed between Macedonia, Egypt, and King Attalos of Pergamon

(*c.* 200 BC). In 133 BC it became subject to Rome. During the Middle Ages it enjoyed independence from 1384–1437, when it fell to Venice. From 1566–1831 it was a Turkish possession.

Ándros (pop.2,000): The capital of the island, also known as *Khóra* ('village'), is situated on the E. coast on a little bay. It was founded in the Middle Ages and endowed with a Venetian fortress (now in ruins). By the old gate (surviving arch) is a bridge joining the fort to the old town (Káto Kástro, 'lower castle'). The church of *Zoodochos Pigí* ('Spring of life') has a carved wooden iconostasis dating from 1717. The Roman Catholic *church of Ágios Andreas* dates from the 15C (restored in 1749). The *city museum* has some ceramic objects and some interesting sculptures from the ancient island town of Palaiópolis.

Environs: Above *Apíkia* (5 km.) is the monastery of *Ágios Nikólaos* dating from 1560. The *Pantokrátor* monastery at Falíka (2 km.) is said to have been founded in the 7C. In the village of *Mesariá* (5 km.) is the *church of St.Michael,* built by the Emperor Manuel I Komnenos in 1158. The port of *Kórthion* (9 km. S.) is overlooked by the impressive ruins of the Venetian cstle of *Palaiokastro* (13C). *Palaiópolis* ('old city'): On the W. coast, 16 km. from Andros, are the ruins of the ancient city of Andros, now a fishing port. There are remains of the city walls, the 3C BC Hellenistic agora, and a sunken mole. The most beautiful find, the 'Hermes of Andros', is now in the National Museum in Athens. High above Palaiópolis rises Mt.Kuvara, nearly 3,300 ft. high (superb panorama). The resort of *Batsí* (24 km. NW) has the nunnery of *Agía (Zoodochos Pigí)* dating from 1325, with manuscripts and reliquaries. Nearby in the village of *Ágios Pétros* is a Hellenistic *round tower* (65 ft.) with several storeys. *Tower houses* (defensive towers) can be seen at *Amolokhos*. The N. harbour of *Gávrion* (34 km. NW of Andros, 8 km. from Batsí) has but few traces of the ancient settlement of the same name. At *Zagóra* on the island's SW promontory are the remains of a settlement of the 10 – 6C BC (temple foundations).

Arákhova / ΑΡΑΧΩΒΑ
Fokís / Phokís / Central Greece   p.294 □ F 7/8

This little mountain town (pop. *c.* 3,000) occupies a picturesque site on the S. slopes of Parnassos above Delphi, and is famed for its attractive hand-woven carpets and quilts, as well as for its red wine, tzipuro and basket-cheeses. This was probably the site of the ancient settlement of *Anemóreia* (no traces have survived). The narrow wynds and steep stairs are picturesque. There are superb views over the gorge and the mountain air is wholesome (health resort).

Environs: The Parnassos road runs NW from Arákhova to the ancient cult-site of the **Korykian Cave** (modern *Saranta Avlí*). The cave lies at an altitude of 4,600 ft. in rugged mountain scenery beneath the peak of Liakura (8,061 ft.). In antiquity it was sacred to the shepherd-god Pan and the mountain nymphs (Muses). It consists of a large chamber (200 ft. x 100 ft.) and several smaller caverns (supposedly 40, hence the modern name '40 halls'). At the entrance is a dedicatory inscription (by Eustratos). Inside and in front of the caves the ecstatic Thyads (Bacchantes) celebrated the frenzied winter festivities of Dionysos (who ruled over Parnassos and Delphi during the winter months) dressed in skins and carrying torches and thyrsos. Recent excavations by the French school (around 1971) have produced valuable finds from the Neolithic, Mycenean and archaic (7C BC) ages, up to the Hellenistic period. The inscriptions, sculptures and terracotta figurines have been taken to the museum in Delphi. From Arákhova it is possible to climb Liakura, a *peak of Parnassos* (with a guide). The peak offers superb views over the whole mountain district and over the sea.

Mérbaka (Árgos), church of the Panagía

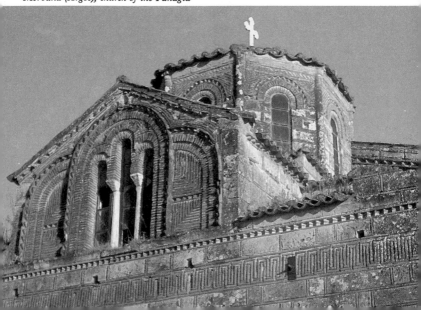

Árgos/ΑΡΓΟΣ
Argolís/Peloponnese   p.294☐F 9

The modern city of Árgos ('The plain') has a population of some 20,000, and is an important commercial and agricultural centre lying in the midst of the fertile Argolís, on the site of the ancient city at the foot of Mt.Larissa (948 ft.).

History: The history of Argos stretches back into the 2nd millennium when the Achaeans occupied the area. Traces of this Middle Helladic settlement have been found on the hill of Aspís. According to legend King Danaos came to the Argolís from Egypt with his 50 daughters after a quarrel with his brother Aigyptos. The Danaid race then drove out the Pelasgians who were the previous inhabitants of the area. In the 13C BC Adrastos and Amphiaraos joined the expedition of the Seven against Thebes, and later took part in the Trojan War. Homer also mentions Diomedes, an Argive and son of Tydeus, who returned uninjured.

Mérbaka (Árgos), church of the Panagía

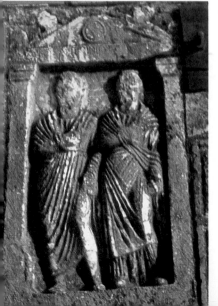

Towards the end of the 12C the Dorians entered the area, took the fort of Lárissa, and spread out across the Argolís.

The 7C was the time of the city's greatest prosperity under King Pheidon, who is supposed to have been the first to introduce coinage. During his time a temple was built to Hera. Doric architecture developed here. In 494 the Argives were defeated at the Battle of Sepeia and subjugated by the Spartans under Kleomenes I. In the succeeding years Argos was a rival of Sparta, finally making a treaty with the Athenians in 460 against the Spartans (Argive victory over Sparta at Oinoe).

Argos blossomed anew during the Roman period. Baths, public buildings and an odeion were built.

During the barbarian invasions of AD 267 and 395 the city was destroyed.

It regained importance during the Middle Ages when the knights of the 4th Crusade built castles in the surrounding territory (1204).

During the Greek War of Independence two national assemblies were held in Argos, in 1821 and 1829. In 1822 Kolokotronis and Ypsilantis defended the fort successfully against Dramali Pasha. The city was plundered and destroyed by Ibrahim Pasha.

In the 5C BC Argos was renowned for its school of sculpture, and leading sculptors like Ageladas (c. 515–460) and most famous of all, Polykleitos (480–420), were Argives. Polykleitos the Younger (435–360), who built the tholos at Epidauros, was also born in Argos.

Agora: This is situated on the road to Trípolis, opposite the Odeon.

A long *portico* (5C) runs along the S. edge of the agora. This was rebuilt in the 4C AD after a Gothic raid. There are remains of a large hypostyle hall (107 ft. 1 in. along the sides) with 16 Ionic columns (of which the bases of 7 survive), probably the *bouleuterion* (last quarter of the 3C BC). A building identified as the *nymphaion* dates from the 2C AD. Beneath the foundations of the agora lies an extensive cemetery.

Baths: These date back to the 2C AD, and were rebuilt in the 4C. The entrance is beneath the Roman aqueduct, where the original entrance also stood. First comes a well-preserved *apsidal room* (75 ft. 6 in. x 34 ft. 9 in.) with a coffered ceiling. This had a crypt with three sarcophagi, built before the baths. Next came the actual entrance to the baths, followed by the *apodyterium* (changing-room) surrounded by benches. From here one came to the *frigidarium* (cold bath) with three plunge-baths, and going right, to the large *caldarium* (heated bath). Two further rooms, one behind another, opened off to the left of this last. They were heated by a hypocaust system and by channels in the walls.

Odeion: This is situated beside the Roman aqueduct S. of the baths. It was built in the 1C AD and rebuilt in the 3C. The orchestra was probably covered since it was paved with mosaics. A row of niches in the proscenium were faced in marble. The first 14 rows of seats can still be seen in front of the cavea. The Odeion was built on the site of an earlier building (5C BC) where the Argive assembly met. 55 yards S. of the Odeion are the remains of a *sanctuary of Aphrodite* (430 – 420), destroyed by the Goths in the 4C AD. According to Pausanias a relief of Telesilla, the famous Argive poetess, stood in front of the temple. A sacrificial altar 19ft. 8 in. long and 5 ft. 9 in. wide also stood in front of the temple; only its core survives.

Theatre: This is an imposing structure with 81 rows of seats on the slope of Mt. Lárissa. It held 20,000 spectators and was the largest Greek theatre. It dates from the end of the 4C BC and was rebuilt in the 2C AD, when the Greek skene was removed and replaced by a Roman construction in brick, and again in the late 4C, when the orchestra was converted into a basin for mock sea-battles. In the centre of the orchestra stood a sacrificial altar and a pedestal. The parodos was decorated with statues of the Dioscuri.

Heraion of Árgos

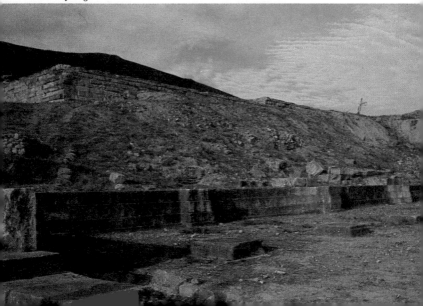

Lárissa fort (about 40 minutes' climb): Here are the few remains of the *temple of Zeus Larisaios and Athena Polias*, which was already a place of asylum in the 2nd millennium BC. The plan of the fortifications dates in the main from Byzantine times (12C); they were enlarged by the Franks and Turks. The double walls follow the line of the ancient enceintes dating from the 6C (outer wall) and 5C BC (inner wall). The fort was at one time joined to the city walls which reached as far as Aspis hill.

Directly below the fort is the monastery Panagia tou Vrachou ('Our Lady of the Cliffs') on the site of the *sanctuary of Hera Akraia*.

Aspis hill: This hill takes its name from its shape which resembles a shield. Here stood the *sanctuary of Apollo Deiradiotes* (or Pythios) on a raised terrace; here too was the seat of an oracle. Near a large cistern was the *sanctuary of Athena Oxyderkes* ('the clearsighted'), also built on a raised terrace. Remains of a tholos can be seen on another terrace.

The French Archaeological School uncovered several Mycenean tombs (14&13C BC) at the foot of the hill, as well as a Middle Helladic settlement (2000–1580).

Next to the church of Agios Ilias at the top of the hill are a few remains of a 2nd millennium settlement. A circular wall of polygonal masonry replaced a prehistoric cyclopean wall (2nd millennium).

Museum: This is rich in finds from the 8 to 6C BC, exhibited in chronological order, starting at the entrance. Of special interest are several vases, almost exclusively from Deira, the area between Mt. Larissa and Aspis hill.

There is an interesting fragment of an earthenware krater (7C BC) with a picture of the blinding of Polyphemos by Odysseus and his companions. Displayed in case 8 are supports for spits in the shape of ships dating from the late Geometric period. Case 9 contains spits.

There is a late Geometric cuirass and helmet from a grave in Árgos. The helmet is conical with two cheek-guards and a crest into which a horsetail was fixed. This is the

Vathýpetro (Arkhánes), aristocratic villa

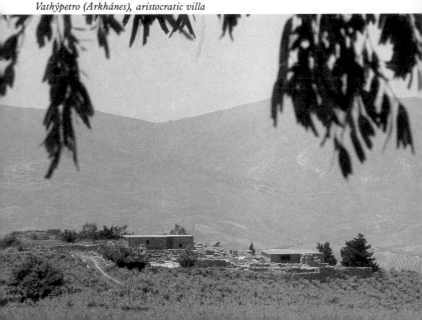

only surviving example of the 'Homeric helmet'.

The second floor houses Roman statues and reliefs, including copies of the statues of Korinna and the Farnese Hercules. In the basement are finds from Lerna, dating from Neolithic times to the late Helladic period.

Beneath a roof in the museum courtyard is a late Roman mosaic from the 5C with personifications of the seasons and months.

Environs: Heraion of Árgos (*c.* 9 km. NE): The site was inhabited from the 3rd millennium, and remains of a Mycenean settlement have been discovered (15–13C). The greatest period of prosperity was during the 5C, but annual festivals in honour of Hera were still held here in Pausanias's time. Originally the shrine lay on two plateaux surrounded by gorges. It was discovered in 1831. Systematic excavations were conducted by the American School (1892&3 and 1925–8) and by the French School (1947–9). At the entrance to the sacred area are *monumental steps* 266 ft. wide

which also served as a supporting wall. The steps led right up to the terrace where the classical temple of Hera stands. At the end of the steps is a small *sacrificial altar*. On the left of the steps is a Doric *columned hall*. The monumental steps, peripteral hall and temple all date from the 5C jBC. Left of the temple is a rectangular building with a central columned court. On the N. side of this are three rooms with couch bases. This permits the identification of the hall with the *banqueting-hall*, dating from the 6C BC. Another peripteral hall of the 5C is opposite the banqueting-hall. In the middle of the platform stands the *temple of Hera* built in 420 by the Argive Eupolemos (peripteral Doric). On the E. pediment the birth of Zeus was depicted, and on the W. pediment the fall of Troy. The metopes bore scenes of battles with Amazons and Giants.

The cella held a seated statue of Hera in chryselephantine by Polykleitos and a xoanon of the goddess which the Argives brought from Tiryns in 468 BC. In front of the temple entrance stood an *altar* (55 ft. 9 in. x 7 ft. 11 in.) from the Hellenistic

Arkhánes, necropolis

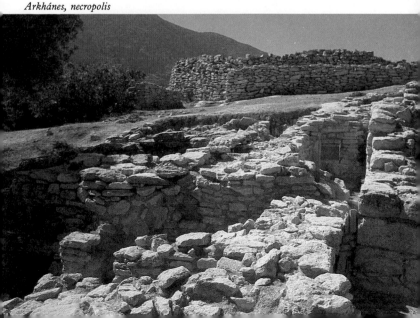

period. E. of the altar was a hypostyle building (94 ft. 10 in. x 56 ft), which may have been a telesterion dating from the middle of the 5C BC.

N. of the classical temple of Hera are two more columned buildings (end of the 7C BC); the E. is smaller than the W., which measures 206 ft. 8 in. x 334 ft. 5 in. The *earlier temple of Hera* (start of the 7C) stood on a higher terrace; it burned down in 423 BC through the carelessness of a priestess. The *baths* date from Roman times and had a mosaic floor in the atrium (E. side) and bathing-pool (W. side). S. of the baths is the *gymnasion* (112 ft. x 112 ft.), surrounded by columned halls. **Midéa** (15 km. E.): From Déndra (13 km.) one can climb to the *acropolis* of Midéa (about half an hour) which has Cyclopean walls (14C BC) and a square tower in the SE. On the summit of the hill are foundations, probably of a palace. The fortress was destroyed at the end of the 12C by fire. Midéa is said to have been founded by Perseus and to have been the birthplace of Alkmene, mother of Herakles. Some 220 yards N. of Déndra is a *Mycenean cemetery* where

bronze implements were found, consisting of linked bronze chains (15C, now in the museum in Nauplia). **Mérbaka** (12 km.): *Church of the Panagía* (12C), a domed church with fragments of the Heraion incorporated into the masonry. The village takes its name from Wilhelm van Moerbeke, who came to Greece as first Latin Bishop of Corinth in 1277. **Kenkhreai** (modern *Ellinikón, c.*10 km. SW): The river Erasinos flows from the rocks at *Kefalári* (5 km.). The caves here were sacred to Pan and Dionysos, and here the Tyrbe festival was held. Beside the source of the Erasinos (3 km. on foot) is the *pyramid of Kenkhreai*, where the Argives buried their fallen after the battle against the Spartans in 669 BC.

Arkhánes/Arkhánai/ΑΡΧΑΝΕΣ

Iráklion/Crete   p.298□H 14

S. of Knossós lies Arkhánes with its two churches, both with 14C frescos. The village occupies the site of a Minoan settle-

Vathýpetro (Arkhánes), olive press

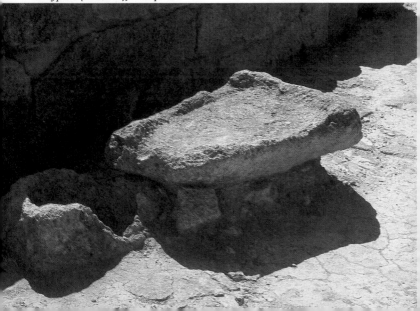

ment dating from *c.* 1600 BC. Remains of a palace, shrine and cemetery have been excavated. Above the village is the hill of Phurni where a cemetery with an ossuary (*c.* 1600 BC) and a Mycenean tholos tomb (*c.* 1400 BC) have been discovered. The finds are now in the Archaeological Museum in Iráklion.

Environs: Iúktas/Youktas: Arkhánes lies on the E. slopes of Mt.Iúktas (2,660 ft.), on whose N. peak there was a Minoan shrine. In post-Homeric times a myth became current that Zeus was buried on Mt.Iúktas. His grave was venerated there until Christian times when the chapel of the Metamórphosis (Transfiguration) was erected there. **Lýkastos:** S. of Iúktas there are a few remains of the ancient settlement of Lýkastos, from which tradition tells us Idomeneus set out with his warriors for Troy. **Vathýpetro:** 15 km. S. of Knossós and 5 km. from Arkhánes is Vathýpetro, where the largest multi-storeyed aristocratic villa of this type so far discovered has been excavated. It was built around 1550 BC and destroyed about 1500

BC. The original megaron had the dimensions of a palace. The inner court contained a shrine. Large columned halls were also discovered, with a cult-niche for sacrifices, a treasury (finds in the Iráklion museum), store-rooms, a 16C BC kiln, and an olive- and wine-press, still workable. **Ágios Vasílios:** 13 km. S. of Arkhánes is Ágios Vasílios with its little chapel of *Agios Ioannis* situated a little outside the village beside a gorge, with very beautiful and well-preserved frescos dating from 1291. Also of interest are *Ágios Antonios, Agia Pelagia, Ágios Georgios* and the *Panagía,* all very close by.

Árta/APTA

Árta/Epirus   p.294☐C/D 6

History: The site of the modern city of Árta was occupied in antiquity by *Ambrakía* founded according to legend by Ambrakos. The city was a Corinthian colony (*c.* 640 BC). During the Peloponnesian War it was an ally of Sparta against Athens.

Árta, Panagia Parigoritissa

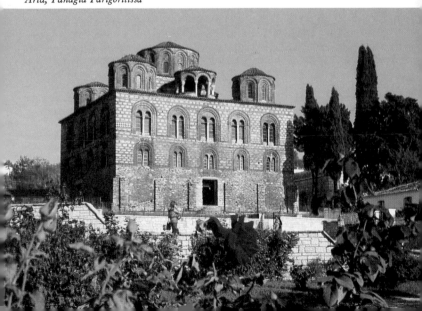

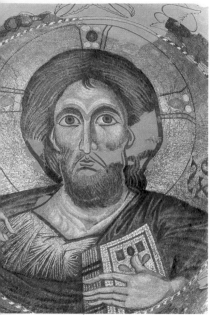

Árta, Panagia Parigoritissa

In 295 BC Pyrrhos, King of Epirus, made Ambrakia his residence, and this was the time of the city's zenith. In 167 BC it was completely destroyed by the Romans. In 31 BC the city of Nikópolis was built nearby, and many inhabitants of Ambrakia settled there. At the end of the 11C the name Árta appears for the first time. Later it became the seat of the Despotate of Epirus. During the reign of Theodoros (1214 –30) the Despotate reached its greatest extent, including not only Aitolia, Akarnania, Epirus, the neighbouring islands, and part of Albania as far as Durazzo, but also Thessaly and S. Macedonia. Theodoros was defeated by the Bulgarians in 1230 and Macedonia was lost to the Despotate. The period 1231–68 was the high point of the Despotate, and during this time many churches were built or altered in Árta and the surrounding area. In the 14C decline

set in, lasting until 1449 when Árta was captured by the Turks who were only driven out in 1878.

Panagia Parigoritissa: This is the largest and most famous church in Árta, built by the Despot Nikephoros and his wife Anna in 1289–96, and dedicated to the Mother of God of Consolation. From the outside the church has the appearance of a three-storeyed palace with five cupolas. The walls are built on the classical Byzantine isodomic system. The ceramic decorations around the windows should be examined. The narthex occupies the whole width of the church, and has five doors leading into the interior. The outermost doors lead into chapels which function as side aisles next to the sanctuary, and end in three-sided niches.

Interior decorations: The capitals of the squinch arches supporting the dome are decorated with carved reliefs of the Nativity of Christ, the Lamb of God, prophets and evangelists. The work is by foreign artists. The dome is decorated with a mosaic roundel of Christ Pantocrator; the face measures 7 ft. 3 in. across, and the image is surrounded by cherubim, seraphim, and powers. Decorative arches spring from the top of the royal doors and end in the sanctuary. The flat surfaces of the arches are decorated with scenes of animals and monsters, with the foundation inscription in between. The mosaics in the Parigoritissa are the work of artists from Constantinople or Thessalonika, and are amongst the finest examples of 13C Byzantine art.

Agia Theodora: The church was founded by Theodora, wife of the Despot Michael II, and has borne her name since her canonization. Her tomb is in the narthex, which also contains numerous reliefs of Theodora and her children between two angels. The church is in the Hellenistic ba-

Árta, Panagia Parigoritissa ▷

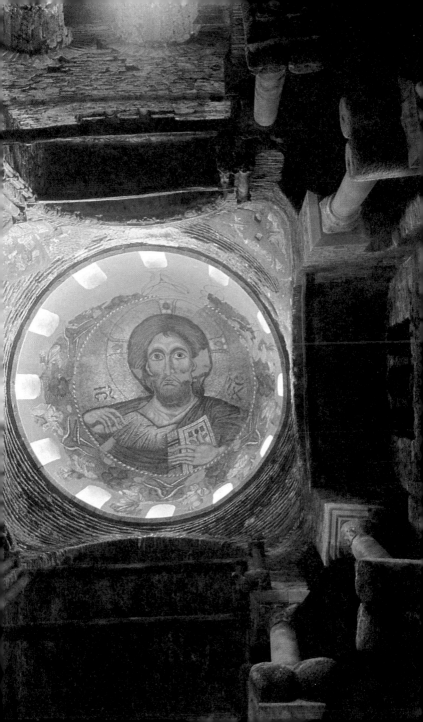

silica style with a nave and two aisles and three three-sided apses on the E. side. The narthex is domed and has an open colonnade on the S. side. The floor of the nave is paved with large marble slabs separated by geometrical motifs in marble and mosaic tesserae.

Agios Vasilios (E. of Agia Theodora): This church is a basilica with a wooden roof. There are side-chapels on the N. and S. which terminate in three-sided apses. To the right and left of the pediment window at the E. end are two ceramic reliefs. The wall paintings in the interior date from around the end of the 17C. Agios Vasilios was probably built in the second half of the 13C.

Fortress (13C): This stands in the N. of the city and was probably erected by Despot Michael II. The castle is an irregular rectangle in shape, measures 558 ft. x 920 ft. and has 18 towers. The Byzantine walls are built of relatively small undressed stones and bricks. A Byzantine structure survives inside the fort.

Bridge: The present bridge was built in 1602–6 and is 466 ft. long and 12 ft. 4 in. wide. It has four large arches and one smaller one. According to legend, the wife of the architect was sacrificed to ensure that the bridge would stand.

Byzantine apse (near Agia Theodora): Today only the arched door survives. It may have been part of a Byzantine villa or palace.

Environs: Ágios Dimítrios Katsúris (5 km. SW): The church was built in the 9C and is the oldest Byzantine monument in the Árta region. It is rectangular, with side walls 36 ft. long, and is surmounted by a cross-dome. The narthex is roofed in wood. At various points in the church and bell tower there are 12&13C sculptures. In-

teresting also are the wall paintings, including scenes from the life of Christ and of the Mother of God.

Ágios Nikólaos tis Rodiás (c. 1 km. W. of Ágios Dimítrios): The church is called *Rodiá* after the old monastery to the Mother of God. It is a two-columned cross-domed church with fine paintings on the N. and S. walls depicting the Three Young Men in the fiery furnace and the Seven Sleepers who hid in a cave during the persecution of Christians.

Ágios Vasílios tis Géfyras (c. 1 km. W.): A 14C church with a single aisle and a beautiful cylindrical drum and dome decorated with zigzag brickwork.

Panagía Vryóni (c. 6 km. SE): This little-known church (1238) has a tripartite sanctuary roofed with a barrel-vault and a dome above the central area decorated with calottes on the sides. The W. part of the church is shaped like a wooden-roofed basilica with a nave and two aisles.

Káto Panagías (1.5 km. S. in the village of *Káto Panagiaá*): The monastery was built in the middle of the 13C, probably by Michael II, and belongs to the same period as the monastery at Vlakhérna. The ceramic ornamentation is especially rich. Káto Panagías has a nave and two aisles but no dome and a raised barrel vault. The sculpted column decorations are not contemporaneous with the building but come from late antique buildings in Ambrakía. The monastic church has wall paintings (1715). Some Byzantine paintings survive in the diaconicon.

Vlakhérna (in the NE): This monastery was founded at the end of the 12C or the beginning of the 13C, probably by Michael II, Despot of Epirus, and his wife Theodora. Many alterations have been made since that time. It is rich in carved

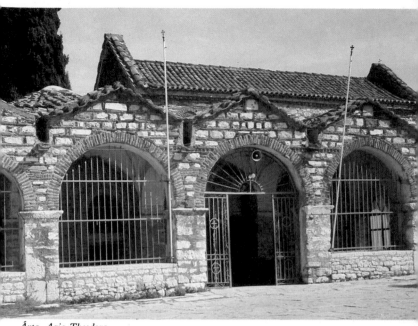

Árta, Agia Theodora

Árta, bridge

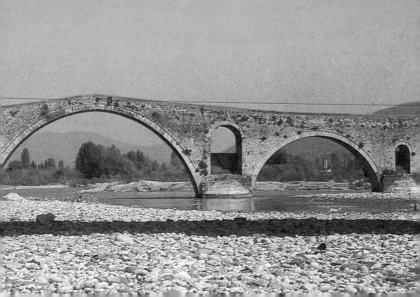

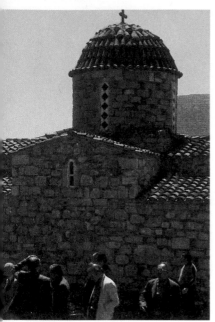

Askri, Byzantine chapel

ornament, and interesting inscriptions and tombs.

Askri/ΑΣΚΡΗ
Boeotia/Central Greece   p.294☐G 8

This village (pop. 800, *c.* 5 km. SW of Thespiaí) used to be called *Palaiopanagiá* until a few years ago. On the W. edge of the modern village of Askri is the cemetery chapel of St.Vlasios (*c.* 16C). Interesting frescos were discovered on the walls of the church and altar.

Valley of the Muses: Some 2 km. away, at the foot of Mt.Helikon (5,742 ft.), a sacred mountain in antiquity famed for its noble trees and healing herbs, lies the valley of the Muses. Here the great poet Hesiod (7C BC) of Askri was initiated into the secrets of the poetic art by the mountain goddesses. The veneration of the Muses is said to have been brought here by Thracian settlers. The Muses were nine in number and were the patronesses of the arts and sciences.

On the E. peak of Helikon (5,007 ft.) stood the altar of Helikonian Zeus. The site of the altar is now occupied by the ruined church of the Prophet Elijah, built from the old polygonal masonry of the altar of Zeus. A few yards away is the ancient spring of Hippokrini (the 'horse spring', now Kryopigádi), said to have sprung up when the rock was struck by the hoof of Pegasos. Those who drank from this spring, as of the other poetic spring of Aganippi, were filled with poetic inspiration. To the left of the path up to Helikon, near a small chapel of the Paraskevi, is the site of the sanctuary of the Muses. There was no temple, only an open altar. Here stood the tripod won by Hesiod in the poetic competition in Khalkís, and the statues of the Nine Muses later carried off to Constantinople by Constantine the Great to decorate the Senate-House of his new capital, where they were eventually destroyed in a fire.

The French excavations conducted some years ago revealed the foundations of a Hellenistic *hall* near the altar, and another *hall* on the left bank of the Permessos. Some 330 yards further on are the remains of the *theatre of the Muses* built in the 2C BC for the quadrennial musical games.

On the right in the direction of Helikon rises a small hill on top of which a *tower* can be seen. This was the site of the small ancient city of Askri or Askra. Tradition dates the tower to the age of Hesiod in the 7C BC, but it is in fact Hellenistic, built of finely dressed blocks.

The valley of the Muses is dotted with the fallen walls of many ruined churches built

Askri, Chapel of St.Vlasios ▷

Ο ΑΓΙΟΣ ΓΡΗΓΟΡΙΟΣ ὁ ΘΕΟΛΟΓΟΣ

Ὁ Θεὸς ὁ ἅγιος ὁ ἐν ἁγίοις ἀναπαυόμενος

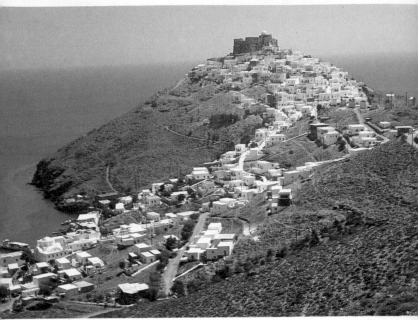

Astypálaia, panorama

from masonry taken from the ancient buildings of Askri. The church of St. Nikólaos a little further off to the S. is supported by columns from the sanctuary of the Muses.

The second small *tower* dates from the period of Catalan domination. It stands to the right on a small elevation in front of the valley of the Muses. Almost a mile to the NW is a lovely 10C Byzantine *chapel*, recently discovered and restored.

Ástros/ΑΣΤΡΟΣ
Arcadia/Peloponnese   p.294□F 10

This little town (pop. 2,675) built on a hill lies 32 km. SE of Trípolis, the capital of Arcadia. Remains of the ancient walls and of a Frankish fort can still be seen.

Environs: Between Ástros and Dolianá is the 12C monastery of **Loukoú** (Lukú), with fine wall paintings and marble floor decorations. Much ancient material was incorporated in the construction, Corinthian capital in the W. door, marble columns in the interior and old ceramics in the outer walls. The area belonged in antiquity to Polemokrates (240 BC), a grandson of Asklepios. In the NE are two granite columns and ancient ruined foundations. Here Herodes Atticus, a rich Athenian of the 2C AD, is said to have had a villa. Finds from the excavations are kept in the little museum in Ástros. **Ágios Andréas** (some 20 km. S.) has remains of Pelasgian walls. Nearby is the *Orthókostas monastery* with fine wall paintings. **Paraléa Tyroú** *(Paralia Tyrú)* (some 40 km. S.) has remains of an ancient acropolis. **Leonídi** (60 km. S.). The village is named after the Byzantine

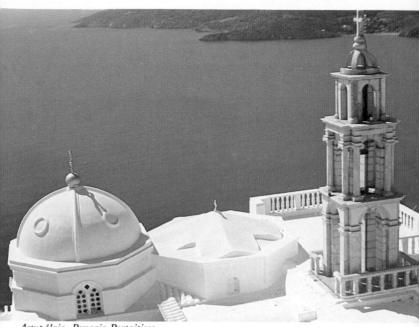

Astypálaia, Panagia Portaitissa

church of Agios Leonidas. Nearby are the *monasteries* of *Síntsa* and *Elóni*.

Astypálaia/ΑΣΤΥΠΑΛΑΙΑ
Dodecanese/E.Aegean Islands
p.300□M/N 11/12

This island (pop. 1200) covers 37.5 sq. miles and consists of two halves joined like the wings of a butterfly by the isthmus of Ágios Andréas which is 7 km. long and in parts only 130 yards wide. This strange, peaceful and picturesque island links the Cyclades with the Dodecanese.

History: The island was settled in the Mycenean period (funerary treasures from the tholos tombs and vases from Armenokhóri). Around 800 BC Dorians from Mégara migrated here. During the Roman period it was autonomous, and in the Middle Ages it was held by the Venetian rulers of Naxos before being taken by the Turks in the 16C. From 1912 it was administered by Italy until it was returned to Greece in 1948.

Astypálaia (also known as *Khóra*): The capital of the island with 800 inhabitants lies on the SW wing of the island on a cape above the port of *Péra Gialós*. It stands on the site of the ancient city of the same name, of which foundations of the *agora* and of various *temples* survive. The church of *Agios Georgios* (the earliest Byzantine island church, with a beautiful carved iconostasis) was built on the remains of an ancient temple. The marble fragments in the church's façade were taken from the ancient acropolis. The *Kastro* was rebuilt around 1240 by the Venetian family of Guerini. It consists of crowded houses backing onto the mountain slope. Outside the fort is the interesting church of the *Panagia Portaitissa* ('Gate church'), one of the loveliest island churches in the Dodecanese. It was founded in 1764 by the monk Anthimos, and contains a carved iconostasis. The miraculous icon of the Portaitissa is a copy of that in the Athonite monastery of Iberon.

Environs: In the village of *Maltesana* (4 km. NE) is a *Roman bath* with well-preserved mosaics. The monastery of *Ágios Ioánnis* lies some 12 km. NE in superb surroundings with fine views over the sea. Not far away are the ruins of the Venetian *castle* of this name dating from the 13C. By the sea is the monastery of Agía Livýa. Near the fishing-village of *Vathý* (25 km. NE) are the interesting *Dragon Caves (Spílaio Dráku)*, and nearby the monastery of the *Panagia* showing eastern influence. Scattered over the whole island are some 200 votive chapels built in thanks for safe returns by sailors.

Atalánti/ΑΤΑΛΑΝΤΗ
Phthiótis (Ftiótis)/Central Greece   p.294☐G 7

This attractive town (pop. *c.* 4,600) lies on the N. slopes of Mt.Khlomo (3,610 ft.), and is named after the Boeotian Amazon and huntress Atalánta. During the Middle Ages (14C) it was the seat of a Catalan governor. Atalánti lies some 75 km. SE of the city of Lamía, and its port of *Skála* (5 km. E.) is connected by ship with Khalkís across the Gulf of Euboea (Évripos). In Skála are the remains of what was probably the ancient Lokrian capital of Opoús. Opposite lies the little island known since antiquity as *Atalánti*, which lent its name to the small bay (Gulf of Atalánti). Fine views.

Environs: Passing through the little towns of *Proskynás* (18 km. SE) and *Malesína* (24 km. SE) one comes to the monastery of **Ágios Geórgios** on the coast. Close by are the *ruins* of the 11C Byzantine monastery with frescos by the 16C painter Kakava in the church. The monastery was rebuilt following the earthquake of 1894 (church 1920). On the Gulf of Atalánti (to the E.) are the ruins of the ancient port of **Halaí** (modern *Alaí*), which flowered in the 4CBC, was destroyed by Sulla in the 1C BC, and inhabited up to Byzantine times. There survive the remains of the *ramparts* with towers and bastions: the earlier of these is in polygonal masonry dating from the 6C BC, the second more extensive set dating from the 4C BC; gates in the NE and NW. The street leading S. goes to the sanctuary of Athena (6C BC) with a temple, cult statue, altar and cultic spring (restored at a later date). The friendly coastal town of **Lárymna** (*c.* 30 km. SE) has harbour-works of the 4C BC, when it was the easternmost port of Lokrís on the Gulf of Euboea. The seaside resort of **Kaména Vúrla** (40 km. NW) has been famed since antiquity for its radioactive healing springs (for arthritis, neuritis and rheumatism). On the neighbouring mountain slopes are the remains of a sanctuary of Asklepios. Nearby is the 16C **Monastery of the Metamórfosis** with *frescos* (*c.* 1725–57).

Athens/Athínai/ΑΘΗΝΑΙ
Attica/Central Greece   p.296☐H 9

Myth and History

3500 BC: The earliest traces of settlement have been found on the S. and N. slopes of the acropolis hill, and are dated by some scholars to 5000 BC. Wells were dug around 3500 BC by these early inhabi-

Athena of Piraeus (Arch.Mus.) ▷

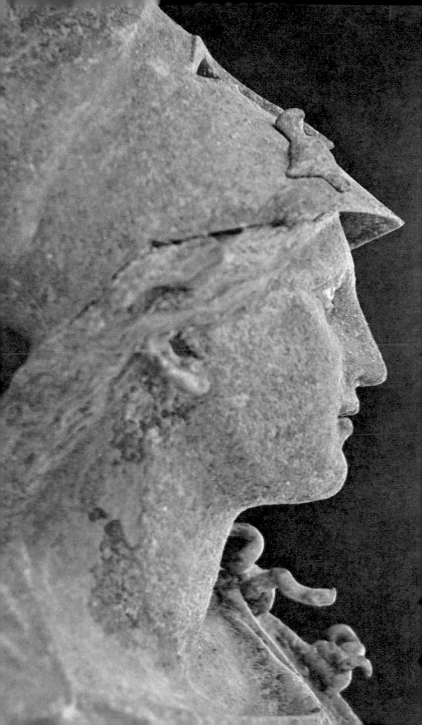

tants, known to tradition as the Pelasgians. The cultivation of olives and vines was also apparently known to them.

2000 BC: In the course of the migrations of populations, Ionians entered Attica around 1900 BC—they also called themselves Hellenes.

The prehistory of Athens is known to us only from myths and legends, including those recorded by Apollodoros. According to these the first king of Athens was called Kekrops, said to have had the body of a snake. He introduced the first laws and took a census of the people. His tomb is in the Caryatid porch of the Erechtheion. The gods Poseidon and Athena are said to have had a contest for the possession of Attica, in which Athena emerged victorious, giving her name to the city.

The rulers who succeeded Kekrops were Kranos, Amphiktyon, and Erichthonios. The latter, son of Hephaistos and Athena, also had the body of a snake. During his reign the wooden cult-statue of Athena was erected. He was succeeded by his son Pandion, and then by Erechtheus, his grandson, who inhabited, according to Homer, Odyssey 7,81, a safe stronghold, a fortress which must have encircled the acropolis with its defensive walls around 1300 BC. Remains of this can still be seen today in the Cyclopean walls behind the E. wing of the Propylaia. He was followed by Kekrops II and Pandion II, and finally by Aigeus, the king who is said by tradition to have cast himself down from the cliffs of the acropolis when he saw his son Theseus's ship returning from Crete set with black sails. Aigeus believed that Theseus was dead, since he had agreed that his ship would return under black sails if his mission failed and the Minotaur had not been overcome. Theseus had forgotten in his triumphant return to hoist the white sails. The Aegean Sea takes its name from the unfortunate Aigeus.

Acropolis with the Odeion of Herodes Atticus ▷

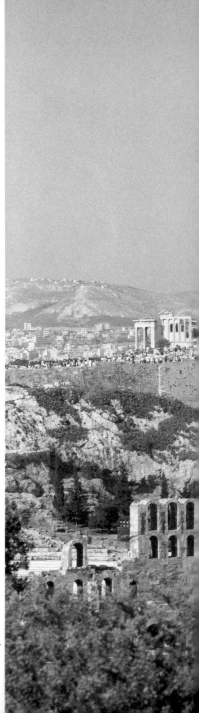

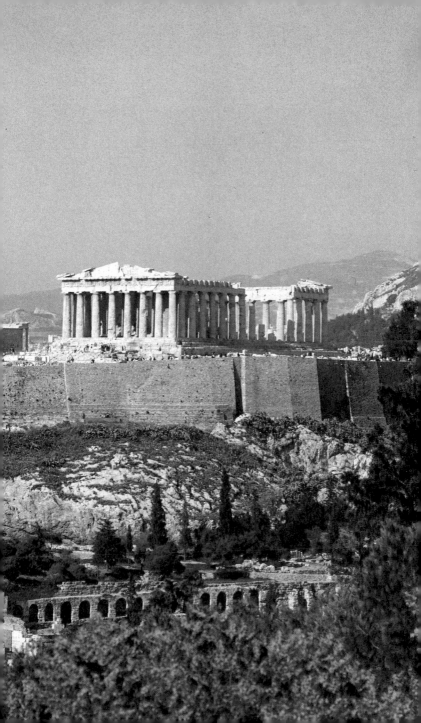

1300 BC: It was during the reign of the legendary Theseus that Attica, then divided into twelve city states engaged in mutual struggle, was unified. This unification (synoecism) occurred in 1259 under the leadership of Athens. Modern historians prefer to date this process early in the 1st millennium BC. In any case, it was upon this that Athens's position of preeminence over many centuries was based. The acropolis, with its cult centres of Athena and Poseidon, became the chief shrine of Attica.

Theseus was the author of many legendary deeds. He killed not only the Minotaur, the bull-headed monster of Crete, to which young Athenian men and maidens had to be sacrificed yearly, but also highwaymen like Prokrustes. He fought against the Centaurs and Amazons, abducted Helen from Sparta, and was eventually murdered by King Lykomedes on the island of Skyros. It was only in 475 that Kimon brought his bones back to Athens and erected the Theseion there in his honour.

Around this time Attica had developed crafts, as evidenced in the grave finds made to the NW of the Greek agora, where the dead had been buried since the 12C BC. Between 950 and 700 vase-painting was dominated by the Geometric style, with the advent of Dipylon vases around 750, and the first monumental sculptures around 700. Works in bronze were chiefly made on the agora hill. From the 7C BC, Athens was exporting vases as well as wine and oil. By the 6C Attic pottery was ever more sought after throughout the Mediterranean, and surpassed Corinthian ware.

683 BC: After the time of Theseus the power of the nobility grew ever greater whilst the kings diminished in authority. The leading families of Attica settled in Athens. The city grew rapidly around the acropolis, and in 683 the kings finally lost all power, which was divided among the nine archons who resided near the Prytaneion in the N. part of the early agora. This must have been the site of the public buildings. Each of the archons had his own sphere of authority—justice, leading the army, and so forth—and they held their offices for the duration of their lives. From 686 various archons were elected annually, but still from the nobility. The rest of the population, particularly the farmers, had to pay taxes and became increasingly oppressed, until they rebelled, one of the principal reasons for this action being that Attica's livelihood was based on agriculture. The money economy was introduced as exports grew, and though this benefited traders, it left the peasantry in a position of complete dependence. The people longed for a new constitution.

624 BC: In 624 Drakon promulgated a new code of laws, in which the code of penalties was overhauled. Their severity remains a byword to this day.

594 BC: Solon promulgated new laws. In particular he broke the power of the nobility through his agrarian reforms. He abolished bondage for debt and introduced reforms in coinage, weights and measures. He divided the people into four classes according to their taxable capacity, and gave all classes a part in the administration of justice. Solon was not successful in internal politics alone. In fact he was only able to conduct internal affairs so successfully because he could point to his considerable achievements in foreign affairs. He defeated the city of Sigeion on the Hellespont, and the island of Salamis. This was the start of Athens's expansion as a naval power. The code of Solon was influential in later times throughout Greece and the Greek colonies, and even on Roman law. The aristocracy who had lost their power under Solon sought constantly to regain their former privileges. Solon introduced the Council of the Four Hundred as a counterbalance to the

Amphora (6C BC, Arch. Mus.) ▷

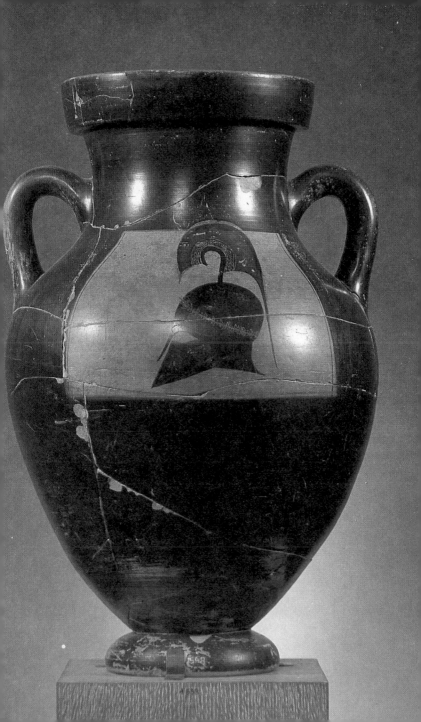

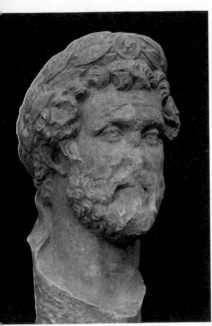

Head of an old man

Head of a young man

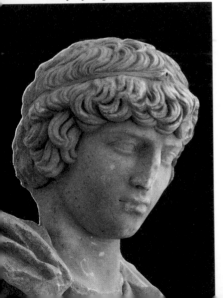

Areopagos. This council guaranteed democracy in Athens at a time when the rest of Greece had already reverted to aristocratic government. When Solon had created order in Athens he left the city. He was later counted among the 'Seven Sages'.

561 BC: After Solon had left the city, troubles once again broke out. The poorest among the population, the small peasant farmers in the surrounding area, revolted. Their leaders were joined by Peisistratos, a nobleman from Brauron, who besieged the acropolis in 561 with the assistance of his bodyguard. He was put to flight, but returned and from 546 until his death in 528 he was an absolute, but according to Aristotle, a democratically-minded, tyrant, to whom Athens owed much. Peisistratos was responsible for building the temple of Athena Polias. The Propylaia was rebuilt, and the Olympieion, one of the largest temples of antiquity, was begun but never completed, as was the temple of Dionysos Eleuthereus near the present theatre of Dionysos. Countless statues were erected. Ionian artists brought marble from Paros and Naxos into Athens. The same period saw the development of the black-figure style of vase-painting (from about 560 onwards), and three decades later the red-figure style. Peisistratos introduced the cult of Dionysos and the Panathenaea festival, as well as the tragic agon (competition) at the greater Dionysia. Thespis was the first tragedian, and with him the age of Greek tragedy was born. Peisistratos's sons Hippias and Hipparchos who succeeded their father as rulers also contributed to the rise of Athenian culture. Hipparchos was murdered in the agora in 514 as a result of the personal enmity of Harmodios and Aristogeiton, who were subsequently celebrated as having freed Athens from the yoke of tyranny. In 510 Hippias, who had finally developed into

Peplos kore (Arch. Mus.) ▷

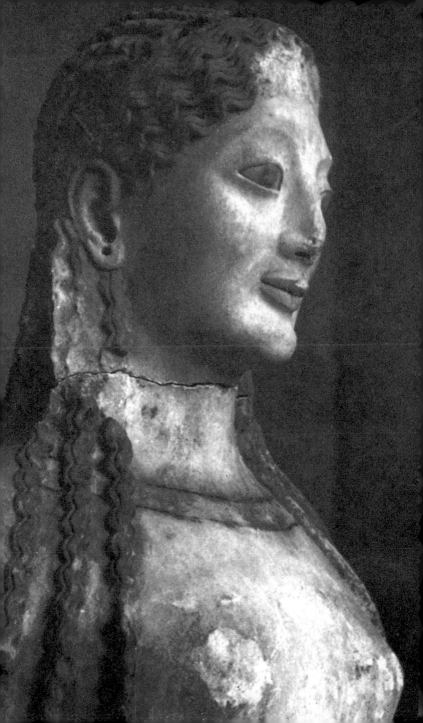

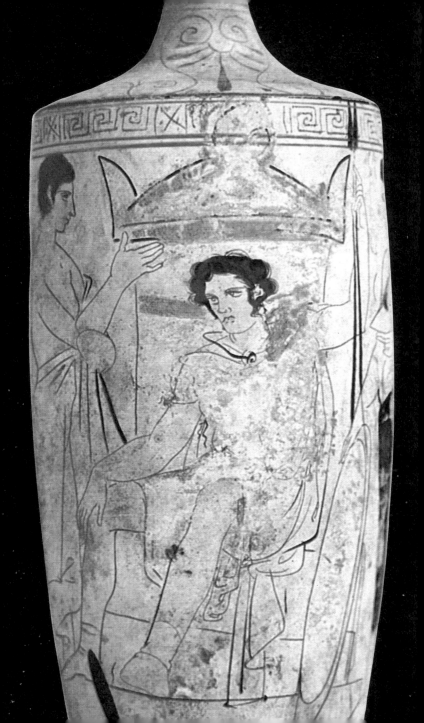

a tyrant in the modern sense, was expelled by the Alkmaionids.

510 BC: The fall of the tyrants provoked a crisis. The alliances with Thessaly, Eretria, Argos, Macedonia, and Sparta collapsed. After the fall of Polykrates in 522 the Persians extended their empire to the W. and laid siege to Samos.

507 BC: In 507 Kleisthenes, the leading representative of the Alkmaionids, proclaimed a new democratic constitution. He divided Attica into 10 phylai (tribes); the Council was formed of 500 members elected by lot, and executive power was wielded by nine archons, also elected by lot. Kleisthenes also introduced ostracism, by means of which enemies of the government could be exiled for ten years.

500 BC: From this time onwards the Persians were attempting to expand their empire. In 499 Athens sent a fleet to the Ionian colonies in order to repel Persian influence. As a result the Persian King Darius attacked Greece itself. In 490 BC the Persians made a landing in the Bay of Marathon, but the Athenians were able to repulse them with the support of troops from Plataia. Meanwhile Themistokles was continuing to build up the Athenian fleet to 200 warships. In 480 the Persians made a second attack under Darius's son Xerxes. The population of Attica was evacuated and the land left to the enemy. The Persian supreme commander Mardonios destroyed the fortress on the acropolis and archaic Athens was completely ravaged, its population having fled to Salamis. In the same year, in the straits of Salamis, Themistokles drew up his fleet against the Persians, who occupied the whole of Attica. The Persians suffered such a serious defeat that Xerxes withdrew into Asia Minor, but his commander Mardonios, with his considerable land force, fell on Plataia in Boeotia in 479, where he suffered a decisive defeat, as did

◁ *Vase from Erétria (Arch. Mus.)*

the Persian fleet at Mykale. With the end of the Persian War Athenian self-consciousness was markedly strengthened. The task of rebuilding the city was immediately taken up; Piraeus was laid out as a port city and the city walls constructed under Themistokles (remains can still be seen in the Kerameikos district). In 478 the first Attic naval league was formed with Athens taking the leading role. Themistokles was exiled by the Athenians in 471, despite all his services to the city. His successor Kimon, a member of the old nobility, and popular with rich and poor alike for his generosity, devoted himself with equal care to building up the city anew. The agora was rebuilt under him, and in 475 two porticoes and the Stoa Poikile (coloured portico) were built. The acropolis wall was also re-erected during his time.

465 BC: Kimon finally succeeded in breaking Persian naval power with his victory at the battle of the Eurymedon, and he died in 449 BC after two naval victories off Cyprus. During Kimon's time Aischylos's drama 'The Persians' was produced in the theatre of Dionysos (471). Pindar composed his odes, and Polygnotos, Mikon and Panainos painted the Stoa Poikile.

461 BC: With Kimon in exile, Perikles became the leading figure in the state, a position which he retained until his death in 429. It was he who entrusted the reconstruction of the buildings on the acropolis to Pheidias, and this period is known as the Periclean age, an age inextricably linked with the highest cultural achievements of Athens, the first high European culture since the time of Crete, and for many the highest point of civilization anywhere. The period is also known as the Golden Age. Between 461 and 429 Athens flourished in foreign affairs, internal politics, and above all in culture.

Kimon had been on friendly terms with Sparta; indeed it was this which led to his downfall. In 462 Perikles broke with the

Peloponnesian city. The struggle against Sparta divided the whole land into two parties and led to numerous wars. Athens was expanding, founding colonies with its fleet. Perikles was also extremely active in home affairs, introducing democratic reforms and many new ordinances such as free entry to the theatre. A third wall alongside the 'Long Walls' linking Athens to Piraeus was built by Kallikrates. Perikles encouraged the arts and sciences, and artists and sages from all over Greece were attracted to Athens. The city was the home of the philosopher Sokrates, the tragedian Sophokles the comedian Aristophanes, the architects Mnesikles, Iktinos, and Kallikrates, the sculptors Myron, Pheidias, Kalamis, Alkamenes and Agorakritos, and the painters Polygnotos and Panainos. Another figure of the day was the historian Herodotos, who was publicly honoured for his work in Athens in 445.

The Odeion of Perikles and the temple of Dionysos arose on the E. slopes of the acropolis, and the temple of Hephaistos was built in the agora. In 448 BC work began on the reconstruction of the temple of Athena on the acropolis, and from 438 to 432 the Propylaia were rebuilt by Mnesikles. The temple of Athena Nike was also built, and in the city the Lykaion gymnasion.

431 BC: This year saw the outbreak of the Second Peloponnesian War, which was to bring about the downfall of Athens. Sparta was no longer willing to recognize Athens's position of predominance, and between 431 and 404 the two city-states were engaged in many battles. Alkibiades and the Athenians won two victories over the Spartans before being defeated. Then in 406 the Athenian fleet under Konon defeated the Spartans. After 405 the Spartans led by Lysander and Nearchos gained the ascendant. In 404 Athens was forced to surrender. Lysander razed the walls of Piraeus and the 'Long Walls'; Athens, which had in the interim been ravaged by plague

(Perikles died of the plague in 429), lost its fleet and its power. Sparta had suffered serious losses during the war also, but took over the hegemony of Greece.

Despite this, the war did not put an abrupt end to the cultural flowering of Athens. In 421 the Hephaisteion was consecrated. Building work continued on the Erechtheion, a new temple arose within the compound of Dionysos, and in 420 the sanctuaries of Asklepios and Hygieia were erected on the S. slopes. Important sculptures and paintings continued to be created and comedy reached its apogee with Aristophanes, as did philosophy with Sokrates and Plato. Nonetheless, Athens's fertile creative period was over, as the trial and conviction of Sokrates in 399 testifies.

404 BC: This year brought the end of the Peloponnesian War and with it the end of democracy. Athens was ruled by the Thirty Tyrants. It was not long, however, before Thrasyboulos reintroduced democracy in 403. Athens gained power once again, and was able to annihilate the Spartan fleet at Knidos in 394.

378 BC: An alliance with Thebes laid the foundations for the Second Attic Sea League. Athens's naval hegemony was once more guaranteed. However, the shifting politics of alliances which Athens now undertook in order to ensure its pre-eminence weakened rather than strengthened the city.

The 4C in Athens was the age of philosophy, with Plato and Aristotle, but it was also the age of the great orators, with Isokrates, Lysias, Isaios and Aischines, and their successor Demosthenes. A new peak of sculptural excellence was reached with Kephisodotos and his son Praxiteles, and with Leochares, Skopas and Euphranor, whilst painting flourished with Pamphilos and Parrhasios. The theatre of Dionysos and the stadion were built in stone under

Zeus or Poseidon, bronze figure (Arch. ▷
Mus.)

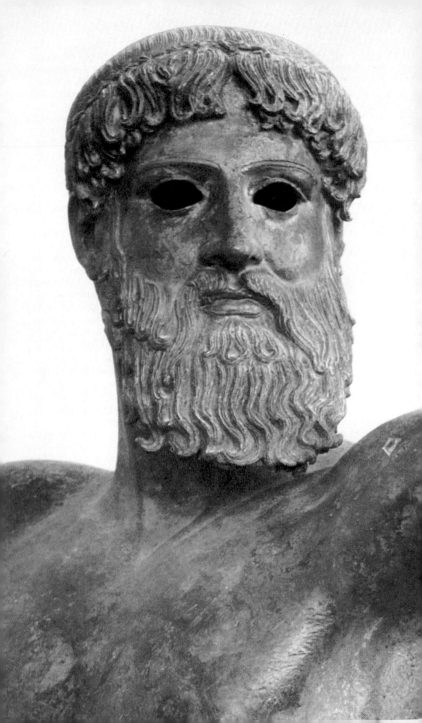

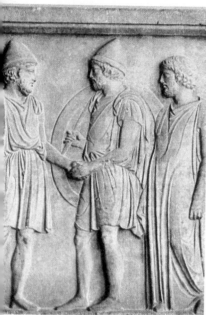

Relief of a Boeotian soldier

Female Tanagra figurine (Kanellópulos Collection)

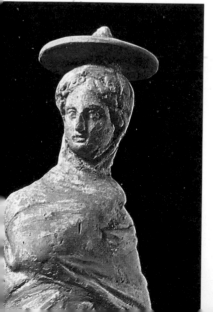

Lykourgos, who was first and foremost an able administrator of finances. Defensive structures arose in Piraeus and in the city. **338 BC:** Meanwhile, however, Macedonia had risen to a position of pre-eminence under Philip II, and in 338 the Athenians were defeated by the Macedonians at Chaironeia. Demosthenes had stood up against Philip II in his speeches (first Philippic, 351), and was subsequently condemned to death. In 336 Philip's son Alexander, later the Great, came to power. He was to influence the destinies not only of Macedonia but of all Greece, not to mention Asia Minor and western Asia as far as India and Tashkent, and part of Africa as well. Athens became ever more dependent on Macedonia, and in 322 was occupied by the Macedonians. However, Alexander proved receptive to Athenian culture, having a little earlier returned to Athens the statue of the 'Tyrannicides' by Antenor, which the Persians had carried off.

300 BC: With the 3C Athens entered the so-called Hellenistic age; in power and cultural influence it was growing ever weaker although it was still independent. But the city's political fortunes were variable, and it fluctuated between dependence and autonomy.

The cult of Serapis was introduced into Athens as a result of the city's friendship with Egypt. After the Khremonidean War Athens once again fell under Macedonian sway, and in 217 was raided by Aitolian and Cretan pirates. In 220 Philip V of Macedon invaded Athens. Then Attalos I of Pergamon and (for the first time) the Romans presented themselves as the city's protectors. From this time on the Romans made themselves the city's patrons and defenders.

168 BC: The Macedonians were defeated by the Romans at Pydna, and Athens was declared a 'libera civitas'. The kings of Pergamon also extended their protection to

Philosopher from Anticythera (Arch.Mus.) ▷

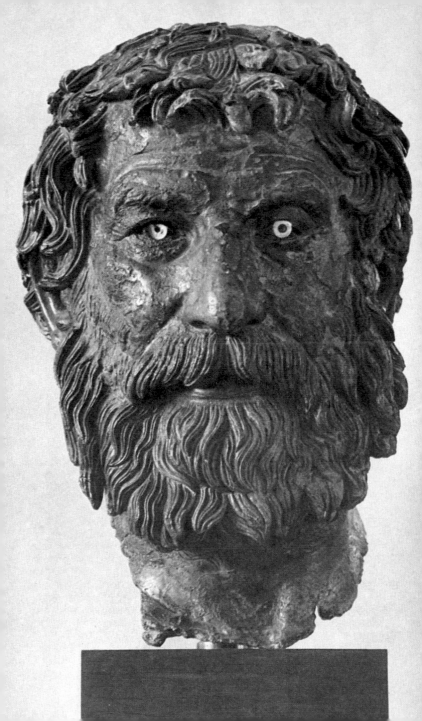

Athens, continuing building works on the Olympieion. The independence of its classical culture was, however, destroyed. **88 BC**: The Council voluntarily submitted to Mithridates VI of Pontus, even lending him support in his war against Rome. His cruelty provoked an angry reaction from Rome, and in 86 BC the Roman general Sulla took Athens and destroyed it. This marked the end of any political importance for Athens, although its cultural importance continued to be great under Roman rule. Roman art and philosophy, indeed its entire civilization developed under strong Athenian influence. The damage caused by Sulla was repaired by donations from Rome, Asia Minor, and Syria. Athens was already living, as indeed it still does, off the memory of the Periklean age and the wonder which the remains and ruins of that age provoked. In 27 BC Athens was given the status of a free city in alliance with Rome by Augustus, who built a new agora near the Tower of the Winds. A little later Agrippa founded a large theatre for the old agora. A round temple dedicated to Roma and Augustus was built on the acropolis. Even Athens was party to the deification of the Roman emperors.

AD 49: The apostle Paul visited Athens; from this time on the adherents of Christianity increased slowly but steadily.

AD 124: Between AD 124 and 131 the Emperor Hadrian paid three visits to Athens. This cultured emperor patronized the city, extending its area by a quarter to the E. of the Hadrian Gate. The speciality of this period was copying classical masterpieces. The next to occupy the role of patron in AD 150 was the orator Herodes Atticus of Marathon. He built the Panathenaic stadion, a temple to Tyche, and a theatre on the SE slopes of the acropolis.

AD 267: In AD 170 the Kostobokoi raided the city, and in 267 Athens and Attica were invaded and ravaged by the Goths and Herulians, who were defeated by Herenios Dexippos. Under Constantine the Great

(306–37) and later under Theodosios II (408–50) works of art were carried off from Athens to Constantinople, which became the capital of the Byzantine empire in 330. In 375 the city was damaged by a severe earthquake, and in 396 Alaric, who was drawn up with his troops before Athens, was so impressed by the sight of the Athena Promachos that he withdrew without attacking the city.

AD 393: The Olympic Games were banned by Theodosios I, but the Panathenaia continued to be held. In the years following 360 the Emperor Julian the Apostate attempted to reintroduce the ancient religion, but Theodosios II, who was married to the daughter of an Athenian philosopher, closed the pagan temples in Athens in 429.

AD 529: Justinian closed the University of Athens. During his reign Greek works of art were removed from Athens, including the Athena Promachos which was still standing in Constantinople in the 9C. Increasing numbers of buildings dedicated to the ancient gods were Christianized. Thus the Parthenon was dedicated first to Hagia Sophia, then to the Panagia. The Erechtheion was turned into a chapel and the temple of Hephaistos into a church of St. George.

733: Athens broke off from the Latin church and became a dependency of Constantinople. In 769 the Athenian Irene became Empress of Constantinople, as did her fellow-townswoman Theophano in 807.

857: Athens became the seat of an Archbishop and the Parthenon his cathedral. From the 11C more and more churches were built in Athens and throughout Attica.

1204: In 1147 the Normans laid siege to Piraeus. In 1204 the French Crusaders took Athens, and Constantinople was taken by the Franks. Athens with Boeotia and

Vase from Erétria (Arch. Mus.) ▷

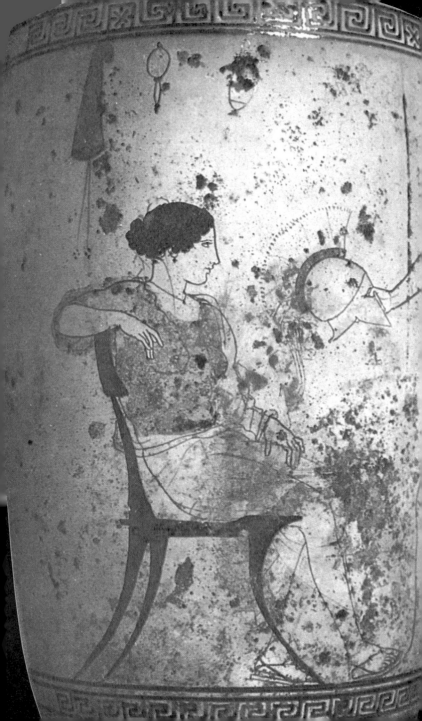

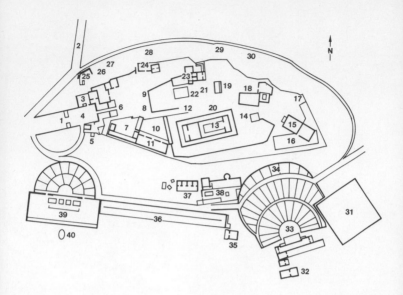

Acropolis (after J.Travlos): The numbers on this plan refer to the sections in the description of the Acropolis in the text.

Megaris was given to the knight Othon de la Roche, and in 1260 became a Frankish duchy.

1311: The Catalans took Athens, and the Florentines captured it in 1387. The Florentine Dukes built their palace in the Propylaia and began new buildings on the acropolis.

1546: Three years after the fall of Constantinople the Turks under Mehmed II conquered Athens, where they remained until the 19C, in spite of Venetian attempts to capture it in 1466 and 1687. The Parthenon was now converted from a cathedral into a mosque, while the Propylaia became the residence of the Turkish governor, and the Erechtheion that of his harem.

1645: During the 16C the buildings on the acropolis suffered two unlucky and serious blows. In 1645 lightning struck the gunpowder magazine in the Propylaia, damaging the whole superstructure. Then in 1687 the Parthenon was destroyed by an exploding gunpowder magazine. Further portions of the works of art were destroyed by collectors or carried off, whilst Athens itself continued to decline in importance. Only two Turkish mosques survive, the Syntrivani on Monastiraki Square and the Fetihie Cami near the Tower of the Winds; and these have lost their minarets.

1821: During the War of Liberation Athens decided for the revolution and in 1822 forced the Turks to capitulate.

1833: After many bitter struggles between Greeks and Turks, King Otho of Bavaria finally entered Athens in triumph. In 1834 he raised Athens to the status of capital of

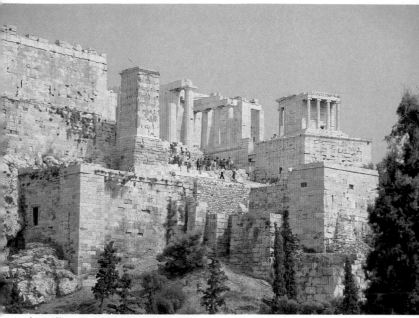

Acropolis, entrance ramp and Propylaia

his new Kingdom of Greece. The population grew rapidly. Otho was interested only in ancient Athens, and allowed many medieval and later buildings to be torn down. K.F. Schinkel was commisioned to build a new royal palace on the acropolis but the archaeologists fought successfully to preserve the ancient ruins inviolate. In 1834 Klenze's design for the city was accepted as the basis of future building.

1863: The Bavarian Wittelsbach line was displaced by the Glücksburgs in the person of King George I. The German architects were succeeded by the Danish architects Chr. and Th. Hansen who continued to build in the classical style. Chr. Hansen drew up the plans for the University built in 1839–49, and Th. Hansen those of the Academy, built 1885–91, which display marked neo-Renaissance and neo-baroque influences. Athens now regained its position as the spiritual, artistic and political capital of Greece. In economic terms too it had developed rapidly. The population was no longer purely Greek, but had elements from every part; it continued to grow rapidly. In 1839 it numbered around 2,500, by 1928 it had risen to 704,247, and today Athens has 2.5 million inhabitants.

20C: The history of Athens in the 19&20C has been no less turbulent than in earlier centuries. Changes of government, revolts, and quarrels with the East have all played their part. The First and Second World Wars brought further unrest to the political scene. In 1924 Greece became a republic, in 1935 the monarchy was restored, in 1936 Metaxas became dictator, in 1940 Mussolini invaded the country, in 1941 Hitler, and in 1944 the Communist resistance movements began hostilities. In 1947 Paul

I ascended the throne. Papagos brought an end to the civil war in 1949, becoming Prime Minister from 1952 to 1955. He was succeeded by Karamanlis, who held the office until 1963 and was re-elected in 1974 in the first democratic elections in the new republic. In 1964–5 G.Papandreou was Prime Minister. In 1967 King Constantine II, who had succeeded his father Paul, was forced into exile by a military coup d'état, and deposed in 1973. Papadopoulos was dictator 1967–73.

During the whole of this period Athens continued to increase in importance as capital. Athens and Piraeus coalesced into a great city with tower blocks and modern buildings. Once again Athens has become world-famous for its ancient culture. Long before the rediscovery of the Minoan Cretan culture Athens was felt to be the cradle of all European culture, and even today it is considered to represent the high point of western cultural achievement.

The Acropolis

The main attraction in Athens is the acropolis or 'High City'. It stands on a limestone cliff 512 ft. high, 885 ft. long and over 512 ft. wide. Seen from the W. the acropolis rises over the plain on top of a steep cliff. This made it a good site for a fortress, and later for the raised site of the temples of the gods. The acropolis seems to have already been settled around 3,000 BC. About 1500 BC this high-lying settlement was surrounded with a defensive wall with its main gate to the W. In the NE of this wall a gate pierced a tower to give access to the fortress within the walls. In the W. of the acropolis, near the clepsydra wells, dwellings from the Mycenean period have been uncovered. Around the end of the 13C the old defensive walls were replaced by the Cylopean walls, also knwon as the Pelasgikon or Pelargikon, remains of which could be seen, e.g. S. of the Parthenon.

Front of the Temple of Athena Nike ▷

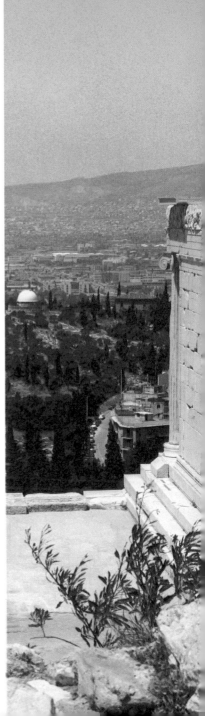

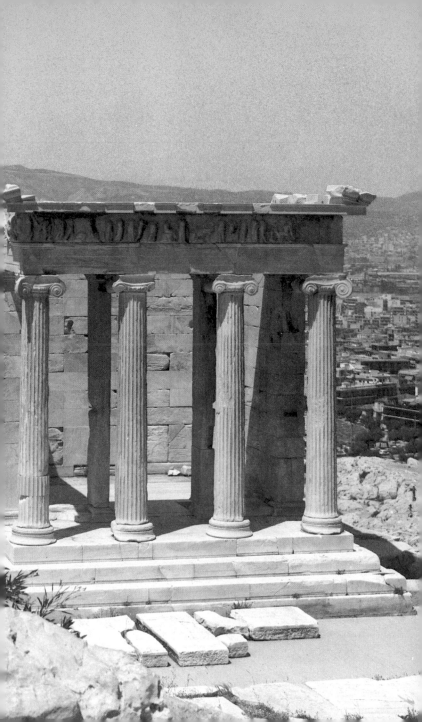

The NE gate was replaced by underground steps on the N. side.

Under Peisistratos and his sons the W. entrance in the Cyclopean walls was converted into a propylon. In 510 the Delphic oracle announced that the Cyclopean walls were unlucky and they were completely razed. When the Persians invaded in 480 the sanctuaries on the acropolis were destroyed. Later Themistokles rebuilt the defensive wall in the W and N. incorporating the ruins of earlier structures. Next Kimon enlarged the acropolis plateau to the S. and built the E. and S. walls. Ruins of earlier buildings from the so-called 'Persian rubble' were once more used. Finally, under Perikles, arose the buildings which have made Athens famous, the Parthenon, Propylaia, temple of Athena Nike, and the Erechtheion.

During the Roman period their survival was ensured by the prevailing respect for classical art. Under Turkish rule they suffered serious damage from the gunpowder explosions, particularly that in the Parthenon in 1687. In the 19&20C the acropolis began to recover its original shape and to be restored under the influence of classicism and growing archaeological knowledge. The latest threat to the ancient buildings in our own day is constituted by the gigantic influx of visitors, the effects of aeroplanes and exhaust pollution, all very serious. UNESCO have undertaken a 15 million dollar programme to save the acropolis, and protected areas have been created which may not be entered. Protective flooring and roofing and protective scaffolding have been installed. Aeroplanes are now forbidden to overfly the acropolis and visitors are required to comply with the conditions of entry.

1. Beulé Gate: The modern entrance to the acropolis is through the Beulé Gate on the S. slopes. It was built from the ruins of earlier buildings after the Herulian invasion in AD 267, and walled up again under the Turks. In 1853 Ernest Beulé removed the masonry to reveal the gate which served originally as an outer bastion of the Propylaia.

2. Panathenaic Way: The Panathenaic

Side of the Temple of Athena Nike

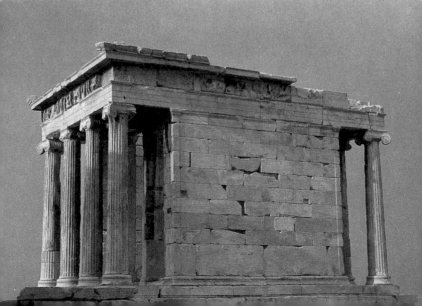

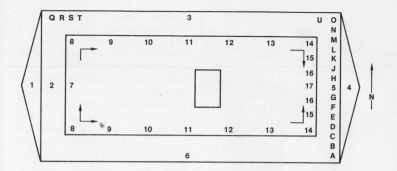

Parthenon, pediment, metopes and frieze

The sculpture on the Parthenon is world famous; it comprises 92 Doric metopes (2,3,5,6) dating from 447–0, which were carved by various sculptors in their workshops and only then added to the temple exterior. There were 14 on both the W. and E. fronts, and 32 on the N. and S., but only 40 of the 92 still survive, and some are seriously damaged; there are now 13 on the N. and only one on the S. 15 are housed in the British Museum in London, one in the Louvre and 3 in the Acropolis Museum. The heavily damaged metopes on the W. side (2) depict the battle against the Amazons.

Those on the E. (5) show the battle of the giants. From S. to N.: Hermes (A), Dionysus (B), Aries and giant (C), Athena (D), Amphitride steering a chariot (E), Poseidon defeating the giant Polybotos (F), Hera steering Zeus's chariot (G), Zeus (H), Apollo fighting (I), Artemis steering Apollo's chariot (K), Herakles (L), Aphrodite fighting a giant (M), Hephaistos (N), Helios's sun chariot (O). The S. side, which depicts the battle with the centaurs, has only one surviving metope, showing a centaur throttling a Greek (P). The N. metopes (3) show the Trojan War, and the surviving sections depict a council of the gods (Q–S) and Selene with a beast of prey, then a few scenes from the Trojan War and a representation of the sun chariot of Helios.

In the interior, Ionic friezes over 3 ft. high decorate the outside walls of the cella; these, also, are only preserved in a fragmentary state. A large section of the original frieze is in the British Museum in London or in the Acropolis Museum, and one piece is in the Louvre in Paris. The friezes probably date from after the metopes and display the illusion of depth introduced by Pheidias, who used his experience as an architect to develop sculpture. It is clear that the work is the product of a number of sculptors, but was created under Pheidias's supervision. The whole frieze depicts the Panathenaic procession, which travelled every four years from the gymnasion at the Dipylon over the agora to the acropolis. It comprised maidens with sacrificial objects (calves and lambs, 13), youths (12), musicians (11), old men with olive branches (10), and finally the splendidly woven Peplos, which was brought on a chariot to the goddess Athena. The Athenian population followed the procession.

The preparations for the Panathenaic procession were depicted on the W. side of the outside cella wall. The images of the horses which have survived are still astonishingly lifelike in their movement. The festival procession was then led round both the N. and S. sides with horsemen (8) and chariots (9) round to the E. side, where a group of deities is depicted in the middle section of the exterior wall waiting to greet the Panathenaic procession.

The two pediments (1 and 4) were the last to be built, dating from 432, and have marble sculptures. Everything points to their having been designed by Pheidias, but there must have been many sculptors involved. The work again uses perspective, with the movement of the figures and their relation to each other playing an important role. Little of the original sculpture still remains on the gables: most of it is in the British Museum in London, in the Louvre in Paris, and in the Vatican in Rome, with some sections in the Acropolis Museum and the National Museum in Athens. What remains on the Parthenon is heavily weathered, and some sections, such as a horse's head and the reclining figure on the E. pediment, are copies. The original work on the W. pediment (1) includes the contest between Athena and Poseidon, and on the E. pediment (4) the birth of Athena from the head of Zeus, her father.

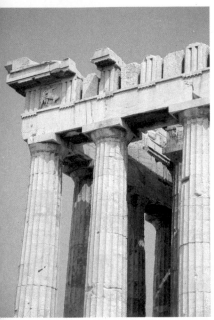

Acropolis, Parthenon, detail

Parthenon, Doric columns and frieze

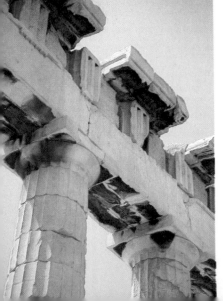

Way was originally supported by steep entrance ramps, the walls of which can be seen at this point. It was Theseus who founded the Great Panathenaia in honour of Athena, patron goddess of the city. In 566 BC Peisistratos refounded the Panathenaic festivals which were held quadrennially thereafter, with the great Panathenaic procession from the agora to the temple of Athena on the acropolis. The Panathenaic Way was built specifically for this when the earlier ways proved too narrow for the thousands of participants in the festival. Today the Way winds up to the Propylaia passing by the temple of Athena Nike.

3. Monument of Agrippa: Opposite the temple of Athena Nike on the left-hand side the plinth of the monument of Agrippa has been discovered on a platform. It is made of Hymettos marble and was erected in the 2C BC. The platform was built in the 5C BC by Mnesikles.

4. Open Staircase: In the 1C AD a monumental staircase to the Propylaia was built. The marble staircase which stretched from the Beulé Gate was removed in the 19C; a few steps can still be seen on this spot.

5. Temple of Athena Nike: On the right stands the perfectly proportioned little temple of Athena Nike, on a projecting spur in the SW of the acropolis called Pyrgos, in front of the S. part of the Propylaia. The Ionic columns and richly decorated frieze are extremely beautiful. The relief on the E. and S. façades has been re-erected, but the slabs constituting the rest of the frieze are now in the British Museum in London and have been replaced by copies. The frieze in the E. shows the assembly of the gods on Mt.Olympus. Originally the temple was richly painted

Parthenon ▷

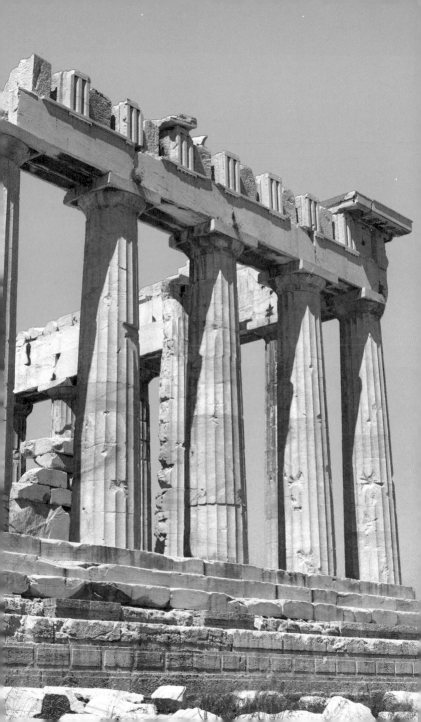

with floral patterns. The whole temple was taken down and rebuilt by the Turks in 1687, and restored to its original state in 1835. Further reconstruction took place in 1935 and 1939. Beneath the surviving temple of Athena Nike a cult site of Athena Nike, the Athenian goddess of victory, must have been built around 550 BC and destroyed by the Persians in 480. The cella paving shows traces of the old altar. The present temple was begun in Pentelic marble in 447 BC with Kallikrates as architect, and work continued until around 427. In 425 or 421 the wooden cult-statue of Athena Nike was dedicated. This statue is described by Pausanias, according to whom the goddess held a pomegranate, symbol of fertility, in her right hand and a helmet in her left. The wings of the Athena Nike were removed to prevent her flying away. Around 410 BC a marble balustrade, now in the Acropolis Museum, was built around the temple. It was from here, according to legend, that Aigeus threw himself down from the cliffs when he saw his son Theseus returning home, his ship flying black sails.

6. Propylaia: The way now leads directly to the famous Propylaia. The word Propylon means a lobby or the entrance to a temple. The original Mycenean gate was a propylon of this type in front of the sanctuary of Athena. It is assumed that a new Propylon was built in the 6C BC for the Panathenaia. From about 490 onwards another Propylon was under construction, and was destroyed by the Persians in 480. Thus it fell to the architect Mnesikles to build yet another new Propylon, and he conceived the monumental entrances or 'Propylaia' to lead up to the Parthenon. In 437 BC he began the construction that was to become the pride of Greece. At the end of the 4C the Theban general

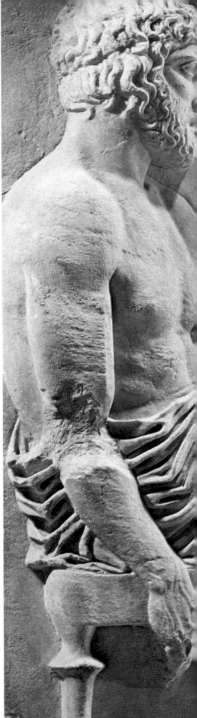

Part of the Parthenon frieze ▷

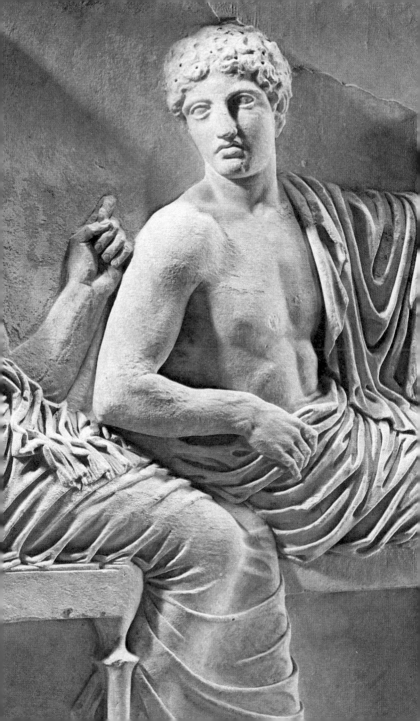

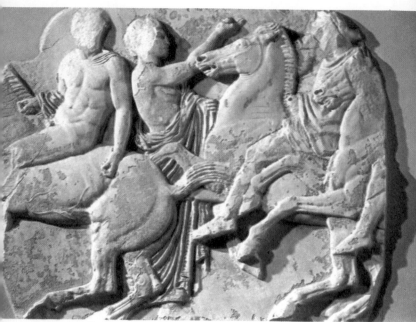

Detail of the Parthenon frieze (Acrop. Mus.)

Epaminondas said that his countrymen would never be able to break the confidence of the Athenian unless they were able to steal the Propylaia and erect them in front of their own acropolis. The proportions of the Propylaia are surprisingly beautiful, and in fact asymmetrical. The S. wing is much narrower than the N. because it is hemmed in by the temple of Athena Nike and the hill of Pyrgos. The total effect, however, is one of an unusually large gate of unsurpassed strength and majesty. It was the largest and most beautiful building of its day, consisting of an entrance façade of Pentelic marble pierced by five openings originally closed by wooden doors. The largest of these was the central entrance, through which the Panathenaic procession passed with priests and sacrificial animals. It stands higher and one metope wider than the pair of entrances to each side. The outermost entances are even smaller. A double staircase of extremely high steps leads through the gates into the temple compound. The steps leading through the largest entrance are flat to allow the sacrificial animals to pass through. Since 1970 they have been covered over with wood to protect them from the throng of visitors. To the W. a hall stands immediately in front of the façade; the front of this consists of 6 Doric columns which originally supported the pediment. The way up to the main entrance was flanked by 3 Ionic columns on each side. The W. hall was monumental in size, and measured 59 ft. 5 in. in width and 42 ft. 6 in. in depth, and was roofed with a coffered marble ceiling painted with gilded designs on a blue background. To the E. the façade of the Propylaia ended in another hall of considerably smaller depth and height, but

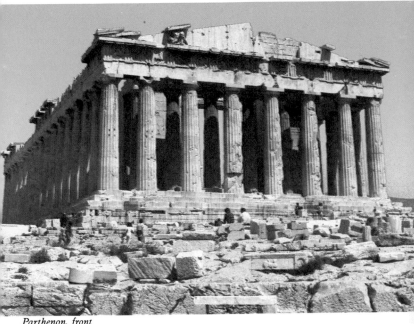

Parthenon, front

with a façade of 6 Doric columns. To the right and left of the W. hall stood adjoining wings, the S. of which consisted of only one room and was the smaller, whilst the N. had an ante-room which led into the so-called picture gallery. Pausanias tells us in his Guide to Greece (I,22,6), written in the 2C AD, that many paintings could be admired here, presumably painted wooden tablets, some of which depicted Homeric themes. All these paintings have been lost. The gallery was evidently originally a kind of rest-room where pilgrims to the acropolis could relax on couches.

In and around the Propylaia there were originally all kinds of cult-sites. Pausanias writes of two equestrian statues in the W. hall. In front of the Propylaia stood Hermes Propylaios, the Graces and a Hekataion. In front of the S. side of the E. hall the round plinth for the bronze statue

of Athena Hygieia has survived along with the ruins of a sacrificial table and a marble altar.

History of the Propylaia: The wonder of the whole world, the Propylaia survived in their original state until the 12C AD, when the Bishop made them his residence; but even so they had been altered little by the 13C. The Duke of Athens were the first to add a new storey to the N. wing. Then the Florentine Nerio Acciaiuoli and his mistress Maria Rendi built a palace in the Propylaia and a tower above the S. wing. Their illegitimate son Antonio ruled Athens for 30 years in peace. In 1458 the Turkish era began. The Turkish commander now occupied the Propylaia palace. The central ante-room was roofed with a dome, and a weapon store and powder house was added. In 1645 the powder

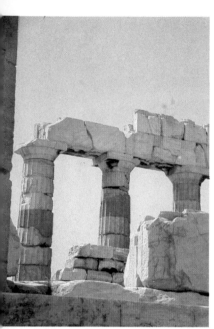

Parthenon, detail

magazine was hit by lightning, destroying the Propylaia and killing Isouf Agha, the commander of the day, and his family. The powder magazine was then moved into the Parthenon, where it exploded in 1687.

When Otho I of Bavaria entered Athens in 1833 the acropolis was in desperate need of restoration. Systematic restoration of the Propylaia began only in 1909, and N.Balanos and A.Orlandos should be mentioned in this regard. A strange feature is that the monuments on the acropolis were originally painted in glowing colours, and having in the interim lost all their colour give a completely false impression—in their bright, colourless appearance—of classical antiquity, at least as regards its delight in colour.

7. Artemis Brauronia: Between the Propylaia, the Parthenon and the Khalkotheke stood the sanctuary of Artemis Brauronia, occupying a trapezoidal plot. The boundary wall standing directly on the cliff survives to a height of three feet above ground level, as do some steps cut into the rock leading to the en-

Section of the Parthenon frieze (Acrop. Mus.)

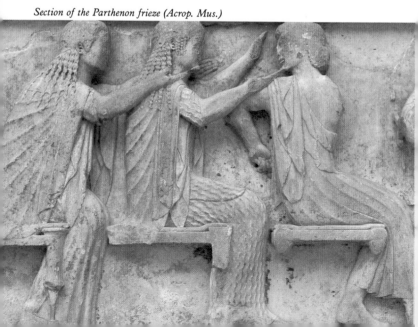

trance. At the base of the wall hollows can still be seen which held stele. The name of Artemis Brauronia implies the 'Bear-goddess'; her cult comes from Brauron, the town from which Peisistratos came. The sanctuary was probably laid out under Kimon and later altered during the construction of the Propylaia. Women in childbed offered sacrifices of jewellery to this Artemis for a safe delivery. Probably in the sanctuary itself stood the Trojan horse, cast in bronze at the end of the 5C, and described by Pausanias. The pedestal, with holes for the hooves, is still visible.

8. Bronze Quadriga: Oppposite the entrance to the sanctuary of Artemis Brauronia stood the bronze Quadriga set up by the Athenians in 506 after their victory over the Boeotians and Chalkidikans. The pedestal survives.

9. Athena Promachos: A few yards further on to the NW, apparently directly in front of the E. main gate of the Propylaia and 125 ft. from it, stood the famous statue of Athena Promachos (the Champion), an early work of Pheidias, consecrated around 454. The square pedestal hewn in the rock is all that is visible today. The fragmentary incription reads 'The Athenians erected her from the Persian booty'. It was probably made as a thanks-offering for the aversion of the Persian peril. Niketas Khomates, a Greek historian, described the statue about AD 1200. According to him it was a huge figure standing 30 ft. high with a helmet and horse-hair plume, a peplos in her left hand and a lance in her right. It was carried off to Constantinople in the 6C during the reign of the Emperor Justinian. In 1204, when the Crusaders were attacking Constantinople, the Byzantines came to believe that Athena was inviting the enemy into Constantinople with her outstretched hand and broke the statue up.

10. Athena Ergane: Next to the foundations of the Parthenon and six feet higher than the Brauronium stood the sanctuary of Athena Ergane (Athena of the craftsmen). From here steps led up to the Parthenon terrace.

Acropolis, Erechtheion

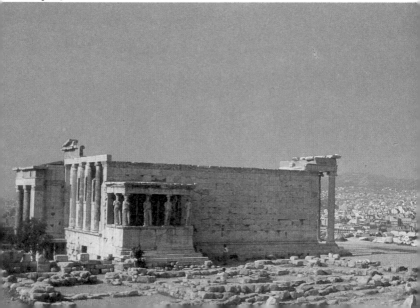

11. Khalkotheke: Further S. on the acropolis wall stood the Khalkotheke, a storeroom and armoury built around 450 BC. Some foundations are visible. Here weapons and bronze sacred implements were stored.

12. The Sacred Way: From the Propylaia the Sacred Way once led to the earlier temple of Athena. Some traces of this way can still be made out N. of the Parthenon, such as a rock inscription on a site dedicated to the goddess of the fruit-bearing earth (Ge Karpophoros) behind a grille to the rear of the 7th column of the Parthenon.

13. Parthenon: The site of the Parthenon, the most famous building in Greece, must long have been a cult site sacred to Athena before the temple was built.
a) There was probably an early archaic temple on the site in the 7 or 6C.
b) A second building known as the Hekatompedon was connected with the introduction of the Panathenaia around 560 BC. The name means 'building a hundred feet long'; remains of this temple, demolished in 488 to make way for the raised foundations of a new temple, can be seen in the N. wall of the acropolis and E. of the present Parthenon. The Hekatompedon was built of poros, with the metopes and cornices of island marble; these last can now be seen in the Acropolis Museum along with the poros pedimental carvings.
c) A new temple was erected to replace the Hekatompedon in years following 488; this stood on a raised foundation built for the temple and entirely in marble. When the Persians destroyed the acropolis in 480 this temple with its 6 x 16 columns was still under construction.
d) In 468 BC during Kimon's rule the restoration of the temple was begun. The supporting terrace was enlarged, and fragments of sculptures from the so-called Persian rubble buried. With the death of Kimon in 450 BC work came to an end.
e) Finally under Perikles a new period of building began in 447 BC. The ground plan was enlarged. The chief architect was Pheidias, with Iktinos and Kallikrates working under him. The numerous figures

Erechtheion, Caryatid Porch

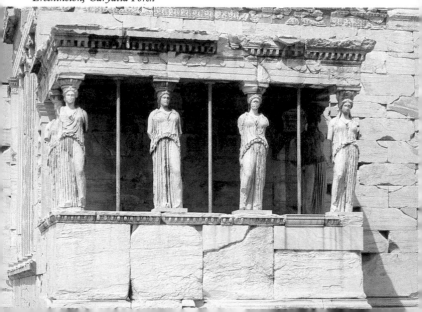

on the pediments, metopes and friezes were executed by the best sculptors in Athens. In the nine years up to 431 BC one of the most magnificent buildings in the world was completed. It is a classical Doric temple in Pentelic marble on a limestone foundation.

It is peripteral in form with a peristasis or columned hall measuring 101 ft. 4 in. by 228 ft. There are 8 x 17 columns standing 34 ft. 3 in. high, making it unusually large. However, it is not at all oppressive but full of power and majesty, and yet clean and almost weightless because of its slender columns.

One of the touches of genius in the design is that the architects did not set the columns perfectly upright but sloping slightly inwards, which combined with the complex construction of the rest of the building to create an illusion of perfect uprightness, an illusion assisted by the slight unevenness of the floor which protected the building from damage by earthquake. The slight raising of the floor in the centre ensured that water would run quickly off. Every part of the Parthenon is calculated to confer solidity and permanence. Optical effects were also employed in the construction, and even optical illusion, as with the columns; thus the corner columns which would otherwise have appeared smaller were given a larger diameter. This was an art which was to achieve its full development only during the baroque in theatrical design and in painting. The chief impression of the Parthenon, however, is of a temple of perfect proportions and beauty.

In front and to the rear of the cella are two 6-columned halls, the pronaos to the E. and the opisthodomos to the W. The cella was unusually large for the period; it was surrounded by solid walls with a remarkable order of columns, and was divided into an E. main room where the cult statue of Athena Parthenos stood, and a smaller W. room with four interior Ionic columns, the actual Parthenon.

The marble architectural ornament on the Parthenon was unusually rich. There were 92 metopes around the entablature representing the battle of the Centaurs, the battle of the gods and giants and so on,

Erechtheion, Caryatid

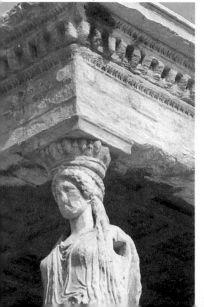
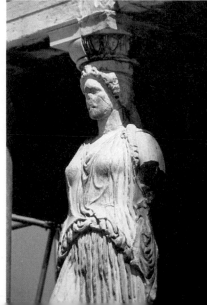

whilst the tympana had reliefs of teams of horses. The E. pediment depicted the birth of Athena and the W. pediment the contest between Athena and Poseidon. The cella entablature was decorated with a frieze of the Panathenaic procession in the presence of the gods.

The overall impression created by the Parthenon in its original form was far more colourful than it now appears. The coffered marble ceiling of the cella was decorated with roses and foliage, whilst the internal walls were painted red. Bronze and gold were employed on the ornamentation, and the triglyphs, metopes, and probably even the columns and capitals on the exterior of the temple were predominantly red and blue.

The chief point of attraction in the Parthenon was the statue of *Athena Parthenos* from the hand of Pheidias, which stood according to some authorities as high as 40 ft. Detailed descriptions of its appearance have come down to us from Pausanias, Plutarch and Lucian. It was made of chryselephantine (ivory and gold) and bore all the mythic attributes of Athena. The statue was erected using the treasury of the Attic-Delian naval league, and over a ton of pure gold was used in it. Not all the allies approved of the Athenians using their gold reserves on works of art, and much of the gold later had to be melted down again. A rumour was put about by jealous tongues that Pheidias had embezzled part of the gold intended for Athena's clothing. The gold plates were taken down from the statue and weighed and Pheidias's innocence established. Nevertheless the Athena Parthenos was to prove Pheidias's undoing. He had perpetuated his own image and that of Perikles in miniature on the statue, and this was taken as sacrilege. According to tradition he was thrown into prison where he eventually died. The statue itself stood unharmed until 298 BC, when the tyrant Lakhares removed its golden clothing. During the 1st half of the 5C AD it was described by the Greek historian Zosimos, and in 426 it was removed to Constantinople, where it is presumed to have been destroyed.

The site where the statue stood in the Parthenon cella can be recognized by the slight rectangular depression paved in tufa on the floor. The national Archaeological Museum has a small and rather crude copy of the statue dating from the 3C AD, the so-called *Varvakion Athena* (Room 20).

The Parthenon's history has been troubled even though it has managed to survive. During the Hellenistic period it was damaged by fire and restored. At this time the Athena Parthenos was given a new plinth and the bases of the cella columns were renewed. Until Roman times the Parthenon was venerated as the temple of the goddess Athena. Alexander the Great presented 300 Persian sets of armour in 334 BC as a thanks-offering for his victory at the river Granikos, and the Parthenon received countless other such votive offerings. Gradually, however, faith in the old gods decayed. In 305 BC King Demetrios, himself venerated as a demi-god, installed his courtesans in the W. part of the temple and held riotous feasts there. In 298 Lakhares stole the temple's golden decorations, whilst in 39 BC the Roman general Antony apparently celebrated a marriage with Athena. Further desecrations followed, until in AD 426 the cult-statue of Athena Parthenos itself was carried off. In 437 Theodosios II ordered the ancient temple to be purified and the idols to be abolished. The Parthenon was consecrated to Holy Wisdom and became the church of Agia Sophia. At this time the E. pediment was destroyed and an apse constructed. In the 10C the Parthenon was dedicated to the Panagia Athiniotissa becoming a church of Our Lady. Christian wall paintings adorned the interior walls. In 1018 the

*Bronze head, Man from Delos (Arch.   ▷
Museum)*

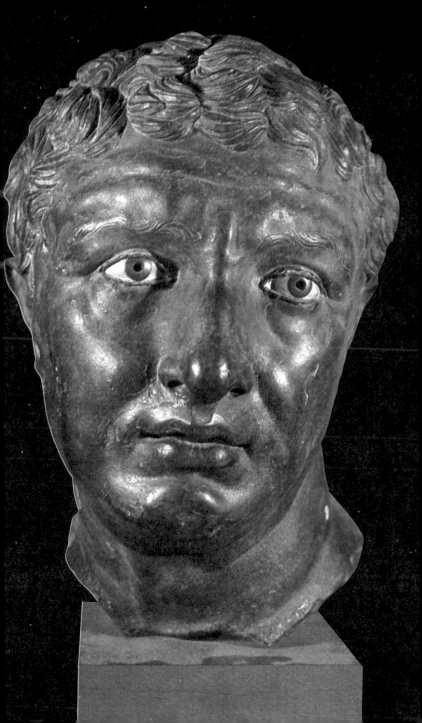

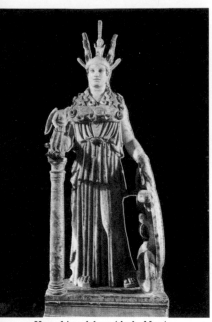

Varvakion Athene (Arch. Mus.)

Byzantine Emperor Basil II presented the Parthenon with a long venerated golden dove and a giant ornate oil-lamp. Under the Franks the Parthenon became the Roman Catholic castle church. After 1466 it was converted to a mosque under Turkish rule, and a minaret was erected at its SW corner. On 26 September 1687 disaster struck. The powder magazine which the Turks kept in the Parthenon was hit by a cannon ball fired by Venetians under F.Morosini. The magazine exploded and the temple was torn apart. A new mosque was built in the ruins. In 1799–1802 Lord Elgin, British ambassador to the Porte, appeared on the scene. He removed a large number of statues, 56 slabs of frieze, among them the most beautiful, and 15 metopes, which he took to England, where they are now kept in the British Museum in London. Finally in 1834 restoration of

the Parthenon was begun under L.von Klenze; important parts were played by E.Beulé and N.Balanos who re-erected the N. row of columns in 1922.

14. Temple of Roma and Augustus: Some 75 ft. E. of the E. façade of the Parthenon is the almost square poros foundation of the temple of Roma and Augustus, a round temple built entirely in white marble between 27 BC and AD 14. It was dedicated to the Roman imperial cult and was the first monument to be built on the acropolis since the age of Perikles, after a gap of 400 years. The central area was open, surrounded only by columns, and had a diameter of 25 ft. 9 in.

15. Ergasterion: SE of the temple of Roma and Augustus are the remains of a rectangular building, the so-called Ergasterion, originally divided into two rooms. This was probably the workshop of Pheidias and his assistants.

16. Acropolis Museum: In 1878 the Acropolis Museum was built diagonally over the foundations of the Ergasterion. The treasures displayed here come chiefly from the Persian rubble; it was enlarged in 1886 and refitted and reopened after the World War 2. For the contents of the museum see the section devoted to museums.

17. Belvedere: N. of the Museum at the NE corner of the acropolis is the Belvedere built by Queen Amalia, wife of Otho I, in the 19C from a Turkish tower. From here there is an extensive view over the city.

18. Zeus Polieus: The remains of a shrine probably dedicated to Zeus Polieus stand betwen the temple of Roma and Augustus and the N. wall of the acropolis. W. of this at the highest point of the acropolis are the tufa foundations of the Temenos of Zeus Polieus which enclosed an altar and a stall for the sacrificial animals. Every summer a great sacrifice was held here in honour of the Father of the Gods.

19. Altar of Athena: Between the sanctuary of Zeus Polieus and the Erechtheion stood the huge altar of Athena. Here cattle were offered to the goddess.

20. Old Temple of Athena: Behind the Hekatompedon described above, and later between the Parthenon and the Erechtheion stood the so-called Old Temple of Athena built around 520 BC to replace an earlier temple to Athena dating from the Geometric period. This was destroyed by the Persians in 480 and then partially rebuilt before finally burning down in 406, after which it was never rebuilt again, since the Parthenon and Erechtheion were by now in existence. Some of its foundations can still be seen. Some poros architectural fragments have been found, and various fragments of carvings, some of them painted, and pedimental sculptures can be seen in the Acropolis Museum. More recent excavations have suggested that the N. ante-hall of the Erechtheion is to be identified with the entrance to the Old Temple of Athena.

21. Royal Palace: Before the Geometric period the site of the Old Temple of Athena was occupied by a Mycenean stronghold, connected with the Pelasgian steps in the N. of the acropolis wall. Pre-archaic ochre-coloured foundations in limestone belonging to this stronghold have been discovered in the Erechtheion. According to ancient written traditions this fortress was the palace of the kings of Athens, and must have been the residence of Kodros, who gave his life for his people.

22. Pandroseion: There are no traces of this sanctuary of Pandrosos, one of the three daughters of Kekrops, whose tomb, the Kekropion, lies partially beneth the Caryatid porch of the Erechtheion. The

shrine was originally connected with the Erechtheion by a small staircase. The complex covered a large area, and had an inner court where legend placed the olive-tree planted by Athena in her contest with Poseidon as evidence of her victorious possession of Attica. Zeus had promised Attica to whichever could make the greatest benefaction to the land, and Athena's tree was judged more beneficial than Poseidon's noble steed. The olive-tree has been continuallly replanted and still stands in front of the Erechtheion. An altar of Zeus Herkaios has also been uncovered here. Probably the Pandroseion also functioned as a sanctuary of the goddess Pandrosos, who was venerated here as far back as 2000 BC.

23. Erechtheion: An archaic Erechtheion of polychrome tufa was destroyed by the Persians in 480. The present building, the principal monument on the acropolis after the Parthenon, is well preserved; it was built entirely of marble, with Philokles as master-architect, in 421–06. Work was interrupted from 415 to 409 by the outbreak of the Peloponnesian War. Like the Parthenon it is one of the most beautiful classical Greek buildings, but unlike the latter it is loosely arranged on an irregular polygonal plan, its slender columns and daring Caryatids being built on more than one level, the foundations of the S. and E. walls being nearly 10 ft. lower than those of the N. and W. walls. Where the Parthenon is compact and powerful, the Erechtheion has a relaxed, almost sentimental beauty. The complexity of the Erechtheion is due to the need to preserve most of the already existing cult sites in the structure. It was probably this which produced the entirely new form of this uniquely graceful solution. Seen from the E. the Erechtheion resembles an Ionic prostyle temple, but behind the facade it turns into a rectangle with halls springing out on either side. Originally the Erechtheion, so called after the tomb of Erechtheus, was called the 'Temple of Athena Polias' or the 'Temple with the old statue'. The ancient xoanon or carved olive-wood statue of Athena Polias said to have fallen from heaven was venerated here after 480 BC. It was to this statue that the Panathenaic procession came to deck it with a new peplos. Previously the xoanon had stood in the Old Temple of Athena.

The year the Erechtheion was completed the Old Temple of Athena burned down. The damage which the fire caused in the Erechtheion was not repaired until 394. The building survived in its original form until the 7C AD when it was converted into a church and considerably rearranged. In 1463 the Turkish governor installed his harem here. In 1801 Lord Elgin removed one of the Caryatids with other material;

Erechtheion (after J. Travlos) **1** E. portico with 6 Ionic columns on a stylobate of 3 marble steps. The pediment bears no sculptures **2** former altar of Zeus Hypatos **3** E. cella **4** formerly: priests' thrones **5** former altar of Hephaistos **6** former altar of the hero Boutes **7** former altar of Poseidon-Erechtheus **8** N. porch with coffered ceiling and 6 slightly inclined Ionic columns. On the pavement is a lightning mark, the mark of Poseidon's trident or a supposed thunderbolt of Zeus—probably a mark left by a bolt of lightning **9** former altar of the Thyechoos **10** from the N. porch there was a way leading to the former Pandroseion, where the olive-tree of Athena still stands **11** Gate, famous for its lavish Ionic decoration (now consists partly of copies) **12** elevated part of the W. cella **13** Puteal (peep-hole), through which one could look into the well, the 'Erechtheus Sea', a salt-water spring, which is supposed to have sprung up beneath Poseidon's trident, which he had hurled in fury after losing his contest with Athena **14** Porch of the Caryatids, situated above

the Tomb of Kekrops perhaps as a sort of canopy. This part of the building, one of the most beautiful architectural monuments of all, has 6 larger than life-size statues of maidens, Caryatids, which support the porch roof with their heads. Gracefully animated, the figures stand clad in long tunics, radiating peace, harmony, grace and nobility. Many individual caryatids, almost all from the 2nd half of the 6 and the early 5C BC, were excavated from the Persian rubble in the vicinity of the former Hekatompedon. These were votive statues, which were also erected to guard the temple, probably in place of the actual temple maidens, who had guarded the temple in earlier times. Many experts have concluded that the caryatids of the Erechtheion were korai **15** Tomb of Kekrops **16** W. cella **17** here stood the Lamp of Kallimachos with the eternal fire **18** repository of booty from the Persian Wars **19** Former adyton or megaron for the cult-statue (xoanon) of Athena Polias **20** site of the cult-statue of Hermes **21** Tomb of Erechtheus

Propylaia from the acropolis

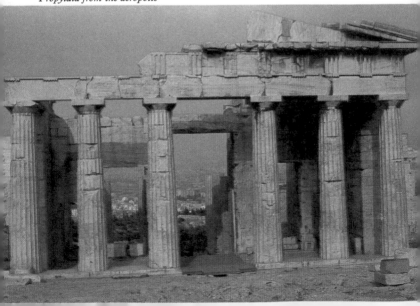

this was later replaced by a cast. The Erechtheion also suffered during the War of Liberation. In 1838 work began on clearing the rubble from its walls, and in 1842 – 4 Paccard restored the Caryatid porch. In 1852 the W. façade was severely damaged in a storm. Finally in 1903–4 it was reconstructed by Balanos.

24. House of the Arrephoroi: Between the Erechtheion and the acropolis wall are the remains of ancient cult sites with tufa supporting walls and the ruins of a Turkish cistern. The conspicuous square foundations date from the 5C BC and belonged to the House of the Arrephoroi. These were young girls (seven to eleven years old) from the best families in Athens who wove the peplos offered each year to the goddess under the direction of the priestess of

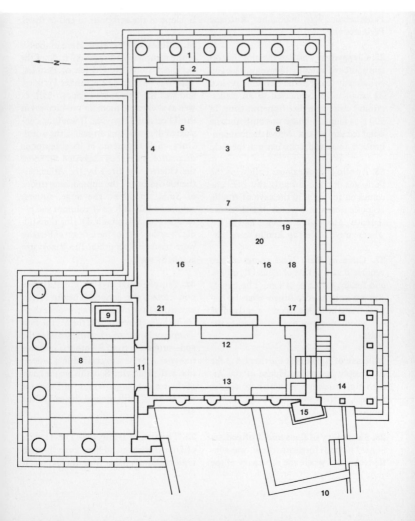

Athena. Two staircases led from the House of the Arrephoroi, one to a very ancient underground cavern, the other probably to the Peripatos, the way leading around the acropolis.

Along the Peripatos

Following the course of the Peripatos NW from near the exit from the acropolis, one quickly reaches, at the spot where the Panathenaic Way debouches into the Peripatos the:

25. Clepsydra: This was the most important source of water in the stronghold, and was already in use in the Neolithic period. 22 small wells connected to an underground water-vein date from this time. In 500 BC a fountain-house was built and the water led into a basin. Above the fountain-house is a cave with steps hewn in the rock.

26. Apollo Hypokraisos: Following the Peripatos further towards the NE one comes on the right to the cave of Apollo Hypokraisos, a title which means 'under the cave'. The walls of the cave had niches where votive tablets to Apollo were left.

27. Cave of Pan: Next comes a cave venerated as a shrine of Zeus Olympios, and finally the Cave of Pan. The cult of Pan was introduced to Athens after the Battle of Marathon. One can still clearly make out where offerings were attached to the walls.

28. Cave of Aglauros: Further on to the E., steeply below the House of the Arrephoroi, and connected with it by a secret passage, is the Cave of Aglauros. It was rediscovered in 1937.

29. Sanctuary of Eros and Aphrodite: Some 110 yards further to the E. was a little rocky area where the sanctuary of the two gods stood, also known as the 'sanctuary of Aphrodite in the garden'. According to Pausanias (I,27, 3) two of the Arrephoroi dwelt in the Old Temple of Athena and had to carry cult-objects on their heads here at night by a subterranean passage.

30. Inscription: There is an inscription on the Peripatos further to the E. on the edge of the path. The Peripatos now leads on past several more cult caves round the E. slope of the acropolis to end in the S.

31. Odeion of Perikles: Here in the SE of the acropolis and some 82 ft. S. of the Peripatos stood the Odeion of Perikles. This was built in 442 BC under Perikles, and was the first roofed concert-hall, as well as a rehearsal room for productions in the Theatre of Dionysos. It was long considered the finest concert-hall in the world. Only small fragments of its sumptuous decoration have been excavated. In 86 BC the Odeion was fired by the Athenians themselves before the approaching troops of Sulla. In 60 BC the huge, square, columned hall with its 90 columns and pyramidal roof, was rebuilt. During the Middle Ages the ruins of the Odeion of Perikles were used to strengthen the Rizokastro acropolis walls.

32. Temple of Dionysos: The Peripatos now crosses the famous Theatre of Dionysos. In front of the entrance to the theatre in the S. there stood in the 6C the first Temple of Dionysos. Here the statue of the god—originally from Eleutherai in Boeotia—was kept; it was carried in a procession at the Dionysia. S. of this are the ruins of the second, larger temple of Dionysos Eleuthereus, built around the end of the 4C.

33. Theatre of Dionysos: The Theatre of Dionysos seems to have gone through nine building phases from the 6C on. It

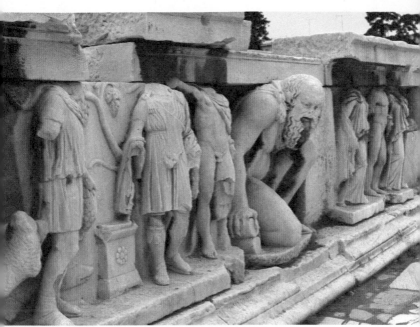

Silenos, a companion of Bacchus, in the Theatre of Dionysos

was the first European theatre and the cradle of ancient tragedy. Tradition makes Thespis the first to have crossed the country in his proverbial cart with his troupe and to have produced the first drama in 534 BC when he brought on a single actor in dialogue with the chorus-leader, probably in the agora. These productions were from the outset held in honour of the god Dionysos.

Dionysos, son of Zeus and Semele, was a god of vegetation, of tumult, ecstasy, metamorphosis, acting and masks. He inspired men with poetic and prophetic utterance. Each year at the Greater Dionysia in the spring dithyrambic dances and chorus works were performed. The festivities were conducted by a leader, and Thespis, one of the earliest, created a new form when he set his actor opposite the chorus, a form which was to culminate in a com-

petition. Increasing numbers of spectators flocked to these contests, and the site was moved from the agora to the temple of Dionysos. At first the spectators sat on the slopes of the hill to watch the festivities taking place on a round, rammed area called the orchestra. Then wooden seats were erectd on the slope, and named the theatron, referring originally only to the spectators' area. The stage now consisted of a wooden structure with an altar and a tomb. Wooden stage flaps and painted scenery were introduced, and more and more competitors began to take part, culminating in Aiskhylos, Sophokles, and Euripides, who won ever more firsts. Around 500 Pratinas staged the stayr-play as a postlude to the tragedies, whilst in 472 Aiskhylos introduced a second actor in his 'Persians', and Sophokles a third. This was the highpoint of tragedy. In 485 comedy was in-

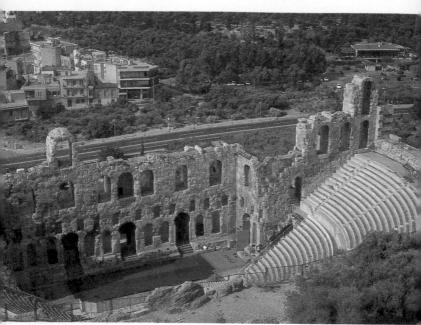

Odeion of Herodes Atticus

troduced, in which Kratinos and Aristophanes excelled. The skene developed into an elongated rectangular stone area, with the altar in the centre of the orchestra, and a wall pierced by three doors behind the skene. The 'Charonic steps' led down into the underworld, and flying apparatus and a crane provided for appearances by the gods. A platform called the theologeion could be let down from the roof to bring the 'deus ex machina' suddenly down from heaven on to the stage. Acoustic and optical effects such as artificial thunder and painted lightning were employed. Masks are traditionally attributed to Thespis, but were probably introduced by Aiskhylos. Drama developed rapidly to its apogee, visible to us chiefly in the quality of its dramatic poets. The ever more favourable reception accorded to the productions in the Theatre of Di-

onysos meant that stage and auditorium had to be enlarged and improved. Under Lykourgos around 330 BC the theatre acquired 67 rows of stone benches seating 17,000 spectators, separated by gangways into three rings, the lower of which was divided by steps into 13 segments. In the middle of the first row the place of honour carved in relief and reserved for the priest of Dionysos Eleuthereus can still be seen; it was probably surmounted with a canopy during the Roman period. Behind it a place of honour was added later for the Emperor Hadrian. In the Roman period the orchestra was paved and separated by a stone barrier from the spectators. The reliefs on the stage house, many times rebuilt, in the S. of the theatre, depicting scenes from the Dionysos myths, date from the 1C AD.

The earliest productions in the 6&5C were

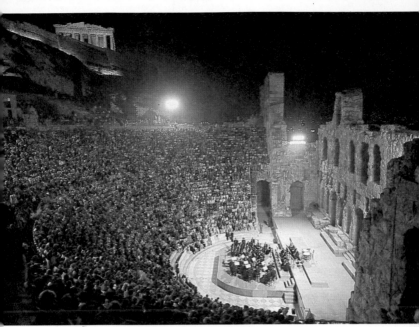

Evening performance in the Odeion of Herodes Atticus

closely linked with the cult, began with processions, and lasted up to 8 hourse. During the Roman period the Theatre was used for dramatic productions, but also drifted from its original purpose. Gladiatorial contests, mock sea-battles and, according to some scholars, wild-beast hunts were held here. At the end of the 5C AD the orchestra was converted into the court of a Christian basilica. In the 17C archaeologists first began to take an interest, and from 1837 the 'Greek Archaeological Company' started excavations here, revealing this important cultural monument once more.

34. Monument of Thrasyllos: N. of the Theatre of Dionysos on a site once occupied by a large number of choregic monuments, set up by victorious chorus-leaders, and right against the acropolis cliffs, stands the Monument of Thrasyllos erected in 320 BC. Beneath it is a cave, the chapel of the Panagia Spiliótissa. In 1827 the monument was destroyed by the Turks. These monuments originally had the tripods which were the prizes won by the choregoi in the competitions set on marble plinths, for both chorus-leader and poet were honoured in this way.

35. Monument of Nikias: W. of the Theatre of Dionysos are the rectangular foundations of the choregic monument of Nikias built in 319 BC and destroyed soon after 267 BC. The stones were used in the construction of the Beulé Gate.

36. Stoa of Eumenes: Adjoining the Theatre further to the W. is the 535 ft. long Stoa of Eumenes, a two-storeyed lobby where theatre visitors could relax. It was the gift of Eumenes II, King of Pergamon around 160 BC. The hall had Doric columns outside, whereas inside it had Ionic columns below, and Pergamene columns on the upper storey. The supporting walls and arcades, originally faced in marble slabs, survive.

37. Old Asklepieion: The site of the Old Asklepieion was originally occupied by a sanctuary dedicated to a water-god. The cult of Asklepios, god of healing, was brought from Epidauros to Athens in 420 BC, and the Old Asklepieion built to the W. of the Theatre of Dionysos, at the foot of the S. slopes of the Propylaia, and N. of the Peripatos. Ruins of the building are now to be seen to the W. of the New Asklepieion. These inclue ruins of a 92 ft. long Ionic stoa which held four square rooms, remains of an ante-temple with ruins of an altar, and the spring with its rectangular basin. The structure survived until the 6C AD. S. of it is another later cistern from the Turkish period.

38. New Asklepieion: The ruins of the New Asklepieion, built around the middle of the 4C between the Old Asklepieion and the Theatre of Dionysos are more impressive. There are remains of walls, an altar pedestal, but barely any remnant of a 164 ft. long portico, once a two-storeyed dormitory for the sick. In the E. there is a cave with a spring, later considered therapeutic, now a chapel, and in the W. a round roofed sacrificial pit, S. of the portico another hall was built in the Roman period; ruins are still visible. Later, in the early Christian period a basilica was built over the ruins of the Asklepieion; only ruined walls can be seen.

39. Odeion of Herodes Atticus: On the SW edge of the acropolis slopes stands this theatre, reconstructed in the 20C, and originally dating from the 2C AD. The father of Herodes Atticus is said to have dis-

covered a treasure in an old house, which he at once presented to the Emperor. The Emperor returned it to him, so that he was able to give his son Herodes a correct education. He attained rank and office, increased his wealth, and spent large sums on the city. In AD 161 he built a huge Odeion capable of seating 5,000 spectators in memory of his dead wife Regilla. The façade alone stood 92 ft. high. The walls were of dressed poros covered with marble slabs. Floors, staircases, and ante-rooms were decorated with mosaics. In front of the three-storeyed theatre stood a columned hall, and lobbies occupied the area in front of the entrances. There were three doors in the stage wall and eight niches. Three steps joined the stage to the orchestra, whilst the steep auditorium was roofed in cedar-wood.

In AD 268 the Herulians burned the Odeion down. Under the Turks it was used as a bastion. Excavations began between 1848 and 1858. In the 20C the theatre was restored, and in 1955 it attained worldwide renown with the establishment of the Athens festival. Here great artists from all over the world performed, danced, and played, whilst the audience enjoyed—as they had done in the days of Herodes Atticus—the unique acoustics which permit the smallest sound to be heard far away without distortion. The Odeion also played an important part in the reawakening of interest in ancient tragedy performed in modern Greek.

In 1960–1 all the seats were renewed in Pentelic marble; and the orchestra was paved with blue and white flags.

40. Sanctuary of the Nymphs: The Peripatos sometimes coincides with the modern way around the acropolis, sometimes follows it, and sometimes crosses it. We leave it at the Odeion of Herodes Atti-

Hill of the Muses, Monument of ▷
Philopappos

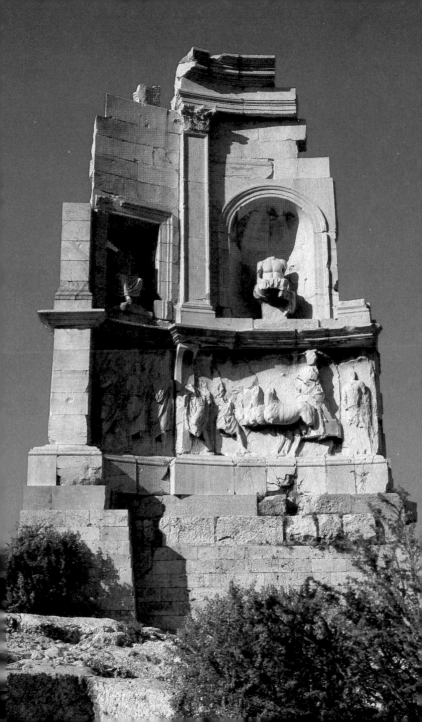

cus for the Sanctuary of the Nymphs to the
S. of the theatre, the remains of which were
uncovered in 1955–9. Jars offered here in
the 7C BC were discovered here, and can
now be seen in the Acropolis Museum.
The jars were used for carrying water for
the marriage bath. After the wedding the
bride brought the jar to the Sanctuary of
the Nymphs as a votive offering.

The Hills of Athens

The hills with the principal cultural
monuments, the Philopappos, Pnyx,
Areopagos, Hill of the Nymphs and Hill
of the Muses, all lie to the W. of the acropolis. Parking is easiest on the Hill of the
Muses, from where one can easily reach the
agora.

1. Areopagos; Directly to the NW of the
acropolis rises the Areopagos (377 ft.). It
can also be reached as an excursion from
the Peripatos, or its modern equivalent, the
acropolis walkway. Between the acropolis
and the Areopagos is a saddle, now a parking place. This is thought to have been the
earliest archaic agora, but the area has not
yet been excavated. Rock-hewn steps lead
up to the Areopagos. The history of the
Areopagos is very ancient. In 1939 and
1947 Mycenean tholos tombs were discovered here, and the wealth of the finds
suggested royal graves from around 1400
BC. Since the earliest times the Areopagos
has been the hill of justice. It is said that
Ares was tried by the gods here for the murder of Halirrhothios. The council of elders
which consisted in the 7C of Eupatrids,
and practised blood justice, was already
known as the Court of the Areopagos. Solon turned the members of the Areopagos
into the guardians of the constitution and
protectors of the laws. Later these rights
were removed, but from the 4C they were

Agora with Byzantine church and ▷
Hephaisteion

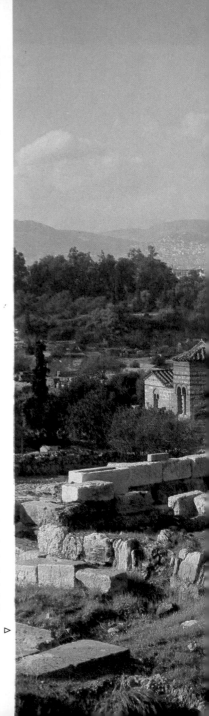

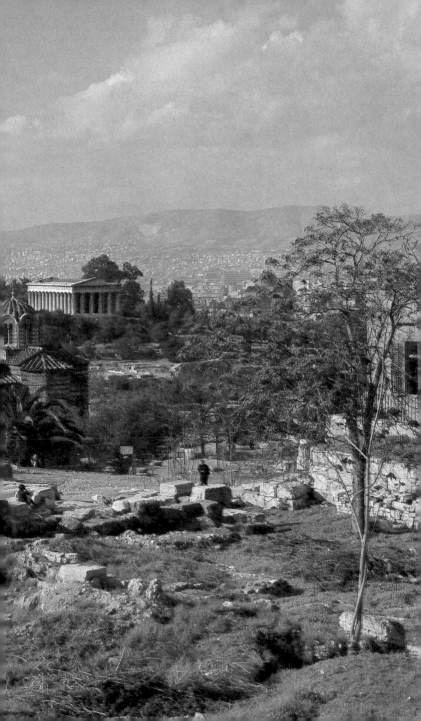

entrusted with the trial of treason and corruption. Here Orestes defended himself against the charge of murdering his mother. The Areopagos is rich in history. Here the Amazons encamped, and from here the Persians launched their attack on the acropolis in 480. In AD 51 the Apostle Paul preached here in the middle of the seat of justice, converting the councillor Dionysios, later to become the patron saint of Athens as Dionysios the Areopagite. The ruins of his 16C church can still be seen by looking from the hill towards the N. slope. The peak of the Areopagos has been artificially levelled, and from here there are superb views over the agora and the Propylaia above. The ruined walls of a small building which stood on the peak were probably connected with the administration of justice. Immediately below the hill to the SW old houses have been uncovered; this is the *Amyneion*, the sanctuary of a god of healing. Investigation of the NW slope produces many finds from earlier settlements, including the elliptical *Geometric House* and a polygonal votive plaque from the 7C BC. The *spring* was believed to have therapeutic qualities, while the hollow area was a place of inviolable *asylum* for murderers and runaway slaves. Here stood the *Tomb of Oedipus*. On the E. side of the Areopagos a path leads to the so-called *Cave of the Furies* (located by some scholars on the NW slopes). From here one can enter the agora excavations by the S. gate or else return to the path up to the acropolis and thence to the Hill of the Muses.

2. Hill of the Muses: This hill (482 ft.) was sacred to the Muses. The Macedonian King Demetrios Poliorketes built a fort here in 294 BC. Today the site is occupied by the *Monument of Philopappos*, a funerary monument built by the Romans in AD 114–16 in memory of a Syrian prince and benefactor of Athens. The view from here over the acropolis is famous.

3. Hill of the Nymphs: From the Hill of the Muses one may proceed to the neighbouring Hill of the Nymphs W. of the Areopagos. Here, between the slopes of four hills, ancient cave-dwellings cut into the rocks were discovered; they were still inhabited in the 5C BC. The so-called *Tomb of Kimon* has been discovered here, as has the alleged *Prison of Sokrates*, which cannot be certainly identified as such. The 'Long Walls' connecting Athens to Piraeus originally ended here. There is also an observatory on the hill.

4. Pnyx: The popular assemblies which made official decisions met in the earliest times in the agora, but later the Pnyx became the place of assembly of the Athenian democracy. The name means 'place where people stand close-packed'. Originally the people looked down on to the orators' tribune on a natural rock stand. At the end of the 5C the people's area was extended northwards and laid out in semicircular terraces with two gangway-stairs. In the 2nd half of the 4C this complex on the NE of the hill with its 280 ft. long protecting wall was again enlarged and rebuilt. Stairs, lobbies, and monumental doors were built, of which only ruins survive. The large terrace resembles an amphitheatre and measures 230 ft. deep by 390 ft. across, and affords a superb view of the acropolis. Behind the orator's tribune is another rocky platform identified by some scholars as the *altar of Zeus Agoraios*. The surviving niches in the cliff-face belonged to a Roman sanctuary of *Zeus Hypsistos*. A little further off are the foundations of a building hewn in the rock and the pedestal of the famous *Sundial of Meton* (433/2 BC. In the 5C BC Meton calculated the length of the year at 365 [5/19] days, overestimating it by only 30 minutes.

The Agora: Following lesser excavations in the 19&20C the ancient Greek marketplace was uncovered by American archaeologists in 1931–41 and 1946–60. To

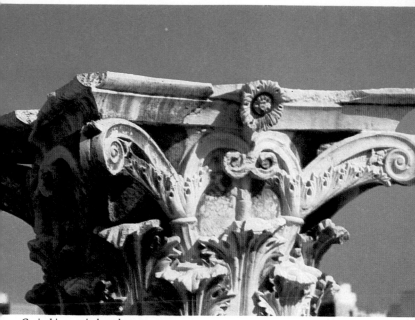

Corinthian capital on the agora

do this a whole quarter of the city had to be evacuated and demolished.

The value of these archaeological discoveries can be understood in a visit to the excavations which now lie in the midst of myrtles, cypresses and olive-trees. Whole historical periods can be reconstructed with the aid of the finds made here and the writings of ancient authors, chief among them Pausanias.

I. History of the Agora: The Old Agora of Theseus, plausibly identified in the S. of the present agora and standing a little higher than it, became too small, and in the 6C Solon commissioned the building of a new city centre. This was laid out NW of the acropolis in an area which had been used as a burial-ground since the Mycenean period. The oldest buildings in the new agora are in the W. at the foot of the acropolis hill. For thousands of years henceforth the area was to be the centre of the city, the seat of popular assemblies, a place of justice, of cult gatherings, athletic contests, dance and choral performances and popular entertainments. Only later did the Pnyx become the seat of the popular assembly, the Areopagos the seat of blood-justice, and the Theatre of Dionysos the centre of the dramatic competitions. The centre of cult activities had long been the Areopagos, but the Panathenaic procession wound along the specially built way from the agora to the statue of Athena Polias. The agora remained the centre for state administration, and the showplace for political, philosophical and artistic contests and judgements, but above all the main commercial centre and market-place to which all the main roads led. It is no surprise that new and often spectacular buildings were

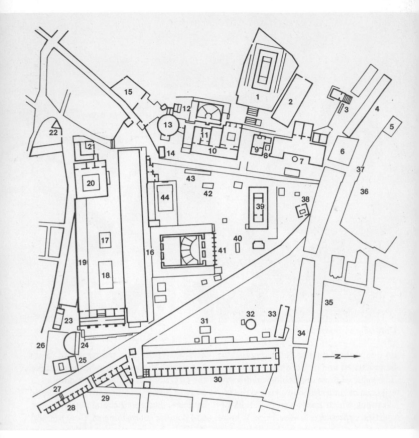

Greek Agora (after J.Travlos): The numbers on the plan are referred to in the description of the agora in the text.

constantly being built here, often at the expense of earlier ones.

In Peisistratos's time, around 530, the Altar of the Twelve Gods was built along with the Residence of the Tyrants in the SW corner and the Enneakrounos fountain in the SE. About 508 BC following the reforms of Kleisthenes, the Heliaia law-courts, the Great Drain in the W., the old Bouleuterion and the small Metroon temple were built. After destruction by the Persians in 480 BC the agora was rebuilt and much altered. The Tholos, and later the Temple of Hephaistos, was built, along with the Hall of Zeus, the Stoa in the S. and after 350 BC the sanctuaries of Apollo Patroos, Zeus Phratrios and Athena Phratria. The Stoa of Attalos, a new Metroon, and the S. and Middle Stoas were built in the Hellenistic period in the 2C BC. In 86 BC much was destroyed during Sulla's cam-

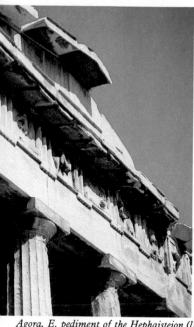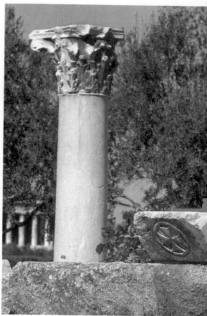

Agora, E. pediment of the Hephaisteion (l) and Corinthian column (r)

paign. Under Augustus around 20 BC the Odeion of Agrippa was rebuilt in the middle of the agora and the Temple of Ares next to it. In the 2C AD the Library of Pantainos was built. In 267 the Herulians occupied Greece and put Athens to the flame. New walls, the Walls of Valerian, were built to replace the Themistoklean ones, and these did not include the agora within their perimeter. For over 100 years the site was no more than ruins, until around 400 a new period of construction began. A gymnasion was built, as was a new tholos. The Temple of Hephaistos was converted to Christian use. In 529 the Emperor Justinian closed the philosophical schools and put an end to instruction in the gymnasion, and by 550 the agora had lost all its importance. From the 11C Byzantines, Franks and Turks succeeded one another, gradually taking the area over as a residential quarter, which it remained until the houses gave way once more to the excavations of the ancient agora.

II. W. Part of the Agora: There are three entrances to the agora ruins. The best is the W. entrance which affords an excellent view over the romantic ruins with Mt.Hymettos in the background. The two most interesting buildings in the agora are the Temple of Hephaistos and the Agora Museum.

1. Temple of Hephaistos: Close to the W. entrance on a rocky plateau overlooking the expanse of ruins is the well-preserved Temple of Hephaistos built in 450–40 BC. The Temple is known as the Theseion by modern Athenians, although it was never dedicated to Theseus, but to Hephaistos, god of smiths and potters, and to the god-

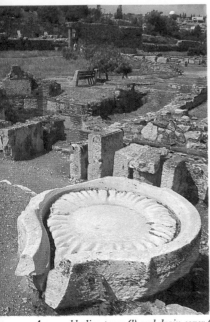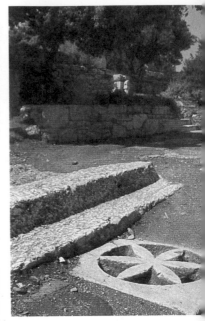

Agora, old olive-press (l) and drain cover (r)

dess Athena. The two cult-statues of Athena and Hephaistos cast together stand, now as before, in the cella of the temple. They were executed by Alkamenes, a pupil of Pheidias in 449–4 BC. The temple has survived wars, invasions and plundering, and its conversion in the 5C AD into the church of St.George; it was restored to its former state without too much difficulty. It was built before the Parthenon, and lacks the beauty of proportion and radiant majesty of the latter building, as well as the ingenious play of perspective, although the 6 x 13 Doric columns of the Temple of Hephaistos are set far apart and lean slightly inwards. The entablature does not sit more heavily on the columns than in the Parthenon. The cella was a two-storeyed peristyle hall of 4 x 7 columns. Some scholars believe that the architect of this temple was the same as the architect of the Temple of Ares on the agora and the Temple of Poseidon on Cape Sounion. Only scanty traces of the ornament and paintwork survive, chief of these are the metopes with their Herakles cycle and the frieze on the E. side. The metopes on the N. and S. depict the deeds of Theseus. Parts of the pedimental carvings in Pentelic marble were discovered in the agora excavations in 1931–48. In the 3C AD the immediate neighbourhood of the Hephaisteion was turned into a garden, with a surrounding wall separating the sacred enclosure from the rest of the area.

2. Hellenistic columned hall: N. of the Hephaisteion stood a Hellenistic columned hall with three aisles.

3. Temple of Aphrodite Krania: Further to the N. of this columned hall on the

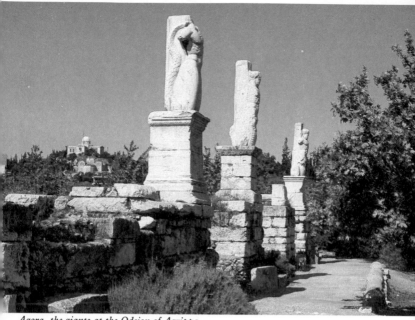

Agora, the giants at the Odeion of Agrippa

N. slope of the hill are the remains of a temple from the early Roman period, the N. part of which has been obliterated by the underground railway. When the railway was being built in 1892 fragments of Doric architecture were discovered from this temple, which was probably dedicated to Aphrodite Krania. The cult statue for an earlier temple on the site was executed by Pheidias, and a copy of this statue can be seen in the Agora Museum, along with an altar of Hymettos marble also found in the neighbourhood of the temple.

4. Roman hall: N. of the temple of Aphrodite Krania stood a Roman hall.

5.Panathenaic Way and Eleusinion: Parallel to this hall and N. of it ran the Panathenaic Way. It was 33 ft. wide and paved in parts. Each year the festal procession of the goddess Athena passed along it. The way began in the W. at the Sacred Gate (Dipylon), and ran diagonally across the whole agora and up to the acropolis. During excavations on the Panathenaic Way the **Eleusinion** was also discovered S. of the agora, some 460 ft. S. of the Stoa of Attalos; this was an archaic shrine from the 6C BC which was rebuilt around 490 and served for a period as the Bouleuterion or council assembly. In AD 267 it was evidently destroyed in the Herulian invasion.

6. Stoa Basileios: E. of the Roman hall the foundations of the stoa of the Archon Basileus were discovered during excavations next to the Piraeus underground railway in 1970. The Doric portico had 8 columns on its façade; it was a public building built around 530 BC and destroyed in AD 267 by the Herulians.

7. Stoa of Zeus Eleutherios: This U-shaped stoa, of which only the plan is visible, lies to the S. of the Stoa Basileios. The N. end of the side-wing has been cut off by the railway. The stoa was built in the second half of the 5C BC and must originally have been adorned with the now lost *murals of Euphranor* which were painted after 362, and depicted the Twelve Gods, Theseus, and the Battle of Mantinea. Beneath the hall a *Temple of Zeus* and an *altar of Zeus* from the 6C BC have been excavated. In the 1C AD rooms were built on to the stoa to house the imperial cult. A carved, mailed torso of the Emperor Hadrian exhibited in front of the hall comes from this cult. E. of the temple is the base of the altar of Zeus.

8. Temple of Zeus Phratrios and Athena Phratria: Between the Stoa of Zeus Eleutherios and the Temple of Apollo Patroos to its S. the little shrine of Zeus Phratrios and Athena Phratria dating from the middle of the 4C has been discovered.

9. Temple of Apollo Patroos: The ancient Athenians believed that they were descended from the Ionians. The mythic progenitor of the Ionians was the god Ion, a son of Apollo. This temple, dedicated to Apollo the Father, was erected around the end of the 4C BC. There were two earlier buildings on this site, a temple to Apollo built in the 6C BC and destroyed by the Persians in 480, and another built in the middle of the 4C, of which the foundations survive almost in their entirety. In the 2C BC the portico in front of the E. cella was added. The *colossal marble statue of Apollo* now in the Agora Museum comes from the last temple and was probably the work of Euphranor. The roomy pronaos probably housed several bronze statues by Leochares and Kalamis which won Pausanias's commendation.

10. Metroon: Tradition relates that in 423

BC a priest of the Mother of the Gods was murdered. The expiation exacted by the Oracle of Delphi was the dedication of a shrine to Kybele in the then bouleuterion. This request suggests that the Metroon or temple of the Mother of the Gods was built inside the bouleuterion area. The last Metroon built in the 2C BC had three halls and stood directly above the old bouleuterion. The N. hall and the forehall were added on. The foundations and some architectural fragments survive. The statue of the Mother of the Gods which formerly stood in the old bouleuterion and then in the Metroon was said to be by Pheidias. The plinth on which the cult image stood has been found along with an altar in front of the temple. In Roman times the N. hall of the Metroon was altered and rebuilt. In AD 267 a basilica was built here following the Herulian destruction. In the 5C AD the floor of the N. hall was decorated with mosaics.

11. Bouleuterion: The old bouleuterion dating from the end of the 6C was destroyed by the Persians. The Metroon was subsequently built on the ruins, which overlie those of two earlier buildings dating from the 7&6C BC.

12. New Bouleuterion: This was built at the end of the 5C and destroyed in AD 267 by the Herulians, but later restored. The bouleuterion was one of the most important buildings in the agora, where the council originally created by Solon met. Of the new bouleuterion only the poros foundations can now be seen. The twelve rows of seats in the orchestra, which had a radius of 8 ft. 8 in., were made of wood, later replaced by stone. The propylon in the E. next to the Metroon portico dates from the 3C BC; the foundations are still visible.

13. Tholos: S. of the bouleuterion was an-

Archaic kouros (Arch. Mus.) ▷

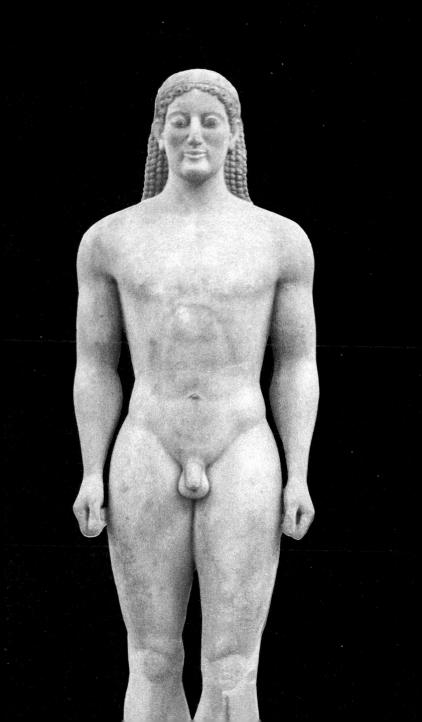

other state building, the tholos, also known as the skias, where the Prytaneis dined under a shady roof. The Tholos was named after an earlier building on the same site often called the *Prytanikon*. This dated from the 6C BC. The Tholos is a round building with a diameter of 60 ft. 1 in. erected in 465 BC and, despite being frequently damaged, always rebuilt, until it was destroyed by the Herulians in AD 267. It was rebuilt for the last time in the 4C AD, when the entry with its paved marble floor and the columns supporting the conical roof were added. Some of the bricks, once painted, are now to be seen in the Agora Museum. The Tholos had a fountain attached, and housed the official weights and measures.

14. Great Drain: E. of the Tholos the course of a drain 3 ft. wide and 3 ft. deep has been discovered; this carried rain-water from the hills in the S. and W. to the Eridanos in the N. The drain was built in the 5C BC and originally lined with marble slabs. It was not the only drain, for 100 years later two more were built in the area of the agora.

15. Strategeion: To the SW of the Tholos a few clues have led to the identification of the Strategeion, the office of the Strategoi or commanders, which was one of the public buildings on a par with the Bouleuterion and Tholos.

III. S. Part of the Agora

16. Middle Stoa: To the SE of the Tholos and precisely aligned E-W stood a great two-storeyed Doric portico, built in the 2C BC and evidently part of a gymnasion.

17. W. Temple / 18. E. Temple: S. of the Middle Stoa and between it and the S. Stoa excavations have revealed two buildings of uncertain identity, known as the E. Temple and beside it the smaller W. Temple.

19. S. Stoa: Parts of the foundations of the S. Stoa survive. This was erected in the Hellenistic period diagonally above a 5C banqueting-hall which had 15 rooms furnished with couches.

20. Heliaia: Only a few portions of the walls of a square enclosure remain of this justice building, along with a columned inner court dating from the archaic period.

21. and 23. Fountain-Houses: To the E. and W. of the 4C BC S. Stoa fountain-houses have been discovered.

22. Abaton: S. of the W. fountain-house a small Abaton from the 5C BC has been discovered.

24. Nymphaion: To the NE of the E. fountain-house is a semicircular Nymphaion dating from the 2C AD.

25. SE temple: Next to this in the SE stood the SE Temple built during the reign of Augustus.

26. Church of the Holy Apostles: This stands above the earlier Nymphaion, and dates from the 11C AD.

27. E. Building: Turning back into the agora to the NW, one comes to a building which linked the S. and Middle Stoas. This consisted of a hall and two columned rooms with a kind of entrance into the square between the S. and Middle Stoas.

IV. E. Part of the Agora

28. SE Stoa: The chief building in the E. is the rebuilt Stoa of Attalos. To the S. of this and adjoining it diagonally stood the Library of Pantainos and next to this and further to the S. the SE Stoa, built in the 1C AD; ruins of it are still visible. It is

Roman agora, Tower of the Winds ▷

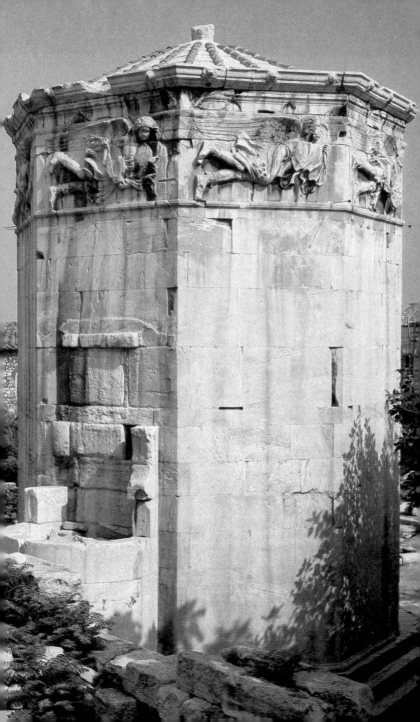

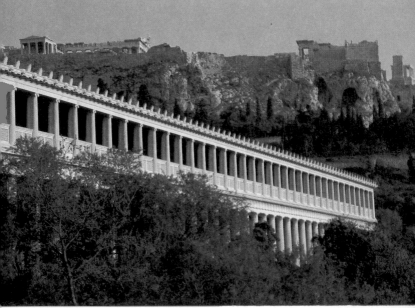

Stoa of Attalos in the E. part of the Agora

thought that the rooms adjoining one another so closely behind the portico were shops.

29. Library of Pantainos: According to an inscription this library was built in AD 100 by Titus Flavius Pantainos and his children. It was destroyed by the Herulians in AD 267.

30. Stoa of Attalos: This two-aisled, double-storeyed building was founded by King Attalos II of Pergamon (159–38 BC). The site was occupied earlier by a Mycenean cemetery, then by 5&4C buildings. The present stoa like the original measures over 367 ft. 4 in. length, 37 ft. 6 in. in height and 64 ft. in depth, and has 45 Doric columns on the lower storey which are fluted only at the top. Inside there are 24 Ionic columns. The upper storey has Ionic columns outside and Pergamene inside. The halls on both floors were flanked by 24 small and almost square rooms probably used as scriptoria and shops. Steps led to the upper storey on both sides of the stoa.

In 1931 American archaeologists decided to rebuild the stoa completely from its ruins and house a museum inside it. A few of the square rooms were kept and the rest were incorporated into a hall. The excavations in the agora had brought so many finds to light that a special Agora Museum was called for, and they were housed here when the reconstruction was complete.

31. Bema: A bema or orator's tribune stood in front of the Stoa of Attalos in Hellenistic times.

32. Fountain-house: A round, roofed Ro-

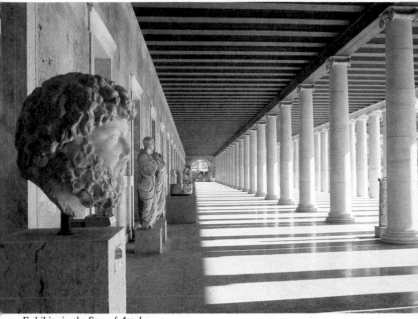

Exhibits in the Stoa of Attalos

man fountain-house has been discovered in front of the Stoa of Attalos near several other monuments.

33. NE Stoa: Forming an oblique angle with the NW corner of the Stoa of Attalos is the so-called NE Stoa.

V. N. Part and Centre of the Agora

34. Basilica: Across the ruins of the NE Stoa where the underground railway buildings now stand there stood a large three-aisled basilica with a columned portico.

35. Stoa Poikile / 36. Stoa of Hermes: N. of the underground railway the foundations of two large buildings have been discovered which both probably date from the 2C AD. These are the Stoa of Hermes and the Stoa Poikile.

37. Hippomachia Gate: SW of the Stoa of Hermes the remains of the Hippomachia Gate have been uncovered.

38. Altar of the Twelve Gods: Around the end of the 6C BC the famous altar of the twelve gods to the S. of the Stoa of Hermes was dedicated. Its ruins were excavated during work on the underground railway in 1891. It was only in 1934 when it had become largely obscured once again that it was identified. In former times the altar was the centre from which distances in Attica were measured. In the Roman period it served as the altar of pity. Here the needy, beggars and foreigners without means gathered and sought asylum.

39. Temple of Ares: S. of the altar of the twelve gods stood the altar of Ares, built 435–20. The archaeologist Dinsmoor sug-

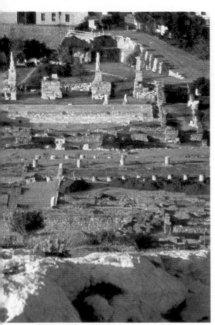

Odeion of Agrippa

sequently executed by Kritios and Nesiotes. Alexander the Great had the original brought back to Athens, and both monuments then stood alongside one another in the middle of the agora.

41. Odeion of Agrippa: According to tradition the dramatic and musical contests which were later held in the theatre of Dionysos were originally held in the agora. Only when the wooden stage on the agora, already too small, had collapsed, was the new auditorium built on the S. slope of the acropolis. Then, in about 15 BC, on the site of the old orchestra, the huge Odeion of Agrippa was erected, measuring 168 ft. 7 in. by 141 ft. 9 in. It was a theatre and concert-hall seating 1,000 in ten rows, entirely surrounded by two-storeyed halls. Today pilasters and the capitals of columns and the orchestra can be seen, as well as walls belonging to surrounding buildings of the 2&5C AD. To the N., at the entrance to the Odeion, are three colossal statues, two tritons and a giant on huge plinths, set up in the 2C AD.

42. Altar of Zeus Agoraios: W. of the N. portico of the Odeion of Agrippa are the foundations and some steps and other remains of a great altar of Zeus dating from the end of the 4C BC. The rich ornamentation is especially interesting. This altar originally stood on the Pnyx and was moved to the agora. Here the archons swore their oaths on taking up office.

43. Monument of the Eponymous Heroes: SW of the altar of Zeus and opposite the Metroon stood the huge monument of the eponymous heroes of Attica. On the walls of this monument laws and legal actions were posted. Two tripods flanked a plinth supporting 10 bronze statues of the heroes. The surviving remains date from the 4C.

44. SW Temple: The so-called SW

gests that the temple originally stood in Akharnai or in the Roman agora and was moved to the present site only around the birth of Christ. Pausanias in AD 165 records that the cult-statue of Ares was made by Alkamenes. The remains of carved ornaments can be seen in the Agora Museum. The only trace of the site today is a slight rise in the ground.

40. Plinth of the Statue of the Tyrannicides: To the N. of the Odeion of Agrippa is the site where the sculptured group of Harmodios and Aristogeiton probably stood. It was they who in 514 BC murdered the tyrant Hipparchos (see history of Athens); they were honoured as liberating heroes by the Athenians and given a monument. The original bronze statue by Antenor was carried off by the Persians in 480, and a new statue was sub-

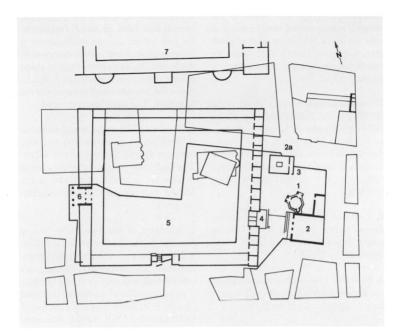

Roman Agora (after J.Travlos): The numbers on the plan are referred to in the description of the agora in the text.

Temple, a building standing in front of the Middle Stoa to the SW of the Odeion of Agrippa and built around 430 BC may have been earlier the temple of the eponymous heroes.

Roman agora and Environs:

The Roman agora was laid out on a rectangular plan measuring 367 ft. 6 in. x 315 ft. It lies not far from the Stoa of Attalos in the Greek agora, between the Library of Hadrian and the Tower of the Winds.

1. Tower of the Winds: The entrance to the Roman agora is in the E. near the Tower of the Winds. This octagonal tower standing 39 ft. 8 in. high was built in the 1C BC and was originally the *Water-clock of Andronikos Kyrrhestes.* The time could be read from the height of water in a pipe. The sides of the tower were oriented to the 8 Athenian cardinal points, and the 8 winds corresponding to these are allegorically depicted on the marble frieze encircling the tower, with Boreas to the N., Kaikias to the NE, Apeliotes to the E., Euros to the SE, Notos to the S., Lips, the Italian Scirocco, to the SE, Zephyros to the W., and Skiron to the NW. A bronze triton revolved on the pyramidal roof and acted as a weather-vane, but has been lost. The tower served not only as a water-clock and sundial, but also probably as a planetarium. Around AD 1750 a sect of Muslim dervishes took over the tower, decorating the interior walls with wooden panels gaily painted with sentences from the Koran.

Medrese: Opposite the Tower of the Winds is a finely worked arched gate which once led into a Muslim medrese or seminary, built by the Turks in 1721. Today the gate is boarded up, and the seminary is closed.

2. Agoranomion: S. of the Tower of the Winds are the foundations of a 1C AD building dedicated to Athena Archegetis and Divus Augustus. The name Agoranomion (market-police, formerly thought to have been situated here) has nothing to do with the function of the building.

3. Latrine: The ruins of a huge marble Roman latrine from the 1C AD, seating nearly 70 people, are to be found N. of the Tower of the Winds.

4. E. Gate: The entrance to the ruins of the Roman agora is through the E. gate, a Roman propylon from the 2C AD.

5. Roman agora: Between 1892 and 1966 the ruins of the Roman agora, probably dating from the end of the Hellenistic period, have been excavated. During the 1st half of the 2C the double-storeyed colonnades were built inside this agora to the S. and W., as were the rows of shops behind these colonnades in the S. and E. A marble fountain is still to be seen in the S. gallery. The inner court is paved.

6. W. Gate: The monumental propylon in the W. of the agora was built with four columns around the end of the 1C BC. The Doric gate was also called the Gate of Athena Archegetis (leader), and in the Middle Ages Porta tu Staropazar (cornmarket gate).

7. Library of Hadrian: The library founded by the Emperor Hadrian in AD 132, and which served not only as a library, but also as a lecture-hall, theatre, and concert-hall, was only identified in 1882. It stands to the N. of the Roman agora and parallel to it, and consists of a columned hall measuring 400 ft. x 269 ft. The outer walls are broken by exedrae. On the W. side a propylon and Corinthian columns sur-

Roman agora: Gate of Athena Archegetis

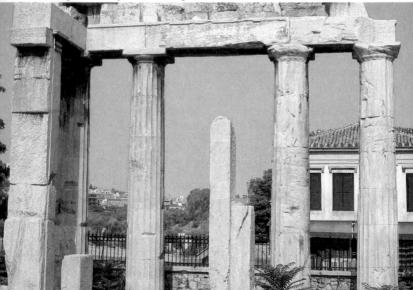

vive, as does the E. side. The library was housed in the central hall, where the niches for the scrolls can be seen. The court contained a huge fountain in the centre of gardens. In 1969 a small theatre with polychrome marble flooring was uncovered. In the 5C AD a building with four apses was erected, and in the 7C a basilica with a nave and two aisles, above the library ruins; the remains of these buildings can still be seen.

8. Plaka: SE of the Roman agora is Plaka, an old quarter of the city. The meaning of the name is disputed; it derives either from the Greek plaka: plaque, flat, or else from an Albanian word meaning old. Supporters of the latter hypothesis maintain that Albanian immigrants brought the name to Athens with them in the 16C. The area contains many old houses and churches (see p.125).

9. Monument of Lysikrates: S. of Plaka, not far from the theatre of Dionysos, is a round marble building (9 ft. 2 in. in diameter) built in the 2nd half of the 4C, with a bronze tripod won by the Choregos Lysikrates in 335/4 BC as the prize at the Dionysia. This is the only fully preserved choregic monument from antiquity. The marble frieze encircling the monument tells the story of a Homeric hymn to Dionysos in its carved figures. The Corinthian columns on the monument are thought to be the earliest such columns in Athens. In 1669 the Capuchins bought the monument for their monastery, which they established there. The monastery fell victim to fire during the War of Independence, and in 1845 the monument was re-excavated by French archaeologists.

10. Syntagma Square: SE of Plaka is Syntagma Square, in whose vicinity is a whole series of early medieval churches. The square itself is chiefly remarkable for its 19C public buildings.

Dipylon and Kerameikos

Monastiraki: Monastiraki Square, to the NE of the Greek agora (close to Hadrian's library), has an early medieval church and

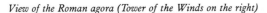

View of the Roman agora (Tower of the Winds on the right)

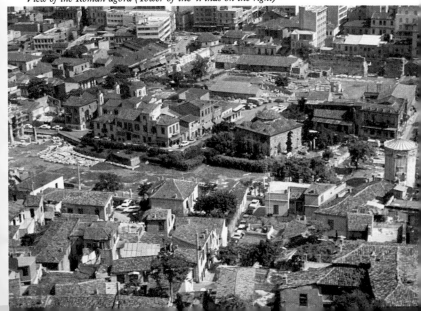

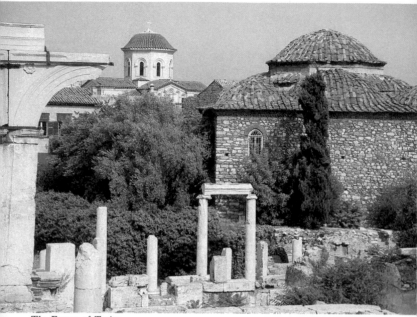

The Forum of Trajan

a mosque dating from 1759, now converted into a Museum of Greek Folklore. Crossing this and walking W. one comes to the Dipylon, and further to the W. of this the Kerameikos.

Dipylon (1): The Dipylon, one of the most impressive ruins in NW Athens, was in antiquity the chief of the 15 city gates. A broad road, now built over, led through it and directly to the agora. Another military road also led from the Dipylon to the Academy, and another fork down to Piraeus harbor, crossing the Sacred Way (2).

Originally the site of the Dipylon was occupied by the *Thriasian* or *Keramic gate*, built in 479 under Themistokles. At the end of the 4C the present Dipylon was built, covering an area of 131 ft. by 65 ft. 6 in. In the NW stood the gate (3) guarded

by two massively built flanking towers covering an area of almost 86 sq. ft. Thick walls surrounded the court. In front of the SE entrance, also flanked by two strong towers, and with two gates, stood the *altar of Zeus Herkaios* (4). E. of the entrance, inside the city walls, stood an ancient *fountain-house* (5), of which a few steps survive.

Pompeion (6): W. of the Dipylon and adjoining it, but within the city walls, stood the Pompeion, a 4C BC building which served as a kind of store-room and preparation chamber for the festal processions. It was built around a court and was surrounded by a columned hall. On the N. and W. sides of the building, ruins of which are still visible, there were diningrooms. The Pompeion was decorated with painted portraits of poets and a bronze

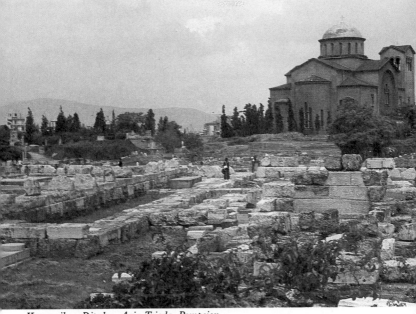

Kerameikos, Dipylon, Agia Triada, Pompeion

statue of Sokrates by Lysippos. Diogenes is also said to have stayed here. To the E. the original Propylon can be made out (7). The Pompeion was destroyed by Sulla in 88 BC when he invested Athens. A new Pompeion was built by Hadrian, and ruins of the *magnificent gate* (8) attached to it can be seen. This new Pompeion was destroyed in AD 267 by the Herulians.

Sacred Gate (9): SW of the Pompeion was the Sacred Gate, which spanned the *Sacred Way* (2) and the Eridanos stream. The complex was 115 ft. long by 40 ft. wide and flanked by two corner turrets, and dated originally from the 5C BC, but was continually rebuilt.

Kerameikos: In the foothills to the NW between the Dipylon and the Sacred Gate lies the site of the ancient funerary monu-

Monument of Lysikrates

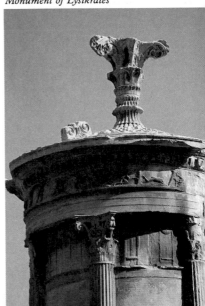

ments. This ancient cemetery is known as the Kerameikos after the original Kerameikos city-quarter, or potters' quarter. Ancient potters' workshops have been discovered there. The area was already serving as a cemetery in the 12C BC, first in the N., later in the S. quarter. At first, during the post-Mycenean period the dead were laid in graves lined with slabs, and small ceramic objects decorated with geometric motifs were laid in with them. After 1100 the Doric custom of cremation prevailed. Pottery funeral relics are still found, and these document the astonishing development of Attic pottery up to the famous huge Dipylon vases of the 8C. Starting in 1871 the graves of the Kerameikos area were uncovered by archaeologists, and despite all the destruction and infilling, they can be reconstructed as far back as the 12C BC. In the 7C the dead were placed in pit-graves. From the 6C they were buried beneath high grave-mounds, and later (after 350) beneath mounds of earth and pebbles. From the 5C the Kerameikos cemetery became renowned for its monumental and splendid funeral treasures. Under Kimon it became the state burial-ground. The best artists made sarcophagi, stele, small temples, funerary tables, statues, epigrams, and other monuments. The cemetery was enlarged in the 4C, and burials began S. of the Eridanos. The appointments of the graves became truly luxurious, so that in the 2nd half of the 5C all grave-goods were required to be cremated, and during the rule of Demetrios of Phaleron (317-07 BC) sumptuous funeral monuments were forbidden by law. From this time onwards only *Kioniskoi* (small, unadorned columns) were permitted. The Kerameikos cemetery was destroyed several times, notably in 480 BC by the Persians, in the 3C BC by Philip V of Macedon, and in 86 BC by Sulla. It was often rebuilt and enlarged. In the 2nd half of the 1C houses were built here, but these quickly gave way once more to graves. The

Kerameikos nonetheless remains impressive, even though the monuments now standing there are copies. The surviving original monuments are in the National Museum and the Kerameikos Museum (11), which should be visited after the cemetery. One should begin one's visit to the quarter in the street which originally ran from the Dipylon to Plato's Academy. This street was 128 ft. wide at its start and was called the Kerameikos even before the name was given to the whole cemetery. Then one should turn off the Sacred Way S. of Agia Triada into the Street of Tombs, and after visiting the monuments there, return to the museum, which is next to the modern entrance to the Kerameikos quarter, in the NW of the complex.

Academy and Kolonos Hill: Further to the NW of the Kerameikos one reaches

Dipylon and Kerameikos 1 Dipylon **2** Sacred Way **3** NW gate of the Dipylon **4** SE gate of the Dipylon **5** fountain-house **6** Pompeion **7** Propylon of the old Pompeion **8** great gate of the new Pompeion **9** Sacred Gate **10** Present entrance to the Kerameikos district **11** Kerameikos Museum **12** Burial mound from the 4C BC **13** Burial mound from the 5C BC **14** tomb of the generals Chairon and Thibrachos, killed in Piraeus in 403 BC **15** Hellenistic tomb **16** state tomb from the 4C BC **17** Agia Triada **18** classical tomb buildings **19** classical bridge **20** Tritopatreion, small temple of the Tritopatreis, probably from the 5C BC **21** Loutrophoros of Olympichos **22** tomb of Antidosis **23** tomb Lekythos of Aristomache **24** tomb of Eukoline, beautiful relief with a figure of a woman holding a bird in her hand **25** Tomb precinct of Lysimachides of Acharnai from the 2nd half of the 4C BC with a relief of Charon and a votive panel depicting a funeral feast **26** funerary column of Bion and base of a stela **27** famous tomb stela of Hegeso (5C BC), the original is in the National Museum **28** Geometric tombs **29** tomb of Dionysios of Kollytos with Naiskos and bull from the 4C BC **30** tomb of a family from Herakleia Pontike **31** funerary altar of Hipparate, c. 500 BC **32** tomb relief for Dexileos of Thorikos, who was killed in the Corinthian War in 394/3 BC **33** tomb plot of Demetria and Pamphile (c. 350 BC with burial mound, the stela of Dorkas of Sikyon and the relief of Pamphile, who is depicted sitting next to her mother Demetria, with the Loutrophoros of Hegetor and the base of the stela of Demetria, the stela of Glykera and the tomb slab of another Demetria **34** tomb of a family from Messene **35** Tomb of Isidoros and Zosime **36** funerary pillar of Sosibios **37** archaic burial mound

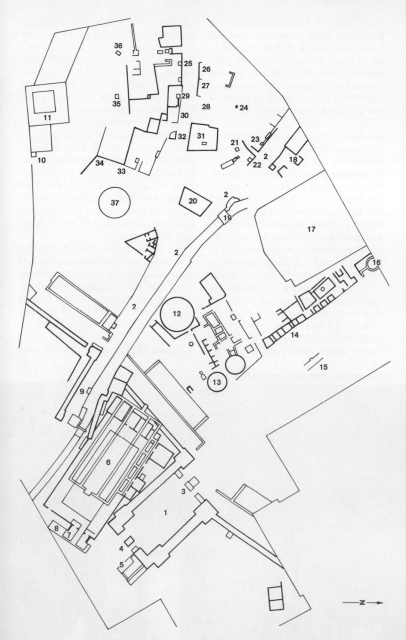

Plato's Academy. The surprisingly broad Kerameikos Road of ancient times led directly over the mile from the Dipylon to the Garden of Epikouros, where the philosopher, born in 341 BC, taught. Here too Plato had started his school, the Academy. This former garden suburb of Athens is now a hideous industrial zone.

Academy: The entrance to the excavations area of the Academy is on the corner of Kratylou and Thinai streets, and is usually closed. Furthermore, the remains of this complex are not particularly impressive. Excavations begun in 1929 revealed that the area was inhabited as early as the Neolithic period. Before the time of the Academy the area was a kind of sanctuary of the hero Hekademos, in whose honour a *heroon* was built. A house dating from around 2000 BC may be connected with the hero. In 1966 evidence of the originial Academy was discovered here, in the form of a boundary stone, the *Horos tes Hekademeias,* from the 5C BC. The name Academy, properly Hekademeia, is traditionally derived from Hekademos. In the 6C Hipparchos built a wall around the Hekademos area. It was said of Kimon that he turned the originally arid site into a well-watered and fertile grove (Plutarch, Kimon, 13). Plato taught here from 387 BC, and his pupil Aristotle used the spot as a gymnasion. The foundations of a Hellenistic gymnasion have been found, along with a Palaistra and bath for athletes, portions of a square court, ruins of long halls in the E., S., and W., bases for pupils' tables, and fragments of honorary decrees and writing-tablets. These remains date from 500 BC to the 6C AD. Here Plato taught, and after him the philosophy schools up to the time of Justinian, who closed the Academy in AD 529. The buildings fell into decay.

Of the 12 sacred *Moriai* (olive-trees) which grew here in honour of Athena, and played a part in her cult and in Greek legislation, one, *Plato's olive,* evidently extremely ancient, survives on the Sacred Way. It is said to be a scion of the olive-tree on the acropolis, and the second oldest in Attica.

Kolonos: Perikles and Sophokles were

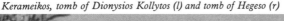
Kerameikos, tomb of Dionysios Kollytos (l) and tomb of Hegeso (r)

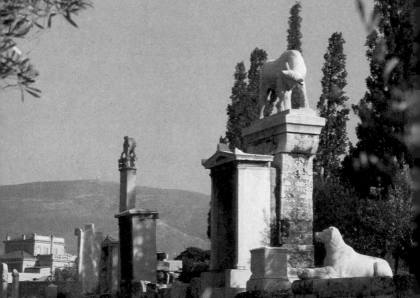

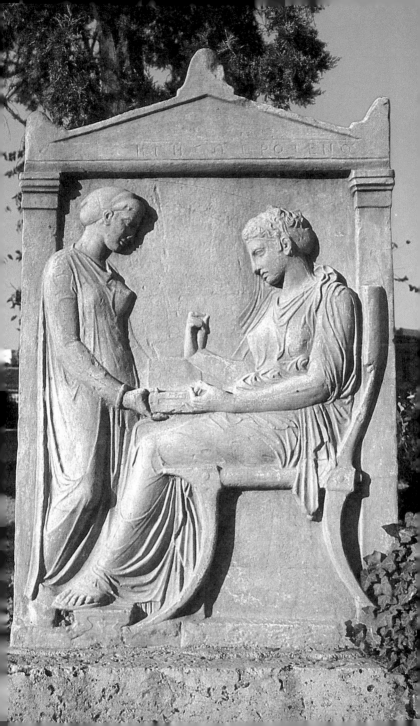

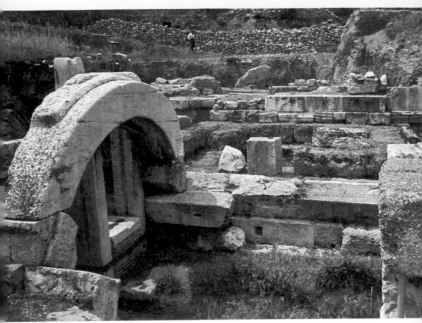

Kerameikos, Sacred Gate

born in the Kolonos quarter of the city E. of the Academy. This was the setting of Sophokles's last tragedy, 'Oedipus in Kolonos'. Two monuments commemorate the archaeologists Chr. Lénormant and K.O. Müller.

The Ilissos Region

Arch of Hadrian (1): Proceeding along the way to the Olympieion and the Ilissos region one comes to the Arch of Hadrian, probably built in the 2C AD to replace a 6C BC city gate. The monument is built in Pentelic marble and reads on the side facing the acropolis, 'This is Athens, ancient city of Theseus', and on the other side, 'The city of Hadrian and not of Theseus'. The region around the river Ilissos which one now enters has been inhabited since prehistoric times, particularly along the

banks of the river. The Ilissos itself has been covered over since the middle of this century to take traffic, and now flows underground. Excavations have brought ruins from every period of Athens's history to light.

Olympieion (5): The remains of the Olympieion are still overwhelming in their size, with the enormous columns with their Corinthian capitals and the vast column drums lying on the ground in the N. of the site. This temple of Zeus was 647 years in construction, and finally completed in AD 131/2 under Hadrian. Peisistratos began work on a monumental limestone temple in 515 BC to replace an earlier structure. In 174 BC Antiochos IV Epiphanes of Syria employed the Roman architect Cossutius to start work afresh. He enlarged the ground plan and altered the

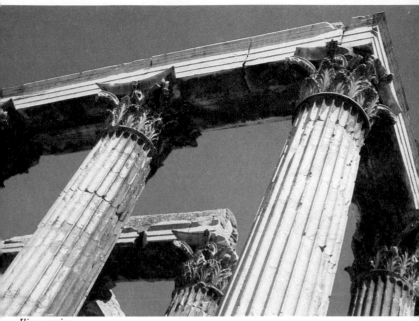

Ilissos region

orientation. The 15 columns which survive today in the SE corner date from this period. There were a total of 104 columns in Pentelic marble, 20 double rows to the N. and S. and three rows of 8 to the E, and W. After the death of Antiochos IV in 165 BC the building was left unfinished. Sulla carried off columns from the temple. Finally Hadrian completed the work, building a temenos wall with a propylon and placing his own chryselephantine statue next to that of Zeus in the cella. The building measures 362 ft. by 143 ft. 4 in.

Stadion (23): The horseshoe-shaped Stadion lies in a natural hollow between two hills. It seats 70,000 spectators and was built 1869–70 with a donation by Averoff (a Greek) as the showplace for the first modern Olympic Games held in 1896, nearly 1500 years after the last ancient

games. It was designed by Baron de Coubertin and built by the German architect E.Ziller. Astonishingly, it is an almost exact copy of the reconstruction of the ancient Greek stadium by Herodes Atticus in 139–43. In many respects the beauty and functional qualities of classical architecture have never been surpassed.

Churches in Athens

Most churches in Athens are closed. The key is usually kept by the sacristan in a neighbouring house.
Many early churches were in ancient temples. The ruins of these churches have been removed during the restoration of the temples, and most of them can be seen in the Byzantine Museum. Thus in the 5C the Panagia Athíniotissa was built in the Parthenon, a church of St.George in the

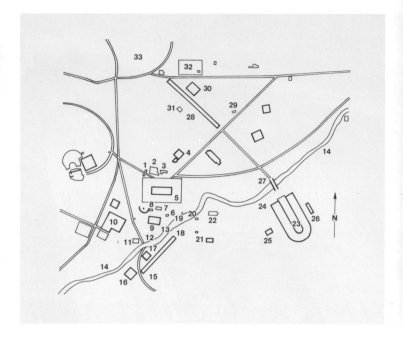

Ilissos region 1 Arch of Hadrian **2** remains of houses **3** Roman bath **4** Roman building with semicircular hall **5** Olympeion **6** precinct of Kronos and Rhea, the Roman ruins of which were excavated in 1892 **7** Temple of Apollo Delphinios. The ruins of the Doric peristyle date from the 5C BC. There was probably already a Mycenean Temple of Apollo on this site, as a few finds have indicated **8** former law court of the Delphinion **9** Panhellenion **10** Kodros **11** former Python, Temple of Apollo Pythios from the 6 or 5C BC **12** Aphrodite in the Garden, a beautiful garden quarter famous in ancient times **13** altar **14** Ilissos. In 1956–67, with long stretches of the river running underground, the banks were examined by archaeologists **15** an inscription bearing the name Kynosarges was discovered here **16-17** Gymnasion from the 6C BC, the Kynosarges Gymnasion, excavated in 1896 and one of the 3 most famous gymnasia in Athens. The philosophical ideas of the Cynics are said to have been developed here **18** relief of Pan, barely recognizable, hewn out of the rock, possibly a shrine to Pan from the 5C BC

19 Kallirrhoe Spring, whnce Sacred Water was once taken for religious rites **20** crossing over the Ilissos **21** small temple of Artemis Agrotera, discovered and identified in 1751–5 and possibly an early work by the architect Kallikrates. Destroyed by the Turks in 1778 **22** Metroon in Agrai **23** Stadium **24** Shrine of Pan **25** Temple of Tyche **26** probable site of Herodes Atticus's tomb **27** Roman bridge **28** area formerly occupied by the Lykeion, which with the Academy and the Kynosarges was one of the three most celebrated gymnasia in Athens **29** foundations of the Temple of Apollo Lykeios, which gave its name to the later gymnasion **30** gymnasion building where Aristotle taught in the 4C BC; the covered colonnade of the building was called the peripatos, hence the naming of Aristotle's school as the Peripatetics **31** Lykeion bath **32** gardens of Theophrastos, the spot where, in the middle of modern Athens, archaeologists uncovered the botanical gardens of Theophrastos, Aristotle's follower **33** Eridanos **VIII–XIII** city gates

Temple of Hephaistos, and the Megáli Panagia in the Library of Hadrian. Two churches are still to be found at the foot of the acropolis cliff:

Ágios Giorgios tu Vrachu (St.George of the cliffs): A small church near Epicharmou street with a vaulted nave probably dating from the Frankish period, and

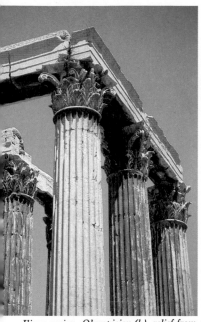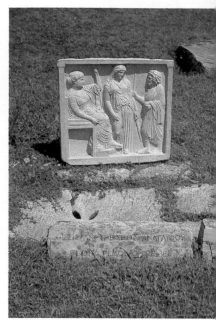

Ilissos region, Olympieion (l.), relief from a house (r.)

Agios Simeon against the acropolis cliffs, dating from the Turkish period.

Sotira Nikodímu (Church of St. Nikodemos): This church built in 1045 (now a Russian church) stands near Plaka, and once belonged to the monastery of St. Nikodemos. There are surviving crypts which to judge from their shape must have been built on a Roman bath-house. In one of these is the grave of the founder. The monks' cells were destroyed in an earthquake in 1701, and in 1780 the church was damaged by the Turks. In 1847 it was bought by the Russian state. It is an octagonal building with a large dome; the interior was rebuilt after 1855 by the Bavarian architect Friedrich von Thiersen.

Church of St.Paul: Close to the church of St.Nikodemos on Leophóros Amalías is the neo-Gothic Anglican church designed in 1840–3 by C.R. Cockerell.

Sotira Kottáki: SW of the latter in Kidathinéon street is a 13C church, originally cross-domed but later converted into a basilica with nave and two aisles and restored.

Agia Rinula: This little church stands almost completely concealed on Navarchor-Nikodemou street. Young girls used to pray here before their school examinations.

Church of St.Katherine: Not far from Sotira Kottáki on Pharmáki street, E. of the monument of Lysikrates is the church of St. Katherine (Ekaterini) in a court with palm-trees behind the ruins of a Roman colonnade. The cupola and apses date from the 13C.

Ágios Nikólaos Rangava: N. of the monument of Lysikrates is this 11C church, subsequently altered, which originally belonged to the residence of the Rangavas — a family which was related to Byzantine emperors and patriarchs.

Monastiri tu Panagíu Táfu: This monastery subject to the Holy Sepulchre in Jerusalem is on Erechtheus street. The monastery church *Agii Anargyri* (of the moneyless saints) originally dates from the 17C. The carved and gilded iconostasis inside is interesting, as is the residence of the exarch (1858) behind the church.

Agios Ioannis Theologos: Further up Erechtheus street, on the corner of Erotokritou street, is this little 13C cross-domed church.

Metamorphosis tu Sotiros: The nearby church of the Transfiguration on Theorias street, with its high cupola built in the 14C during the reign of the Florentine Acciaiuoli, is well worth a visit. There is a little side chapel cut into the rock, perhaps originally a cave. The altar is an early Christian capital. Fragments of paintings are to be found in the apse.

Panagia Chrysokastriotissa: The church of Our Golden Lady of the Castle stands at the S. end of Markou-Avriliou street. It is said that when the Turks were taking the acropolis the women and children threw themselves down from the cliffs. The wonder-working icon of the Chrysokastriotissa, which came from the acropolis, saved them all and conducted them unharmed back to their houses. Since then the church has been a refuge for women and children in peril.

Pantanassa church: The sunken 10C ba-

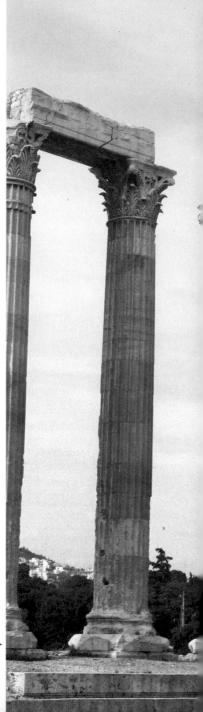

Ilissos region, Olympieion ▷

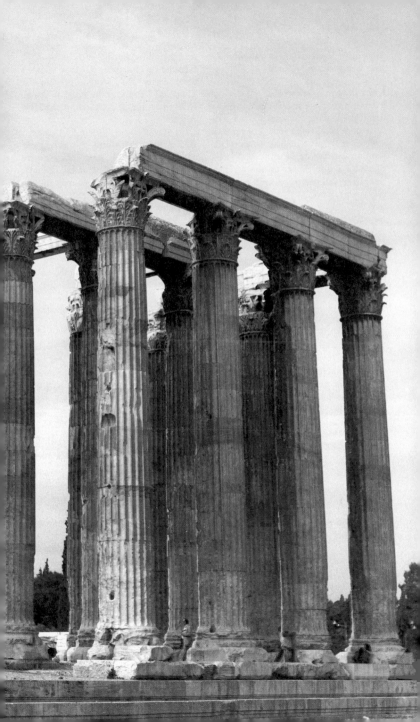

silica of the Pantanassa is on Monastiráki square; it was restored in 1911.

Kapnikarea church: Leaving Monastiráki square and proceeding E. up Ermu street in the direction of Syntagma square one comes after some 220 yards to a beautiful 11C cross-domed church which was later enlarged by the addition of a narthex and a side chapel on the N. The Byzantine wall paintings inside are especially remarkable.

New Metropolis: Close by to the SE of the Kapnikarea is Metropolis square with the old and new Metropolitan churches. The large cathedral was built 1842–62 to plans by Schaubert.

Old Metropolis: Behind this lies the smaller building of the Old Metropolis, also known as the *Panagia Gorgoepikoos* and *Agios Eleftherios*. It was built in the 12C as a four-columned cross-domed church with a narthex; ancient carvings were used, including a frieze of the calendar, pilaster capitals, pediment carvings, funerary aediculae, and so on. Here the Middle Ages and antiquity have been blended into a unity of great charm.

Church of St.Philip: W. of Monastiráki square is the church of St.Philip, and next to this to the S. on the old agora the church of the Apostles, probably built around 1000.

Church of the Apostles: This was restored during the excavations in the agora. It was built over a 2C BC Nymphaion and originally had 4 conches. The interior, surmounted by 4 large and 4 smaller domes, is beautifully proportioned and has fine Byzantine paintings. The outer walls of undressed stone with brick decorations are equally worth seeing.

Agion Asomaton: Proceeding W. out of

Monastiráki square in the direction of the Kerameikos along Ermu street one comes after some 330 yards, opposite the Theseion station on the right, to the recently restored 11C church of the Holy Angels.

Agios Ioannis Kolona: Euripides street runs parallel to Ermu street some 330 yard further to the N. Here stands the little chapel of St.John with a Roman column projecting from its roof. John the Baptist is venerated here for his healing powers against all ailments of the head.

Agii Theodori: Also on Euripides street where it runs into Klafthmonos square is the Church of the Sts.Theodore, an 11C building of dressed stone and brick.

Athens in the 19 and 20C.

The splendour of Athens which had been renowned throughout the ancient world became gradually more and more obscured through the course of history. Even through the long centuries of Turkish rule, however, the monuments on the acropolis were never quite forgotten, though the city itself sank during the Middle Ages into an unimportant provincial town. When the Turks were expelled in 1833 the city had a population of barely 3,000. In 1834 King Otho made his residennce in Athens, which he named capital of Greece. Neoclassical architects inspired by the abundant antiquities of the city set to work. Amidst the little, old, half decayed houses arose a royal palace, streets, gardens, and great commercial buildings. In 1899 the population had risen to 110,000. In 1896 the first Olympic Games in modern times were held in the newly built Stadion. Museums, business houses and factories

Ilissos region, Hadrian's Arch ▷

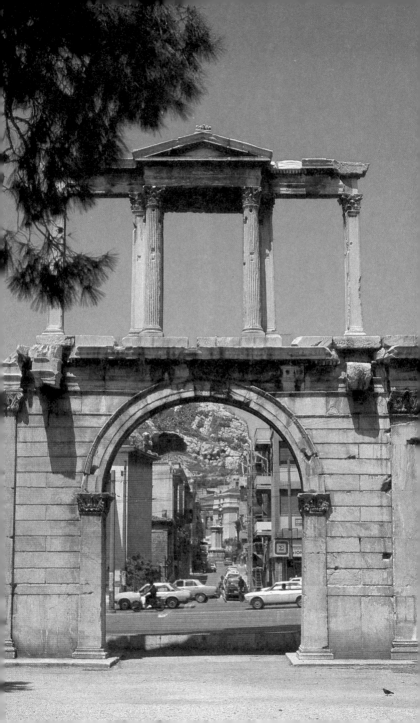

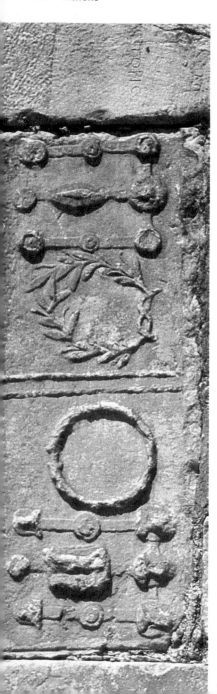

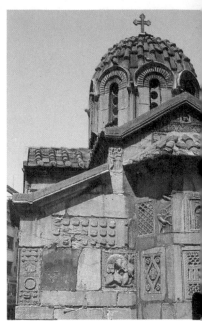

*Old (small) Metropolis, E. façade,
ancient and Byzantine reliefs on the E.
façade*

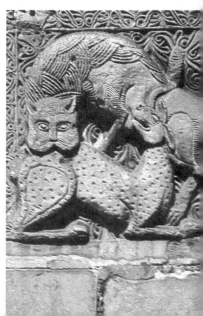

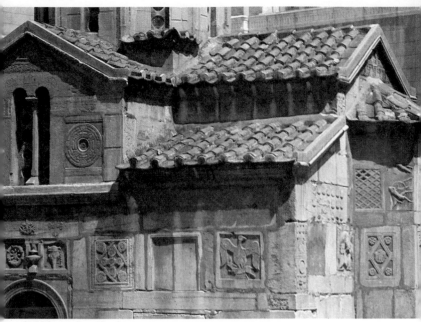

Old Metropolis, side view

sprung up. Foreign trade grew to enormous dimensions, and in the 20C the ever growing number of inhabitants had to be housed in rapidly constructed high-rise blocks. Today Athens and its suburbs have a population of 2.54 million, and it is the largest and in every respect the greatest city in Greece.

The visitor who wishes to follow Athens's rise in the 19C should visit the two squares which were laid out at the time when the new street network was being planned, *Omonia Square* to the N. of the city centre and *Syntagma Square* to the E. Under the Bavarian Wittelsbach King Otho I, who ruled in Athens 1834–62, the new Athens was created by two Danish, one French, and several German architects. The plan of the new street network had already been laid out by Schaubert of Breslau and the Greek Kleanthes in 1832–3.

In 1834 Leo von Klenze undertook the continuation of this large-scale work. On the square now called Syntagma Square, Friedrich von Gärtner built the **Royal Palace** in 1834–8, now the seat of the Parliament. S. and E. of the palace the botanist Karl Froos laid out the **National Gardens** to the design of Queen Amalia, which was planted and tended for decades by the Head Court Gardener Friedrich Schmidt. In the S. part of this garden the Zappa brothers subsequently built an exhibition hall. In 1867 the Danish architect Hansen built the **Hotel Grand Bretagne** on Syntagma Square. The façade of the lower storey, originally designed as a private house, has survived unchanged, although the building was converted into a hotel in 1874, and upper storeys were added in 1960.

Leaving Syntagma Square by Venizelos

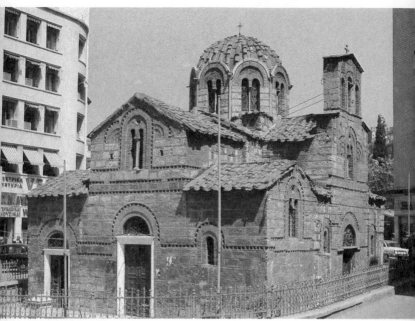

Church of Agii Theodori

street in a NW direction and heading towards Omonia Square one comes first on the right-hand side to **Schliemann's House** with its loggias on the right-hand side, built by Ernst Ziller as the 'Iliu melathron'. It is now the seat of the Supreme Court. Next comes the **eye hospital** in Byzantine style, then Leo von Klenze's **church of St.Dionysios**. A few paces further on is the spacious **Academy of Sciences** and the **University**, begun in 1837 by Christian Hansen of Copenhagen, and finally the **National Library**, built, like the Academy, by Theophil Hansen, Christian's younger brother. Parallel to Venizelos street in the SE runs Stadiu street. Here on a level with the University is the **Old Parliament**, built by Boulanger in 1871, and now the home of the Historical Museum. Finally NE of the Zappeion on Herodes-Atticus street is the

Crown Prince's Palace built by Ziller in 1890–8.

Theatres in Athens

Athens is the cradle of the theatre, and is still home to a considerable number of productions, particularly the Athens festival in the *theatre of Herodes Atticus* (see p.90). During the winter the State Opera plays in the *Olympia theatre* (59 Odos Akademias). National Theatre productions can be seen in the winter in the *Royal Theatre* (Odos Agiu Konstantinu). During the summer the Arts Theatre (Theatro Technis) plays in the theatre of Herodes Atticus or in the *Attikon* (16 Odos Kodrigtonos), and in the winter in the *Theatro Technis* (52 Odos Stadiu).

There is also a large number of small

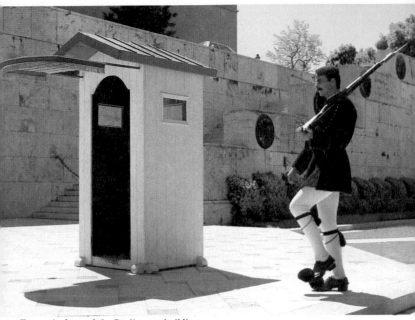

Evzone in front of the Parliament building

theatres, especially on Syntagma Square, Omonia Square, and near the National Museum. Here modern and folk plays are performed. There are a few summer theatres along Leoforos Alexandras. Classical tragedies in modern Greek are also of interest to the non-Greek visitor. Ballet and folk-dancing are performed on Philopappos Hill, whilst the chief venues for concerts are the *Kotopuli theatre* (Odos Panepistimiu) and the *Parnassus hall* (Platia Karytsi).

Museums in Athens

National Archaeological Museum (1 Tositsa street): The National Museum is one of the world's most famous museums and has a precious collection of sculptures and pottery from archaic, classical and Hellenistic Greece. The present building is by Ludwig Lange of Darmstdt (1808–68); it was begun in 1860 and finished in 1889 in the neo-Greek style. It was enlarged and extended in 1925, then in 1935–8, and finally after the Second World War. On the ground floor, rooms 4–6 exhibit the prehistoric collection, Mycenean art and Cycladic art. In rooms 7–13 archaic art, including the Geometric period, is displayed. Rooms 14–21 exhibit early and high classical art, rooms 22–31 late classical and Hellenistic art. Room 32 houses the A. and H.Stathatos collection, and room 35 the K.Karapanos collection with finds from Dodona. There are small bronzes in room 36, art of the Roman period in rooms 38–43, and large bronze statues in room 40. On the upper floor there are collections of vases, wall paintings (from Santorini), and exhibits from

National Archaeological Museum, Ground Floor (from 4 onwards the numbers of the key match the room numbers) **1** entrance **2** sales kiosk **3** entrance hall **4** Mycenean art with finds from Mycene, Argos and Pylos, the frescos from Tiryns, the golden goblet from Vaphio and Agamemnon's gold death mask **5** Neolithic art **6** Cycladic art with idols, ceramics and frescos; Parian marble flute- and lyre-players (2400-2200 BC) **7** Dipylon vase and Dipylon head ivory statue (8C BC) and statue of Artemis from around 650 BC **8** larger than life size Kouros from Cape Sounion, from about 600 BC **9** kouroi; winged Nike figure from Delos, about 550 BC; tomb kouros (Melos, about 500 BC); kore from Markopoulon **10** sculptures from the mid-6C, including a kouros from Markopoulon, a tomb kouros (about 550 BC) and a tomb stela from Attica dating from around 560 BC **11** sculptures from the second half of the 6C, including a tomb stela of Pentelic marble by Aristokles, the base of a kouros statue depicting games and fights between cats and dogs (Attic, about 510 BC), and the base of an Attic statue from around 490 BC depicting a ball game **12** late-6C and early-5C sculptures including warriors' heads from the Temple of Aphaia on Aegina (c. 500) and a stela from Athens (c. 510 BC) **13** statue of Aristodikos (Attic, about 500 BC), a high point in the development of kouros statues; tomb kouros of Croesus (Attic, about 520 BC), one of the finest examples from this period **14** sculptures, 1st half of the 5C, including a votive relief of the goddess Aphrodite (?) from Melos (c. 470) **15** 5C sculptures, including a votive relief of the goddesses of Eleusis, and a bronze statue of Poseidon 6 ft. 10 in. high **16** Classical tomb reliefs: tomb stela of a young man holding a bird (around 420 BC, Attic) **17** late-5C sculptures: head of Hera by Polykleitos and statue of Athena (Athena Lenormant) **18** 5&4C tomb reliefs: Hegeso stela (Kerameikos, c. 400) **21** Diadumenos room with Roman copies of classical sculptures; Diadumenos of Delos, horse and rider by Artemision (2C BC, bronze, original) **22** 4C BC sculptures from Epidauros **23/24** 4C BC tombs **25–27** religious reliefs, 4C **28** tombs and sculptures from Attica: huge 4&3C relief with horse and negro squires; Ephebe from Antikythera (bronze, c. 340); head of the goddess Hygieia, Tegea c. 360 **29/30** Hellenistic sculptures: early-3C BC statue of Themis, 2C portrait of a beardless man, Olympic victor **32** Stathatos collection, given to the museum in 1957, with some interesting bronzes and ancient and Byzantine jewellery **34** votive reliefs and sculptures **35** Karapanos collection **36** collection of bronze figures **37–39** Roman sculptures **40** huge bronze statues: statue of Athena (7 ft. 9 in. high), armed and with a plumed helmet, about 375 BC and probably by Kephisodotos, Praxiteles's father; and the oldest known bronze kouros, a statue of Apollo from the late 6C.

National Archaeological Museum, 1st Floor A Thera room, housing frescos and finds from Thera **49–56** Ceramics collection, displayed in chronological order to offer an impression of the development of Greek ceramics from the 3rd millennium through to the end of the 5C BC. The paintings depict scenes from ancient life. Room 50 contains the celebrated Nessos amphora, which dates from the 2nd half of the 7C BC.

Zappeion from the public garden

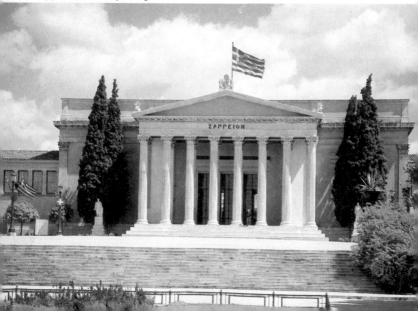

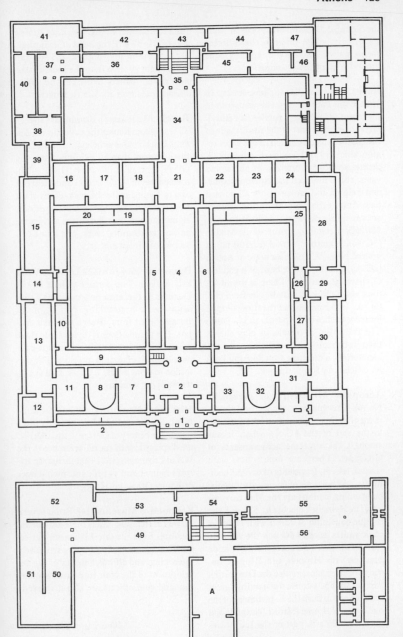

the National Museum of Cyprus in Nicosia. A brief guide through the different rooms may be found in the captions to the ground plan of the museum.

Agora Museum (24 Adrianu street): In 1956 King Paul opened this museum in the rooms of the Stoa of Attalos (see entry). Here the greater part of the finds made in the excavations conducted in the agora region since 1931 have been assembled. Statues, terracottas, bronzes, amphorae and vases, not to mention inscriptions, coins, and weights and measures are all housed here. Among the most interesting exhibits are a standing statue of Apollo Patroos (*c.* 320 BC), a standing statue of Aphrodite (2C BC), a marble Nereid (*c.* 400 BC), a winged Nike (5C BC), a statuette of Apollo (2C BC), and the bronze head of a goddess of victory (*c.* 430 BC). There is an intriguing water-clock (clepsydra) in fired clay (5C BC) which measured the time allotted for the speeches of the parties in law cases. The collection of ostraka or clay sherds used in ostracism is interesting, and the kleroterion, a machine for choosing public officials by lot, is unique.

Acropolis Museum (see acropolis, No.16): This museum records the development of Attic sculpture from the early 5C to the end of the 6C BC, when it was amongst the supreme achievements of Greek art. There are nine rooms with statues, reliefs, fragments of carved pediments, and portions of friezes. Among the outstanding exhibits are the *Man carrying a calf* in Hymettos marble (*c.* 570 BC), the unique collection of *Korai* with their archaic smiles (mostly 6C BC), the *Rampin rider*, with part of a second rider beside him (perhaps Hippias and Hipparchos, sons of Peisistratos, or else the Dioscuri?), from about 550 BC, the outstanding great sculpted group from the E. pediment of the old *Temple of Athena* (battle of the gods and giants, *c.* 525 BC), part of the sculptures

from the parapet of the *Temple of Athena Nike* (421–07 BC), the head of a youth (*c.* 485 BC), a standing youth (*c.* 485 BC), and as highlight 20 slabs from the Ionic *Parthenon frieze*, which depicted the Great Panathenaia over its 525 ft. length.

Benaki Museum (1 Koumbrari street): This museum houses the collection of Antonis Benaki in his neoclassical home. The three storeys display exhibits from the Greek War of Liberation (1821 – 30), mementoes of King Otho I and George I and of Byron, ancient Greek works of art from the Mycenean to Hellenistic periods, Byzantine and post-Byzantine art, icons, ancient goldsmiths' work, and a fine collection of Greek folk art.

Byzantine Museum (22 Leoforos Vassilisis Sofias): The former palace of the Duchess of Piacenza now contains a museum with a precious collection of Byzantine art from Greece and Asia Minor. The ground floor is divided into three rooms arranged as churches illustrating the development of church interiors. The collection of icons on the 1st floor with 9–17C works is outstanding.

Historical Museum (in the Old Parliament, Stadiu street): Here exhibits illustrating the history of Greece in the 18&19C are displayed, with special reference to the War of Liberation (1821–30), including Byron's helmet and sword, and mementoes of Kings Otho and George I.

Kerameikos Museum (148 Ermu street): As well as stele and reliefs there are funeral treasures from the late Mycenean period on. The collection of pottery is particularly interesting, and affords a survey of the development of the craft in Attica. Bronze, iron and gold objects are also displayed.

Illisos Area, Olympieion ▷

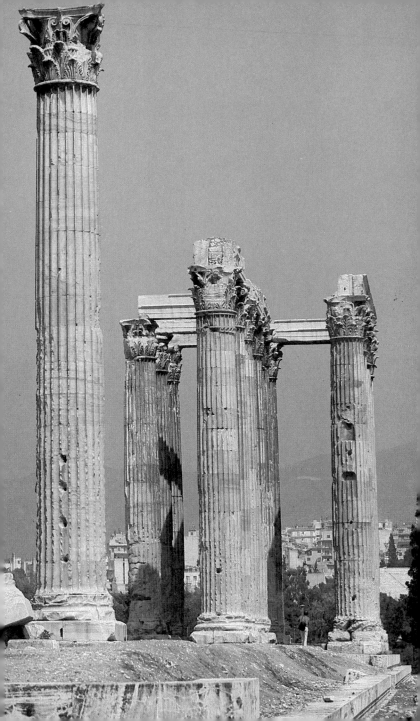

Museum of War (Leoforos Vasilissis Sofias): This museum was established during the military dictatorship to display exhibits intended to throw a proper light on Greek armies over the centuries.

Museum of Greek Folk Art / Museum of Folklore (17 Vidathinaion street): A superb collection of embroidery (Coptic clothing from the 2C AD to the present day), processional litter cloths from the 17C, gold and silver objects from Asia Minor, pottery, icons and jewellery.

National Art Gallery (60 Vasileos-Konstantinou street): This museum opposite the Hilton houses paintings from every period, including four works attributed to El Greco, and 19&20C works in particular.

Kanellópulos Collection (Plaka / Corner of Theoria and Panu): The collection of Paul and Alexandra Kanellópulos was acquired by the State in 1972 and opened as a museum in 1976. This family collection includes antiquities from every period, with some notable sculptures, pots, and icons.

Áthos/Ághion Óros/Mount Athos/ΑΘΟΣ

Macedonia   p.292☐H/I 3/4

The Athos peninsula is the easternmost of the fingers of the Chalkidike peninsula in northern Greece, (some 150 km. SE of Thessaloníki). It is 28 miles long but only 3–6 miles wide and covers an area of 130 square miles. A ridge of mountains runs down the length of the peninsula, rising to its highest point at the SE end, with Mount Athos (6,670 ft.). Today it is the site of the world famous monastic republic of the Holy Mountain (Aghion Oros).

History: In antiquity, the remote peninsula was famous only because of the unsuccessful attempt to build a canal by Xerxes (483 BC) across the narrow neck of land at the NW end of the peninsula (E. of Trypití). The Persian general, Mardonius, had lost the greater part of his fleet in 493 BC when he attempted to sail round Athos (Cape Akrathos). The King of the Persians, Xerxes, therefore decided to cut a canal through the peninsula to allow ships to pass; but it eventually proved to be too shallow.

Mount Athos was mentioned as early as Homer and Aiskhylos as being the Throne of Zeus and was equated with the giant of the same name, Athos, who was said to have raised the peak during his struggle with Poseidon.

In early Christian times (6&7C) this bare and isolated region soon became a place of refuge for hermits, anchorites and ascetics like, for example, the famous monk Peter the Athonite. In the 8&9C, these hermits settled together in small monastic communities under the guidance of a Protos ('First'). The era of the major monastic foundations began in the 10C: in 963 the monk, St. Athanasius the Athonite, with the support of his friend, the Emperor Nikephoras II Phokas (963–9), founded the first and most renowned of the monasteries, the Great Lavra (*Moni Megístis Lavras*) at the SE end of Athos. Following the constitution of the monastery of Studion in Constantinople, he wrote the first monastic rule of Athos (the *Typikon* or 'Exemplar'), which was officially recognized in 972 by the Emperor John Tsimiskis as the constitution of the autonomous monastic republic. This Rule established the communal life and self- government of the monks and further imposed the vows of abstinence (from marriage and eating meat), obedience and poverty. In the supplementary Typikon of 1045 (2nd. Typikon), it was forbidden for any female creature (even animals such as hens) to remain on Athos; this still holds true today.

In 1060, the monastic republic, which by then had grown considerably, was confirmed as independent from the Patriarch in Constantinople. More monasteries were founded in the 12C, even during the period of Frankish rule (from 1204) and especially during the revival under the Palaiologoi (1261–1453). Under the Turkish occupation (from 1453) and during the Wars of Independence (1821), the Holy Mountain was a stronghold of Greek Orthodoxy and nationalism (the Turks respected most of the monastic privileges). At this time, many smaller settlements, known as *Sketes* (ascetics' dwellings), *Kellia* (cell dwellings), *Kalyves* (huts) etc., came into being and were looked after by the bigger monasteries. At the same period, most of the monasteries of the E. side and many of those on the W. abandoned the strict (coenobitic) rule of common life of the old Typikon and chose instead a laxer (idiorrhythmic) rule of individual discipline. This idiorrhythmic Rule allows not only greater freedom of life-style and ownership of property, but also allows the eating of meat, except in Holy Week.

Of the 20 major monasteries, only 12 still follow the strict rule of common life (C) while the remaining 8 follow the more recent rule of individual discipline (I).

In the following table the 20 major monasteries are listed in their hierarchical order together with the date of their foundation and their rule of life:

1. Great Lavra (Megisti Lavra), 963 (I)
2. Vatopedi monastery (Vatopedíu), 972 (I)
3. Iberer monastery (Ivíron), 976 (I)
4. Khilandari monastery (Khilandaríu), 1076 (I)
5. Dionysos monastery (Dionysíu), 1374 (C)
6. Kutlumusi monastery (Kutlumusíu),1283 (C)
7. Pantokrator monastery (Pantokratoros), 1363 (I)

8. Xiropotamos monastery (Xiropotamu), 956 (I)
9. Zografos monastery (Zografu), 1270 (C)
10. Dochiarios monastery (Dochiariu), 1046 (I)
11. Karakallos monastery (Karakallu), 1033 (C)
12. Philotheos monastery (Philotheu), 992 (I)
13. Simon-Petra museum (Simonos Petra), 1300 (C)
14. Paulus monastery (Agíu Pavlu), 1050 (C)
15. Stavronikita monastery 1001–1542 (I)
16. Xenophon monastery (Xenophontos), 1033 (C)
17. Gregorius monastery (Grigoríu), 1345 (C)
18. Esfigmenu monastery, 1035 (C)
19. Russian monastery (Rossikon), 1169–1765 (C)
20. Kostamonítu monastery, 1086 (C)

Organization and Administration of the Monasteries: The monks have many tasks (more than 50 different posts) all of which, from abbot to novice, are hierarchically organized. At the head of the monastery is the abbot (Igoumenos) or president (Proigoumenos) assisted by counsellors (Epitropoi) and a council of elders (Synaxis). After the senior monks (Megaloskimoi) come the junior ones (Mikroskimoi), and lastly the inferior monks (Paramikroi) who do all the heavy manual labour. The novice (Rasophoros: wearer of the cowl) graduates to the rank of senior novice (Stavrophoros: carrier of the cross). All monks (Kalogeroi) have a long beard (Ghenia) and long hair which is tied in a bun under a black cap (Skouphia). Their normal dress is the black belted habit (Zostiko). The monk's daily round is encapsulated in the following words: 'Ghraphi, meleta, psalli, stenasi, prosevkhou, siopa!' ('Write, read, sing much, sigh, pray, keep silent!').

The monks spend about 8 hours per day

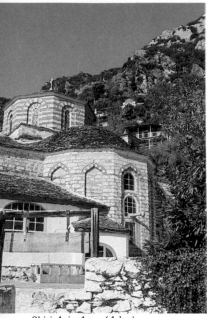

Skiti Agia Anna (Athos)

into 5 Tetrads (groups of four) under the leadership of the 5 major monasteries: Lavra, Vatopedíu, Ivíron, Khilandaríu Dionysíu. The four Epistates (supervisors) and the Protepistatis (chief-supervisor) or Protos (first) are elected every five years. The administrative council has chiefly financial and judicial jurisdiction, as established in the Greek State's official recognition in 1920–6 of the *Theocratic Republic of Athos*. Nevertheless, Greek suzerainty is represented by the accredited Governor and the police station in Karyes. Here the tourist's letters of introduction (obtained from the relevant consulate in Thessaloníki) are examined and residence permits (Diamonitírion) are issued for a limited period. Accommodation and food are not charged for, but visitors are expected to offer some donation.

Architecture and art: The external architecture of the larger monasteries is largely the same. The complex is approximately square and surrounded by a wall with towers (monastery fortress). In the *monastery courtyard* (perívolos, also square) is the central *monastery church,* the katholikon or *katholikos naos,* as it is the main building. The adjacent *monastery buildings* look into the central courtyard and their exterior façades are often sombre and fortress-like, with parapets and machicolations for defensive purposes. The detached *katholikon* (main church) is always a *cross-in-square church* (often with numerous side domes) with shell-like apses (usually triconchal) various side chapels and a bipartite narthex. The architectural multiplicity of the various parts of the katholikon is a magnificent demonstration of the medieval and Byzantine search for God. The focal point of the architectural and pictorial design is the Ruler of the World, Christ Pantocrator, in the main dome.

praying. The daily routine looks something like this in detail (Vatopedi monastery):
4 a.m.: wake up (Eghersis).
4–7a.m.: Orthros (matins), Liturgía (mass), breakfast (Proghevma)
7 – 10 a.m.: chores (Diakonima)10 – 12 noon: household chores, study
12–3 p.m.: lunch, siesta
3–4 p.m.: Esperinós (vespers)
4–6p.m.: walks, social calls
6–7 p.m.: prepare the evening meal
7–9 p.m.: evening meal (Dípnon), study
9–12 midnight: evening prayer (Kanón), private prayer, sleep.
The administration of the monastic repulic is the responsibility of the appointed representatives (Antiprosopoi) of the 20 major monasteries who meet in the capital Karyés (Karyai) in the Iera Kinotis (sacred congregation). These are subdivided

Skiti Agia Anna (Athos), dome ▷

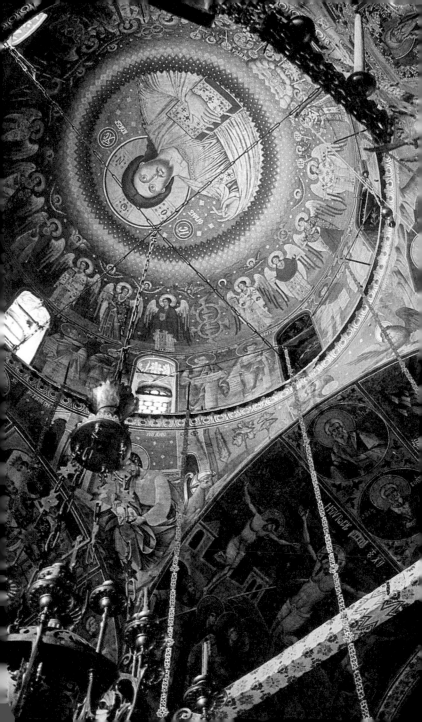

The *trapeza* (trapezi: 'table'), which is usually cruciform with apses, serves as the monks' *refectory* (refektorium); after the church (katholikon) this is the most important communal space and is decorated with lavish *wall paintings* of saints, wooden ceilings and often enormous *marble tables*. In the monasteries of the strict (coenobite) orders the monks process after the liturgy in hierarchical order from the katholikon to the trapeza, where they take the Christian 'love feast' (agape). In the idiorrhythmic monasteries this only happens on certain feast days. The reading during the meal (anagosma) is from the *ambon* (lectern).

Near the trapeza are the service rooms such as the *kitchen* (estia), the *bakery* (magnipiíon) and the underground *stores* for provisions and wine.

Near the katholikon is the *holy water building* (phiali:'vessel'), usually a small, rectangular building with peristyle, fountain and painted dome.

The *bell towers* (kampanarió) are usually square with massive walls and arched openings in the upper storeys. They are sometimes connected with the narthex or the katholikon.

The *monks' cells* (kellia:'cells') are housed in the multi-storeyed buildings of the *chordai* ('strings' of the building) with their broad façades. The fortress-like complexes were equipped with protruding *upper storeys* (wooden constructions) and *balconies* in the last few centuries and are suspended over the gorges in a picturesque fashion (e.g. Simon-Petra, monastery of Dionysos). The multi-storeyed *watch towers* with embrasures, battlements and parapets add to the fortress-like appearance.

Each of the coastal monasteries has a *quay* (arsanas) of its own with boat houses, some with their own watch towers.

The so-called *skítai* (derived from 'asketeien') are ascetics' villages, mostly in the S. of Athos); each has its own small *church* (kyriakon) and they still look like early Christian lavra (ancient monks' settlements). Guests are accommodated with the leader (díkaios: 'the just one') in the guest house (archontariki). Many of these small settlements (skítai, kalyves, kellia, kathísmata) are now deserted because of the

Karyés (Athos), Protaton monastery

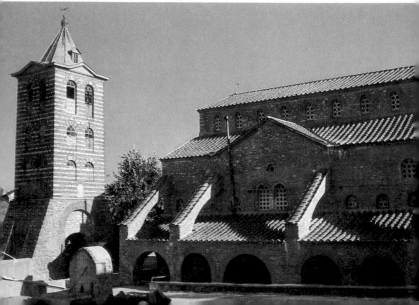

relatively small number of monks (c. 1,500); formerly there were over 10,000 monks on Athos.

The members of the strictest order, the ascetics, live in isolated mountain caves and huts in the so-called *erimitíria* (hermitages), *isychastíria* (rest places) and *askitíria* (ascetics' huts).

Wall paintings *(tichografíes):* The wall paintings are probably the most important artistic feature of Mount Athos. In the 14&15C particularly the churches and refectories of the monasteries were frescoed by the so-called Macedonian school in the Byzantine style; they cover an area of over a million sq. ft. of painted wall. The oldest and most famous painter is the 14C Manuel Panselinos ('full moon'). He and his pupils created the finest examples of Byzantine frescos (portraits) on the Holy Mountain. The second phase of wall paintings is that of the post-Byzantine Cretan school of the 16&17C, of which the principal representative is Theophanes the Cretan (c. 1535), and his school, which includes Frankos Kastellanos of Thebes

(16C); they were followed in the 18&19C by powerful painters in the popular style. The decoration of the katholikon followed a clearly defined iconographic programme (see also under Dafní): at the top of the dome the Pantocrator, as his retinue the Theotokos (Panagia, Madonna), John the Baptist and various prophets and angels. In the apse the life of the patron saint and in the conch of the main apse 'Madonna and Child' with Christ above them. In the apsidal chapels Death and Resurrection with figures from the Old Testament and the Trinity. Above the sanctuary (bema) Christ with a Crown of Thorns, in the nave and the side choirs the great liturgical festivals of the church year (Dodekaeorton: 'cycle of twelve festivals'), and also Councils, lives of the Martyrs and the last Judgement.

The refectory (trapeza) is decorated with pictures of the saints and of eating and drinking.

Icons: The numerous portable Byzantine icons on Mount Athos (there are said to be roughly 20,000) are predominantly gifts

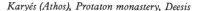

Karyés (Athos), Protaton monastery, Deesis

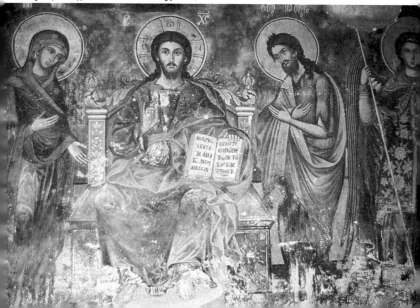

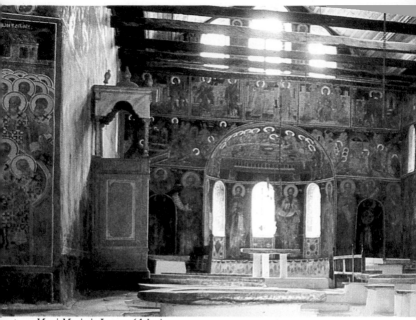

Moni Megistis Lavras (Athos)

from the capital cities Constantinople and Thessaloníki; indigenous monastic painting schools (agiografos: 'hagiograph') did not appear until the 17C. The painter monk Dionysos wrote his famous 'Hermeneia' of hagiography *c.* 1730.

Icons were usually placed on the iconostasis (also called ikonostasion or templon), which separated the congregation from the Holy of Holies (ieron). In the 16C wooden iconostases, some decorated with carving, developed from the original low choir screens consisting of marble columns with a protective balustrade; the icons placed there symbolize the 'holy window' to the other 'cosmos' (Holy of Holies). Frequently Mary, revered as the Mother of God, appears as the miracle-working Panagia; she has many other epithets: Tricherusa ('three-armed'), Portaitissa ('keeper of the gate'), Odigítra ('she who points the way'), Fovera Prostasía ('the protection which deters'), Paramythía ('comfortress'), Vrefokratusa ('the bearer of the child') and many others. Christ (Pantocrator), the Archangel Michael (Taxiarchis), St. George, the Apostles Peter and Paul, St. Nicholas, St. Stephen, etc. are also themes for icons.

Miniatures: Numerous old manuscripts decorated with excellent miniature paintings and calligraphy are also an important feature of Mount Athos.

Kayrés *(Karyai):* Because of its central postion in the middle of the peninsula this fairly small place (450 inhabitants) became very important to the early monastic communities and the later monastic state as early as the 9–10C. Here the Holy Community meets under the Protos (First) in

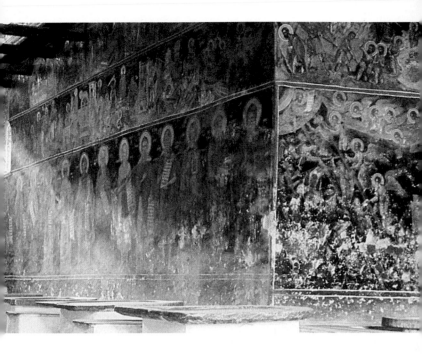

the Protaton Monastery; the first church built on Athos is also here and likewise named after the Protos. The 10C *monastery church* (built on older foundations) is a three-aisled basilica with three E. apses. The square interior with four corner chapels has a narthex in the W. and a narrow porch in the N. The *bell tower* has walls in layers of two colours and dates from the 14C, when the whole church was rebuilt. The excellent Macedonian school frescos in the nave are by the famous painter Manuel Panselinos (*c.* 1300, restored in 1955). The frescos in the narthex and the N. porch date from the 16C. In the sanctuary is the venerable *Ikone Axion estín* ('Dignum est') of the Mother of God with the Christ Child, ostensibly 8C. As well as the administrative buildings in Karyés and the police station which issues residence permits there are also numerous monastic buildings closely connected with the W. coast harbour of *Dáfni* (*c.* 2 hours on foot). Near to Karyés to the N. is the *Skiti Ágios Andreas* (ascetics' settlement) of 1849 with an interesting *main church* (kyriakon). It belongs to the monastery of Vatopédi and is considered to be Russian in origin.

The monasteries: The 10 monasteries on the W. coast are separated from the 10 on the E. coast by the mountain ridge running the length of the peninsula. The monasteries are described in sequence from the oldest, Moni Megístis Lávras (Great Lávra Monastery) at the SE tip, moving up the E. coast to the N. and down the W. side from N. to S., in other words as a long circular tour.

Moni Megístis Lávras (Great Lávra

Monastery): This monastery in the SE of the peninsula was founded c.963 by the holy monk Athanasios and is both the oldest and the most famous monastery on Athos. The founder of the monastery brought together the ascetics who were living in informal association into the first Great Lávra (monks' community); he established firm rules for the order (typikon) which were recorded on the tragos (goat parchment) of 971; the document is now in Karyés). The *katholikon* was built c. 1000 as a three-apsed Greek cross with naos, lití (eso-narthex) and exo-narthex in the W. The two smaller churches in the N. and S. (side chapels) have the same ground plan as the katholikon. The porch in the W. is a later addition and was altered in the 19C. The Lávra church served as a pattern for the design of the other churches of Athos. St. Athanasios is said to have been killed during the vaulting of the main dome c. 1004 and his richly decorated *shrine* in the N. chapel of the '40 martyrs' is still a popular place of pilgrimage.

The wonderful *frescos* in the *naos* are by Theophánes (Strelitsas) of Crete (c. 1535), one of the principal representatives of the so-called Cretan school (16C) with Italian and Venetian influence. His sons Symeón and Neophytos were also involved in the decoration of the side chapel *Ágios Nikolaos* (1560) and the *Agía Triada* chapel (c.1570), along with the famous fresco painter Frankos Kastellanos (Katelanos). The great *trapeza* (refectory) of the formerly coenobitic house (idiorrhythmic from the 16C) is cruciform with an apse in the W. (former abbot's seat) and a transept in the E., which was also added c. 1000; it has a fine *marble tables* and a dark wooden ceiling dating from 1512. The *frescos* in the refectory are presumed to be by Frankos Kastellanos (1512, 1560); the themes are the 'Last Judgement' in the E. with the hosts of the saved and the damned; the 'ancestry of Christ' (Tree of Jesse) with the 'wise men of Greece' (Sokrates, Pythagoras, Homer, Aristotle, Plato, Plutarch, Philon etc.); paintings of the saints; representations of martyrs; the Life of the Virgin etc.

Between the katholikon and the trapeza is the fine old *phiale* (holy water fountain);

Moni Ivíron (Athos)

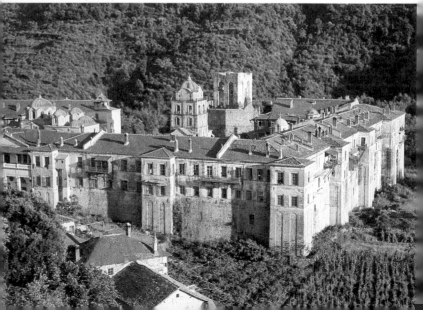

the *balustrade* with marble slabs in the parapet dates from the 10C and has early Christian healing symbols as decoration, and the decorative high-vaulted *dome* has 17C *frescos*. The fountain symbolizes the word of God (Logos) and the Mother of God (Theotokos) as the sources of life (Zoodochos Pigí).

The *treasury* (Thisavros: 'Thesaurus') contains the *robe* and *evangelistary* of the Emperor Nikephoros Phokas (10C), valuable old *icons* (for example mosaic icons by Joannis Prodromos), fine *reliquaries* with a relic of the True Cross) old documents and *decrees*, jewellery with precious stones, liturgical vestments etc.

In the library are numerous old *parchment manuscripts* with copies of the Gospels and ancient Greek texts.

Environs: The original home of the hermits is the rugged S. tip of the peninsula, between the capes of Akrathos and Pínnes. In the numerous caves and rocky gorges S. of the peak of Athos were the hermitages (eremitria) of the earliest Athonites (hermits of Athos) Petros and Nilos (7&8C). This barely accessible region with its numerous Skítes (ascetics' villages) and kellia (living cells) is still a paradise for the search for God away from the distractions of the world, and the painting of icons (agiographie). Most of the settlements were refounded in the 17&18C and are loosely connected with the idiorrhythmic monastery of Great Lávra. The most notable are the Skíten *Agia Anna* of 1689, *Nea Skíti* of 1760 (both in the SW), *Prodromos* of 1852 (by Cape Akrathos in the SE), *Kavsokalyvia* (18C), the Kellia of *Kerasia* (the highest monastic settlement (2,296 ft.) at the S. foot of Mount Athos), the hut settlements (Kalyvia) of *Ágios Vasilios*, *Katunakia* and *Karulia* etc. It is possible to climb the 6,669 ft. Mount Athos from here (particularly from the monastery of Lavra); on the summit is the small *Metamorfosis chapel* ('Transfiguration of Christ') and the *Panagia chapel* is 4,921 ft. below the summit. There is a very fine view.

Moni Karakallu (monastery of Karakallu): This monastery is still coenobitic and is about 4 hours on foot N.

Moni Megistis Lavras (Athos)

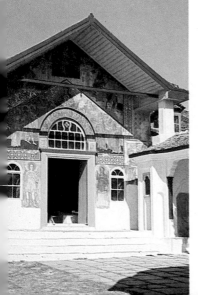

Moni Vatopedíu (Athos)

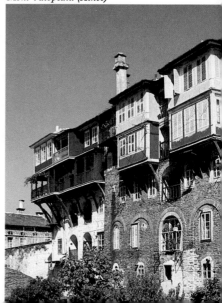

of the Lávra monastery. The modest complex with its massive defensive tower (16C) has a 16C church dedicated to St. Peter and St. Paul. The frescos are 18C and there is a fine cycle in the exonarthex on the Revelation. In the *library* is a notable 13C *evangelistary*.

Moni Philotheu (monastery of Philotheos): The little idiorrhythmic monastery is said to have been founded in the 10C by the monk Philotheos, a contemporary of St.Athanasios of Lavra. The *monastery church* (katholikon), which survived the fire of 1871, has 16C frescos ('Apocalypse') in the exo-narthex. The monastery is dedicated to the Annunciation (Evangelismos) and possesses a miraculous icon of the *Panagía Glykofilusa*, one of the oldest on Athos, and also a hand of the teacher St.John Chrysostom as a *relic*; this dates from the 4C, and was a gift of the Emperor Nikephoros III (1079–81), who lived here as a monk.

Moni Iviron (monastery of the Iberians): This high-ranking idiorrhythmic monastery was founded *c.* 980 by three 'Iberians' (i.e. Georgians) and is near Karyés (SE, about 1½ hours). The founder of the monastery, Thorníkios, was generously supported by the Byzantine emperors. The monastery was occupied by Georgian monks until *c.* 1350 and was a centre of E. Georgian writing (numerous translations into Greek). It was of great importance for Tsarist Russia and Rumania. The miraculous 9C icon of the *Panagia Portaitissa* ('Mother of God of the Gate') is surrounded by legend; it is housed in the *chapel* (1680) of the same name (with a fine inlaid door) and protects the monastery from harm. Even so the whole complex was destroyed by a great fire in 1865, with the sole exception of the *defensive tower* and the fortress-like foundations; the monastery has been rebuilt. The monastery is occupied today exclusively by Greeks and has

a katholikon dedicated to the Dormition of Mary (Kimisis Theotoku); it was built in 976 and extended in 1513 with fine Nicaean *tiles, portals* and *frescos* (1592), restored in 1848; in it are various gifts from Russian Tsars, including a magnificent evangelistary presented by Peter the Great *c.* 1720.

The **library** contains numerous valuable 13&14C *manuscripts* and old 11 – 13C *Gospels*, and also 15C Venetian first editions of Greek classics.

In the *treasury* are the gold-embroidered *vestments* of the Emperor John I Tsimiskís (968–76), valuable old icons and a sculpted crucifix (1607) among other items.

Moni Kutlumusiu (Kutlumusiu monastery): This little monastery lies SE of Karyés about 1 hour inland and was founded in 1283 by Kutlumu, a Turkish prince who had been converted to Christianity. The Metamorfosis church ('Transfiguration of Christ') of the coenobitic monastery has *frescos* from 1540, a fine *iconostasis*, and also an old *icon of Nikólaos* above the abbot's seat.

Moni Stavronikita (monastery of Stavronikíta): This small, battlemented monastery with a *defensive tower* is E. of Karyés on a rocky outcrop towering out of the sea. The monastery is dedicated to St. Nicholas and was first mentioned *c.* 1000 but refounded in 1542 by Patriarch Jeremías of Constantinople. In the *katholikon* of 1546 there are fine *frescos* by the Cretan Theophanes (see Moni Megístis Lávras) A 14C *mosaic icon* of St. Nicholas of Myra which was rescued from the sea is worshipped as a miraculous image; it is nicknamed 'Stridi', the 'oyster'. In the *library* are fine 11&12C manuscripts, including a *psalter* with lavish *miniatures*.

Moni Vatopedíu (Athos), kathilikon

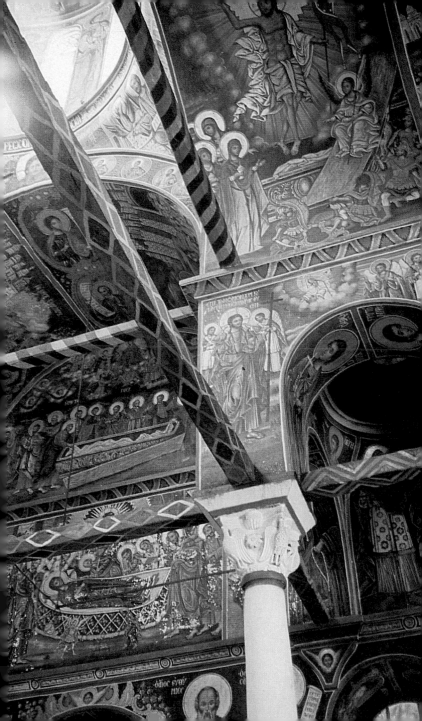

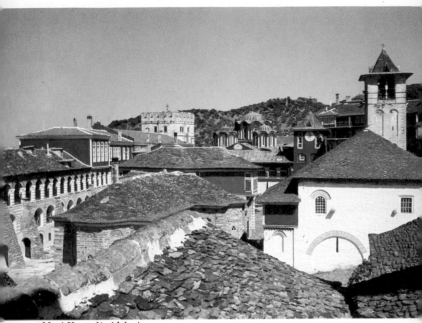

Moni Vatopedíu (Athos)

Moni Pantokratoros (Monastery of the Pantokrator): The monastery with its many balconies and sturdy defensive tower has a picturesque site on a cliff on the E. coast. It is about an hour on foot N. of Stavronikita or 2 hours NE of Karyés. The monastery was founded by two brothers, Alexios and Ioannis Stratigopulos (*c.*1270), the former being the Byzantine general who in 1216 won back Constantinople from the Latins for Emperor Michael VIII Palaiologos (beginning of the Palaiologoi period). The *Metamorfosis church* ('Transfiguration of Christ') has a fine 14C *icon of Christ.* Alexios and Ioannis Stratigopulos are buried in the narthex.

The *library* has a collection of valuable old *manuscripts* including a *psalter* with 11C miniatures of the Annunciation and an *evangelistary* by Ioannis Kalyvitis (parchment codex with 13C miniatures in an old Slav metal binding). There is a splendid view to the S. across the E. coast.

Environs: The small skiti *Profítis Ilias* (Prophet Elias) to the NW is attached to the Pantokrator monastery. The neighbouring Skiti of *Bogoroditsa,* also to the NW, is attached to the Panteleimon monastery on the W. coast. It was founded in the 19C by Russian monks, and its name is the Russian for 'Mother of God'.

Moni Vatopediu (Vatopedi monastery): This monastery on the N. of the E. coast (NE of Karyés, about 3 hours on foot) ranks next to the Lávra monastery and was founded from there *c.* 972. It is today one of the most prosperous and open-minded of the Athos monasteries (idiorrhythmic, electricity, telephone, modern guest-rooms etc.). It differs from all the other monaster-

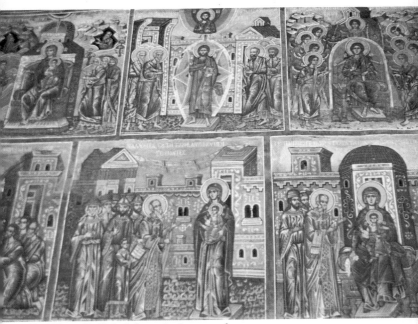

Moni Vatopedíu (Athos), frescos in the exo-narthex

ies on the Holy Mountain by working to the Western (Roman) Gregorian Calendar. The Julian (Eastern) Calendar is 13 days behind ours, a fact which should be borne in mind when calculating patronal feasts. According to legend the son (Paidí) of Emperor Theodosios I (391 – 5) was shipwrecked here and found in a blackberry bush (vatos); this was said to have given the monastery its name 'vatopaidion' ('blackberry child'); another version suggests that it simply means 'blackberry ground' ('vatopedion').

The monastery, which is surrounded by battlemented *walls* and has an old *defensive tower* (now the library), was rebuilt after a fire in 1966. The *katholikon* was built as a three-apsed church with side chapels and an exo-narthex in the 10&11C and has been much rebuilt. The splendid 15C *bronze doors* are said to have come from the church of Agia Sophia in Thessaloníki as a consecration gift. They are decorated with *reliefs* of the Annunciation, to which the whole church is dedicated ('Evangelismós': Annunciation: 25 March). There are fine 11C *wall mosaics* of an unusual kind covering a large area above the *katholikon doorway*. Their themes are the Evangelismós and the Deesis (Adoration of Christ). On the Deesis are Christ Enthroned, the Madonna and John the Baptist (as a symbol of the worship of the Emperor). Inside the katholikon are fine Macedonian school *frescos c.* 1312, restored in 1819. In the exonarthex is a fine representation of the Last Judgement (*c.* 1426). In the chapel of *Ágios Dimitrios* (added in the 18C) are unusual 13&14C *mosaic icons*, of which the finest is the 13C *Crucifixion* with reliefs of the 12 festivals of the Church (Dodekaeorton) in a 14C silver frame; also 'St.Anne with the Child of Mary' (13&14C) in another fine silver frame; icons of Peter and Paul and the Panagía Odigítria ('Mother of God pointing the way') in a fine frame; there is also a soapstone relief of St.George and the 12 Apostles (15&16C).

The *treasury* (thesauros) contains valuable Byzantine *metalwork*, including the 15C *goblet* of Michael Palaiologos (jasper goblet on a silver base with incised dragon handles); fine decorative crosses including an *altar cross* (Stavrothíki) with fragments of the True Cross; the silver-mounted head of St.Gregory of Nazianzus and a 9C reliquary shrine with scenes from the life of St.Demetrios; there is also a small museum of Byzantine art.

The large *library* in the fortified tower has over 8,000 volumes and valuable *manuscripts*, many on parchment, including an Octateuch (the first eight books of the Old Testament) with 162 11C *miniatures*; manuscripts (*c.*1200) on the maps in the 'Geography' by the Greek geographer Strabo (1C AD) and the Alexandrian geographer Ptolemy (2C AD). The only copy so far discovered of the Pausanias's 'Perie-gesis' or Description of Greece (2C AD).

Environs: Nearby are the ruins of the *Athos Academy*, which was founded in the 18C but soon abandoned because of resistance from the monks. The neighbouring skíti of *Ágios Dimítrios* (to the S.) and the skíti of *Ágios Andreas* to the N. of Karyés (also known as Skíti Seraí) with its fine 19C kyriakon belong to the monastery of Vatopédi.

Moni Esfigmenu (monastery of Esfigmenu): The handsome coenobite monastery with red and white *outer walls* and two battlemented *towers* was founded in 1030. It was subsequently damaged, destroyed in the 16C, then rebuilt in the 18C. The katholikon, which is dedicated to the Ascension of Christ (Analipsis) was rebuilt *c.* 1805; the frescos are 19C.

The principal treasure of the *library* is an 11C *Minologion* (book of months). The parchment manuscript is lavishly illuminated and contains the first four months of the orthodox church year (September to December) with a saint's life for each day. The 14C *mosaic icon* of the Crucifixion,

Moni Panteleimonos (Athos)

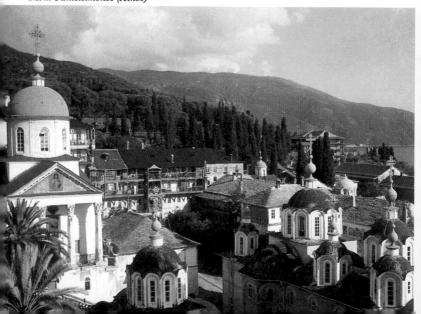

15C Epitaphios and a fine *carved iconostasis* are also worth seeing.

Moni Khilandaríu (monastery of khilandari): This old Serbian idiorrythmic monastery in the N. of the peninsula is about 45 minutes on foot W. of Esfigmenu. It was founded *c.* 1197 on the site of an abandoned older monastery by the Serbian prince Stefan Nemanja. His son, St.Savas, made it a centre of Serbian culture with the help of lavish gifts from Serbian princes and kings. The *katholikon* is a three-apsed building in coloured brick with a roomy liti (eso-narthex as a simple room for prayer) and an exo-narthex with a fine geometrical floor pattern. The 13&14C *frescos* were restored *c.* 1804, and are a baptismal cycle; there is a fine carved iconostasis.

By the abbot's throne is the famous miraculous *icon*, the Panagía Tricherusa ('Mother of God with three hands') with a lavish cover in gilded lead, said to be the work of John Damaskinos (*c.* 670–750); it was brought to the monastery of Khilandari in 1371.

In the *trapeza* (dining room), which is T-shaped with apses, are 17C *frescos* (Akathistos Hymnos, Life of St. Savas, 'Jacob's ladder'). In the inner courtyard is a fine *phiali* (holy water fountain) with 8 small columns, fountain and domed vaulting with frescos (Old Testament scenes on the theme of the 'Water of Life').

The *library* in the fortified tower has many old *manuscripts*, the best of which is the 13C 'Tetraevangelon' with the four Gospels; there are also documents, decrees, and sealed edicts of Serbian and Byzantine rulers.

The collection of 14&15C *icons* is worth seeing: ('Four Evangelists', 'Deesis' of Christ with Mary and John the Baptist, the Archangels Michael and Gabriel and a rare 13C *mosaic icon* 'Mother of God and Child'; also a 14C *altar cloth*, 13&14C *crystal vessels*, 6–14C capitals and sculptures and valuable embroidery.

Moni Zografu (Monastery of Zografos): The 'painter's monastery' (zografos: 'painter') is in the N. of the peninsula on the W. of the ridge. The

Moni Panteleimonos (Athos)

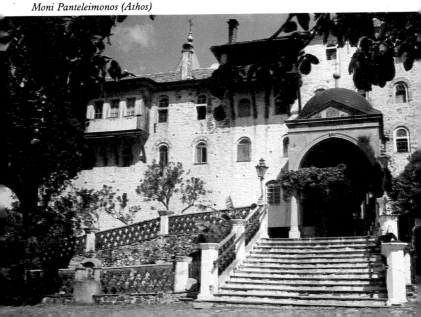

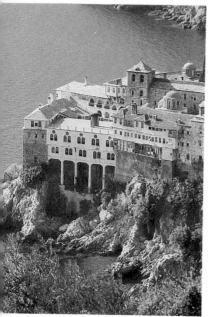

Moni Grigoríu (Athos)

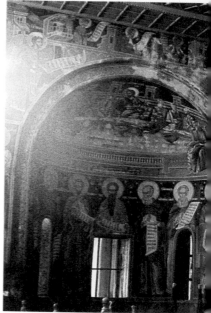

Moni Doinysíu (Athos), trapeza

coenobitic Bulgarian monastery was founded in 1270 and is dedicated to St. George. It was extensively rebuilt in the 19C. It has a miraculous *icon* of St.George (13&14C) in the old Slavonic style. It is said to be by the anonymous painter (Zografos) who gave the monastery its name. In the *Chapel of St.George* are 16C frescos of the Cretan school.

The *library* has Greek, old Serbian and old Bulgarian codices, including the 13C *Radomir Psalter* with fine old Bulgarian illuminations.

Moni Konstamonitu (Monastery of Konstamonítu): The monastery was founded *c.* 1080 and is inland in the NW of the peninsula, S. of Zografos. The monastery was named after its founder, a monk from Kastamón, in Asia Minor.

The *frescos* in the katholikon are 15C. The

miraculaous icon of St.Stephanos, the patron of the monastery and the *Panagía icon* (both 13&14C) are worth seeing.

Moni Dochiariu (monastery of Dochiarios): The monastery is charmingly set on a rocky plateau on the W. coast; it is idiorrhythmic and is said to have been founded *c.* 976 by the Dochiarios (cellar master) of the monastery of Lávra. The beautifully built fortress monastery was first mentioned in documents *c.* 1040 (Chrysobull). The *katholikon* is dedicated to the archangels and was rebuilt *c.* 1568 and decorated with fine *frescos* of the Cretan school in the same century: in the exonarthex representations of hermits, in the eso-narthex Old Testament cycles (Tree of Jesse, Paradise, Ejection from Paradise, the prophet Jonah among others). There are lavish frescos in the naos which has a cen-

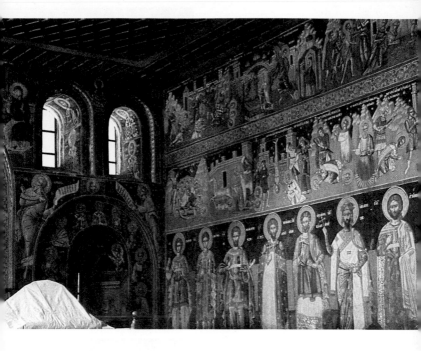

tral dome on four granite pillars (Pantocrator, Resurrection, Descent to Hell etc.). In the *chapel* is the miraculous image of the *Panagía Gorgoypíkoos* ('Mother of God of the rapid aid') which is contemporary with the foundation of the monastery.

The trapeza of 1547 is painted with 21 interesting *fresco cycles* of the Apocalypse in the 16C Cretan style. In the inner ccourtyard is a fine *phiali* with slate roof, arches, vaulted ceiling and fountain niche with frescos. The powerful *fortified tower* rises near the coast.

The *library* contains fine *manuscripts*, including a Tetraevangelon (evangelistary) with *miniatures* and a minologion (book of months) for the month of November (both 12C).

Moni Xenophontos (monastery of Xenophon): Founded *c.* 1010 by the

monk Xenophon on the W. coast and dedicated to St.George (23 April). It was rebuilt in 1544–63 after being plundered and destroyed. The dome of the *old katholikon* was painted with *frescos* of the Cretan school (Master Antonios) *c.* 1545; the same master was responsible for the frescos in the eso-narthex (*c.* 1563). The frescos in the exo-narthex date from *c.* 1650 (Apocalypse).

At the beginning of the 19C a plain *new katholikon* was built of stuccoed marble without frescos. It contains two fine old *mosaic icons* (probably originally wall mosaics) of the martyrs Demetrios and Georgios (11C). There is also an icon of St. George (said to be 9C) and the miraculous icon of the *Panagía Odigitria* ('Mother of God as Leader'), who was much honoured in Byzantium (the old copy is probably 13 or 14C. In the trapeza (1700) there is a fine

Moni Dionysíu (Athos), fresco ▷

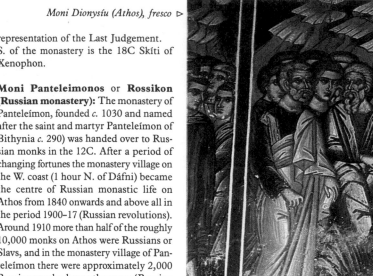

representation of the Last Judgement.
S. of the monastery is the 18C Skíti of
Xenophon.

Moni Panteleímonos or **Rossikon
(Russian monastery):** The monastery of
Panteleímon, founded *c.* 1030 and named
after the saint and martyr Panteleímon of
Bithynia *c.* 290) was handed over to Russian monks in the 12C. After a period of
changing fortunes the monastery village on
the W. coast (1 hour N. of Dáfni) became
the centre of Russian monastic life on
Athos from 1840 onwards and above all in
the period 1900–17 (Russian revolutions).
Around 1910 more than half of the roughly
10,000 monks on Athos were Russians or
Slavs, and in the monastery village of Panteleímon there were approximately 2,000
Russian monks, hence the name 'Russian
monastery'. Important buildings, including the Romanov Hall, were destroyed by
fire in 1968.
The *old katholikon* (*c.* 1450) has fine frescos
in the popular style. The *new katholikon*
of 1888 has two aisles, two main altars and
a gilded iconostasis. One wing of the
church is dedicated to the Agia Skepi
('Mother of God of the Protecting Cloak')
and the other to the Russian national saint
Alexander Nevsky (13C). The *miraculous
icon* of St. Panteleímon is worth seeing.
Even today the liturgy is sung in Russian
and Greek, although only a few monks remain; once the choir was world famous.
The *library* has valuable *manuscripts*
(parchments) from the 9–15C, including
a copy of the famous 'Homilies' of Gregory
of Nazianzus (4C) with 11C illuminations.

**Moni Xiropotamu (monastery of
Xiropotamos):** The monastery on the
'dry river' (Xiropotamos) is between the

Moni Dionysíu (Athos), fresco in the   ▷
trapeza

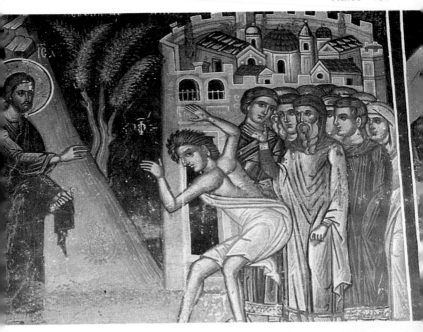

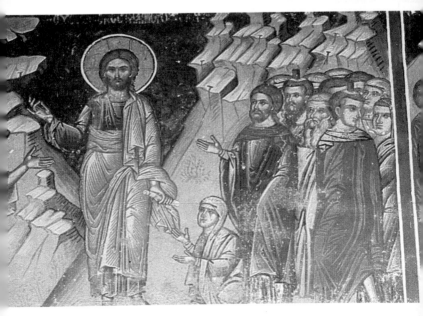

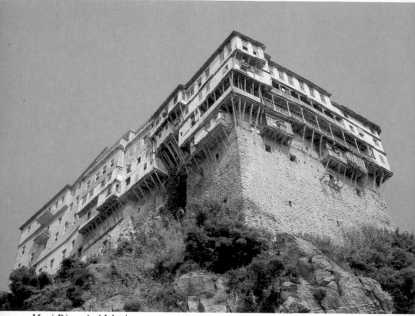

Moni Dionysíu (Athos)

small port of Dáfni and the town of Karyés; there is a fine view. It is said to have been founded in 956, before the monastery of Lávra, as a loosely-knit monastic community. Possible founders are St.Irene or the hermit Pavlos (Paul), an opponent of St. Athanasios. In the katholikon there are *frescos* (1730), a *reliquary* with a splinter from the True Cross and interesting *stone sculptures* (bas-relief on the statue of St. Demetrios); also two *busts* in the *bell tower*. The *treasury* contains a fine 14C *communion dish* (patene) in dark green serpentine with relief (Mother of God with angels). The dish is said to have come from Pulchéria, the sister of Emperor Theodosios II (5C).

Moni Simonos Petra (Monastery of Simon Petra): The monastery, romantically set on a cliff on the W. coast, was founded

c. 1300 by Símon the Hermit, hence the name Símonos Petra ('Simon's rock'). The towering building with 7–10 storeys and balconies looks like a fortress and is only connected to the mountain side to the NE by an arched bridge. The monastery, which stood under the special protection of the kings of Rumania, was frequently damaged by fires, which also destroyed the collection of ancient manuscripts. It was rebuilt in 1893 after the fire of 1891. The new katholikon, dedicated to the Nativity of Christ, dates from this period.

Moni Grigoríu (monastery of Gregory): This monastery is right on the coast and has old *fortified walls*; it is in the SW of the peninsula and was founded *c.* 1345 by the monk Gregory. It was rebuilt *c.* 1780 after a fire and the katholikon was decorated with splendidly-coloured

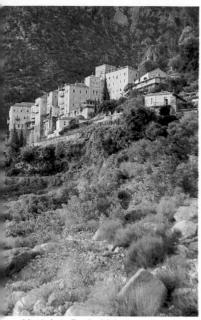

Moni Agíu Pavlu (Athos)

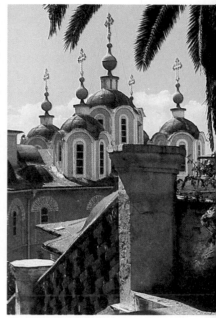

Moni Panteleimonos (Athos)

frescos. In the *naos* is the miraculous *icon of the Panagía Galaktotrofusa* ('calming Mother of God'), a 15C theme seldom found in the Eastern Church; there is also an *icon* of St.Nicholas, the patron saint of the church.

Moni Dionysíu (monastery of Diony-sios): This splendid monastery on a cliff-top on the SW coast was founded in 1366 by the hermit Dionysos. In 1376 Emperor Alexios III of Trebizond (Komnenos) built a towering monastery with many storeys; the balconies were added later; it was rebuilt on several occasions after fires in the 16C. The *katholikon*, dedicated to John the Baptist, was built in the 16C and decorated *c.* 1547 with impressive *frescos* by the Cretan painter Zorzi (derived from Giorgio: George) (Pantocrator in the dome, the Evangelist, the Birth of Christ, John the

Baptist, Transfiguration on Mount Tabor, Purgatory, Death of Mary among others). The same artist was responsible for the *frescos* in the *trapeza* of the Last Judgement (including the rejection of the 'Eosforos' Lucifer, and the angelic host of the 'Asomati') representations of martyrs and the monastic Ladder to Heaven (Ladder of Life). The trapeza of the coenobytic monastery is T-shaped with an abbot's throne and *ambo* with sculpted decoration. In the *porch* are fine *frescos* (1568) with scenes from the Apocalypse.

The *library* has valuable old *manuscripts*, including a splendid *Gospel* of *c.* 1200 with fine *illuminations* and a *binding in relief*; also a 13C codex with scenes from the Dodekaeorton (12 Festivals of the Christian year) and above all the *golden bull* (Chrysobullon) of Emperor Alexios III Komnenos recording the foundation of the monastery in 1374 (with fine illuminations of blessing by John the Baptist). The 7C *wax icon* of the miraculous Panagia Myrrovlotissa ('Fragrant Mother of God') with a fine gold binding (1786) is also worth seeing.

Moni Agiu Pavlu (monastery of Paul): This monastery is said to have been founded *c.* 980 by the monk Pavlos, the founder of the Xiropotamos monastery. In the 15C the monastery, which occupies a picturesque site above the SW coast, was supported by the princes of Rumania and Serbia; the fine *chapel of St.George* and the old katholikon date from this period. The katholikon was destroyed by fire *c.* 1900; the chapel was decorated with fine frescos of the Macedonian school *c.* 1430 (Lives of Christ and the Mother of God, Transfiguration on Mount Tabor with Moses and Elias, Peter and Paul, the Mother of God as a Source of Life etc.).

The rebuilt katholikon of 1844 is dedicated to Christ's Presentation in the Temple (Ypanti, Candlemas; 2 Febraury).

Treasures in the monastery include a portable altar in one piece with miniature paintings (Deesis of Christ), a portable altar with two panels (cycle of the 12 feasts) and a portable cross.

Avlis/Aulis/ΑΥΛΙΣ
Boeotia/Central Greece   p.294□H 8

An old Boeotian town about 70 km. from Athens on the Gulf of Euboia. Agamemnon used the harbour as the starting point for his Trojan expedition and, according to legend, sacrificed his daughter Iphigenia to the goddess Artemis here. Later King Agesilaos of Sparta mustered his army in the town at the beginning of his campaign against the Persians.

Temple of Artemis: A few years ago Greek excavations on the SW side of the harbour of Mikró Vathý revealed the remains of this famous temple; there are signs of worship as early as the 8C BC. Mycenean remains have been found on the hill of Jeladovuni, S. of the harbour. There used to be a well in front of the temple, which can still be seen and bears the name of the Agamemnon.

Moni Agíu Pavlu (Athos), Peter and Paul ▷

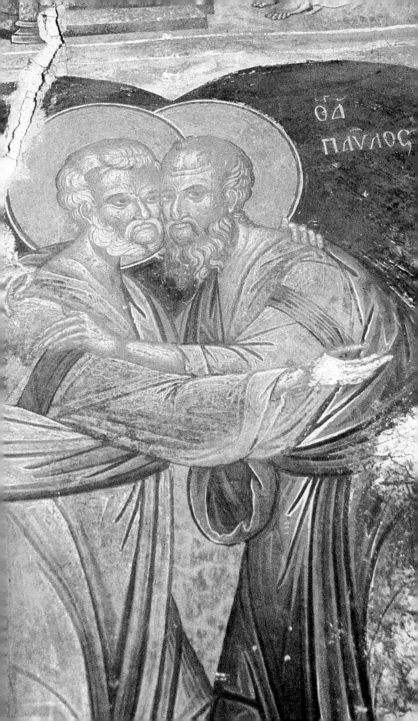

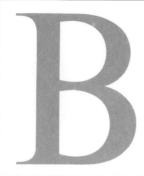

Bizarianó Pediádos/Bitzariáno Pedhiádha/ΠΕΔΙΑΔΟΣ

Iráklion/Crete   p.298□H 14

30 km. SE of Knossós is the town of Bizarianó with a beautiful 12C basilica, Ágios Panteleimon, with a nave and two aisles. This church, built on the ruins of an early Christian basilica, contains antique tomb stele incorporated in the S. wall. Large frescos from the 12&13C are well preserved in part.

Environs: Sklaverokhóri Pediádos: Near Bizarianó lies Sklaverokhóri with the little church of Kimesis tis Theotoku, in which beautiful, expressive 14C frescos, painted in warm colours, survive. Of particular interest is the 'Arrival in Jerusalem'. **Episkopí:** S. of Bizarianó is the village of Episkopí with the chapel of Ágios Ioannis and the church of Agia Paraskevi. Both contain well-preserved frescos, similar in style to those in Sklaverokhóri.

Boeotia/Viotía/ BOIOTIA

Boeotia/Central Greece   p.294□F 6/H 7/8

The name of this region on the E. side of the Greek mainland goes back to the founding of the Boeotian capital, Thebes. Its name was derived from the lowing of a cow which knelt down on the spot where Kadmos later founded Thebes.

Boeotia was famous even in antiquity for the fertility of its soil. The region is the most famous dancing-ground of war, as the Boeotian hero Epaminondas once remarked. But it is also the land of the Muses, and the home of Pindar, Hesiod and Plutarch.

Today Boeotia is a nome (pop. *c.* 105,000, capital Levádia). Nobel Prize winner Odysseas Elytis sang the praises of Boeotia's soil, which today produces corn, cotton, olives, tobacco, citrus fruits and, on the plateaux, wine (the well-known retsína).

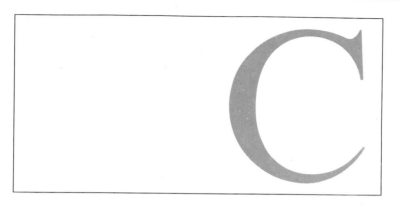

Chaironeia/ΧΑΙΠΟΝΕΙΑ
Boeotia/Central Greece   p.294☐G 7/8

A few km. W. of Orchómenos and 144 km. from Athens lies the village of Chaironeia, home of Plutarch.

History: Near the present village there stood, in antiquity, the little town of the same name, which rose to fame as the site of several famous battles. It lies on a small plain between Mounts Akontion and Thurion. The most important battle took place here on an August day in 338 BC, and decided the futures of the Greek states of the time. King Philip of Macedon and his son Alexander, with their well-organized and equipped troops, clashed with the Greek army, consisting mostly of Athenians and Thebans, on the plain of the river Kiphissos. Philip was victorious,

Episkopi (Bizariano Perd.), St. George

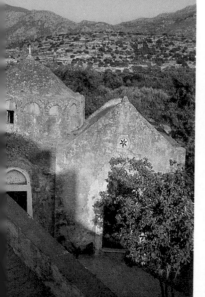

Lion of Chaironeia

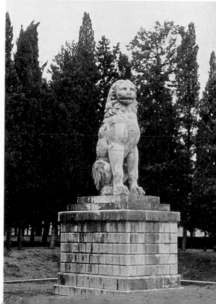

thus ensuring his sway over old Hellas. In honour of the fallen Thebans, who were annihilated by Alexander's cavalry, there stands over the mass grave of the Sacred Band the Lion of Chaironeia, as a symbol of their bravery and as a guardian of the dead. This monument (20 ft. tall), standing at the S. entrance to the village, was re-erected in 1904 after its destruction during the War of Liberation.

Another famous battle took place in 86 BC, when the army of Mithridates suffered a disastrous defeat at the hands of the Romans under Sulla. On 15 March AD 1311 Chaironeia was once more the scene of a battle. This time it was between two foreign armies, the Franks and the Catalans, for the domination of Greece. At the head of the Franks, accompanied by cavalry, stood Duke Gautier de Brienne. The swampy area around the Kiphissos, which was unsuitable for cavalry, sealed the Franks' fate. The Byzantine historian Nikephoros Gregoras reported that the Franks' horses sank to their bellies in mud and were unable to move. The Catalans were victorious and ruled central Greece until 1380, when the Florentines succeeded them.

Museum: This contains an important collection of ceramics from prehistoric to the end of Mycenean times. There are also sculptures and vases from the classical and Roman periods, as well as a recently discovered early Christian sculpture of the Lamb of God.

Chalkidike/ ΧΑΛΚΙΔΙΚΗ

Chalkidike/Macedonia   p.292☐G-I 3/4

Chalkidike is a peninsula SE of Saloniki and S. of the lakes of Volvi and Agios Vasilios. It consists of three finger-shaped spits of land: *Kassándra, Sithonia* and *Agion Oros* (Mount Athos).

The peninsula was settled early on, as the skull of *Petrálona* (Homo neanderthalensis) indicates. Pelasgians and Thracians later settled in Chalkidike. In the 8C BC the Eretrians and the Chalkidikians (inhabitants of Chalkís in Euboea) established colonies here. Other cities, like Athens, Corinth and Andros then followed the example of the Eretrians. At the end of the 4C BC Philip II of Macedon founded towns in Chalkidike. During the Persian Wars some towns were forced to support the Persians. Chalkidike then joined the Athenian league of states. During the Peloponnesian War 32 towns united (Koinon ton Chalkidaion). In 348 BC Philip II of Macedon occupied Chalkidike. From 1430 to 1912 the peninsula was under Turkish rule. In 1821 the people rose unsuccessfully against the Turks.

Polýgyros: Capital of Chalkidike (69 km. SE of Saloniki, pop. 3,700), situated on a mountain slope. The town is famous for its hand-woven textiles. The *museum (Neo Musio)* of Polýgyros contains finds from an extensive area.

Òlynthos (15 km. SW of Polýgyros): This town was inhabited even during Neolithic times. In 348 BC Òlynthos was captured and destroyed by Philip II. Excavations on the hills where the old town stood have so far revealed streets, houses, an *agora* and an *acropolis*. One of the houses has a mosaic pavement. On one hill the remains of a Neolithic settlement were discovered. Excavations of the *necropolis* revealed a tomb from the late 5C or early 4C BC.

Stágira (61 km. NE of Polýgyros): Birthplace of Aristotle. On the site of the ancient town there now stands the village of *Stratóni* (7 km. from the present Stágira). Stágira was a colony of the island of Andros and of Chalkis. Philip II destroyed the town, but later let it be rebuilt in recognition of Aristotle's services as tutor to his

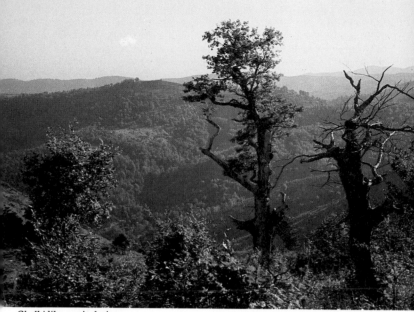

Chalkidike, typical view

son Alexander. Stágira was destroyed once and for all by the Goths in the 4C AD.

Petrálona (*c.*57 km. SE of Saloniki): It was here that in 1960 Professor Poulianos discovered a Neanderthal skull and other bone fragments in a grotto. This cave is of particular interest to anthropologists and is still being excavated.

Kassándra Peninsula: Potídaia: This town stands on the narrow isthmus which joins Kassándra to the mainland (76 km. from Saloniki). It was founded by the Corinthians towards the end of the 7C BC. In 432 BC the inhabitants of Potídaia rose against Athens. This was one of the events which led to the outbreak of the Peloponnesian War. The town was besieged for two years and finally taken by the Athenians. In the following century the

town was occupied and destroyed by Philip II. It was later rebuilt by King Kassandros, Alexander's successor. All that remains to be seen of the ancient town are sparse *remnants of walls.*

Ágios Mámas (10 km. N. of Potídaia): Small village near Mudania. A Copper Age *settlement* was discovered here.

Néa Skióni: Small village on the W. coast with remains of the ancient town of the same name.

Kalándra (*c.*25 km. S. of Potídaia): Remains of the ancient town of *Méndi.*

Sithonía Peninsula: Batopédion: On the N. side of the peninsula with an old monastery, still occupied, which contains valuable manuscripts.

Athos Peninsula: Ierissós: Little fishing village (pop. 2,400), in the bay of the same name. A few km. S. of Ierissós the peninsula is at its narrowest. Here Xerxes, King of Persia, had a canal cut for his fleet. Ancient foundations are to be found at the jetty and by the ruins of a *medieval castle* on a crag.

Old Ákanthos *(Archáia Ákanthos):* On the inner side of the gulf, opposite Ierissós, remains of the old town of Ákanthos are to be seen.

Mount Athos see Athos.

Chaniá/XANIA
Chaniá/Crete   p.298☐F 13

History: Chaniá was originally a Minoan settlement. Subsequently, Samian immigrants founded a new town on the same site in 520 BC. This was Kydonía, which, after several feuds with its neighbours, grew to be the most important settlement in W. Crete. In 1252 Kydonía was captured by the Venetians, who named it 'Canea'. The Genoese ruled the town from 1267– 90, when it was recaptured by the Venetians, who built a wall around the principal district of Kastelli (mostly still extant) and also fortified a suburb with a ring of walls. The relatively small harbour was built in the 14C. Turkish corsairs raided the town in 1537 and in 1538 the master military architect Michele Sanmicheli of Venice built new defences, some of which are enormous, but which nevertheless could only withstand a Turkish siege for 55 days in 1645. In spite of constant uprisings by the Cretans with losses on both sides, the Turks maintained control of Chaniá, which meanwhile declined in importance. It was, however, named capital of Crete in 1841 and remained so until 1971, when it was replaced by Iráklion. In 1898 Chaniá, together with the whole of Crete, was incorporated into Greece. In 1941, following heavy damage by air raids, the city was taken by German troops.

Old Town: Although the old town, which shows marked Venetian influence, suffered particularly badly during the air raids, it is still as charming as ever. Down little alleys are beautiful houses of nobles, with flights of steps and loggias, coats of arms, marble portals and stone fountains decorated with reliefs.

San Francesco: Chaniá has 23 churches, the largest and most beautiful of which is San Francesco, a 14C Gothic building with a nave and two aisles, which for a time served as a mosque. The fountain in the inner court dates from that time. Since 1962 San Francesco has been a *museum,* containing an interesting collection of finds from W. Crete: late Minoan sarcophagi, architectural fragments from the periods of Roman, Venetian and Turkish occupation and many small objects.

San Salvatore: This 13C church by the Bastion of San Salvatore (1538–40) was also a mosque under Turkish rule.

Ágios Nikolaos: Standing to the S. of the Arsenal, this church originally belonged to a Dominican monastery and later became imperial mosque to Sultan Ibrahim, when the tower was converted into a minaret. Since 1918 Ágios Nikolaos has again been an Orthodox church.

Mosque of the Janissaries: This little mosque (1645) stands near the Venetian harbour and is now used for tourists. The Turkish minaret (Chadzi Michali Daliani) stood SE of the covered market.

Harbour: The small Venetian harbour with its old lighthouse is most picturesque. The 7 Venetian arsenals can still be seen here.

Kastelli: On a hill in the city centre stands a Venetian citadel (Kastelli). A Minoan palace was also excavated here.

Market: The large covered market was modelled on the one in Marseilles.

Museums: Apart from the Archaeological Museum in San Franceso, there is also the *Naval Museum* by the harbour and the *Historical Museum* outside the city walls to the S.

Environs: Agía Triáda: NE of Chaniá is the Akrotíri peninsula with the monastery of Agía Triáda, 17 km. from Chaniá, which was founded by a Venetian of the Zangarólo family in 1632 (hence it is sometimes called Moni Tsangarólu). The monastery, now a priests' school, has a monumental portal with beautiful steps and a Venetian-style campanile. **Guvernéto / Gouvernéto:** About an hour's walk to the N. of Agía Triáda is the 16C monastery of Guvernéto. The lavish masonry of the walls and the bases of the columns in the courtyard displays Asiatic influence. The carving on the façade of the church of the Virgin is equally unusual. The monastery, whose monks often rebelled — against the Turks for example — is striking for its fortress-like appearance. Throughout the whole of Crete the monks frequently joined with the people to resist invaders. The icons in the monastery library are of interest. **Panagía:** About 1 km. further N. is the *stalagmite cave* which in antiquity was the cult grotto of Artemis and is now called the *Panagía Cave.* **Ágios Ioánnis/Katholikó:** A few steps further NW lies the cave church of the hermit John with an abandoned monastery above a steep ravine. In the 16C a Venetian portal wall with two bell towers was built in front of the church. The monks originally lived in the Katholikó, some even in the little caves in the rock face. After being constantly raided by pirates they finally withdrew to Guvernéto. A 50 ft. bridge spans the ravine. Still discernible on the shore are the ruins of the old monastery harbour.

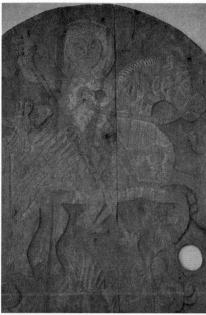

Chaniá, St. George (Hist. Mus.)

Chersonesos/Chersónisos/ΧΕΡΣ-ΟΝΗΣΟΣ
Iráklion/Crete   p.298□H 14

The village of Chersonesos lies on the N. coast of Crete, 26 km. E. of Iráklion. On a peninsula there are the ruins of an early Christian basilica with a partly preserved mosaic pavement from the 5 or 6C AD.

Ágios Nikolaos: Dating from around 1800, this church was built over an earlier basilica, also dating from the 5 or 6C, of which the apse and mosaics in the narthex and nave have survived.

Roman Fountain: Chersonesos, formerly the seat of a bishop, still has a Roman fountain with mosaics.

Environs: Kastélli Pediádos: 10 km. S. of Chersonesos lies Kastélli, with a square Venetian fortress dominated by two towers. **Lýttos / Lýktos:** Some 5 km. E. of Kastélli are the ruins of the ancient city of *Lýttos*, which lay on a slope of Mt. Diktys. Traces from Greek and Roman times were discovered here. **Arkalokhóri:** 9 km. S. of Kastélli, hidden at the foot of Mt. Diktys, is a *grotto* which was a place of worship in the Minoan age. It was discovered by archaeologists in 1912, who dug up, apart from bronzes and ceramics, numerous double-headed axes. It was not until 1934 that some children chanced upon a new entrance to the grotto, which had apparently been shut off for 3,500 years (probably following a cave-in during an earthquake). Unfortunately most of the finds were plundered. Scientists could only save a few things from the treasure that lay here, including heavy, double-headed gold axes. Since the Greek poet Hesiod wrote in 700 BC that the cave of Zeus and Hera was to be found in Lýttos, it was thought that the cave in which Zeus grew up had been discovered at Arkalokhóri rather than at Psik-

hró. In fact there were obviously several grottoes where Zeus was worshipped. **Ano Viánnos:** 30 km. SE of Arkalokhóri one comes to the idyllically situated village of Viánnos, *Agia Pelagia*, a small single-aisled church with barrel vaulting and beautiful, well preserved frescos (1360), stands at the highest point in the village. the chapel of *Ágios Georgios* contains frescos painted by Ioánnis Mousóuros (Musúros) in 1401. The *fort of Belvedere* was originally built by the Genoese. A shrine from Minoan times was recently excavated near the village.

Chios/Khíos/ΧΙΟΣ
East Aegean Islands   p.296□M 7/8

This island (331 sq. m., *c.* 54,000 inhab.) lies just off the Turkish mainland (5 miles from the Cesme peninsula). The 'craggy' island (Homer) has luxuriant vegetation.

History: In prehistoric times Chios was part of the same cultural group as the

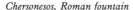

Chersonesos, Roman fountain

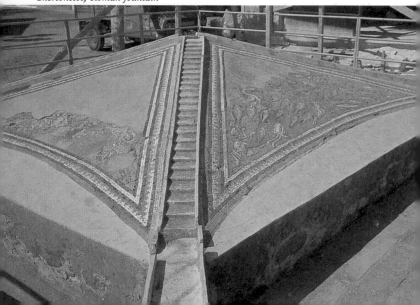

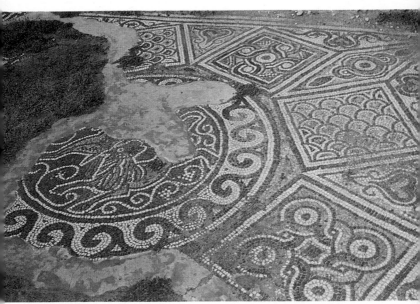

Chersonesos, fragment of a mosaic

neighbouring islands of Lesbos and Lemnos and the area around Troy. Around 1000 BC the island was settled by Ionian Greeks from Euboea. Homer (*c.* 800 BC) is supposed to have been born on Chios. The island enjoyed its great heyday in the 7/6C BC (trade, ceramics, sculpture). Ruled by the Persians from 512–479 BC, Chios then became a member of the Delian Confederacy from 477 BC onwards and was independent for a short time in the 3C BC. From 190 BC it was subject to Rome. Occupied by Venice, 1204 – 1304, and by Genoa, for the first time, from 1304–29. From 1346 the island was ruled by a Genoese mastic company (Giustiniani), before being taken by the Turks in 1566. After an unsuccessful revolt the Turks killed around 30,000 islanders (Massacre of Chios). Final annexation to Greece, 1912.

Khíos (pop. *c.* 24,000): The island's capital

Arkalokhóri, golden double axe

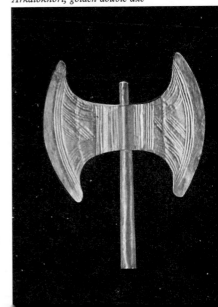

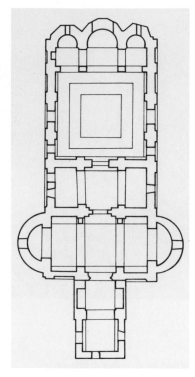

Chios, monastery church of Néa Moni: ground plan of the 18C monastery church of Néa Moni on Chios

is on the E. coast on the site of the ancient city of the same name (few extant remains)—note the Genoese fortress of *Kastro* (founded by the Byzantines, considerably extended by the Genoese after 1433) with massive walls and towers. The fortress area served the Turkish garrison as a safe place of residence (16–19C). The city itself has few points of interest (due to the devastation of 1822 and the earthquake of 1881). *Archaeological Museum* (former mosque on Plateia Vounaki): Local finds and works of art from prehistoric times up to the modern age, above all fragments of sculptures (including two archaic korai) and ceramics; also architectural fragments from early Christian and Byzantine churches. There are also finds from the village of Emporió (early Helladic beaked vases and protogeometric vessels). Next to the 19C *cathedral* stands the interesting *Korais Library* with over 130,000 volumes (from 1792), named after the famous scholar Korais (born on Chios). Adjacent is the *Folklore Museum (Laografico Musio)* with old instruments, fabrics, embroideries and carvings. Also of interest is the *Picture Gallery (Pinakothiki)* in the house of Korais, with old engravings, watercolours, historic panel paintings and old Chian family portraits. In the public park stands the bronze statue of the hero of the War of Independence of 1821, Admiral Kanaris. Nearby is a Turkish marble fountain (1768).

Environs: Near the town of *Vrontádos* (4 km. N.), by the *Pasa spring* is the *Teacher's Rock (Dhaskalópetra)*, where Homer is supposed to have taught ('School of Homer'). This rock throne with a circle of seats hewn out of the stone was an early shrine of the Phrygian deity Cybele. Nearby is the tomb of the modern Greek poet Jannis Psycharis (1854–1929), who came from Chios. At the village of *Vávila*, 7 km. S. of Khíos, is the interesting church of the *Panagia Krina*, a cruciform domed basilica of 1287 with old frescos. In the main church are works by the painter Michael Chomatzas (1734) in the Cretan post-Byzantine style. In the neighbouring village of *Neokhóri* (8 km. S.) is the 19C church of the Panagia and the monastery of *Ágios Minas,* where thousands of Chiots were massacred by the Turks in 1822. In the village of *Karyés* (6 km. W. of Khíos) are two monasteries: *Ágios Markos* and *Agion Pateron.*

Convent of Néa Moni ('New Convent'): This interesting convent of the Virgin, fa-

Chios, monastery of Néa Moni ▷

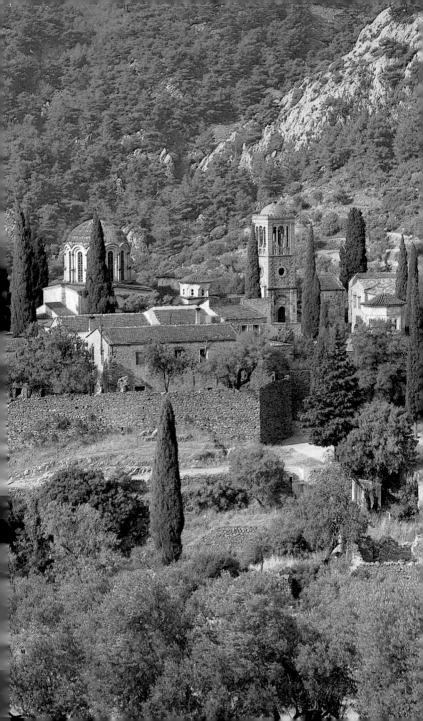

mous for its mid-Byzantine mosaics, lies 10 km. inland, to the W. of Khíos. Néa Moní was founded around 1050 by Emperor Constantine IX Monomachos (1042 –54) on the site of the discovery of a miraculous icon. Frescos and mosaics date from the same period. It is reputed that the Emperor summoned the artists from Constantinople himself. The Turks in 1822 (pillaging, theft of relics, destruction of library) and the earthquake of 1881 (collapse of dome) did much damage. After decades of neglect it is now being restored. The convent once had extensive lands and was a great influence in the island. The church katholikon has two porches, the exonarthex and esonarthex, the domed naos and the apsidal sanctuary. The exonarthex is frescoed, the esonarthex and naos contain important *mosaics*. In the former there are, amongst others, the 'Washing of Feet', 'Judas's Betrayal of Christ', and saints. In the latter the 'Baptism', 'Crucifixion', 'Descent from the Cross' and the impressive 'Resurrection' are preserved. Unfortunately the 'Pantocrator' in the dome was destroyed by the earthquake of 1881 (dome

restored). The inner cladding is largely of red stone (partly marble), and there remain only fragments of the mosaic pavement. Other surviving parts of the convent are the *refectory* with marble table and stone benches, and the *cistern,* with three aisles and a flat dome. The *bell tower* dates from 1900. At the entrance, next to the watch tower, stands the cemetery chapel with an *ossuary,* containing the bones of thousands of Chiots slaughtered in the massacre of 1822.

Environs: In the small mountain village of *Anávatos* (*c.* 4 km. NW) is the chapel of *Ágios Georgios* with Cretan-Venetian frescos (16C).

Pyrgíon (28 km S. of Khíos): The charming main town (pop. *c.* 1,500) of the S. part of the island still displays its medieval character with interesting *house fronts:* black and white geometrical sgraffito ornamentation, particularly in the main square. Of interest is the late Byzantine church of *Agii Apostoloi* (church of the apostles), a 13C domed church with 18C

Chios, the Kalo Petra

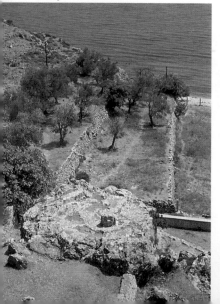

Néa Moní (Chios), charnel house

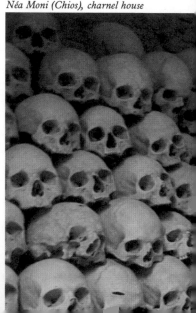

frescos (e.g. the 'Pantocrator' in the dome). The town is dominated by the ruins of a 14C Genoese *fortress* .

Environs: At the village of *Emporió* (6 km. SE) are the remains of a *prehistoric settlement* of the West Anatolian cultural group (Trojan culture), which was later built over in ancient and early Christian times (e.g. a late antique fortress, destroyed around AD 670). On the slopes lay a Greek *settlement* of the 8/7C BC with traces of various *temples* to Athena, Apollo, Artemis, Hera and Aphrodite and several megarons. At the southern tip of the island, at *Káto Fána* (8 km. SW) the shrine of *Apollo Phanaios* from ancient *Phánai,* founded in the 9C BC, was discovered. Above the 6C Temple of Apollo (few traces), the remains of a *basilica* from the time of the Emperor Justinian (527–65) have been excavated. Also of interest is the *fortified village of Mestá* (c. 10 km. NW) with old walls and gates at the foot of a Genoese *keep* (a refuge in case of pirates). The *Taxiárch church* (Archangel) has interesting Byzantine (island) architecture. The area between Pyrgíon and Mestá

has been known for centuries as a centre for mastic (Mastikhokhória, 'mastic villages'). Mastic, valued even in ancient times as chewing gum, is derived from the resin of the lentisk tree *Pistacia Lentiscus,* which grows up to 7 ft. The mastic region was protected by the Genoese in the 14C with a series of *fortresses* and *watch towers* (e.g. fortress of *Armólia,* 20 km. SW of Khíos).

Volissós (40 km. NE of Khíos): Picturesque coastal village (pop. about 700); medieval in character lying at the foot of a hill with a ruined Byzantine fortress (good view).

Environs: Nearby (4.5 km.) is a church with an interesting 17C iconostasis (village of Piramía). Near the coast is the convent of *Agía Markélla* with a famous pilgrimage on the 22 July. At *Ágios Gálas* (57 km. NW of Khíos) Neolithic finds were made in a *cave* (known locally as the 'Bed of the Mother of God').

Kardámyla (25 km. N. of Khíos): The

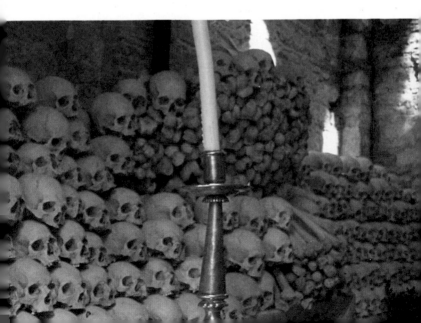

beautifully situated little harbour (pop. 2,600) of *Mármaro* (on the N. coast) lies above ancient *Kardámila* (barely any traces). It is here that Homer's saga is supposed to have been born around 800 BC.

Environs: At the village of *Langádes* (*c.* 7 km. SE) are the few remains of the Athenian military base of *Delphínion* (412 BC).

Island of Psará (*c.* 16 sq. m., pop. 400): This little island, known as *Psyría* in antiquity, lies about 18 km. NW of the main island of Chios. At the start of the 19C it had a flourishing merchant fleet (about 6000 inhabitants in 1820) and fought with Admiral Kanaris against the Turks. In 1824, however, it was totally defeated by the Turks. The entire population was massacred or driven out to Néa Psará on Euboea. The present town of *Psará* is dominated by the ruins of a medieval *fort (Kastro).* To the N., on the slopes of Profitis Ilias, lies the monastery of the Virgin *Kímisis Theotóku* (18C).

Corfu: see **Kérkyra**

Corinth: see **Kórinthos**

Crete: see **Kríti**

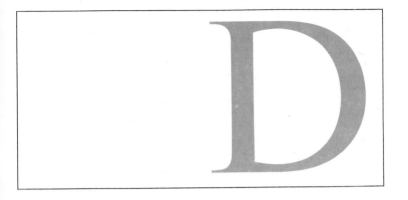

D

Dafní/Daphní/ΔΑΦΝΙ
Attica/Central Greece   p.294☐H 8

On the hill of Aigaleos, some 10 km. outside Athens on the former Sacred Way to Eleusis (NW), lies the interesting Byzantine **monastery church of Dafní**. The name of the monastery, founded as early as the 5/6C (remains of foundations to the W. of the present building), is derived from the former *Temple of Apollo Daphnephoros*, which once stood here (no traces). The temple of 'Apollo amongst the Laurels' was destroyed in AD 395. Around 1080 a new church and monastery were built (under the house of Comnenus). The domed cross-in-square basilica was decorated with marvellous Byzantine *mosaics*. Under Frankish rule (1204–1456) the mon-

Dafní, Byzantine monastery church with remains of the monastery foundations

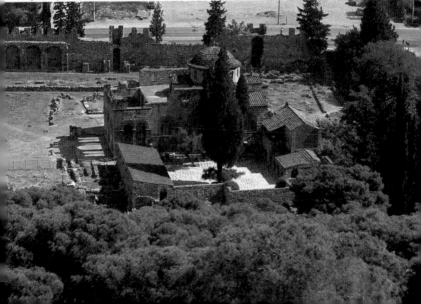

astery of the *Kimisis Theotoku* ('Dormition of the Virgin') was taken over by Burgundian Cistercians around 1211, who added a Gothic exo-narthex. The pointed arches of the W. façade and the battlements also date from this time. Various Frankish dukes were buried here. Following the conquest of Attica, the Turks returned the monastery to the Orthodox church. The present *monastery court* around the *well* originated in the 16C. The monastery was abandoned during the uprisings against the Turks at the end of the 18C, when it was used for a time as a fortress. Restoration of the church and the partly destroyed mosaics did not begin until 1890. Neither the original flagging of the floor, nor the marble facing are preserved. The mosaics have also suffered badly. Nevertheless, the church is a model example of Byzantine mosaic. The central naos has an imposing mosaic of the *Pantocrator* in the dome: the dome itself represents heaven, where Christ rules as a strict and judicial lord of the world (comparable with the Byzantine emperor as his representative on earth). He is surrounded by the 16 Old Testament prophets who foretold Christ's coming (clockwise: Moses, David, Isaiah, Solomon, Elijah, Elisha, Jonah, Habakkuk, Zephaniah, Malachi, Daniel, Micah, Joel, Zachariah, Ezekiel, Jeremiah). The pendentives depict the *Annunciation* and *Nativity* (E.), and the *Baptism* and *Transfiguration* (W.) of the Saviour. The dome of the *sanctuary* (bema) depicts the *Resurrected Christ* together with the Archangels Gabriel and Michael. Depicted in the vault of the *apse* (sanctuary), behind the iconostasis, is the *Virgin* (Panagia Theotokos) and Child. In the *prothesis* (left) is *John the Baptist* with Orthodox saints; in the *Diakonikon* (right) is *St. Nicholas.* In the left arm of the cross is *Lazarus Raised from the Dead* above the *Entry into Jerusalem;* the *Birth of the Virgin* above the *Crucifixion.* In the right one is the depiction *Christ in the Temple* above *Doubting Thomas;* the *Magi*

above *'Christ's Descent into Limbo'* (hell). The Virgin enthroned (Theotokos) in the bema contrasts with the Assumption over the entrance (narthex) to the W. There are further mosaics in the *S. section* of the narthex: The *Life of the Virgin* (the Presentation of the Virgin, the Benediction, Joachim and Anna). In the *N. section* is the *Life of Christ* (Judas's Betrayal, Washing of the Feet, Last Supper). All these important works of art were created by an unknown medieval Greek artist, who here provided (particularly for the illiterate) a convincing portrayal of the fundamental truths of Orthodox Christianity. Apart from the biblical scenes, the church interior is also adorned with numerous pictures of Orthodox saints. The original entrance was on the W. side (through the exo-narthex and narthex); it is now in the right side arm.

Of the other monastery buildings, the substructure of an 11C *refectory* with an apse (N.), and the *cloister* adjoining the church to the S. are preserved. The 16C *monks' cells* surround the square *court,* which has cisterns. Here there are *sarcophagi* with western symbols (fleurs-de-lys, Latin crosses) from the time of the Frankish de la Roche dukes.

Beneath the *arcades* are further Byzantine fragments of the former *crypt;* a few antique finds from the nearby Sacred Way are also to be seen.

Environs: The famous *Wine Festival of Dafní* takes place annually in the autumn near the monastery, with the tasting of wine from all the wine-growing areas of Greece, and folk dancing etc. Some 2 km. NW on the Sacred Way, at the foot of a rock face, is a former *shrine of Aphrodite* (niches for votive statues). Part of the *Sacred Way* to Eleusis is still visible.

Dafní, Christ Pantocrator ▷

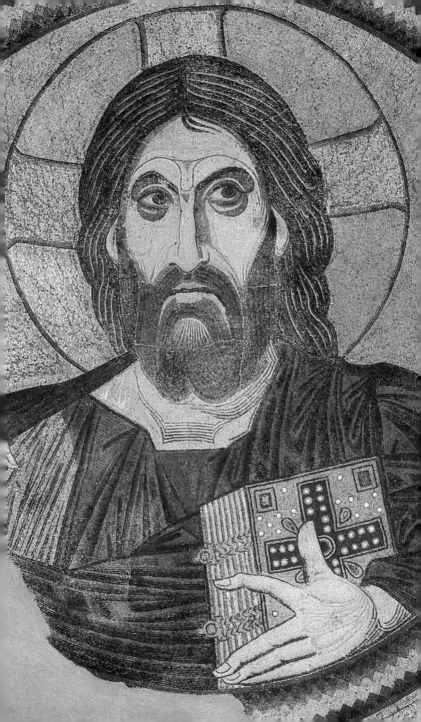

Delfí / Delphi / ΔΕΛΦΟΙ
Fokís/Central Greece　　　　　　p.294□F 7/8

About 3 km. E. of the little town of Delfí, which was only transferred here in 1892 (pop. *c.* 1,200), lies the *Temenos of Apollo* of the same name (excavation site). The most famous religious site in all antiquity, considered the 'navel of the world', is to be found in a unique setting on a southern spur of Parnassos, which rises to 8,150 ft. The shrine, at an altitude of 1,800 ft., is dominated by the precipice of the Phaidriades above the deep ravine of the Pleistos valley, covered with ancient olive-trees. It provides a beautiful view of the Giona mountains to the NW (7,820 ft.), the Helikons to the SE and the bay of Itéa to the S.

History: The area was already inhabited in the 3/2 millennium BC, and on the site of the Temenos of Apollo there was an old shrine to the Chthonic Mother Earth Gaia, who was worshipped under the symbol of the dragon or the python as 'Pytho'. Probably dating back to this time is the role of the Pythia priestess, who had an oracle above the ravine of the earth goddess (mountain goddess). When the Dorians arrived here around 1000 BC, their (shepherd) god Apollo came with them and displaced the Chthonic Mother Earth cult with his symbols of light, strength and wisdom (male principle). The role of the Pythia oracle was kept (now as a priestess of Apollo) and expanded by the male priesthood of Apollo into the Oracle of Delphi, soon to become world-famous. The ecstatic cries of the Pythia were phrased into ambiguous aphorisms (distich couplets) and for centuries they dictated social and political undertakings (foundations of colonies, wars, revolts).
Originally Delphi lay in the territory of its

Delfí, Treasury of the Athenians ▷

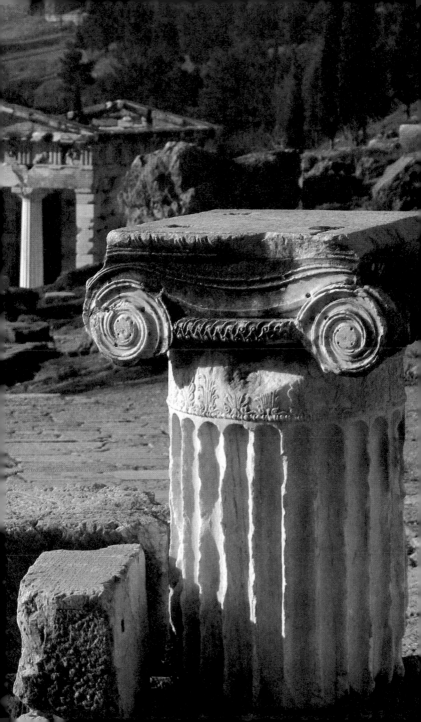

ancient neighbour, the city and port of Kírrha, or Krísa (now Itéa), and was freed from its jurisdiction by the First Sacred War (600–590 BC). From then on the Amphictyonic League (an alliance of nearly every Greek tribe) guaranteed the independence and inviolability of the 'sacred state' of Delphi, which was administered by a sort of 'Order' of priests, prophets, holy people and exegetes. During this prosperous period the great Temple of Apollo was built (around 514 BC) with funds from all over the world (the wooden temple had burned down in 548 BC), and the 'treasuries' constructed. After its ambiguous stance in the Persian Wars, the oracle's prestige gradually declined (growing influence of Athens) and there was a disastrous series of Sacred Wars (448, 356–46 and 339 BC) over the shrine and the Sacred Plain (olive-groves below Delphi). King Philip of Macedon was called to assist (338 BC) and he defeated the Greek states. In 191 BC the Romans occupied the nominally independent shrine. After the repulse of the Gauls (109 BC) numerous treasures were taken by Sulla (86 BC) and, particularly, by Nero (AD 54–68). Plutarch was still High Priest here in AD 105–26. It was not until Theodosius's Edict (381) that it was finally abolished. The medieval village of Kastrí, which grew up over the ruins, was transferred to the site of modern Delfí when intensive excavations were begun in 1892 by the French School.

Temple of Apollo: At the centre of the *Pythian Sanctuary* (c. 440 x 620 ft., with the highest part some 228 ft. further up the slope than the lowest) are the ruins of the great Temple of Apollo. After the first wooden temple of the 7C BC burned down around 548 BC a Doric *peripteral temple* 28 x 195 ft. was built on a specially constructed terrace (walls preserved) in 514–05 BC. This so-called *Alkmaeonid temple* (funded by the Athenian Alkmaeonids)

was destroyed by an earthquake in 373 BC (architectural fragments in the museum). A new Doric peripteral temple was built in 370 – 30 BC to the same plans as its predecessor, with stuccoed tufa columns (6 at each end and 15 on either side). 6 of these columns have been re-erected on the foundations. The interior is known from ancient descriptions by Pausanias and others. On the E. side was the *Pronaos* (remains of paving) with statues of Hermes and wise sayings ('Know Yourself', 'Nothing in Excess'). The *interior* (Naos or Megaron) contained the Hearth of Hospitality (Hestia) with the eternal fire. There was also a lavish collection of votive gifts (weapons, vases, statues). The partly underground *Adyton* (inner sanctum) on the W. side was the actual chamber of the Pythia and the Oracle. This contained the sacred *navel-stone* 'Omphalos' (copy in the museum), the golden statue of Apollo, the monument to Dionysos (he ruled here during the winter, while Apollo was on Delos), the sacred laurel-tree and—over an undiscovered chasm—the *tripod* of the Pythia or prophetess. Those seeking advice sat in a *side-room* (Oikos) separated by a curtain. From the ruins of the Temple of Apollo there is a magnificent view over the lower-lying area of the sanctuary and the whole of the Pleistos valley up to the Bay of Itéa. *Great Altar of Apollo:* In front of the E. end of the Temple of Apollo is the partly reconstructed *Sacrificial Altar,* built of layers of black and white marble (26 x 16 ft.). This was donated by the island of Chios in 475 BC. Next to it stood a *pillar* from the 2C BC, which bore the gilt statue of King Eumenes II of Pergamon (Aetolian donation). The whole *temple forecourt* was once bordered by splendid votive gifts (sparse remains).

Retaining wall of the Temple of Apollo: The terrace of the temple is supported on the S. side by a massive 295 ft. long retaining wall of polygonal masonry built in about 548 BC (prime example of an archaic pol-

Sacred precinct of Delfí (archaeological excavation area) **1** main entrance **2** base of the bronze bull of Kérkyra **3** Arcadian victory monuments **4** Lacedaimonian monument **5** monument of the Athenians **6** Argive monument **7** horse **8** Seven Epigones **9** Kings of Argos **10** Offerings of the Tarentines **11** Treasury of the Sikyonians **12** Treasury of the Siphnians **13** Treasury of the Thebans **14** Treasury of Potidaia **15** Treasury of the Athenians **16** Bouleuterion (council chamber) **17** Treasury of the Knidians **18** Aiolian Treasury **19** rock of the Sibyl **20** column of the Naxians **21** Stoa of the Athenians **22** Treasury of the Corinthians **23** Treasury of Kyrene **24** Prytaneion **25** tripod of Plataia **26** Chariot of Rhodes **27** Great Altar of Apollo **28** offering of Gelon **29** offerings, including the Eurymedon Palm **30** Temple of Apollo **31** offering of Polyzalos, spot where the Charioteer was found **32** Lion Hunt of Alexander **33** theatre skene **34** theatre **35** offering of Daochos (Thessalian monument) **36** Temenos of Neoptolemos **37** Stoa of Attalos **38** Lesche of the Knidians **39** walls of the Temenos

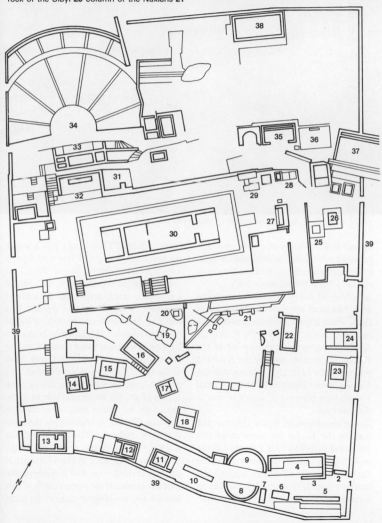

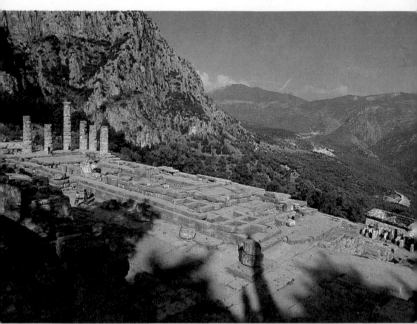

Delfí, Temple of Apollo, the centre of the sacred precinct

ygonal wall). It is covered with over 800 (official) *inscriptions,* which provide valuable information about the sanctuary (particularly from 200 BC to AD 200).

Sanctuary of Earth: Below the retaining wall, blocks of stone mark the shrine of Gaia, where a spring was the centre of the pre-Greek oracle. Nearby is the *Rock of the Sibyl,* the legendary predecessor of the Pythia. On another rock by the retaining wall stood the 32 ft. high column with the *Naxian Sphinx* (donated by Naxos around 550 BC, base preserved), which is now in the museum.

Stoa of the Athenians: Below the retaining wall to the E. lie the remains of this columned hall (92 x 13 ft.). It was built after 478 BC to contain the booty following the victory over the Persians, with 8 Ionic marble columns (3 of which have been re-erected). In front of the Stoa was the *Sanc-*

tuary of Halos ('Threshing Floor'), where the mythical killing of Python by Apollo was depicted in dance. *Sacred Way:* This led from the main entrance (to the S.) along a relatively steep, serpentine path to the forecourt of the Temple of Apollo. It is about 12-16 ft. wide and its original course has been retained. It is lined on both sides by *votive monuments* and about 20 *treasuries* belonging to the richest Greek cities of the time. This sort of 'victory walk' testified to inter-Greek feuding through the means of art: the victorious side in a war would site its victory monument directly opposite the hall (or treasury) of the loser (Syracuse–Athens *c.* 413, Sparta–Athens *c.* 430, Arcadia–Sparta *c.* 369 BC). Right by the main entrance in the SE corner is the base of the *Bronze Bull of Kérkyra,* donated in gratitude for a great catch of fish around 480 BC. Next to this (to the right

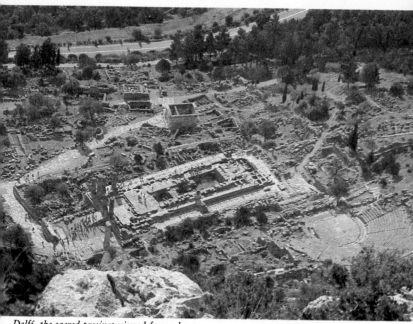

Delfí, the sacred precinct viewed from above

of the Way) is the *Monument of the Admirals* (65 x 20 ft.) in memory of the Peloponnesian War (431–404 BC); in front of this are two Arcadian *victory monuments* (marble bases survive) from around 370 BC. Opposite (left side of the Way) are the remains of the *Monument of the Athenians*, made by Pheidias in 464 BC for the victory of Marathon (to hold their Persian booty). Adjacent, on both sides of the Way, are the foundations of two Argive *exedrae*, which had a series of statues connected with the history of Argos (*c.* 369 BC. This is followed on the left by the *Offerings of the Tarentines* for a victory over the Messapians (473 BC). It consisted of bronze statues of horses and prisoners; four bases survive, some with inscriptions. There now follow the *Treasuries* (20 in all), which not only contained votive gifts, but were also actual votive gifts in themselves: On

the left is the *Treasury of the Sikyonians* with a clearly evident ground plan. It was built in the 6C BC with stone blocks from a circular building (tholos) and a rectangular building (monopteros) (5 small metopes from this in the museum). Next is the *Treasury of the Siphnians* (*c.* 525 BC). This was financed by the gold mined on the small island of Siphnos and was particularly lavishly decorated in Ionic style (frieze of figures in museum). Opposite (right side) are the remains of foundations of smaller (unidentified) *treasuries*. Set back from the bend in the Way (in the SW corner) are remains of the *Treasury of the Thebans*, built for the victory of Leuktra in 371 BC. Nearby is the rubble of other buildings or treasuries (including that of Potidaia). *Treasury of the Athenians:* A Parian marble building *in antis*, with two columns at the front and a Doric *pediment* with triglyphs and metopes (copies). The metopes (originals in the museum) treat themes from the myths of Herakles and Theseus. The building was erected around 490 BC in gratitude for the victory over the Persians at Marathon (inscription on a statue-base in front of the S. wall). Numerous other *wall inscriptions* (on the S. side), mostly from the 3C BC onwards, are preserved (including hymns to Apollo with musical notation, now in the museum). The building lies on older *tufa foundations* from 580 BC (traces inside). The monument was rebuilt with the old stones by the city of Athens in 1904. Opposite are remains probably of the *Treasury of the Syracusans* (Alkibiades led an unsuccessful Athenian expedition against Syracuse in 414 BC) and the *Treasury of the Knidians*. Next to the Treasury of the Athenians lie the remains of the *Bouleuterion* (Senate House) from the 6C BC. On the E. side of the sacred precinct (below the temple), on the other side of the Sacred Way, there are still the ruins of various treasuries and other buildings (Treasury of Kyrene, Prytaneion and so on).

After another bend the Sacred Way opens on to the *temple forecourt* (to the E.). Here lie the remains of famous votive offerings, above all the *Tripod of Plataia* erected in memory of the battle fought there (479 BC). This was a bronze column of intertwined snakes with a gold tripod (financed from Persian spoils); the column now stands in At Meydani Square in Istanbul. Behind this stood the *Votive Offering of Rhodes* (gold Chariot of Helios) and nearby the statues of the Attalos I and Eumenes II, kings of Pergamon. The *Stoa of Attalos* extends outside the temple precinct. *Crossroads of the Tripods:* On the N. side of the temple forecourt are the remains of various *votive offerings*. That of the tyrant Gelon of Syracuse (victory over Carthage) consisted of gold tripods and victory goddesses, and weighed nearly two tons. Further remains of monuments and stele

(sockets survive), including a large square base (N. side) for a statue of Apollo, the base of the *Eurymedon Palm* (victory over the Persians, 468 BC), and the restored *pillars* (for an equestrian statue) of King Prusias of Bithynia. *Ischegaon Wall:* The Sacred Way on the N. side of the temple (leading to the theatre) was bounded by a *retaining wall* (for the upper terrace) in the 4C BC (as was the theatre staircase). Next to the staircase there is an *exedra* dedicated to Alexander the Great (*c.* 330 BC). This is the spot were the famous *Charioteer of Delphi* (now in the museum) was found—the Charioteer was part of an offering of Polyzalos. To the W., outside the sanctuary wall (same level as temple), lie the remains of a long *Stoa* from Hellenistic times (4C BC). Above the retaining wall to the E. is a horseshoe-shaped statue-base, next to which is the *Monument of the Thessalians* (under King Daochos *c.* 336 BC) with well-preserved statues of the king's great-grandfather and others in the museum. Adjacent is the *Temenos of Neoptolemos* (son of Achilles), endowed by the Thessalians. *Mycenean finds* were made here, including a large filled Pithos for sacrifices. Near the sparse remains of the *Kérkyra Monument* (base inscription). W. of the temple are further ruins: a *treasury* with a re-erected archaic *tufa column* (and column drum).

Theatre: This lies to the NW above the Temple of Apollo and was built in the 4C BC and restored under King Eumenes II in 159 BC. The 35 tiers of grey stone seated about 5,000 spectators (the Theatre of Dionysos in Athens held 17,000). The well-preserved *orchestra* is paved with polygonal slabs and surrounded by a covered water conduit. The *Proskenion* had a frieze relief (1C AD, now in the museum) depicting the Labours of Herakles. From the upper tiers there is a wonderful view

Delfí, Tholos of Marmaria

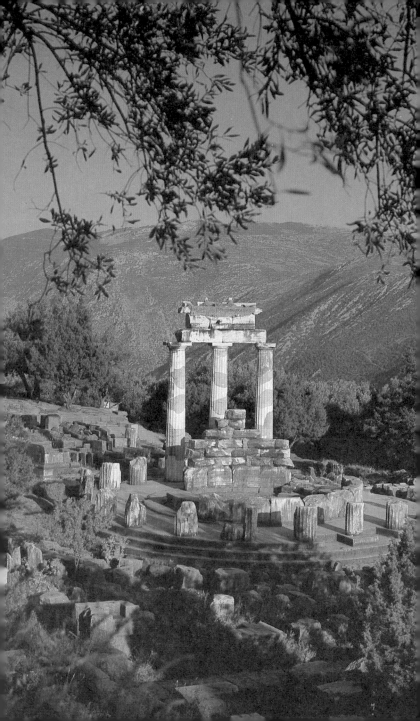

of the Sacred Precinct and the magnificent mountain scenery. The Pythian Games were regularly held here every 4 years (between the Olympic Games) and the theatre was the venue for the musical (flute, kithara, singing) and dramatic contests (tragedy, comedy). Held under the patronage of Apollo, the God of Art, the victors in these contests received the Pythian laurel wreath. Nearby (to the E.) is the supposed site of the *Fountain of Kassotis* (paved terrace), whose water was carried to the temple. Not far away was the *Lesche of the Knidians* (club-house) with works by the famous painter Polygnotos of Thasos (*c.* 450 BC).

Stadium: NW of the theatre (outside the Sacred Precinct) lies the *Stadium,* also built in the 4C BC but altered by Herodes Atticus in the 2C AD. The 12 tiers of seats for about 7,000 spectators were cut into the slope to the N. (preserved), and supported on the valley side by a rampart and retaining wall (now collapsed). It is on the site of an earlier 5C stadium BC with simple earth tiers (stone inscription). To the NE

stood a Roman *Triumphal Arch* (4 pillars preserved) for the entrance of the contestants and on the N. side a *tribune* with stone seats and back-rests for the judges (Proedria). The *track* was nearly 600 ft. long (up to 90 ft. wide). Starting and finishing lines (Aphesis and Terma) are marked by grooved marble sills and there are sockets for the posts separating the tracks. The sporting events of the Pythian Games, which were almost as important as the Olympics, were all held here, with the exception of the chariot race, which took place on the plain of Krisa. The first four-yearly contests go back to around 590 BC, although before that they had been held irregularly or every 8 years.

Temenos Walls: The Sacred Precinct (Temenos) was surrounded in early times by a partly polygonal (6C BC) wall (Peribolos). W. and E. walls were rebuilt in the 4C BC. Near the E. wall (main entrance) are ruins of Roman buildings (3C AD baths): the Roman Agora. In this area interesting finds were recently made from early archaic times (8–6C BC, possibly old shrine of Dionysos).

Delfí, theatre with Temple of Apollo

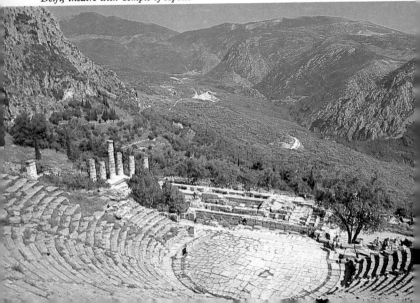

Sacred Fountain of Kastalia: This famous fountain wells up between the deeply cleft precipices of the Phaidriades (ancient name: Hyampeia) to the E. of the Temple Precinct. In antiquity it was used for purification and a nymph of the same name was worshipped in it. The Roman poets saw it as a source of poetic inspiration. This is where the *Cave of the Python* is supposed to have been and remains of an old shrine of the Earth-Mother Gaia (Ge: 'Earth') have been discovered. The spring water flows out of the living rock, which has been carved into a fountain house, into a narrow reservoir (originally covered) and from there into a large rock-hewn basin. Above the fountain and basin is a façade with niches for statues (the nymph Kastalia) and votive offerings.

The older archaic-classical fountain house lies directly on the present road. It was a square surrounded by benches, into which water flowed from 3 lions' heads on the rock face. Here and, later, at the upper fountain, the pilgrims ritually cleansed themselves before entering the Temenos of Apollo.

Gymnasion: Right on the road to Arákhova (SE of the Kastalian Fountain) lie the remains of the gymnasion (4C BC, on the site of an earlier building). On the *upper terrace* there was a covered *colonnade* (Xystos) and next to it an open *track* (Paradromís), both of exactly stadium-length (200 yards), for running practice. On the *lower terrace are remains of a round bath* (32 ft. in diameter), a *Palaestra* for the wrestling competitions, with a peristyle court (for rest periods), changing rooms (Apodyterion) and massage rooms (Elaioterion). The complex was altered during Roman times.

Sanctuary of Athena: This is SE of the gymnasion, below the road to Arákhova. *Old Temple of Athena* (in the SE of the precinct): This was built around 510 BC as a Doric peripteral temple, but was destroyed several times by rock falls from the Phaidriades (the last landslide on the 25.3.1905 demolished 12 of the remaining columns). There was a shrine here as far back as the 7C BC. Further traces of a Mycenean shrine. S. of the temple there are remains

Delfí, sacred fountain of Kastalia

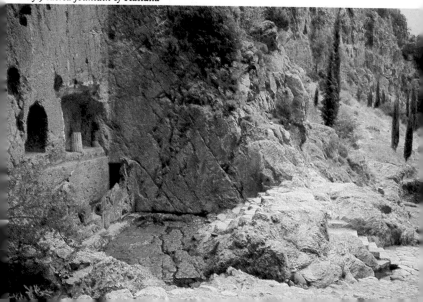

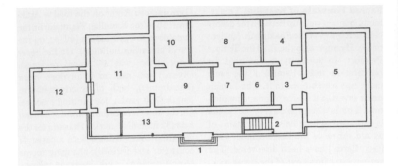

Archaeological Museum in Delfí 1 entrance
2 main staircase **3** early bronze sculptures **4**
Cleobis and Biton **5** Siphnian friezes **6** metope
room **7** small figures from pediment of the archaic
Temple of Apollo **8** figures from the pediment of
the new Temple of Apollo **9** early classical figures
10 Tholos room **11** late classical and early
Hellenistic sculptures **12** hall of the Charioteer **13**
Roman sculptures, with statue of Antinoos

of an archaic *Peribolos* (enclosing wall). To
the E. are remains of *altars* and a *monumental gate*. Next to these is a small *Heroon* for
the Delphic hero Phylakos (*c.* 480 BC victory over the Persians). There are also the
remains of a Heroon commemorating the
battles against the Gauls 279 BC. To the E.
are archaic inscriptions to Athena and
others on a wall.

New Temple of Athena: This was built in
the 4C BC as a Doric Prostylos (with open
colonnade) on a site at the NW end of the
precinct, which was less threatened by rock
falls than that of the old temple. It was
dedicated to Athena Pronaia ('in front of
the temple'), as her temple lay below the
great Temple of Apollo. Built of the finest
Parnassos limestone (many remains), it
stood on a foundation of rubble. Immediately to the NW of the temple are the traces
of priests' dwellings.

Tholos: This marble rotunda (Tholos:
'round building, dome') in Attic-Doric
style (purpose unknown) was built around
380 BC by the architect Theodoros. The
Tholos, one of Delphi's most beautiful
monuments, was enclosed by a *peristyle*

with 20 Doric columns (today 3 have been
re-erected with copies of the metopes). On
the stylobate of three steps, within the circle of columns, there was a round *cella*
(with Corinthian half-columns and black
marble paving inside). On the outside the
cella wall was adorned with a Doric frieze
with triglyphs and metopes (now in the
museum); on the roof were lion's head
water spouts. The present cornice is copied
from models. E. of the Tholos are the remains of two treasuries. The *Treasury of
Massalia* (now the city of Marseilles) was
built around 530 BC in Ionic-Aeolian style
(columns with palm capitals). Next to it is
an unidentified treasury (Doric *c.* 490 BC).
There is a splendid view from the Sanctuary of Athena of the Temenos of Apollo,
the cliffs of the Phaidriades, the Pleistos
ravine and the surrounding mountains.

Archaeological Museum: This lies SW
of the excavation area on the road to the village of Delfí. The collections of the fourth
largest museum in Greece are all from the
Temenos of Apollo and offer an impressive
survey of the development of Greek art.
Room 1 (upstairs): On the landing is a Roman marble copy of the *Navel Stone 'Omphalos'.* The original Omphalos stood in
the Temple of Apollo and was wrapped in
holy bands (here chiselled into the stone).

Delfí, Charioteer (museum) ▷

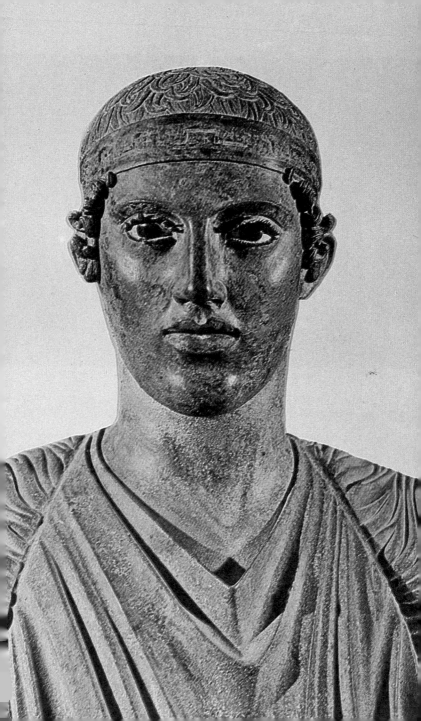

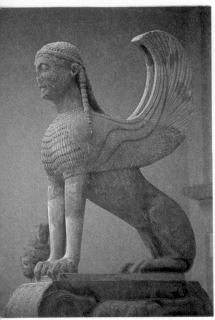

Delfí, Naxian sphinx (museum)

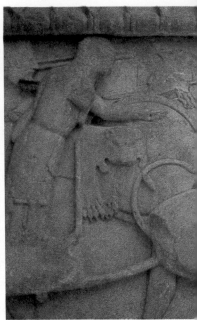

Delfí, N. frieze on the Síphnian Treasury

According to myth Zeus sent two eagles from both ends of the world (E. and W.) who met at the 'Navel of the World' in Delphi. It is also meant to be the tombstone of the serpent Python. Also note a small relief of the Omphalos between Athena and Apollo, a proscenium frieze from the theatre (1C AD) with the Labours of Herakles and a tripod. Below the stairs (entrance on the right) is a *marble sarcophagus* with a bust of Herakles and battle scenes. Early Christian mosaic pavement (4C) from the village of Delfí.

Room 2: In the 'Hall of the Shields' there are interesting *bronze shields* from the 7C BC (with lions' heads, circles), two *bronze griffins* on tripod cauldrons (7/6C BC), a small Daedalic bronze Kouros (7C BC).

Room 3 ('Kouroi Room'): Of particular interest are the 2 colossal statues (about 6 ft. 6 ins.) of *Cleobis and Biton* by the Argive sculptor Polymedes (*c.* 600 BC). The myth relates that the two sons of the Priestess of Hera Kydíppe yoked themselves to her chariot, as the animals were missing, and pulled it some 6 miles up to the temple. Their mother asked Hera to grant them the best in life and the goddess thereupon let the youths (Kouroi) slumber and die (an example of the pessimistic world-view of the ancients). A feature of the statues (a votive gift of the Argives) is the so-called 'archaic pose', the foot thrust forward and the arms rigid, which still betrays the influence of large-scale Egyptian sculpture. On the walls are five *metopes* from the *Treasury of Sikyón* (*c.* 560 BC): Motifs from the story of the Argonauts (Europa and Zeus as a bull, Deeds of the Dioscuri, the Calydonian Boar and others). Also a small *bronze Kouros* (Apollo) *c.* 540 BC.

Room 4 ('Síphnos Room'): Here, above all,

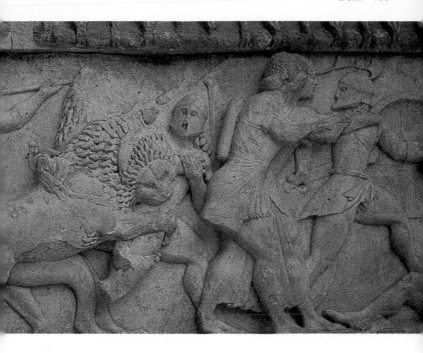

are the *friezes* from the *Siphnian Treasury* (built around 525 BC). On the left (of the door) is the famous *East Frieze* with the *Assembly of Gods* during the Trojan War. To the left are the 'supporters of Troy': Ares, Aphrodite, Artemis and Apollo, enthroned in the middle is Zeus and on the right the 'supporters of the Greeks': Poseidon (destroyed), Athena, Hera and Demeter. The right side of the frieze depicts another Trojan scene (Nestor). Above it is the *East Pediment:* Dispute between Herakles and Apollo over the Delphic tripod; Zeus as mediator. On the wall opposite is the *West Frieze* with the *Judgement of Paris:* victorious Aphrodite alighting from a chariot. Next to it is the chariot of Athene with the god Hermes (fragments). The equally fragmentary *South Frieze* depicts the rape of the daughters of Leukippos by the Dioscuri. On the side wall is the famous

North Frieze with scenes from the battle of the Olympian Gods against the Giants. The Giants are depicted as heavily armed hoplites grouped around 3 chariots; on the left is Hephaistos with storm-blowing bellows, then Herakles with a lion's skin, Artemis and Apollo, Zeus's war chariot, bearded Ares, Hermes with his cap and Poseidon; and, in between them, the Giants. On the right side of the room stands the *Naxian Sphinx* (c. 560 BC), the oldest votive gift in Delphi. This stood on a 30 ft. column in front of the polygonal wall below the Temple of Apollo. There is also a *caryatid* from the *portico* of the Siphnian Treasury, and next to it the *capital* which it bore. At the door is an Aeolian *capital* from the *Treasury of Massalia* in the Sanctuary of Athena.

Room 5: Displayed here are remains of the *Athenian Treasury* (c. 490 BC). The 24

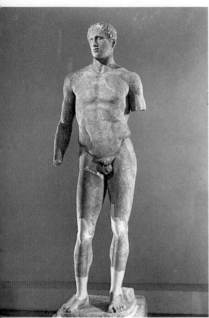

Delfí, kuros (museum)

marble metopes depict scenes from the *Labours of Herakles* (N. side): Nemean lion, hind, Kyknos, centaur etc.; *Deeds of Theseus* (S. side) with Athena, Sinis, Prokrustes, Minotaur, Amazons, Bull of Marathon etc.

Room 6: This contains the *sculptural fragments* from the west pediment of the *Archaic Temple of Apollo* (*c.* 510 BC), depicting the Battle of the Gods and Giants (fragment: *Athena charging into battle*). Next to this are a small *Kouros* (5C BC) and a walking *Peploskore* (vestal virgin) from 470 BC. Incised on a stone slab (from the Athenian Treasury) are *Hymns to Apollo* in letters and musical notation from the 2C BC.

Room 7: Sculptures from the east pediment of the *Archaic Temple of Apollo* (Alkmaeonid Temple) *c.* 510 BC. The theme is Apollo's entry into Delphi (animal groups:

lion devouring deer or bull; women and man with cart and horses; remnants of painting discernible). Also a *Kouros* from around 450 BC and a small *bronze cow* (statuette from 500 BC). Votive inscription by Emperor Domitian from AD 84.

Room 8: ('Tomb Room'): In the middle is the early classical *tomb* of an athlete with servants (465 BC); a few other *grave stele.* Three Demeter Kore masks (glass showcase). In front of these are 2 bronze hydras (4C BC). *Figure of Dionysos* (from the New Temple of Apollo). *Round altar* (1C BC) with depictions of girls. Fine athlete's torso (4C BC).

Room 9 ('Tholos Room'): Reconstructed here are parts of the entablature of the *Tholos* (from the Sanctuary of Athena) with Doric outer columns and Corinthian inner ones. The *fragments of metopes* depict fighting Greeks, Amazons and centaurs.

Room 10: Three dancing *Korai* (daughters of Kekrops) around a large *acanthus column* (a votive offering of the Athenians *c.* 335 BC). The original 36 ft. high column bore a tripod. Note the *Offering by Daochos* (statues, *c.* 338 BC). The well-preserved statue of the athlete *Agias* is by the famous sculptor Lysippos (time of Alexandria). In the corner is a *figure of a philosopher* (*c.* 270 BC).

Room 11: This contains the finest exhibit in the museum, the *Charioteer,* an early classical bronze statue (474 BC) donated by the tyrant Gelon of Syracuse to mark his victory (chariot race) at the Pythian Games of 478 BC. There are other fragments in the showcases. Note the expressive hand, the feet, the eyes of coloured stone, the fine eyelashes and the mouth with its smile of victory. The sculptor is unknown (possibly Sotades of Thespiai). The room also contains a bronze *votive flask* depicting women and an offering cup (*c.* 460 BC.

Room 12: Statue of Antinous (favourite of the Emperor Hadrian) from the 2C AD, *heads,* particularly that of the Consul *Flaminius,* who, in 196 BC, ended

Macedonian supremacy. In the showcases are interesting Helladic and early archaic finds from the immediate vicinity.

Environs: Throughout the environs of the Temenos of Apollo (to the E., S. and SW) there are remains of antique **tombs**, including **cave tombs** (to the S.). The **Spring of Sybaris**, famous since antiquity (now the *Zaleska Spring*) lies in the vicinity of the Pleistos ravine to the S. of the shrines. The spring can be reached via a bridle-path from the village of Delfí. The monster Lamía or Sybaris is supposed to have lived in the *cave* by the spring (former hermitage), until it was killed by the Delphic hero Eurybatos. From here one descends to the ravine and the little monastery of the *Panagía* (climb back up to the road by the Sanctuary of Athena). 8 km. W. of Delphi lies the village of **Krisó,** which is descended from the prehistoric settlement of Krisa. By the chapel of *Ágios Georgios* are traces of a mid-Helladic settlement (surrounded by a wall in Mycenean times). According to legend Krisa even took part in the Trojan War (under King Strophios and his son Pylades, the friend of Orestes). The town was destroyed in 590 BC during the First Sacred War.

Dílesi/ΔΗΛΕΣΙ
Boeotia/Central Greece   p.294 □ H 8

In ancient times Dílesi was called *Délion* and had a shrine of Apollo erected by Ionians from the island of Delos, hence the name Délion. In the year 424 BC a great battle in which the Boetians defeated the Athenians took place here.

Dílos/Delos (I)/ΔΗΛΟΣ
Cyclades/Aegean Islands   p.296 □ L 10

This infertile island in the middle of the Cyclades, only 1.4 sq. miles in area and

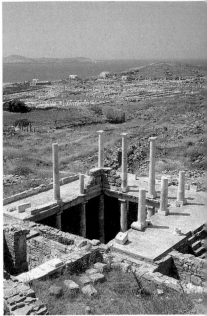
Dílos, House of Hermes

uninhabited to this day, was the most important religious place in the Aegean in ancient times. Today, the island, which lies some 3 km. from Mykonos, is a superb open-air museum of ancient culture.

History: According to the myth, the twin gods Apollo and Artemis were born on the island, which was also called *Ortygía* ('Quail Island'). The earliest traces of settlement date back to the 3rd millennium BC and to a Mycenean settlement between 1400 and 1200 BC. The first Ionian settlers colonized the island around 1000 BC, probably bringing the cult of Apollo with them. By the 7C BC Delos was already the centre of the Ionian League under the supremacy of Naxos and later of Athens. From that time onwards the Delian Games (music, dance, sport) were held every four years, and large embassies (Theoria) from

Athens. After the victory over the Persians, Athens founded the Delian Confederacy, a maritime league (477 BC) based in Delos. Delos lost its importance when the treasury of the League was transferred to Athens in 454 BC and through the subsequent decrees forbidding child-bearing, burial and, finally, living on the island ('Purification Decree' of 425 BC. Only when released from Athens in 314 BC (by the Macedonians) and later under Roman protectorate (from 168 BC) did the island enjoy independant economic growth as a free Aegaean port and trading centre. Merchants from all over the ancient world settled here and built secular and religious buildings, particularly following the destruction of Corinth (146 BC). Thousands of slaves changed hands here daily. The island finally declined after being captured and plundered by King Mithridates of Pontos in 88 BC.

Archaeological Area: The excavation area, about one mile x 1100 yards, where the French Archaeological School of Athens has been working since 1872, can be divided into several areas: a) *Sacred Precinct* around the Hieron of Apollo; b) the *area around the around the Sacred Lake*; c) *ancient town* and theatre quarter S. of the Sacred Precinct; d) *religious sites on Mount Kynthos.*

a) *Sacred Precinct:* Ships arriving for the festivals were moored in the *Sacred Harbour* on the W. side of the island (near the present moles). At the main landing place stood the south *Festival Gate* to the Sacred Precinct. In the 2C BC the gate was enlarged by the Athenians into a marble propylaia with Doric columns. From the 9 or 8C BC, the adjoining area was the centre of the worship of Apollo, with its 3 *Temples of Apollo.* The smallest and oldest of these was the *Porinos Naos,* built of chalky sandstone (poros), it dates from around the middle of the 6C and contained

a 26 ft. metal statue of Apollo (by Tektaios, *c.* 540 BC). The treasury of the Delian Confederacy was housed here until 454 BC. The foundations of the rectangular temple, about 33 x 52 ft. (in antis), survive. The *Temple of Apollo* (*c.* 480 BC) was built by the Athenians and was the largest (44 x 97 ft.) and southernmost of the temples, although it was not completed until the 3C BC. It is a classical Doric temple with 6 x 13 columns (peripteros), a narrow cella with a pronaos and opisthodomos; gneiss foundations and marble steps survive. **Temple of the Athenians:** Around 420 BC the Athenians built a third, smaller Doric temple (*c.* 58 ft 6 in. x 37 ft. 6 in.), between the Porinos Naos and the 'Great Temple', with 6 columns at each end and 7 statues in the cella ('Temple of the Seven Statues'). It is interesting that all three temples are orientated to the W. (Ionic-Asia Minor style). The oldest identifiable building in the sanctuary, the early-6C BC *Oikos of the Naxians,,* lies SE of the old festival square, which probably goes back to an old Mycenean religious site and settlement (*c.* 1400 – 1200 BC). It is an elongated Ionic columned hall, 33 x 82 ft., on the site of an older building of the 8 or 7C BC. In front of the N. wall is the massive *marble base,* 16 ft. 5 in. x 11 ft. 6 in., which bore a 29 ft. 6 in. statue of Apollo, the *'Colossus of the Naxians'* (pieces of the torso and of the basin are to be found further N. near the Artemísion). The *Stoa of the Naxians* was built SW of the Sacred Precinct, near the Propylaia, around 550 BC. The precinct itself was paved with bluish marble and played an important role in sacred rites (Delia). In the corner of the stoa stood the *Bronze Palm-Tree* donated by Nikias of Athens in about 417 BC (granite base survives), which is reputed to have brought down the Statue of Apollo in a storm (Plutarch). To the NE of the Stoa of the Naxians are the poros foundations of a rectangular building, the *Keraton,* preceded by columns (*c.* 350 BC). It is an almost

Dílos, archaeological excavation area 1 Agora of the Competialists **2** Stoa of Philipp **3** S. Agora **4** Naxian hall **5** Stoa of the Naxians **6** Keraton **7** Temple of Artemis **8** Temple of Apollo **9** Treasuries **10** Prytaneion **11** Monument of the Bulls **12** Sanctuary of Dionysus **13** Stoa **14** Thesmophorion **15** Agora of Theophrastos **16** columned hall **17** temple (of Leto) **18** store **19** Agora of the Italians **20** Lion Terrace **21** Sacred Lake **22** House of the Poseidoniasts **23** lake palaistra **24** granite palaistra **25** House of the Diadumenos **26** House of the Comedians **27** Archaeological Museum **28** House of Hermes **29** Sanctuary of the Syrian Gods **30** Serapeion **31** Temple of Hera **32** House of the Dolphins **33** House of the Masks **34** theatre **35** House of the Trident **36** House of Dionysos **37** House of Cleopatra **38** Triarius wall **39** ancient path **40** hieron (B,C) **41** Kynthion

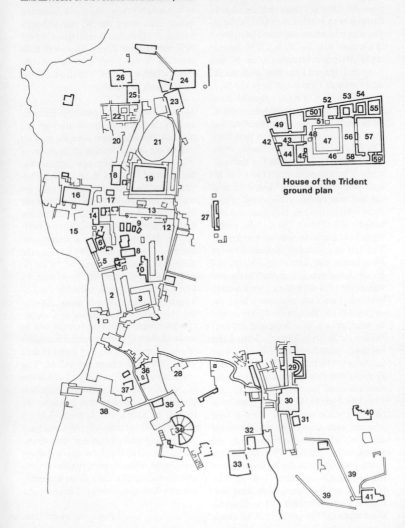

House of the Trident ground plan

square hall, 52 ft.6 in. x 55 ft.9 in. and the *Horned Altar* (keratinos bomos) of Apollo, around which the 'Crane Dance' (Geranos) was performed, is supposed to have stood here. NE of the Keraton are the foundations of the *Artemísion* (2C BC), the Temple of Artemis. As early as Mycenean times (*c.* 1200 BC) there was an altar of Artemis here, making it probably the oldest religious site on the island (also traces of a temple from the 7C BC). The Sanctuary of Artemis is bordered to the N. and E. by an L-shaped Ionic stoa from the 2C BC. Five small *'Treasuries'* lie to the N. of the Porinos Naos. They are probably from the 5C BC. Adjoining the temple to the W. are an archaic building (Bouleuterion?) and the *Prytaneion* (administrative building). The *Hall of the Ship* or Monument of the Bulls forms the E. boundary of the sanctuary. It is an elongated hall (30 x 220 ft.) with an entrance to the S. The interior of the hall was probably decorated with a frieze relief (mermaids, dolphins) and contained a sort of basin, 151 x 16 ft., probably to hold a trireme dedicated to Apollo. The hall was probably dedicated by the Macedonian king Demetrios (3C BC) and his son Antigonos. The *capitals* in the passage to the cella are adorned with recumbent bulls (hence the misnomer). Near the entrance to the Hall (to the SE) is a *granite altar*, which was dedicated to Zeus Polieus (or Soter) (*c.* 280 BC). Behind this lies the E. boundary wall of the sanctuary (*c.* 280 BC), which leads NE to the former *E. Gate, where the remains of the foundations of a small Temple of Dionysos* (*c.* 26 x 13 ft.) lie. Next to this are the remains of two choregic monuments with a base adorned with reliefs (3C BC). Depicted upon one is Dionysos with maenads and a cock with a phallus. The *Stoa of Antigonos*, which forms the N. boundary of the sanctuary, is a columned hall, 390 x 66 ft., built by the Macedonian king Antigonos Gonatas around 253 BC (foundations survive). The portico has 47 Doric

columns; remains of the bluish Tinos marble *frieze* with bull's heads are preserved. Before the central section of the Stoa are the remains of a Mycenean *tomb*, which is thought to be the tomb of the Hyperborean maidens Arge and Opis. At the W. end of the Stoa are the foundations of an assembly room, the *Ekklesiasterion,* which dates from the 5C BC, although subsequently altered several times. In the NW corner is the *Thesmophorion* (2 halls about 40 ft. wide) with a 5C BC peristyle court, which was probably dedicated to the fertility cult of Demeter.

b)Area to the N. of the Sanctuary: Immediately N. and NW of the sanctuary are the markets and complexes used for trading and by the administration. The *Agora of Theophrastos* (now a large open square) was built around 126 BC by the Athenian Theophrastos; the base of his statue survives with an inscription. N. of this stood the *hypostyle hall* (columned), built by the Delians around 208 BC and later rebuilt by the Athenians. It was a rectangular building measuring about 184 x 112 ft.; the ceiling of which was borne by 24 Doric and 20 Ionic columns (S. front with 15 Doric columns). It was probably used as a corn exchange and trade room. Adjoining this are the foundations of a *temple* (Dodekatheon) dedicated around 280 BC to the 12 Gods of Olympos and the remains of a small archaic *Temple of Leto* (29 ft. 6 in. x 39 ft. 4 in.) from the 6C BC. The whole area around the Sacred Lake in the N., whence leads a *Processional Way,* was probably dedicated to this goddess, the mother of Apollo and Artemis. Later a granite building containing *shops* was built on what was open pasture and towards the end of the 2C BC the *Agora of the Italians* was erected. This complex, the most extensive on Delos, was used as an assembly place by Roman merchants. The rectangu-

Dílos, one of the lions ▷

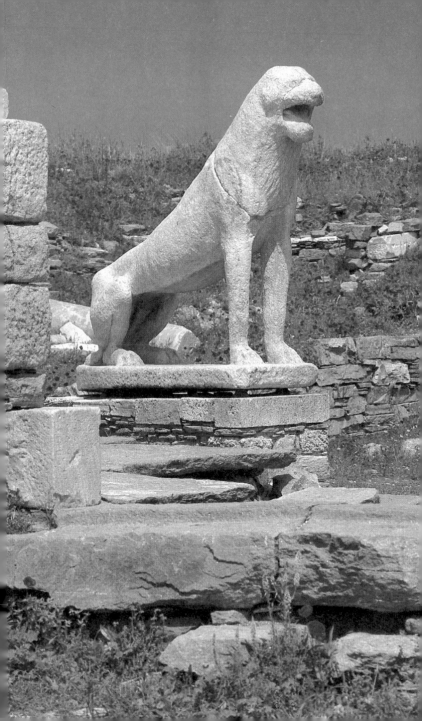

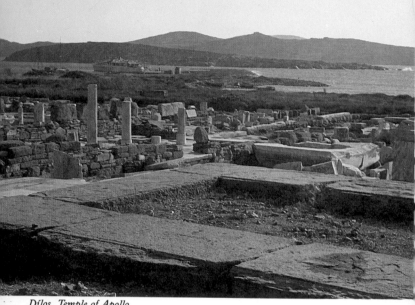

Dílos, Temple of Apollo

lar *inner court* (227 x 328 ft.) was surrounded by a two-storeyed *peristyle* (Doric
columns, Ionic upper storey). Behind the
colonnades lay the still partly preserved
trading rooms with beautiful *mosaic pavements* (e.g. the cell of Satricanius and the
cell of Ofellius with a beautiful statue by
the Athenian sculptors Dionysios and
Timarkhides). The Agora itself is Roman;
the W. entrance is a gate with 4 Doric
columns. Adjoining the Agora of the
Italians to the N. is the *Sacred Lake*. This
was fed in ancient times by a tributary of
the river Inopos and upon it swam the
swans of Apollo and the geese of Leto. In
1926 the lake was closed off because of the
danger of disease (the surrounding wall is
visible). To the W. of the lake is the famous
Terrace of the Lions, now the emblems of
Delos: On a 164 ft. long terrace at the end
of the *Processional Way* there once stood

at least 9 (possibly 16) archaic marble lions
from Naxos (7C BC), probably acting as
guardians of the Sanctuary of Leto. The
lions sit with very straight upper bodies
and open mouths on rectangular or oval
plinths. The bodies are strikingly slender.
Four of these, the oldest monumental
Greek animal figures, are well preserved,
three only partly so. One was taken to
Venice in the 17C (now in front of the Arsenal) and one disappeared without trace.
The intrinsic relationship of the row of
lions with the birthplace of the goddess
Leto (or the connection with the Asian or
Egyptian lion symbolism) has still not
been exactly explained. NW of the Sacred
Lake (behind the Terrace of the Lions) was
the complex of the *Poseidoniasts.* This was
built by a group of Merchants from Berytos
(now Beirut), who settled here under the
protection of the sea-god Poseidon. A few

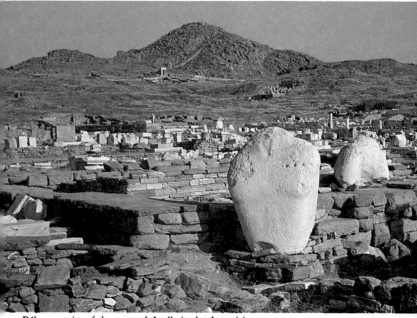

Dílos, remains of the statue of Apollo in the Artemision

interesting remains are still preserved from the building, which was completed around 110 BC (peristyle court, wells, mosaic pavement and bases of statues). Just N. of the Sacred Lake lie the remains of the *Lake Palaistra* from the 3C BC (destroyed in 69 BC, E. part concealed by the *Wall of Triarius*). The Palaistra as well as the wall stand on the foundations of earlier secular and religious buildings. The *Old Palaistra* (Granite Palaistra) to the N. of the Lake Palaistra was built of granite blocks around 166 BC (large peristyle court, 52 ft. 6 in. x 69 ft., with cistern). E. of this is the granite substructure of the *Hippodrome,* the Well of the Maltese and the remains of the city wall built in 69 BC by the Roman legate Triarius as a protection against pirate attacks. In the N. district of the Sacred Lake the foundations of several large *houses* were also excavated. The *Lake House* (next

to the Granite Palaistra) with a portal giving on to the lake; the *House of the Diadumenos* (N. by the complex of the Poseidoniasts), where a marble copy of the metal statue of the same name by Polykleitos was discovered (now in Athens). NW of this is a block of houses with the *House of the Comedians* (named after the discovery there of a painted frieze depicting actors of comedy and tragedy). In the adjacent *House of the Tritons* is a floor mosaic depicting Tritons and Eros; further W. is *Hill House* with a vestibule and back-and-white paved court. In the NE of the island there are yet more ruins, which were connected by a road to the sanctuary. These include the *Shrine of Archegetes* (Archegesion) named after the founding king (Archegetes) Anios, c. 600 BC; the shrine comprises a paved court without a temple. The *Gymnasion* (3C BC) with

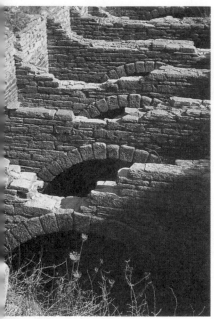

Dílos, theatre, cisterns

Dílos, relief

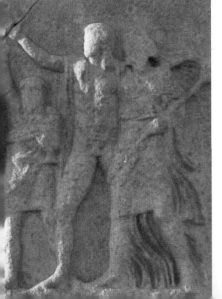

Ionic peristyle court, rooms for washing and instruction. The *Stadium* (*c.* 200 BC) with a 550 ft. long running track, built on the rock in the N., and remains of a residential area. Nearby are the ruins of a *synagogue* from the 1C BC.

c) Ancient town (and theatre quarter) to the S. of the sanctuaries: The remains of the ancient town largely date from the time of the island's greatest economic growth (2&1C BC). The N. boundary of the town is formed, on the edge of the Sanctuary of Apollo, by the *Agora of the Delians,* the *South Stoa,* the *Dromos* (Sacred Way) and the *Stoa of Philip.* The Agora of the Delians is a rectangular paved square bounded to the N. and E. by an L-shaped stoa of the 2C and to the S. by a portico from the 3C BC. This was the island's first trading centre (shops, later Roman baths as well). Adjoining to the E. was the *South Stoa* (217 x 43 ft.) with a front of 28 Doric columns (3C BC). The base of an equestrian statue (to the SW) commemorates the general of King Attalos I of Pergamon, who probably funded the building of the stoa. Opposite, on the 43 ft. wide, stone-paved *Dromos* lie the remains of the *Stoa of Philip,* founded in 210 BC by Philip V of Macedon (votive inscription on the remains of the architrave). The front (236 ft. long) had 16 Doric columns; it was later completed by a *West Stoa* on the harbour side. The W. boundary (harbour side) is formed by the *Agora of the Hermaists* (or Competialists). This was the assembly place of the Italian merchant-guild of the 2C BC (under the protection of Hermes), particularly prior to the building of the Agora of the Italians. Here are remains of votive altars, bases of statues and smaller buildings. Nearby lay the *ancient harbour* (now sanded up), which was protected by two moles built of granite blocks. The alleys between the Agora of the Hermaists

Dílos, theatre ▷

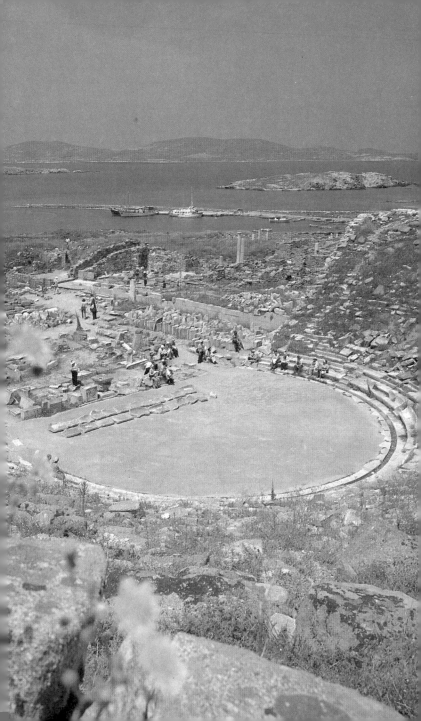

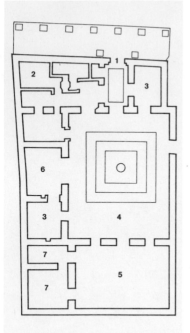

Dílos, House of the Dolphins 1 entrance **2** kitchen **3** room **4** peristyle court **5** oikos (living room) **6** andron **7** sleeping chambers

and the S. part of the Wall of Triarius are narrow and irregular ('Theatre Alley', about 6 ft. wide). The houses themselves were up to 40 ft. high (13–16 ft. high remains of walls survive). By the Theatre Alley lie the interesting *House of Cleopatra* (named after the statues of the Athenian couple Cleopatra and Dioscourides, around 138 BC) and the *House of Dionysos* with a beautiful *mosaic* in the inner court depicting Dionysos astride a panther. The peristyle court is surrounded by columns about 18 ft. 4 in. high. Graffiti (pictures of ships) on the walls. On the outer wall is a relief (Herakles's Club?). Near the theatre is the interesting *House of the Trident* (named after the trident motif in the

mosaic pavement). It is a typical, large house of the island (vestibule, kitchen, dining-room, oikos, inner court with gallery and peristyle and impluvium with well). Of interest is the *impluvium mosaic* (dolphin with trident). The fronts of these houses were predominantly window-less, life being conducted in the inner court and interior. On the upper floor were sleeping quarters and ladies' chambers. In the SE of the town lies the badly preserved *theatre* (*c.* 220 BC) with seating for about 5,000 spectators (26 rows of seats), round orchestra with a water channel and a large *cistern* (72 x 20 ft.) with a surviving granite arch behind the stage. Rainwater was collected here in 9 chambers. Somewhat further SE are traces of 3 *sanctuaries:* One to *Dionysos* (Hermes and Pan), a *Temple of Apollo,* a temple to Artemis-Hekate. E. of the theatre is the *House of the Dolphins* (2C BC. This occupies an 'insula' (residential block) with an upper storey (side-rooms). The peristyle court had 12 Doric columns; the sunken pavement of the columned court (impluvium) above the well has a beautiful *mosaic.* In the middle is a rosette, in the four corners are Erotes on dolphins with divine attributes (trident of Poseidon, thyrsos staff of Dionysos, herald's staff of Hermes). In the hall is a black-and-white mosaic with Phoenician Tanit symbols to ward off evil spirits. Across the street lies the *House of the Masks* (2C BC). In four rooms there are particularly beautiful *mosaics:* Dionysos with thyrsos and tambourine riding a panther between two centaurs; in the main room (oikos) is the depiction of the 9 masks (types) of the 'new' comody (Pollux, 2C AD describes it); dancing Silenus with flute players; a decorated amphora with palm-frond. On the slope of the dried-up Inopos (NE of theatre) lies the well preserved terraced *House of Hermes,* built in the 2C BC and named after the head of a statue of Hermes, which was found here. Further NE is the *House of the Inopos,* named after the main

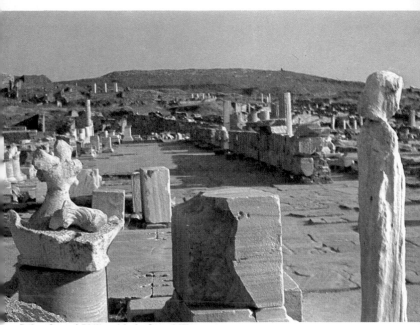

Dílos, Stoa of Philip with the Sacred Way

Dílos, temple and treasury

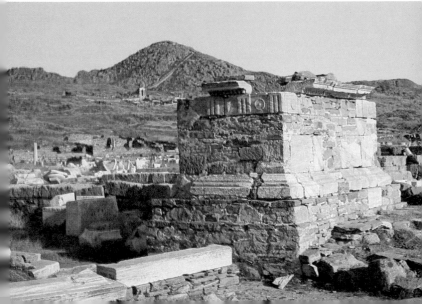

stream of ancient Delos. It has two entrances on the street side, a peristyle court
and a mosaic of a dove (from the upper
floor).

d) Sanctuaries on Mount Kynthos: E. of the
ancient town is another area of cult buildings. Near the SE part of the Wall of Triarius lie the remains of a *Temple of Aphrodite* from the 4C BC. Below Mount
Kynthos on the E. slope of the bed of the
Inopos is the *Terrace of the Foreign Gods*
(Syrian and Egyptian gods) from the 2C
BC. The badly damaged *Serapeion A* (by
the House of the Inopos) was the oldest
(private) sanctuary of the Egyptian god
Serapis on Delos (worshipped together
with Isis and Anubis). Nearby is a
Samothrokeion, which was dedicated to the
Kabeiroi of the island of Samothráke
(temple remains from the 4C BC). Above
the water reservoir (3C BC) lie the remains
of *Serapeion B* and the *Sanctuary of the
Egyptian* (S. part) *and Syrian Gods* (N.
part) Atargatis (Aphrodite) and Hadad
(weather god), founded around 128 BC.
This includes a propylon, inner court, 3
chapels and colonnades (stoa). Also belonging to it was a small *theatre* with 12 rows
of seats (about 500 seats). The complex adjoining to the S., *Serapeion C* (2C BC was
the official shrine of the gods Serapis, Isis
and Anubis. The main building includes
a court with Ionic porticoes, which was
surrounded by cult buildings and votive
gifts. To the E. is the rebuilt marble façade
of the *Temple of Isis* from 135 BC (large
statue of the goddess preserved). To the S.
is a long square (Dromos) with a sphinx
gallery of Egyptian design (traces survives).
Nearby are the foundations of the Sanctuary of Hera *(Heraion)* from the 7 or 6C BC.
Two columns from the small temple (23 ft.
x 42 ft. 8 in.) have survived. S. of the Heraion on the ancient path to the summit of
Mount Kynthos lie the remains of the
shrine of *Agatha Tyche* ('Good Fortune')
from the 3C BC with court, peristyle halls

and a small temple. On the summit of
Mount Kynthos (368 ft.) are the remains
of the *Kynthion:* This was the sanctuary
of Zeus Kynthios and Athena Kynthia
with a temple from the 3C BC. The summit (with a superb view) was already occupied in the 3C BC (votive inscriptions to
Zeus from the 7C BC). On the W. slope is
the *Kynthos Grotto* (for Apollo?) with the
base of a statue of Herakles. There were
further shrines in the Kynthos area including one to Zeus Hypsistos (lord) in the S.
and the *Hieron* of the gods of Askalon in
the E., also the Terrace of Artemis Locheia
(temple substructure). In the S. of the island (near the coast) lay granaries and
docks and a few smaller insignificant
shrines: the *Sanctuary of the Dioscouri* with
a peribolos, the *Sanctuary of Asklepios* (3C
BC) with propylon, oikos and temple remains; the sanctuary of the sea-goddess
Leukothea (few traces).

Archaeological Museum (NE of the Hieron
of Apollo): One of the most important
Greek collections of archaic art (although
the best finds on Delos were taken to the
National Museum in Athens). The *Central Hall* contains works from the 7&6C
BC: triangular base (marble) with a ram's
head and Gorgon masks from a statue of
Apollo (Eutychides of Naxos); Naxian
sphinx; marble relief (procession of gods);
marble stele from the Temple of Good Fortune (Artemis with torches); numerous
kouroi and korai. In the *First Room* to the
left are fragments of paintings from houses:
seated statue of Dionysos; actor dressed as
Silenus (Roman); statues of Muses, and
Artemis; tomb stele; fragments of acroteria,
pediment decorations (*c.* 420 BC) from the
Temple of Apollo and numerous herms,
etc. The *2nd Room* to the left contains,
among other things, finds from the Heraion (in glass cases), small sculptures, terracottas, vessels, vases, Hellenistic pottery

Dílos, Dionysos on a panther ▷

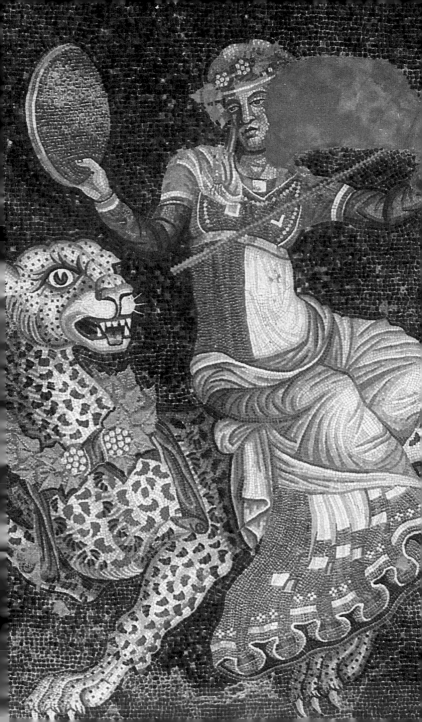

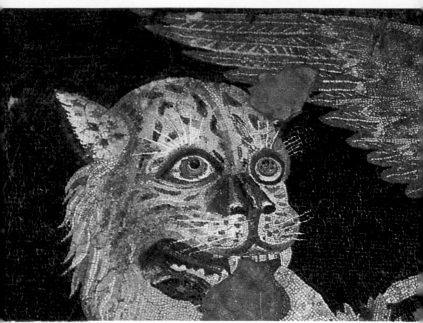

Dílos, Hellenistic wall painting in a house

and figurines (from the houses) and household objects. In the *room to the right* are fragments of sculptures and inscriptions, votive gifts from the Artemísion (ivory, bronze); also Mycenean ivories and so on.

Environs: The neighbouring island of *Rínia,* also uninhabited and lying to the W. of Delos, provided burial grounds and shelter for women about to give birth after the purification of Delos (now also known as *Megáli Dílos:* 'Greater Delos'). The ancient settlement lay on the W. coast (remains of a *Temple of Herakles* from the 2C BC). To the E. are the burial grounds with numerous tomb finds (now in the Museum of Mykonos). Note the *'Purification Ditch',* a mass grave for coffins transferred from Delos, also the Hellenistic *'Columbarium',* a passage tomb with burial niches and gneiss slabs.

Diónysos/ΔΙΟΝΞΣΟΣ
Attica   p.296☐H 8

This little town on the N. slope of the Pentelikon range (lovely excursions from Athens), about 30 km. NE of Athens. Nearby are the marble quarries, still important today.

History: As its name indicates, the town has, since antiquity, been closely linked with the god of wine and ecstasy, Dionysos (Bacchus). It is here that the Athenian Ikarios is supposed to have received the first vine from Dionysos in thanks for his hospitality. When he introduced the unusual plant to the peasants of Attica they, drunk with wine, beat him to death (a reflection of the difficulties experienced in introducing the cult of Dionysos). In anti-

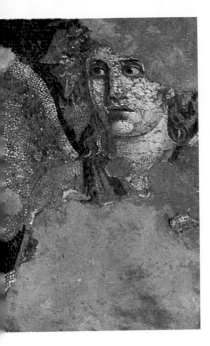

corner is what was probably a *Priest's house*. In the N. part of the precinct are remains of a further building and a Temenos wall. Next to this is a semicircular *Exedra* with a pedestal.

Environs: About 2 km. E. in the direction of Marathon is the **German Military Cemetery** (from World War 2) with the graves of nearly 10,000 dead. From here the plain of *Marathon* (see Marathónas) can also be seen, where, in 490 BC the Athenian army marched to the battle on the coast (shortest route to Marathon or Néa Mákri) and from which the messenger ran to Athens with news of the victory.

Dístomon/ΔΙΣΤΟΜΟΝ
Boeotia/Central Greece   p.294□F 8

A village 20 km. W. of Levádia (about 2, 500 inhab.). Just before the village is a crossroads where, according to mythology, Oedipus is supposed to have killed his father Laios—having failed to recognize him. Dístomon was built on the site of the ancient *Ámbrosos*. Only a few visible traces remain of the old wall. During the Greek War of Liberation it was the site of two battles (1825 and 1827).

Environs: Antíkyra (*c.* 8 km. SW of Dístomon): According to mythology Antíkyra was founded by Antikyréus, who, with the help of the hellebore growing here, is supposed to have cured Herakles of his madness.
Not far to the E. is a small Byzantine chapel, founded by the neighbouring monastery of Hósios Lukás.

quity it was known as *Ikária*. The *Rustic Dionysia*, which were a kind of winter solstice carnival, probably started here. Here or at the *City Dionysia* (Anthesteria spring festival) the poet actor Thespis of Ikária is supposed to produced the first tragedy with actors and chorus.

Excavation area: This is a small precinct of Apollo-Dionysos (such as in Delphi), the remains of which are, however, less well preserved.
At the entrance are *stone seats of honour* from the old **theatre** (6&5C BC). The *orchestra* was supported to the NE by a straight terrace wall. It lacked its own stage house. On the left are the remains of an *altar* and adjoining to the NW are the foundations of a small **Temple of Apollo** (*c.* 30 ft. x 23 ft.) with the surviving base of the cult figure in the *cella*. Built on to the

---

Dodóni/Dodóna/ΔΟΔΟΝΗ
Epirus/Ioánnina   p.290□C 5

Dodóna lies in a narrow valley (3 miles long and 440–1300 yards wide) 22 km. S.

of Ioánnina. To the W. rise the Tomoros Mountains (Olytsika), at the feet of which are the villages of Dramési, Dodóni, Néon Mantíon and Melígi. The ancient settlement and the sanctuary lie on 3 level areas. At the top of the hill is the acropolis, at the foot the sanctuary and to the S., on a lower level, are a few colonnades and the main entrance at the SW corner.

Sanctuary: This is the oldest and one of the most important sanctuaries of antiquity. The first inhabitants were of pre-Hellenic extraction, as excavations and the names Dodóna and Tómaros indicate. They were probably Pelasgians, as they were called by Homer and Hesiod. The chthonic cult of the pre-Grecian goddess Gaia (goddess of the Earth), who was also known as 'Great Mother', is linked with these inhabitants. Their sacred animals were the bull, boar and dove, their symbol the double axe. When the Thesproti, an Indo-European race, arrived in Epirus at the start of the 2 millennium BC they brought the worship of the oak tree with them. The goddess and the oak were then honoured together, the tree becoming the home of the goddess. When the cult of Zeus spread in Dodóna, the goddess became the wife of the god and acquired the name Dioni. Thus the tree became his home and the symbols of the goddess were transferred to him. The god became Naios Zeus (Naios: 'He who dwells on Earth') and Phegonaios ('The god who dwells in the oak'). The priests, the Selloi or Elloi, from whom the Hellenes probably derived their name, slept on the ground near the tree and drew prophetic powers from the ground where Zeus lived. Until the end of the 5C BC Zeus was worshipped in the open, beneath his oak. Tripods and kettles were set up under the tree to guard him. At the end of the 5C a temple, the Sacred House (Hiera Oikia), was built for the cult figure of Zeus and for the votive gifts. Later the tripods and kettles were replaced by a

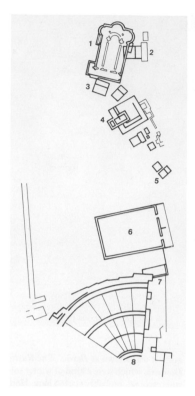

Dodóna 1 Christian basilica **2** Temple of Herakles **3** old Temple of Dione **4** Temple of Zeus (sacred precinct) **5** Temple of Aphrodite **6** Bouleuterion **7** Prytaneion **8** theatre

low stone wall. The inhabitants of Korfú (Kérkyra) built two columns. Upon one stood a small bronze boy with a whip in his hand, on the other was a kettle. When the wind blew the whip clanged against the kettle.

At the start of the 4C BC the Molossians attempted to increase the splendour of the oracle. Alexander the Great showed great interest in Dodóna and wished to make the sanctuary larger and more beautiful. This project was later realized by King Pyrrhus. During the 4C BC the walls of the *Acrop-*

olis were built. The fortress had a circumference of 2,460 ft. At the SW corner was a large gate leading to the theatre and in the middle of the E. side another gate opening on to the Plain of Ioánnina. Numerous buildings date from the time of King Pyrrhus. The low wall of the Hiera Oikia was replaced by 3 Ionic colonnades. The *Theatre* was also built at this time and had 20,000 seats.

The *Stadium,* only partly excavated today, is 820 ft. long and has 22 rows of seats on the N. side. At the same time the *Bouleuterion* and the *Prytaneion* were built, as well as temples for Dioni, Aphrodite and Herakles, the mythical forbear of King Pyrrhus.

In 167 BC Dodóna was destroyed by the Romans. At the time of Augustus the theatre was converted into an arena. The end of the cult of Dodóna came as Christianity asserted itself. In AD 392 the oak was felled and uprooted. In the 5C AD a basilica with a nave and two aisles was built to the E. of the Hiera Oikia. The history of Dodóna ended with the invasions of the Goths and a great earthquake. In 1875 Dodóna was rediscovered through excavations led by K.Karapanos. Work was then continued by Professors Sotiriadis, Evangelidis and Dakaris. Professor Dakaris rebuilt the theatre and each August since 1960 the *Dodonaia* have been celebrated in it, with productions of ancient drama.

The Oracle: The priests determined the will of Zeus from the rustling of the leaves of the oak, the flight of the doves, which nested in the oak and later also from the sounds of the brass kettle. The priests replied verbally to the spoken questions of the visitor. Later (6C BC) the questions were inscribed on a rectangular piece of lead. Many such inscriptions were discovered during the excavations and are now displayed in the Archaeological Museum of Ioánnina. The contents vary; Theris and Onasimos, for example, wanted to know if

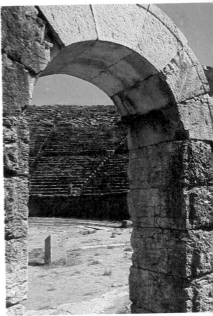

Dodóna, entrance to theatre

they should marry a woman. Another wanted to know if he was the father of the child his wife had borne.

The Naia: This festival was held every four years in honour of Zeus with athletic, musical and dramatic contests.

Ancient tradition: Homer was the first to mention the the sanctuary of Dodóna. In the 'Iliad' Achilles addresses Zeus thus: 'Zeus, King of Dodóna...'. In the 'Odyssey' he relates that Odysseus visited the sanctuary of Dodóna to ask the oak how he would return to Ithaca. Hesiod calls Dodóna the 'Seat of the Pelasgians' and reports that Zeus lived in the roots of the sacred oak and that his priests, the Selloi, gathered their powers of prophecy from the earth. The goddess Athena collected a piece of the Dodóna oak, when the Argonauts were building their ship, and incorporated it into the bow, in order that the ship might give the Argonauts advice in difficult situations.

Dráma/ΔPAMA
Dráma/Macedonia   p.292□I 2

Capital of the nome of the same name (34, 000 inhab., 166 km. from Thessaloníki). This was a flourishing town even in classical and post-classical times. It was mentioned by the ancient Greek authors Thucydides and Pausanias under the name of *Dráviskos*.

Archaeological excavations revealed remains of settlements from the Neolithic and Bronze Ages.

Byzantine Wall *(Byzantino tichos):* Built in 1205. Remains of this wall are to be found in the centre of the town.

The Anastenária: An annual religious festival held every autumn; amongst other things dances on glowing coals are performed.

Environs: Moní Ikosiphiníssis (30 km. S.): Occupied, 5C monastery, situated on the N. side of Mount Pangaion. The Patriarch Gregorius V lived here as a refugee for 9 months. **Prosotsáni** (20 km. W.): In the vicinity of this little village are healing springs and the *Cave of Rhodolivos,* famous for its stalactites and stalagmites.

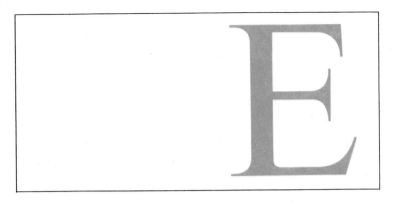

Édessa/ΕΔΕΣΣΑ
Pélla/Macedonia   p.290☐E 3

This picturesque town (15,000 inhabitants), some 90 km. from Thessaloníki, is
the capital of the nome of Pélla and a centre of fruit-growing and trading. It used to
be thought that it was the pre-classical
Aigaí. Under King Perdikkas this was the
first capital of the Macedonian state (Kingdom of Imathía), which Perdikkas welded
out of a number of smaller states. In the
5C BC, King Arkhelaos made Pélla the
capital of Macedonia, and it was there that
Alexander the Great's father, King Philip
II, was born. Recent excavations by Professor Andronikos of Thessaloníki have established, however, that it is the modern
village of Vergína, rather than Édessa,
which occupies the site of the ancient
Aigaí.

Town wall: Recent excavations have revealed parts of a town wall in the lower
town, with three *towers*, remains of a *town
gate* , and dwellings dating from the 4C
BC.

Old bridge: At the N. end of the town is
the arch of a bridge dating from Roman or
Byzantine times, across which the old Via
Egnatia is supposed to have passed.

Church of Kimisis tis Theotoku: This
Byzantine funerary church stands on the
site of an ancient temple. It still contains
old columns and beautiful *wall paintings*.

Museum: Archaeological finds from the
surrounding district are on display in a
15C building which used to be a mosque.

Folklore Museum: Typical traditional
costumes and folk art from the period of
the Turkish occupation.

Also worth seeing: S. of the town there
are two *waterfalls* down which the river
Edessaios cascades. Behind the waterfalls
there is a small cave with stalactites and
stalagmites. *Anthestiria* (festival of flowers):
Every May, Édessa hosts a popular flower
festival with folk dancing and other events.

Environs: Lake Vegorítis (20 km. W.)
On an island in the lake two prehistoric settlements and *walls* dating from the Roman
period have been discovered.

Elassóna/ΕΛΑΣΣΟΝΑ
Lárisa/Thessaly   p.290☐E 5

This attractively situated small country
town (7,000 inhabitants, 61 km. NW of

Lárisa) lies in the basin of the river Elassonítikos, SW of the Olympos massif. It is mentioned in Homer as Oloossón, which stood in the middle of the then region of Perraibía. There are scant remains from prehistoric and ancient times on the acropolis above the gorge through which the Elassonítikos flows. A pretty Byzantine stone bridge spans the river, which runs through the town.

Panagia Olympiotissa ('The Olympian Mother of God'): 13C Monastery on the Acropolis with an *arched bridge* over the deep ravine. The monastery was endowed by the Emperor Andronikos II. (1282–1328). Cruciform domed church, high drum with flat cupola, richly varied patterns in the brickwork, carved wooden door of 1300, beautiful marble columns in the narthex and frescos dating from the Palaiologoi dynasty. The iconostasis is 19C and is an example of wood carving from Epirus. The icon of the Mother of God (1296) is supposed to be miraculous.

Town Museum *(Musio):* Finds from the surrounding area (inscriptions, gravestones, Mycenean vases from N. Thessaly) are shown here.

Environs: Tsaritsáni *(c.* 5 km. SE): This village was founded by Bulgarians in the 10C in the foothills of Kato Olympos ('Low Olympos', about 4,921 ft.). It contains several attractive Byzantine churches: *Ágios Panteleimon* (1007, Byzantine), which has frescos and carved wood, the *Taxiarkhis church* (16C), *Ágios Nikolaos* (17C), and *Agii Anargyri* (18C). Nearby (to the SE) is the monastery of *Ágios Athanasios,* and, further E., the (Bulgarian) monastery of *Valetsiko* . From Elassóna a winding road passes over the wooded massif of **Mt. Olympos** to Kateríni; glorious view over the various peaks of what is, at over 9,000 ft., the highest mountain in Greece. This colossal, bell-shaped lime-

stone massif, frequently shrouded in cloud, was believed in ancient times to be the home, high above the earth, of the Olympian gods, and above all the throne of 'cloud-collecting Zeus' (Homer). The W. ascent to the main summit of the 'Three Brothers' (9,570 ft.) can be made in 11 hours from the mountain village of *Kokkinoplós* (about 25 km. N.); the E. ascent is also possible, starting from *Litókhoro* .

Elevsína/Eleusis/ΕΛΕΥΣΙΝΑ
Attica/Central Greece   p.294☐H 8

This busy industrial town with 20,000 inhabitants lies 20 km. NW of Athens on the Bay of Eleusis, in the Saronic Gulf. It is famous for the festivities (the Eleusinian Mysteries) which were held here annually in antiquity, at the beginning of autumn.

History: The area was settled by the Helladic period. Near the sanctuary on the E. side of the Acropolis there are remains of a temple which date from the Mycenean and Geometric period (early Attic cult site). While Athens acquired a political supremacy in the 7C BC, Eleusis gained increasing importance as a 'holy place'. It became the centre of a kind of popular religion which, in its worship of the chief goddess Demeter (Mother Earth), derived from ancient Aegean forms of the matriarchal fertility cult. Demeter, the sister of Zeus, was looked upon as the 'thesmophoros' ('founder','law-giver'), of agricultural society and of the settled population (village and town). She and her daughter Persephone (also called Kore, meaning 'maiden') were worshipped as the epitome of all growth, especially of cultivated grain. A series of festivals and rituals grew up around her which followed the natural course of the year (the agricultural calender, comparable in this context with our ecclesiastical year), and which were meant to guarantee and increase the crop.

Eleusis, Shrine of Demeter (archaeological excavation site) **1** entrance **2** Temple of Artemis, altars and eschara **3** portico **4** spring house **5** triumphal arch **6** Kallichoron well **7** Roman baths **8** Great Propylaia **9** triumphal arch **10** Gate and old streets **11** area of ancient houses **12** Roman cisterns **13** Roman houses **14** inner, Lesser Propylaia **15** Wall of Peisistratos (6C BC) **16** Shrine of Pluto (Plutonium) **17** altar **18** Sacred Way **19** the Panagia chapel **20** Roman megaron **21** Temple of Kore (Persephone) **22** House of the Heralds **23** medieval fortifications **24** acropolis **26** Portico of Philo **27** terrace with steps carved in the rock **28** Periklean wall **29** round tower **30** Bouleterion (council chamber) **31** Hiera Oikia **32** Mithraium **33** gymnasion **34** portico **35** Archaeological Museum

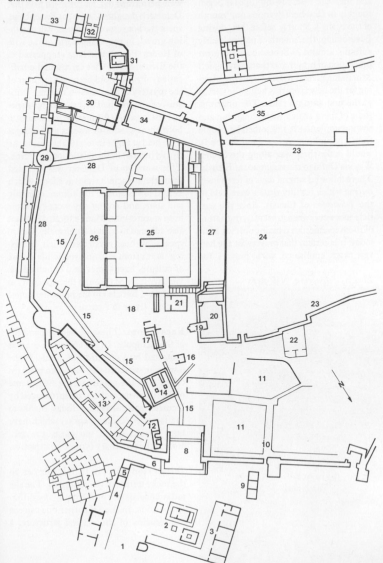

The agricultural year ended with the bringing in of the harvest in June (month of Skirophorion). The new year began on the first new moon after midsummer's day (at the beginning of July). The fields would lie fallow during the heat of the summer, and then the next sowing (Spora) began roughly in October (Pyanopsion, 'month of the beans'). Shortly before that, during Boedromion, the 'month of prayers' (early autumn, around 21 September), the great procession of prayer and thanksgiving left Athens for Eleusis to beg for divine blessing for the new crop, this being the period of the first autumn rains. The pilgrims, some of them armed with ploughing and sowing implements and joined by people from throughout Attica (and beyond), would make their way along the Sacred Way via Dafní to the sanctuary at Eleusis. There followed several days of festivities, during which fertility rituals were held in the *Telesterion* of Eleusis; since the participants were sworn to secrecy, the nature of these ceremonies remains obscure even today. It is certain that prayers for the harvest were combined with prayers for

Eleusis, Telesterion, NW steps

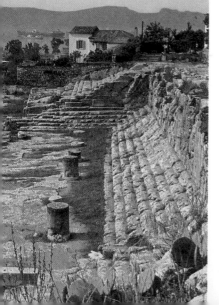

progeny and healthy procreation. For the people of that time, the sowing of the fields in furrows was a symbol of human procreation (ritual orgasm). Rituals connected with the after-life (ritual funeral processions) and prayers for happiness after death were performed too, for the myth held that Demeter's daughter, 'Kore', or Persephone, spent the hot summer months, when nothing grows, in the underworld as the wife of Hades (Pluto), and later reappeared to the Eleusinians. After ceremonial purification, anyone could become a member of the mystery ceremonies—a mystes. 'Initiates', or epoptai, had first to undergo a special test (askesis). Admission ceremonies to both these grades of mystes and epoptes were held at night in torchlight during the rituals (teletai) in the telesterion, or shrine. This worship of Demeter was regarded throughout ancient times as a force which helped to sustain the institutions of family and state, and not by any means as some bizarre secret cult. Many educated Romans also adhered to it, at least formally. Cicero speaks 'of those mysteries which, in raising us up from a brutal rustic life to one of culture, have tamed and ennobled us. We have learned through them not only to live in joy, but also to die in greater hope.' (Cicero, letter to Atticus).

Excavations: These lie beneath and SE of the Acropolis. In the 6C BC the site was protected by a *fortifed wall*. Outside the town gate stretched the Thriasian plain (so called after the neighbouring Attic deme of Thrias), where the grain introduced by Demeter was cultivated. Today, thanks to the factories (cement works) which have been placed much too close, the area around the sanctuary is most unattractive.

Telesterion (shrine): Its NE side lies on the rocky terrace of the Acropolis. The site today consists of ruins from many different periods. In the SE corner one can see the remains of the earliest structure, a

Mycenean *megaron* (about 1400 BC) whose walls contain antai and periboloi; there are also wall fragments from the Geometric and archaic period (8/7C BC). Over the years the shrine changed and expanded more and more; these fragments indicate how early it first acquired importance. The tyrant Peisistratos (about 540 BC) built a square structure (each side being 88 ft. 7 in., with 5 rows of 5 columns) on the site and fragments of paving remain. After this was destroyed by the Persians (about 480 BC, Kimon erected a rectangular hall (88 ft. 7 in. x 144 ft. 4 in.) with 3 rows of 7 columns. Perikles added another hall of equal dimensions, thus restoring a square ground plan. It was designed by Iktinos, the architect of the Parthenon, about 440 BC. During the 4C BC the architect Philo constructed an uncompleted *portico* along the SE front. The inner colonnade was standardized by the Roman emperors. Two doorways opened into each of the three free sides. The pillars, some nearly 20 ft. high, stood on tufa pavement and supported an upper floor where the 'sacred objects' (hiera) were kept. Around the columned hall

there were eight terraced rows providing space for about 3,000 people to take part in the ceremony. The *outer wall* of Peisistratos (roughly to the SE, sections survive) had to be moved due to the enlargement undertaken by Perikles (there is an interesting *round tower* in the SE corner). In the second half of the 4C BC the semicircle of walls was extended to the S. by Lykurgos. Here there are ruins of shops and of a *bouleuterion* (council chamber) from the same period. It was altered by the Romans into a columned hall. Next to it, on the other side of a gate, is a *portico* by the side of the rampart, together with more fragments of the walls of Peisistratos and Perikles. A massive foundation structure S. of the Telesterion used to support a Lykurgan gallery. Outside the wall there is a *Peribolos* (enclosure) of polygonal masonry (6C BC, which surrounds the remains of a small, late Geometric *temple* (the so-called 'Sacred House') from the 8C BC. There are ruins of Roman buildings nearby. The *wall of the Temenos* wound around the sacred precinct in an arc from the E to the NW, right up to the ancient *town gate*.

Eleusis, Plutonium

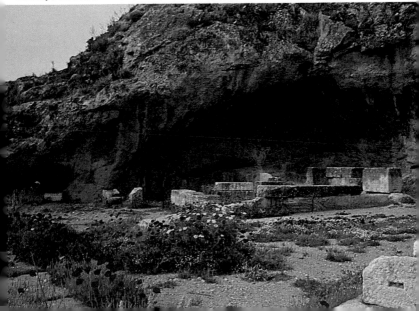

Precinct of Demeter-Kore: To the NE of the Telesterion, on a terrace hewn out of the rock there are traces of a *temple* which was presumably dedicated to Kore. Next to it, and to the left of the Sacred Way, there is a *flight of steps* cut into the rock, leading up to another *terrace*. There would probably have been an altar here with statues of both goddesses. Further up still, above the remains of a *Roman megaron* (doubtless a temple of Demeter in earlier times), there now stands the small *chapel of the Virgin Mary Panagítsa* (indicating that the cult of the mother-goddess Demeter has lived on in the worship of Mary the Mother of God, for the one presumably influenced the other).

Precinct of Hades or **Plutonion:** At the end of the Sacred Way, in the rock to the left of the Lesser Propylaia, there are two **grottoes**, in front of which the remains of a wall and a terrace can be seen. This was the site of the sanctuary of Hades, god of the underworld, who as Pluto (derived from 'plutos', meaning 'wealth') also guarded food supplies and the treasures of the earth. Kore, or Persephone, was supposed to disappear into the underworld every year through one of the grottoes and to re-appear at the beginning of every autumn out of the other, symbolizing the cycle of death and rebirth.

Lesser Propylaia: These enclosed the inner precinct of the temple. The structure was erected with a Doric **frieze** in Roman times (about 54 BC) on the site of an earlier gate dating from the 6C BC. Parts of the frieze now lie by the gateway and bear recognizable images of corn and other subjects connected with the cult of Demeter. There are also traces on the ground of the double doors. On both sides, fragments of the *wall of Peisistratos* (6C BC) can still be seen clearly. Its foundations of polygonal masonry were about 4 ft. high and supported an embankment of unbaked brick. Between it and the outer wall (5C BC) lie the remains of late Roman buildings (living quarters, shops, etc.), and, to the SE, the well-preserved *stone pillars* of a *storehouse* for the sacrificial wheat (tithes).

Great Propylaia: These are in the Doric style and make a magnificent outer entrance; they were built from Pentelic marble in the 2C BC by Antoninus Pius. They are faithfully modelled on the central portion of the Propylaia in the Acropolis at Athens. The *façade* comprised a portico with six columns, of which there are fragments in the forecourt. The *pediment* of the structure was reassembled here with its *medallion bust* of Marcus Aurelius, the successor of Antoninus Pius. There are partially preserved thresholds and an inscription. The inner enclosure also consisted of a *portico* with six Doric columns. The gateway replaced an earlier entrance and stands next to the remains of the outer wall and the town wall (5C BC). Nearby are the remains of Roman *cistern* (with a row of steps). In the NW part of the inner portion of the excavations (inside the wall of Peisistratos) there are various remains of priests' living quarters with many separate rooms (foundations preserved), including the *prytaneion* and *pompeion*, which were respectively the premises of the *prytaneis* and the place where the objects used in the procession were kept safe. Above these are remains of the *priests' house* which belonged to the Kerykes (meaning 'heralds'), who, together with the Eumolpids, were one of the hereditary priestly families to serve at the sanctuary. The **house of the heralds** has fragments of Roman painting and a large pithos.

Great Forecourt: The Sacred Way from Athens ended in a paved forecourt; the buildings here are predominantly Roman. The most important site, near the Propylaia, was the legendary *Kallichoron*, or well of the dancing ground. This is where Demeter was supposed to have mourned during her search for her kidnapped daughter, while the young maidens of Eleusis comforted her with their dances. The deeply set *well-head* dates from the time of Peisistratos (6C BC) and was not touched even by the Romans, out of respect for the cult. In the background is the fine polygonal substructure of the *wall of Kimon*,with Roman squared stones. Nearby are the remains of a rectangular *tower*, part of the outer wall. In the corner is the NE *triumphal arch* which led towards the harbour. The arch was built by Antoninus Pius in the Corinthian style; its inscription survives. A large part of its marble superstructure has been reassembled nearby. The pilgrims purified themselves here in a *fountain* whose basin has been preserved. In the middle of the forecourt stood the *Temple of Artemis and Poseidon*, which was built in the Doric style in the 2C AD, on the site of an earlier sanctuary dating from the 8C BC; in front of its remains are the *plinths* of two *altars*. To the NW of the temple are the remains of a Roman *sacrificial site* with a peribolos (surrounding wall)

and traces of an earlier sanctuary (7C BC). Behind that are the ruins of a Roman *portico* with a three-sided gallery. Next to it, to the NW, are the remains of a second *triumphal arch*, on the road to Mégara, which matches the first one.

The sanctuary, which is of real interest, was the religious centre of antiquity; it was eventually suppressed by the unpredictable Emperor Theodosius (AD 392) and shortly afterwards plundered by the Goths under Alaric (AD 395). The site has been systematically excavated and investigated by the Greek Archaeological Society.

Museum: This is situated to the SW of the excavations, near the ancient *terrace* which led to the upper floor of the Telesterion. The numerous sculptures and architectural pieces are mostly from the buildings at Eleusis (there are copies of the sculptures which have been transferred to the National Museum in Athens).

Entrance hall: Statue of Demeter by Agorakritos, a pupil of Pheidias, dating from 420 BC. Copy of the famous *telesterion relief*, dating from 440 BC,

Eleusis, museum: relief (l) and relief with Demeter and Persephone (r)

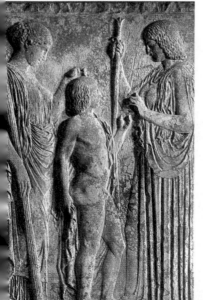
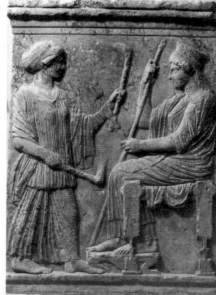

which is in the National Museum. It shows Demeter handing Triptolemos, an Eleusinian, the first ear of wheat; her daughter Kore, or Persephone, stands behind her carrying a torch. A Roman *Persephone*, and a relief dating from the 1C BC (showing the priest Lakratides).

Room to the right: Copy of a *panel painting* representing 'Demeter, Kore, Iakchos, and mystai' (4C BC). *Marble boars* (typical votive offerings). *Statue of Kore (480 BC).* 4C BC *relief* showing 'Persephone purifying young mystai'. *Dedication relief* showing Athena with citizens of Athens and, on the left, Kore or Persephone (421 BC). *Pediment decorations* from the Telesterion (6C BC). Archaic *torso of kouros* from Mégara (about 530 BC). Reliefs showing Demeter and Kore. *Stele* depicting battle scenes between Athenians and Spartans (late 5C BC). In the centre of the room, a large protoattic *amphora* (7C BC, Eleusis). The neck of the vase shows Odysseus blinding the cyclops Polyphemos, while the main part represents Perseus killing the Gorgon Medusa with Athena's help.

First room to left (left of entrance): *Statue*

of ephebe by Lysippos; archaic *Kore* (6C BC); archaic-type woman carrying bowl (3C BC); statue of *Dionysos* (2C BC); statue of Asklepios dating from 320 BC; two Roman statuettes of Poseidon (copies of a 4C BC statue).

Second room to left: Roman sculptures of Hadrian's friend *Antinoos* (2C AD) and of the Emperor *Tiberius* (1C AD); also a reconstruction of the sacred precinct of Eleusis.

Third room to left: Caryatid from the Lesser Propylaia (1C AD). *Terracotta coffin* containing skeleton of a child. *Bronze vessel* with partially burnt human bones (500 BC). Above it, the *remnant* of an ancient garment. Corinthian *vase* from the 7C BC showing Chimaera (in the display case); also *sacrificial vessels* for the cult of Demeter.

Fourth room to left: Collection of ceramics from various periods. Display cases 1 and 2: Minoan vases (*c.* 2000–1600 BC). Also, statuette of a woman (Neolithic *c.* 2800 BC). Cases 3 – 5: Mycenean ceramics (1600– 1100 BC). Cases 6 – 8: Geometric ceramics (1000–750 BC). Case 9: Bronze

Epídavros, abaton with Temple of Asklepios

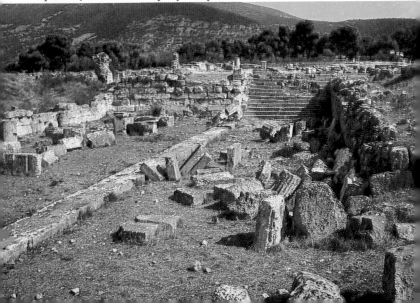

vases from the 5C BC. Case 12: Corinthian oriental-style vases (750–600 BC). Case 14: Black figure ceramics (600 – 500 BC). Case 21: Mycenean bronze weapons and jewellery from a tomb near Mégara dating from about 1600 BC.

Environs: To the W. of the excavations begins the long slope of the **Acropolis**. At its foot, to the NE, near the *Chapel of the Panagia* (which is in the vicinity of the Telesterion) there are traces of a *Mycenean structure* of unknown purpose. To its N., there are medieval *walls* which defended the summit of the Acropolis. The whole range of hills above the roads to Corinth, Thebes, and Athens had been secured from ancient times by *watch-towers*. The ancient town lay to the N. and W. of the range of hills; remains of the town wall have survived. To the S. of the Acropolis, about 1 km. W. of the Museum, traces have been discovered of a *prehistoric settlement* (1700 – 1200 BC) and, nearby, of a large *necropolis* (8C BC). The six huge *grave furrows* may be the graves of the Seven against Thebes (Helladic period) mentioned by

Pausanias and Plutarch. The remains of a *Roman bridge* can be seen near the village of *Káto Pigádi* (*c.* 2 km. W., towards Athens). The remains of its four large arches date from the reign of Hadrian, AD 124.

Epídavros/Epidauros/ ΕΠΙΔΑΥΡΟΣ
Argolís/Peleponnese   p.294□G 9

History: In ancient times, the god Asklepios was worshipped here. According to legend, he was the son of Apollo and Koronis, the daughter of King Phlegyas of Orchomenos. Asklepios was nurtured by a goat after his mother died in childbirth and was brought up by the centaur Chiron, who taught him the art of healing.
However, Asklepios is also a chthonic deity, closely connected with the earth, as his symbol, the snake, indicates. In Epidauros he was worshipped together with Apollo Maleatas, a local manifestation of Apollo, who in turn had replaced Maleatas, an earlier deity.

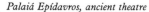

Palaiá Epídavros, ancient theatre

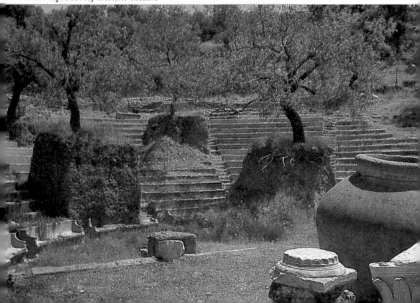

The oldest remains of the sanctuary date from the 6C BC. It became famous at the end of the 4C BC. Sick people streamed here from all over Greece to pray for healing. After various purification ceremonies, they had to spend a night in the abaton, where the god would appear to them in a dream and indicate the appropriate therapy.

Every four years, panhellenic games with musical and sporting competitions known as the Asklepieia were held. However, these never attained the celebrity of the Olympic or the Pythian Games. The sanctuary was suppressed by the Emperor Theodosius in AD 426.

The excavations were conducted by the Greek archaeologists Kavadias and Papadimitriou in 1948–51 in the sanctuary of Maleatas.

Theatre: This is the most famous and best preserved of antiquity and is still used for performances. It was most probably built at the beginning of the 3C BC. Originally, it had 34 rows of seats, carved from limestone, and was divided into twelve wedges. In the 2C BC, it was expanded; 21 extra rows of seats were added and the audience capacity was increased from 12,000 instead of the earlier 6,200. Guests of honour sat in the first row (prohedria), whose seats had backrests.

The *orchestra* was 66 ft. 7 in. in diameter and was surrounded by a low marble enclosure; the floor was of beaten loam. In the centre stood the altar of Dionysos, of which today only the foundations are recognisable. Access to the orchestra was provided by two *parodoi* (entrances), each having a door which could be closed; parts of both parodoi have been used to reassemble the W. one. Behind the orchestra was the *skene* (stagehouse) which had four interior supports, each with two small rooms beside it. The *proskenion* (front stage) was 72 ft. 2 in. wide and 7 ft. 2 in. deep and had two wings coming forward

at the sides. The façade comprised fourteen Ionic half-columns, and between these were placed the periakta, movable wooden boards with painted scenery. Later, when the chorus began to perform in the orchestra in addition to the individual actors, the periakta were fastened to the walls of the skene. The theatre was rebuilt after the invading Goths had destroyed it, together with the sanctuary, in AD 267. Parts of the sanctuary were used in this reconstruction.

Sanctuary of Maleatas (about 15 minutes' climb from the theatre): This site was inhabited as early as the third millennium BC. Remains have been discovered of an altar for burnt sacrifices dating from the 7C BC. At the beginning of the 4C, a small temple was erected, and towards the end of the same century a stoa was added with 17 or 19 columns.

Remains from the Roman period comprise a well, a cistern, and a house for priests. According to Pausanias, this was founded by the senator Antoninus.

Katagogion: Moving away from the theatre and past the museum, we come first to the guest-house (known as the *Xenon* or *Katagogion*) where travellers stayed. This is a square building (250 ft. 4 in. square) dating from the 4C BC. It had 160 rooms on two storeys, arranged around four courtyards with Doric pillars.

Greek bath (W. of the Katagogion): Ruins of a structure dating from the 3C BC.

Gymnasion (N. of the Greek bath): A large structure (249 ft. 4 in. x 229 ft. 7 in.) with tufa plinths which can still be seen. In its original form, it had an inner courtyard surrounded by 60 columns, halls, and rooms in the corners. The entrance (to the NW) had a propylon with six Doric columns. The Romans converted the propylon into a *sanctuary of Hygieia* and the inner courtyard into an *odeion*.

Palaestra (N. of the Gymnasion): An almost square structure (112 ft. 2 in. x 96 ft. 4 in.) which has rooms on three sides and a stoa to the N. The outer walls are of hewn stone. The stoa can be identified with the *Stoa of Kotys*, while the building as a whole is considered to be the Palaestra.

Temple of Artemis (43 ft. 7 in. x 30 ft. 10 in.): This was built at the end of the 4C BC and had six Doric columns at the front and two in front of the antae. The cult image was kept in the cella, surrounded by ten pillars.

Temple of Themis (next to the Stoa of Kotys): This also dates from the 4C BC. It measures 23 ft. 9 in. x 15 ft. 10 in. and had two entrances, one from the E. and one from the W.

Temple of Asklepios and Egyptian Apollo (NE): Built by Antoninus in Roman times. On the S. side, there is a villa with two atria.

In the sacred precinct, which was surrounded by boundary marks, and to the N. of the Temple of Artemis, there is a rectangular structure (79 ft. 9 in. x 67 ft. 10 in.) which is the oldest in the sanctuary. At its NW corner there stood a temple and altar of Apollo. In the middle of the 6C BC, the structure was used as a dormitory. This could be the **old Abaton**, where Asklepios appeared in a dream to those seeking healing. In Roman times, it was used as a house for priests. To the W. of this building there was an altar dedicated to Apollo.

Temple of Asklepios: Doric peripteros (79 ft. 9 in. x 43 ft. 4 in.) built of tufa. The architect was Theodoros of Phokaia. The floor was paved with tufa flagstones. The cult statue, which was the work of Thrasymedes of Paros, was of gold and ivory and dated from 350 BC. It was kept in a niche in the cella (1 ft. 8 in. beneath ground level). The acroteria and pedimental figures were copied from the models supplied by the sculptor Timotheos (390/80 BC).

Tholos (W of temple of Asklepios): Only the foundations remain (diameter 69 ft. 10 in.). It was supposedly built by Polykleitos the younger (about 360 BC). It is a rotunda which comprised six concentric round walls, the first three being continuous, while the next three were interrupted by gateways and connected to each other by transverse walls. The outermost wall supported 26 Doric columns, and 14 Corinthian columns stood on the third wall from the outside. The door was on the E. side and had lavish carved decorations (now in the museum). The coffered ceiling was decorated with a plant motif. The floor was covered with black-and-white flagstones and had a round opening in the middle, which was covered over with a flagstone and through which one could reach the lower floor.

It is not known exactly what the building was used for. The original accounts, which are in the museum, refer to it as a *Thymele* (place of sacrifice). It is also surmised that the sacred snakes of Asklepios were kept on the lower floor.

Abaton (N. of the Tholon): A columned hall, 229 ft. 8 in. by 31 ft. 2 in., with 29 Ionic columns on the façade and 13 columns on the inside. Because of the steep slope on which it stood, the W. part of the building had two storeys, while the E. part, which was older (dating from the 4C BC), only had one. A staircase of 14 steps connected the two storeys. To the E of the Abaton there is a *well*, 56 ft. deep, which dates from the 6C BC. Nearby stood tablets on which were inscribed records of cures. These were the so-called pinakes which are now in the museum.

Well house (W. of the Abaton and outside the sacred precinct): This rests on tufa

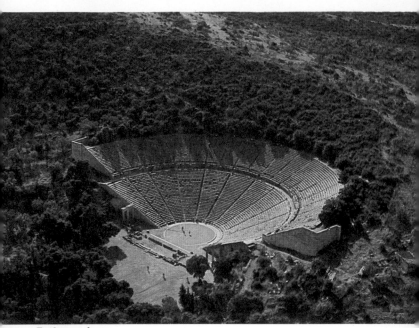

Epídavros, theatre

foundations dating from classical times and is divided into small areas which may have been used as water tanks.

Next to the NE side of the Abaton there were a **library** (S.) and a **thermal establishment** (N.) which dated from the 2C BC and which stood on the foundations of older buildings.

Stoa (further NE): Long building dating from the 3C BC.

Thermal establishment (on the E. side of the Stoa): Of Roman origin. The brick walls are preserved to a height of 3 to 6 ft. The central area had four columns and a mosaic floor. before being converted into baths, the building is supposed to have been used as a large cistern which supplied the sanctuary with water.

To the S. is the **Epidoteion**, a building with a stoa, which was erected in the 4C BC and rebuilt in the 2C AD. To the W. of the long stoa are the remains of a small **Temple of Aphrodite** built at the end of the 4C BC. To the N. of the Stoa there was a 5C BC **villa** which has left some visible remains.

Propylaia (W. of the small Temple of Aphrodite): These date from 340–30 BC. The ramps on the narrow sides of the propylaia can still be seen. There was an *early Christian basilica* (4 or 5C AD) to the E. of the Propylaia which was covered with beautiful mosaics.

Stadium (W. of the Gymnasion): This was built in the hollow between two hills and was 644 ft. 6 in. in length and 75 ft. 6 in. wide. The running track was 594 ft.

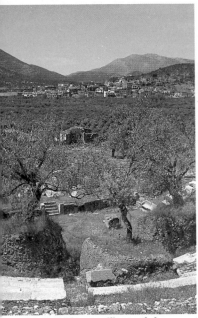

Palaiá Epídavros, village and theatre

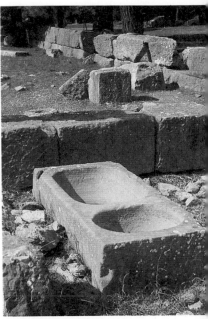

Epídavros, Katagogion

10 in. long. Stone seats have been preserved on both of the long sides of the rectangle and on one of the short sides. A tunnel was constructed in Hellenistic times which passed beneath the N. side of the stadium to the *athletes' living quarters* and a *palaestra*.

Museum: *First Room:* A tablet recording the accounts for the construction of the Temple of Asklepios and the Tholos; a collection of bronze surgical instruments; and inscriptions listing cures from such ailments as infertility, tapeworm, and eye, kidney, and gall-bladder complaints.
Second Room: Statues of Asklepios and Hygieia; reconstruction of the entablature of the propylon of the Gymnasion and pedimental acroteria (originals in the Epidauros room in the National Museum in Athens).

Third Room: Fragments of sculptures from the Temple of Asklepios; reconstruction of the Temple of Asklepios and the Tholos; Corinthian capital (from the Tholos) attributed to Polykleitos the younger; parts of the coffered ceiling and of the doorframe of the Tholos.

Environs: Palaiá Epídavros (Old Epidauros, *c.* 10 km. NE): Remains of the ancient harbour, which is partly flooded, can still be identified. Remains of a theatre and an early Christian church.

Évia/Euboea/ΕΥΒΟΙΑ
Évia/Aegean Islands   p.296☐H/I 7/9

Euboea (population 165,000) is the second largest Greek island after Crete. It measures 109 miles by between 4 and 19 miles across and its area of 1,468 sq. m. compares with Crete's 3,206 sq. m. Geologically and geographically, it forms part of the mainland of central Greece, from whose E. coast it is separated by the narrow Gulf of Euboia (which at Chalkís is only 130 ft. wide). The scenery is unusually attractive, and includes abundant woodland, both coniferous and deciduous (principally in the N.) and a mountain range, running from N. to S. and rising to 5,725 ft. (at the summit of Mt. Dírfys); there are also fertile plains around Chalkís and Kymí which produce fruit and olives. Thanks to its proximity to Athens (which is only 81 km. from Chalkís), the island has become a popular destination for excursions. (There are 429 miles of coastline).

History: Euboea (in modern Greek, Évia) was in very ancient times called *Abantís* after its legendary original inhabitants, the Abantes. Its classical name, Euboea, indicates that it was once rich in cattle ('eúboos'). There are finds from the Neolithic and early and middle Helladic periods (2600–1600 BC) and from the Mycenean period (1400–1200 BC). Around 800 BC it was settled by Ionians from Attica. The capitals of Chalkís and Erétria reached the peak of their prosperity in the 8–6C BC, thanks to sea trade and travel. These two cities founded important colonies, including Cumae and Neapolis in southern Italy and others in Sicily, Kerkyra, and Chalkidike. The Chalkidian script was a model for the later Latin alphabet. But in the following centuries Euboea was more and more eclipsed by the rising power of Athens, virtually becoming its granary; and a settlement of Athenian farmers was established there in 447/6 BC. The bridging of the Straits of Euripos at Chalkís in 410 BC effectively made the island part of Boeotia and the mainland. Its power grew after it had joined the Athenians' second maritime league in 378 BC; in 338 BC it

was annexed by Macedonia; in 194 BC it became a Roman possession. It was conquered by the Franks in AD 1207, and was under Venice from 1306 until 1470, when 360 years of Turkish rule began. The island was restored to Greek sovereignty in 1830.

Chalkís (population 36,000): Capital of the nome or province of Euboea. Its flourishing commercial and industrial life has been due, ever since ancient times, to the bridge which links it with the mainland, spanning the Euripos (Evripos) at its narrowest point. Today's iron swing bridge, dating from 1856, was preceded by a number of wooden bridges which were built in antiquity and under the Turks; the first in 410 BC. The fact that the current of the Euripos changes direction several times a day is an interesting natural phenomenon (the sea-level rises and falls by over 3 ft.). Because of the bridge, the Venetians gave the name of *Negroponte* ('black bridge') both to the town and the island. On the shore of the mainland opposite stands the *Karababa* (meaning 'black father'), a Turkish fort of 1686 called after the Sultan of the same name. In the old city, the *Kastro*, near the few remains of the old Venetian-Turkish fort, stands the *Turkish mosque* (in Platía Pesónton Oplitón). It originates from what was the principal Venetian church, San Marco di Negroponte. Inside the mosque, there is a collection of Venetian and Turkish architectural fragments. On the square in front of it is a small *Turkish fountain*. Nearby (about a hundred yards away) is the former early Christian basilica of *Agia Paraskevi* (5–8C), altered in the 14C into a Gothic church. The interior has interesting capitals and cipollino columns. It is thought that this was formerly the site of a temple to Leto or Apollo. Near the old Venetian *Governor's Palace* (Spiti tu Bailu), now a prison, are the final arches of a Turkish *aqueduct*, of which some remains survive. The *ancient city*, of which virtually nothing remains (though there are fragments of a temple in the museum), was situated to the E. of the modern one. The harbour and agora were on Ágios Stéfanos Bay. The industrial suburb of *Proástio* contains the church of *Ágios Dimitrios*, which was previously a mosque and has a *bell tower* converted from a minaret. On Vathrovuni hill, at the SE end of the town and in the direction of Erétria, are the remains of an *Acropolis* with the *foundations of towers* and the remnants of a Pelasgian *settlement* including walls, houses, paths, and rock tombs. Not far from there, near the chapel of Ágios Stéfanos, was the ancient *spring of Arethusa* (whose modern name is *Mikra Vrysi*), by which stand the remains of a *Roman gymnasion* with *baths* and a *mosaic pavement*. Some Neolithic sites have been discovered on the *Maníka* peninsula N. of Chalkís, including a cemetery of beehive tombs with votive offerings.*Archaeological Museum* (Odos Aristotelus): Of particular interest are the late archaic *pediment sculptures* from the Temple of Apollo in Erétria (about 510 BC), especially that depicting 'Theseus carrying off Antiope, queen of the Amazons'; there is also a scene representing Athena with the Gorgon's head, and various fragments showing Amazons. These are masterpieces of Greek art, and have its characteristic smile. In the main room there is also a *votive relief* from the 5C BC, and *torsoes* of a man and of a youth. Near the entrance is the statue (from Aidipsos) of Hadrian's favourite, Antinous, as *Dionysos*, as well as a *statue of Hermes*, a female *tomb statue* (from Aidipsos), a *statue of Apollo*, the so-called *Persephone* from Erétria (about 330 BC), and others. The display cases contain Mycenean, Geometric, archaic, and classical *vases* and *ceramics* (as well as bronze statuettes). In the courtyard of the museum there are architectural fragments including capitals from the Temple of Zeus in Chalkís (about

500 BC) and from the Temple of Artemis in Aulís, together with reliefs and fragments of statues. The *Museum of Popular Art* has some rare exhibits of popular art. Works of art from the Byzantine, Venetian, and Turkish periods are to be found in the *Old Mosque* on the Platía Oplitón, which houses a museum of medieval art including mosaic pavements, sculptures, reliefs, and other pieces.

Environs: Past *Néa Artáki* (9 km. N.) is the ancient *Lelantine Plain* (much disputed between Chalkís and Erétria), where one can see Venetian *watch towers* and the remains of a Venetian-Turkish *watercourse*. 35 km. NE is the mountain village of *Stení* (population 1,000); from here one can climb the delightful Mt. Dirfys (5,719 ft.) and enjoy its glorious views (there are thick woods of chestnut, lime, and pine below). *Psakhná* (16 km. N; population 5,000) contains a Byzantine church, *Agia Triada*, and, to the S., the ruins of an early Christian church with an atrium and a narthex. Not far from Psakhná is the *Monastery of the Dormition* (Kímisis), which was important in the 18C and was rebuilt in 1908, and, to the NW, the *Monastery of Ioánnes*, which has frescos from the 13C. Near *Politiká* (c. 26 km. NW) there is an old 12C *Monastery of the Panagía* which has a cruciform domed church dating from the 15C (the frescos were added in 1668). SE of Chalkís is the village of *Fýlla* which boasts Venetian *watch towers* and the house in which Miaulis, a hero of the struggle for independence, was born. Nearby is the well-preserved Venetian *Kastello* of Lilanto. To the E. is the Monastery of *Ágios Georgios*, which has a church dating from the 13/14C (rebuilt in the 17C). Near *Levkándi* (c. 14 km. SE), on Mágula hill, there are interesting excavations of sites dating from the early Helladic, Mycenean, and Geometric (700 BC) periods. Near *Prokópion* (51 km. N.) is the *church of Ágios Ioannis* which has a popular church festival every 24 August. Further E., on the coast, (c. 60 km. N.) is the remote but attractive monastery of *Ágios Ioánnis*, dating from the 17C. 4 km. NE of *Mantúdion* (*c.* 63 km. NW), near the village of *Kimási*, which lies on the E. coast of the island on the Bay of Peléki, one can still see the remains of the outer walls of the ancient city of *Kérinthos* (6C BC).

Erétria (also known as *Néa Psará*): A small coastal town (population *c.* 2,000) which lies 22 km. SE of Chalkís. Here, on the site of the much bigger *ancient city of Erétria*, which flourished in the 8–6C and again in the 3C BC, are the most important excavations in Euboea, carried out by Greek and Swiss archaeologists. A strong *wall*, which is still well preserved in parts, surrounded the city, which was nonetheless repeatedly destroyed, notably by the Persians in 490 BC and the Romans in 198 BC, and rebuilt. After it was devastated in 87 BC, it fell more and more into decline, until it was eventually resettled in 1834 by refugees from the island of Psará (near Chios). Its spacious street layout was the work of the Bavarian architect Schaubert, who also designed Athens and Piraeus under King Otto I. Best preserved is the ancient *theatre* dating from the 4C BC, which had several later extensions, including an underground passage leading from the hyposkenion (the lower part of the stage) to the middle of the orchestra, which was used for surprising entries such as that of a deus ex machina. The theatre had about 6,500 seats. Due SW of the theatre are the foundations of the *Temple of Dionysos*, a late classical Doric *peripteros* with 6 by 11 columns. There are bases of monuments and *altar foundations* nearby. Near here are the ruins of an imposing *West Gate* with cyclopean walls dating from the 7C BC (there were also several later stages of construction). Beneath the gate the *vault* of an underground stream is preserved. From the West Gate, the city wall continues southwards with three Hellenistic *towers*. By these there are finds from a 4C BC

necropolis. To the S. of the West Gate and near the wall is the so-called *palace*, which has a peristyle courtyard and was built around 400 BC as a place of worship for the nobility. This incorporated a *sacred precinct* (from about 700BC) and the remains of a *heroon* dating from the 8C BC (it is a triangular cult site with flagstones). A little farther S. is another *palace* dating from 400 BC, together with other ruins including those of a house and 5 rooms used for worship. Its structure is an enlarged version of the design used for Delian houses. Both palaces were destroyed by the Romans in 198 BC and later restored. Opposite are the remains of a *Temple of Ares and Aphrodite*. The most important place of worship was the *Temple of Apollo Daphnephoros* ('Apollo wearing his laurel crown'), which is in the city centre, on Odos Apollonos. This is a late archaic *peripteral temple* with 6 by 14 Doric columns dating from the end of the 6C BC. The foundations are preserved. Its tympana on the W. side were decorated with sculptures depicting Theseus's fight against the Amazons (now in the museum in Chalkís). Inside the structure are the remains of an early archaic temple built in the style of the Temple of Hera in Samos; some traces remain of the foundations of its 6 by 19 *wooden columns*. There are also the ruins of some even older buildings, including a Geometric hecatompedos temple and an *apsidal building* dating from 800 BC which may well have been comparable to the legendary *laurel sanctuary*, in legend the first temple of Apollo at Delphi (Erétria lay halfway on the journey between the two cult sites of Delphi and Delos). Passing to the S. along Odos Apollonos in the direction of the *ancient harbour* we see the remains of the foundations of a *tholos*, which housed the administration, on the ancient *agora*, now built over by houses. Nearby are the remains of *baths* which had swimming pools. To the SE, on the site which was once occupied by the harbour (which is now dry land), are the remains of a *gymnasion* with a *palaestra* dating from the 5C BC (this has been repeatedly rebuilt—for example in the 2C BC). Nearby are the foundation walls of a *Sanctuary of Isis* (about 300 BC). It is worth seeing the well-preserved *city wall* to the E., with its nine *towers*. To the N. of the excavations is the ancient *Acropolis* (443 ft. high) on which stand ruins of the *North Wall*; there are some other poorly-preserved remains. Beneath the Acropolis are the remains of a *Thesmophorion* which had a flight of stairs as well as halls around the cella. Nearby is a *Sanctuary of Artemis* from the 5C BC of which remains of temple walls, an altar, and a temenos survive. To the W. there is a hill with a *Macedonian chamber tomb* (about 300 BC) which has a dromos, sarcophagi, thrones, and wall paintings representing symposia. *Archaeological Museum* (S. of the excavations): Finds from Erétria and Levkándi from the Mycenean and Geometric periods, including the protogeometric clay figure of a centaur from the 10C BC; *vases* from the Geometric, archaic, classical and Hellenistic periods; burial objects, idols, bronze vessels, weapons, and ornaments; numerous tombstone inscriptions and votive offerings; and various stele and reliefs (partly fragments) from tombs dating from the classical and late classical periods.

Environs: Amárynthos (11 km. E.) is on the site of the ancient settlement of the same name (of which virtually nothing survives). Nearby is the Monastery of *Ágios Nikolaos* which has a church dating from 1565 with attractive 16C frescos, and is decorated with colourful faience tiles on the outside. *Alivéri* (population 4,700) is on the site of the ancient *Tamýnai*, of which there are virtually no remains, *c.* 28 km. E. of Erétria. There is an attractive *church of the Panagía* here, dating from 1393, which has pointed arches and incorporates pieces of ancient architecture.

Dýstos (*c.* 63 km. SE of Chalkís): The ruins of the *ancient city* of the same name stand in the plain of Dýstos. (The lake here drains off into underground outlets called katavothrae and in the summer dries out

Kymi (Évia)

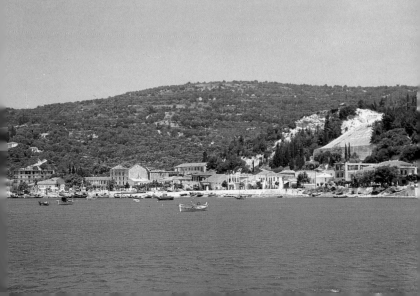

completely). The 5C BC *city wall*, which is built of polygonal masonry and has 11 *towers*, is well-preserved in parts. The *main gate* (to the E.) leads to what was once the *agora*. It is still possible to identify the outlines and supporting walls of the, generally two-storeyed, terraced *houses* of this classical city, which was set on the slopes of the hill. The *Acropolis*, which now includes the ruins of a Venetian *fortress (Kastro)*, was on the top of the hill.

Environs: Near the village of *Zárakes (c.* 12 km. SE) there are the remains of an *ancient settlement*.

Kými (*c.* 93 km. NE of Chalkís): This town (population *c.* 3,000) stands on a cliff 820 ft. high on the E. coast. It has inherited the name of the famous ancient city of Kýme, which established the colony of *Cumae* in southern Italy and subsequently developed the Latin alphabet there. No remains have as yet been discovered of the ancient city. The modern town contains the attractive *church of the Panagía* and the remains of a Venetian *fortress*.

Environs: 3 km. to the N., on the headland, is the *Monastery of the Saviour* (Moni Sotiros); this dates from the 16/17C and has a (restored) wooden iconostasis dating from 1874. 4 km. to the S. is the port of *Paralía Kýmis* (whence connections are made to the Sporades). Near *Vrýsi (c.* 10 km. S.) are the ruins of a medieval castle. *Avlonri (c.* 15 km. S.) contains the *church of Ágios Dimitrios* which dates from the 12C and incorporates the remains of ancient columns in its walls. There are also the ruins of Frankish and Venetian fortresses and towers in the vicinity. To the E. is the convent of *Ágios Charálampos*, which has a church dating from the 11/12C and the remains of some frescos. To the N. of Avlonári is the *monastery of the Mother of God (Kimisis Theotoku)*, which has a 14C church and icons dating from the 16–18C.

Kárystos (126 km. SE of Chalkís): This port (population *c.* 3,500) is situated in the S. of the island, beneath the lovely, wooded Mt.Ókhi. It was founded in 1833. Ferries depart from here for Rafína in Attica and for the island of Andros. The ruins of the ancient city of the same name (now called *Palaiochóra)* and its *Acropolis* (razed by Themistokles in 467 BC) are 3 km. inland. Today this is the site of the Venetian fortress *Castel Rosso* ('Red Castle'). An ancient *stone bridge* over the Megalorevma is still preserved. The *stone quarries* to the SE of the ancient city (near Mýli/Aetós) are also interesting and contain the remains of some columns. This is where the green cipollino marble, which was famous in Roman times, was quarried. Nearby there is a *cave with stalactites* called Agia Trias. The town *Museum* has a collection of ancient sculptures, fragments of architecture, and incriptions from the surrounding area. *Environs:* There is a medieval *aqueduct* (arches preserved) near *Grabiá*, beneath Mt.Ókhi (which has two summits: the N. one is 4,019 ft. high, and the one to the S., called Ágios Ilias, is 4,586 ft. Beneath Ágios Ilias is the so-called *house of the dragon (drakospito)* (late Geometric), which may have been a cult site. Near Platanistó (2 km. E.) are the rather scanty remains of a sanctuary of Poseidon. At the southern end of the island is *Cape Kaphereús* (Kafiréas), which was notorious in ancient times (the Venetians renamed it *Capo d'Oro* (Gold Cape). To the W. of *Stýra (c.* 30 km. NW) are the remains of the *ancient city* of that name which was mentioned by Homer (only one tower on the Acropolis is preserved). There are green cipollino *marble quarries* on the neighbouring Mt.Ágios Nikolaos and, on its summit, the *Frankish fort of Larmena*. On its slope are the so-called *dragons' houses (drakospita)*, buildings made of stone slabs with smoke outlets which may have been either archaic cult sites or living quarters for the stonecutters.

Aidipsós (*c.* 150 km. NW of Chalkís): This spa (population *c.* 5,000) has been well-known since the time of the ancients (who knew it by the same name) and it stands on an idyllic bay in the NW of the island. Its hot springs contain a number of minerals, including sodium chloride, iodine, calcium, and calcium chloride, and vary between 34 and 71 degrees C. The remains of the *Roman bath houses* are interesting, as are the ancient surrounds of the springs and streams, notably the Agiu Anagyru spring. The existence here of some 60 springs was described by Aristotle (in his 'Meteorologika'); and Sulla and the Emperors Hadrian and Constantine were among those who came here. The archaeological finds (statues, inscriptions, etc.) are housed in the *parish hall*.

Environs: Beneath Mt. Balanti (3,205 ft.), the summit of the ancient Mt. Teléthrion, is the Monastery of *Ágios Geórgios*, dating from the 18C, which contains a 15/16C church and a wooden iconostasis made in 1834 (as well as an interesting collection of church utensils). Near the village of *Ágios* are the ruins of a Byzantine *church of Demetrios*.

Istiaía (131 km. NW of Chalkís): This town on the N. slopes of Mt. Teléthrion, now an agricultural centre, dates back to the ancient town of *Histiaía* mentioned by Homer in the Iliad. Its inhabitants were driven out by the Athenians in 447 BC during the rule of Perikles, but they returned later. They settled in the area between the modern town and the neighbouring port of *Oreós* (now called *Oraií*) which looks across the straits to Thessaly. There are remains of two citadels dating from ancient times. The first, the *maritime acropolis*, has the ruins of an ancient wall and a *Venetian fort*; to the S. are the foundations of a single-aisled *Byzantine church*. Opposite it is the second, inland acropolis (Apano Oreos), of which little is left. Between the two are the foundations of a large *marble temple*. In the area around Oraií, early Helladic and Mycenean remains have been excavated. On the village square there is a colossal *marble bull* dating from the 4C BC which was recovered from the sea. The *town hall* in Istiaía contains an interesting *archaeological collection* including votive reliefs, tomb inscriptions, fragments of sculptures, and ceramics. (There is a similar collection in the town hall at Oraií). A small *hunting museum (Kynigitiko Musion)* in Istiaía gives information about the indigenous birds and animals.

Environs: Near the coastal town of *Artemísion* (13 km. NE) are the remains of a famous *Sanctuary of Artemis.* Cape Artemísion was the site of a sea-battle in 480 BC between the Athenians and the Persians. This is also where one of the showpieces of the National Museum in Athens, the bronze statue of Poseidon or Zeus hurling his trident, was recovered from the sea.

Límni (86 km. NW of Chalkís): This lovely seaside town on the W. coast (population 2,800) probably dates back to the ancient *Elýmnion* (of which nothing is left). It contains the remains of a 5C early Christian *basilica* which has a *pavement mosaic*. The 19C *Mitropolis church* and the church of *Ágios Athanásios*, which has 17C rustic frescos, are also interesting.

Environs: Near the coastal monastery of *Ágios Nikoláos (Galatáki)*, 6 km. S, the remains have been discovered of a *Temple of Poseidon* dating from the 5C BC. The monastery was built over it in the 10C and rebuilt in 1556. It has beautiful 17C frescos in the narthex and valuable church utensils (as well as some old manuscripts). The interesting *monastery of Ósios Davíd* is situated to the NE of the coastal village of *Roviés* (*c.* 10 km. NW). This dates from the 16C and contains beautiful 18C frescos.

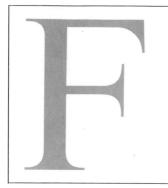

Fársala/Phársala/ΦΑΡΣΑΛΑ
Lárisa/Thessaly   p.294☐F 6

This agricultural, tobacco-growing centre (population 7,000) lies to the SE of the plain of Thessaly on the foothills of the Narthakion mountains (part of the Othrys massif). The region has been settled since Neolithic and Mycenean times. Finds from Mycenean tombs reveal that ancient *Pharsalos* was the main town, and possibly even the seat, of the Mycenean Myrmidons, whose king was Achilles. Whether or not Homer's *Phthía,* capital of *Phthiótis,* with the 'Castle of Achilles' lay here is still unclear. Sparse remains of the antique (Hellenistic-Roman) Agora were uncovered in the town (main square). Further remains of the Acropolis are to be seen on the 1,140 ft. high Kastro hill to the S. of the town. The plain of the river Enipeus (Enipeas) N. of the town was the site of the decisive battle between Pompey and Caesar for the control of Rome which took place in 48 BC. Pompey's numerically superior army (*c.* 40,000 men) was totally annihilated in one day by Caesar's tactics (pincer movement). With a few followers, the defeated Pompey managed to reach the sea and thence Egypt. As a consequence of the Battle of Pharsalos, Caesar held power by him-

self, the Republic came to an end and the Empire began.

The town, destroyed by the earthquake of 1954 and rebuilt in modern style, has little of interest apart from a late archaic *domed tomb* (8/7C) above a Mycenean tomb to the W. of the town.

Environs: To the E. and NE are various excavation sites, including *Palaiókastro* (Ano Deréngli), *c.* 5 km. NE, a settlement which was constantly inhabited from 2500 to 500 BC *(Palaió-Phársala).* Nearby are remains of a *Shrine of Thetis (Thetideion)* and a few ruins of the ancient town of *Skotússa* with a *Shrine of Zeus* (remains of Acropolis and broken pottery finds). Further NE is the Kynos-Kephalai range (2,362 ft.), the so-called 'Dog's Head' (now known by its Turkish name of Karadag: 'Black Mountain'), where in 364 BC and 197 BC important battles took place: the Roman general Flaminius besieged Philip V of Macedon here in 197 BC (end of Macedonian supremacy). Lying on a height at *Néon Monastírion* (14 km. SW) are the remains of the medieval fortress of *Gynaikokastro* ('Women's Castle', walls of dressed masonry survive) on the site of ancient *Proerna,* where a famous *Temple of Demeter* stood. At the town of *Domokós* (*c.* 29 km. SW), with the ruins of a medieval *castle,*

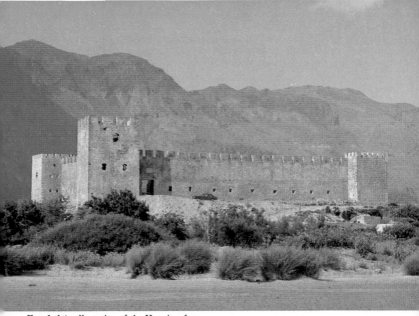

Frankokástello, ruins of the Venetian fortress

are the remains of the ancient town of *Thaumákoi*, traces of which are to be found to the W. of the castle. On the S. slope of the *Acropolis* there are remains of a *Gymnasion* and of a bastion with polygonal masonry. To the N. of the town is a tower with broad ramparts.

Flórina/ΦΛΟΡΙΝΑ
Flórina/Macedonia   p.290☐D 3

Capital of the area bordering Albania and Yugoslavia (population 12,000, 164 km. from Thessaloníki). This area was settled by early classical times. It later became part of the Macedonian state at the time of Arkhelaos (5C BC). The town is now known for its agricultural products (peanuts, cherries, paprika).

Archaeological Museum: Displayed here are the remains of tombstones and numerous Roman sculptures.

Picture Gallery *(Pinakothiki):* Works by painters native to Flórina.

Environs: Ágios Germanós (*c.* 50 km. NW): Little village lying to the E. of Lake Préspa. The village church of the same name was built in the 11C. It is cruciform, with 4 columns and a dome. The church also contains the completely preserved body of St. Germanos (miracle worker). **Amýnteon** (32 km. E.): Little town with famous *healing springs (Xyno Nero)*. **Préspes:** In this area there are several villages and the two *Prespa lakes* (Great and Little Prespa). These lakes became famous for their abundant and rare flora and fauna. There are numerous Byzantine churches to be seen here: the church of *Ágios Markos* in the village of *Próti*, the *Panagia* in the village of *Kladorákhi*, the churches of the *12 Apostles*, *Ágios Dimitrios* and *Ágios Georgios*. On the small island of **Ágios Achillios** (on Little Prespa lake) lies the 11C *basilica* of the same name, with a nave and two aisles. On Great Prespa lake lies the church of *Panagia Eleusa*, which was built in a natural cave in 1410.

**Frankokástello/
Frango Kástello/Frangokástello/
ΦΡΑΓΚΟΚΑΣΤΣΛΛΟ**

Chaniá/Crete   p.298□F 14

On the S. coast of Crete rise the ruins of this massive Venetian fortress, built in 1371. The rectangular curtain walls still stand. Above the entrance gate on the S. side is a relief with the lion of Venice.

Environs: Komitádes: 6 km. N. of Frankokástello is the village of Komitádes with the church of *Ágios Georgios*, which contains beautiful frescos (1314) by J.Pagoménos. **Alíkampos:** 30 km. N. of Komitádes lies the village of Alíkampos. In a cemetery in front of the town stands the little single-aisled church of *Panagia Dhexámini* with barrel vaulting and beautiful, vibrant frescos by J.Pagoménos (1315/16). **Khóra Sfakíon:** 18 km. further W. of Frankokástello, most charmingly situated on a hill, also on the S. coast, is the village of Khóra Sphakíon. Due to its position in the White Mountains (Lefká Óri) it was a secure base for attacks and uprisings against foreign rulers. Also of interest is a small, originally Venetian, *fortress* altered by the Turks. The village, which in the 16C was a wealthy Venetian town, still has the ruins of *45 old churches* from that time. **Anápolis:** About 10 km. NW of Khóra Sphakíon lies Anápolis, an ancient settlement of which only the odd remnant survives. Daskalojánnis, the famous resistance fighter of 1770, lived here. **Arádena:** About 2 hours NE by foot, lying on the far side of a gorge, is the little community of Arádena with the *church of the Archangel Michael*, which has a dome with a drum and remarkable frescos (1546).

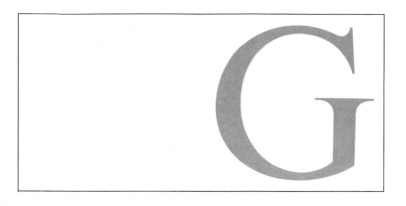

Gastúni/ΓΑΣΤΟΥΝΗ
Elis/Peloponnese   p.294☐D 9

This village (population 4,200), 26 km. N.
of Pyrgos, owes its name to the Frankish
Baron Gastogne. In the village are remains
of a Frankish fortress and of the Byzantine
church of the *Panagia Katholokí* (12C).

Environs: Elis (*c.* 12 km. NE): The ancient town where Herakles, according to
legend, cleaned out the Augeian stables.
During excavations by the Austrian and
Greek Schools the *Agora,* the *Gymnasion*
and remains of a *theatre* from Hellenistic
times were discovered. Also Roman
mosaics, including one of the attributes of
the Muses. In the gymnasion the athletes
trained for the Olympic Games.

Geraki/Yeráki/ΓΕΡΑΚΙ
Lakonia/Peloponnese   p.298☐F 11

This village (population 1,606), 42 km. SE
of Sparta, has been inhabited for 6,000
years (first settled in the Middle Helladic
Age). Remains of Pelasgian walls from
1100 BC are well-preserved. In ancient
times the village was called Geronthrai,
and annual feasts were held in honour of

the god of War. It was a barony in Frankish
times and Guy de Nivelet built a castle in
1254, which can still be seen. After the battle of Pelagonia (1263) the village fell to the
Byzantines and remained a strategic base.
Most of Geráki's churches were built during this period.

Ágios Ioannis Chrysostomos: 13C
church, built of stone slabs and pieces of
broken, ancient reliefs (one with a Roman
inscription serves as a lintel). Inside is the
'Adoration of the Archangels'.

Ágios-Sostis: Church (*c.* 1200), also built
from old fragments.

Evangelistria: Church from the mid-12C
with well- preserved, good-quality frescos
(Pantocrator in the dome, 'Transfiguration'
over the sanctuary).

Ágios-Georgios: Basilica (13C) with a
nave, two aisles and a Frankish coat-of-
arms above the entrance arch.

Goniás/Gonia/ΓΟΝΙΑΣ
Chaniá/Crete   p.298☐E 13

Rodopú (Rodopós) is a rough, mountainous, sparsely-populated peninsula in

NW Crete. Consequently it has become the breeding-ground for countless numbers of birds, giving it the name 'Island of Birds'. In antiquity Rodopú was called 'Tityros'.

In the SE of the peninsula, near the N. coast of Crete and N. of the village of Kolimvári, lies *Moní Gonias,* a massive monastery with a beautiful view over the Gulf of Chaniá. The monastery was founded in 1618 under the name of Moni Odigitrías; destroyed in 1645 and rebuilt in 1661. It was restored and extended in 1798, 1874 and 1884. Of particular interest are the monastery's baroque portals. The monastery church contains a collection of valuable icons from the 16–18C. Today the monastery is the seat of the Greek Orthodox Academy of Crete.

Environs: Diktynnaíon: In 1942, at the N. end of the Rodopú peninsula, on the S. rock plateau above the Bay of Meniés on the E. coast, German archaeologists discovered the ruins of an ancient shrine, the Diktynnaíon. The shrine of the Diktynna is best reached by boat from Kolimvári, but it can also be approached by foot from the village of Rodopú, 15 km. S, which lies about 3 km. NW of Goniás in the middle of the peninsula. *Diktynna,* actually Britomartis (daughter of Zeus and the Karme, born on Crete), was worshipped as a goddess in antiquity. She was credited with the invention of the hunting net, hence her name Diktynna (meaning 'net'). The place where the shrine was discovered reveals traces of dwellings going back to the 9C BC. The first temple appears to have originated towards the end of the 7C BC. The temple excavated this century was originally built under Hadrian in AD 123. The Temple of Diktynna stood in a court surrounded by columned halls. Propylaia in the NW provided the entrance to the temple. On the W. side of the court a terrace and barrel-vaulted cisterns were dis-

covered. In the vicinity further buildings were excavated, the purpose of which is not entirely certain. A larger building originally served as a pilgrims' hostel. In 1913 further ruins, a Roman emperor's head, a statue of Hadrian and a marble statue of Diktynna were discovered in the area. These finds are now to be seen in the Museum in Chaniá. Earlier a paved Roman road had led from the Temple of Diktynna via Rodopú to the coastal road leading from Chaniá to Kastélli. Individual walls and supporting walls, paving and a milestone in the village of Rodopú still testify to its existence. The ancient building materials, particularly those of the Temple of Diktynna, was for the most part removed and used for new buildings in Chaniá and elsewhere—an occurrence that has not helped the archaeological research.

Górtyna/Górtys/Górtyn/
ΓΟΡΤΞΝΑ
Iráklion/Crete   p.298□G 14

History: Górtys, in the middle of Crete in the fertile Messara region, was—as excavations have shown—already populated in the Minoan age, but was under the rule of Phaistós. With the arrival of the Dorians it rose to importance, conquered Phaistós and Mátala in the 3C BC and finally became capital of Crete under the Romans from AD 67 to 395.

In AD 59 St.Paul the Apostle, on his voyage to Rome, also came to Crete. His companion Titus, who became the first bishop of the island, appears to have built a church here, which may have been the building which preceded the still extant early Christian *Ágios Titos.* Górtys became the centre of Christian Crete. In 824, after the Arabs had invaded the island, the inhabitants of Górtys abandoned it and founded

Górtys, the Odeion ▷

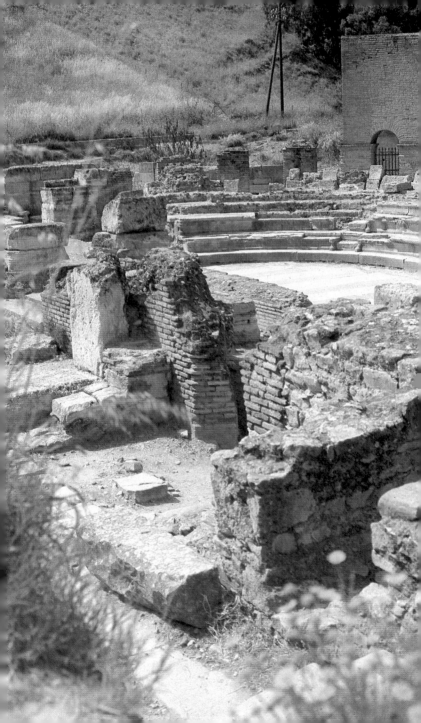

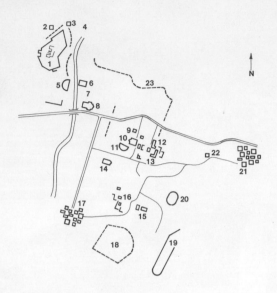

Górtys, area of ruins 1 Isolated remains of the acropolis. Remains of an archaic goddess were found here (now in the Archaeological Museum in Iráklion) **2** foundations of a massive temple, altered many times **3** remains of a 43 ft. long sacrificial altar **4** remains of an aqueduct **5** seats of a theatre **6** Odeion (partly rebuilt) with the Code of Laws of Górtys **7** Agora, where the Temple of Asklepios originally stood (the statue of the god Asklepios, now in the Arch. Mus. in Iráklion, was found here) **8** Ágios Titos basilica (6C), of which the apse and parts of the transept still remain. It was originally cruciform with a nave and two aisles and is one of Crete's most important monuments. It is considered to be the first resting-place of St. Paul's companion Titus **9** Temple of the Egyptian Gods Isis and Serapis. The original statues are still partly preserved, as are the foundations of the columns and walls **10** Pythion, archaic Temple of Apollo Pythios, which, as a few finds have indicated, was built above a Minoan structure. NE of the Greek temple (6C BC), restored by the Romans in the 2C BC, was a treasury. The ruins of the three-aisled temple still create an impression of massiveness, with the bases of Corinthian columns and a Roman apse in the central aisle. Here was found the statue of Apollo Pythios and beautiful archaic reliefs (now in the Arch. Mus. in Iráklion) **11** Roman theatre **12** Nymphaeum with fragments of Roman statues **13** Praetorium, originally the centre of Roman Górtys, dates from the 2C AD and was rebuilt in the 4C AD following an earthquake **14** foundations of a Byzantine basilica **15** Nymphaeum (2C AD) with cisterns and 2 elongated, originally roofed, rooms **16** remains of Roman baths **17** Mitropolis, a small township, where a Minoan mansion and a smaller house were excavated **18** burial ground **19** stadium **20** ruins of an amphitheatre (2C AD) **21** Agii Deka, village with the church of Agii Deka, built in memory of the 10 martyrs. Antique columns from Górtys were used in the building of the Byzantine basilica with a nave and two aisles **22** museum on the edge of Agii Deka with architectural fragments, sculptures and inscriptions

a new settlement outside their city, Agii Dheka, meaning 'Ten Saints' after 10 priests, later canonized, who were martyred in Górtys on 23 December AD 250 during the Christian persecutions. Górtys declined, and olives grew between the ruins. In 1880 two German archaeologists

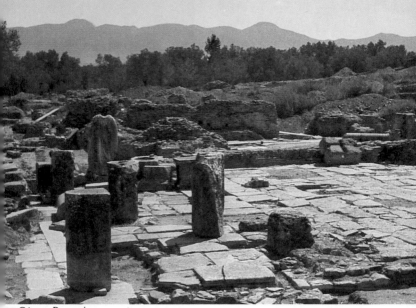

Górtys, Praetorium

came across the few remains of the town visible amongst the extensive olive grove. They began excavating and discovered the *Roman and early Christian monuments.*

The Górtys Code of Laws: During the excavations an *Odeion* was discovered together with 42 numbered stone blocks, on which a total of 12 law texts were inscribed. The first of these blocks was discovered in 1857, but could not be properly deciphered. The tablets, which under the Romans — as now, following their re-assembly—occupied a place on the N. wall of the Odeion, were originally in the 5C BC from the Bouleuterion of the then Agora. The Odeion was built around 100 BC over the ruins of the Bouleuterion. The N. wall, with the inscribed tablets was preserved, however. The text, which could only be deciphered when all the tablets were avail-

able, is written in Cretan-Dorian dialect alternately from left to right and from right to left and contains the complete code of laws for the city, controlling all the rights of the citizens of Górtys—rights of freemen and of slaves, laws concerning administration, marriage, punishment and trial.The now excavated and widely scattered area of ruins shows the former importance of the city, particularly under the Romans.

Environs: Ampelórisa: W. of Agii Dheka, an hour's walk away, is a quarry with halls at Ampelórisa. Some experts think that this was the actual labyrinth of the Minotaur. **Plátanos:** About 6 km. S. of Górtys lies Plátanos. In 1915 a Cretan discovered 2 *Tholoi* (round tombs) nearby. One of these is the largest beehive tomb on the whole island. Such Cretan tombs—

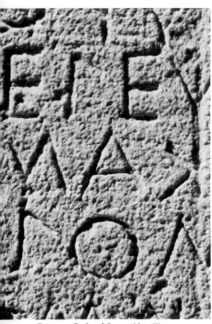

Górtys, Code of Laws (detail)

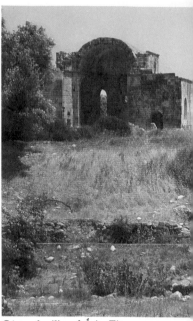

Górtys, basilica of Ágios Titos

mostly family tombs—date from around 2600 BC to 1500 BC. The ceremonies were held on a paved square in front of the tomb. **Léntas/Lendas:** About 10 km. S. of Plátanos on the S. coast of the island lies Léntas. To the E., near Lebéna round tombs from the pre-palatial age (2400–2200 BC) were discovered. These contained many sculptures and painted ceramics (animals, fruit, ships, etc.)from that time. Minoan arts and crafts of this kind will henceforth be described as Lebéna Style. The commonest feature of this style (white painting on dark ground) is a reddish base, while a brown colour is predominant in the contemporary Ágios-Onúfrios Style. **Rhizenía:** About 10 km. N. of Górtys towards Iráklion, turning W. at Agia Varvára and travelling another 5 km., one comes to the village of *Priniás*. In 1906–8, on the table mountain of *Patéla*, 1.5 km. before the village, Italian archaeologists excavated the *antique city* of Rhizenía. Of particular interest are two *temples,* which were discovered here and date from around 700 BC. The relief slabs and sculptures can now be seen in the Museum in Iráklion. W. of the two temples is a fortress dating from Hellenistic times.

Grevená/ΓΡΕΘΕΝΑ
Grevená/Macedonia   p.290☐D 4

Capital (population 8,000) of the nome of the same name, lying at the foot of the Pindos and Khasia mountains.

Environs: Spílaion (17 km. W.): Little village with remains of an older settlement, including remains of the town walls,

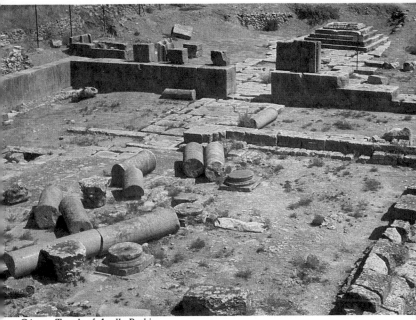

Górtys, Temple of Apollo Pythios

necropolis, monastery with fine Byzantine items.

Gúrnia/Gournia/Gurnjá/
ΓΟΞΝΙΑ
Lasithi/Crete   p.298□I 14

In 1901 a farmer working in a field found an old seal stone and this discovery led the American archaeologist Harriet Boyd to dig with colleagues for further treasures at the site of the find. What this work revealed were the foundation walls of an entire Minoan town.

Gúrnia, at the island's narrowest point in the E. of Crete near the Gulf of Mirabello, 19 km. SE of Ágios Nikólaos, is the only entire Minoan town to have been excavated

so far. The area of ruins gives a good impression of the urban culture of the time. It was obviously not quite so refined and sophisticated as in the palaces, but nevertheless just as astonishingly advanced and diverse. Gúrnia proves what the palaces of Knossós, Phaistós and Mália had already suggested: Crete was the home of the earliest advanced European civilization. The citizens of Gúrnia were traders, fishermen, farmers and craftsmen. Many of the smaller finds from Gúrnia are now to be found in the museum in Iráklion. Of particular interest is what was found in the workshops: Millstones, potter's wheels and clay lids, carpentry workshops with saws, axes, chisels, drills and bronze tools, oil presses and tubs for cleaning the oil, wine-press houses and copper smithies with moulds, chisels and awls. Near Gúrnia there were rectangular *chamber tombs*.

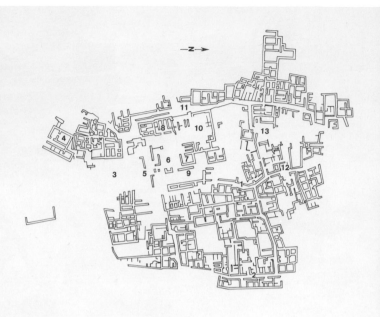

Gúrnia, Minoan town 1 and **2** 2 parallel paved main streets **3** Agora **4** South House (from the time of the later Minoan settlement) **5** staircase **6** court of a small palace, perhaps the residence of the local ruler **7** store, in which containers of oil, wine, honey and corn were kept **8** smaller magazines **9** women's chambers **10** Men's chambers **11** further parallel streets, probably connected to street 1 **12** well preserved house **13** small shrine with sacrificial altar, where a snake godesss (similar to the one in Knossós) was found, along with other religious objects

walls up to 8 ft. high were excavated in 1904. However, by the time of the Palatial age this two-storeyed villa was no longer inhabited.

The ceramics which were found here (now in Iráklion) are called 'mottled ware' after their black-and-red flecked colouring and characterized as Vasilikí Style. These are mainly jugs and pots with beak-like spouts.

It is now known that the town dates from around 1600 BC. Between 1500 and 1450 the town appears to have been annihilated. The next finds, which confirm the resettlement and enlargement of the town, only date back to around 1300 BC. Thereafter it was totally forgotten for centuries.

Environs: Vasilikí: About 4 km. S. of Gúrnia is Vasilikí, where the remains of an early Minoan mansion with foundation

Gýthion/ΓΥΘΕΙΟΝ

Lakonia/Peloponnese   p.298□F 11

Old town (population 4,910) with interesting neoclassical buildings. Today it is the main port for exports from Máni and Sparta. The town lies at the foot of Mt. Larysion, on the summit of which are the ruins of a castle. The area is dedicated to the worship of Dionysos and Praxidikai.

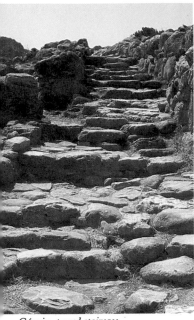

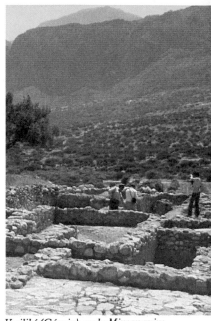

Gúrnia, paved staircase

Vasilikí (Gúrnia), early Minoan ruins

Gýthion, ancient theatre

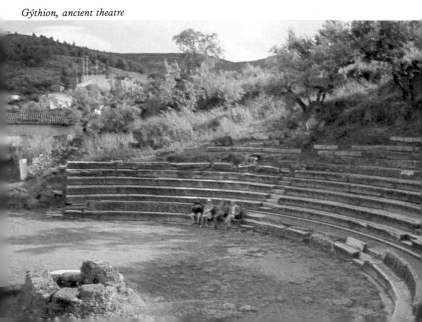

In ancient times too Gýthion was used as a port and base by the Spartans. The little island of *Marathonísi,* the ancient *Kranái,* lying opposite, is now joined to the mainland by a causeway. Kranái was a Phoenician trading post, dealing in costly purple dye. Marathonísi is supposed to have provided refuge for Paris as he was making his way to Troy with Helen. On the tip of the island are the ruins of the town of *Las.* This was a Spartan holy place and has many temples and votive offerings. On the island there was a shrine to Aphrodite, which the Phoenician traders had founded (perhaps on the site of the church of Ágios Georgios. There is also a refuge tower of the Mavromichalis, a Máni family, on the island.

Towards Sparta (now the site of Pelekitó to the NW) at the foot of Mt. Larysion there is an *altar* hewn into the rock, dedicated to Zeus Kappotas, where Orestes was cured of madness. This altar belonged to the shrine of Zeus Terastios (protected by inscriptions).

The ancient town was about 250 yards further N. Remains of the *Acropolis,* the *Roman theatre* and (2C AD) a *temple* of Tiberius and Augustus.

Gýthion, island of Marathonisi

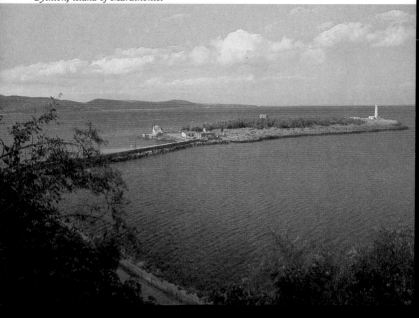

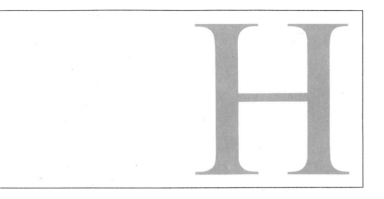

Hósios Lukás/Ósios Lukás/MONH
OΣIOY ΛOYKA
Boeotia/Central Greece   p.294☐F 8

Monastery: Hósios Lukás is one of the most beautiful Byzantine monasteries in Greece.

The miraculous saint, the Blessed Luke (Hosios Lukas), to whom the church is dedicated, was a hermit from the immediate vicinity. Born in AD 896 in the village of Kastrí (today Delfí), he led an adventurous life and later moved to a place near the present village of Stíri (this is why it is also called 'Stiriotis'). He was subsequently joined by a crowd of young people coming from nearby who wished to put into effect the ideals of Byzantine monasti-

Hósios Lukás, dome of the monastery church

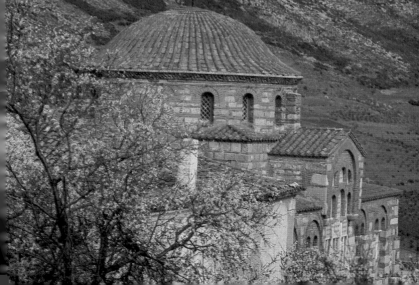

cism. The holy man's great intellectual gifts, miracles and prophecies made him famous all over the Byzantine empire. He attracted the attention of the Byzantine court by prophesying that Emperor Romanos Lekapenos would recapture the island of Crete from the Saracens (this prophecy was fulfilled AD 961). It is said that Romanos Lekapenos began the monastery church after the saint's death in 953. Emperor Basíleios Bulgaroktonos ('Killer of Bulgarians') later completed this work at the request of Theophano, his mother. A flight of stone steps leads from the square above the monastery southwards across the forecourt to the monastery courtyard proper. On the left, by the entrance, is a spring whose water possesses healing properties. This is the original spring which the Blessed Luke discovered. A few steps further on, on the E. side, are the two churches, while the cells are on the W. side. The smaller of the two churches, which stands beside the main one, is dedicated to Theotókos, the Mother of God. It is older than the Katholikon and was most probably built in the second half of the 10C AD.

Its architectural form is that of a cross-in-square basilica of the kind usual in Constantinople at that time. The dome is supported by four columns. Inside, the decoration of the church is plain. It has a beautiful pavement consisting of large mosaic slabs. Traces of interesting frescos from the 11&12C can be seen below the white limestone layer at various points on the walls around the altar. The outer walls of

Hósios Lukás, Main church 1 entrance **2** narthex decorated with mosaics on a gold ground **3** The Washing of the Feet, in the niche **4, 5** Crucifixion **6** Resurrection **7** Doubting Thomas, in the S. niche. On the ceiling are busts of saints and archangels **8** John the Baptist **9** the Mother of God **10** Michael **11** Gabriel **12** Christ Pantocrator above the entrance to the Naos **13, 14** Baptistery **15** nave **16** Dome, painting of Christ Pantocrator, mosaic destroyed, replaced at the end of the 16C; below are depictions of the **17** Mother of God, the archangels **18** Gabriel **19** Uriel **20** Raphael **21** Michael and **22** Ioannis Prodromos. Mosaics on the squinches **23** Birth of Christ **24** Christ in the Temple **25** Baptism **26** Annunciation (no longer survives) **27** aisles **28** St. Luke Stíris **29** tomb **30** Prothesis **31** Diakonikon **32** treasury **33** dome of the sanctuary **34** Descent of the Holy Ghost with astonishingly expressionistic figures of youths seated in a circle **35** apse vault **36** Mother of God enthroned

Hósios Lukás, church of Theotókos

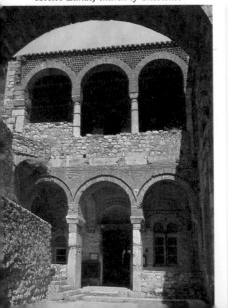

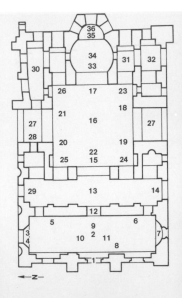

the church are decorated with sculptures which show an Oriental influence.

The first church of the monastery was dedicated to St. Barbara and it contained the tomb of the Blessed Luke. The main church, dedicated to Luke, was later built on the site of this first church.

The *main church (Katholikon),* which was founded by Abbot Philotheos in the early 11C AD, is a monumental example of a Byzantine Greek-cross-octagon church. Its dome is supported by eight pillars. Small marble columns subdivide the windows into two and three arches.

The visitor entering the church is confronted by a majestic array of mosaics on a gold ground. The artists very probably came from Constantinople.

The floor, whose architectural focus is the cross, consists of large marble slabs in various shades of colour. The walls have a splendid, polychrome marble facing.

Saints and scenes from the Bible are depicted in the three main sections of the church—narthex, naos and bema.

There is a tremendous mosaic of Christ above the entrance to the Naos. Just to the left of this is a Crucifixion, and to the right a Resurrection; both of these are markedly expressive. The same also applies to the figures of the two Apostles, St. Peter on the E. wall and St. Andrew on the W. wall.

The naos contains a multitude of mosaics, although they appear somewhat stiff compared to those in the Dafní monastery near Athens. As was noted by André Grabar, they 'have not been influenced by the 10C Renaissance'. The arrangement of images in the naos appears to be based on a programme which was developed in Constantinople in the 9C AD for use in cross-in-square churches.

The dome and its original Christ Pantocrator were destroyed by an earthquake in the 16C. An impression of the lost Pantocrator may be gained from the small head-and-shoulder image of Christ in the SE arch of the cross below the gallery. A fresco of the Pantocrator now occupies the dome instead of the mosaic. The Madonna and Child adorn the vault of the apse. In the dome of the bema there is a Descent of the Holy Ghost. In the corner niches below the dome there are representations of three of

Hósios Lukás, mosaic of Christ Pantocrator

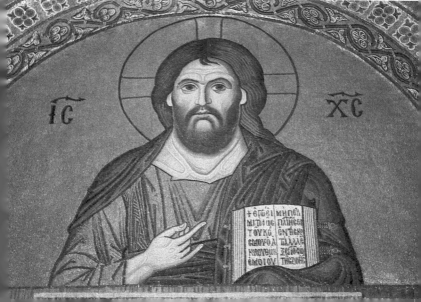

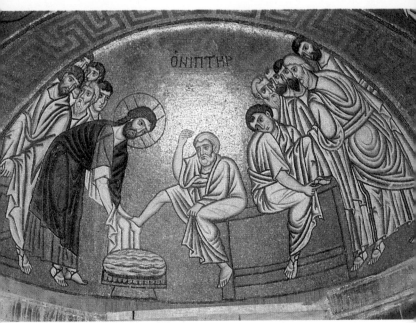

Hósios Lukás, the Washing of Feet

the main events in Christ's life: the Nativity, Presentation in the Temple, and Baptism. The fourth scene, the Annunciation, has unfortunately not survived.

The figure of the Blessed Luke, the monastery's founder, is to be found in the N. transept and is especially impressive. The hands raised solemnly in prayer, the strict ascetic facial features and the large, expressive eyes are characteristic of Byzantine art in the 11C AD.

The wall paintings on the side walls and galleries date from the same period as the mosaics, are of a popular and didactic nature and come from the Cappadocian peasants' school. The empty reliquary of the Blessed Luke is in the N. part of the church. Geoffrey II Villehardouin, the Frankish lord (1218–45), ordered the saint's relics to be removed in order to present them to the then Pope.

The marble templon is also notable. The movable icons by the famous Cretan artist Michael Damaskenos (16C) formerly hung here.

The walls of the small lower church, which is the crypt of St.Barbara, is decorated with frescos similar to those mentioned above. These wall paintings date from the same period.

The entrance to this crypt is between the outer S. wall of the main church and the restored old refectory of the monastery. The tomb of the Blessed Luke is on the N. wall of the crypt.

A small collection of the once important treasures of the monastery is on display in the rebuilt refectory. Most of the treasures were removed from the country during Frankish rule.

A secret pit was found under the marble chairs of the altar during restoration work

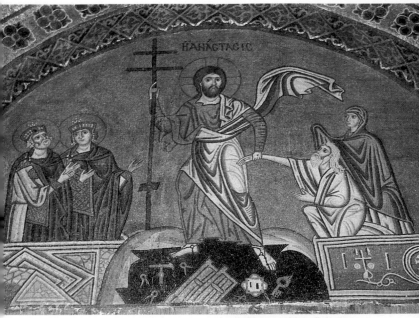

Hósios Lukás, Resurrection (above), icon of Christ by M.Damaskinos (below)

carried out in 1957. In it there were 18 small sacks filled with mosaic tesserae. They most probably came from the monastery dome, which collapsed in the 16C. The monastery had an important role to play during Turkish rule and the later struggle for independence. On 27 March 1821, the uprising of Central Greece was proclaimed here after a solemn liturgy by Bishop Jesaias of Sálona.

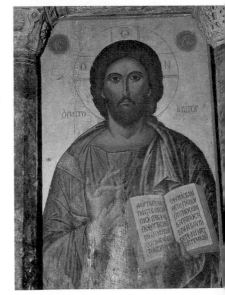

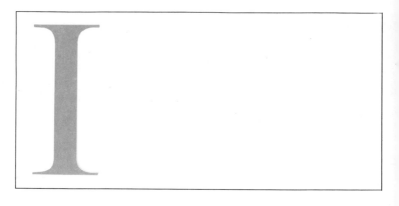

Ierápetra/Hierápetra/
ΙΕΡΑΠΕΤΡΑ
Lasíthi/Crete   p.298☐J 14

This small old harbour on the S. coast of
the island, opposite Gúrnia, was established by the Minoans for trade with
Africa. The best way to reach it is to travel
by bus from Ágios Nikólaos.

In the 2C BC the ancient harbour of Her-
apytna was here. Today it is almost completely silted up. During the period of
Roman rule it enjoyed its heyday, being the
port for trade with Kyrenaika. In the early
13C it was occupied by Genoese and then
by Venetians.

This small, charming town, which makes
a very African impression, occupies a
horseshoe site and is surrounded by mountain scenery. Some of the buildings are
Turkish, others Venetian in origin. However, here the styles form a charming
amalgam.

Church on the harbour square: The
little church by the harbour, with its small
bell tower and the twin octagonal domes,
makes more of a Byzantine than an Islamic
impression.

Turkish mosque: The Turkish mosque,
which was built on a square ground plan
with rectangular windows above a beautiful octagonal cleaning fountain in the foreground, makes a very different impression
from the typical mosque. The fountain
combines every style from Greek to Moorish. Only the wooden minaret with its octagonal lantern is what one would expect.

Ágios Ioánnis: The church of St. John,
which was formerly also a mosque, was
likewise built on a square ground plan.

Harbour castle: The beautifully situated
Venetian fortress by the harbour is well
worth seeing. The fortress displays less
Venetian than Moorish stylistic elements
(e.g. the bright red building stone and the
rounded-off battlements). It was erected in
1508 and was rebuilt by Morosini in 1626.

Museum: The small museum in Ierápetra
displays some very interesting finds from
the environs (tomb stele, sculptures etc.).
A Cretan-Mycenean sarcophagus is outstanding. It was made between 1450 and
1350 BC and was decorated with
paintings.

Amphitheatre: To the W., a little way
outside the town, there are some ruins
which originate from a Roman amphitheatre.

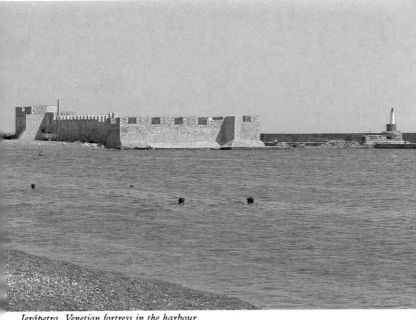

Ierápetra, Venetian fortress in the harbour

Environs: Mýrtos: 16 km. from Ierápetra, there is an early Minoan settlement (it can be reached via the new National road on the S. coast), which was not excavated until 1967&8. It was originally established in 2500 BC. A second excavation site located next to this and dating from the Middle Minoan period was uncovered in 1970–3.

Igumenítsa/ΗΓΟΥΜΕΝΙΤΣΑ
Thesprotía/Epirus   p.290□B 5

This small harbour town, with its 4,500 inhabitants, is regarded as the Western gate to Greece because of the ferry connection with Italy (Brindisi, Bari, Ancona) and Korfú.

Environs: Paramythiá (about 24 km.

SE): A medieval town probably bearing the name of the old monastery of Panagia Paramythiá. Nearby are the ruins of the Byzantine fortress of Ágios Donatos (named after a bishop of Évria). Many old tombs with important finds have been discovered in Paramythiá, and these are today exhibited in the museum of Ioánnina.

Fotikí/Photike: An inscription defining the site of the ancient town of Photike has been discovered near to Paramythiá, at Limpóni. Excavations carried out here have brought to light numerous finds dating from the Roman period. Especially worth mentioning is the marble sarcophagus discovered near to Lampovíthra in 1872. Today this sarcophagus is on display in the museum of Ioánnina (Room B). This town was the seat of a bishop in Byzantine times. Its decline began in the

11C AD with the Slav invasions, which devastated Photike along with many other towns.

Ikaría (I)/IKAPIA
East Aegean Islands/Aegean Islands
p.296□M 9

This isolated, fertile island with an area of 100 sq. m. and some 8,000 inhabitants is some 42 km. between both Mykonos and Samos. Known as *Íkaros* in ancient times, the island takes its name from Icarus, the son of the Cretan architect Daedalus. The former is said to have fallen into the 'Icarian Sea' to the S. of the island when attempting to fly with the aid of birds' wings.

History: The island was colonized by Icarians in *c.* 800 BC and was allied with Samos. It was later a member of the Athenian Naval League, but was of no particular importance in classical times. The Venetians controlled it in 1207-1333, and from 1362 to 1481 they were followed by the Giustinianis of Chíos. It was conquered by the Turks in 1567 and was returned to Greece in 1912.

Ágios Kírykos (1100 inhabitants): The main town of the island, named after its patron Kirykos, is on a mountain slope on the SE coast. The *cathedral* (Mitrópolis) of *Ágios Kírykos* dating from the 18C, and the church of *Ágios Nikólaos* (17C) with old icons and a beautiful iconostasis, are both worth seeing. The small *Archaeological Museum* (in the gymnasion) has various ancient finds from the island, including vases, ceramics and fragments of sculpture. *Environs:* The health resort of *Thérma* (3 km. NE), which has been known for its hot sulphurous springs since antiquity, was attributed to Asklepios, the god of medicine. Some remains of the site of the Hellenistic-Roman *thermal springs* are to be found at the edge of the town. Near the village of

Perdíki (6 km. NE) are the ruins of a 13C Venetian *castle (kastro)*. Ancient *sculptures* from the 6C BC have been discovered near the village of *Katafýgio* (8 km. NE), and they include the *tombstone relief* of Palion of Paros, and also some 6C BC *tombs* below the acropolis, scarcely any of which survives (good panoramic view). The church of *Ágios Dimitrios*, with its escape route below the sacristy, is also of interest. The 18C monastery of *Levkada*, and also some radioactive springs in the sea, are to be found in *Levkáda* (3 km. SE). The ancient town of *Drákanon* (today *Fanárion*), with a well-preserved Hellenistic *tower* (3C BC) and a 14C ruined fortress, stood on the NE tip of the island.

Évdilos: This charming fishing village (about 600 inhabitants) is 26 km. NW of the main town on the NW coast. Nearby, about 2 km. to the W. near the village of *Kámpos*, the remains of *Oinóe*, the capital of the island in ancient times, have been uncovered: ancient marble slabs, reliefs, inscriptions and stele dating from the 5&4C BC from the ancient cemetery. In addition, some remains of the ancient *town walls* and *fortifications*, mixed with Byzantine ruins, have survived. *Agia Irini* ('St.Irene') is the oldest church on the island. Dating from the 11C, it stands above the foundations of an early Christian *basilica* (the apse and parts of the marble floor still survive), and is worth visiting. Medieval walls (with arches), and houses (palatia). Classical marble fragments have been incorporated in the outer walls of the church of *Ágios Georgios* in *Palaiókastro*.

Armenistís: The remnants of a well-known *Shrine of Artemis* have been discovered near the small harbour of Armenistís (some 38 km. W. of the main town): to the W., at *Na* (from naos: 'temple'), on a rocky plateau, are the remains of the foundations of the *Temple of Artemis Tauropulos* ('Goddess of the Bull') with the altar pedestals surviving, parts of statues from the 5C BC, and fragments of vases. *Tombs* from the 5C BC, with funerary objects, have also been found nearby, and so have some foundations of ancient walls (between Armenistís and Khristós).

Ioánnina/ΙΩΑΝΝΙΝΑ
Ioánnina/Epirus   p.290☐C 5

History: Ioánnina, the main town of Epirus (40,000 inhabitants) was founded under the Emperor Justinian (AD 527–65). The town takes its name from the monastery of Ágios Ioánnis, which stood by the walls, near the Aslan Pasha mosque. When Michael I. Angelos Komnenos founded the despotate of Epirus in 1204, Ioánnina became the capital. The town fell to the Serbs in the 14C and was conquered by the Turks in 1431. Dionysios, the bishop of Tríkki, who is known as 'Skylosophos', attempted to liberate the town in 1611. However, the Turks were the victors. The Christians lost the privileges which they still possessed, and the two mosques which were built in this period are signs of the Turks' absolute domination of the town. Ali Pasha came to power in Ioánnina in 1788. He was an upstart from a poor family, a cruel despot with a conflicting personality. It was under his domination that Epirus became the most important province of the Ottoman Empire. In 1820, Ali Pasha attempted to found a state which was independent of the Sublime Porte. When Ioánnina was besieged by the troops of Hursit Pasha, Ali Pasha and Vassiliki, his mistress, fled to the monastery of Ágios Panteleímon on the island in the lake of Ioánnina, where he was killed in January 1822. Despite the tyranny, the town rapidly continued to develop and enjoyed a cultural and economic heyday. During the Turkish period, Ioánnina was one of the centres of Greek spiritual life and had

some famous schools. Turkish rule continued until 1913.

Ágios Athanásios: This 19C cathedral has a beautiful iconostasis. The tomb of Ágios Georgios of Ioánnina is to be found here. He died a martyr on 17 January 1833.

Fortress: The walls date from the 11C and have been rebuilt several times.

Aslan Pasha Mosque (built 1618): Since 1933 it has been used as a *museum of popular art (dimotikon)* with very beautiful historical, folklore and archaeological collections. Underneath the mosque there are catacombs and prisons in which many resistance fighters died a martyr's death under Turkish rule. The Koranic school, the mausoleum of Aslan Pasha, and the sundial, are in the courtyard.

Fetiche Pasha Mosque: The tomb of Ali Pasha survives in the courtyard.

Archaeological Museum (in the centre of the town): Various finds from the ancient towns of Epirus (Dodóni, Vítsa, Nekromanteíon and others) are on display in room A. There are ancient Greek and Roman reliefs in room B. Rooms C and E are used as an art gallery. The Byzantine and late Byzantine finds are exhibited in room D.

Turistikon Peripteron (in the S. of the town): Works of popular art are exhibited in a hall here.

Association of Epirot Studies *(Etairía Ipirotikon Meletón):* Located in the town centre, with a library and a folklore collection.

Lake Pamvotis (10–43 ft. deep, 5 miles long, 1 to 3 miles wide): It lies at the foot of the Mitsikeli range and extends to the N. of the town. It became famous through

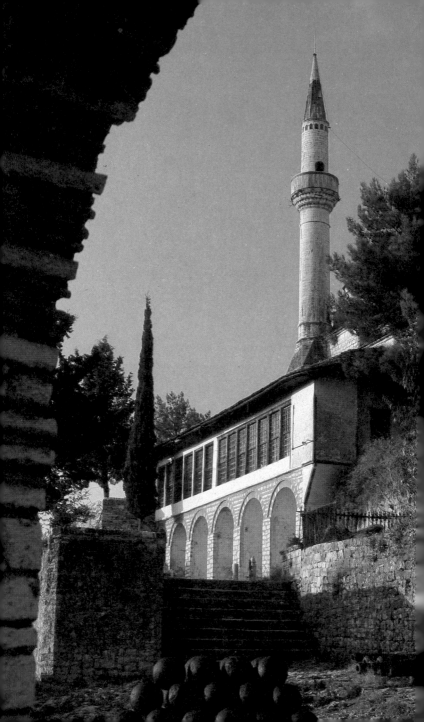

the story of Kyra Frossini, whom Ali Pasha had drowned in the lake in 1801, along with seventeen other women from Ioánnina. This episode is still sung of today in various versions of folk songs.

Environs: Island of Nisí (550 yards wide, 880 yards long): The inhabitants of the island were originally from the Máni (Peloponnese), settling here in the 17C. The island is much frequented for its famous monasteries and the beautiful scenery.

Ágios Ioánnis Prodromos: This monastery was built by the brothers Apsarades in 1506. Underneath the altar is a subterranean corridor leading to the lake. *Ágios Panteleímon* (17C): This church is a small basilica (one nave, two aisles) with a carved wooden templon. Nearby is the house in which Ali Pasha was killed. Today it is used as a historical museum. *Ágios Nikólaos Philanthropinon* (or *Spanú*): The monastery was built in 1292. The church is a single-aisled basilica with a narthex on three sides. On the SW wall of the narthex there are 16C pictures of ancient thinkers (from the left: Plato, Apollonius, Solon, Aristotle, Plutarch, Thucydides, Kheilon). *Ágios Nikólaos Díliu* (11C): This is the oldest monastery on the island, with frescos and inscriptions from the 15C. *Agia Eleusis* (16C): A single-aisled basilica with wall paintings. **Pérama** (4 km. NE): One of the most beautiful stalactite caves in Europe (daily tours lasting 45 min.). **Kastrítsa** (14 km. SE): The town of Tékmon stood here in ancient times (4C BC). There are two caves on the hill. One is Palaeolithic, the other Neolithic. The finds discovered during excavations indicate that the caves of Kastrítsa were inhabited between 22000 and 9000 BC. The finds are stone tools which are exhibited in hall A of the museum of Ioánnina. **Zítsa** (28 km. NW): Beautiful mountain village whose spar-

◁ *Ioánnina, Aslan Pasha Mosque*

kling wine is known far and wide. The 14C monastery of *Prophitis Ilias* has a rich library. Lord Byron stayed in the monastery for a considerable period in 1806. **Moní Vellá** (32 km. NW): Vellá was an old town on a hill on the bank of the river Kalamas (1 km. SW of the monastery). It was at its zenith under the Byzantines. In the 18C, Vellá was only a small village. Today the monastery of Moní Vellá, with its beautiful wall paintings, is to be found here. There are interesting pictures of ancient philosophers (Thucydides, Aristotle, Xenophon, Plato). **Kónitsa** (64 km. N.): Pouqueville claims that Kónitsa stands on the site of the ancient town of *Ekatómpedon*, which was known as *Glavinítsa* in Byzantine times. Under Turkish domination, Kónitsa was an important trading centre between Albania and Macedonia. The *Mosque of Sultan Suleiman* has survived, as has a Venetian *castle*. Outside Kónitsa there is an old bridge across the river Aoos. This is the largest and highest stone bridge in Greece.

Íos/Ios (I)/ΙΟΣ
Cyclades/Aegean Islands   p.300□L 11

This small mountainous island (40 sq. miles, about 1300 inhabitants) is half way from Naxos to Thíra: together with the neighbouring islands of Síkinos and Folégandros, it forms the S. row of islands extending from E. to W. in the Cyclades. The island only played a small role in ancient times. It was part of the Duchy of Naxos in the Middle Ages, and was conquered by the Turks in 1537. Albanians settled on the island in the 17&18C.

Íos/Ios (also *Khóra*, 'town'): The main town is in the W. of the island, some 2 km. above the port of *Órmos Íu*. Its charm derives from its pretty little churches and picturesque *windmills*. Near the harbour is the beautiful church of *Agia Irini* (St.Irene), with a dome and bell towers dating from the 18C. Excavations of the Cycladic culture are to be found near *Manganári* to the S. To the E. are the ruins of the 14C Venetian castle of *Katákorfa* (Crispo). *Profítis Ilias* (2,340 ft.), the highest mountain in the island with a monastery of the same name, is also here. Nearby, to the NE, is the alleged *tomb of Homer,* who is said to have died here.

Environs: Some 6 km. W. of Ios is the small island of *Síkinos* (15 sq. miles, 330 inhabitants), with the port of *Aloprónia* in the SE and the island's main village, *Khorió* ('village'), a charming Cycladic village situated on a hill with a square 14C *kastro*. Nearby (4 km. W.), is the 5C church of *Episkopi* (Panagia), which dates back to a cult building from the 2C BC (popularly known as *Naos Apollonos,* 'Temple of Apollo'). Only scant remains, to be found near *Agía Marína* (to the W.), still survive of the ancient town. The barren little marble island of *Folégandros* (map p.298 □ K 11) is 6 miles SW of Síkinos. Settled by Dorians in ancient times, it was used as a place of banish-

ment by the Romans. Inland from the port of *Karavostásis* (in the SE) is the romantic main town of *Folégandros* (also known as *Khóra*, 'village'), which is typical of the islands in its arrangement, with the medieval *kastro* (13C) in the centre. Further E. are the ruins of the Venetian castle of *Palaiokastro* (13&14C). The ancient town, of which only some slight traces survive, lay between these two. Some parts of the remains are in the *Panagia church.*

Iráklion/Herakleion/ ΗΡΑΚΛΕΙΟΝ
Iráklion/Crete   p.298□H 14

Iráklion, with its 85,000 inhabitants, is the largest town in Crete and since 1971 has once again been its capital. It stands in the middle of the N. coast of the island. The Arabs founded the town in AD 824, giving it the name Rabd-el-Kandak. The Byzantines took it in 941. It 1204 it fell to Venice and was named *Candia*. The Cretans constantly struggled against the Venetian oc-

Íos (Ios), view of the island's capital

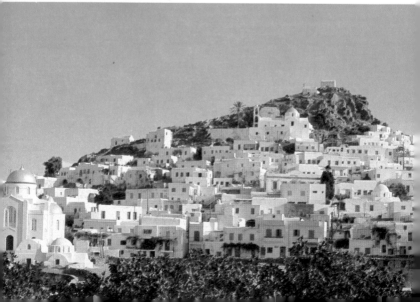

cupation and, in an insurrection in 1274, murdered the Duke of Crete and many of his followers. In 1458–60 mainland Greeks who had fled to Crete rebelled. The Venetians expanded the town into a strong fortress from 1492 onwards. The defensive walls were reinforced by Michele Sammicheli, the Venetian military architect, in 1526. In 1648 the Turks first besieged the town, which they had tried in vain to storm several times. In 1660, 1668 and 1669, troops were sent from France to support Candia. Finally, on 5 September 1669, the town was, in spite of everything, forced to surrender to the Turks, who had lost over 100,000 men during the siege. Candia was given the name of *Megalo Kastro* under Turkish rule. It declined in importance, the harbour silted up, and Khaniá became the capital of Crete. In 1913, after the union with Greece, the town was named *Herakleion* (in modern Greek 'Iráklion'), after an ancient port nearby. The town developed a new impetus, and despite the earthquake in 1926 and the destruction and occupation during World War 2, it has continually gained in importance, especially as a result of tourism (Iráklion has a harbour and an airport).

Cathedral of Ágios Minas: This 19C neo-Byzantine cathedral is in the centre of the town. In the right transept there are four icons by Michael Damaskinos, who is regarded as El Greco's teacher.

Ágios Minas and **Agia Ekaterini:** Near the cathedral are the 18C church of Ágios Minas and the small 17C **Agia Ekaterini**. The latter was built as early as 1555 and was formerly part of the Sinai monastery. Once a centre of learning, it had a painting school whose pupils included Damaskinos and El Greco. In the 16C a second church was associated with it but this later became a mosque. Today, Agia Ekaterini is an *icon museum*. The late Byzantine paintings and five icons by Damaskinos are outstanding.

Ágios Markos: The church of Ágios Markos is by the Morosini fountain, on the way to the Venetian port. Originally built

Iráklion, view of the modern town

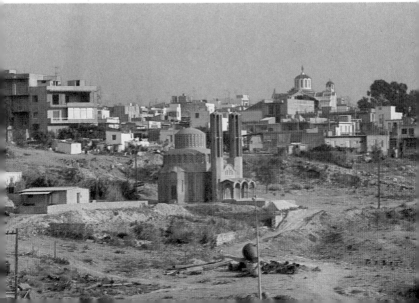

Iráklion, Archaeological Museum: Ground Floor:

Room I: Neolithic and Prepalatial Period till around 2000 BC (e.g. finds from the Eileithya Cave).

Room II: Middle Minoan Protopalatial Period, 2000 – 1700 BC (e.g. pottery from Mália and Knossós, masks from Týlissos).

Room III: Protopalatial Period, 2000 – 1700 BC (mostly finds from the First Palace of Phaistós, e.g. Phaistos Disk).

Room IV: Neopalatial Period, 1700 – 1400 BC (finds from the palaces of Phaistós, Knossós and Mália, e.g. snake goddesses, bull's head from Knossós, the famous ivory acrobat and the gaming table from Knossós).

Room V: Finds from the Neopalatial Period of the Late Minoan Age (1450 – 1400 BC) from the Palace of Knossós.

Room VI: Postpalatial Period (1400 – 1100 BC), mostly tomb finds from necropoles in the vicinity of Knossós and Phaistós.

Room VII: Neopalatial Period (1700 – 1400 BC), finds from central Crete, e.g. rhyton and the Chieftain Cup from Agía Triáda.

Room VIII: Neopalatial Period (1700 – 1400 BC), finds from the Palace of Káto Z kros, e.g. steatite sacrificial drinking vessel.

Room IX: Neopalatial Period (1700 – 1400 BC), with finds E. Crete.

Room X: Postpalatial Period (1400 – 1100 BC), finds from central and E. Crete.

Room XI: Post-Minoan and Geometric Period (1100 – 650 BC), finds from various locations on the island during the time of the Dorian conquest, e.g. vases and pottery from the shrine of Karphi.

Room XII: Geometric and Orientalizing Period (800 – 600 BC), finds from central Crete, e.g. bronzes from the Idaian Cave.

Room XIII: Room of the Sarcophagi. Minoan terracotta sarcophagi (1400 – 1100 BC), e.g. sarcophagus from Agía Triáda.

Upper Floor: Frescos from Minoan palaces and villas.

Room XIV: Neopalatial Period (1700 – 1400 BC), frescos from central and E. Crete, e.g. 'The Procession', 'Prince of the Lillies', 'The Blue Ladies' and 'The Dolphins' from the Palace of Knossós. In the middle of the room is a painted sarcophagus from Agía Triáda.

Room XV: Neopalatial Period (1700 – 1400 BC). Frescos from Knossós and Týlissos, e.g. 'La Parisienne' from Knossós.

Room XVI: Neopalatial Period (1700 – 1400 BC). Smaller frescos, e.g. 'The Saffron Gatherer'.

Room XVII: Giamalakis Collection, finds from Minoan, Greek, Roman and Byzantine periods.

Room XVIII: Archaic, Hellenistic and Roman periods (700 – 400 BC), minor works.

The adjoining gallery then leads back down to two more rooms on the Ground Floor:

Room XIX: Archaic Monumental Art (700–550 BC), e.g. relief of the archaic Temple of Górtyna and frieze of the Riders from Rhizenia.

Room XX: Sculptures from the Greek, Hellenistic and Roman epochs (5 and 4C BC).

Iráklion, Venetian harbour with the old Arsenal

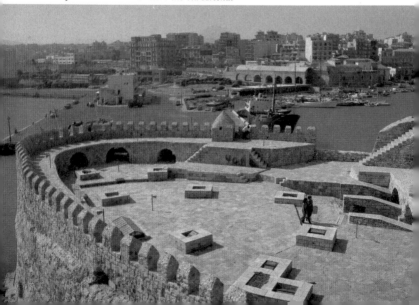

in 1239, it was formerly used as a Roman Catholic church and was rebuilt by the Venetians after two earthquakes (1303 and 1508). The Turks transformed the church into a mosque. It later housed a bank and finally served as a hall for lectures and concerts. It too houses an *icon museum* at present, which exhibits copies of 13&14C Byzantine frescos from various Cretan churches, some of them being in Kritsa, Potamiés, Avdú, Ágios, Vassílios, Selniou and Mesklá.

Ágios Titos: Near the Loggia is the church of Ágios Titos, named after Titus, the companion of the Apostle Paul. Paul came to Crete in AD 59 in order to establish Christianity, and installed Titus as the island's first bishop. The relics of St.Titus are preserved in the church. Originally Byzantine, the church was rebuilt after two earthquakes in 1446 and 1508. Further rebuilding became necessary in 1577 after a fire in 1544. The Turks later used the church as a mosque. It had to be rebuilt once again after another earthquake in 1856.

Loggia: The former exchange of the Venetian traders is between Ágios Markos and Ágios Titos and was rebuilt after being destroyed in World War 2. This two-storeyed building dating from 1628 has Doric columns on the ground floor and Ionic ones on the first floor.

Sagredo Fountain: The fountain at the NE corner of the loggia was built in 1602.

Morosini Fountain (near Ágios Markos): This fountain was built in 1628 under Morosini, the Venetian governor. The eight basins are decorated with reliefs. Four lions, which bear the upper basin, are probably from an older, 14C fountain. Morosini was also responsible for supplying Iráklion with water by means of an aqueduct from Mt.Yuktas.

Bembo Fountain/San Salvatore Fountain: Some 220 yards S. of the cathedral is a restored Renaissance fountain. The marble basin was probably an ancient sarcophagus. The headless Roman statue

Iráklion, Venetian fortress (Kastell Koules)

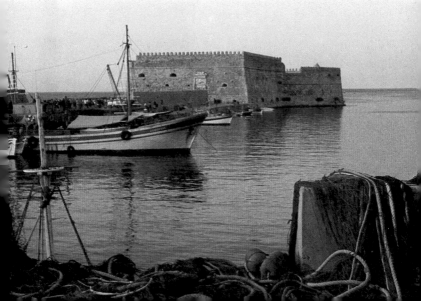

Iráklion, Morosini Fountain (detail) ▷

standing between four columns comes from Ierápetra.

Venetian walls: The entire old town is still surrounded by the massive Venetian walls. The Ágios Georgios gate to the E., with its image of the Saint and the inscription dating from 1565, is especially noteworthy, as is the particularly beautiful Gesú gate (Kainúria gate) in the SE, with stone-carvings and inscriptions dating from 1567 and 1587. The Martinengo bastion, including the tomb of the famous Cretan writer Nikos Kazantzakis, who came from Iráklion and died in Freiburg in 1957, is in the extreme S. His tomb bears the following inscription: 'I do not hope for anything, I am free.' From here there is a clear view of the massive ramparts and gates, and a fine vista of the Yuktas mountains. To the W. is the Pantocrator gate, whose large arch dates from the 20C, while the smaller arch on the N. side is from 1567.

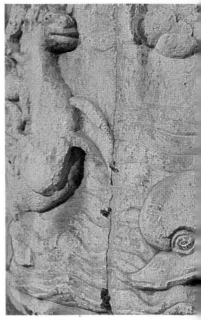

Venetian harbour: In the E. of the town, to the W. of the New Harbour, we find the Old Harbour which dates from 1303 and still has a late-13C mole to the E. The main section of this complex dates from 1523–40.

Venetian fortress: The 16C Venetian fortress (Castle Koules) guards the entrance to the harbour from the sea, and it still has beautiful winged lions of St. Mark on its W. and N. façades. The base of a minaret survives from the Turkish period.

Historical museum: The Historical and Ethnographical Museum of Crete is near the mole in the N. of the town, by the Leoforos Makariou promenade. The museum's exhibits range from early Chris-

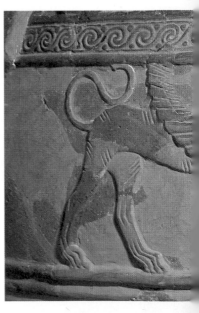

Detail of a vase (Arch. Mus.) ▷

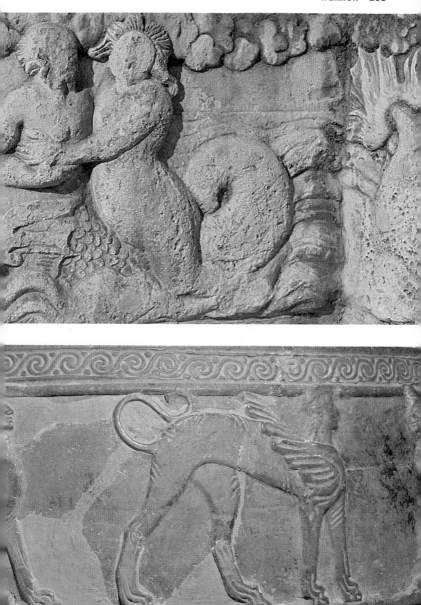

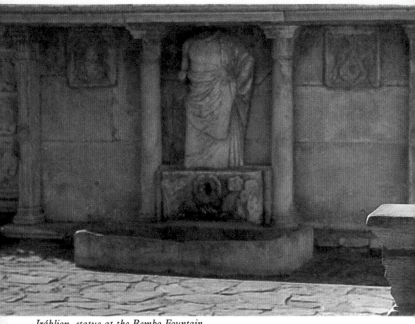

Iráklion, statue at the Bembo Fountain

tian times to the present: parts of ships, architectural fragments, parts of windows and fountains, tombstones, sculptures, coats-of-arms, inscriptions and manuscripts, cult relics, frescos, jewels, ceramics, garments, coins, seals, folk art, and an exhibition in memory of Nikos Kasantzakis.

Archaeological museum (AMI)/Arkhaiologikó Musio: To the S. of the harbour, near the Sabbionera bastion, is one of the most important museums of its kind, the showpiece of Europe's first culture pure and simple. Anyone interested in the independent beginnings of Europe, fed by only a few Asian or African influences and by art at a time long before the archaic Greek influences arrived, must visit this museum. Indeed it is best to do so before visiting the ruins of Knossós, Mália,

Phaistós and Agia Triáda, because the museum will provide an idea of the original size and perfection of the ruins. It is in the museum that the treasures of Crete are to be found.

In the second half of the 19C, some Cretans endeavoured to preserve the ancient treasures of their country. The 'Association of the Friends of Culture' was founded in Iráklion in 1878. With the agreement of the Turkish government of the time, an official archaeological body was established in 1883 and endeavoured to preserve and salvage the country's historical and archaeological property. The destruction of the ancient architectural monuments was finally halted. Purchases were made and foreign researchers were granted permission to carry out excavations. The result of this was a collection which was initially housed in the cathedral of Ágios Minas.

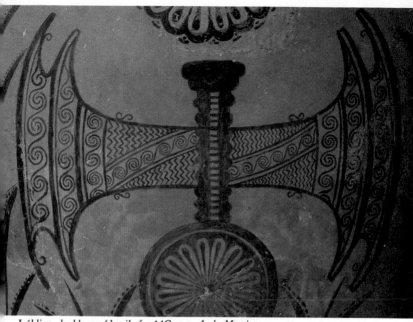

Iráklion, double axe (detail of a 14C vase, Arch. Mus.)

After the Turks had left Crete, the extent of the excavations and collections increased considerably. In 1904 it was deemed necessary to start building a museum in which large numbers of finds could be housed. After the earthquakes of 1911, 1926, 1930 and 1935, work on building the present museum was begun by the initiative of the archaeologist Sp. Marinátos in 1937. The collection was kept in cellars during World War 2 and went on show again in 1951, having suffered little damage. It has been systematically organized since 1952 and is open to the public. The museum building was expanded in 1964 and almost 70 per cent of all the Minoan finds can be seen here.

Gallery of folk art: The folk art gallery of Eva and Helmut Grimm, which is mainly devoted to 19C Cretan folk art, has an interesting collection of richly patterned woven wall tapestries. Extremely beautiful, they sometimes appear almost Minoan.

Environs: Iráklion provides an ideal starting point for a trip round Crete. Knossós (q.v.) is only 5 km. SE, and Týlissos, Ámnissos (q.v.), with the Eileithya cave (q.v.), are less than 30 km. distant. **Phódele/Fódele:** Phódele, in a charming location in a gorge W. of Iráklion, is the birthplace of El Greco, Crete's most celebrated painter, who became famous in Spain and died there. However, in his home town he grew up under the name of Domenikos Theotokopoulos and also learned the art of painting. The house where El Greco was born is near the 12C Panagia church. **Savathianóu:** 17 km. from Iráklion in the direction of Phódele a small side road branches off and runs for 4 km. to the Savathianóu convent. Some very fine, lively icons of an earthen colour are on display in the small rock church of Ágios Savos (1741).

Isthmus of Corinth
Corinth/Peloponnese   p.294□G 9

The isthmus of Corinth is the only connection between the mainland and the Peloponnese. Even in antiquity there were plans to dig through the isthmus, but these were never ventured upon. In AD 40, Caligula sent some engineers to the site. However, they were disuaded by Egyptian engineers, who claimed that the sea level in the Gulf of Corinth was higher than that in the Saronic Gulf and that the island of Aegina would thus inevitably be flooded. Nero made an attempt in AD 67 with several thousand workers who cut in from both sides at the narrowest point. The plan was abandoned when Nero died. It was not until 1882 that the work was resumed and it was completed in 1893.

The overall length of the canal is 4 miles, the width 82 ft. and the depth 26 ft. The remains of the ancient *Diolkos* were found during excavations in 1956. This was the 10–16 ft. wide paved road along which the boats were pulled on carts from one gulf to the other. Estimates of the date when the Diolkos was built vary between the 7C and 5C BC.

Environs: Ísthmia (S. of the isthmus of Corinth near the village of Kyrá-Vrísi). The Isthmian Games were held every two years from 582 BC onwards near the shrine of Poseidon in honour of a dead hero, Palaimon. Poseidon was thought to be the founder, but so too was the Attic hero Theseus. From AD 228 onwards, Romans were also allowed to take part in the Games. *Shrine of Poseidon:* The oldest ex-

cavated foundations are part of a 7C BC temple, which had columns of wood. To the E. of the temple are the remains of an *altar* where various consecration gifts from the archaic period were found. In about the mid 5C the old temple was replaced by a peripteros with 6 x 13 columns. In the Corinthian War in 390 BC, the temple burned down, but was rebuilt and survived until Corinth was devastated (AD 146). In 44 BC, when Corinth was rebuilt, so too was the Temple of Poseidon. It was enclosed by a *peribolos* whose dimensions changed over the years. The *Palaimonion* was built on the site of the start line of the old stadium in the Roman period when that stadium was no longer in use. It is a monopteros temple which is depicted on coins from Corinth from the imperial period. Stairs on the E. side led to the adyton below the temple, which was intended for the cult of Palaimon. The *theatre*, NE of the shrine, was built in the early 4C BC and extended in the late 4C. Further rebuilding was carried out under Nero on the occasion of the Games in AD 66. Some of the rows of seats, and also the skene and proskenion from the 4C, have survived. *Stadium:* The paved starting line, at which 16 contestants could start, has survived. A little way to the S. of this is the start line of a second, Hellenistic stadium (the overall length of the stadium is 594 ft.). To the N. of the shrine are some Roman *baths* which border on the wall *(Hexamilion)* that ran 40 km. and connected Corinth with the port of Kenchreai. To the E. of the baths is the *fortress of Justinian* (6C AD), which was built from ancient building materials. The S. gate was flanked by two octagonal towers. There are numerous excavation finds in the *museum* of Ísthmia, including glass mosaics with a reproduction of the harbour of Kenchreai, a perirrhanterion (holy-water stoup) from the Temple of Poseidon (7C) and others. **Kenchreai:** This was once the Eastern port of Corinth and appeared on Corinthian coins. It had two moles which are today almost covered by water. The foundations of a Hellenistic temple of Isis were discovered on the S. mole, and further out into the sea those of an early Christian basilica are to be found. On the N. mole are the ruins of a tower and the foundations of buildings from the Roman and early Christian periods. **Bath of Helena** (*Lutron Elenis,* 2 km. from Kenchreai). This is on the site of the ancient *Solygeia* with some remains of an early archaic temple.

Itéa/ITEA
Fokis/Central Greece   p.294□F 8

The harbour of Itéa ('pastures') is to be found on the edge of the olive-groves of the Holy Plain below Delphi. It has some 3,000 inhabitants. The remains of the mole of the ancient town of *Kírra* are at the edge of the town to the SE. The town where the pilgrim ships travelling to Delphi landed was destroyed in *c.* 590 BC (1st Holy War) and was abandoned. The quiet Gulf of Itéa is also known as the Krisaian Gulf, a name which it takes from *Krísa*, a form of Kírra.

Environs: Some 5 km. further inland, below Delphi, is the small village of **Krisó** (also: *Khrysó*). It was settled from the early Helladic period and has some remains of *Mycenaen walls*. It takes its name from the ancient town of *Krísa* (a form of *Kírra*), which was destroyed in *c.* 590 BC. Below Krisó, in the valley of Plístos (Pleistos), was the *hippodrome,* where the famous chariot races were organized during the Pythian Games (the precise site has not been discovered). On the bare W. coast of the Gulf of Itéa (20 km. SW) is the charming little harbour of **Galaxídi(on)** with a few traces of the ancient settlement of *Oiántheia* (remains of ramparts). This town of shipbuilders and sailors played a part in the War of Liberation of 1821 (naval base). The 13C Byzantine church of *Ágios Sotir* (church of the Saviour) with remains of wall paintings and reliefs in the apse, 3 km. outside the town. The small *museum* contains finds and historical documents on the history of the town. The remnants of the

Iráklion, La Parisienne (Arch. Mus.)

Isthmus of Corinth

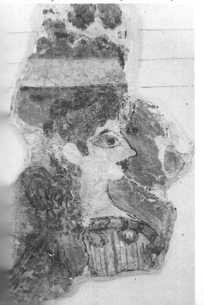

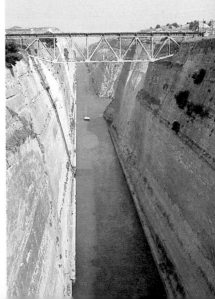

town of *Tolophón* are near to *Eratiní* (36 km. SW) and have a rather well-preserved ancient *fortress*.

Itháki/Ithaka (I)/IΘAKH
Ionian Islands   p.294□C 7/8

The rocky island (38 sq. miles, about 5,000 inhabitants) is 15 miles long and only 660 yards wide in the middle, at the isthmus of Aetos ('Eagle's Isthmus'). To the W., it is separated from the neighbouring island of Kefallinia by a strait only 1 to 2.5 miles wide.

History: In Homer's 'Odyssey', the hero Odysseus is the king of Ithaka and the neighbouring islands (Sami, Dulikhion, Zakynthos). Excavations of Mycenean sites (at Pelikáta, Stavrós, Pólis, Frikés and on Mt.Aetos) seem to confirm this statement. From the beginning, the history of Ithaka was closely associated with that of its neighbouring island of Kefallinía. The island was almost deserted under the Turks and it was not until the 16C that it was repopulated by the Venetians.

Vathý ('Depth'): The main town of the island (about 2,500 inhabitants) is a charming natural harbour located on the deeply indented Molos bay, with the remains of a Venetian *castle*. The town was badly damaged by the earthquake of 1953. A small *museum* contains an interesting collection of Mycenean vases.
Environs: The interesting nymph's grotto of *Marmarospilia* 3 km. SW of Vathý is said to be the cave in which Odysseus concealed his treasures ('Odyssey', XIII). The grotto is probably an old *nymph's shrine.* Finds from the 9&8C BC were made here. *Fountain of Arethusa* (Perapigadi): Some 10 km. S. of Vathý. The spring which is still flowing today, and the nearby 'raven's rock' *(Korakas),* are the most easily located of those places in Ithaka which are mentioned in the Odyssey. Nearby is the *Marathia* plateau (S. tip of the island) where the pigsties of Eumaios were to be found ('Odyssey', XIV). *Mt.Aetos* ('Eagle mountain', 6 km. W.): The remains of the ancient town of *Alalkomenaí* are on the peak of this mountain (1, 250 ft.) near the isthmus. Some traces of the *rampart* with polygonal masonry (7C), of the small *acropolis* and of the houses of the lower town still survive. Remains of a Corinthian shrine and of a tower dating from the 5C BC stand on the slope. Aetos is popularly referred to as the 'Mountain of Odysseus' (Kástro Odysséa). *Katharón Monastery* (8 km. N.) on Mt.Neritos (1,950 ft.) with a splendid view of the whole island and the Ionian Sea. The church of *Anogí* (15 km. NW), with 17C frescos, is also worth seeing. It is at present thought that the site of the Mycenean Ithaka is near the village of *Stavrós* ('Cross', 20 km. NW). Near *Pelikáta* (1 km. N.) the British School uncovered some remains of a *settlement* which was probably founded in *c.* 2200 BC and which was occupied until Mycenean times. There are also some Hellenistic tombs. The palace (acropolis) of Odysseus is most likely to have been here. The finds of Pelikáta can be inspected in the small *Odysseus Museum* of Stavrós (pottery, including a clay shard bearing the inscription 'To Odysseus' and dating from the 2C BC). Below Stavrós is the ancient port of *Pólis*, whose name is reminiscent of the Homeric capital of the island. The remains of a sunken town may be seen here below the surface of the sea. On the W. shore of Pólis there was an important *cult grotto* which was visited from the Mycenean period until the 1C BC (Geometric bronze finds in the museum of Stavrós). The church of *Exogi* (22 km. N.) with medieval frescos. Nearby is the *chapel of Ágios Athanasios,* which was built on the square base of an ancient tower (6C), referred to popularly as the 'School of Homer'.

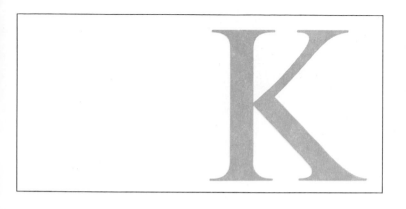

K

Kaisarianí/ΚΑΙΣΑΡΙΑΝΗ
Attica/Central Greece   p.296☐H 9

Monastery: Some 7 km. SE of Athens is the famous monastery church of Kaisarianí, which is situated on the slopes of Mt.Hymettos (now Ymittos) among plane trees, cypresses and pines. Its name comes from the nearby *spring of Kaisarianí Pigí* ('royal spring'), whose water the Emperor Hadrian conducted down to Athens in the 2C AD. The mouth of the spring, which is in the shape of a ram's head, has been preserved, and dates from the 6C BC. This was the site of a temple of Aphrodite, of which there are no remains. An early Christian *basilica* was built on the site of the temple in the 5C, and there are some fragments from it in the monastery courtyard; around 1000 the present *Panagia Kaisarianí* was built: it is a domed cross-

Kaisarianí, monastery garden, walk

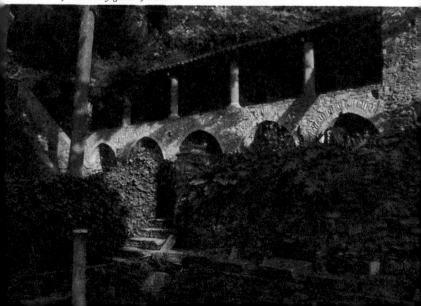

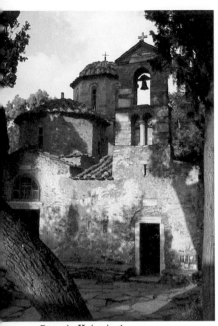

Panagía Kaisarianí

in-square church with four supporting columns bearing ancient Ionic capitals. The cornice is twice as high and the dome four times as high as the distance between the columns, which are based on ancient models. The *narthex* has a flat dome and the *parekklésion* (right) with *bell tower* is 17C. The columns with Ionic capitals in front of the entrance were part of the old temple of Aphrodite.

Wall paintings: Apart from those in the narthex, the interesting wall paintings in the church date from the 16C, and are the work of a monk of the Macedonian School from Mt.Athos. In the *dome* is Christ *Pantocrator,* and beneath him the *Prophets* and four *Evangelists.* In the *vault of the apse* is the *Mother of God (Panagía Theotókos)* as the Queen of Heaven with the archangels *Michael* and *Gabriel.* Underneath is *Christ as High Priest* with the Eucharist, and the orthodox teachers Chrysostom, Basil and Gregory. Also depicted is the *life of Jesus,* beginning in the S. of the sanctuary: birth, presentation in the temple, baptism, annunciation, raising of Lazarus, entry into Jerusalem, last supper, resurrection of the dead, mourning of Christ, doubting Thomas, ascension and descent of the Holy Ghost. The wall paintings in the *narthex* are by the Peloponnesian artist Ioánnis Ypatos and date from 1682 (according to the inscription over the door); they depict the *life of Mary* and seven *allegories.* In the *side chapel,* which is dedicated to St. Antony, is a 14C *Madonna.*

Also worth seeing: Near the church (left from the entrance of the monastery courtyard) are the remnants of a *bath house* from the 5C, constructed along Roman lines. It consists of a sweat bath (sudatorium) with a warm air hypocaust, a central room with a vaulted dome for the warm bath (caldarium) and a cold bath (frigidarium) with the *original floor* still preserved. Near the bath house is a *cell building* and, to the W. of the courtyard, a *refectory* with pointed arch-vaulting and a small apse. Nearby (some 330 yards SW) is the old *monks' cemetery* with a 17C *church of the archangels* (Taxiarchis). Also nearby are the remains of an interesting *basilica,* which had a nave and two aisles (of the same name). It was built in the 6C, rebuilt in the 10C and contains some *ancient sections.*

Environs: Some 4 km. further, half way up Mt.Ymettos (1,788 ft.), is the interesting Byzantine monastery of *Astéri* ('star monastery'), with a well-preserved monastery church dating from the 11C. It has a dome borne on four columns with ancient *capitals,* and partially damaged 16C wall paintings. The remnants of frescos in the *refectory,* which include an interesting Madonna, are 17C. The summit of *Ymettos* (3,366 ft., *c.* 18 km. from Athens): In antiquity, there was a shrine to Zeus on this spot, with a statue. There is a nearby *cave* which contains *religious remains* from the 10–6C BC, including *altar fragments*. The bee-keepers of Hymettos were well-known in antiquity, and Hymettos honey is still a delicacy. The peak of Ymettos has sparse vegetation and is now barred from public access as a military radar station, but there is a splendid view over Attica and the Saronic Gulf from just below the peak. The plateau extends for over 18 km. from the NW to NE, and is separated by the Pirnari ravine.

The ancient *stone quarries* are situated S. of Kaisarianí (30 minutes by foot) by the old *Karyes monastery* below the Kakorevma gulley. Between the villages of Kará, Trachónes and Chasáni are a number of remains of old *grave sites*.

Kalabáka/Kalambáka/ ΚΑΛΑΜΠΑΚΑ
Tríkala/Thessaly   p.290□E 5

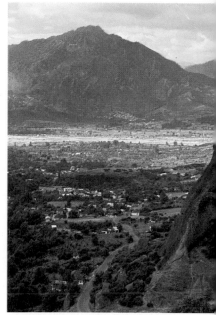

Kalabáka, Pinios valley

This is a small inland town with some 6,000 inhabitants; its names are Turkish, and it is situated on the N. edge of the plain of Thessaly under the strange rocks of Meteora. Behind it is the Pindos mountain range, from which the Pinios river (Peneios in antiquity) emerges. It is on the site of the ancient town of *Aigínion*, which was mentioned by Livy. In the Middle Ages it was a bishop's seat, and was known as *Stági* or *Stágus*.

Mitropolis Church: This Byzantine church dates from the 10&11C and was restored under Emperor Andronikos Palaiologos in 1309.

In the *apse* are the remains of the original 11C *mosaic pavement*, and the priests' *sýnthronon*. There are some interesting *decorations* on the altar, in the marble *ambo* and the nave. On the S. wall of the ambo are some ancient *funerary stele*. The narthex

is 16C, and the *wall paintings* are by Neofytos (Cretan School); they date from 1573 and depict the *Crucifixion* and the *Ascension of Elijah*.

Environs: On the **Kastro Hill**, which lies 1 km. N., are the remains of the ancient acropolis of *Aigínon*. The *Metéora monasteries* (see entry) can be visited from the small village of **Kastráki**.

Kalamáta/ΚΑΛΑΜΑΤΑ
Messenia/Peloponnese   p.298□E 11

Main town of the district of Messenia and with a population of 39,000, this is the most important port in the Peloponnese. The present town is built on the site of the old Homeric *Pharaí* or *Pheraí*, which was one of Menelaus's towns, and was offered to Achilles along with six others in an attempt to appease his wrath.

History: In 1208 *Kastro Chalemate* was mentioned in the Chronicle of the Fourth Crusade, which was written by Geoffroy de Villehardouin. Geoffroy and his followers ruled Kalamáta and the surrounding area, which was then known as Achaea, for over a century. In 1587 Marie de Bourbon acquired the city; it had been in the hands of the Despots of Mystrás from 1430, and the Turks from 1460. From 1685–1715 Kalamáta was under Venetian rule, and later again under the Turks, until 1827 when it was won back after the naval battle of Navarino.

Kastro: This was built by Villehardouin in 1208 on the site of a Mycenean acropolis and a Byzantine fortress. There is a Lion of St. Mark over the entrance.

Benaki Museum: A fine collection of excavated finds from various regions of Messenia.

Picture gallery: 350 works by Greek and foreign painters.

Also worth seeing: The churches of *Agioi Apostoloi* (10C) and *Ágios Charalambos* (12C) are in the graveyard directly beneath the Church of the Assumption.

Environs: Akovítika (2 km.) has some Mycenean tombs and **Peristeriá** has a temple to Apollo. **Thuría** (8 km. N.): 5 km. away from the modern village are the remains of the old town of the same name, which was destroyed by the Spartans and rebuilt by Epameinondas. **Andrúsa** (11 km. NW): This was an important Peloponnesian trading centre in the Middle Ages; interesting places to visit include the Frankish *castle*, the 12C *Andromonastiro monastery* and the monastery

at *Samarína*, which was built on the foundations of an ancient temple and includes traces of wall paintings.

Kalávryta / ΚΑΛΑΒΡΥΤΑ
Achaia / Peloponnese   p.294 □ E 8

This is a small resort with some 2,000 inhabitants at an altitude of 2,296 ft. on the edge of the rugged Chelmos range, which rises to 7,546 ft. This was the site of the ancient city of *Kýthaina*, which was destroyed in 220 BC but flourished again under Hadrian.

Necropolis: To the SE is *Salména*, with the remains of an ancient necropolis.

Kastro Tremolo: This was built by the Franks in the 13C on a steep cliff to the NE (3,904 ft. high); it was once a massive castle, which served as the seat of the barony of Tremouille, but it is now a ruin.

Environs: The **Agía Lávra** monastery is some 7 km. to the SW; it was founded as a daughter monastery to the one on Mt. Athos in 961 and is now the national shrine for the Greek War of Liberation of 1821. This is where Archbishop Germanós of Patras is said to have given the signal to attack the Turks on the 25 March 1821 (25 March is now a national holiday in Greece). The monastery was destroyed on several occasions (by Ibrahim Pasha in 1826; by the Germans in 1943, because of its support for the partisans) and has since been rebuilt. The 17C cross-in-square church of the *Kimisis* (Dormition of the Virgin) is interesting. There is a small *monastery museum* in the treasury, which contains 11&12C manuscripts, the cover of an Evangelistary of Catherine the Great, and mementoes of the War of Liberation. Near to the mountain village of **Méga Spílaion** (11 km. N.), in the impressive, wooded

Vuraikos gorge, is the old monastery of *Mega Spilaion* ('great cave'), which was supposedly founded in the 8C by carving a hole in the precipitous cliff (hence the name). It is here that the legend of Euphrosyne ('Joy'), the devout shepherdess with royal blood, originated with a miracleworking *icon of the Virgin*, which still survives. The *monastery* was the object of pilgrimages and, during the Middle Ages, was one of the richest monasteries in the land. It was destroyed three times by fire (1400, 1640 and 1934) and rebuilt each time. The cave church of the *Panagía Chrysospiliotissa* ('Mother of God in the Gold Cave') is interesting, with a miraculous 8 or 9C wax icon (attributed to the apostle Luke). There is a *door* with *reliefs* in silvered copper, and numerous *reliquaries* and *plaques*. The inlaid *floor*, with images of a royal eagle, sun, moon and stars dates from the 17C. The *treasury* houses the skull of St.Euphrosyne in a silver reliquary shrine, and also the skull of St. Theodore. The refectory, the bakery, the gallery running along the façade with cells opening off it and the library are all interesting, although unfortunately the majority of the manuscripts have been burnt or otherwise lost. The old wine cellars in the lower grotto contain 20,000 litre bottles. Nearby, by the village of **Sólos** (about 6 hours on foot) in the Chelmos massif, is the small mountain waterfall of the *Styx* (today known as the *Mavronero* or 'black water'). This stream and waterfall played an important role in ancient mythology as the River of the Underworld (River of the Dead); there was another Underworld River, the Acheron in Epiros. Some 30 km. W. of Kalávryta is the small mountain village of **Káto Vlasía**, with a medieval monastery of the same name. From this point there is a climb up to the Erimanthos massif (7,290 ft.) to the SW. *C.* 3 km. NW of Káto Vlasia are the remains of the ancient town of **Leóntion**, which was excavated in 1958. The *NE door*

and other sections of the *theatre*, which was built in the 4C BC, have survived; it has rows of seats, parodoi and a skene support.

Kálymnos/Kalymnos (I)/
ΚΑΛΥΜΝΟΣ
East Aegean Islands (Dodecanese)/
Aegean Islands   p.300☐N/O 10/11

This island is famous for its sponges; it is 43 sq. miles in area, has a population of some 14,000 and lies between the islands of Leros (to the NW) and Kos (to the SE, 12 km. distant). It is mountainous with a sheer coastline, but its interior is fertile, and it has mineral springs and limestone caves.

History: Kalymnos has been inhabited since Neolithic times, and prehistoric tools and ceramics have been found in the grottoes; later finds are rich, and display Minoan and Mycenean influence. Around 800 BC it was colonized by Dorians from Epidavros. It was a member of the Athenian maritime leagues of 478 and 378 BC, after which its sovereignty changed regularly. During the Middle Ages it was held by the Knights Hospitallers of Rhodes, until it was captured by the Turks in 1522. From 1912 until its return to Greek sovereignty in 1948 it was under Italian rule.

Kálymnos (also known as *Pothiá*): The island's capital, it was founded around 1850 and is situated on the S. coast with a population of some 9,500. Excavations have revealed that the site has been inhabited since Neolithic and Mycenean times, especially in the *Neolithic grottoes* by the small church of *Agia Varvara*. There are some remains from an *early Christian basilica* built of ancient stone blocks (near the school), with an *apse* which is still standing; near to that is a classical *burial site*. There are traces of ancient remains in the foundations of the church of *Palia Panagia*. The churches of

Ágios Sotir and the *Christ Church* on the beach are also interesting, with a fine *iconostasis* by Chalepas and paintings by local artists (including 'Christ with God the Father' by Manglís). The *Archaeological Museum* houses an interesting collection of finds from the island from Neolithic (caves of Daskalió), Mycenean, classical (from the shrine of Apollo) and post-Byzantine times, including a torso of Asklepios, Mycenean vases, fragments of pottery, Geometric and archaic ceramics. The *town library* contains an interesting archive with some rare editions.

Other interesting island villages: 2 km. W. of the town are the ruins of the Crusader castle of *Péra Kastro (Palaiokastro)*, which includes the church of the *Panagia Chrysocheria* ('gold hand'), wih the remains of some old frescos and icons. The coat-of-arms of the 14C head of the order is on the wall. It is possible that there was an acropolis here as early as Mycenean times, as some fragmentary finds suggest. Nearby is a small church, and also some windmills. The village of *Khorió* is some 4 km. to the NW and has a population of 2,300; it was the medieval capital and citadel. The ruins of the 9–14C Byzantine-Venetian fortress of *Kastro*, with its coat-of-arms of the Hospitallers, tower above it. The houses, cisterns and chapels of the old citadel have mostly collapsed. Ancient remains and *tombs* have also been found in and around Khorió. To the S. of Khorió lies the church of the *Twelve Apostles*, which is 11C in origin. Near the village of *Dámos* are the remains of the early Christian basilica of *Christos (tis Jerusalem)*, which dates from the 6C; it has some ancient sections, such as the W. wall of the *apse* and the *synthronon*. The basilica was built on the site of an ancient shrine to Apollo Delios (Delian Apollo), which was built in the 5 or 4C BC and was the main religious centre of the island at the time. There are remnants nearby of a *theatre* from the 3C BC, and

another *basilica* dedicated to the *Evangelists* and containing mosaics and ancient fragments; this is where the statue of Asklepios was found. There are also traces of *Mycenean rock tombs*, not only here but in the neighbouring area of *Pánormos* (8 km.) on the W. coast and *Myrtiés*, where the ancient district of *Pothaía* lay. There are traces of chamber tombs, house foundations and walls. Near *Myrtiés* (9 km. NW) is another well-preserved early Christian *basilica*, *Ágios Ioánnis*, which has a nave and two aisles, and *mosaics* in the narthex. Close by is the small medieval castle of *Kasteli (Palaiokastro)*, whose walls and structure are still partially standing from the 9C. There is a small church of the Panagia nearby. Across from Myrtiés is the small island of *Télendos*, which was separated from the mainland during the earthquakes of 535 BC. There are some ruins of a medieval (14C) *castle* and church situated on the island's peak of *Ágios Konstantinos*, and also a few remains from ancient and Roman times. Lower down are a number of early Christian buildings, including the basilica of *Ag[aqc]ios Basilios*, with a baptistery, domed section and cemetery. Near the port of *Arginóntas* (*c.* 12 km. NW) are the ruins of a 13C Venetian *castle*. The fertile coastal settlement of *Vathý* on the E. coast, 12 km. NE, which is protected by a bay, has some 6,000 inhabitants and has produced numerous ancient finds; in particular, the grotto of *Daskalio*, with its hazardous access, has provided important Neolithic and Bronze Age discoveries. The village of *Empolás* has a well-preserved *wall* from the Hellenistic period, and the church of the *Archangel Michael* is 17C with old elements. Near *Rína* are the remains of a Hellenistic *watch-tower*; the area also has ruined medieval houses and the Byzantine church of *Panagia Khosti* with 12 or 13C *frescos*. Other monasteries on the island include *Ágios Ioánnis*, 17C with frescos in Cretan-Venetian style, the nunnery of *Agia Sarva*, with a 16C Last Supper in the apse, and *Agia Ekaterini* from the 17C, which is near a limestone cave. There is a Mycenean beehive tomb in the NW of the island near the port of *Emporió*, with traces of an ancient settlement.

Kardítsa/ΚΑΡΔΙΤΣΑ
Kardítsa/Thessaly   p.290☐E 6

This is an agricultural centre with a population of around 25,000, situated in the plain of Thessaly facing the S. slopes of the Pindos range, which rises up to 7,218 ft. Founded under the Turks, it is a trading centre for tobacco, grain, cotton, silk and cattle.

Environs: The ruins of the ancient town of **Metrópolis** (now *Mitrópolis*) are 10 km. to the SW, and include the remnants of the *walls* and the *acropolis*. It was captured by Flaminius in 191 BC. To the SW are the ruins of two *fortresses*: *Vunési* and *Portísta* on the 3,773 ft. Mt.Koróna. The remains of the ancient city of **Ithóme** are close to the village of *Fanárion*, 17 km. to the NW. This was the centre of the old region of Hestiaiótis (Estiaiótis), and there are Hellenistic walls to the NW and a Byzantine *fortress* on a hill. Near the village of **Georgikón**, to the S. of Kardítsa, a Mycenean tomb has been excavated. To the N. of **Sofádes** (*c.* 15 km. SE, a rural centre with 4,500 inhabitants) are the sparse remains of the ancient town of *Árne*. To the S. of Sofádes (*c.* 30 km. S. of Kardítsa), a *shrine to Athena* was uncovered in 1963, and traces from Hellenistic and Roman times have been found. The village of **Lutropigí** (with its neighbouring village of Lutrá Smokóvu) some 34 km. to the SE, is a celebrated mountain and thermal spa, with sulphur springs effective against rheumatism and skin complaints. Nearby is the Byzantine monastery of *Rentína*, which has some impressive *frescos*.

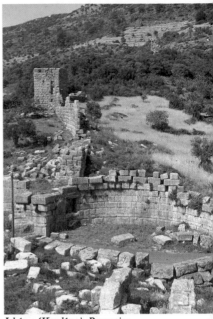

Ithóme (Kardítsa), Byzantine fortifications

Kárpathos/Karpathos (I)/ΚΑΡΠΑΘΟΣ
East Aegean Islands (Dodecanese)/
Aegean Islands   p.300☐O 13/14

This is the second-largest island of the Dodecanese, with an area of 116 sq. miles, but is thinly populated (only 6,000 inhabitants); it is situated half way between Crete and Rhodes. It is some 35 miles. long and 5 or 6 miles wide, and is mountainous, with a highest peak of 3,937 ft. It is moist, wooded and fertile, and its inhabitants still practise many of their old (Doric) customs.

History: In ancient times, the island was colonized by Dorians, around 800 BC, and was closely linked originally to Crete and later to Rhodes. In the Middle Ages, it came under the rule of the Venetians and Knights Hospitallers (1306–1538), and was then occupied by the Turks from 1539–1912; from 1912 until its return to Greece in 1948 it was held by the Italians.

Kárpathos (also known as *Pigádia*): This is the island's capital, with a population of 1,400, and a port. It stands on a bay in the SE of the island and was built in 1912 on the site of the ancient city of *Poseidón*, of which there are a few scattered remains.

Other island sites: The former capital was the neighbouring town of *Apéri* (9 km. NW), which now has a population of around 600. Close to it is the 16C monastery of *Kyra Panagia* (13 km. NW). There are the remains of an old *acropolis (palaiokastro)* in *Arkása*, 16 km. to the SW on the SW coast, and also the ruins of the early Christian basilica of *Agia Anastasia* (whose mosaics are housed in the museum at Rhodes). The village of *Óthos* (13 km. NW) contains the *Stavrakis house*, a classic example of island architecture. The attractively situated mountain village of

Karýtaina, Ágios Nikólaos

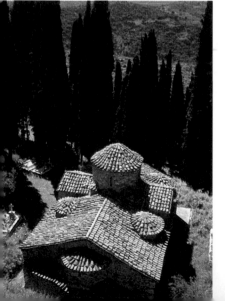

Ólympos (*c.* 50 km. N.) in the north of the island is known for its ancient customs and habits (costume, dance). The picturesque port of *Diafáni* (60 km. N.) is close to Ólympos. Nearby, by *Vrychónta*, are remnants of an old *temple*. To the N. of the island is the small (6 sq. miles) island of *Sariá (Sáros)*, which is separated by a channel only 100 yards wide, with Byzantine ruins on the shore.

Karpenísion/ΚΑΡΠΕΝΗΣΙΟΝ
Evrytanía/Central Greece   p.294☐E 7

This mountain town with a population of 4,500 is situated 3,281 ft. up, 82 km. W. of Lamía. It is dominated by the 7,546 ft. high mountain of Tymfristos and is set in wooded mountain countryside, in a popular skiing area.

Environs: Above Megálo Khorió (15 km. S.) is the interesting mountain monastery of **Prusós** (31 km. S.), which is 11C with an icon of the Virgin and fine iconostases. E. of Karpenísion are the charming mountain villages of Tymfristós (2,762 ft., 22 km.) and Ágios Geórgios (35 km.), and near the village of Vitóli (42 km.) are the remains of the ancient city of **Spércheia**. The hill of *Kastrorachi* has remains of a wall with square towers from the old Hellenistic *fortress* above the river Spercheios (Sperchios).

Karýtaina/ΚΑΡΥΤΑΙΝΑ
Arkadía/Peloponnese   p.294☐E 10

This attractive village (50 km. W. of Trípolis) in the Lykaion range is situated by the gorge of the Alphaios. In the Middle Ages it was the seat of one of the five baronies of Arkadia.

Church of the Panagia: This is an 11C

church with an iconostasis painted with ornamental designs and birds.

Ágios Nikolaos: This church has a cruciform ground plan and five domes. Its frescos have unfortunately been somewhat damaged. The chapel of *Ágios Andreas* is basilican at its W. end, and takes the form of a half-cross to the E.

Castle: This was built in 1209 by the Bruyères family and ceded to the Palaiologoi in 1320. In 1460 it was taken over by the Turks. The arched gateway leads through to a courtyard, to the S. of which is a huge hall; there is a square tower on the N. side.

Environs: The beautiful but still unexplored **grottoes of Kówia** (1 hour by foot). **Górtys** (2 hours by foot from Karýtaina): French excavations here have revealed two *shrines to Asklepios*, one on the left bank of the Gortynios (now Lousios) which was begun in the middle of the 4C but was never completed; it has a late-4C thermal bath which was altered in the 3C.

There are some Hellenistic and Roman houses to the SE. The Asklepieíon, of which little remains, was built in the late 5C or early 4C as a Doric peripteros, to the SW of the acropolis. The late-3C Asklepios bath has a stoá which served as an abaton.

Kásos (I)/ΚΑΣΟΣ

East Aegean Islands (Dodecanese)/
Aegean Islands   p.300☐N/O 4

This is the most southerly of the islands in the Dodecanese; it has an area of 25 sq. miles and a population of 1,400 and is only three nautical miles SW of Kárpathos. It is mountainous and barren, but rich in water. Historically, it has been under the sway of Kárpathos since antiquity. In the 18C it became an important shipbuilding and seafaring centre through its Albanian immigrant population.

Fry (460 inhabitants): The main port and capital is situated in a bay on the NW, and was founded in 1840. There was an ancient

Karýtaina, view of the picturesque village

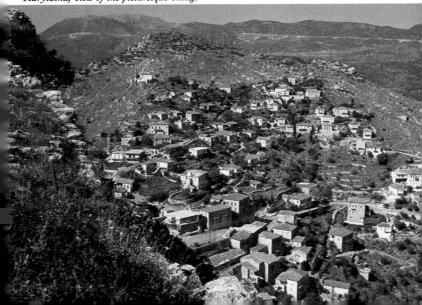

city called *Óphrys* on the same site, but few traces of it survive.

Environs: Near the village of *Póli,* 2 km. S., are some *remains* of walls from an ancient settlement. There is a church of the *Agia Triada* in the village, and a monastery of *Ágios Geórgios.* To the SE is the picturesque monastery village of *Panagía.* The *limestone caves of Ellinokamara* at Sellái are interesting, and contain the remains of a walled Pelasgian *cult-site,* which is near the cave of Fotokamara.

Kastélli Kissámu/
ΚΑΣΤΕΛΛΙ ΚΙΣΣΑΜΟΥ

Chaniá/Crete   p.298□E 13

The small town of Kastélli is situated on a beautiful bay at W. tip of Crete, on the N. coast in between the peninsulas of Gramvúsa and Rodopú; it stands on the site of the ancient town of Kissamos.

Antiquity: Some sections of the town fortifications date from antiquity; the later work is Venetian (16C), restored by the Turks. They were built in part using material from the important Roman harbour of Polyrrhéneia. There are also remains of a Roman viaduct, a temple and a theatre.

Venetian rule: Kissámu was also important under Venice, this time as a bishop's seat. The small Venetian castle near the church remains from this period.

Turkish rule: The castle was rebuilt during this period; there are also a number of Byzantine churches with fine frescos in the town and its surrounding area, e.g. in Kefáli, Lousakiés and Voukoliés.

Museum: There is a small but interesting museum, with exhibits from various periods from the area around Kissámu. The most interesting piece is the magnifi-

cent sculpture of a satyr, probably Hellenistic, which was only discovered in 1966.

Environs: Polyrrhéneia (now Polyrrínia): 6 km. S., by the village of Anó Palaiókastro, are the remains of this important old Dorian settlement from the 8C BC; it is situated on top of a 1,000 ft. hill, which affords a splendid view in all directions. The remnants of walls, temples and rock tombs are still clearly visible, and there is an acropolis on the highest point of the hill. There are broad walls leading up to the top. The town was once comparatively large and the Venetians added a castle, whose walls are still standing. The church at the foot of the acropolis is built of ancient materials. *Phalásarna:* This was Polyrrhéneia's rival in ancient times; it is some 14 km. W. of Kissámu, and was once one of Crete's major cities. The remains of a port are still visible today, but since the earthquakes of the 5C they have been thrust 165 yards inland from the W. coast; also as a result of the earthquake, the city rose over 30 ft., and a section of the E. coast, which included the town of Olús, sank into the sea. The site where the town was founded in the 5C BC has some remains of buildings, rock tombs and a throne-like seat. The prolonged enmity between Polyrrhéneia and Phalásarna seems to have been bitter and violent. **Gramvúsa:** This is Crete's most north-westerly peninsula, and is only accessible on foot, and then only to experienced hikers; it is easier to sail round to the peninsula in a boat. Shortly before the tip of the peninsula, on the E.coast, is a Temple of Apollo known as the Agníon ruins. Further on is the small island of Gramvúsa, which lies directly off the N. end of the peninsula. It is the site of the ruins of a huge old Venetian fortress, and a small church with Byzantine frescos.

Kastoriá, Ágios Nikólaos, fresco ▷

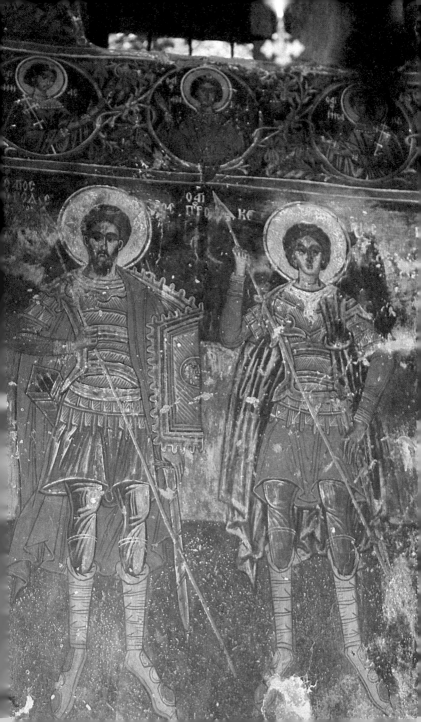

Kastellóriso (I)/ΚΑΣΤΕΛΛΟΡΙΖΟ
East Aegean Islands/Aegean Islands
p.300☐P 14

This small island is also known as *Megísti*, and is the most south-easterly of all the Greek islands. The barren red cliff with the mighty *Hospitallers' castle* dating from 1380 lies only 1.5 miles from the mainland of Asia Minor and the port of Kas. The island takes its name, which means *Castello Rosso* ('red castle'), from this cliff-top castle. The small fortified harbour is interesting, as are the ruins of the ancient fortress on the *palaiokastro* (acropolis). Stone Age and Mycenean finds indicate early settlement along the same pattern as the nearby mainland.

Kastoriá/ΚΑΣΤΟΡΙΑ
Kastoriá/Macedonia   p.290☐D 3

Kastoriá is situated in the NW part of Macedonia and has some 20,000 inhabitants; it is the main city of the nome of the

Kastoriá, Panagia Kumbelidiki

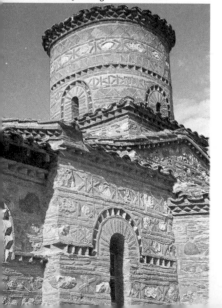

Kastoriá, Panagia Kumbelidiki, frescos ▷ over the portal

same name, and a centre of the fur trade. It lies on a small peninsula projecting into a lake, which shares its name. It was mentioned by Livy under the name of *Kéletron* and was taken by Rome in 200 BC. During Byzantine times it served as a refuge for deposed Byzantine kings. Kastoriá is famous for its numerous Byzantine churches (75), some of which date back to the 10C.

Byzantine city walls: The remains of the walls can be found in Omonoia Square (the highest point in the city) and the marketplace (also known as General van Fleet Square).

Ágios Athanasios (built 1384–5): This church has 14C frescos.

Agios Nikolaos tú Kasnitzi: This is a single-aisled basilica built around 1000, with 10&11C frescos and a 9C painting of the founder. Nearby is the chapel of **Ágios Panteleimon**.

Panagia Kumbelidiki: This is a small 11C church with a high dome; the exterior frescos over the portal date from the 13C.

Taxiarchis Chapel: Built 11–13C, with 14C icons.

Taxiarchis Church (*Ágios Michaelos*) (12C): The frescos inside are 14C and depict Christ's Passion. Nearby is the chapel of **Agia Triada**.

Agii Anargiri: A 10C basilica; recent restoration has revealed 11C wall paintings: on the left, Christ between Mary and St. John, and on the right, a Madonna in prayer between two angels, behind the All Holy: a Madonna and Child.

Kastoriá, basilica of Agii Anargiri ▷

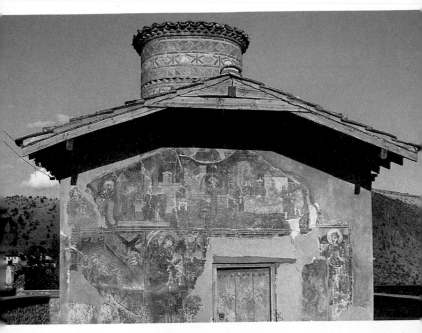

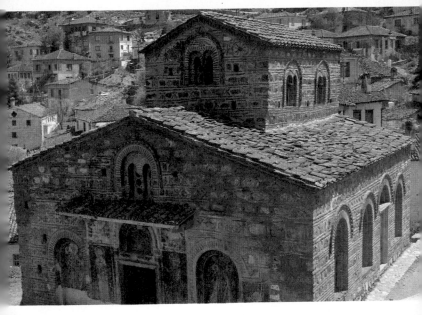

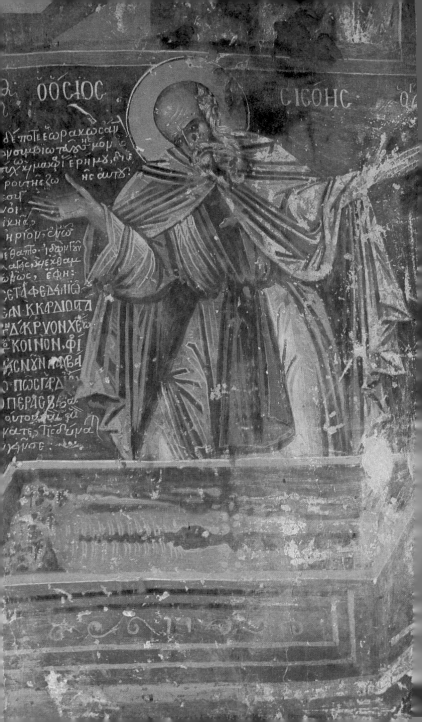

Ο ΟCΙΟC   CΙCΟΗC

ν ποτεεωρακωσαν
γουνιωτάλυ μόν
Αχυμαφϊερημω,λ
ροιτης εω
ουζ
νοϊ
ϊχνα
ηρϊον,ενω
εθαπο,ϊδωμεν
αϊς,ανεχθαι
ωως,εφη:
ϲεταφεδαλιω
ϲμκκρδιοτα
ρδακρυονχεω
εκοινον,φι
ϲενχναμβα
οπωϲϲραϊ
οπεραϲβϊδα
αϊτου,αλεϊ
κωτεϲτιϲθυμα
ηανϲε:

Panagía Mavriótissa: This monastery has two old chapels from the 11&12C: the *Panagia Chapel* has 11&12C frescos, and the *Ágios Ioánnis Prodomos Chapel* has some remarkable 16C paintings.

Archontiká (town houses/mansions): These are wooden houses dating from the 17&18C, most of which are situated in the SE district of the city and are built from traditional old materials. The most impressive, *Archontiko Adelphon Emmanuel*, belonged to the two Emmanuel brothers who were executed by the Turks in 1800; it is now a museum. *Archontiko tu Natzi* is an interesting mansion in the W. of the city. Others include *Sapuntzi* and *Tsiatsiapa*.

Museum of Local History (*Laografico Musio*): This is situated in the courtyard of the monastery of Panagia Mavriótissa at the end of the peninsula.

Also worth seeing: Kursum-Tzami: This mosque is in the market place; it has a number of small domes and a large courtyard. It is the only mosque still standing, where once there were seven.

Environs: Dispílion (*c.* 10 km. S.): Two prehistoric houses have been uncovered here, by the shores of the lake. **Klisúra** (*c.* 30 km. E.): This is a mountain village situated at an altitude of 3,940 ft. with the famous church of *Ágios Dimitrios*, which has fine sculptures and an iconostasis from the 15C.

Katerini/KATEPINH
Piería/Macedonia   p.290□F 4

This is the capital of the nome of Piería, and is located on the coast, close to Mt.Olympos; it has 30,000 inhabitants and

◁ *Kastoriá, sarcophagus, P. Mavriótissa*

is 98 km. SW of Thessaloníki. The grape festival is worth seeing; it takes place during the last ten days of September, and is an important traditional event.

Environs: Díon (15 km. S.): This is an old Macedonian town which flourished at the end of the 5C BC. King Archelaos of Macedonia established a *shrine to Zeus* in the early 4C BC, and the town used to have a *stadium*. The *theatre* is still standing. The *Olympos Festival* takes place here in autumn, and consists of the performance of old plays and customs events. The remnants of the old town also include some *tombs* from the 3&2C BC in *Maláthria*, to the N., a *fortification wall* from the time of Philip II, sections of the old stadium and the ruins of a 6C early Christian basilica with a well-preserved *mosaic floor*. Díon has a small museum with an exhibition of *sculptures*, mostly Hellenistic, and some early Christian finds. **Litókhoron** (24 km. S.): This village at the foot of Mt.Olympos is the starting point for any attempt to scale the mountain, which is the highest in Greece and which, in antiquity, was believed to be the seat of the 12 Olympian gods. **Platamón:** This is a tourist resort by the sea (85 km. S.), not far from the main road from Larissa to Thessaloníki, with a medieval *castle* (Kastro tis Orias) on a hill, which is the site of some of the events of the Olympos Festival. **Pýdna** (14 km. N.): The ancient settlement was founded in the 8 or 7C BC, and was an important harbour and trading centre; *tombs* are still being found, dating back to classical, Hellenistic and Roman times, and also *inscriptions* and *sculptures*. Near the town, the oldest known Macedonian tomb was uncovered, and proved to be rich in treasures, which are now in the museum of Thessaloníki. Olympias, the mother of Alexander the Great, was murdered in Pýdna at the command of the Diadocian king Cassander. In 168 BC, the last Macedonian king, Perseus, lost the deci-

Káto Zákros, lay-out of the Palace: 1 entrance from the S. **2** workshops **3** well with staircase **4** central court, also used as arena for bull-games **5** probable altar **6** columned portico **7** vestibule **8** private room of the Lady of the Palace with brick pavement **9** magazines **10** paved inner court **11** to **15** ante-rooms, finding-place of the talents (bronze basin and elephant tusks, the largest of which was 23 ft. long) **16** cult objects were kept here **17** sacred precinct with cult basin **18** audience chambers of the Lords of the Palace **19** banquet hall **20** treasury, where rock-crystal vase was found **21** workshop **22** workshop, probably dye-house **23** kitchen and dining-room **24** kitchen magazines **25** late Minoan settlement **26** great court between palace and settlement **27** bathrooms **28** magazine **29** Lord's megaron **30** Lady's megaron **31** court with large water basin **32** square well **33** well or spring-house with square basin **34** passage linking central court and harbour **35** rooms with drainage pipes, possible bath

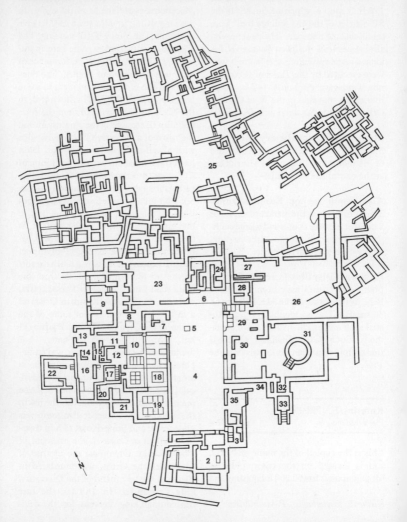

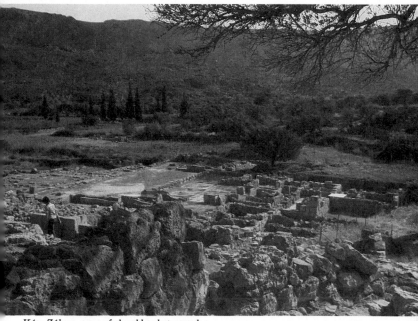

Káto Zákros, part of the old palace complex

sive battle against the Romans. There is still a small fishing port on the site of the classical harbour.

Káto Zákros/Káto Sákros/
ΚΑΤΟ ΖΑΚΡΟΣ
Lasíthi/Crete   p.298□I 14

Since 1960 excavation of a palace has been in progress some 330 yards outside the village of Káto Zácros, on the E. coast of Crete in an area which has been inhabited since 2500 BC; it dates from around 1700 BC and had three storeys and some 200 rooms.

The palace was probably destroyed by the volcanic eruption of Santorini in about 1450 BC. The archaeologists, who were clearly the first to explore the site, found relatively little of the tufa masonry, but an amazing number of treasures: some 2,000 pottery vases, exquisite hand-carved works in gilded slate, quartz crystal and marble, tools, bronze tree-saws and kettles with double axe emblems, religious objects and pithoi (huge pithoi with Linear A script), and numerous reliefs and sculptures with depictions of animals, especially wild goats and sea creatures, plants and ornamental decoration. The most famous are a bull's head phyton made of steatite, and a small vase of breathtaking beauty made of quartz. The most valuable finds from the treasury are now housed in the Archaeological Museum in Iráklion.

Harbour: The palace of Káto Zákros was a major naval base and the most important trading centre in Crete, importing raw materials such as gold, copper, bronze and

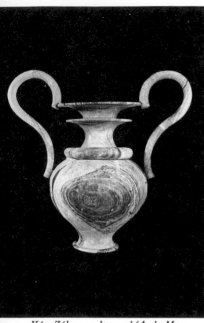

Káto Zákros, cult vessel (Arch. Mus. Iráklion)

ivory and probably exporting highly-crafted Minoan work. The port belonged to the palace, and a paved street led to it from the W. front of the palace. There are only a few scattered remains of the harbour itself.

Valley of the Dead: The palace is built on a hill, with a view over the whole bay and over the 'Valley of the Dead', a deep gorge which leads down to the sea. The niches and caves in the ravine's sides contain graves from an even earlier period: some of them date back to 2400 BC, and this gorge has served as a burial site for centuries.

Palace: The palace itself is reminiscent of Knossós, Phaistós or Mália: the various sections of the palace are built round a central courtyard, which is 98 ft. x 39 ft., and the wings are well-suited in their lay out to their purposes, as is the case at Knossós. In both cases, the E. section contains the private chambers. The W. wing housed the religious chambers and state rooms, and, as in Knossós, the main storerooms were

Káto Zákros, treasury

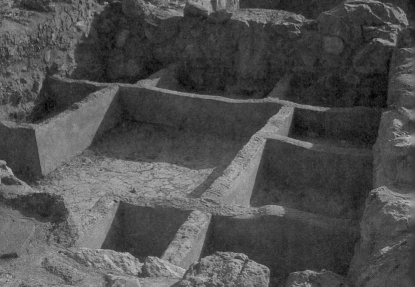

to the NW. The N. wing had more private and business rooms, and the S. wing was primarily workshops. The sanitary arrangements are also of especial interest: there were three wells which supplied the palace with fresh spring water, a drainage system and toilet facilities, and a proper sewerage system.

Environs: Áno Zácros: This is 7 km. W. of Káto Zákros, and in 1965 was the site of the discovery of a late Minoan house, a wine press and a pithos with Linear A script, which is now in the Archaeological Museum in Iráklion. **Agía Fotía:** Between Káto Zákros and Sitía, a huge Minoan burial site was discovered here in 1971, with 252 shaft and chamber tombs. The treasures which came to light, including copper daggers and amulets, are on display in the museum at Ágios Nikólaos.

Kavála/ΚΑΒΑΛΑ
Kavála/Macedonia   p.292☐I 2

Kavála has a population of 50,000 and is one of the most beautiful towns in Greece; it was built as a colony of Thasos, and originally known as *Skávala*. The Apostle Paul came here and founded the first Christian church in Europe, in the village which is now called *Krinídes*. Kavála is known for its many fine beaches.

Kastro tís Panagías: This is a well-preserved 14C Byzantine castle, built on the highest point in the town (Panagía).

Kamares or **Hydragogeion:** This is a two-storey 16C aqueduct built along Roman lines; it is an impressive structure, which once provided Kavála with its water supply.

House of Mohammed Ali: The birthplace of Mohammed Ali (1769–1849), the founder of the Khedive dynasty, this house is still in good condition and there is a bronze equestrian statue of him in front of the house.

Archaeological Museum *(Archaiologico Musio):* This displays a number of sculp-

Kavála, two-tiered aqueduct, built on Roman lines

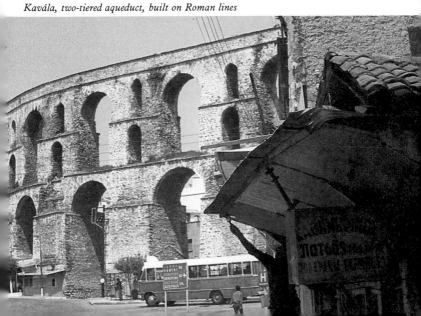

tures, gold jewellery and glass from Roman times. The finds are from the surrounding area and include frescos, friezes, terracotta figures, vases and sculptures from classical, Hellenistic and early Christian times.

Kavírio/Shrine of Kaveira/
IEPON TON KABEIPON
Boeotia/Central Greece   p.294☐ G 8

This shrine lies some 8 km. W. of Thebes, and was where the Kaveira, or 'Great Gods', were worshipped. The name is connected in mythology with the original home of the gods, the Phrygian mountain of Kaveiros. The details of their cult worship, which is referred to by the great Theban poet Pindar, are unclear; originating in Samothráki, it appeared in the Boeotian town of Anthedón, during the 6C BC. The site of the original shrine is surrounded by olive trees, and excavation work in 1887 brought a number of significant finds to light, notably black figure vases with images of Kaveiros. They are now housed in

Fiskárdon (Kef), typical landscape

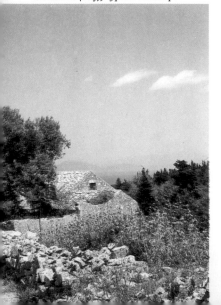

the National Museum in Athens and the Archaeological Museum in Thebes.

The shrine was at its peak in the 4C BC, when the temple was rebuilt. The auditorium, the side halls and a shrine to the Kaveira Demeter date from Hellenistic times. The German excavations which have taken place in recent years have revealed the Hellenistic structures.

On the edge of the shrine, to the W., is a small house which was built during the most recent German excavations and which houses numerous fragments and remains of the shrine.

Kéa/Kéos/Kea (I)/KEA
Cyclades/Aegean Islands   p.296☐ I 9

This is the largest and the most northerly of the western Cyclades, with an area of *c.* 46 sq. miles and a population of 1,700. It is separated from the SE point of Attica by the Kea Channel.

History: The island, which has been inhabited since the 3rd millennium BC, had links with Crete and the Mycenean world and played an important part in ancient history, largely because of its mineral riches, which included iron, silver and bronze ore. It was colonized by Ionians around 900 BC, and built up strong diplomatic ties with Athens, including membership of the Athenian maritime league. The remains of the four ancient cities (Tetrápolis) are still visible. It fell to Rome in 50 BC, and was Venetian (Ghizzi, Michieli) during the Middle Ages. It was taken by the Turks in 1566.

Kéa (or *Khóra*, 'village'): The capital is tiny, with a population of only 700, and is situated inland on the site of the ancient city of *Iulís*, of which there are scattered remains. There are also remnants of a 13C Venetian *Kastro*, built with material from the ancient acropolis. About 1 km. NE is the huge ancient figure of a lion carved in a cliff (23 ft. long, 10 ft. high), which dates from the 6C BC.

Environs: Near the monastery of *Agía Marina*, 6 km. SE, are the remains of an ancient three-storeyed *tower* (4C BC). Near the harbour of *Livádi* (*c.* 5 km. to the NW) are some scattered remnants of the ancient village of *Korissía*. The peninsula of *Agía Iríni* ('St.Irene') has the remnants of a prehistoric Bronze Age settlement near *Vurkári*, where a number of interesting finds have been made, including ceramics, weapons, jewellery. Some 10 km. S. of Kéa are the remains of the ancient village of *Karthaía*, with the foundations of three 5C Doric marble temples still standing on the acropolis.

Kefallinía/Kefallonía/Kefallinia (I)/
ΚΕΦΑΛΟΝΙΑ
Ionian Islands   p.294☐B/C 8

This rich and fertile island, with an area of 297 sq. miles and a population of around 37,000, is the largest of the Ionian Islands.

History: The island's original name was *Sáme* or *Sámos*, which is the name used in Homer's 'Odyssey'; this is now the name of a town on the E. coast. Subsequently the island took its name from the Kephallonian tribe. In antiquity, it had four towns (Tetrápolis): Kráne, Pále, Prónnoi and Sáme. Remnants of all four have been excavated, and a number of Mycenean (beehive) tombs suggest that the island was highly significant at that time (most of the suitors in the 'Odyssey' were from Sáme). In historical sequence, the island next came under the sway of Corinth, but was later subject to Athens. In 189 BC it was taken by the Romans. It changed hands through the early Middle Ages, and in 1500 it became Venetian, with the Turks having controlled it for only twenty years (1479–99). After an English protectorate between 1814 and 1864, it was returned to Greece. In 1953 a large number of the buildings were destroyed by an earthquake, but they have since been rebuilt.

Argostólion/Argostóli: The capital of the island, with a population of 8,000; it is situated on the Bay of Livádi on the W. coast and was founded by the Venetians in 1757. Since the earthquake of 1953, much of it has been rebuilt. The harbour is attractive, and has an *Archaeological Museum* with Mycenean pieces found on the island, mostly from the necropoles of Metaxáta and Mazakaráta; they include jewellery, weapons, tools, vases and sarcophagi. The *cathedral* is also interesting, with some fine icons, and there is a small *local history museum*.

Environs: 3 km. S. is the ancient town of *Kráne*, which still has parts of its old *wall*, the ancient settlement, a *temple*, a small *altar* and a *water system*. 10 km. SE is a medieval *Kastro* on the site of the old capital of *Ágios Andréas*, which was abandoned in favour of Argostólion in 1757. There are remains of churches, houses and a monastery on the cliffs. On the 1,000 ft. peak are the remains of a 12&13C *castle* with a moat and drawbridge, with the remnants of a church and other buildings in its interior. It affords a fine view. Nearby is the monastery of *Ágios Andréas*, which has fine frescos and icons by the Cretan School, and also from the 17C. 12 km. S. is the *necropolis of Mazarakáta*, where Cavvadias discovered numerous *Mycenean tombs* in 1908, including a *beehive tomb*. Three rock tombs have been found, along with the remains of a temple of the dead, near *Metaxáta* (13 km. S.). There are also Mycenean tombs near *Lakkíthra*, 10 km. to the S., with rock caves housing treasure chambers. These Mycenean finds to the S. of Argostólion are the most culturally interesting on the island, and are all on display in

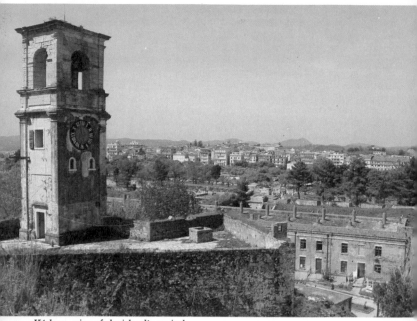

Kérkyra, view of the island's capital

the local museum. They are family tombs of the nobility, housed in domed vaults, rock chambers, grottoes and caves. Before they were found, no Mycenean castles or palaces had been discovered. 3 km. N. are the celebrated *sea mills*, with 'katavothres' ('gullets') through which the sea water drove the mill. The earthquake of 1953 dried up the 100 ft. channels. On the southernmost point of the island, which is accessible from Argostólion, are the remains of a Roman villa dating from the 2C AD, near the village of *Skála* (20 km. S.). It has a fine mosaic pavement with a motif of envy. The main room was later converted into a church (Chapel of St. Athanasius). Nearby (by Cape George) are the remains of the pillars of an 6C Doric temple, which was converted into a church and whose capitals survive. N. of Skála was the ancient town of *Prónnoi*, of which

nothing is left. On the neighbouring peak of *Ainos* (5,400 ft.) are the remnants of an old *sacrificial altar*, which was once dedicated to the weather god Zeus (Megas Zeus). Close by is the *monastery* of the island's patron saint, *Ágios Gerásimos*, which dates from the 16C.

Sámi (23 km. N. of Argostólion): This lively port on the E. coast is opposite the island of Ithaka. It is dominated by the ancient *acropolis*, and also the remains of a polygonal wall with towers and another castle hill. The town was taken by the Romans in 189 BC (there is a bath by the port of *Agía Evfimía* dating from the period of Roman occupation, around the 3C AD). So far no traces of Mycenean civilisation have been found.
Environs: The nearby *Drogarati caves* are interesting: they are a system of limestone

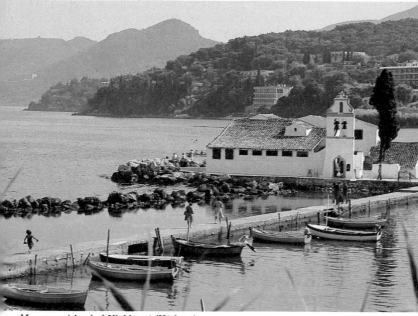

Monastery island of Vlakherná (Kérkyra)

caves, water passages and underground lakes in between Sámi and Argostólion, where the sea disappears underground and then reappears. (There are entrances near Khaliotáta and Vlakháta.) To the NW of Sámi lies the picturesque harbour of *Ásos* (*c.* 25 km. NW), which has a Venetian *fortress* dating from 1595. The fishing village of *Fiskàrdon* (50 km. N.) is also worth visiting, at the N. tip of the island. It is named after the Norman lord Robert Guiscard, who died there in 1085 after the island's conquest.

Lixúri (*c.* 30 km. from Argostólion): This is the second largest town on the island, on the W. coast bay of Livádi opposite Argostólion. There is little to see in the town itself, apart from a *local history museum*, but nearby are the scattered remains of the ancient town of *Pále* (now Palaiókastro).

Kérkyra/Corfu (I)/ΚΕΡΚΞΡΑ

Ionian Islands p.290☐A/B 5

This is the most northerly and the second-largest of the Ionian Islands (229 sq. miles) and is shaped in the form of a sickle, 39 miles long and 4–15 miles wide. The N. of the island comes within two miles of the coast of Albania. It is fertile and well-populated, with some 100, 000 inhabitants).

History: Corfu is reputed to have been the kingdom of the legendary Phaiacian king Alkínoos, which was Odysseus's last stop on his voyage home to Ithaka (Homer, 'Odyssey' V–VII). It was also known as *Skería* and *Drepáne* ('sickle'). It was not until medieval times that it became known as *(Stus) Korfus* ('with the peaks'), which evolved into the modern name of Corfu. Around 734 BC Corinth established a base here as a stop en route to Sicily (near what is now Palaiópolis, 'old city'). This settlement was called Kérkyra, or Kórkyra. The colony soon became a significant port in its own right, and clashed with its mother city of Corinth in a naval battle in 665 BC. Its struggle with Corinth was also the cause of the Peloponnesian War (431–404 BC), in which Kérkyra remained faithful to the Athenian maritime league. It also joined the second Athenian maritime league, and withstood the resulting Spartan siege in 372 BC. After falling occasionally under the sway of Syracuse, Kerkyra belonged to Macedonia and Epeiros, until in 229 BC it came under the Illyrian protectorate of Rome. In the 4C AD it was part of the Eastern Roman Empire, and was the victim of numerous raids during the Dark Ages from the Vandals, Ostrogoths, Slavs and others. It came into Venetian hands during the 4th Crusade in 1205, and from 1386–1797 it belonged, along with the other Ionian islands, to the Doges of Venice. While the rest of Greece was under Turkish rule, Kérkyra flourished culturally with the Italian Renaissance (painting and poetry). In 1797, Napoleon founded the Republic of the Ionian Islands (Septinsular Republic), and in 1815 Corfu was placed under the protection of England as an independent state by the first English Lord High Commissioner. In 1864 the Heptánisos ('republic of seven islands') finally became part of the Kingdom of Greece.

Kérkyra/Corfu: The island's capital has a population of some 30,000 and is situated amidst hills on the E. coast facing Albania. Its lay-out and character are reminiscent of a southern Italian town. The ancient port of *Palaiopolis* was abandoned in early Byzantine times, and the modern city was established further to the N.

Church of Ágios Spyrídon: This was built in 1589 and houses the relics of St. Spyridon, which were brought from Constantinople to Corfu in 1456 (he was the archbishop of Cyprus in around 325, and is the patron saint of the town and island of Corfu). His shrine, surrounded by candles and icons, is situated to the right of the sacristy, and is borne through the church four times a year in a holy procession; the most important day is 11 August. There are some fine Italianate wall paintings in the church interior, which were restored in about 1830. The 17C white marble *iconostasis* represents a Latin church façade. The 16C *Orthodox Cathedral* (Mitropolis Church) is also interesting: it contains a row of Byzantine icons and works from the Ionian islands, including the headless mummy of St.Theodora Augusta. Opposite the town hall is the *Latin Cathedral*, which was built in 1658 and seriously damaged in 1944. The small church of *Panagía Mandrakina* (1700) is situated on the N. of the Spianada. The *Platytera monastery* in the W. of the city has some rare post-Byzantine icons. The *Church of St.Iason and St.Sosipatros*, in the southern suburb of Anemomylos, is a remarkable 12C Byzantine domed cross-in-square church, with open arms and delicate arcades, supported by three ancient monolithic columns with capitals. There is a fresco of the Dormition of the Virgin in the narthex, and one of St.George in the naos, which has been rebuilt. 1.5 km. S. of the city are the ruins of the church of *Agia Kerkyra*, or the church of Palaiopolis; it is a basilica which was built out of ashlars from the ancient city in the 5C AD and it stands on the site of a 5C BC temple. It had a nave, four aisles and a double narthex. After being burned to the ground in a Vandal invasion, it was rebuilt with a nave and two aisles in the 6C and later destroyed by Arabs in the 11C. The triple *doorway* in the façade, with a lion of St. Mark, has survived the waves of destruc-

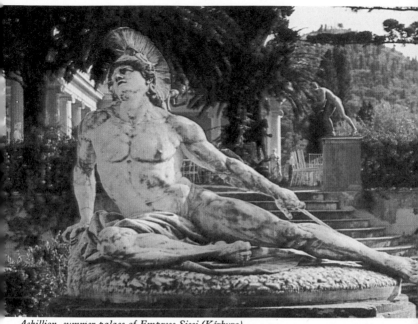

Achillion, summer palace of Empress Sissi (Kérkyra)

tion. *Old Fortress (Frurion)*: This was built by the Venetians in 1550 on a double peak on the coast, and was known as the 'Fortezza Vecchia' ('Old Fortress'). It is separated from the mainland by an artificial ditch, the Contrafossa, which is 50 ft. deep and about 100 ft. wide. The fortress now serves as a military academy, and includes the Castel di Terra with a lighthouse and the Castel de Mar with a powder magazine. At the end of the bridge is the statue of Marshal Schulenburg, who defended the town against the Turks in 1716; the statue dates from 1717 and is by the Italian sculptor Corradini. *Esplanade (Spianada)*: The largest and most impressive square in Greece is situated on the mainland just opposite the old fortress. It was formerly a military parade ground and firing range in front of the fortress, but was turned into a park by the British in the 19C. On one

side of the square is a row of *arcaded houses* in French Empire style dating from 1807 –14. *New Fortress:* This was built by the Venetians in 1576–89 after the first Turkish siege of 1537, and has massive walls and towers. There is a winged Lion of St.Mark over the Spilia Square entrance. The upper section of the structure was added by the British in 1815. *Town Hall:* This was built by the Venetians as an assembly room and converted into a theatre in 1693. It has been the town hall since 1902. There is a plaque to Morosini, who recovered the Moréa in 1687, on the narrow side. The *Royal Palace* was built in 1816 by the British, and stands on the N. side of the esplanade. It is a neoclassical building, and was the residence of the British High Commissioner. Today the E. wing houses ancient Christian relics and icons, including mosaics from the early

Christian basilica of Palaiopolis and some 16C icons. There is also a collection of Chinese and Japanese art. The *Archaeological Museum* houses prehistoric, ancient and other finds from excavations on the island. The most significant exhibit is the celebrated *Gorgon pediment, c.* 590 BC, from the W. façade of the Temple of Artemis from the ancient city of Kérkyra (Palaiopolis). It is the oldest known Greek monumental relief, and is almost perfectly preserved. In the middle section is the hideous gorgon Medusa depicted in flight, with a panther by her side and her two children nearby, Pegasus the flying horse and the hero Chrysaor. Medusa was the only one of the three gorgons who was mortal. Her hair consisted of snakes, and anyone who caught sight of her turned to stone. In the right corner of the pediment is Zeus, sending a thunderbolt against the Giants. The left hand panel shows the young Neoptolemos, son of Achilles, killing the Trojan king Priam. The ancient *lioness* on Menekrates' tomb, in the next room, is also interesting; it is a carved figure dating from between 625 and 540 BC. There are other ancient fragments which are of interest, including the head of another *gorgon* from the late 6C, and a copy of a head of the playwright Menander (342–293 BC), as well as vases and fragments of statues.

The *ancient city of Kérkyra* (now *Palaiopolis*) is situated to the S. of the modern town, on the isthmus of the peninsula. Near the nunnery of *Agii Theodori* (St. Theodora), the remains of a *Temple of Artemis* have been uncovered; the *Gorgon Pediment* in the museum is from here. The temple was some 150 ft. long and 70 ft. wide, and was founded in the early 6C BC. Immediately behind the nunnery, there is still an altar with an archaic triglyph. Excavations were begun here in 1911 at the instigation of Kaiser Wilhelm II, under W. Dörpfeld, and remains of ancient temples, shrines, baths, houses and town walls were all discovered in the same area. The ancient city had two harbours: the Alkinoos harbour on bay of Garitsa to the E., and the Hyllaikós harbour on the bay of Khalikiópulo to the W. The *agora* and the wealthy quarter were to the NE, and the labourers' quarter to the W. NE of the town walls were the *necropoles*, and the *Tomb of Menekrates* survives from around 590 BC to the N. of Anemómylos. The remains of the circular *cenotaph*, consisting of six stone tiers, are preserved; it was once crowned with a lion, which is now in the museum. The hexameter inscription tells that it is dedicated to the memory of Menekrates, son of Tlasias, from Lokris, near Corinth. This form of hero's burial was reserved for city founders and distinguished citizens.

Environs: S. of the suburb of *Anemómylos* is the *Villa Mon Repos*, which was built in 1824 as the summer residence of the British High Commissioner. On the most southerly point of the *Palaiopolis* peninsula is the vantage point of *Kanoni* (*c.* 4 km.), which owes its name to an old French bastion. It is fertile and affords a fine view over to the two small islands of *Pontikonísi* ('mouse island'), which is supposedly Odysseus's Phaeacian ship which was turned to stone, and the monastery island of *Vlakherná*. This is linked to the mainland by a footbridge. The monastery of *Panagía Vlakhernon* dates from the 17C. The summer palace of *Achíllion*, former residence of Queen Elizabeth of Austria, is situated on the road to *Benítses*, 11 km. to the S. It was built in neo-Renaissance style by the Italian architect Carita in 1890 and is set in a delightful park. Kaiser Wilhelm II bought it and spent his holidays here until 1914; it is now a casino. It was named *Achilles* after the Austrian queen's favourite hero, and is highly ornate and decorated with thematic paintings on the walls and ceilings (e.g. 'Achilles in Troy'). The park contains numerous copies of ancient statues (e.g. 'Dying Achilles', a bronze statue by Herter, a sculptor from Berlin,

1884, and 'Achilles Victorious', a bronze statue by Goetz). There are also statues of Muses and busts of Greek poets. The interior contains a Byzantine style chapel, a monumental fresco, a Renaissance style dining room and an Ionic peristyle decorated with frescos. There is a splendid panorama of Corfu and the Palaiopolis peninsula from the park. Near *Guviá* (8 km. N. on Guviá Bay) are the remains of the Venetian *arsenals*, which were built in 1716. This is where the Venetian galleys anchored, in a covered shelter.

Palaiokastrítsa: On the W. coast of the island (24 km. NW) is the site, according to V.Bérard, of the Phaeacian king Alkínoos's city, at the tip of the peninsula of Ágios Nikólaos, at the foot of Mt.Arakli, with a fine view from the neighbouring village of Lákones. Nearby is the *Palaiokastrítsa monastery*, which has some interesting icons and a splendid array of terraces. During the Middle Ages it was linked to the fortress of *Angelokastro* situated at the top of a steep hill (1,000 ft.). The remains of the fortress are interesting; it was allegedly built by the Despot of Epiros, Angelos Komnenos, in the 13C. Further S. is the bay of Ermones, where, according to V.Bérard's theory, Odysseus was stranded when he was found by Nausicaa.

Kasíopi (35 km. N.): This is a small port in the N., on the straits between Corfu and Albania, with the ruins of an Angevin *fortress* on a hill (1267–1386), probably built on the site of a Hellenistic *castle*. By *Róda* (37 km. N.), at the N. end of the Pantokrator range, are the foundations of a 5C temple. On the highest mountain on the island, *Pantokrator* (3,000 ft.), is a monastery of the same name, which was founded in 1347.

Páxos/Paxí: Páxos is a small, flat island with an area of 7 sq. miles and some 2,300 inhabitants; it lies 15 miles off the coast of Epirus and nearly 40 miles S. of Corfu. Apart from the ruins of a Venetian *fortress* in the bay of Gaíos, it has little of cultural interest. The sea *grottoes*, however, are interesting; one of them, the *Ypopanti grotto*, was believed to be the site of the marble palace of Poseidon, the sea-god. Páxos, and its neighbouring island of *Antípaxos* (2.3 sq. miles), have been treated as part of Corfu since antiquity.

Khrísafa/ΧΡΞΣΑΦΑ
Lakonia/Peloponnese   p.294□F 10

A small town, about 15 km. E. of Sparta on the road to Monemvasía, with interesting churches (guide brings the keys to the churches).

Church of Kimisis: 14C, with well-preserved frescos.

Ágios Dimitrios: 17C church with a cruciform ground plan. Icon, *Christos Elkomenos* ('Christ Flagellated').

Ágios Ioannis-Prodromos (about half an hour's walk): The S. transept has a Transfiguration of Christ.

Chrysafiótissa: This church, built in 1290, was formerly a monastery, the foundations of which can still be seen. Badly damaged frescos. The famous 'Flying Icon' is now to be seen in the Chrysafiótissa in Monemvasía. It is reported that this image of the Virgin flew of its own accord from Khrísafa to Monemvasía. A church was then built on the spot where it came to rest. The inhabitants of Khrísafa, not really believing the truth of this amazing flight, went to Monemvasía and took the image back, whereupon it flew back to Monemvasía.

Kifisiá / ΚΗΦΙΣΙΑ
Attica   p.296 □ H 8

This town has a population of around 15,000 and is situated in fertile countryside at the foot of Mt.Penteli amidst pine and plane trees; it is a popular summer retreat for Athenians, lying 14 km. NE of the city. Even in late antiquity *Kephisía* was known as a desirable villa suburb, much as it is today. The rich Athenian Herodes Atticus possessed estates here which are described in Gellius' book 'Noctes Atticae' (2C AD). This was also the home town of the playwright Menander (342–293 BC), a writer of the New Comedy.

Roman Burial Chamber (town centre): This is the only remnant from ancient times; it dates from the 2C BC and contains a *garlanded sarcophagus*, with a sarcophagus bearing a relief of Eros in front of it and another with a depiction of the myth of Leda.

Also worth seeing: The *Botanical Garden* has rare Mediterranean plants and the *Gulandris Museum* (Levidu 13) has a natural history collection.

Environs: Amarúsion, now known as *Marúsi*, is a village some 2 km. to the SW, and is the penultimate station on the metro line from Athens. In ancient times it was the important Attic deme of *Athmonon*, which had a famous shrine to Artemis Amarysia, of which there are no remains. (Amarysia is the root of the name Amarúsion.) The shrine was linked to the sanctuary of Artemis in Vravróna (Braurón). Today the town is best known for its pottery and ceramic industries, and there is a permanent exhibition of ceramic craft and folklore (Ekthesi Keramikís), with exhibits from all over Greece, especially the 'pottery island', Sífnos. The neighbouring village of **Chalándri(on)**, between the

mountains of Ymittos (Hymettos) and Penteli and *c.* 8 km. from Athens, has a late Roman *burial chamber*, the only remnant of the ancient deme of *Phlýa*, which is situated in the chapel of *Panagía Marmariotissa*; the apse has replaced the door front of the chamber, but the remainder has survived. It dates from the time of Herodes Atticus, the 2C AD. The outlying industrial area of *Néa Ionía* (*c.* 7 km. from the centre of Athens) can be reached through the suburbs of *Psychikó* and *Filothéi*; it includes the interesting Byzantine church of *Omorfi Ekklisía* ('beautiful church'), a 12C cross-in-square church with a narthex and S. chapel with rib-vaulting; fine masonry, relief-like decoration. The *octagonal dome* is interesting, with fine columns and ornate marble arches. There are some beautiful 13&14C *frescos* on the dome, including an impressive youthful Pantocrator (Macedonian School), and the walls. Near the suburb of **Agía Paraskeví** (*c.* 8 km. NE of Athens), on the N. slopes of Ymettos, is the monastery of *Ágios Ioánnis (Kynigos)*, which is visible from afar. It dates from the 13C, as does the small *monastery church* with its fine *dome* supported by two columns and pilasters. The domed narthex was built during the 16&17C Turkish occupation, and the surrounding buildings date from the 18&19C. It offers a fine view over the Athenian plain and the plain of Mesogia to the E.

Kilkís / ΚΙΛΚΙΣ
Kilkís / Macedonia   p.292 □ G 2

This is the capital of the nome of the same name on Greece's northern border, which was established in 1922 by Greeks who arrived from Asia Minor after the Balkan War; it has some 15,000 inhabitants and is 50 km. N. of Thessaloníki. The broad, fertile plains around the river Axios are heavily cultivated.

Museum: There is a small archaeological museum with a number of interesting finds from various periods.

Also worth seeing: A *cave* with stalactites and stalagmites has been discovered in the hill of Ágios Georgios, not far from the town.

Knossós/Knossos/ΚΝΩΣΟΣ
Iráklion/Crete   p.298☐H 14

Crete has a claim to be regarded as the birthplace of European culture, for that is how the Minoan civilization, named after the legendary king Minos, has been perceived; and Knossós, 5 km. S. of Iráklion, is the most important site on the island. It was believed that the excavations in Knossos had revealed King Minos's palace. Minos was originally a general term for priest-king, but according to the legend Minos is said to have lived around 1500 BC, and to have been the son of Zeus and Europa. He married Pasiphae, who was a daughter of Helios, the sun god, and she bore him seven children. Minos's oldest son, Katreus, succeeded his father on the throne, but was murdered by his own son, Althaimenes. Minos's second son, Deukalion, then acceeded to the throne. Whilst Minos was still on the throne, his fourth son, Androgeos, was seriously injured in a sword-fight with Aegeus, the king of Athens, and died of his wounds. Minos consequently attacked Athens and subjugated it. He then exacted a tribute from Athens every seven or nine years of seven young men and seven maidens; these victims never returned to Athens; and the legend said that they were fed to Pasiphae's seventh child, a hideous monster known as the Minotaur.

This minotaur, half man and half bull, was said to be the result of Pasiphae's degenerate love for a white bull. The story runs

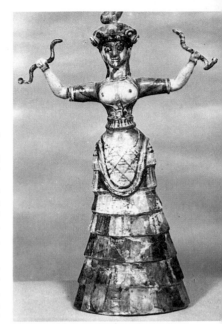

Knossós, small snake godess (Arch. Mus. Iráklion)

Knossós, corridor of the W. magazine

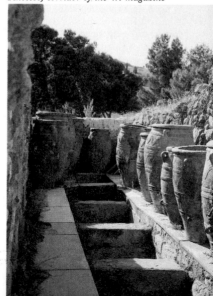

Knossós, bull-fight (mosaic, Arch. Mus. ▷
Iráklion)

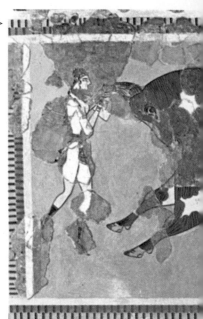

that it was kept in a labyrinth built by Daedalus, the famous Greek architect who Minos protected from the Greeks who wanted him for the murder of his nephew. It was Daedalus who later, with his son Icarus, flew away from Crete with the help of artificial wings which he made himself. He managed to cross the sea, but Icarus, despite his father's warning, flew too close to the sun, which melted the wax holding the feathers together, and he fell into the sea.

The legend continues that Theseus, a son of the king of Athens, came to Crete with the seven youths and seven maidens who were to be sacrificed to the minotaur. Ariadne, a daughter of King Minos, fell in love with him. Theseus killed the minotaur and Ariadne helped him to find his way out of the labyrinth with a thread. Theseus took Ariadne off with him to Naxos, but then left her to marry her sister Phaedra.

Excavations: When a merchant from Iráklion, who was coincidentally called Minos Kalokairinos, found the first traces of ancient Knossós in 1878, the Minoan culture had long since been forgotten. Kalokairinos found six chambers with 12 large storage vases (pithoi) on the hill of Kephala, and in 1880 the American W.Stielman recognized the connection between Kephala and the legendary labyrinth of Knossós. In 1889 Heinrich Schliemann became involved, and in 1895 the Frenchman J.Joubert unsuccessfully attempted further excavation. In 1900, after the end of Turkish rule, the English archaeologist Arthur Evans began work, and unearthed an incredible array of ancient buildings and treasures, which established that there had been a palace on the site around 2000

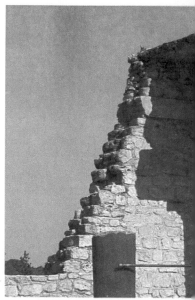

Knossós, N. entrance (restored) ▷

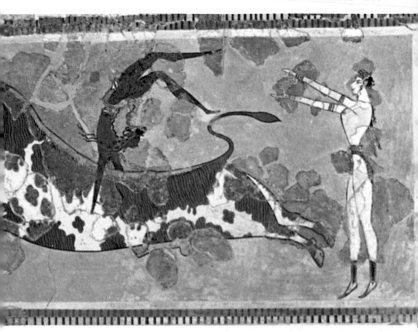

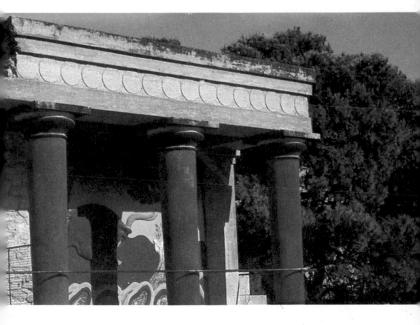

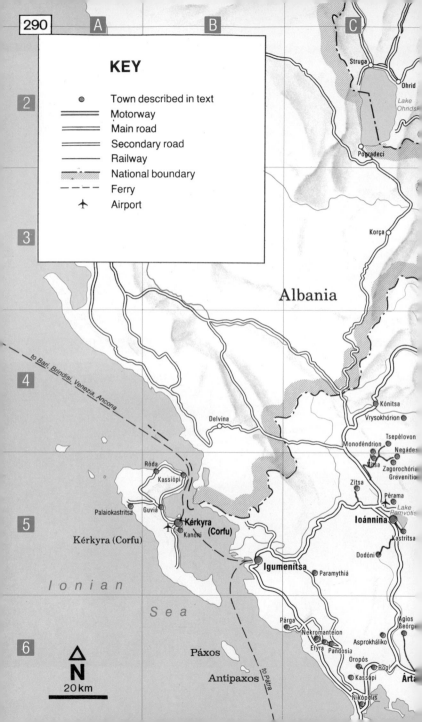

290

A · B · C

KEY

- ● Town described in text
- ═══ Motorway
- ═══ Main road
- ─── Secondary road
- ─── Railway
- ░░░ National boundary
- ─ ─ Ferry
- ✈ Airport

2

3

Struga
Ohrid
Lake Ohridsk

Pogradeci

Korça

Albania

4

to Bari, Brindisi, Venezia, Ancona

Delvina

Kónitsa
Vrysokhórion

Tsepélovon
Monodéndrion Negádes
Vítsa Zagorochória
Grevenítio

Róda
Kassiópi

Zitsa
Pérama
Lake Pamvotis

5

Palaiokastritsa
Guviá
Kérkyra (Corfu)
Kanóni

Ioánnina
Kastritsa

Kérkyra (Corfu)

Dodóni

Igumenítsa
Paramythiá

Ionian

Sea

Párga
Nekromanteíon
Efýra Pandosía
Oropós
Kassópi
Nikópolis

Asprokháliko

Rógi
Árta

Agios
Geórge

Páxos

Antipaxos

to Pátra

△
N
▬▬▬
20 km

6

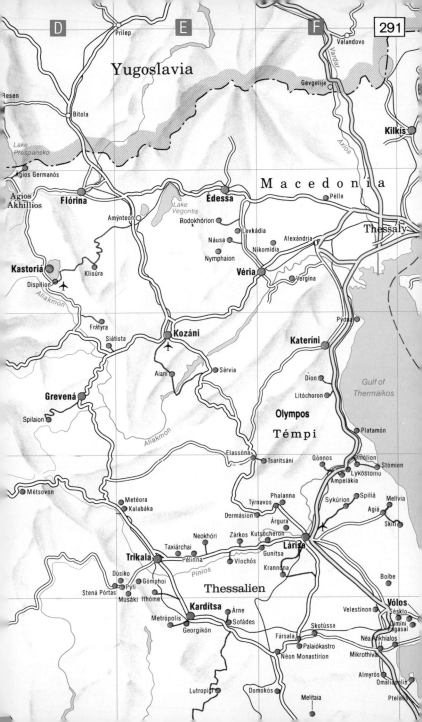

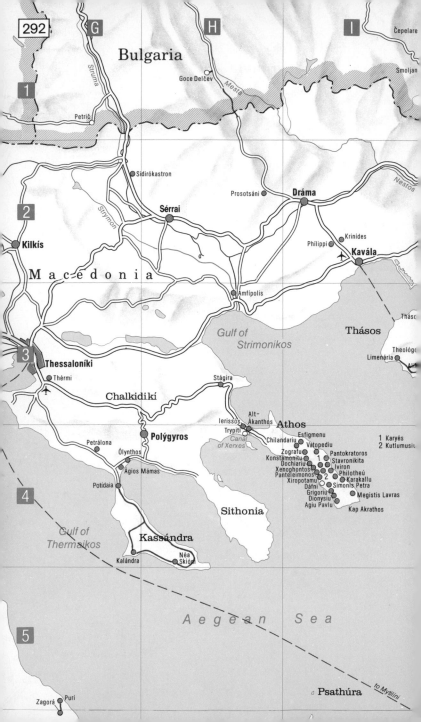

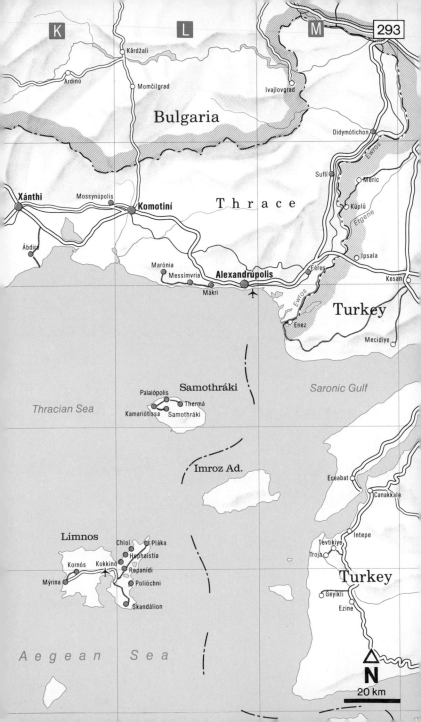

K　　　L　　　M

Bulgaria

Kărdžali

Ardino

Momčilgrad

Ivajlovgrad

Didymótichon

T　h　r　a　c　e

Suflí

Meric

Küplü

Xánthi

Mossynúpolis

Komotiní

Ergene

Ábdira

Marónia

Messímvria

Alexandrúpolis

Mákri

Féres

Ewros

Ipsala

Kesan

Turkey

Énez

Mecidiye

Samothráki

Saronic Gulf

Palaiópolis

Thermá

Thracian Sea

Kamariótissa

Samothráki

Imroz Ad.

Eceabat

Canakkale

Límnos

Chloí

Pláka

Intepe

Tevtikiye

Kornós

Kokkinó

Hephaïstia

Repanídi

Trojá

Mýrina

Polióchni

Turkey

Skandálion

Geyiklı

Ezine

A　e　g　e　a　n　　S　e　a

△
N

20 km

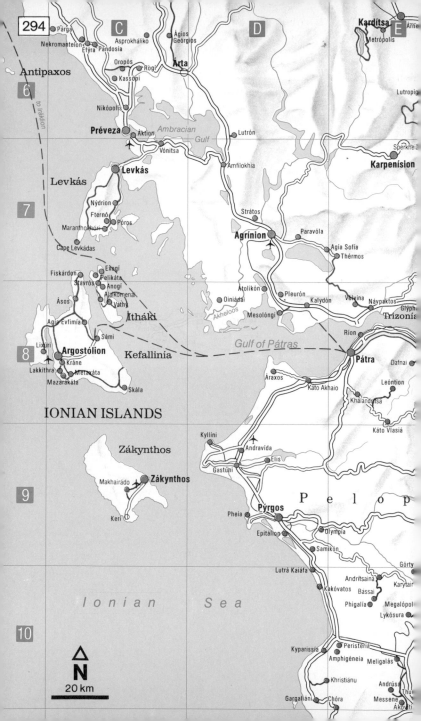

IONIAN ISLANDS

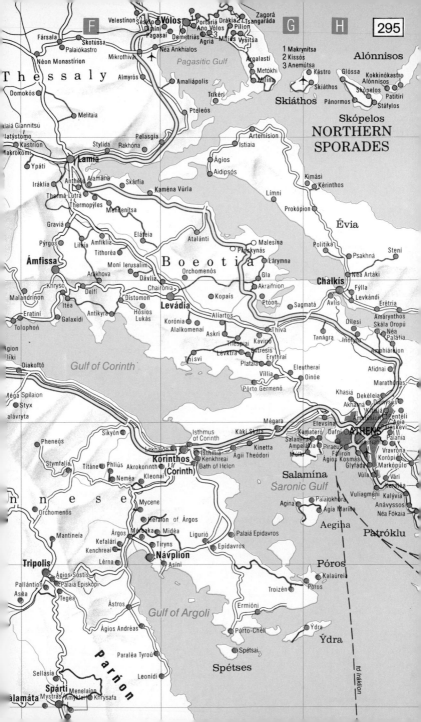

Velestínon
Séskio
Vólos
Portariá Drákia Zagorá
Tsangaráda

1 Makrynitsa
2 Kissós
3 Anemútsa

Alónnisos

Fársala
Skotússa
Palaiókastro
Néon Monastírion
Mikrothíva

Dimini
Pagasai
Demetriás
Ano Vólos
Agriá
Mliés Vysitsa

Pilion

Kástro
Glóssa
Kokkinókastro
Alónnisos
Skópelos
Patitíri

T h e s s a l y
Almyrós
Néa Ankhialos
Pagasitic Gulf
Argalastí
Metókhi
Mílina

Skiáthos
Skiáthos
Pánormos
Stáfylos

Domokós
Amaliápolis
Skiáthos

Melitaia
Trikéri
Skópelos

NORTHERN
SPORADES

alaiá Giannitsú
latýstomo
Kastríon
Makrokómi
Ypáti

Pelasgia
Stylida
Rakhóna
Lamía

Artemísion
Istiaia

Agios
Aidipsós

Kimási
Kérinthos

Evia

Iráklia
Antheia Alamána
Anthela
Thermá Lutrá
Thermopýles
Mendenitsa

Skárfia
Kaména Vúrla

Límni

Prokópion

Graviá
Eláfeia
Atalánti
Politiká
Psakhná
Steni

Pýrgos
Ámfissa
Lilaia
Amfíklia
Tithoréa
Moní Ierusalim
Ankhova
Dávlia

B o e o t i a
Orchomenós
Ploskynás
Lárymna
Malesína

Néa Artáki
Chalkís
Fýlla
Levkándi
Erétria

Khrysó
Delfí
Malandrínon
Itéa
Antíkyra
Distomon
Hósios
Lukás
Chairónia

Gla
Akraifnion
Ptóon

Sagmatá
Avlís

Dílesi
Skála Oropú
Néa
Palátia

Eratiní
Galaxídi
Tolophón

Korónia
Alalkomenai
Kopaís
Aliartos
Kavíno
Thíva
Erythraí

Amárynthos

Tanágra
Inóvia
Amphiárion

Agion
liki
Diakoftó

Thespiai
Sýtresis
Leyktra
Plataiá
Askri

Eleutherai
Oinóe

Afídnai

Marathónas

Megá Spílaion
Styx
alávryta

Gulf of Corinth
Thisvi

Vília
Pórto Germenó

Khasiá
Dekéleia
Akharná
Dionysos
Pentéli

Marathónas

Sikyón

Mégara
Káki Skála
Etevsína
Kamateró
Dafní
ATHENS

Pheneós

Isthmus
of Corinth
Lekhaíon
Isthmía
Kenchreai
Bath of Helen

Kinetta
Agii Theódori
Salamína
Ampelákia
Múlki

Piraeus
Fáliron
Agios Kosmás
Glyfáda

Agia
Paraskeví
Palaiá

Vravróna
Koropí
Markópulo
Vári

Stymfalía
Titáne
Phliús
Akrokorinth
Neméa
Kleonai
Kórinthos
(Corinth)

Salamína
Saronic Gulf

Vuliagméni
Kerátea
Kalývia
Anávyssos
Néa Fókaia

n n e s e
Orchomenós

Mycene
Heraíon of Árgos
Mídea
Ligurió

Palaiókhora
Agina
Agia Marína
Aegina

Patróklu

Mantineia
Kefalári
Kenchreai
Lérna
Árgos
Merbaka
Tíryns
Návplion
Asíni

Palaiá Epidavros
Epídavros

Póros
Kalaúreia

Tripolis
Ágios Sóstis
Palaiá Episkópi
Aséa
Pallántion
Tegéa

Ástros
Ágios Andréas

Ermióni
Pórto-Chéli

Troizén
Póros

Ýdra

Gulf of Argoli

Spétsai
Ýdra

Parnon

Paraléa Tyroú
Leonídi

Sellasía
Spárti
Mystrás
Menelaion
Amyklaio
Khrysafa
alamáta

Spétses

to Iraklion

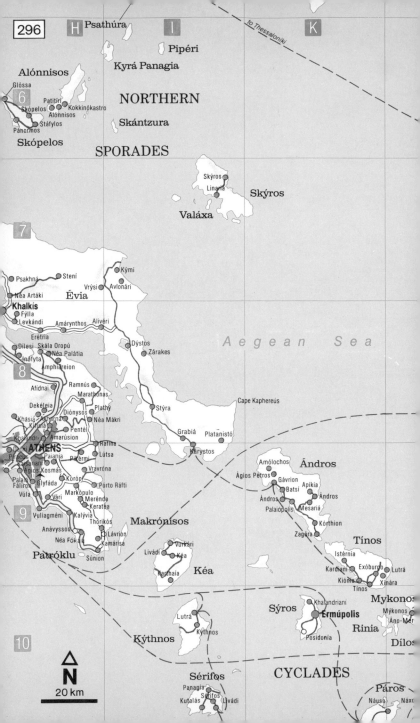

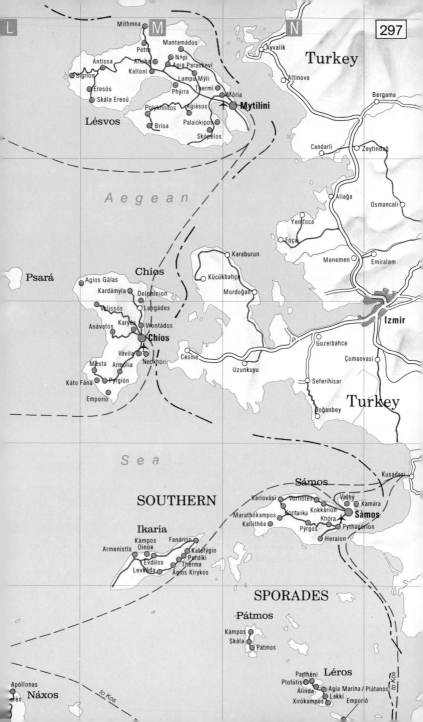

Mithmna
Mantamádos
Pétra
Ayvalik
Ántissa
Nápi
Arísha
Altinova
 Agia Paraskeví
Sigrion
Kallóni
Lampú Mýli
Bergama
Eresós
Phýrra
Thermí
Skála Eresú
Agiásos
Polýknitos
Palaiókipos
Candarli
Zeytindağ
Brísa
Skópelos
Lésvos
Mória
Mytilíni

Aegean

Aliağa
Osmancali
Yenifoca
Foça
Karaburun
Menemen
Emiralem

Psará
Agios Gálas
Chios
Kardámyla
Delphínion
Vlissós
Langádes
Küçükbahçe
Mordoğan
Anávatos
Karyes
Vrontádos
Chíos
Izmír
Vávila
Mestá
Neokhóri
Armólia
Cesme
Guzelbahçe
Káto Fána
Pyrgíon
Uzunkuyu
Çumaovasi
Emporió
Seferihisar
Doğanbey
Turkey

Sea

Kusadasi
Sámos
Karlovási
Vurlíotes
Vathý
Kamára
SOUTHERN
Marathókampos
Kontaiika
Kokkárion
Sámos
Kallithéa
Khóra
Pythagórion
Pýrgos
Heraíon
Ikaría
Fanárion
Kámpos
Armenistís
Oinóe
Kaléfygio
Evdilos
Perdíki
Therma
Levkáda
Ágios Kírykos

SPORADES

Pátmos
Kámpos
Skála
Pátmos

Apóllonas
etés
Náxos
to Kos
Léros
Parthéni
Plofútis
Agía Marína / Plátanos
Álinda
Lakkí
Xirókampos
Emporió

Turkey

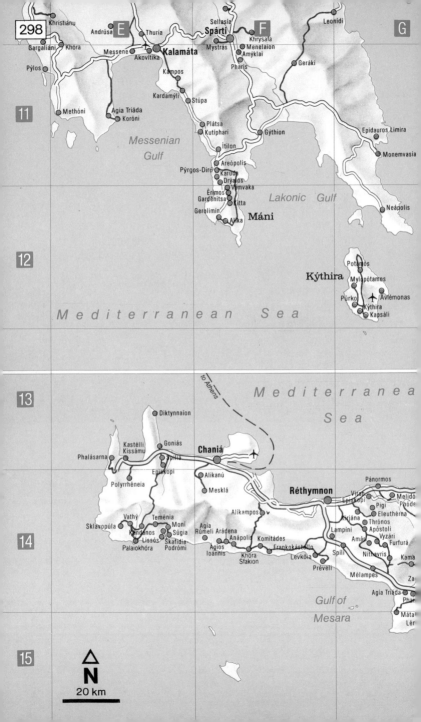

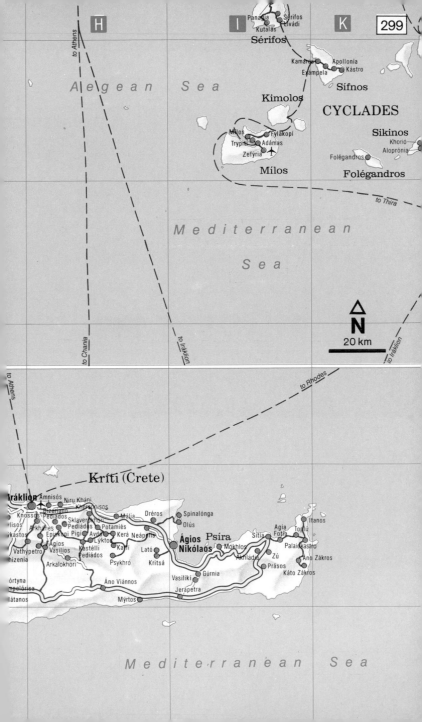

to Athens

A e g e a n   S e a

Panagía
Sérifos
Kutalás — Livádi
Sérifos

Kamáres — Apollonía
Exámpela — Kástro

Sífnos

Kímolos

CYCLADES

Sikinos

Mílos — Fylakopí
Trypití — Adámas
Zefyría

Khorió
Aloprónia

Folégandros

Mílos

Folégandros

M e d i t e r r a n e a n

S e a

to Thíra

△
N
20 km

to Chaniá

to Iráklion

to Iráklion

to Athens

to Rhodes

Kríti (Crete)

Iráklion — Amnisós — Nírou Kháni
Piezanós — Khóra — Psinós
Knossós — Pediádos — Spinalónga — Itanos
Sklaverokhóri — Mália — Dréros — Toplú
Arkhánes — Pediádos — Potamiés — Olús — Agía — Palaíkastro
Epískopi — Pigi — Avdú — Kerá — Neápolis — Foteiá
Ágios — Lýktos — Psíra — Sitía
Vathýpetro — Vasílios — Kastélli — Kafú — Lató — **Ágios** — Mókhlos
Chizenía — Pediádos — Kritsá — **Nikólaos** — Akhládi — Zú
Arkalokhóri — Psykhró — Prásos — Áno Zákros
órtyna — Vasilikí — Gúrnia — Káto Zákros
mpelóusa — Áno Viánnos — Jerápetra
látanos — Mýrtos

M e d i t e r r a n e a n   S e a

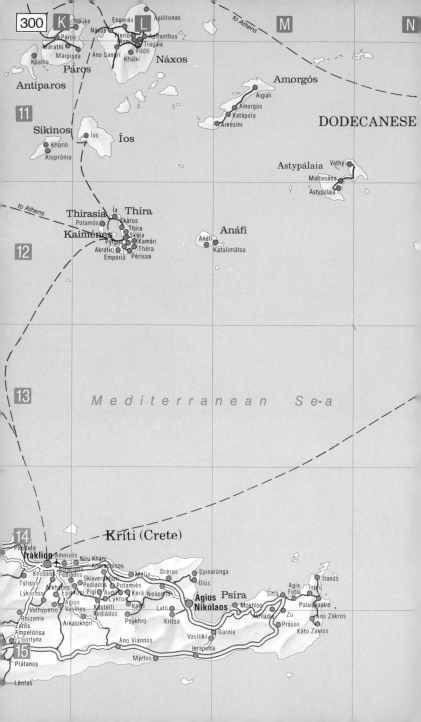

11

12

13

14

15

Páros

Antíparos

Náousa
Páros
Maráthi
Márpissa
Kástro

Náxos
Engarés
Apóllonas
Mérion
Monís
Apíranthos
Filóti
Áno Sangrí
Tragaía
Khálki
Náxos

Amorgós
Aigiáli
Amorgós
Katápola
Arkesíni

DODECANESE

Síkinos

Khorió
Aloprónia

Íos
Íos

to Athens

Astypálaia
Vathý
Maltesána
Astypálaia

Thirasía
Ía
Thíra
Potamós
Skáros
Thíra
Kaiménes
Pýrgos
Skála
Kamári
Akrotíri
Théra
Emporió
Périssa

Anáfi
Anáfi
Katalimátsa

Mediterranean Sea

Kríti (Crete)

Phódele
Amnisós
Iráklion
Niru Kháni
Bizarianu
Khersónisos
Knossós
Pediádos
Sklaverokhóri
Tylisos
Arkhánes
Pediádos
Potamiés
Mália
Dréros
Spinalónga
Lýkastos
Epískopí Pigí
Avdóu
Lýktos
Kerá
Neápoli
Ólus
Agía
Fotiá
Itanós
Vathýpetro
Ágios
Vasílios
Kastélli
Pediádos
Kamí
Lató
Ágios
Nikólaos
Sittía
Palaíokastro
Rhizenía
Arkalokhóri
Psykhró
Kritsá
Mókhlos
Zú
Áno Zákros
Zarós
Ampelórisa
Górtyna
Vasilikí
Gúrnia
Prásos
Káto Zákros
Áno Viánnos
Ierápetra
Plátanos
Mýrtos
Léntas
Akhládia
Psíra
Topu

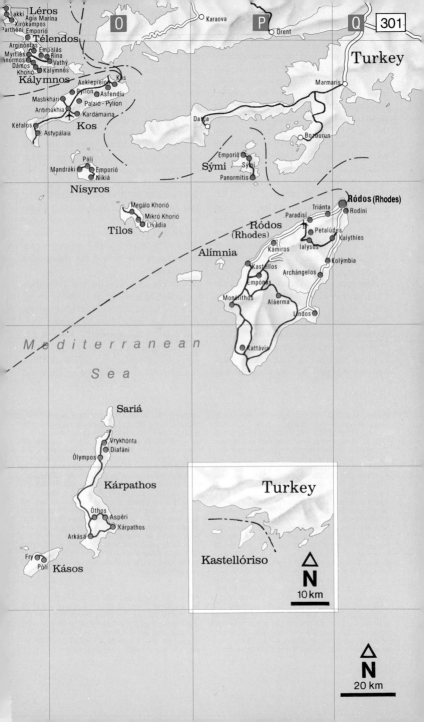

BC, and that it had been destroyed by earthquakes in around 1700 BC. The palace had been rebuilt (at that time the population of Knossós may have been around 50,000) in about 1600, partly destroyed and again rebuilt in around 1500 BC, and finally, according to recent scientific discoveries, destroyed in 1375 BC after being damaged by the violent volcanic eruption of Santorini in 1450.

It was then overrun by a number of peoples from the Greek mainland until 1100 BC. In the 4C Knossós was still the most important settlement in Crete. It was ruled by Egyptians and mainland Greeks in turn until the Romans took it, and the whole of Crete, in 69-7. Knossós was later occupied by Byzantines, Venetians and Turks, and in more recent times Germans, Americans and finally NATO troops have been stationed here.

The continual succession of new occupants, new settlements and wars left the country ravaged, with its ancient culture forgotten; but since 1900 it has been laboriously uncovered. Evans excavated in Crete

for 25 years and, with the help of improving scientific techniques, rebuilt the huge royal palace with concrete, plaster and paint.

The question was then asked, whether the huge, labyrinthine series of interconnected rooms and passages was a royal palace at all. Professor Dr.Hans Georg Wunderlich identified it as a type of necropolis, but his hypothesis was extensively refuted. Earthenware tablets with Linear B script dating from around 1450 BC were deciphered by two Englishmen, M.Ventris and J.Chadwick (although their findings were disputed), but gave no definitive information. Meanwhile, other evidence seemed to confirm that it was indeed the palace of a priest-king.

A number of multi-storeyed complexes seemed to be grouped around an open, 90 ft. x 200 ft. rectangular courtyard: yards, passageways, halls, stairs, workshops, storage, admimistration and reception rooms, as well as royal living quarters (separated for men and women). The arrangement of the rooms was determined by light and

Palace of Knossós according to the reconstruction and sub-division of Evans. **1** W. court with 3 round buildings for sacrificial offerings (2000-1750 BC) **2** altar base **3** main portal **4** guard-room **5** processional corridor, formerly frescoed with life-size depictions of gift-bearers - now in the Archaeological Museum, Iráklion **6** corridor of the Prince of the Lilies **7** S. propylaia **8** to **9** magazines which once contained 400 pithoi, each of which held 78 litres **10** administration room **11** archive, it was here that clay tablets with Linear B script were found **12** staircase to upper floor **13** central court **14** open vestibule **15** throne-room, originally with alabaster throne, there are frescos above the alabaster benches, these are copies, the originals are in the Archaeological Museum, Iráklion **16** sanctuary (the original, small altar is in Archaeological Museum, Iráklion) **17** tripartite shrine **18** treasury pit of the central shrine (three snake goddesses and a fine ceramic plates - all now in Iráklion - were found **19** Greek temple **20** shrine, originally with miniature fresco **21** cult room, originally with fresco of the 'Crocus Gatherer'? **22** N. propylaia **23** the Royal Road linking the palace with the harbour of Knossós **24** state staircase **25** court with cult basin **26** shaft staircase **27** corridor of the chess game, in which a valuable Minoan board game was found, made from lapis lazuli,

rock crystal, silver and gold, the pieces being made of ivory **28** royal pottery **29** magazine with giant pithoi **30** court with bull-game fresco **31** pottery **32** lapidary workshop **33** E. portico **34** queen's boudoir **35** megaron of the queen, the fresco of the dolphins was found here **36** residential section with double axes **37** bathroom **38** shrine of the double axe, a cult room with the sacred symbols of the bull's horns and the double axe, as well as a small pottery 'goddess with raised hands' (the deaf goddess) **39** cult basin **40** enclave, in the room to the W. on the entrance side was the 'Fresco with the Three Blue Ladies' **41** main staircase, entrance to the private royal apartments **42** side staircase, place where the ivory 'little ski-jumper' was found, now in Iráklion **43** Stepped Portico, leading to a Minoan viaduct to the road to the Caravanserei and Phaistós **44** residential building

Palace of Knossós, 1st floor: 1 upper propylon **2** Hall of Three Columns **3** treasury **4** large columned hall **5** room once decorated with the 'Parisienne' fresco **6** frescoed room which today has the Bull-game fresco, the 'Blue Bird', the 'Blue Ape', the 'Three Blue Ladies', the 'Captain and the Negro' and miniature frescos

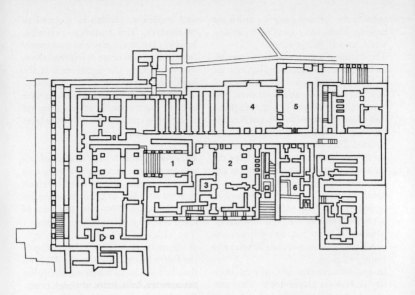

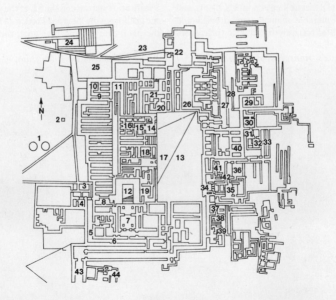

temperature. Sanitary systems, warm water heating, baths and closets with running water can still be identified.

The building is extraordinarily large for such an early structure; it displays extreme technical sophistication and architectural skill, and frescos of high artistic merit. The amazingly lifelike and ornate wall paintings which decorated the palace of Knossós have been partially uncovered and reconstructed. They suggest an epoch of cultural development which must have been the highest in Europe, long before the art and culture of classical Greece.

Some aspects of Minoan culture seem to be derived from Asia, and the construction of the labyrinth from Egypt. Essentially, however, it is unique, and displays unparalleled sophistication, joie de vivre and courtly elegance.

In contrast to the rest of Greek art, military themes are played down. The commonest motifs are religious details (bull horns, double axes), games (the 'bull game'), theatre scenes, animals, plants, and innumerable women, well-dressed and with attractively-styled hair (priestesses and goddesses, painted or sculpted in miniature). The masonry, ceramics, jewellery and miniatures, which are mostly housed in the museum at Iráklion, show, like the frescos, the significance of the highly-developed Minoan civilization.

236,806 sq. ft. of the Palace of Knossós are open to visitors (see the ground plan and its key); it is situated on a hill on the bank of the Kairátos.

Private houses: A large number of private houses have been excavated in the area around the palace, some of which date back to 2000 BC. Most of them, however, are from the period 1700–1400, and some of them contain remains of great interest: The 'House of the Sacrificial Oxen' is S. of the centre of the palace; the 'House of the Fallen Blocks', nearby to the W. (44 on the plan), is a house which was clearly the three-storeyed residence of a high priest. It contained a small shrine with a crypt.

Viaduct: A staircase in the SE of the palace leads from the 'Stepped Portico' (43 on the plan) over a Minoan viaduct, the re-

Knossós, ruins (Prepalatial period)   *Knossós, Prince of the Lilies (Mus. of Ir.)* ▷

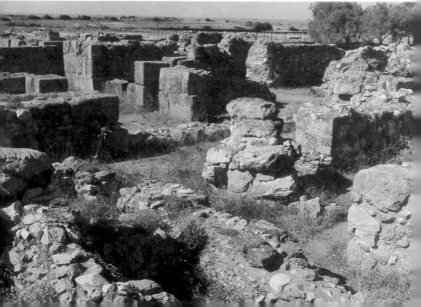

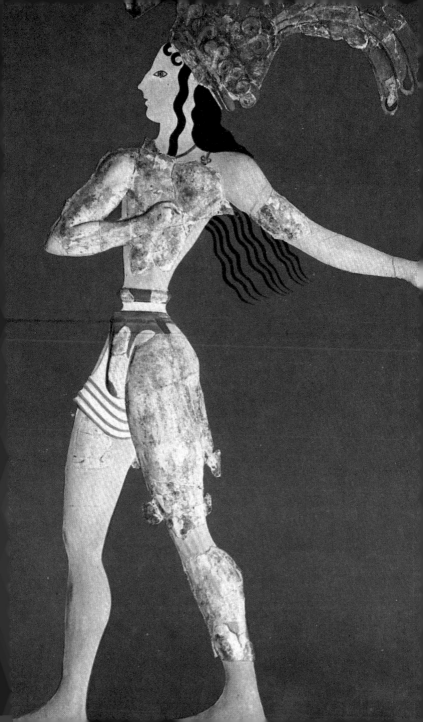

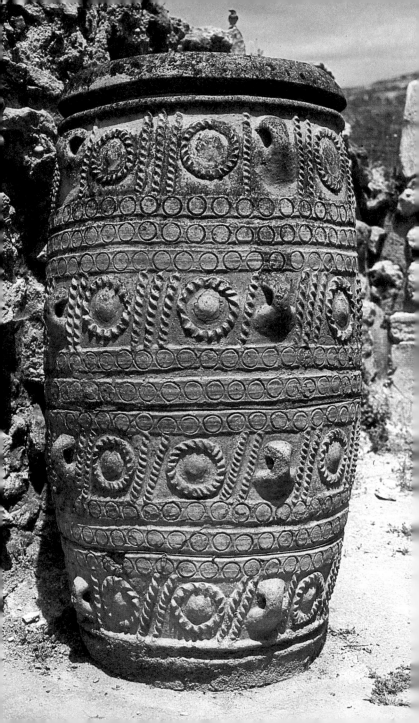

mains of which are still identifiable, which traverses the Vlychiá gorge to the Caravanserai.

Caravanserai: Little of this large structure still stands; it had baths and was used by travellers to clean and refresh themselves before entering the palace.

The frescos from the former main hall, which depict hoopoes and partridges, are now in the Archaeological Museum at Iráklion.

Small Palace: To the NW of the great palace of Knossós is the 'Small Palace', which was the second largest building in the old town. Private rooms, cult rooms and a crypt shrine with pillars have been uncovered.

A number of cult objects have been found here, including a very impressive and realistic sacrificial cup in the form of a bull's head, fashioned from black steatite and dating from 1550–1500 BC. They are on display in the Archaeological Museum in Iráklion.

Royal Villa: This is situated to the NE of the large palace, and used to be a small private house with an open central courtyard.

The main room has a niche which suggests that there was once a royal throne here; there is also a crypt supported by pillars, a shaft staircase, a main staircase and private rooms including a bath and lavatory.

House of Frescos: To the S. of the royal street of the Knossós palace is the 'House of Frescos', where various Minoan frescos were discovered, including the 'blue monkey' and the 'blue bird'.

Temple Tomb: Some 875 yards S. of the palace, near the road to Akhárnes and on the slopes of the Gypsade hill, is a temple tomb dating from 1700–1600 BC. It consists of a cult room, an open courtyard, an open and a roofed terrace, a crypt supported by pillars and a burial chamber which housed the wooden and clay sarcophagi.

◁ *Knossós, large pithos*   *Dolphin mosaic, fragment*

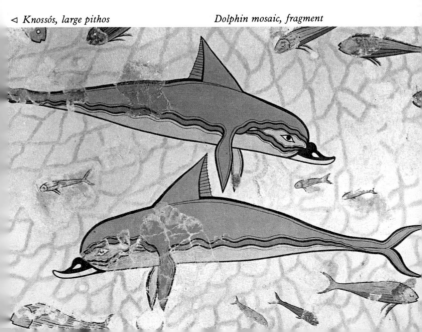

Komotiní/KOMOTHNH
Rodópi/Thrace   p.292☐I 2

This is the capital of the deme of Rodó-
pi, and has a population of 30,000. The
Roman *Via Egnatia* passes through it.
This was once an important route from
Italy to the Orient.

Small Fortress (inside the city): These
are the well-preserved remains of a 4C AD
building.

Archaeological Museum (*New Museum*,
situated in the town park): This houses
sculptures, Greek and Roman tomb
inscriptions, coins and rare gold busts of
a Roman emperor.

Byzantine Museum (*Byzantino Musio*):
Numerous icons, priests' vestments and
vessels.

Local Craft Museum (*Laografiko-istoriko
Musio*, 6 Bakali St.): Thracian costume,
jewellery and historical documents.

Environs: Marónia (32 km. SE): Near
this village is a field of ruins, which
excavations have revealed to be the site of
an *ancient acropolis* from the 13&12C BC.
Mossynúpolis (8 km. W.): This was once
a prosperous Byzantine town, of which
little is still standing. S. of Mossynúpolis
is the prehistoric *Tomb of Parathimi*.

Kopaís/Lake Kopaís/ΚΟΠΑΙΣ
Boeotia/Central Greece   p.294☐G 8

According to Strabo, the lake at Kopaís was
drained in ancient times by the inhabitants
of Orchomenos to create a fertile plain for
development; recent excavations have confirmed Strabo's assertion. Under the supervision of Prof. Dr. S.Lauffer of

Munich, ancient channels have been discovered which diverted the lake water into
holes (katavothres), allowing the water from
Lake Kopaís to flow out into the Straits of
Euboea. The excavations also revealed a
larger channel, which was commissioned
by Alexander the Great and built by the
engineer Krates.
There are a number of ancient sites on the
plain of Kopaís, such as the Pýrgos (castle) of St.Marina NE from Gla over the
Melas bridge, which dates from Mycenean
times, and foundations from a classical heroon on the island of Strowiki (7.5 km. SE
of Pýrgos).

Environs: Ptóon (*c.* 26 km. N. of
Thebes): at the foot of Mt.Pelagia is the famous shrine of Ptóon-Apollo, which is
built on three levels. This was the site of
an ancient oracle, which was later linked
to Apollo; Mardonios questioned this oracle for its advice before the battle of Plataia.
French excavations have revealed the ruins
of the shrine: on the third level are the remains of a Doric Temple of Apollo from
the 3C BC, which was built on the foundations of an older temple (7C BC). This is
where the great Kouros, which is on display in the National Museum in Athens,
was found. **Akraifnion** (*c.* 30 km. NW of
Thebes): This is where the Thebans are
said to have sought refuge after their town
was destroyed by Alexander the Great. On
the outskirts of the town is a small chapel
consecrated to St.George which, according to an inscription on the wall dated
1311, was founded by the Frankish lord of
the region, Antonius le Flamenk, probably as a votive offering to St.George, the
patron saint of military commanders, before the battle against the Catalans at
Khairónia (1311). **Gla:** The village of Kástro (Topólia) is not far from Akraifnion, and
2.5 km. outside it is the old island of Gla,
visible across the open fields of Kopaís. It
was known to Homer as *Arne*, and was the
site of one of Greece's most important pre-

historic settlements. The Cyclopean walls of this 14C BC Mycenean fortress are 2 miles long, and the acropolis is on the N. side; the palace stands on the highest point of the hill, and was the seat of the Mycenean lords. Recent Greek excavations have brought pieces of the Mycenean settlement and palace to light. **Alíartos** (31 km. W. of Thebes): ½ a mile from the present-day village, on the right hand side of the road to Levádia, are the remains of the ancient settlement; this is where the Spartan general Lysander was killed by a brave Alíartian soldier during the Boeotian War in 395 BC. According to legend, the famous blind prophet of Thebes, Teiresias, also died here. **Evangelístria nunnery** (8 km. from Alíartos): This was founded in the late Byzantine period, and rebuilt around 1665, according to an inscription over the entrance.

The walls of the main church are covered with fine 17C frescos. In the templon (sanctuary) are magnificent icons representing the Annunciation, which is why the nunnery is known as the Evangelístria ('Angel of the Annunciation'). The church is a famous pilgrimage destination, visited by pilgrims from all over Greece. There are 20 nuns living here at present, and they produce superb weaving and embroidery.

Kórinthos/Corinth/ΚΟΡΙΝΘΟΣ
Corinth/Peloponnese   p.294□G 9

The ancient city of Corinth lay some 6 km. S. of the modern one, which has a population of 16,000 but no points of particular interest to the sightseer.

Kórinthos, ancient city centre 1 Temple of Octavia **2** museum **3** Glauke fountain **4** shrine of Hera Akraia **5** W. shops **6** Temple of Hermes **7** Babbius monument **8** Temple of Poseidon **9** Temple of Herakles **10** Temple of Apollo Klarios **11** Pantheon **12** Temple of Venus **13** Dionysos shrine **14** shops **15** Bouleuterion **16** S. basilica **17** fountain **18** office of the Agonothetes (mosaics) **19** SE building **20** round building **21** S. stoa **22** central shops **23** Bema **24** Julian Basilica **25** starting line of the Greek stadium **26** retaining wall **27** altar **28** agora **29** underground entrance **30** triglyph wall **31** NW shops **32** sacred springs **33** Propylon **34** Fountain of Peirene **35** peripteral temple **36** Baths of Eurykles **37** 4C Greek temple **38** façade of the Captive Barbarians **39** Lechaion road **40** oracular shrine **41** basilica **42** Greek market **43** Roman market **44** N. stoa **45** N. market **46** Temple of Apollo **47** theatre **48** Odeion

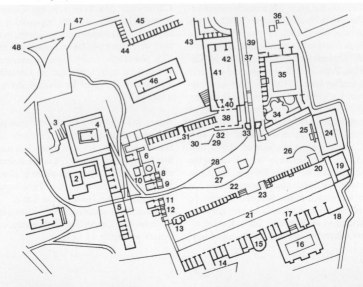

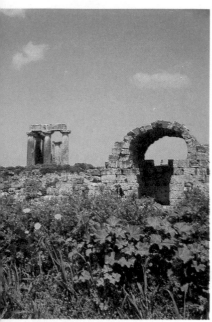
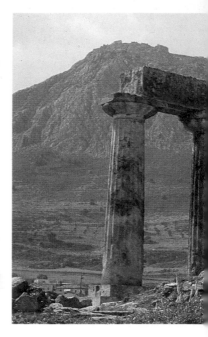

Kórinthos, agora, Temple of Apollo

History: Sisyphos and Ephyra were the legendary founders of the city in around 1000 BC, but there was a much earlier settlement in Neolithic times (5000) and the Bronze Age (3000), of which traces have been found in the surrounding area. In the 8C Corinth founded the colonies of Kérkyra, Poteidea and Syracuse, and just over a century later (657 BC) the reign of the tyrant Kypselos and later his son Periander (627–585) began, which was to lead the city into its period of greatest prosperity. During the Peloponnesian War of 431–404, Corinth was on the side of Sparta, but changed allegiances in 395 and began the Corinthian War (395–387). In 335 it was conquered by the Macedonians, and in 224 it was united to the Achaean League. In 146 BC it was destroyed by the Romans, and in 44 BC rebuilt by Julius Caesar, after which the city enjoyed a second hey-

day. The Apostle Paul founded a community there in 51–2 and preached Christianity (the Letters to the Corinthians). Hadrian (117–38) improved the city with some magnificent buildings, but they were destroyed by an earthquake in 375. The Goths, under Alaric, conquered and razed it in 395, and ancient Corinth was finally destroyed by another earthquake in 551.

Agora (837 x 39 ft.): By the entrance to the excavation area is the *Fountain of Glauke*, which is carved in the rock; it has four basins, each of which was the source of a spring. To the E. is the *shrine of Hera Akraia*, whose cult came from Perachora. The temple dates from Roman times.
SW from the museum is a *peripteral temple*, commissioned, according to Pausanis, as a mark of respect by Octavia.

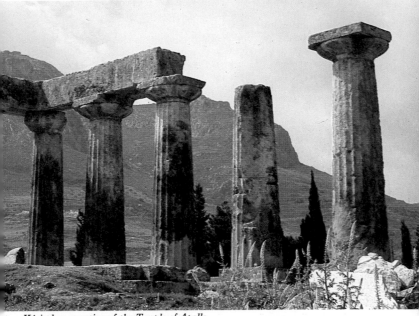

Kórinthos, remains of the Temple of Apollo

The path from the museum leads to the *W. buildings* of the agora from the 1C BC. Directly opposite are the *foundations of six temples* from Roman times, and the round monument of Babbius Philinus. According to Pausanias's account, the most southerly of the temples was dedicated to the goddess Tyche. Next is the Pantheon, then the Temple of Hercules and Neptune (Poseidon). The last two date from around 160 BC. In front of the Babbius monument is the Temple of Apollo Klarios, which had a bronze statue of the god, and lastly a Temple of Hermes. The northern edge of the agora is formed by the *NW buildings*, 16 in all. One of the E. structures was an *oracular shrine*, which had an underground connection to the 'sacred spring' in the centre of the agora. This spring ran below floor level and the only access to it was down a series of steps. The fountain house is stillstanding, and has a triglyph wall with traces of wall paintings. Two bronze lions' heads serve as waterspouts. To the E. is the façade of a Roman basilica, which is known as the *Façade of the Captive Barbarians*; it was a two-storeyed Corinthian basilica and the central four columns on the second storey were larger than life size atlantes of barbarians, two of which are now in the museum.

On the E. side of the agora is the *Julian Basilica*, which was used as a law court and built by the family of Augustus.

The *Greek stadium* is S. of the Fountain of Peirene; the starting lines and holes in the tufa for the runners can still be seen. There are traces of chariot tracks, which suggest that the stadium was also used for chariot races. Near a supporting wall further to the S. are the remains of a *Greek agora* with a pebbled surface.

A row of buildings separates the smaller section of the agora from the higher section to the S. In the middle stands the *Bema*, the monumental rostrum from which the Roman consuls delivered their speeches to the assembled citizens. In 52 BC the Apostle Paul appeared on the Bema in front of the Consul L.I. Gallio, accused by the Jews of Corinth.

Temple of Apollo: This is a Doric peripteros from the mid 6C (built between 550 and 525), with 6 x 15 columns. It has a pronaos and an opisthodomos with two columns between the ante. Two inner rows of columns supported the roof. It was built on the site of an older, 7C temple.

NW Stoa (S. of the temple): This dates from the 3C BC and has rows of Doric columns on the exterior, with Corinthian columns inside.

Further to the E., past a 1C BC propylon which bore a gilded bronze chariot carrying Helios and Phaeton, is the *Fountain of Peirene*, which is on a lower level than the surrounding area and dates, in the form we see it today, from the 2C AD. It was built by Herodes Atticus. The façade had six recesses behind which there were six basins which were filled from an underground water supply. The façade was marble, and the other three sides had exedrae with three niches containing statues of Herodes Atticus's family.

Lechaion Road (W. of the spring): The W. side of this road had a number of porticoes which led to houses, above which was an extended terrace which supported a Roman basilica from the 1C BC. Further to the N. is a semicircular building on the site of a Roman agora. On the opposite side, beginning from the N., are the *Baths of Eurykles* (2C AD), which were replaced by hot water system in Byzantine times; the *latrines* and the *Peribolos of Apollo* with a peristyled court (Ionic columns). On the

W. side of the Peribolos is a small *Temple of Apollo* from the 4C BC.

S. Stoa: This extends behind the shops and dates from the 4C BC. 500 ft. long and two storeys high, with 71 Doric columns along the front and 34 Ionic columns inside, it was restored when Corinth was rebuilt. A row of 33 shops stood behind the Stoa, each divided into two square rooms. The front rooms were supplied from the Fountain of Peirene, and water-pipes ran under the Stoa at the level of the shops. Most of them appear to have been wine shops, on the evidence of what has been found (pitchers and goblets), and were destroyed in the 1C BC.

There are *mosaics* under a protective roof, which depict a crowned athlete with a palm branch in front of a seated female figure, the personification of happiness (Eutychia). Another room contains two mosaics, Dionysos on a chariot which is being pulled by panthers, and Nereids with a Triton; both date from about 200 AD.

S. Basilica (behind the Stoa): This has an inner courtyard surrounded by colonnades. The council chamber, the *Bouleuterion*, is attached to the shops of the S. Stoa and is semicircular in shape. Between it and the E. row of shops in the S. Stoa there is a gap for the road to the port of Kenchreai (1C AD).

Theatre (NW of the Temple of Apollo): There are remnants of the Roman as well as the 5C Greek theatre. The tiers of seats are from the Greek theatre. These have survived because they were concealed by the supporting walls of the Roman cavea. The wall which separated the cavea from the orchestra was covered with paintings, and some of it is still standing. The theatre was destroyed during the invasion of the Goths in AD 396.

Shops, Temple of Apollo ▷

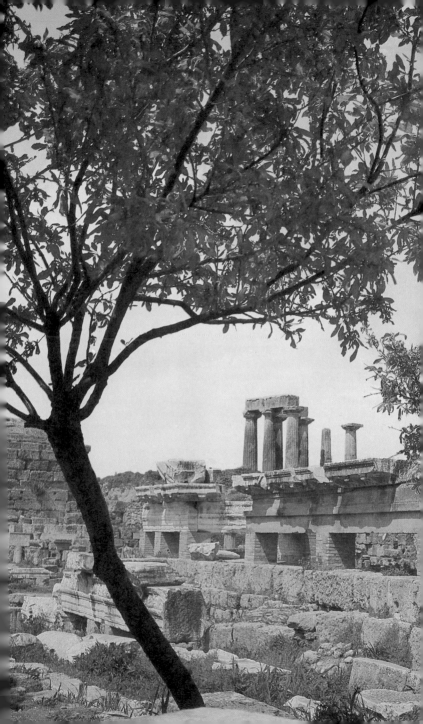

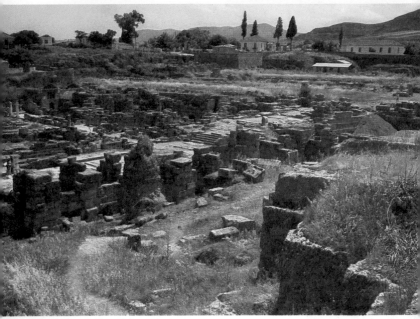

Kórinthos, section of the ancient agora

Odeion (S. of the theatre): This was built in the 1C AD, and could hold 3,000 spectators. It was destroyed by fire in the middle of the 2C, and later rebuilt and used for gladiator fights. It was eventually destroyed by the Goths.

To the E. of the Odeion is the *Shrine of Athena Khalinitis* (with the reins), which takes its name from the magnificent reins with which Bellerophon caught Pegasus, the horse.

Asklepieion (N. of the theatre): 4C BC; a Peribolos encloses a prostyle temple with four columns (50 x 28 ft.). There was an *enkoimiterion* (dormitory) adjacent to the W., in which the sick waited for gods to appear in their dreams and offer them healing advice. The Asklepieion was linked to the *Spring of Lerna* by a staircase. It was a square building with a courtyard surrounded on all sides by colonnades, and was used as a hospitality area for the sick. S. of the Asklepieion are the remains of a *Doric stoa* (1C AD), which may have been part of a gymnasion.

Roman Villa (SW of the Odeion on the Anaploja site): The ruins of a 1C AD villa with a mosaic pavement.

Museum: This houses archaeological finds from Corinth and its environs. Opposite the entrance in the vestibule is a 4C mosaic with griffins; also a Roman relief with the head of Athena Parthenos. *First Room:* Vessels from Neolithic to late Helladic times (4th millenium–1200 BC); obsidian blades; tools; remnants of wall paintings; a proto-Cycladic idol. *Second Room:* A number of proto-Geometric (11&10C), Geometric (10–8C),

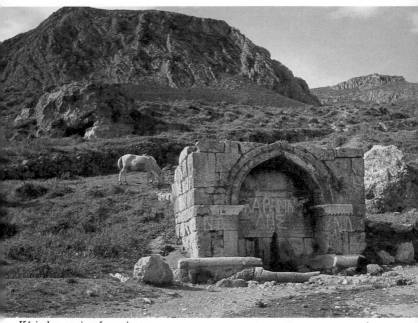

Kórinthos, ancient fountain

proto-Corinthian (8&7C) and Corinthian (7&6C) vases, and black and red figures ceramics; the 5C sarcophagus of an athlete; a terracotta group (Amazon battle, late 6C); sphynx with traces of colour on the wings; 8C terracotta tablet with the Greek alphabet.

Third Room: Statues of the Julian family, including Augustus (27 BC–AD 14); head of Doryphoros, Roman copy of a work by Polyclitus; Roman statue of Demeter; statue of the Emperor Hadrian; statues of the captive barbarians; 2C Roman mosaics; Byzantine ceramics; coins etc.

Asklepieion Room: Finds from the Asklepieion, including metopes, offerings and inscriptions.

The *colonnade* around the courtyard houses reliefs from the theatre from the 2C AD depicting battles of Amazons and giants and the labours of Herakles.

Environs: Acrocorinth: This was Corinth's acropolis from ancient to medieval times, and is situated on a hill almost 2,000 ft. high. The only access is from the W. On the cliff beneath the entrance to the ruins is a *Temple to Demeter and Kore*, which stood from the 7C BC to the 4C AD, and the remains of a *theatre*.

The fortress seems to have existed in archaic times (7C BC); some sections of the wall were rebuilt by the Byzantines. It was taken by the Franks in 1210, and handed over to the Despot of Mystrás in 1394. Six years later it passed to the Hospitallers of Rhodes, and in 1485 it was captured by the Turks before coming under Venetian rule from 1687–1715.

The way into the fortress leads past a Venetian ditch and three gates: the first, like the curtain wall, is Frankish, but was rebuilt by the Venetians after 1687. The second wall is partially Byzantine and partially Venetian, and the third is Byzantine but incorporates parts of an ancient structure from the 4C BC.

The *Shrine of Aphrodite* was known for its large number of temple prostitutes (over 1000), but only a few fragments of it are identifiable in the E. section of the fortress. By the S. wall is the upper *Peirene Spring*, which was roofed and enclosed in Hellenistic times, with the S. section serving as a collecting basin. There is a staircase leading to the underground N. chamber.

Lechaion (3 km. W.): This was once Corinth's northern port, and the harbour is mostly artificial. According to Pausanias there was a shrine to Poseidon here, and Plutarch also mentions a shrine to Aphrodite.

There are remains of an extensive *basilica* (600 ft. long) with three aisles, dating from the 5C AD and built under Anastasius I (491–518) and Justin I (518–27). It was destroyed in 551 by an earthquake.

man II, Andrea Doria of Genoa captured, but was unable to keep hold of it, and the next year the Turks won it back. In 1662 it was conquered by the Spanish, and then the Venetians in 1685 under the command of Morosini, who slaughtered all the Turks there, some 1500.

Fortress: This was built by the Byzantines and enlarged by the Venetians; the entrance consists of a 13C Venetian gate, and there are small churches inside the walls. There are two round towers of differing heights in the NE corner, and in the 16C the Turks made additions. Further round the fortress are a Byzantine structure and to the W. a Venetian bastion built in 1463 with a domed roof and supporting arches.

Environs: The remains of the **Shrine of Apollo Corinthos** are near Kandianika, with the foundations of various temples from the 7&6C BC. Near **Agía Triáda** (5 km. N.) are the remnants of a Roman villa with a mosaic floor (Dionysiac themes) from the mid 2C AD; the mosaic is in the museum at Kalamáta.

Koróni/ΚΟΡΩΝΗ

Messenia/Peloponnese   p.298□E 11

This is situated on the W. coast of the Messenian Gulf, some 50 km. SW of Kalamáta, and has a population of 1,607. Above the town is a Venetian-Turkish fortress.

History: The first inhabitants were settlers from Asini (Argolís); later the inhabitants of the nearby town of Koróni (Petalídion) incorporated the town and adopted the name. Koróni was known for the export of cochineal, a dye obtained from a scale insect, and olive oil. In 1205 it was occupied by Guillaume de Champlitte and Geoffroy de Villehardouin, and one year later by the Venetians. In 1209 the Byzantines took control, and in 1500 the Turks. In 1532, during the rule of Sulei-

---

Kos (I)/ΚΩΣ

East Aegean Islands (Dodecanese)/
Aegean Islands   p.300□N/O 11

Kos is the second-largest island of the Dodecanese after Rhodes, with a size of 112. sq. miles and a population of around 18,000. It is some 27 miles long and 6 miles wide at points, and is only 2.5 miles from the Turkish coast, opposite the ancient town of Halikarnassós, which is now Bodrum. It is a hilly island covered in vegetation, fertile and a popular destination since Roman times.

History: There have been numerous finds suggesting that the island played a significant role in the Mycenean-Achaean epoch of the 15-12C BC, and took part in the Trojan War (see the 'Iliad'). Around 800 BC it was re-colonized by Dorians from Thessaly. During the 6C it belonged to the League of Six Cities (Hexápolis), along with Halikarnassós, Knídos and Rhodes. After the defeat of the Persians in 479 BC, it became a member of the Attic maritime league (479–378), and then changed hands several times (Athens, Rhodes, Macedonia, Ptolemy). Under the Ptolemys (Ptolemy II was born in Kos in 308 BC) the new capital, which was founded in 366, was decorated with both religious and secular buildings, as was the nearby Asklepieion. The Asklepieion area and the medical school of Hippocrates became world famous (coins depict the rod and snake of Asklepios). From 190 BC the island came under Roman rule, and was subject to a succession of earthquakes, most notably in the 6C AD, when the Asklepieion was destroyed. In 431 it became the seat of a bishop, with a number of early Christian basilicas, and from 1309–1522 it fell into the hands of the Hospitallers of Rhodes, subsequently becoming a Turkish posses-sion (1523–1912). It was then under Italian rule until 1948.

Kos (population: 9,000): The modern capital is situated on a bay in the NE of the island, on the same site as the old Hellenis-tic capital of the same name which was founded in 366 BC. The earthquakes of 1933 brought down some of the modern buildings and allowed Italian archaeolo-gists to uncover the foundations of sections of the *ancient city*, which had a population of 100,000. These began near the port of *Mandráki*, which dates from late anti-quity/medieval times: to the SE are the re-mains of the Hellenistic *agora* (4C BC), which includes the remnants of various *temples*. To the E. are some excavated sec-tions of the old *town walls* (366 BC). There are traces of a Hellenistic *stoa* in the E., dat-ing from the 4 or 3C, on the same site as a 5 or 6C AD early Christian *basilica* (St. John) with *baptistery*. The *colonnade* below the 18C *Defterdar Mosque* is also from the stoá. The basilica and the baptistery are connected by a huge *marble door*, and the font in the baptistery is set into the marble

Kos (Kos), Asklepieion

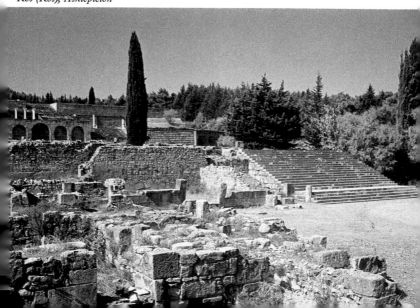

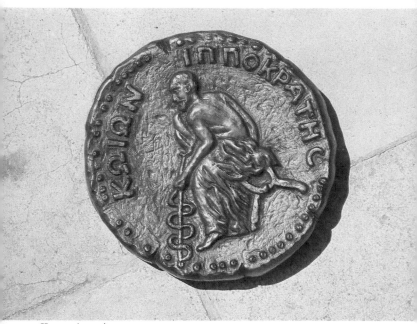

Kos, ancient coin

flags of the pavement. Inside the stoa area are the remains of the foundations of a 3C BC *Temple of Herakles*, including fragments of the stylobate, column bases and capitals, and also a *Temple of Aphrodite* from the 2C BC and a *Roman temple* from the 2C AD. Adjacent are the remains of an *agora* from the 2C BC with a *W. stoa* (market) 500 ft. long and 200 ft. wide, with two columns which have been re-erected. To the S. are the remains of the foundations of a *temple* and *altar to Dionysos*. This area, the Roman agora, was splendidly laid out in Roman times, with wide steps leading from the harbour to the *city gate* to the N. There are traces of paving from *ancient streets*, and blocks from marble walls near the church of *Ágios Konstantinos*, a 15C building with fine frescos.

The second largest excavation area is in the W. of the town, around Megalu-

Konstantinu Street: there are *Roman streets* in this area with paving which is still identifiable, especially the W-E street. There are remains of the *houses* on each side of the street, many of which contain *mosaic floors* (e.g. 'Judgement of Paris') and *wall paintings* dating from the 3C AD. Nearby are the ruins of some large (heated) *baths* with numerous fragments of *mosaics*. One room was partially converted into a church in the 5C AD. The area also has the ruins of a *Roman house*, with fine 3C AD *mosaics*, and the remains of a row of columns from a Roman *gymnasion*, some of which have been re-assembled; it includes *mosaics of gladiators*, and the *stadium* is nearby. An architecturally interesting *Roman house* has also been restored. Nearby is the *Roman odeion*, which has 14 rows of seats made from Kos marble, and a *vaulted building* behind the

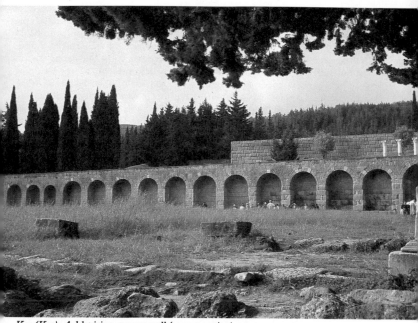

Kos (Kos), Asklepieion, terrace wall (reconstruction)

pentagonal *skene* (stage) and two flights of steps. Further to the W. are the scattered remains of a *Temple of Demeter*. Near the odeion are the remains of a basilica dedicated to John the Baptist (5&6C), from which a baptistery and chapel survive. *Hospitallers' Castle (Kastro):* To the E. of the port of Mandráki is the *fortress* built in 1391 by the Hospitallers of Rhodes on ancient foundations and using ancient building materials. It is separated from the town by a deep moat, and the entrance is reached by an arched bridge from the main square, in which is the *Plane Tree of Hippocrates* (Hippocrates is said to have taught here). The fortress has a *double curtain wall*: the outer one is 15C and bears the coat-of-arms of the Grand Master Pierre d'Aubusson, dating from 1489, on the W. side, above an antique marble lion. The inner wall dates from at least the 14C, but was

strengthened by d'Aubusson. The *Archaeological Museum* is near the port, and the W. wing (ground floor) mainly houses *sculptures* from classical, Hellenistic and Roman times, including a classical-style *statue of Hippocrates* from the 3 or 2C, and a *mosaic* 'Hippocrates meets Asklepios, the God of Healing' from the 2 or 3C AD; there are further fragments and inscriptions from all periods. The first floor houses an interesting collection of *vases* and *small figures*, mostly finds from the Asclepieion. Many finds, however, especially the mosaics, have been taken to the museum in Rhodes.

The Asklepieion (modern Greek *Asklipi-ion*): Some 4 km. SW of the town is the famous *Sanctuary of Asklepios*, which dates from the 4C BC and was built on the site of a still older *Temple to Apollo*. The Asklepieion is one of the most beautifully-appointed island shrines in the Aegean; it was discovered by the German archaeologist Herzog in 1901 and systematically excavated by the Italians. A cypress alley leads to the *lower terrace*, whose courtyard was surrounded on three sides by *colonnades*. The ancient entrance was a central staircase with a *gatehouse* (propylon), flanked by the exterior walls of the halls. In front of this to the left are the remains of *Roman baths* from the 1C AD with a well-preserved hypocaust. This lower terrace was the medicinal and therapeutic centre, and has various *springs* and *fountains*, and also a room for votive tablets. There is also a small temple (naiskos) dedicated by the Emperor Nero's personal physician (1C AD) Xenophon (left by the staircase); Nero was worshipped as a second Asklepios. The *middle terrace* was the centre of the old shrine, and housed the *sacrificial altar* to the god Asklepios. Similar to the one at Pergamon, it dated from the 2C BC and was built on top of an old 4C one. To its right is a simple Ionic *temple in antis*, 30 ft. x 40 ft., dedicated to Asklepios and built around 300 BC. The two columns between the ante have been re-erected. This was the site of the temple treasury, and the vestibule probably housed the famous painting of the 'Sacrificial Procession to the Shrine', by the artist Apelles, the son of the sculptor Praxiteles, to whom the 'Family of Asklepios' group of statues is also attributed. To the left of the altar is a *Roman peripteral temple* dating from the 2C AD with 9 Corinthian columns along the side, 7 of which have been re-erected. The building behind it was some sort of store (lesche), which was built at the same time as the Asklepieion, along with the *exedra* and the *abaton*. The *upper terrace* has a central staircase, and was the site of the great *Temple of Asklepios* from the 2C BC. A peripteral temple whose walls are only standing up to ground level; it had 6 x 11 white marble Doric columns and was a larger version of the Temple of Asklepios at Epídavros, the other main centre of the Asklepios cult in Greece. The upper terrace offers a splendid panorama and was surrounded on three sides by porticoes of Doric columns, like those of the lower terrace. They date from

Kos (Kos), Asklepieion, columns of the Roman peripteral temple

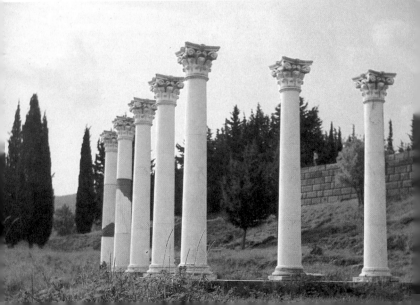

a later period than the temple and housed the sick. Every year the festival of Asklepios (festival of the raising of the rod) was held here, incorporating processions and cock sacrifices by those who had been healed. The sanctuary, seriously damaged by earthquake in the 6C, was finally destroyed and ceased to be of importance. Hippocrates (*c.* 460 – *c.*370 BC), the founder of the science of medicine (his collected knowledge is to be found in the 'Corpus Hippocraticum'), worked on the island of Kos before the founding of the Asklepieion. He came from an old local priestly family and travelled extensively before dying in Larissa, Thessaly. His pupils originally established a centre of healing here after his death, using the old Hippocratic methods (anamnesis, diagnosis, therapy), and the Hippocratic Oath has become the ethical maxim of the medical profession.

Other points of interest on the island: S. of the Asklepieion is the oldest building on the island, a 20 ft. high *Tholos* with a 100 ft. covered passageway leading to it whose purpose is still a mystery. Near *Asfendíu*, some 12 km. from Kos, are the ruins of a medieval Hospitaller *fortress*. The village of *Pylíon* (*c.* 16 km. SW of Kos) has three fine Byzantine churches, and S. of the village are the ruins of the medieval settlement of *Palaio-Pylíon*: the churches of *Ágios Nikolaos*, *Panagia* and *Ágios Antonios* have partially preserved frescos from the 15C. The Byzantine *fortress*, which was restored by the Hospitallers, is situated on the *Kastro hill*. Nearby are the remains of an ancient *Temple of Demeter* and the *Heroon of Kharmylion*, a vaulted room from the 4C BC over which a small church was built from ancient building materials. The harbour of *Kardámaina* has remnants of a *Hospitaller fortress* 25 km. SE of Kos, and to the W. are the ruins of an *Temple of Apollo* and a *Hellenistic theatre* with six rows of tufa seats and a skene podium. Near *Antimákhia*, 24 km. SW of Kos, is an interesting and well-preserved *Hospitaller fortress* (1494) with the bastion of the Grand Master del Caretto. Near the port of Mastikhári, some 30 km. W. of Kos, are the ruins of a 5C early Christian *ba-*

Kos (Kos), Asklepieion, peripteral temple and collection house

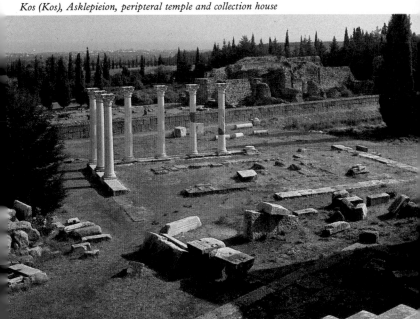

silica with a nave and two aisles, and the remains of a *mosaic floor* and a *baptistery*. There are remnants of a medieval *fortress* near the port of *Kéfalos*, 40 km. from Kos on the SW tip of the island, and the ruins of the early Christian *basilica* of St.Stéfanos are situated on the coast. Some 2 km. to the SE are the remains of the island's ancient capital of *Astypálaia* ('old town'), which is also now known as *Palátia* ('palaces'). This was Kos's predecessor prior to 366 BC; it is in the NE of the island and was destroyed by Sparta in the Peloponnesian War (412 BC). So far excavations have revealed a *Sanctuary of Demeter* from the 4C BC, a *Hellenistic temple* and a 4C *theatre* with well-preserved rows of seats. This may have been the town where Hippocrates first worked, since it was destroyed during his lifetime.

Kozáni/KOZANH
Kozáni/Macedonia   p.290□E 4

This is the capital of the nome of the same name, and has a population of around 24,000; it was built in the 14C, but earlier settlement is suggested by a Stone Age axe found here and on display in the Archaeological Museum at Véria. Further excavations in an old graveyard just outside the modern town have produced a large number of classical finds from the 5C BC.

Acropolis: There are still some remains of this 2C BC structure.

Ágios Nikolaos: Church from 1664 with frescos and numerous wood-carvings.

Museum: A large collection, particularly bronze statues from 1000–500 BC.

Town Library: This contains numerous 17C manuscripts from the 'School of Kozáni', which was celebrated at the time.

It also houses a number of rare German 18C manuscripts.

Also worth seeing: The splendid *mansions* of Wurka, Lassani and Gartzuli are worth a visit.

Environs: Aianí (21 km. S.): This is a small village near the Aliákomon river which was well known in classical and Roman times, and contains Byzantine churches with wall paintings. **Erátyra** (60 km. W.): This is a small village with Byzantine churches and a small *museum* containing finds from the Stone and Bronze Ages. There is a hill near the village with the remains of a prehistoric *acropolis*. **Sérvia** (26 km. SE): This was built under the Byzantine Emperor Herakleios in the 7C; it contains Byzantine *churches* from the 11–16C and a 13C Byzantine *fortress* with a triple wall. **Siátista** (25 km. W.): This is a medieval town situated on a hill, and it contains some interesting Byzantine churches. An important trading centre in the 16–18C, the town had business links with Vienna. *Agía Paraskeví* is a church dating from 1677 with frescos and carved wooden icons. The *Library* contains some interesting manuscripts. Most of the exhibits in the *Prehistory Museum* are from the Stone and Bronze Ages. The town's *houses* are also worth seeing.

Kríti/Crete (I)/KPHTH
                              p.298□E/I 13/15

Crete is Greece's largest island, and is the fifth largest in the entire Mediterranean; it lies to the S. of the Greek mainland and might be viewed, in terms of its culture and the character of its people, as a separate country.

Beaked pitcher with grass decoration, (M. ▷ *Ir.)*

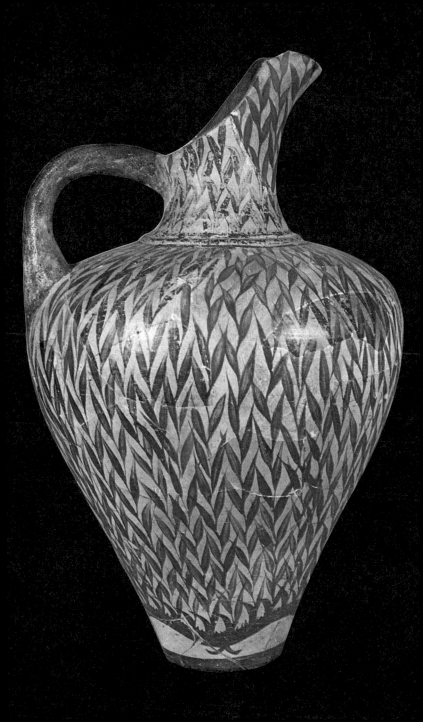

The island is long and thin, extending 162 miles from W. to E. and varying between 9 and 37 miles in width. It is unusually mountainous, with the Léfka Ori (the 'White Mountains') in the W., the Dikte massif in the E. and the Psiloritis (with the 8,000 ft. Mt.Ida) in the centre. These ranges are riddled with cult caves. In between the ranges are fertile valleys, the Lasithi plateau in the E. and the Messará plain in the S. and centre. There are some unusually deep gorges on the island, of which the best known is the Samania gorge in the W.

History: Crete's ancient history mirrors the myths and legends about the island which have been brought to us by the Greeks. It is where Zeus is said to have been born, and, so the legend goes, to have seduced Europa, the daughter of King Tyros of Phoenicia, in the form of a bull, and raised the sons Minos, Rhadamanthus and Sarpedon. Crete is said to be populated by these sons and their descendants, about whom there are innumerable further myths.

Since 1900 Crete has been explored by archaeologists, above all by Sir Arthur Evans, who discovered and reconstructed Knossós, and these archaeologists have established that the stories are more than mere myth. They have found traces of old cult caves claimed to be the birthplace of Zeus (the grottoes on Ida and the caves near Arkalokhóri), the palaces of Zeus and Europa's three sons have been excavated (see Knossós, Phaistós and Mália), and they have uncovered numerous traces of a culture that is both older than any other so far discovered in Europe and so sophisticated and varied that it can only be compared to Europe's more highly-developed cultures. It is known as the Minoan culture after the lord of Knossós, suggesting that Minos was not the name of a single ruler but was in fact a title of the order of priest-king.

The chronology of the cultures of Crete, which has been calculated from Minoan culture, may generally be divided into the following periods:

5500–2600	Neolithic
2700	Prepalatial period or

Quartz rhyton (l.), beaked cult vessel (r.), (Arch. Mus. Ir.)

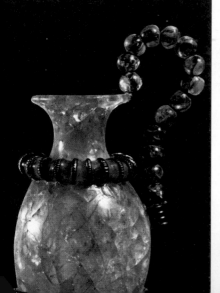
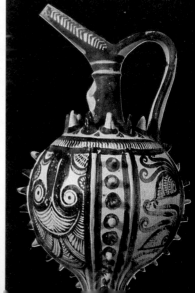

2600–2000	early Minoan period
2000–1700	Protopalatial period (or middle Minoan period, 2000–1580)
1700–1400	Neopalatial period
1400–1100	Postpalatial period (or late Minoan period, 1520–1200)

Even though the experts are not entirely in agreement with regard to this dating system, it still gives a good idea of the various stages of Cretan culture.

Neolithic settlement in Crete, as far as we can tell, seems to have been African in origin. The inhabitants lived in caves, many of which were later converted into religious sanctuaries, and in simple stone buildings. They lived by hunting and fishing, to which they later added agriculture and stock breeding. Their tools were made of bones and stone, and they frequently worshipped female deities. Around 2700 or 2600 settlers arrived, probably from Asia Minor, and slowly began to construct a unique culture on the island. Round tombs, cult objects and ceramics, such as those in the Vassilikí style, have been found from around this period.

Around 2000 BC the palaces at Knossós, Phaistós and Mália were built; polychrome Kamares-style pottery fragments have been found dating from the same period, along with stone fragments, bronze statuettes, seals, and cult objects, mostly double axes, figure-of-eight shields, trees and animals, but also goddesses in human form.

Around 1700 BC the palaces were destroyed by a disaster which affected the entire island; many experts have suggested that it was a series of earthquakes, although some maintain it was an invasion from mainland Greece. However, the palaces were rebuilt even more impressively and with more sophisticated techniques, the cities became larger (e.g. Gúrnia) and more sumptuous villas appeared (e.g. Týlisos or Niru Khani). Linear A script, which has still not been deciphered, also dates from this period. Craft, industry and trade throughout the eastern Mediterranean all

Krater with flower relief (l.), late Minoan ceramic vase (r.), (Arch. Mus. Ir.)

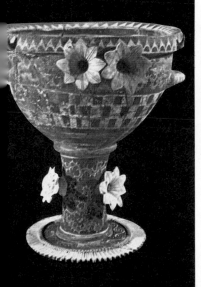
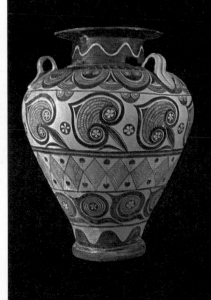

developed dramatically, to the extent that the surrounding mainlands, especially Greece (e.g. Mycene) were strongly influenced by Crete. The king of Knossós seems to have established superiority over those of Mália and Phaistós, and to have ruled the entire island. Huge paved roads were laid. Shrines were built in the palaces, and the significance of the Cretan bull, and the role it played in Cretan games, Cretan myths and especially Cretan religion, can be clearly recognized. Elaborately decorated bulls' horns with ritual significance have been found everywhere. A wide range of magnificent and highly realistic figurines have been found, made of steatite, alabaster, marble, lapis lazuli, bronze, silver, gold, quartz and ivory. The paintings on the interior walls of the buildings and on the sarcophagi display a wide range and their delicacy and harmony make them extraordinarily high cultural achievements for such an early civilisation.

Around 1450 BC the whole of Crete was affected by a great catastrophe which destroyed both cities and palaces. The historian Spyridon Marinatos linked it with the eruption of the volcanic island of Santorini, which destroyed Crete in conjunction with earthquakes and tidal waves. Wolfgang Schiering, however, maintains that it was a regional, tectonic earthquake which did not shake the whole island at the same time with the same force. This would imply that Knossós was not destroyed for good in 1450, but, as recent research suggests, was eventually destroyed in about 1375. Other experts, however, claim that the Achaeans attacked and destroyed the island, and an Achaean took Minos's throne. There had been Achaean immigrants to Crete since 1500 BC.

After 1400 BC the Minoan culture lost its influence for good, and a heavy influx of Dorians around 1100 forced the Minoans to retreat still further. They referred to themselves as Eteocretans ('true Cretans') and built new towns in the E. of Crete, such as Lató, Dréros, Priniás and Górtyna. The Dorians became the ruling class and increased their trade with the mainland, and Cretan sculptors continued to distinguish themselves with larger figures.

In 67 BC the Romans arrived in Crete, making Górtyna the capital.

In AD 395, after the division of the Roman Empire, Crete came under the influence of Byzantium. Christianity was introduced by the Apostle Paul and his companion Titus, and in time the number of churches and monasteries on the island rose, particularly during the late Byzantine period, and they were frequently decorated with beautiful wall paintings. Crete remained under the sway of Byzantium until 824.

In AD 824 it was taken by the Arabs, who founded Rabd-el-Kandak (Candia, later Iráklion). In 961 the Byzantines arrived, and in 1204 the Venetians, who fought continuously for supremacy over the island with the Genoese. Italian style and culture took hold of the island, especially Venetian, at the time when Venice's own style was developing.

For 450 years the Venetians ruled the island, tyrannically at first and later with more temperance. But the Cretans rebelled again and again, and the Turks finally managed to conquer Crete in 1669, when they took Iráklion and exercised cruel and inflexible control over the island. The monasteries, which the Cretans used as bases for uprisings and revolts, saw the most barbaric bloodbaths (see Arkádi).
The Turks, too, brought their culture to Crete, but were largely content with converting Christian churches into mosques and building a few attractive minarets (Chaniá and Réthymnon). Most of their houses were built of wood.

After two centuries Turkish rule was ended by Prince Georgios and Crete became independent; it has been part of Greece since 1913. In 1923 the Muslims were expelled, and Greek refugees from Asia Minor took their place.

20C: Crete has become progressively more modern and prosperous, largely through a thriving tourist industry supported by the excavation work of the archaeologists. The southern climate, attractive landscapes and unique ancient culture makes it an increasingly popular holiday destination. The Cretans are still a very individual people: they love festivals, processions, music and dance but are suspicious of outside infulences. Their motto 'better dead than under subjection' spurred them on to centuries of bloody uprisings against the Venetians and the Turks despite their relatively small numbers and placid temperament (there have been no Minoan fortresses discovered, and few weapons). They displayed a similar resistance to the presence of British soldiers, which was repeated in 1941 when German paratroops landed on Crete and took control of the island. It was eventually freed in 1944 and divided into four administrative regions: Chaniá, Réthymnon, Iráklion and Lasíthi. Iráklion became the island's capital again in 1971.

It is also the best town from which to appreciate the magical country and rich culture the island has to offer. All the places on the island which are mentioned in this book can be found at a glance on the map on page 298.

Kritsá/ΚΡΙΤΣΑ
Lasíthi/Crete   p.298☐H 14

Kritsá lies 11 km. SW of Ágios Nikólaos,

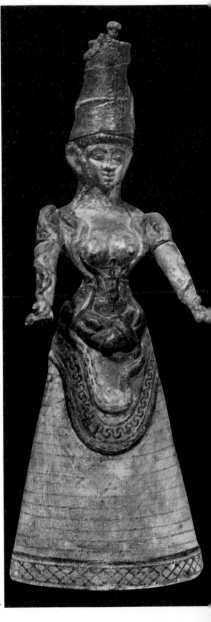

Great snake goddess ▷

and is an attractive market town with extensive olive groves and some fine Byzantine churches; it was the location for the film of 'Zorba the Greek'. There are some fine 14C frescos in the churches of *Ágios Georgios* and *Ágios Konstantínos*, and *Agia Paraskevi*, *Agion Pneuma*, *Ágios Ioánnis* are also worth seeing.

Panagia: 550 yards outside the village is one of Crete's finest churches, the Panagia-Kera, a broad, finely vaulted whitewashed building with a nave and two aisles and built in four separate phases in the 13–15C. The interior is astonishingly richly painted, with frescos which include some extraordinarily delicate, artistic and harmonious examples of colour and structure, offering perhaps the finest example of Byzantine art in the whole of Crete. The nave, which has a high drum and dome, is dedicated to the theme of the Virgin Mary, with 55 frescos. The paintings in the central apse are from the mid 13C, and those on the side wall of the nave are late-13C. The finest frescos are the 43 early-14C ones of St. Anne, in the S. aisle. The

27 frescos in the N. aisle are devoted to St. Antony and date from the mid 14C.

Environs: Lató Between Ágios Nikólaos and Kritsá, on a slope with a view over the Gulf of Mirabello, is the site of the ruins of Lató, which was originally built in the 18C BC and was one of the most magnificent settlements in Crete. The remains of a pentagonal agora from the 8C BC are especially interesting; they are situated on a slope and include a massive staircase. There is also a 3C BC Prytanáon, and a sanctuary which is still identifiable. A cistern and a watch-tower have both been discovered, from which any possible danger from the sea could clearly be seen. The ancient harbour of Lató was on the present-day site of Ágios Nikólaos, and recent excavations of the Doric city have revealed living quarters, shops and a small temple.

Lató (Kritsá), steps

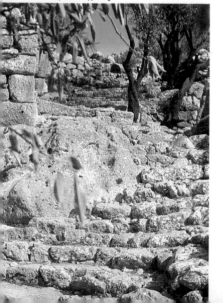

Kyllíni/ΚΥΛΛΗΝΗ
Elis/Peloponnese   p.294☐D 9

This small coastal village, with a population of some 600, is a departure point for the ferry to the island of Zacynthos.
During the Middle Ages it was known as *Glaréntsa* or *Clair-Mont*, and was under the control of Villehardouin, trading with Italian towns. Little remains of the medieval town, apart from some scattered remains of the fortifications, a citadel and a mole.

Environs: Castle of Chlemútsi (5 km. S.): This was built by the Franks in about 1220 and was the residence of Geoffroy II and Guillaume de Villehardouin. It was controlled by the Byzantines in the 15C, but they lost it to the Turks in 1460. In 1825 it was badly damaged by the Egyptian Ibrahim Pasha.

Panagia (Kritsá), Panagia Kera ▷

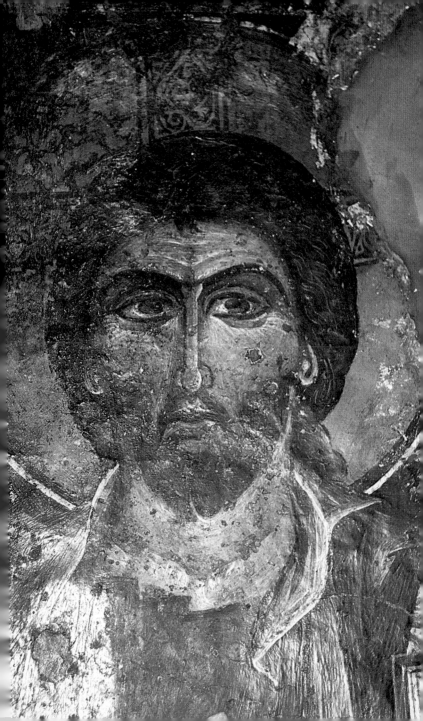

A gateway in the N. side leads through into the *outer castle*; the hexagonal *keep* can be entered through a door in the N.

Kyparissía/ΚΥΠΑΡΙΣΣΙΑ
Messenia/Peloponnese   p.294☐D 10

This town, with its population of around 5,500, is situated on the W. coast of the Peloponnese, and was known as *Arkadia* in the Middle Ages.

History: It was founded in the 4C BC by Epameinondas, along with Megalópolis and Messene. It was an important harbour during the Byzantine period, and was taken in 1205 by Guillaume de Champlitte, occupied by the Genoese family of Zaccaria in 1391, taken by the Turks in 1460, captured by Morosini in 1686 and destroyed by Ibrahim Pasha in 1826.

Fortress: This has a double wall; on the top of the hill is a tower dating from the Byzantine period. *Kalamiá*, between the

town and the sea, has the remains of a Temple of Apollo, a wall and the foundations of some Roman houses.

Environs: Amphigéneia (9 km. E.): There are Cyclopean buildings and a palace with a megaron and numerous columns on the peak of the hill by the modern village of *Muriatáda*. 220 yards N. is a tholos tomb. **Peristeriá** (10 km. NE): Three tholos tombs, one of which is very well-preserved and bears a Minoan double axe and branch on the jamb, dating from the 16C BC. It was used right through to the Hellenistic period. Gold goblets from this tomb are on display in the museum at Khóra. **Christiánu** (29 km. S.): This village is on the site of the ancient *Christianúpolis*, which has an 11C Byzantine church, *Ágios Sotíras*. There are fragments of an old iconostasis.

Kýthira/Kythera/ΚΥΤΗΡΑ
Aegean Islands   p.298☐G 12

This island is relatively barren and undeve-

Chlemútsi (Kyllíni), fortress

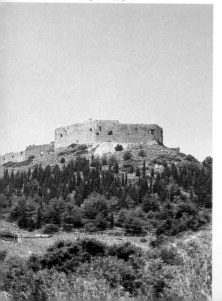

Chlemútsi, fortress interior

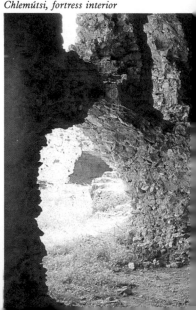

loped with regard to tourism; it is 107 sq. miles in area, with some 4,000 inhabitants, and is only 9 miles from the SE tip of the Peloponnese.

History: Kythera has been considered the birthplace and home of Aphrodite, the goddess of love, since ancient times; traces of Minoan-Mycenean civilization have been found here, dating from around 1600 BC. Politically, the island, inhabited by Dorians, belonged to Sparta, but was occupied by Athens on many occasions. From 1207 it was incorporated into the Venetian empire, and in 1814 it came under the British protectorate of the Ionian islands (Corfu). In 1864 it became part of Greece.

Ký́thira/Kythera (pop: *c.* 350): The romantic capital, also known as *Khóra*, is situated in the S. of the island above the port of *Kapsáli* and is dominated by an imposing 13C Venetian fortress. It has some interesting Byzantine churches decorated with frescos: the 12C *Ágios Theodoros*, *Ágios Ioánnis (Chrysostomos), with 15–18C* *frescos, and Ágios Athanasios* with 17C wall paintings. The *Archaeological Museum* houses finds from the Minoan-Mycenean period, ceramics from all epochs and various Byzantine and post-Byzantine icons. *Environs:* The village of *Púrko* (3 km. NW) contains the interesting church of *Ágios Dimitrios*, which consists of four chapels and has some fine 12C frescos. There is another church of *Ágios Dimitrios* in the neighbouring village of *Kampánika*, which also has 12C frescos. On the E. coast of the island, some 15 km. from the capital, near the village of *Avlémonas*, are the medieval remains of *Palaiokhóra* (Kastrí), built over an ancient *acropolis* of which a few traces remain. Traces of a Minoan or Mycenean settlement have also been found here, dating from about 1600 BC. In the SW of the island, 9 km. S. of the capital, is *Panagía Myrtidiótissa, a picturesque 17C nunnery. Near the village of Mylopótamos, 17 km. NW*, is another ruined town from the Byzantine and Venetian period with a 13C castle and a 17C church, *Ágios Athanasios*, with icons of the Ionian School. Close by is a limestone cave with

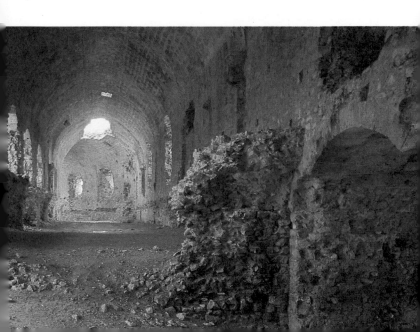

a *chapel* and 11&12C icons. There are ancient tombs and and the remains of a Minoan settlement and an underground *necropolis* by the village of *Potamós*, 22 km. to the N.

Kýthnos (I)/ΚΥΤΝΟΣ
Cyclades/Aegean Islands   p.296☐I 10

This island is in the western Cyclades, 6 miles S. of Kéa; it is 33 sq. miles in area and has a population of 1600. Its hot springs have led to its alternative name of *Thermiá*. It played little part in ancient history, and in medieval and modern times has shared the fate of its neighbouring is-land of Kéa, to which it is attached for administrative purposes.

Kýthnos (or *Khóra*, 'village'): This is situated in the centre of the island, and has blue houses and windmills. The church of *Ágios Savás* was built in 1613 by the island's governor, Gozzadini, and it bears his family crest on the exterior.
Environs: The scanty remains of the ancient Kythnos are on the W. coast, 5 km. W. of the modern town, near *Evraiókastro*. To the N., by the small harbour of *Agía Iríni* (5 km. N. of Kynthos), is the ancient spa of *Lutrá* ('bath'), which was known in antiquity. Nearby, on the northern tip of the island, are the remains of the citadel of *Kastro Orias*, which include ruined chapels, houses and cisterns.

Kyparissía, view over the village

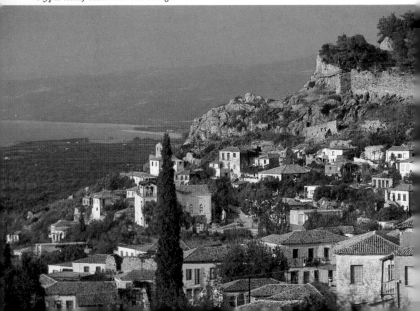

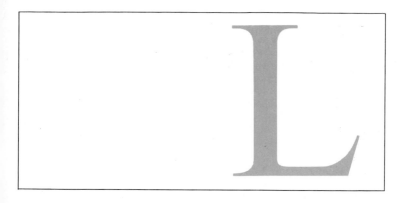

Lamía/ΛΑΜΙΑ
Phthiótis (Ftiótis)/Central Greece

p.294□F 7

This is the capital town of the district of Ftiótis, with a population of 38,000, and is situated at the mouth of the river Sperchios (Spercheios) by the Gulf of Malia. It is an agricultural centre for cotton, tobacco, oil, wine and grain.

Historically, Lamia played a role as the capital of the Thessalian Malians in the 'Lamian War' against the Macedonians in 323 BC. It ceased to be of importance after it was taken by the Romans in 190 BC. The 14C Frankish/Catalan *kastro*, which is now ruined, was built on the site of the *ancient acropolis*, of which there are remains in the NE of the town. To the W. of the fortress are some remnants of the old walls (formerly double walls), and traces of the classical *Isodomos wall* in the NE, SW and E.

Environs: Moní Antinítsa (*c*. 14 km. NW) dates from about 1500 with an old katholikon; it is attractively situated near the *Furka Pass*, 2,500 ft. up on the slopes of the Othrys mountains, with a fine view over the Thessalian plain. Near the village of **Melitáia** (40 km. N.) are the remains of the ancient settlement of *Melíteia* (sections of wall), dating back to prehistoric times. The original name for this area was *Hellás*, which became the ancient name for the whole of Greece. According to legend, this is where Deukalion, the son of Prometheus, and his wife Pyrrha are buried. They landed on Mt.Parnassos in their ark after the flood, and founded a new race of men, with Hellen as the patriarch of the Hellenes. The Homeric hero Achilles was also lord of Phthía (Phthiótis) and its inhabitants, the Myrmidons. 18 km. W. is the celebrated spa of **Lutrá Ypátis** which has sulphur springs. Nearby, close to the village of *Ypáti* on the northern slopes of the Iti mountains, are the remnants of the ancient settlement of *Hýpata*. Its *acropolis*, which is situated on a plateau in the S., is dominated by a Genoese *watch-tower*, and has the ruins of ancient and medieval walls. Nearby are the remains of a 13&14C *castle* and the 15C monastery of *Moni Agathonos*. *Mt.Iti* (ancient name Oita) can be climbed from Ypati; it is where Herakles's funeral pyre was said to have been, and the remains of a Doric *temple* and other structures are visible. Herakles let himself be burnt by the hero Philoctetes to rid himself of the unbearable pain of a poisoned shirt which had been soaked in the blood of the centaur Nessos. For this act Philoctetes received a magic bow, which he used in the Trojan War. Further W. in the Spercheios valley, are the charming villages of **Makrokómi**, 31 km. W., and **Platýstomo** (36 km. W.), which is known for its mineral springs. The area contains traces of ancient settlements, such as the ruined castle near **Kastrión** 23 km. to the W. Near Palaiá Giannitsú (40 km. W.) is the ancient **fortress of Kydonía**, at an altitude of 2,400 ft., with three surrounding walls. On the N. shore of the Gulf of Malia is the small harbour of **Stylída** (*Stylís*), with traces of ancient *fortifications* around its edges (the wall of Leosthenes from 323 BC). There are two old monasteries in the area: *Ágios Blasios* with a single-aisled domed church and narthex with 18C frescos, and *Ágios Georgios* with a fine monastery church dating from 1753.

Lárisa/Larissa/ΛΑΡΙΣΑ
Lárisa/Thessaly   p.290☐F 5

This is the capital of the region, with a population of 73,000, and it is situated in the middle of the E. Thessalian plain ('the granary of Greece'); it is an important industrial, trading and communications centre.

History: The area around Larissa has yielded Palaeolithic finds and numerous remnants from Neolithic times; it was the main area inhabited by the pre-Greek Pelasgians (the old name for Greece was Pelasgía), who probably founded Larissa in the 2nd millennium BC. After the Dorian settlement around 1200 BC, the royal house of the Aleuadai took control, inviting important artists to their court (e.g. Pindar). The doctor Hippocrates also worked here, and died here in 370 BC. It was the centre of the Thessalian Confederation and went through a chequered period (invaded by the Persians in 480, incorpo-

rated into Macedonia in 344, conquered by the Romans in 196 BC). In the Middle Ages the area, being fertile, was occupied and besieged by Goths, Huns, Bulgarians, Serbs, Vlachs and, finally, Turks (1389–1881), leading to a mixed population. It was returned to Greece by the Treaty of Berlin in 1881, when the frontier was moved to the Tempe valley.

The town which was built on top of the ancient ruins has little of interest to see, partly due to the earthquakes of 1941. The *ancient acropolis* was situated on the hill by the modern *Mitropolis church*. Scattered remains of a large *temple* have been found around the park, and parts of an ancient theatre to the E. In the S. of the city are the remains of the Turkish *fortifications*, with *bastions*.

Archaeological Museum (Arkhaiologiko Musio): This is situated in a former Turkish mosque on the main square (Platia), and houses some of the finds from Palaeolithic and Neolithic times which have been discovered in the area, e.g. from the Magúla of Gremnós: stone tools, fossils including elephants' teeth, ceramic fragments from the 5–3 millennia, 4&3 millennia terracotta idols, 'Larissa ceramics' on a black ground and Bronze Age vases (in the glass cases). There is also a *menhir*, a Neolithic stone column, with a coarse relief of a warrior; an *animal frieze* (Larissa temple); a variety of *funerary stele* from the 5–3 C; fragments of Thessalian sculptures from the 4C BC; tomb fragments from the 2–4 C; and early Christian sculptures and choir screens from basilicas.

Environs: On the site of the *Magúla of Gremnós*, some 11 km. NW on the steep banks of the Pinios river, are the remains of the ancient city of **Árgura** (or *Árgeisa*), which has been excavated since 1955. It was settled from the Neolithic onwards, and has ancient and Hellenistic *walls*. In the NW of the plain of Larissa, some 17

m. NW, is the agricultural centre of **Týrnavos**, a small town known for its fine ouzo. It was founded in the 12C and has some attractive 17&18C churches (Ágios Athanasios, Agia Triada). 3 km. away are traces of an *ancient settlement* (Phalanna) and the remains of a *Turkish castle*. The valley of the Titarisios (or Xynias) river, which is mentioned by Homer and flows into the Pinios (Peneios), is the site of the village of **Damásion** (*c.* 25 km. NW), with the remains of the ancient settlement of *Mýlas* to its N. **Kutsókheron** (19 km. W.): This is a village with an interesting *fountain* which emerges from a Doric column base. A short distance to the W. is the spectacular *Kalamáki Gorge* (*c.* 25 km. W.) over the Pinios river. The village of *Gunítsa*, at the entrance to the gorge, has a *graveyard church* built of ancient stone blocks with medieval frescos. The gorge divides *Mt.Titanos* (S., 2,300 ft.) and *Mt.Zárkos* (N., 2,500 ft.), on the latter's slopes there is a village of the same name which includes the attractive medieval churches of *Panagía* and *Ágios Vissaríon*; there are the ruins of a church of *Ágios Nikólaos*, and close by are the remains of an ancient settlement. In the SW of the plain of Larissa (*c.* 18 km. SW), near the village of **Krannóna**, are the remains of the old Thessalian town of *Krannón*, which was ruled by the dynasty of the Skopadai (descendants of Skopas). They were rivals of the Aleuadai of Larissa and the Ekhekratidai of Pharsalos (Fársala) for the position of ruler (Tagos) of Thessaly in the 6&5C.

Lávrion/Laúrion/ΛΑΥΡΙΟΝ
Attica   p.296☐H/I 9

This small port and industrial centre has a population of around 8,000 and is situated on the SE coast of Attica. It is the terminus of the Attic railway line, some 54 km. SE of Athens.

History: In ancient times Laúrion (now Lávrion) was not only the name of the port, but also of the whole surrounding area. It was settled in around 1000 BC and was known from early times for its deposits of metal, especially silver ore. Its mines, which were Athenian from the 6C onwards, were most important in the time of the Persian War, as Themistocles paid for a great number of ships (triremes) with Laurion silver, and it was these ships which defeated the Persian fleet at Salamis. Much of the Athenian coinage was made of Laurion silver. Athens later leased the mines out to private concerns (against a return of about 4%), which led to large-scale and arduous slave labour, with thousands of slaves, including children, involved. To the S. and SE of Lávrion, especially in the Verseko valley, are numerous ancient galleries. After the 2C BC, the mines became less important, due to their over-exploitation and the influx of Macedonian (Thracian) gold. Mining has only been resumed since 1860, in an attempt to extract zinc, iron and manganese from the ancient slagheaps.

Ancient Mines (*Metallía*): Most of the remains of the ancient mines are near *Kamárisa*, the ancient *Maronéa*, or else in the neighbouring Verseko valley (Megala Pevka) to the S., or the Legrena or Botsari valleys. Altogether there are some 2,000 steep tunnel shafts, from 6 x 6 ft. and 100–150 ft. deep (occasionally as much as 300 ft). The slaves worked in a crouching position, and it was frequently children who carried the ore to the surface. It was then cut into small pieces, cleaned in a washing system (known as the Ergasteria, or 'workshop'), and sometimes smelted in an oven. The miners (of whom there were said to be some 20,000 under Perikles in about 430 BC) had to remain unmarried for reasons of cost, and lived in hostels. The countryside round Lávrion has been spoiled by the hand of man since ancient

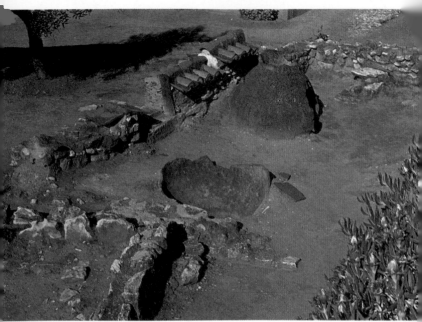

Lérna, middle Helladic kitchen and store

times, and is probably the oldest example of environmental pollution.

Environs: Makrónisos ('long island'): This is a long, thin island opposite Lávrion, which was formerly used as a prison island for political detainees (most recently during the military dictatorship of 1967–74). According to legend, Paris rested here on his flight back to Troy with Helen, which led to its being known as 'Helena' (Eléni).

Lérna/ΛΕΡΝΑ
Argolís/Peloponnese   p.294☐ F 9/10

The prehistoric settlement of Lérna is situated next to the modern village of Myloi, to the left of the road leading to Trípolis.

In antiquity the area was full of marshes, watered by the river Pontinos and numerous springs. It is where Herakles performed his second labour, the killing of the nine-headed Lernaean hydra, perhaps a reference to the difficulty of draining the swamp.

Excavation Area: The work of the American Archaeological Mission has brought traces of Neolithic houses and early and mid Helladic settlements to light. The S. section of the excavation area includes a surrounding wall from early Helladic times (2300–2200), a double wall with two semicircular towers and steps near the W. one. The lower section of the tower consists of large undressed stones, the upper section of unbaked bricks. The W. section of the early Helladic wall is built above a Neolithic structure, built of small stones. The E. section comprises the remains of apsidal houses from the middle Helladic period (1900–1600), built almost on top of each other; other buildings from the same period include a shop and a kitchen, to the left of which is a square structure which may have been the original palace.

The most important building was the *House of the Tiles* (40 x 80 ft.), the royal residence, whose entrance is on the E. side. It leads into a large square hall, then a long thin room, with a further area and a smaller room leading off it. The interior corridors run down the long side; there were probably *staircases* leading to an upper floor. The lower sections of the house's walls were stone, and the upper sections plastered brick.

There are two graves near the N. entrance; the one by the corner of the house is late middle Helladic, the other Mycenean.

The house was destroyed by fire in early Helladic times, and the rubble was piled into a round tumulus, part of which can still be identified.

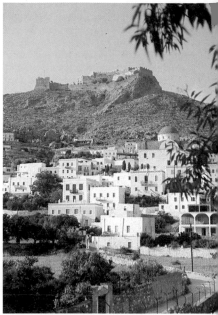

Plátanos (Léros), kastro

Léros/Leros (I)/ΛΕΡΟΣ
East Aegean Islands/Dodecanese/
Aegean Islands   p.296☐N 10

This is a fertile island of varied landscapes with numerous bays, some extending nearly a mile inland, and harbours. It is 21 sq. miles in area, has a population of around 9, 000 and lies to the NW of Kalymnos, separated by a channel only a mile wide. Many of its old local customs have survived.

History: Leros was colonized by the Ionians in around 900 BC, and later became a dependancy of Miletos (Asia Minor). The Byzantines gave it to the monastery on Patmos in 1087, and from 1319–1522 it was under the control of the Hospitallers of Rhodes.

After being held by Turkey (1522–1912), it remained under Italian protection until it was returned to Greece in 1948.

Plátanos/Agía Marína: The capital Plátanos, with its associated port of *Agía Marína*, has a population of around 2,500 and is situated on the W. coast. It is dominated by the massive 11C Byzantine *kastro*, which was restored and extended in the 15&16C by the Hospitallers, and has a 16C coat-of-arms. It contains the small Byzantine church of the *Panagia (tu Kastru)*. The basilica of *Ágios Theologos*, which has a nave and two aisles, is also interesting. The port of Agía Marína has some substantial 19C houses, which were built by returning emigrants. The area around Plátanos has some *ancient remains*, mostly foundations. There is a small *Roman aqueduct* near Agía Marína.

Environs: The island's main port is *Lakki* (4 km. S.), which has 2,400 inhabitants and one of the safest anchorages in the Aegean. Between Lakki and *Xirócampos*, 7 km. to the S., are the remains of an ancient *fortress* (palaiokastro) from the 4C BC, with *sections of wall* still standing and some badly damaged *mosaic floors*. There is an ancient *well* by the village of *Plofútis*. An old *temple of Artemis* has been discovered in the N. of the island by the village of *Parthéni* (12 km. NW of Plátanos); nearby is the monastery of *Kiurí*. The monastery of *Ágios Sideris* is near the village of *Álinda*, 5 km. NE.

Lésvos/Lesbos (I)/ΛΕΣΒΟΣ
East Aegean Islands/Aegean Islands
p.296☐M 6

This island is only 10–13 miles from the coast of Asia Minor, and its area of 630 sq. miles makes it the third largest Aegean island after Crete and Euboea. Its landscape is picturesque, with deeply indented bays, and fertile, with numerous olive-groves. It is relatively densely populated, with some 120,000 inhabitants.

History: The island's original inhabitants belonged to the same racial group of West Anatolians as the founders of Troy. The earliest traces of civilization date back to the 4&3 millennia, and the first Greek settlers (Aiolians from Thessaly) landed in about 1000 BC. Lesbos flourished in the 7&6C under the peacemaker Pittakos (*c.* 590 BC), one of the Seven Sages. Among his contemporaries were the poets Alkaios, from Mytiléne, and Sappho, and the musicians Terpandros and Arion. The concept of 'lesbian' love comes from an inaccurate interpretation of the female school of Sappho. From 546–479 Lesbos was under the control of the Persians. After their liberation the island states of Méthymna and Mytiléne clashed, even though Lesbos was a member of the Athenian maritime league. It was later subjugated by the Macedonians, and then the Romans under Pompey, when it was divided into latifundia and became a popu-

Mytiléne (Lésvos), kastro

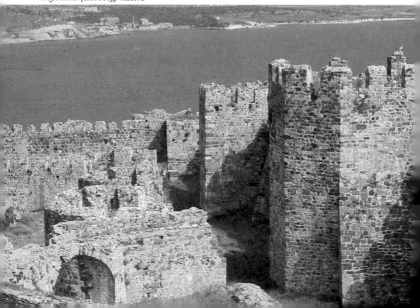

lar holiday resort. In the 2&3C it was the setting for the pastoral story 'Daphnis and Chloe' by Longus. It was invaded frequently in the Byzantine times, and eventually became the seat of the Gattelusi family from Genoa in the 13C; they held the island until 1462, after which it remained Turkish until 1912.

Mytilíni/Mytiléne: This is the capital of the island, with a population of around 24,000; it is situated on the E. coast, with a view over to the Turkish mainland. There is a massive *kastro* fortress on a spit of land in the harbour which was once separated from the town by a channel; it was built in 1373 by the Gattelusi family, whose coat-of-arms is on the wall. The ancient acropolis (6C BC) was situated on the town's highest point. On the town side, to the NW of the harbour, are the remains of the ancient city, which include an interesting Hellenistic *theatre*: it dates from the 3C BC, and was extended by the Romans to seat 10,000, and the *orchestra* was enlarged for lion fights. It is said to have been the model for the first Roman stone theatre,

which was built under Pompey in 55 BC. Nearby are the remains of some ancient fortifications. Below the theatre is the *'House of Menander'*, where impressive *floor mosaics* from the 3C BC, which depict scenes from 4C BC comedies of Menander, have been exposed. They are now housed in the *Archaeological Museum*, which also has Aiolian column capitals and other finds, as well as Byzantine icons and ceramics. The main church of *Ágios Athanasios* is 16&17C and has some interesting wood carvings, and the church of *Ágios Therapon* has Byzantine icons. The *Local Museum (Laografiko Musio*, in the town theatre) has exhibits from the Middle Ages through to the present day, and includes a library with some rare volumes. The suburb of *Variá* has a *museum* with works by the famous folk painter Theophilos (d.1934).

Environs: Near the village of *Mória* (*c.* 4 km. NW) are the remnants of a Roman *aqueduct* from late imperial times (3C AD), which provided Mytiléne with water from 16 miles away. There are more remains 18 km. to the NW, near *Lámpu Mýli.* 6 km.

Eresós (Lésvos), peacock mosaic in museum

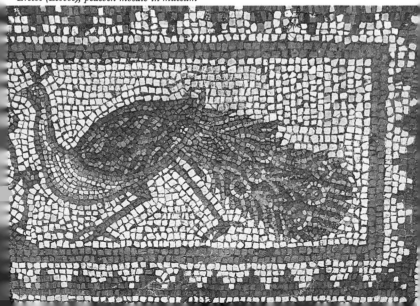

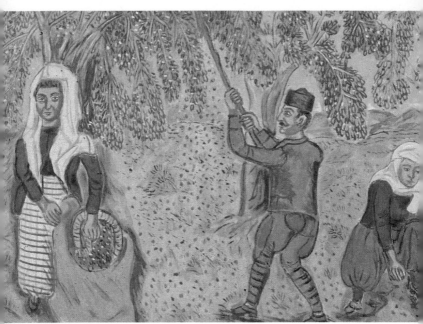

Mytiléne (Lésvos)

W. is the monastery of *Agia Paraskevi*, dating from 1315.

Thermí (9 km. N. of Mytiléne): Close to this small spa, which has a population of around 1000, the remains of a significant *prehistoric settlement* have been excavated by the British. It dates back to Neolithic times, before the founding of Troy, and goes through five phases of development; the remains of the fortifications from the fifth phase (2400–2000) are still visible. It was abandoned in around 2000 but resettled in about 1400 BC, before its eventual destruction at the same time as Troy (see Homer's 'Iliad', IX, 270).

Agiásos (28 km. W. of Mytiléne): This is a charming little town, with a population of around 4,000; it is situated on the N. slopes of the highest mountain on the island, Olympos (3,200 ft.) and affords a fine view over the Gulf of Géra (Jéra). It was a place of retreat for the Turks. The pilgrimage monastery of *Panagia* is worth seeing: it dates from 1170 and contains the icon 'Agai Sion' ('Holy Mt.Zion'). There are also some traditional crafts (weaving, pottery) to watch.
Environs: SW of the Gulf of Géra are the villages of *Skópelos*, which has 2,500 inhabitants and some interesting 17C churches including Ananásios, which is frescoed, and *Palaiókipos*, which has a ruined 14C castle.

Polýkhnitos (45 km. W. of Mytiléne): This is a small inland town with some 4,000 inhabitants; it is known for its hot springs and is situated SE of the Gulf of Kalloní. It includes the interesting monastery of *Dramandri*, which has frescos dat-

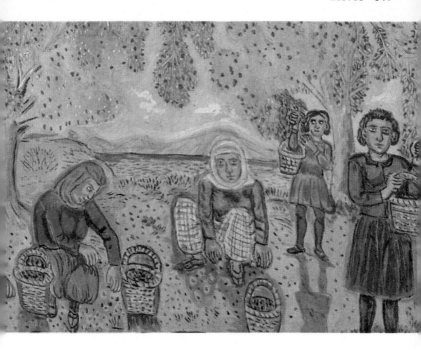

ing from 1580. Nearby (5 km. SE) are the ruins of the ancient town of *Brísa (Vrísa)*, which include a small 3C BC *temple of Dionysos* on the peak.

Kalloní (40 km. NW of Mytiléne): This is a village with a population of some 1,700 situated on the N. edge of the Gulf of Kalloní, which is 13 miles long and, at points, 5 miles across. The area has numerous salt water lagoons.

Environs: 4 km. N. are the ruins of the ancient city of *Arísba (Arísvi)*, which include remains of temples from the 6C BC and sections of a double Genoese *castle wall* (1355). Nearby are the monasteries of *Limonos*, with a local museum and an old library, and the *Panagia Myrsiniotissa*. In the NE of Kalloní bay are the remains of the town of *Phýrra*, which has been ruined since antiquity. It was the religious centre

of the state of Lesbos, and had a shrine to Méson (Hellenistic, 2C BC). The limestone foundations of a temple measuring 110 ft. x 50 ft. have been uncovered. In the N. of the bay, near *Agía Paraskeví*, which has 3,000 inhabitants and is the second largest town on the island, is the site of an ancient temple to Apollo. It dates from the 6C BC, and two sides of foundations (90 ft. x 60 ft.) and a *peripteros* from 530 BC (120 ft. x 50 ft.) have been uncovered, and there are a number of *capitals* on display in the museum at Mytiléne. The town itself includes the 19C *Taxiarchis* church (archangels) and the small cave church of *Agía Paraskeví*, which was probably an old shrine of Asklepios. 3 km. away, in the village of *Nápi*, are the remains of a 6C early Christian *basilica*. The fertile area between Agía Paraskeví (Nápi) and Thermí is the setting for 'Daphnis and Chloe'.

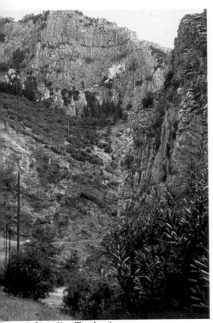

Levádia, Trophonios gorge

Mantamádos (36 km. N. of Mytiléne): This is a small harbour (the port is called *Skála*) on the NE coast, facing Asia Minor, with a population of 1800. The *Taxiarchon monastery* is interesting, and includes some old reliefs of angels. Nearby are the remains of some ancient *tombs* (with reliefs), a medieval *fortress (kastro)*, and the early Christian basilica of *Ágios Stephanos*.

Míthymna (64 km. NE of Mytiléne): This is an attractive port with a population of around 1,500; it is on the NW coast of the island, picturesquely situated on the slopes below the Genoese *fortress* built by the Gattelusi in the 14C on the site of the ancient acropolis of *Méthymna* (now *Mólyvos*, 'lead'). There are traces of the old *fortifications*, some foundations of houses, sarcophagi, ditches and remnants of buildings from Roman times. The ancient finds are on display in the *museum* in the town hall.
Environs: The neighbouring village of *Pétra* has an 18C church, which is built on a cliff. According to legend, this was the area where the head of the mythical singer Orpheus, who was lynched by angry Thracian women, was washed ashore.

Ántissa (73 km. NW of Mytiléne): The present village was built some 4 miles inland because of the fear of piracy.
Environs: Some 7 km. to the NE are the ruins of the *ancient town of Antissa*, which consist of traces of the *acropolis* and remains of a polygonal wall. There are apsidal buildings from the 10 – 8C at the acropolis's foot, and the remains of a Genoese *fortress* on a rocky outcrop are still standing. 5 km. SW of Ántissa, on Mt.Ordymnos, is the interesting monastery of *Ágios Ioánnis* (Theológu Ypsilú), which was founded in the 9C, repeatedly destroyed, rebuilt in the 12C and restored in 1971. It contains valuable Byzantine *icons*, embroidery and gold items, and a library with valuable manuscripts. Close by is the monastery of *Perivólis*, which has 17C frescos. Near the fishing village of *Sigríon* on the W. coast (92 km. NW of Mytiléne) is a *petrified forest*, which was covered by volcanic ash about a million years ago and has since been exposed by rain.

Eresós (88 km. NW of Mytiléne): Because of its vulnerability to pirates, the modern town, which has some 1,800 inhabitants, was built farther N. than the *ancient town* of the same name, whose remains are near the fishing village of *Skála Eresú*, 3 km. to the S. They include traces of the ancient *fortifications* and the ruins of an early Christian *galleried church* from about 500, which is also locally known as the 'school of Theophrastos', a pupil of Aristotle (372–287) who, like the poetess Sappho, was from Eresós. Nearby are the foundations of the 5C former *bishop's church of*

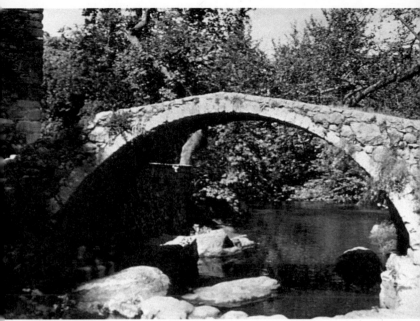

Levádia, Turkish bridge over the Erkyna spring

Ágios Andreas. The small Eresós *Archaeological Museum* houses Hellenistic, Roman and early Christian finds from the area, including sculptures and mosiacs.

Levádia/ΛΕΒΑΔΕΙΑ
Boeotia/Central Greece   p.294☐G 8

According to Pausanias, Levádia, which now has a population of 16,000 and is 46 km. from Thebes, was built on the site of the older town of Mídeia. According to myth, it was founded by the hero Levados, and Homer tells that it took part in the Trojan War. But despite Pausanias's description of it as a wealthy and powerful city, it played little part in classical history, coming to the fore only in the Middle Ages and during the Turkish occupation. Its name was connected with the Greek War of Liberation from the Turks; in ancient times it was best known as the location of the Oracle of Trophonios.

Levádia is separated from the grove of Trophonios by the Erkyna river, which was named after a nymph who was said to inhabit it. By the fortress hill on the S. side of the town is a bridge which dates from the Turkish occupation, which leads over the river to a terrace with huge plane trees. The Erkyna river comes from two springs, Lethe and Mnemosyne, which are closely connected to the Oracle of Trophonios; the first is the spring of forgetfulness and the second of memory. The exact site of the oracle has still not been established, but the most reasonable assumption places the grove on the E. bank of the Erkyna. The gorge near the springs is said to have been the underground entrance to the Oracle of Trophonios. The petitioner had to wait in the dark chamber of a fissure in the grove, perform a detailed ritual and then drink from the spring of Lethe in order to forget everything which had happened. Later he drank from the spring of Mnemosýne in order to remember what the oracle had said.

Levádia's later history was somewhat chequered; it was sacked by the Goths, and then, during the Frankish domination of Greece, was occupied by the Frankish Duke of Athens, Othon de la Roche, and his successors. In 1311, after the defeat of the Franks on the Kiphisso plain near the historic town of Chaironeia, Levádia fell without resistance into the hands of the Catalans, who built the kastro or castle of Phrurio, which is to the S. on the slopes above the city. The square Boeotian watchtowers are also Catalan. It was later conquered by the Florentines under Acciaiuoli, and then fell under Turkish rule from 1460–1829. During this period it was the most important town in Central Greece, and its wealth and flourishing trade led the Turks to give it a number of privileges, the most important being that, despite being under Turkish rule, it remained under Greek administration. Many rich archons (citizens) in Levádia were able to do much to free not just Levádia but the whole of Greece from the yoke of Turkish oppression; these included Georgandai, Nakos and Philon. At the time of the national uprising, a number of legendary heroes were working here, including Athanasios Diakos, who for a short while was a monk at the monastery of Hósios Lukás. He fanned the revolutionary spirit by fighting the Turks and died a martyr after the battle of Alamana, having fallen into the hands of the Turks. He was put on a spit and turned over a fire, while being repeatedly asked 'Jinesai Turkos Diakos min tin pisti su n'allaxis?' ('Will you become a Turk, Diakon, and change your beliefs?'), to which he repeatedly answered 'Egho ghraikos ghenithika ghraikas, the na pethano' ('I was born a Greek and I will die a Greek'). There is a bronze bust to Athanasios Diakos in the cathedral square in Levádia. During the eight year battle for liberation, the town was destroyed by the Turks.

Levádia was also the home town of a great naval hero, Admiral Lambros Katsonis, whose marble bust is situated in the square which bears his name. He did not forget his homeland while he was fighting in the Crimea, and named the town he founded on the S. Crimean coast Levádia.

The heroes of Levádia are famous throughout Greece, and have been celebrated with beautiful folk songs, which are still sung today: 'Saranda Palliraria apo tin Levadhiá Pane ghia na patisun tin Tripolitsia...' ('forty brave young men are leaving Levádia to conquer Trípolis..').

Today Levádia is the capital of Boeotia, and its situation, in the middle of the fertile Kopaís plain makes it a busy industrial and trading centre.

An important local event is the Easter festival which is held every other year in the traditional manner.

Levkás/Leukás/Levkas (I)/
ΛΕΥΚΑΣ
Ionian Islands   p.294☐C 7

Levkas (116 sq. miles, about 25,000 inhabitants) is actually an artificial island, which has been separated from the Akarnanian mainland by a ship canal since antiquity. Today there is a bridge over the narrowest point of the channel, which ranges in width from 660 yards to 3 miles.

History: Levkas continued to be treated as a peninsula, a part of Akarnania. The thesis of the German archaeologist Dörpfeld, that Levkas was in reality the Homeric

Ithaka, has since been refuted. After Corfu was colonised, the Corinthians founded the city of Levkas in 640 BC and cut a canal through the isthmus. The canal, however, silted up easily and had to be frequently cleared and re-dug (under Caesar Augustus, for example, in 31 BC, and most recently in 1905). In 197 BC the Romans anchored their fleet there; the Byzantines were later to do the same.

Levkas was occupied by a number of different powers until 1331, when it was taken by the Venetians. From 1362 to 1467 it was known as *Santa Maura* and belonged to the Angevin dukedom. From 1467–1684 the Turks controlled it (the only Ionian island they occupied), until Morosini won it back for Venice in 1684. It eventually passed to Greece with the other Ionian islands in 1863.

Levkás/Levkas (population *c.* 7,000): The capital town is picturesque, with attractively coloured wooden buildings, and is situated on the N. end of the island. The churches of *Ágios Dimitrios*, which has four paintings by P.Doxaras (d.1729), and *Ágios Minas* (1707), with a ceiling painted by N.Doxaras (d.1761), are both interesting. The Venetian *fortress* of *Santa Maura (Agia Mavra)* on the island opposite was built by Orsini in about 1300; there are two other fortresses in the area, *Alexander* and *Konstantin*, which were built during the Russian protectorate in 1807 to guard the channel.
Environs: The remains of *ancient Levkas* are situated 3 km. to the S. and include defensive walls (polygonal masonry), theatre and acropolis walls (Cyclopean), and traces of a *Roman bridge* over the canal (built under Augustus) near Rouga on the opposite, Akarnanian side.

Nýdrion/Nýdri: This is a small fishing village 18 km. W. of Levkas, where in 1905–10 the German archaeologist Dörpfeld excavated the prehistoric *round build-*

ings of an early Bronze Age culture from around 2000 BC. His residence near the site has been turned into a *museum* containing some of his finds.
Environs: The church of *Fternó*, 29 km. S., has some 18C frescos; the Analipsis (Assumption) church near *Póros* (29 km. S.) has some 17C frescos of the Virgin; the monastery of *Ágios Ioánnis (sto Rodaki)* has 17C frescos of the Ascension and 18C hierarchical ones. The church of *Ágios Geórgios* near *Marantokhóri*, 30 km. to the S., has 15&16C frescos. All the 17&18C frescos in these churches are from the Ionian school, whose centres were Corfu and Zakynthos.

Leukadian cliffs (Cape Levkadas): The southernmost point of the island has the 200 ft. high *white cliff (Petra Levkas)*, on the summit of which there was once a *temple of Apollo*, the remains of which are next to the modern lighthouse. Apollo's priests, wearing birds' wings (first attempt at flight?) used to dive from this point into the sea below, and men in boats used nets to fish the brave divers out of the water. This *katapontismos* ('diving under') formed a sort of religious judgement: unhappy lovers, among whom legend includes the poetess Sappho in about 600 BC, are said to have quelled their passion with this leap.

Lévktra/Leuktra/ΛΕΥΚΤΡΑ
Boeotia/Central Greece   p.294☐G 8

Leuktra lies a few miles NW of Thebes, and was the site of a famous battle in 371 BC in which the Thebans defeated the Spartans and assured their primacy in the Boeotian League. The leaders of the Theban army, which numbered some 7,000 men, were the legendary heroes Epameinondas and Pelopidas, and the victory was largely due to Epameinondas's

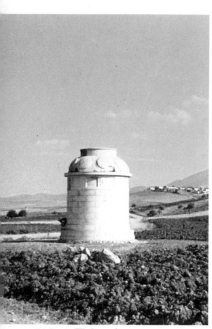

Lévktra, Theban victory monument

American-excavated remains of this Neolithic and Bronze Age settlement are to be found near the Acropodi spring. According to mythology, Évtresis was founded by Zethus and Amphion before they came to Thebes.

Límnos/Lemnos (I)/ΛΗΜΝΟΣ
East Aegean Islands/Aegean Islands
p.292☐K/L 4/5

This is a relatively fertile island, formed partly of volcanic rock, which is almost bisected by two deep bays which leave an isthmus only 2.5 miles across in the middle of the island. It is the eighth largest of the Greek islands, with an area of 184 sq. miles and a population of around 20,000.

History: Límnos (ancient *Lemnos*) was known as the home of the god of fire and the foundry, Hephaistos (Vulcan), probably due to its volcanic origin. Lemnos's culture, like that of Lesbos and Chios, is connected with Troy; skills such as metal and iron working seem to have developed here early. There are a number of dark myths surrounding the island: about Hephaistos, who is said to have slipped on the island and to have been lame ever since; about the wives of Lemnos who murdered their husbands (the 'Lemnian sin'); about the arrival of the Argonauts in Lemnos, and the founding of a new dynasty, and about the Trojan hero Philoctetes (with the magic bow) being marooned here in Homer's 'Iliad' (cf. also the Sophocles play 'Philoctetes on Lemnos'). In historical times (it was settled by the Ionians around 800 BC), Lemnos played a less substantial role, and in the Middle Ages was occupied by the Genoese family of Gattelusi (13&14C), until its capture by the Turks in 1478 and its eventual return to Greece in 1913.

strategy—he tried the celebrated oblique (loxi phalanx) manoeuvre for the first time (it has often been used since, right through to the present day). he strengthened the left wing of his army and used it to break through the enemy front lines, a tactic which brought him victory just as he had anticipated. The Thebans later erected a monument (tropaion) on the site of the battle. A burial mound can still be identified, which presumably contained the bodies of the slaughtered Spartans, and in front of the modern church of Ágios Ioánnis (known as 'tá mármar' after the local marble) are the remains of the foundations of the original Theban victory monument, which was recently rebuilt.

Modern Leuktra has a population of about 1100, mostly engaged farmers.

Environs: Évtresis (3 km. SE): The

Mýrina (*c.* 4,000 inhabitants): The is-

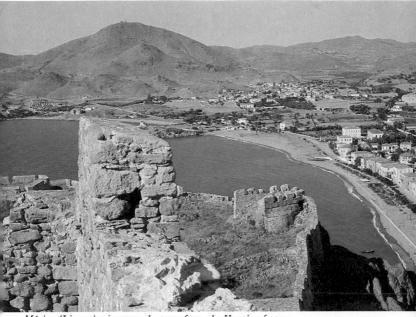

Mýrina (Limnos), view over the town from the Venetian fortress

land's capital is situated on the W. coast, on the site of the ancient settlement of the same name, of which remains are still identifiable, including a *town wall* built by the Athenians, the foundations of *ancient houses*, and underground cellars and *cisterns* on the slopes of the city. The town is dominated by a ruined Venetian *fortress (kastro)*, which dates from the 13C and whose tower affords a fine view over the bay. *Archaeological Museum:* This is where many of the island finds from the areas around Mýrina, Poliókhini and Hephaístia (Ifäistia) are housed; they include Stone and Bronze Age objects, Geometric vases from the first Greek period, early 7&6C ceramics, and Attic style finds from the Kabira shrine of Khlói in an adjacent room. The top floor houses finds from the prehistoric settlement of Poliókhni (Kamínia), and includes a plan and pho-

tographs. The celebrated *funerary stela* of Lemnos/Kamínia bears an inscription which has still not been deciphered, and is displayed in the National Museum in Athens. The *cathedral* (Mitropolis) houses a finely carved 18C wooden iconostasis.

Environs: Nearby (5 km. N.) is a famous mineral spring (rheumatism) on the slopes of *Profitis Ilias*, which has an 18C church of the same name. The picturesque village of *Kornós* (8 km. NE) has a church of the Virgin Mary, *Kímisis Theotoku*, and a church of *Ágios Sosontas*, both 19C.

Repanídi (30 km. NE): Remains of a huge 13C Venetian fortress (*kastro*), and the churches of *Ágios Georgios* and *Ágios Athanasios*, which has a carved wooden choir screen and 17C post-Byzantine icons.

Poliókhni (*c.* 35 km. E. of Mýrina): On the island's SE coast, near the village of

Kamínia (pop. 500), Italian archaeologists have exposed the *ancient settlement* of Poliókhni (3000–1800), one of the oldest and best-preserved Aegean settlements. Its three main phases from the Stone and Bronze Ages show marked similarities to ancient Troy, suggesting a dynastic link. The walled *third settlement* is situated on a slope which runs down to the sea, and covers an area of 600 x 300 ft. The *funerary stela* which was found here and whose inscription is not Greek suggests that its 6C inhabitants may not have been of Greek origin.

Environs: There is a small village called *Skandálion* on the SE cape of the island, which has the fine 18C monastery of *Ágios Sosontas*, which commands a fine view.

Hephaístia (now *Ifáistia*): The ruins of the *ancient city of Hephaístia* are situated on the NE of the Gulf of Purniás, some 33 km. N. of Mýrina; the site is also known as *Palaiopolis*. It is the oldest Greek island town, dating from the 8C BC, and was inhabited by the original Pelasgian peoples. A huge 8–6C *necropolis* has been uncovered, and so have traces of a *temple of Athena* and an early Hellenistic *theatre* from the 4C BC. Other remains include early Christian and Byzantine churches from the medieval town which was destroyed by the Turks in 1395. The ruins of the *Kabira shrine* (cf. Samothrake) near *Khloí* were excavated on a mountain slope near the port of Hephaístia in 1937. It was probably built during the Hellenistic period, but consists of older building materials: there is an old *telesterion* built over the remains of a 7&6C Tyrrhenian building dedicated to the Thracian Aphrodite (wife of Hephaistos), and a more recent Hellenistic *telesterion* with a *temple*, of which only traces of the foundations survive. Nearby are traces of a Roman basilica with a nave and two aisles.

Environs: The ruins of *Kokkinó* (3 km. SW) include a 14C *fortress* built with stones from Hephaístia and a double ring of walls. Near the harbour of *Pláka* (*c.* 10 km. NE) are traces of an ancient settlement (Methonen) and an important radioactive spring, which was the ancient source of 'Lemnian (healing) earth'.

Lutrá Kaiáfa/ΛΟΥΤΡΑ ΚΑΙΑΦΑ
Elis/Peloponnese   p.294☐D 10

This spring, 28 km. SE of Pýrgos, comes from the mountain of Lapithos; it was well known in ancient times, and was dedicated to the Anigrian nymphs. It is situated on the small island of Agia Aikateríni, and its sulphurous and radioactive waters help cure rheumatism, asthma and skin complaints.

Environs:Samikón (5 km. N.): The ancient town of Samikón, or Mákistos, was known for its Temple of Poseidon; the remains of 6C polygonal fortifications are still standing, which were rebuilt in the 4C by the Elians to secure the pass to Arkadia. **Kakóvatos** (8 km. S.): There are traces of a late Helladic palace from epoch I or II, and three tholos tombs from Mycenean times. The finds from the tholos tombs are housed in the National Museum in Athens.

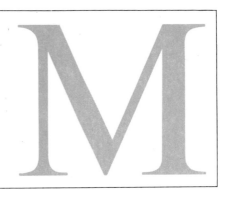

M

Mália/Mallia/ΜΑΛΙΑ
Iráklion/Crete   p.298☐H 14

Mália is a little inland from the N. coast
of Crete and 35 km. NE of Iráklion. It was
near here in 1921 that French and Greek
archaeologists began their excavation of a
Minoan palace whose oldest parts date
from about 2000 BC. In the process, they
discovered the remains of a Minoan city,
which are still being excavated. Not far
from the palace is the Chrysolakkos
necropolis where, among other finds, a
golden pendant of considerable artistic
value was discovered in 1945; it depicts
two bees on a honeycomb.

According to myth, Mália was the palace
of Sarpedon, who, like Minos and
Rhadamanthys, was believed to be the son
of Zeus and Europa. Sarpedon was said to
have won Zeus's promise that he could rule

Mália, store-rooms

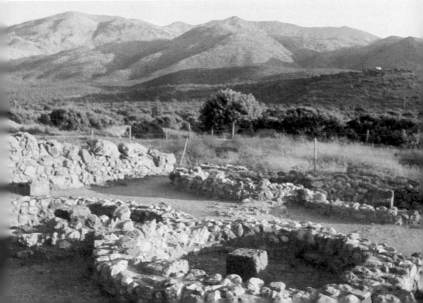

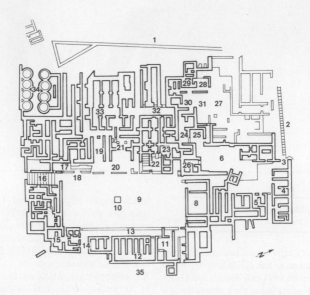

Málic, ground plan of the palace 1 W. courtyard, partially paved with blue limestone **2** paved street leading to the Minoan town **3** main entrance **4** and **5** store-rooms **6** N. courtyard **7** small Mycenean room used for cult purposes and built around the time of the second palace **8** hypostyle room with ante-room which probably seved as a banqueting hall **9** central courtyard **10** sacrificial altar **11** kitchens **12** store-room **13** open hall with pillars and columns **14** E. entrance of the palace **15** royal treasury **16** S. entrance **17** kernos (sacrificial table) with **34** symmetrically arranged niches carved round the edges and one larger one in the centre. The carved niches were used to receive sacrificial grain and fruit. The use of this large round table for sacrifices has been determined by the existence of another smaller table with fewer niches which is still used today by Eastern Orthodox priests for receiving offerings of oil, corn and wine **18** main staircase **19** corridor between the W. and central courtyards **20** open hall **21** pillared crypt **22** throne room of the priest-king **23** spot where royal sceptre in the form of a panther's head was found (now housed in the Archaeological Museum in Iráklion) **24** queen's megaron **25** link between N. and central courtyard **26** archive room **27** king's megaron **28** ante-room to a sacred pool, under the paving traces of the first palace and two fine swords from the time of the first palace were found (Iráklion) **29** sacred pool or bath **30** open columned hall **31** paved courtyard **32** store-rooms **33** store-rooms **34** eight round grain silos which were originally protected by a roof supported by a central pillar **35** E. courtyard

for three generations- which, in those days, presumably meant for three periods of eight years. In any case, the treasures discovered in Málic argue that Sarpedon must have been a wealthy ruler. This is attested for example by the ancient ceramics and by a fine dagger with a golden handle and seal which date from the palace's earliest period.

Unprotected and unfortified, like all Minoan palaces, Málic is set on a plain which looks on one side to the Gulf of Málic and on the other to the mountains and Mt.Dikte. That the Minoan people enjoyed an unusually long period of peace is indicated not only by all the Minoan sites, but also by every Minoan work of art, none of which represents the theme of war, in

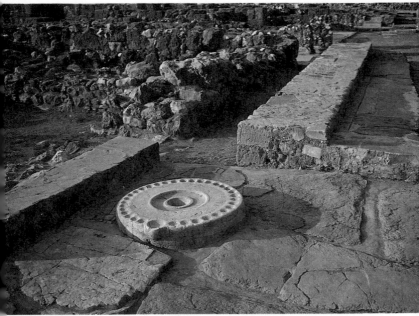

Mália, kernos

complete contrast to nearly every other period and culture. The leisure and tranquillity which this people consequently enjoyed must certainly be one of the reasons for that incredibly high cultural development which has so often caused Crete to be called the 'cradle of European culture'.

Like the other great Cretan palaces, this one is built around a central courtyard. Nonetheless, it does have many individual features, if compared, for example, with Knossós. There have been none of those reconstructions here which impose an image of the past on one's attention; instead, one is able to let the imagination play and recreate for itself what the ruins merely hint at.

There is, though, one concrete structure. This shelters the remains of a hypostyle crypt excavated in 1960–1. Evidently dating from the palace's earliest period, it originally served, together with several secondary rooms, as a kind of council chamber. The accompanying plan of the palace, like all plans of the Minoan sites, only gives what is assumed to be the most likely function of the rooms. To what extent all this remains an unsolved puzzle is shown by the discussion of H.G.Wunderlich's assertion, since largely discredited, that all the Minoan palaces were in fact necropoles. Despite all research, Crete's ancient culture remains, for the time being, a mystery, or at least until the Linear-A script, perhaps even Linear-B, are deciphered definitively. The palace at Mália was built around 2000 BC, rebuilt between 1700 and 1550, and abandoned about 1450, after the eruption of the volcano on Santorín and the great earthquake. It ranks as one of the three great Minoan

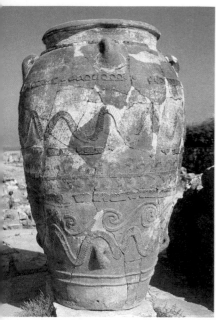

Málta, large pithos

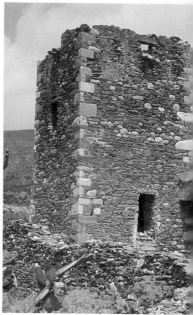

Máni, Alika family tower

palaces in Crete, together with those of Knossós and Phaistós.

Máni/Maina/ΜΑΝΗ
Lakonia/Peloponnese   p.298□ F 12

The Máni, or Maina, is the middle of the Peloponnese's three peninsulas. Its inhabitants consider themselves the direct descendants of the ancient Spartans, and are famous for their bravery and drive for independence, as well as for their blood feuds. After the Slav invasions (7–9C), they withdrew into the impassable regions around Mt.Taygetos. Even the Turks feared them, and they succeeded as early as the 18C in winning autonomy and privileges not granted to the Greeks under Turkish rule.

The Máni divides naturally into two parts, the *Outer Máni* which is fertile and extends from the towns of Kardamýli, Gýtheion and Ageranós in the N. as far S. as Ítilon, and the *Deep Máni*, which is bleak and rocky and occupies the S. half of the peninsula.

Areópolis (pop. *c.* 1,000): Capital of the Máni; previously called *Tsimova*.
The church of the *Taxiarchis* is a single-aisled basilica set in the town centre and built in 1798. The relief above the main portal shows, in the middle, a Byzantine eagle with an escutcheon on its breast. To its right and left are two lions underneath two suns. On both sides of the lions are the archangels. The relief above the S. portal places the archangels in the middle. At their sides are St.Theodore and St.George. Above are depicted the Hand of God and

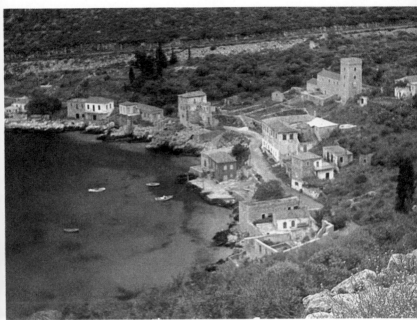

Areópolis (Máni), view over Oitylon

the Holy Spirit as a dove. The church of *Ioánnis Pródromos* has well-preserved frescos, including one of Peter crucified upside down, on a red background.

Environs: Fortress of Kelefá (*c.* 5 km. NE): A 17C structure dating from the Turkish occupation. This was the southernmost point of the Turks' advance into the Máni. Morosini captured the fortress in 1685. **Fortress of Passavá** (*c.* 15 km. NE): A Frankish building which takes its name from the French 'pas avant' or 'passe avant'. The fortress was built in 1254 by Jean de Neuilly, Marshal of Morea. It was captured by the Byzantines in the 14C and later by the Turks and the Venetians, who razed it. **Pýrgos-Dirú** (*c.* 5 km. S.): 12C church of *Ágios Ioánnis,* and the small, cross-in-square church of *Ágios Petros.* The *caverns of Dyrós* are 5 km. from here. The

first of these, called *Vlycháda* after the osprey, can be visited by boat, and it is possible to travel up to a mile into it (1 [3/4] miles have been explored). The water is 23–30 ft. deep. The stalactites and stalagmites are very beautiful. In the second cave, *Alepótrypa* (492 ft. deep), burials and idols have been found dating from the late Neolithic period (4000 – 2800/2700 BC; they are now in the museum in Sparta). There is a third cavern, *Katafýgi,* which can be visited on foot and which has two levels. *Karúda* (*c.* 10 km. S.): 11C church. *Drýalos* (*c.* 11 km. SE): Towers typical of the Mani. The 19C church of *Ágios Geórgios* has been built on an earlier structure dating from the 14C. **Vámvaka** (*c.* 15 km. SE): Church of *Agioi Theodoroi,* built in 1075. Nearby is the village of **Érimos** which contains the *Agia Varvara,* one of the most beautiful churches in the Máni,

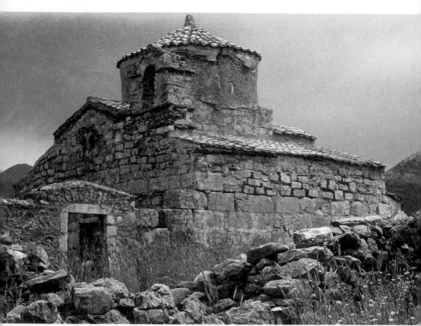

Alika (Máni), Ágios Pétros

dating from the 12C. **Gardénitsa** (*c.* 18 km. SE): Church of the *Ágios Sotir* from the 11 or 12C. **Kítta** (*c.* 20 km. SE): Seat of the Niklians. The region S. of Pýrgos Dirú was called the 'country of the Niklians'—a Frankish-Greek people who fled to the Máni in the 13C after the defeat of the knights near Nikli (in the Tegéa area). They then ruled the region, building towers which only had one window on each side of the upper storey. There were frequent clashes between neighbouring villages, generally as a result of territorial disputes, which invariably ended in the destruction of the enemy's tower. Today, Kítta is effectively abandoned. Nearby is the church of *Ágios Geórgios*, previously dedicated to Saints Sergios and Bakchos. It is a 12C cross-in-square church with four capitals decorated with acanthus vines. **Gerolimín** (*c.* 25 km. S.): This is a fish-

ing village on the Bay of Gerolimín which was once a pirates' hide-out. Nearby is **Alika,** whose old name was Kainipolis, which has the ruins of three 5C basilicas. **Cape Matapán** (*Tainaron, c.* 37 km. SE): This was believed by the ancients to be one of the entrances to Hades. According to myth, Herakles descended from here into the underworld on his mission to overpower Cerberus, the three-headed watchdog of Hades. There are some slight remains of a temple of Poseidon. On *Pórto Cáyo Bay* there are some traces of a Frankish fort. **Itilon/Oitylon** (*c.* 4 km. NE): The ancient Oitilos. The *Monastery of Dekulos* has a church with frescos dating from 1765 and a gilded iconostasis. Some 730 Maniotes set out from here in 1675 to settle in Corsica because they were unwilling to pay taxes to the Turks. **Kutíphari** (*Thalamai, c.* 26 km. NW) con-

tains a 13C church of *Agia Sofia*. **Plátsa**
(*c.* 29 km. NW) contains the churches of
Agia Paraskevi and *Ágios Nikólaos*, both
dating from the 13C, and *Ágios Ioánnis*
which dates from the 15 or 16C. All three
have interesting paintings and icons.
Stúpa: This is the ancient Leuktra; it contains the ruins of a Frankish fortress.
Kardamýli (*c.* 46 km. NW) has a Venetian
fortress built on the ruins of the ancient
acropolis. There is a small offshore island
on which Neoptolemos is supposed to have
landed on his journey to Menelaos. Many
towers are preserved here. In Ano-
Kardamýli, the church of Ágios Spyridon
has a tower which is decorated by a relief
and is crowned by a spire. **Kámpos** (*c.* 60
km. NW): Near here is the 17C *Castle of
Zarnata* which was built on the site of the
ancient Alagonia and has an imposing rampart. Mycenean tombs, and the foundations of a temple, have been discovered in
the castle. It belonged originally to the
Palaiologoi, and was captured, first by the
Turks, and later, in 1685, by Morosini.
The church of *Zoodóchos-Pigí* has a carved
iconostasis.

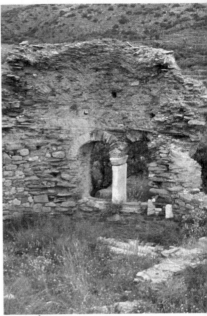

Máni, Ágios Nikólaos, Plátsa

Marathónas/Marathon/ΜΑΡΑΘΩΝ
Attica   p.296□H 8

Marathónas (Marathon), today a small rural community, lies some 42 km. NE of
Athens, inland from the Gulf of Petalion
(Kolpos Petalion). The ancient deme, or
community, of Marathon was closer to the
coast, on the Bay of Marathon.

History: According to myth, the hero
Theseus slew the 'Marathonian bull' on
the Plain of Marathon. The region was settled as early as prehistoric and Mycenean
times and was one of the oldest Ionian settlement areas in Attica. Its lasting fame
derives from the Battle of Marathon which
the Greeks and Persians fought here in 490
BC. The numerically inferior Greek phal-

anx made up of Athenians and Plataians
(the Spartans having been delayed by a festival) faced the Persians along a line running from NW to SE. The Strategos
Miltiades strengthened his right and left
wings, placing the Plataians on the left and
the Athenians on the right, attacked the
Persian army in a pincer movement, and
defeated it. Thanks to these successful tactics (a pincer movement on both wings,
leaving the centre weak) the Athenians lost
a mere 192 hoplites (heavily armed infan-
trymen). Despite their superior force, the
Persians were forced back into their ships
which were lying ready in the bay; of these,
they lost seven to the Athenians (see the
description in Herodotus 6, 107 ff.). Thus
was Athens saved, for the time being. A
young soldier, Diomedon, ran from the
battle-field to Athens, still fully armed,
broke the news of victory with his cry of

'Enikesamen!' ('We won!'), and then fell dead. It was in commemoration of his feat that the modern Olympic games introduced the long-distance marathon, which is roughly 42 km.

Ancient battle-field: This lies on the Bay of Marathon, near the modern coastal road between the villages of *Marathónas* and *Néa Mákri*. The Greek camp was close to the present-day church of Ágios Dimitrios (Vrana), and the Persian camp was on a stream called Charadros, near the modern church of Panagia Mesosporitissa. It was here that the two armies advanced against each other.

The Athenians' burial mound: The 192 Athenian dead were cremated and buried in a mound (which was either a soros or a tymbos) some 550 yards E. of the modern road, close to the sea. The Athenians considered this a national monument, and marked it with a stela made about 490 BC by the sculptor Aristion (it depicts an Attic hoplite and is now in Room 11 of the National Museum in Athens). Excavations carried out in 1890 uncovered skeletons of soldiers killed in the battle, bones of sacrificial animals, fragments of vases, and Persian arrowheads. Today the mound is 29 ft. 6 in. high and roughly 590 ft. round, and is marked by a copy of Aristion's stela.

The Plataians' burial-mound: The burial-mound of the Plataians killed in battle was excavated in 1970 by the Greek archaeologist Marinatos. It lies a little way inland and close to the church of Ágios Dimitrios. (It has a diameter of about 100 ft. and is some 10 ft. high). Skeletons of the fallen soldiers, who were about 20 years old, and their 40-year-old commander, together with fragments of vases which were buried with them as grave offerings, can be seen.

Also worth seeing: Near the tomb of the

Plataians there is a necropolis comprising four *burial mounds* dating from the middle Helladic (2000–1500 BC) and Mycenean (1500–1100 BC) periods, and in particular a restored *Mycenean tholos* with a *dromos* (entrance to the tomb) 82 ft. long, in which were discovered two skeletons of horses—the guardians of the place. The tombs are partly protected by a hall. It is significant that these tombs show an uninterrupted development from the late Helladic to the Mycenean period. Nearby, towards the road, are the remains of an *early Helladic burial ground* (the Tsépi site) with burial chambers one yard square, dating from the third millennium BC.

Archaeological Museum (Archaiologiko Musio): This small museum, near the church of Ágios Dimitrios and close to the Mycenean tombs, contains many archaeological discoveries from the Marathon district. These are arranged in chronological order from Neolithic up to Byzantine times. *Room A:* The display cases contain interesting fragments of Neolithic ceramics from the Cave of Pan at Oinóe (Inói). *Room B:* Ceramics found in the Tsépi early Helladic graveyard. *Room C:* Burial objects (notably black-figure ceramics) from the two burial mounds at Marathon. *Room D:* Tomb reliefs, marble tomb monuments, and ceramics from Néa Mákri, Ágios Andréas, and Marathon. *Room E:* Statues and tomb reliefs (also glass and lamps) from the Roman and Byzantine periods.

Environs: The remains of a **Mycenean acropolis** have been discovered on *Mt.Agriliki* (to the SE of the Plain of Marathon). The ancient town of **Marathon** is presumed to have been situated on the coast itself, near the site of *Plathý* (Ágios Panteleímon, to the NE of the Athenians' burial-mound), where the traces of a prehistoric settlement have been discovered.

Marathónas, Ephebe (Nat.Mus.Athens) ▷

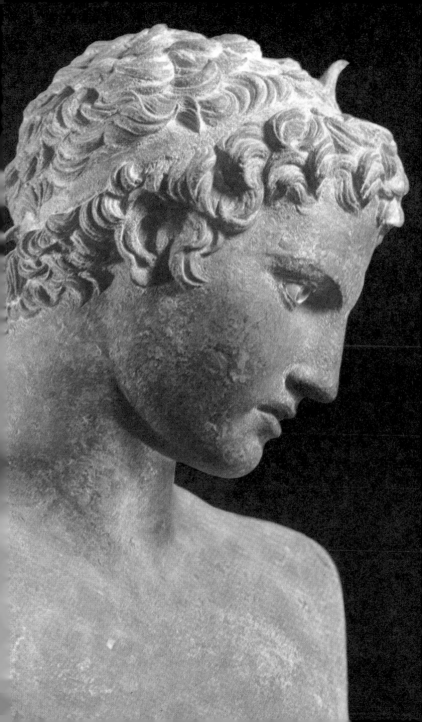

In the 2C AD, the rich Athenian Herodes Atticus possesssed extensive estates nearby. **Néa Mákri** (*c.* 6 km. S.): Popular bathing resort. It was near here that a significant Neolithic-Helladic settlement was discovered (the finds are in the museum at Marathon). Remains of the ancient deme of Oinóe were discovered to the W. of the modern village of Marathon. Not far from there is the so-called **Cave of Pan**, with the remains of a Sanctuary of Pan which was important in classical times. Church of the **Panagia Mesosporitissa** (near the coast): Near here are the remains of a medieval *watch-tower* incorporating a fragment of an Ionic capital (a monument to the battle stood here in classical times). Some 8 km. to the W. of the village of Marathon, in lovely wooded country, is **Marathon Lake**, a reservoir dammed in 1930. The dam is 312 yards long and 236 ft. high. This is the main water reservoir for Athens, which lies 40 km. to the SW. To the NW of the Marathon Lake and some 12 km. NW of Marathon itself, near the modern motorway, there are some slight remains of the early Attic deme of **Aphíd-nai** (now called *Afídnai).* This town, and indeed the whole area, was already settled in Mycenean times. It was incorporated, supposedly by Theseus, into the Attic league of twelve townships (the Dodekapolis) around 1000 BC. According to Attic myth, Helen, the daughter of Zeus and Leda who was born from an egg (her parents had taken the form of swans when they conceived her), was taken from Sparta to Aphídnai. She was then freed by her brothers, the dioscuri Castor and Polydeukes (Pollux).

Markópulo/ΜΑΡΚΟΠΟΥΛΟ
Attica/Central Greece   p.296□H 9

This is the agricultural centre of the fertile interior of central Attica (the name of this area, the (*Mesogia,* means 'the inland') and is some 30 km. SE of Athens. It is worth seeing the small churches of Ágios Konstantinos, Agia Triada, the Panagia (pointed arches), Agia Kyriaki, and Agia Paraskevi; some of these contain *frescos* by Georgios Markos, the 17C Argive painter.

Megalópolis, remains of the ancient theatre

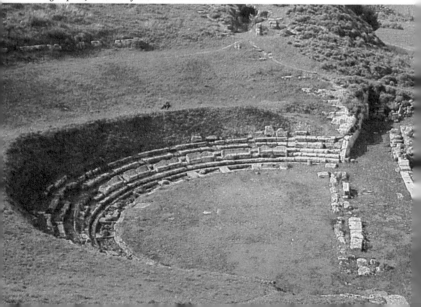

Environs: Some 3 km. to the SE, near *Merénda*, the **necropolis** of the ancient town of *Myrrinús* was excavated near an ancient *well*. The tombs, in which vases were discovered, date from the 8–4C BC, i.e. from the Geometric to the Hellenistic period. The finds are displayed in the museum at Vravróna (Braurón). The remains of an ancient *road* (10 ft. wide) were also discovered here, as were those of two archaic *sculptures* (a kouros and kore), which are now in the National Museum in Athens. The neighbouring village of **Kalývia** (5 km. to the S.) also has some church frescos by the school of Georgios Markos of Argos. A short distance towards the sea near the village of **Keratéa** in the Mesogia (10 km. SE) is the convent of *Moni Kerateas*.

Megalópolis/ΜΕΓΑΛΟΠΟΛΙΣ
Arkadia/Peloponnese   p.294 □ E 10

Megalópolis lies 36 km. to the SW of Trípolis and has a population of about 3,500.

History: After Epameinondas's victory at Leuktra in 371 BC, Megalópolis was founded as the centre and capital of the Arkadian Confederacy. Forty Arkadian villages, as well as larger towns like Mantineía, provided the new city with its population, in a process called synoikismos. By 318, it had a male population of 15,000. It extended on both sides of the river Elisson and had a double wall over 5 miles in length. Aristodamos established a tyranny and ruled here from 266–255 BC; he was followed shortly afterwards by Lydiadas (250–235). In 235, Megalópolis joined the Achaean Confederacy. It was sacked in 223 BC by the Spartans under Kleomenes III.

Some building was certainly carried out in Roman times; for example, a Roman forum was built here during the reign of Diocletian (AD 284–305). Pausanias has left us a detailed description of the city from which its topography can be reconstructed.

Megalópolis produced two important figures, the historian Polybios, who was born about 200 BC, and Philopoimen the general (253–183 BC), who succeeded in

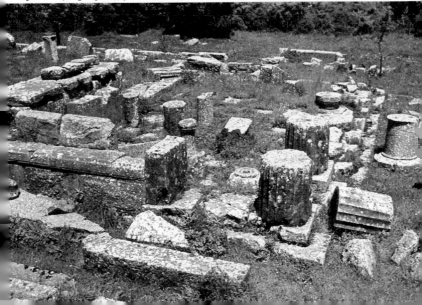

Lykósura (Megalópolis), foundations of the Temple of Despoina

bringing Sparta into the Achaean Confederacy.

Theatre: According to Pausanias, this was once the largest theatre in Greece, and was able to accommodate 20,000 spectators. It had more than 50 rows of seats, and the orchestra had a diameter of just under 100 ft.

Thersileion (behind the skene of the theatre): Named after Thersilos, who built this huge hall for the meetings of the synedrion or assembly, called the Ten Thousand, of the Arkadian Confederacy. It could actually accommodate some ten thousand men. Its roof was supported by 67 pillars. It was destroyed in 223 BC, an event which in fact provided the impulse for the construction of a stone skene—until then a moveable wooden skene had been used. The *stadium* and the *Sanctuary of Dionysos* are to the W. of the Thersileion, and the *Sanctuary of Asklepios* lies to its E.

Sanctuary of Zeus Soter (on the N. bank of the river Elisson): This stood on the river-bank, and had an altar measuring 37 ft. by 16 ft. 10 in., which was surrounded on three sides by a stoa, like the altar of Pergamon (which is in the museum in East Berlin). The cult-image, which according to Pausanias was made by Kephistodotes and Xenophon, was kept in the naos. It represented Zeus enthroned between a personification of the city and the goddess Artemis Soteira.

Agora: To the E. is the *Stoa Myropolis* (built *c.* 250 BC by Aristodemos); to the N. is the *Stoa Philippeios* (338 BC) which was named after Philip II of Macedon (its front was 512 ft. long with 83 Doric columns). To the E. of the Stoa Philippeios there are the foundations of several administrative buildings.

Environs:Lykósura (12 km. SW): Well-known in antiquity because of its 4C

Temple of Despoina. There are the foundations of a Doric stoa which had three altars in front of it to Demeter, Despoina, and Gaia. The small museum contains cult-statues of these three goddesses and of the giant Anytos which were fashioned by the sculptor Damophon in the 2C BC.

Mégara/ΜΕΓΑΡΑ
Attica/Central Greece   p.294□G 9

Mégara (pop. 16,000), a lovely little town with colourful flat-roofed houses, lies at the N. end of the Saronic Gulf, on the road between Athens and Corinth (some 44 km. NW of Athens). Today it is an agricultural centre known for its poultry breeding, wine making, and fruit and vegetable production.

History: Mégara was a Cretan stronghold as early as 1700 BC. Following the Dorian settlement (around 1000 BC), it acquired importance as an independent city-state in the 8&7C. The Megarians founded important colonies including Mégara Hyblaia and Selinús in Sicily, and Chalkedón and Byzántion, the future Constantinople, in the E., the last-named being established in 658 BC. The tyrant Theagenes enlarged the city in about 640 BC. However, the ensuing period saw numerous conflicts with the rising power of Athens (notably, for example, for the possession of the island of Salamis in 570 BC), which Athens finally won. The Peloponnesian Wars harmed Mégara greatly, and it lost virtually all its importance after that. It was the birthplace of the lyric poet Theognis (about 500 BC) and of Euclid, pupil of Socrates and founder of the Megarian school of philosophy.

Ancient remains: Only some slight traces are preserved of the city's brilliant past, including the remains of two *acropoles*

on its two hills to E. and W. The main square, or platia, is actually situated on top of the ancient *agora*, of which virtually nothing is left. Some 320 yards N. of the church the remains of an ancient *aqueduct* (ydragogion) can be seen in the rock together with those of a *fountain*, both dating from the time of the tyrant Theagenes, about 620 BC. There is a large *reservoir*, made of limestone blocks, whose walls have survived, in parts, up to a height of 16 ft. 6 in. The *cistern* (*c.* 60 ft. by 43 ft.) was supported by 5 rows of octagonal columns.

Environs: Kakí Skála ('Evil Staircase', *c.* 7 km. W): Near here are the famous Skironian Rocks. According to the myth, the legendary robber Skiron would intercept people travelling from the Peloponnese to Athens on the narrow rocky path above and hurl them down into the sea, where they were eaten by giant turtles. He met the same fate at the hands of the hero Theseus. Nearby are the beautiful bathing resorts of *Kinétta* (12 km. NW) and *Ágii Theódori* (18 km. SW), which have pebbly beaches and clear water. This was the site of the ancient **Krómyon** (of which nothing remains), where Theseus is said to have slain the man-eating pig Phaia. **Ósios Melétios** (*c.* 15 km. NE): This isolated monastery (*c.* 35 km. NW of Athens), a Byzantine foundation, lies on the footills of Mt.Pateras. Its complex of buildings includes chapels, living quarters, and, notably, a small (restored) *cross-in-square church* with 4 columns dating from the 11 or 12C and *frescos* dating from the 16 or 17C; there is also a two-storeyed stoa with beautiful arches.

Melidóni/Melidónion/
ΜΕΛΙΔΟΝΙΟΝ
Réthymnon/Crete   p. 298 □ G 14

Near this village, which is situated some 3 km. from the N. coast of Crete, between Réthymnon and Iráklion, there is a beautiful cave with *stalactites*. Legend relates that Talos, the bronze monster made by Hephaistos which passed into the possession of Minos, lived here. Talos was supposed to have guarded the Cretan coast. But the historical events which took place in 1824 were much more dreadful. 300 Cretans, mainly women and children, took refuge here from the Turks. The Turks lit a fire in front of the cave, and everyone inside suffocated. There is an altar in the front part of the cave which was used in antiquity for the cult of Hermes and now serves as a memorial to this tragedy.

Environs: Pánormos: Some 5 km. from Melidóni, near the coast, is Pánormos, where a *basilica* with a nave and two aisles dating from the beginning of the 5C was excavated. Evidently the seat of the bishopric of the ancient Eleuthérna had been transferred here. **Eleuthérna** is some 10 km. S. of Pánormos; there is a footpath leading here from the monastery of Arkádi some 6 km. away. Of the ancient town itself (which was important until the 8C BC) there remain the acropolis, which has had a Byzantine tower added to it, Roman cisterns, and above all a beautiful old bridge. The limestone torso of an archaic kouros (630 – 620 BC) which was found here is now kept in the Archaeological Museum in Iráklion. **Pigí:** Near Eleuthérna, and close to Grambelaa, is the village of Pigí. An underground tomb was discovered here in 1971 which contained eight sarcophagi and 42 vases from late Minoan times. **Viran Episkopí:** About 5 km. from Pérama (which is between Melidóni and Eleuthérna), heading towards Plataniés and Réthymnon, one discovers Viran Episkopí, which contains a Catholic church with a fine 16C portal. A Byzantine basilica dating from about AD 1100 was excavated here which had been partly constructed with ancient building material.

Arsáni: Near to Plataniés is the Arsáni monastery, dating from the 17C.

Mesolóngi(on) / Missolúngi / ΜΕΣΟΛΟΓΓΙ
Aetolia / Central Greece   p.294☐ D 8

This, the capital of the nome of Aetolia and Akarnania (pop. *c.* 12,000), lies in the flat alluvial basin formed by the rivers Acheloos to its W. and Evinos to the E. It is a quiet town on the banks of a lagoon (whence its name) which became famous for its heroic resistance during the War of Liberation. Lord Byron landed here in 1824 to fight with the Greeks, but died of malaria the same year. Two years later, in 1826, the bulk of the population was massacred by the Turks in a desperate attempt to break free of the siege; while some of the defenders blew themselves up with the enemy.

In the so-called *park of the heroes*, by the old *town wall*, is the *heroes' memorial (heroon)*, with the busts of the leaders of the struggle for independence (notably Markos Botsaris). Lord Byron's heart lies at rest here too in a tomb of honour.

The *town museum* contains a collection of documents and memoirs relating to the part played by the town in 1821–6 during the War of Liberation.

Environs: Ágios Symeón (4 km. NE): Monastery with a cross commemorating the women and children killed in the War of Liberation. **Pleurón** (*Plevróna, c.* 5 km. NW): The ruins of the ancient city lie on the slopes of Mt.Arakynthos (which is some 3,280 ft. high). Near its SW wall are the remains of a *theatre* whose *stage* rested against the city wall. To the SE there is a well-preserved *cistern* which has doors and basins. Near the E. wall is the ancient *agora* which has a portico, exedrae, and the remains of pedestals. To the N. is the fortified *wall of the acropolis* with square towers (it was destroyed in 234 BC). **Kástro Kyrá Iríni** (*c.* 8 km. NW: Named after Irene, a medieval lady of the castle. Well-preserved *rampart* (2 km. round; the entrance is to the SW) with many towers

Messene, remains of the agora

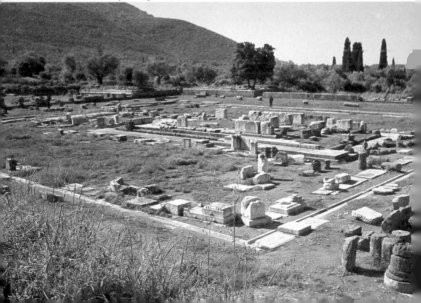

and gateways. **Kalydón** (*c.* 12 km. NE): The ancient city stood at the foot of and to the S. of Mt.Arakynthos. Its legendary king, Meleager (son of Oineus, king of Aetolia), was the subject of the myth of the Kalydonian boar-hunt. This related that Meleager, having managed to kill the wild boar which Artemis had sent to punish him, then quarrelled with his uncles and killed them. His mother Althaia promptly threw on to the fire the brand on which his life depended (for he could remain alive only as long as it remained intact), and he died. The remains of the ancient city, which worshipped Artemis, goddess of the hunt, comprise *walls* dating from the 3C BC and the ruins of a *heroon* (2C BC) which includes parts of a stoa. At a slight distance (820 ft. to the W.), on a hill, stand the remains of the foundations of the *Temple of Artemis Laphria* which dates from the 4C BC and was built on the site of an earlier temple dating from the 6/7C BC. There are also remains of a *columned hall* and several treasuries and fragments of terracotta metopes. There was a *Temple of Apollo* to the W. of the Temple of Artemis.

Messene/ΜΕΣΣΗΝΗ

Messenia / Peloponnese   p.298 □ E 11

The ancient city of Messene stood at the foot of Mt.Ithomi, 29 km. from modern Kalamata and close to the modern village of Mavromáti (which means 'black eye'). It was founded by Epameinondas after his victory over the Spartans at Leuktra in 371 BC. Together with the fortified cities of Árgos, Mantineía and Megalópolis, the purpose of the new city was to defend Messenia. It withstood two sieges at the end of the 3C BC, the first mounted by the Macedonian army led by Demetrios of Pharos, and the second by Nabis, the tyrant of Sparta.

Walls: Over 5 miles long, the walls have square or semicircular watch-towers at regular intervals. At the N. end, where the road from Mavromáti ends, is the *Arkadian Gate*, one of the best preserved city gates in Greece. Two square towers, of which only the foundations remain, formed the outer gate. A forecourt narrowed into a pas-

Messene, the small theatre in the agora

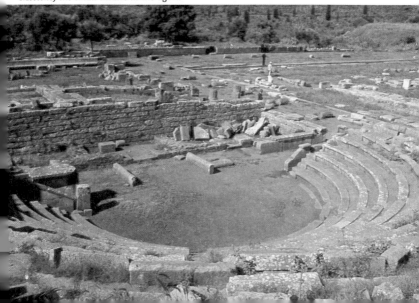

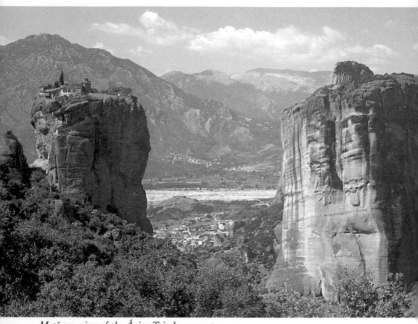

Metéora, view of the Ágios Triada monastery

sage which passed through this gateway, which could be closed. Once through this gate there were niches for statues, a round courtyard, the inner gate and access to the parapet walk.

The wall runs along the slope of Mt.Ithomi from E. to W. It was 6 ft. 6 in. to 8 ft. thick, some 13 ft. high, and consisted of two stone walls, the space between which was filled with earth. The wall which we see today is not the original one dating from the foundation of the city, but was built *c.* 240 BC, at the onset of the conflict between the Macedonians and Aetolians over Messene.

Agora: This is an extensive site which was surrounded by colonnades. At the E. end, a small *theatre* with Doric half-columns joined the proskenion. The orchestra had a polychrome marble pavement. Immedi-

ately to the S. of the theatre is a *propylon* which constituted the E. entrance to the agora, and S. of it again there was an almost square structure, probably the *synedrion* or popular assembly, which had stone benches along three sides. At the S. end of the agora there are a *heroon* and a peristyled house which was perhaps the *prytaneion*. At the N. end of the agora there is a *chamber* between two pillars, which, during the time of the Caesars, housed a colossal statue (of which parts have been found). Also at the N. end of the agora, between this chamber and the propylon, there was a monumental staircase, 23 ft. wide, which led to an upper platform. Here there were two rooms which constituted the *sebasteion*, which was used for the cult of the Emperors. On the W. side of the agora there was an *exedra* in front of a stoa dating from the second half of the 4C. Still on the W. side, there is a *Temple of Artemis* made up of three parts; the base of the cult statue was discovered here. Statues of the priestesses of Artemis were arranged in a semicircle; six of these have been discovered and are now in the town museum.

Mt.Ithomi: According to legend, Zeus was born by a spring on Mt.Ithomi, where he was brought up by two nymphs, Ithomi and Neda. Here were held the *Ithomaea*, festivals in honour of Zeus which included musical competitions. Near the 16C monastery of Voulkánou was the *Sanctuary of Zeus Ithomatas* which consisted of just a single altar and witnessed human sacrifices. On the S. slope was the *Sanctuary of Artemis Limnatis* (Ionic temple in antis, measuring 56 ft. 6 in. by 32 ft. 10 in). On the summit is the site of a fortification dating from the times of the Messenian wars. On the summit of Mt.Eva was the *Sanctuary of Dionysos.*

Museum: There is a small museum in Mavromáti which contains finds from local excavations.

Environs: Meligalás (*c.* 10 km. NE): This town was originally built in the Byzantine period. To its W. is the Mavrozumena Bridge which occupies the site of an ancient bridge and spans the confluence of the Amphitos and Leukasia rivers. 5 km. away can be seen the ruins of the ancient Stenykláros, which was the seat of the first Dorian dynasty in Messenia (12C BC).

Metéora/Metéora
Monasteries/ΜΕΤΕΩΡΑ
Tríkala/Thessaly   p.290☐E 5

Some 3–5 km. to the N. of **Kalabáka** (see entry), at the NW end of the Thessalian plain, rise the precipitous and weirdly

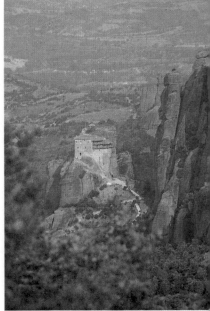

Metéora, monastery and surroundings

shaped rocks, some of which are nearly 1,000 ft. high, which are known as the Meteora. These conglomerate rock formations, whose steepness makes them difficult of access, resulted from the erosion caused by once mighty mountain rivers, notably the Pinios (Peneios), which poured down into the valley from the S. end of the neighbouring Pindos Mountains.

History: The rugged inaccessibility of these rocks made them a refuge down the ages for the local populations. The first ascetics, who were hermits, settled here in caves around 950. After the Serbs had established their rule in Tríkala in 1340, the first hermitage, Panagia Dupianí, was founded (about 1350) by a monk called Kyr Nilos on the top of the *Dupiani* rock; today it is in ruins. The first monastery,

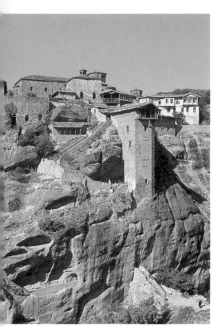

Metéora, Moni Meteoron

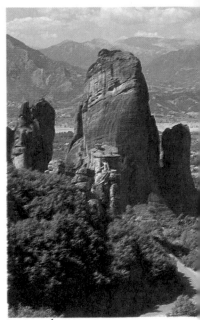

Metéora, Ágios Russánu

Megalon Meteoron, was founded here between 1356 and 1372 by Athanasios Meteoritis on the Platys Lithos ('broad rock'); donations enabled it to be enlarged, around 1388, by Iosaf, a monk descended from the Serbian emperors. New monasteries (all closely linked with Mt.Athos) continued to be established on the other rocks up until the 16C. These gradually fell into dispute with each other over questions of land ownership. Today the monasteries are impoverished, and, of the original 24, only five or six are occupied.

Moni ('Monastery') Meteoron: This, the oldest and largest of all the monasteries here, is set on top of the *Platys Lithos* ('broad rock'), which stands at an altitude 1,752 ft. at the end of the road (*c.* 7.5 km. N. of Kalabáka). It was founded and built

in the 14C and dedicated to the *Metamorphosis* (Transfiguration). Soon, however, its appearance of being suspended above the earth gave it the nickname of *Meteoron* ('floating'), which then passed to the other monasteries as well. The small, original *cross-in-square* of around 1388 was extended in 1550 to become the much larger *Church of the Transfiguration*. The *apse* (part of the old church) has *frescos* dating from 1483 which include a representation of Athanasios, the monastery's founder, in the post-Byzantine Macedonian style (which was influenced by Mt.Athos). The 16C frescos in the *main church* (katholikon) portray the themes of the 'Nativity of Christ', 'Transfiguration', ('Metamorphosis'), 'Crucifixion', and 'Resurrection' in the Cretan Venetian style. Inside, there is a richly carved, gilded *iconostasis*, icon stands, candelabra, and a carved *abbot's throne.* It is also worth seeing the vaulted *refectory* (trapeza) dating from 1557 and the interesting *museum*, which contains 14C icons and pictures, old church utensils, reliquaries, gospels, wood carvings, and a number of old manuscripts, notably those recording the history of the Meteora monasteries. Also of interest are the sacristy, the library, the cloister (with 50 cells off it), cisterns, the Chapel of John the Forerunner (Prodromos), and the Chapel of Ágios Konstantinos (dating from the 18C).

Moni Varlaam: On the next rock to the E. This monastery was erected by the brothers Theophanis and Nektarios of Ioánnina in 1517 on the site of the hermitage built by Varlaam (Barlaam) the monk around 1350. The *monastery church* Agion Panton (All Saints) is a cross-in-square structure with a beautifully *frescoed* narthex painted around 1565 by Frankos Katclanos of Thebes and restored in 1870. The *museum* contains objects used in liturgy, manuscripts, interesting icons, and a gospel which belonged to the Emperor Constantine VII Porphyrogennitos (912–59). Also of interest are the refectory, the monastery kitchens, the library, and the fortified garden, which offers a beautiful view.

Russánu Monastery: This is now a convent, and stands on an inaccessible rock. It dates from around 1639 and is on the site of an earlier hermitage (dating from 1388). The *monastery church* is decorated with well-preserved *frescos* (1566).

Monastery of Ágios Nikolaos: Near the Dupiani rock. Built around 1388 and enlarged in 1628.
The small basilica contains interesting *frescos* (1527) by the Cretan painter Theophanis (Strelitsas). These exemplify the onset of the post-Byzantine Cretan style (16&17C), which superseded the Macedonian school of Athos.

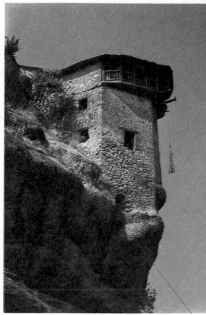

Metéora, hoist

Agia Triada Monastery (Holy Trinity Monastery): Founded in 1438. The monastery church dates from 1476 and has a beautiful façade; parts of its *frescos*, painted in 1692, are damaged. It is also worth seeing the *Chapel of Ágios Ioánnis* (1682) which was hewn out of the rock and stands at the top of the narrow staircase leading up from the valley; this too is carved into the rock and dates from 1888. There is an impressive view from the top over the plain of Thessaly.

Nunnery of Ágios Stefanos: This was founded in 1312 and built by the Emperor Andronikos III Palaiologos (1328–41) with the help of munificent donations. It originally included a small basilica. Its main church, *Ágios Charalampos*, was built in 1798 and has three conches and a main dome together with subsidiary domes. In-

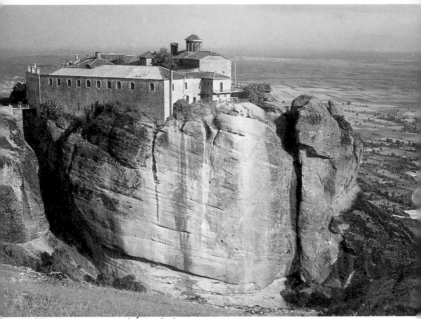

Metéora, monastery of Ágios Stefanos

side, it contains a wealth of wood carvings; of these, the iconostasis (which is decorated with sculptures), the abbot's throne, choir stalls, and the lecterns are fine examples of the carving of Epirus. The small Chapel of St. Stephen has frescos dating from around 1500. The *treasury* (monastery museum) testifies to an earlier opulence, with its old manuscripts, icons, silver, and reliquaries, including the skull, set in silver, of Charalampos, the patron saint of the church. The view over the plain of Thessaly is glorious.

Also worth seeing: The other monasteries and hermitages in the Meteora are today uninhabited, and some of them are ruined (e.g. the Ypapanti Monastery and the Pantokrator Monastery). At one time, the only access to the monasteries consisted of rope ladders and baskets drawn up by rope. Since about 1880, it has been possible to reach the main monasteries by means of staircases carved into the rock.

Methóni/ΜΕΘΩΝΗ
Messenia/Peloponnese   p.298□E 11

A small medieval town 65 km. SW. of Kalamáta (pop. 1300). It has a very well preserved fortified wall built by the Venetians.
Methóni was famous in the Middle Ages for its silk production and export of wine.

History: Methóni is mentioned in Homer under the name of *Pidasos*. It was relinquished to Nauplia by Sparta in ancient times, and was the object of an unsucccessful Athenian siege in 431 BC. Under the

Romans, it was fortified by Antonius, who installed the king of Mauretania as commander of the garrison. The Doge Domenico Michiele destroyed the fortress in 1125. In 1204, after the conquest of Constantinople, Geoffroy de Villehardouin came to Methóni to make sure of his share of the booty. Together with Guillaume de Champlitte, he conquered Moréa.

Sultan Bajezid II took the town in 1500. It was only freed from Turkish rule in 1686 and then remained Venetian until 1715, when the Turks reconquered it.

Fortress: The sea-girt fortress is entered by means of a bridge built by the French General Maison in 1828. There are two massive bastions, the Bembo bastion, built in 1480, and the Loredan bastion, which dates from 1714. One has to pass through three gates before coming to an ancient granite column with a Byzantine capital, which is known as the Morosini column. Inside the walls, there is a small Turkish bath, as well as the remains of a small minaret and cisterns.

The walls on the W. side were built by the Venetians in the 15C and are defended by five towers.

On the S. side is the Sea Gate, which is flanked by two towers. It was linked by a causeway to the octagonal Bourzi tower, which was built by the Turks in the 16C.

Environs: 2 km. along the road to Pýlos is the early Christian cemetery of *Ágios Onuphrios*.

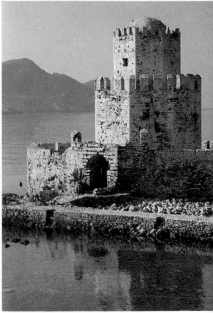

Methóni, Bourzi tower

Of interest: The church of *Agia Paraskevi* (15C) contains mosaics and a beautiful iconostasis. The monastery of *Ágios Nikolaos* has 17C frescos. Métsovon is one of the few places in Greece where people still wear traditional costume.

Mílos/Mélos/Milos (I)/
ΜΗΛΟΣ
Cyclades/Aegean Islands   p.298☐I 11

This, the southernmost of the Western Cyclades (62 sq. miles, pop. *c.*5,000) is an especially charming place to visit, with its deeply indented bay—once a crater—and the island's volcanic origin.

History: The island was inhabited as early as the third millennium BC, serving as a

---

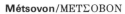

Métsovon/ΜΕΤΣΟΒΟΝ
Ioánnina/Epirus   p.290☐D 5

Métsovon is a small town in the mountains, 64 km. NE. of Ioánnina, with a population of 3,000. It was established by the Romans.

naval base for Crete, and because of its rich supplies of volcanic stone (obsidian), which was suitable for making knives and swords, it conducted a flourishing trade in the Mediterranean. After a period of Mycenean sway (1500–1100 BC), it was settled by Dorian migrants from Lakonia. Later, it took part in the Persian Wars and was a member of the Attic maritime league. In 426 BC, it was besieged by the Athenians, who devastated it in 416. The Macedonians took it in 336 BC, followed by the Romans in 146 BC. During the Middle Ages, it belonged to the Duchy of Naxos, sharing that island's subsequent fate.

Mílos/Milos (also *Pláka*, 'place'): To the NW. of the Bay of *Adámas*, which is a lovely natural harbour, is the island capital, Milos, standing beneath the ruins of the Venetian fortress, *Kastro* (13&14C). Part of the modern town is built on the site of the ancient *Mélos* (founded about 700 BC). The village of *Trypití* (1 km. SE. of Milos) contains the remains of archaic polygonal walls (from the ancient harbour of *Klíma*), the foundations of a Temple of Di-

onysos and a gymnasion, and a small Roman theatre dating from the 1C BC. It was here that the famous *Venus de Milo*, now in the Louvre in Paris, was found in 1820. Nearby (15 minutes' walk) are the interesting *catacombs* which were used as burial places by the early Christian community of Milos in the 2&3C AD; they comprise extensive rock chambers with enough niches for about 2,000 burials. Near the catacombs there is an early Christian *baptistery*. The small *Archaeological Museum* in Trypití contains prehistoric obsidian tools, Greek sculptures, early Christian sarcophagi, and other exhibits. The *Church of the Dormition* (Kimisis) in *Adámas* (17C) is interesting and has a beautiful icon called 'The Beheading of St. John' by Scordili (Cretan school, about 1639). The other churches in Milos also contain some old icons by the Cretan school. The Church of Korfiatissa, built in 1810, has a fine panoramic view.

Environs: It was at the NE tip of the island (15 km. NE), near the village of *Fylakopí*, that the remains of two large *Minoan cit-*

Methóni, bridge and fortress

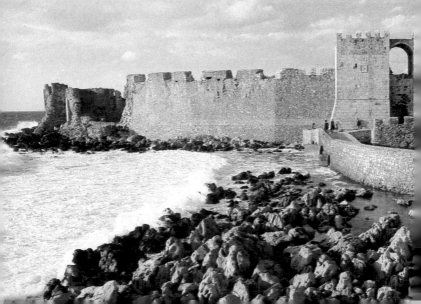

ies (which traded in goods made from obsidian) were excavated by British archaeologists. The ruins of a third, unwalled settlement are Mycenean (1500–1100 BC). The Mycenean *palace* contains superb *fragments of frescos*. There is also a megaron, between the foundation walls of Cycladic houses, and a *double wall* (328 ft. long and up to 13 ft. high) which is divided into chambers. This settlement was destroyed by the Dorian invaders about 1100 BC. Inland from the bay and about 7 km. SE. of Adámas, is the medieval town of *Zefýria* (or *Palaiokhóra*), which was inhabited from the 8C AD until about 1793 (graves and the ruins of houses have survived). To the NE of Milos is the neighbouring island of *Kímolos* (13.5 sq. miles, pop. about 1000), which was famous in antiquity for its chalky earth which was used as a substitute for soap. The ancient city of *Kímolos* (now called *Ellinikó* and in ruins) was independent of Milos. There is a 14C ruined Venetian fort, called *Palaiokastro* (or 'old fort') on a hill in the island, where ancient objects have been discovered.

Mókhlos (I)/ΜΟΧΛΟΣ
Lasíthi/Crete   p.298□I 14

The island of Mókhlos can be reached by boat either from Ágios Nikólaos or, even more conveniently, from the town of Mókhlos, which is on the E. side of the Gulf of Mirabello and lies 130 yards across the water from the island. In Minoan times, this little island was actually a peninsula and possessed a harbour which was possibly the most important in Crete. The archaeological investigations begun in 1908 made some interesting discoveries including some amazingly beautiful artefacts, the remains of the harbour town, and some Minoan tombs, which must have belonged to rich and distinguished families, since they contained gold jewellery, costly vases, precious stones, and ivory. These are chamber tombs, and there are six of them dug into the cliffs on the W. side of the island; each tomb is spacious and rectangular and is approached by a long, curving passage. It was here that archaeologists found the oldest of the Cre-

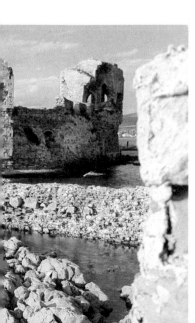

Métsovon, Ágios Paraskevi, iconostasis

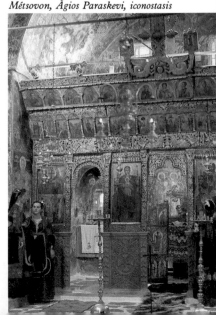

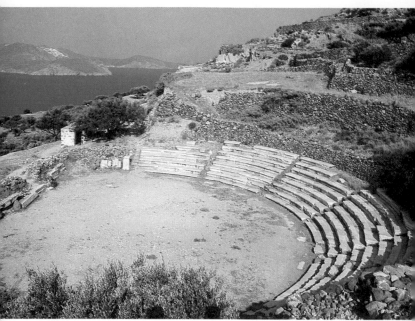

Milos (Milos), small theatre near Trypiti

tan stone seals, the images on which provide some information as to how the early Cretan rowing boats were made. The excavations also uncovered the lid of a jug on which a dog is portrayed, with such finesse and realism that it is hard today to realise that it must have been made about 2500 BC.

Environs: Psíra/Pseira: To the W. of the island is the Island of Psíra, which is slightly larger but, today, no less bleak and lifeless. Here too the same American archaeologists who excavated Mókhlos made some amazing finds. These included the remains of large and small houses, and it was in one of the small houses that fragments were discovered of a lovely fresco similar in style to those of Knossós. The painted ceramics, dating from around 1500 BC, are particularly beautiful.

Monemvasía/ΜΟΝΕΜΒΑΣΙΑ
Lakonia/Peloponnese   p.298□G 11

This town stands on a promontory on the E. coast of Lakonia which is linked to the mainland by a bridge. It began as a Minoan port and was called *Minoa* in ancient times. Its modern name derives from the words *Moni Emvasis*, which means 'the only entrance'. The famous Malvasian wine, a sweet white dessert wine, was produced in these parts.

History: After the Slav invasion, Monemvasía became a place of refuge for the Lakonians, who proceeded to fortify the 1,000 ft. high cliffs. The inhabitants warded off an attack by the Normans in 1149. In 1249, after a three-year siege, Guillaume de Villehardouin took the town with the help of

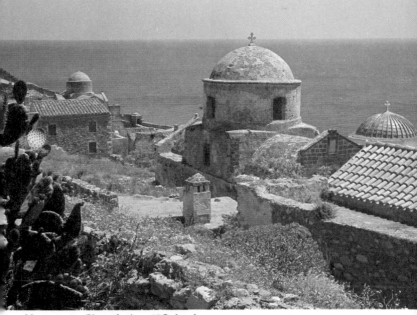

Monemvasía, Chrysafiotissa, 17C church

the Venetian fleet; fourteen years later, after his defeat at Pelagonia in 1263, he ceded it to the Byzantine Emperor. Between 1460 and 1464, it came under the control, first of Pope Pius II, and then of the Republic of Venice, which held it from 1464 until 1540. The Turks conquered Monemvasía in 1540 and kept it until 1690, when the Venetians recaptured it. They held it a second time from 1690 to 1715, when it fell to the Turks again and remained in their hands until 1821.

Town walls: Monemvasía was defended by two parallel walls which reach down the steep slope of the hill to the shore. The rampart is Turkish and was built on a Byzantine site.

Christos Elkomenos: 16C church built in the Italian-Byzantine style on top of a 12C structure. It once contained a famous icon of Christ being flogged, which was carried away by the Byzantines. The main portal is framed by two Corinthian capitals. There is a relief above the lintel which depicts two peacocks.

Ágios Nikólaos: This church, dating from 1703, shows western influence.

Chrysafiotissa: Built at the beginning of the 17C, this church contains the famous 'flying icon' of Chrýsafa.

Church of Agia Sofía: Built in the 13C by Andronikos II (1287–1328) along the lines of the church at Dafní. It contains the remains of 13C frescos which depict Christ (in the central apse) and various martyrs.

Environs: Epidavros Limira (*c.* 8 km.

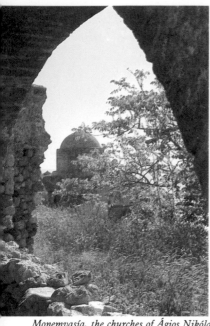 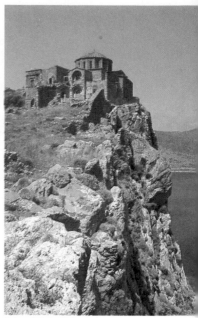

Monemvasía, the churches of Ágios Nikólaos (l.) and Agia Sofía (r.)

N.): A colony of Epídavros (in the Argolís) in the Hellenistic period. It contains some walls and the remains of temples. **Neápolis** (*c.* 30 km. S.): Departure point for the island of Kýthera. The town hall contains a small archaeological collection. The site of the ancient city of Voiés is nearby. The town of **Kastaniá** (8 km.) has a cave with interesting stalactites and stalagmites.

Moní Ierusalím/
ΜΟΝΗ ΙΕΡΟΥΣΑΛΗΜ
Boeotia/Central Greece   p.294□F 7

This monastery, which is dedicated to the Mother of God, is picturesquely situated among pine trees on the slope of Mt.Parnassos, a few miles from the village of *Dáv-*

lia. Its name derives from its earlier connection with the Patriarchate of Jerusalem. This connection was confirmed by the discovery in 1884 of a large marble stone (7 ft. 6 in. long by 2 ft. wide) on which there is an inscription from the 5C AD. According to the inscription, the stone comes from Cana in Galilee.

The monastery is set on a slight hill, a situation which enabled it to become a famous national stronghold during the War of Liberation. Greek freedom fighters also found refuge and support here.

Mykíne/Mycene/ΜΥΚΗΝΑΙ
Argolís/Peloponnese   p.294□F 9

The palace occupies an extensive site which is set on a hill 164 ft. high. Two deep

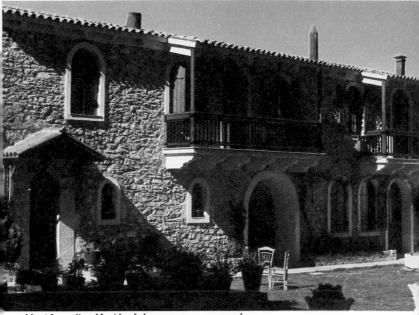

Moní Ierusalim, N. side of the monastery courtyard

ravines, one to the N. and one to the S., render access possible only from the W. Legend has it that Mycene was founded by Perseus, the son of Zeus and Danae, who built the citadel, with its 'Cyclopean walls', with the help of the Cyclopes from Lycia. King Atreus, the son of Pelops, ruled justly, but lived in enmity with his brother Thyestes and eventually invited him to a banquet at which he committed the crime of serving him the flesh of his own children. Thyestes's subsequent curse brought ruin to the next two generations: Agamemnon, the son of Atreus, was killed, at his wife Klytemnestra's instigation, by her lover Aigisthos; and Orestes, Agamemnon's son, himself murdered both Aigisthos and his mother Klytemnestra. Certain remains indicate a Neolithic settlement here. The Achaeans arrived at the beginning of the second millennium BC

and settled in their turn. Around 1600 (Mycenean period) Mycene came into contact with Cretan civilization. The oldest significant excavations are of the first Mycenean royal tombs, which date from the middle of the second millennium BC. The first fortification appeared about 1350, and acquired its final shape about 1200. This was Mycene's heyday.

The site remained inhabited in the Geometric period, and a large temple was erected on the acropolis. In 468 BC, Mycene was taken by the Argives, who partially destroyed its walls. A new settlement was built in the 3C BC, which survived into Roman times. By the time Pausanias saw it, the acropolis had been destroyed. The first excavations were made by Schliemann in 1874–6. He was followed by Stamatakis (1877–8) and the Greek Archaeological Society led by Tsountas

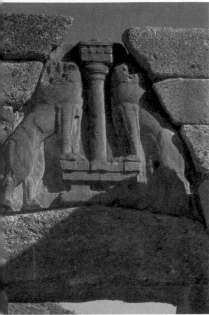

Mycene, Lion Gate

Mycene, steps to Perseia Spring

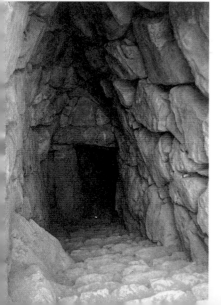

(1886–1902). From 1919 to 1966, the excavation work was conducted by the British School in Athens, and has been continued, since 1966, by Professor Mylonas.

Acropolis: The wall was built in three phases. Of the oldest part, built round 1350 BC, only the N. wall is preserved: the rest was dismantled. The Lion Gate, and the S. and W. walls, which surrounded the royal tombs, were erected about 1250. Finally, the NE wall, which enclosed an underground well, was put up around 1200. The thickness of the wall varies between 10 and 26 ft., although it no longer reaches its full height.

Two styles of construction can be distinguished: the Lion Gate and N. Gate were built from amygdalite ashlars which were laid on top of each other in a regular pattern, while the walls themselves are made of rough-hewn blocks of rock. In the Hellenistic period, the S. wall (in front of Tsountas' house) and the NE wall were repaired with blocks of polygonal masonry.

Lion Gate: This is composed of four monoliths, and is 10 ft. 2 in. high by 9 ft. 1 in. to 9 ft. 8 in. wide. Three grooves have been carved into the pavement by chariot wheels; in later times they were used for drainage. Above the gate is the oldest monumental sculpture in Europe, which shows two lions, erect and facing one another, with their front legs resting on two altars. Between them is a column supporting an entablature. Perhaps this represents the palace, which the lions guarded. To the right of the gate is the so-called *granary* which, however, was more probably used for guarding the gate.

Royal cemetery: The six royal tombs were once enclosed by a double ring of slabs which formed a kind of balustrade. Other tombs were also found here, which however differed in form: the royal tombs were shaft tombs and each was used for several burials. The burial furnishings were particularly precious. No less than 33 lb. of gold was unearthed, in the form of masks, vases, and jewellery. Above the tombs there were sculpted stele. (All these finds are in the National Museum in Athens). Altogether, 19 skeletons were discovered (comprising 8 men, 9 women, and 2 children). In the 13C they must have been reburied, for another circle of tombs was then constructed.

To the S. of the royal cemetery is the *House of the Warrior Vase*, named after the vase depicting six warriors which was found here and is now in the National Museum in Athens. Somewhat higher up is the *Ramp House*, in which the remains of wall paintings were discovered. These two buildings fit the supporting wall and so must be of a later date than the grave circle. Next come the *South House* and the *Mycene sanctuaries* with their sacrificial altar and adyton. At a lower level we see *Tsountas House* and the *Temple of the Idols* (named after the terracotta idols depicting chthonic deities which are now in the museum in Návplion). Wall paintings from these various houses are to be found in the Návplion museum and also in Athens.

Palace: A ramp led to the palace from the inner court of the Lion Gate. This was widened around 1200 BC, and a smaller ramp added in order to retain access to the grave circle (this ramp also led to the South houses). One came first to the *propylon* or entrance hall. To the N. was the old way up to the palace and the *N. corridor* which gave access to the chambers or the *N. gate*. To the right of the propylon there was a long corridor leading to the actual palace. To the S. of this corridor was the *great court* (49 ft. by 39 ft.) bounded to the S. by a large staircase which led into the ante-room. To the W. of the great court there was a square room, possibly a guest room. The megaron was approached through a *prodromos*

or vestibule (14 ft. 1 in. by 37 ft. 9 in.) whose floor was made of ornamental plaster. The *domos* (42 ft. 6 in. x 37 ft. 9 in.) was the throne room. It boasted paintings both on the walls and on the floor (now in the National Museum in Athens). In the centre of the throne room was a hearth enclosed by four wooden pillars which supported the roof.

To the E. of the palace, near the way down from the highest part of the plateau, are the *workshops of the artists and artisans* (92 ft. by 98 ft. 6 in.) who worked for the king. Farther E. is the *House of Columns*, whose function is not clear. There are some other remains (known as the Gamma and Delta Houses) in the E. part of the site. Within the extension of the acropolis at its NE end, which was carried out at the end of the 12C BC for the sake of the water supply, there was an *underground staircase* leading down to the *Perseia spring*. There were two sally-ports, one in the N. wall and one in the S. wall, which could easily be barricaded in times of danger. Also within the extension are the foundations of two Mycenean houses.

To the S. of the N. gate there was a row of store-rooms. There were some more Mycenean houses (known as house M and house N) to the left of the Lion Gate.

Tombs outside the acropolis: The *Lion Tomb* is situated outside the wall, to the right of the Lion Gate. It is a bee-hive tomb with a long entrance passage (72 ft. 2 in. long and 17 ft. 9 in. wide), and contains three depressions. The so-called *tombs of Aigisthos and Klytemnestra* are found to the left of the entrance to the acropolis. The former is one of the oldest tombs and was constructed about 1500 BC (it also contains a depression), while the latter, which is more to the W., dates from about 1220 BC. The dromos is 121 ft. 5 in. long and 19 ft. 8 in. wide and leads up to the doorway, which supported an ornamented relieving triangle. In Hellenistic times

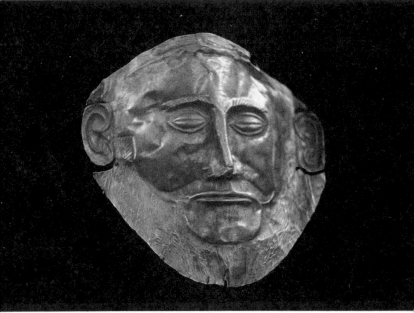

Mycene, gold mask of Agamemnon, Arch.Mus.Athens

there was a small theatre above the dromos (a row of seats survives).

Grave circle B belongs to the same period as the royal tombs inside the acropolis. It has a diameter of 92 ft. Unlike the royal tombs, it contained other graves which were possibly those of other members of the royal family. The grave furnishings discovered here were less sumptuous than those found in the royal tombs. They included a mask, a stone seal, a golden scabbard, some beakers and various other small objects; these are now in the National Museum in Athens.

The *Treasury of Atreus* was built about 1250 BC. The dromos is 118 ft. long, and the large doorway is 17 ft. 8 in. high by 8 ft. 10 in. wide. The massive lintel (31 ft. 2 in. x 3 ft. 11 in.) weighs 118 tons. On each side of the door stood a half-column fashioned from green marble and decorated

with spiral patterns (the remains are in the National museum in Athens). The dome of the tholos is composed of 33 concentric circles of breccia blocks which project upwards. To the right of the tomb chamber there is a square chamber whose walls were lined with stone slabs.

There are five more beehive tombs in the vicinity: the Panagitsa tomb, the Epano Phournos and Kato Phournos tombs, the tomb of the Cyclopes, and the tomb of Orestes, also known as the tomb of the daimons.

Lower town: To the S. of Grave Circle B, on a terrace, are the remains of some Mycenean houses dating from the 13C BC. First is the *House of Shields* which was named after the carved ivories in the form of shields which it contained. It is adjacent to the larger *House of the Oil Merchant*,

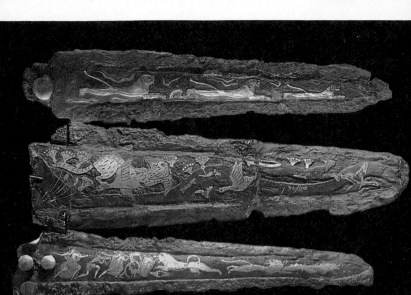

Mycene, bronze dagger with gold and silver decoration (Arch.Mus.Athens)

where Linear B clay tablets were found which give information about staff, oils, and spices—perhaps this was a workshop producing fragrant oils? To the S. is the *House of the Sphinxes* in which precious ivories were found.

All these houses were destroyed by fire at the end of the 13C BC.

There were some other Mycenean houses near the Treasury of Atreus; these were destroyed in an earthquake around 1230 BC.

Mýkonos/Mykonos (I)/ΜΥΚΟΝΟΣ
Cyclades/Aegean Islands   p.296☐L 10

This barren rocky island (34 sq. miles; pop. about 4, 000) is now a popular tourist resort.

History: The island was settled by the Io-

nians around 900 BC. In ancient times it was completely overshadowed by its neighbour Delos, which was a cult-site. In the Middle Ages, it belonged, together with Tinos, to the principality of Ghizzi, and remained Venetian from 1390 until 1718. The Turkish occupation here was short-lived.

Mýkonos/Mykonos (pop. 2,700): This is a picturesque harbour town on the W. coast, with windmills and white, cube-shaped, flat-roofed houses which frequently incorporate pieces of ancient marble from nearby Delos. Along the shore there are 17&18C arcaded houses (Italian influence). It is worth seeing the *Paraportianí* church, which, standing close to the sea, looks like a blinding-white limestone rock. It consists of four chapels vaulted by a dome. Apart from these rec-

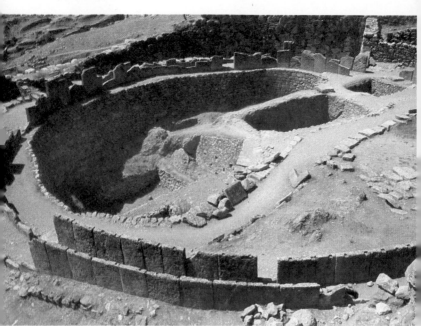

Mycene, gravecircle

tangular chapels, it contains another room at basement level and a cruciform area beneath the dome. This church typifies Greek island architecture which likes to have regularly shaped rooms freely combined into a whole; on the outside, this somehow gives the buildings the appearance of sculptures. On the sea-front there is the 17C *Town Hall* and other beautiful, arcaded 17C buildings. Nearby, there is a small *private museum* of folklore. The *Archaeological Museum* (near the harbour) contains an interesting *collection of vases* ranging from the Geometric to the classical period, as well as tomb stele and inscriptions. These come predominantly from tombs discovered in the neighbouring island of Rínia (Rhéneia), to which the dead buried on the cult island of Delos had been transferred, together with their grave furnishings, after Delos had been 'purified'

by the Athenians in 426BC. The showpiece of the collection is a two-handled *clay pithos* which is 4 ft. 5 in. high and was used to store provisions. It depicts various scenes from the capture of Troy: on the neck of the vessel we see the Greeks emerging from the wooden horse, and, on the main part, the plunder of Troy by Greek warriors. The pithos was found on Mykonos and dates from the 7C BC (thus it is the oldest representation of the Trojan horse). Also worth seeing is the torso of a *statue of Herakles* (5C BC).

Environs: There are supposed to be roughly 365 small churches and chapels in the town and on the island, most of which were endowed by sailors as an act of gratitude for their safe homecoming (they date from the 17&18C but are undecorated). There are also many windmills and dovecotes. In the eastern part of the island, near

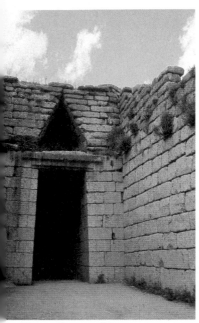

Mycene, Treasury of Atreus

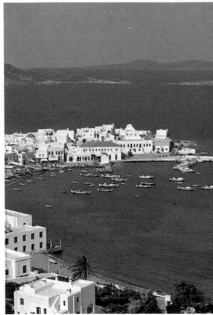

Mýkonos (Mýkonos), harbour

Áno-Merá (10 km.), are the ruins of the 14C Venetian fortress of *Palaiokastro*, among which there are also some traces of an ancient settlement. It is worth seeing the 17C *Turliani* convent nearby (its bell tower is decorated with a relief). On the promontory of *Anavólusa* in the SW of the island there are slight traces of a Bronze-Age Cycladic settlement.

Mystrás/Mistrás/ΜΥΣΤΡΑΣ
Lakonia/Peloponnese   p.298☐F 10/11

A Byzantine town, once capital of Moréa. It contains many churches with middle- and late-Byzantine frescos, as well as the Palace of the Despots and various houses of rich Byzantine families.

History: The fortress of Mystrás was built by Guillaume de Villehardouin in 1249, after his capture of Monemvasía, in order to protect the area from the Slavs in the Eurotas valley and the Lakonians around Taygetos. It was originally called *Myzithras*, but this name was later corrupted into Mystrás ('mistress'). In 1259, after his defeat at the battle of Pelagonia, Guillaume de Villehardouin was captured by Michael Palaiologos, and in 1263, as the price for his release, he was forced to cede Mystrás and Máni to Byzantium. In 1265 the Byzantines were besieged by the Franks, and, because of the constant disturbances, the people of Lakonia withdrew into the fortress. In this way the town gradually grew up. When the Emperor John VI Katakousinos (1347–54) appointed his son Manuel as governor of Mystrás, he also gave him the title of despot, which was retained by all the subsequent rulers of Mystrás (namely, Matthew, 1380–3, and then the Palaiologoi, Theodore I, 1383–1407; Theodore II, 1407 – 43; Constantine, 1443–8; and Demetrios, 1448–60). The town was captured by the Turks in 1459; during 1687–1715 it was ruled by the Venetians. In 1770 the Albanians invaded and destroyed the town, which was deserted thereafter.

Some important scholars lived in Mystrás in the first half of the 15C, including Vissarion, who later became a cardinal, Georgios Gemistos Plithon, the neoplatonic philosopher, and Hieronymos Charitonomos, a scientist who lived in Paris.

Mitrópolis: This is the church of St. Demetrios, which, according to an inscription dated 1309, was built by the Metropolitan Nikiphoros Moschopoulos. It must nonetheless have been built on to an earlier church dating from the 12 or 13C—a three-aisled basilica with a later cruciform, domed upper storey and four domes above the arms of the cross. There is a marble plaque in the floor depicting

the double-headed eagle, which marks the spot where the last Palaiologos stood at his coronation. There are interesting 14C wall paintings; one of them in the right aisle shows the life of St.Demetrios, and two of those in the left aisle depict the life of the Virgin Mary and Christ in Galilee. In the narthex there is an early-14C Last Judgement, with Christ in between the damned and the elect.

Near the church there is a small *museum* which contains finds from the ruins of Mystrás.

Peribleptos Monastery: The buildings are mid-14C and are partly built into the rock. Above the entrance there are two lions—the emblem of Venice. The frescos, which are by two artists, are the most beautiful in Mystrás and herald the kind of style which became known in the 16C as the 'Cretan school'. Above the sanctuary is the Ascension of Christ; the central apse has the Virgin and Child, framed by two archangels; the N. apse shows the 'Divine Liturgy'. The scenes of the dodekaeorton, or 'twelve festivals', include the Descent

Mystrás, Mitrópolis, church of St. Demetrios

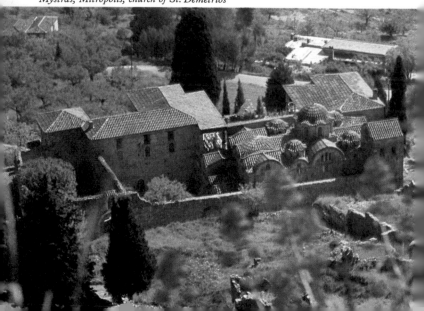

Mystrás, ruined Byzantine city
A. Lower city
 1. Peribleptos monastery
 2. St. George
 3. house of Krevates (18C)
 4. house of Frangopulos (15C)
 5. church of the archangels
 6. Agia Kyriaki
 7. Ágios Christophoros
 8. Marmara fountain (ancient sarcophagus)
 9. Ágios Ioánnis
10. lower entrance
11. Episcopal Palace (museum)
12. Mitrópolis
13. Evangelistria church
14. Agii Theodori
15. Brontochion monastery
16. refectory
17. church
18. Afendiko
B. Upper City
19. Upper entrance
20. Agia Sofia
21. Nauplia Gate
22. Palace of the Despots
23. Turkish baths
24. mosque
25. Monemvasía Gate
26. Ágios Nikólaos
27. Small Palace
28. Pantanassa monastery
29. Frankish citadel of Villehardouin

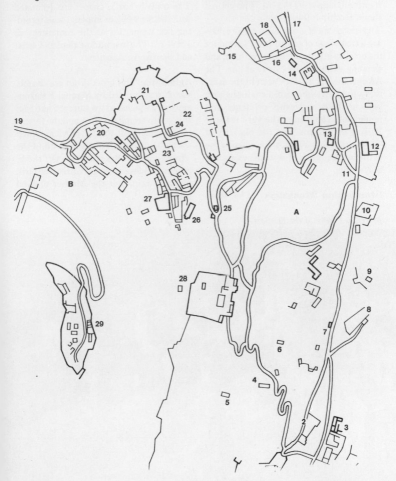

from the Cross, the Transfiguration, and, in the S. transept, the Nativity of Christ. The S. aisle has scenes from the life of the Virgin. The central dome shows the Pantocrator. Opposite the altar are the two founders of the church holding a model of the Peribleptos Monastery.

Pantanassa Convent: Founded in 1428 by Ioánnis Frankopoulos, who was the minister of the last despot of Mystrás, Constantine Dragatsis (1443–8). The church shows Gothic influence.

The frescos are of a very high quality, having a rich range of colour (they introduce the colours green and lemon-yellow), and showing an impressive clarity of line. The Ascension which can be seen in the sanctuary, the Entry into Jerusalem in the nave (which shows a wealth of detail and remarkable colouring), the very realistic Raising of Lazarus, and the Nativity of Christ in the S. transept, all represent some of the best examples of Byzantine painting in the 15C.

Brontóchion Monastery: The main church, the *Afendiko*, is in the form of a basilica with five domes, and was built before 1311. Several chapels have been added to the narthex; of these, the N. chapel contains the tombs of noble families, including that of the despot Theodore II, who died in 1444. The walls are faced with marble on which frescos have been painted. Those in the N. chapel include the Wedding at Cana, Christ with the woman of Samaria, and a group of martyrs. The walls in the S. chapel are decorated with the *chrysobuls* or imperial seals recording the properties of the monastery in 1313–23. The main dome depicts Christ and the twelve Apostles.

Agia Sofía: This cross-in-square church, which was founded by Manuel Katakousinos in 1350, has a two-storeyed narthex. It is worth seeing the floor and the frescos in the chapel off the N. portico, which show the Annunciation, the death of the Virgin, and the Resurrection. Off the S. portico there are images of Christ, the birth of the Virgin, and the Mother of God praying.

Mystrás, Palace of the Despots

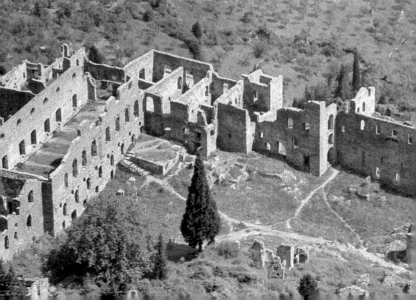

Evangelistria Church (about 1400): Frescos preserved from the same period.

Agii Theodori: This is the oldest church in Mystrás, and was built before 1296. In the chapel on the left there is a depiction of Michael Palaiologos kneeling before the Virgin Mary. The right-hand chapel shows scenes from Mary's life.

Palace of the Despots: This is an extensive L-shaped structure. The N. wing probably dates from the period of Guillaume de Villehardouin (1249–63). Next to this, there are kitchens built over two cisterns. The palace was enlarged during the reign of Manuel Katakousinos, when a four-storeyed building was erected in front of the kitchens to house servants. During the same period, the main building was extended northwards to provide the despot's residence.

The large transverse wing and the throne room (125 ft. x 39 ft.) date from the time of the Palaiologoi (1380–1460).

Small Palace *(Palatáki):* Manor house dating from the second half of the 13C. The older structure is farther down. 14C keep with balcony.

Monemvasía Gate: 13C. The upper part of the town lay beyond this gate and was reserved for the privileged classes.

Frankish fortress (2,037 ft.; about 30 minutes' climb): This was built by the Franks but almost entirely rebuilt by the Turks. After passing through the gate on the NW side, one enters the outer courtyard, then, after a short climb, the inner one. The bastions inside date from the Frankish period. There is a keep in the middle of the courtyard.

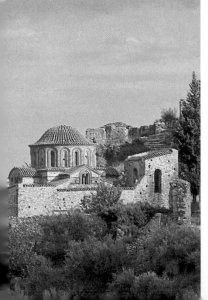

Mystrás, Pantanassa Convent

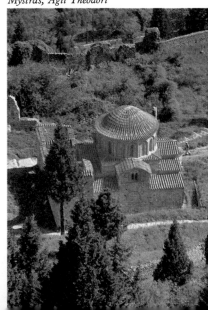

Mystrás, Agii Theodori

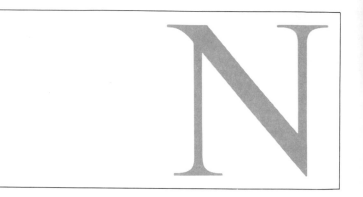

Náusa / Náussa / ΝΑΟΥΣΑ
Imathía / Macedonia   p.290 □ E 3

This is the second largest town in Imathía after Véria; it has a population of 15,000 and is situated 96 km. from Thessaloníki and 22 km. from Véria, 1,000 ft. above sea-level and half way up Mt.Vermion. The river Arapitsa, which has some impressive waterfalls, flows through it. In spring there is the celebrated Náusa carnival, a feature of which is a dance (Choros tis Bulas) performed by men with unusual masks; it is nationalist in origin and stems from the time of the Turkish occupation. On the N. edge of the town are the *Saranta Ontades* ('forty chamber') caves, which contain stalactites and stalagmites.

Environs: Nympháion (*Nymfáion*): This is a village below Náusa where recent excavations have revealed a *temple (iero ton nymfon)*, which was where Alexander the Great was schooled. A large number of Macedonian *tombs* have been found in this area, including one from the 3C BC, which is built like a small temple, with four Doric columns supporting a flat roof, and a frieze incorporating *sculptures* depicting battle scenes between the Macedonians and the Persians. **Rodokhórion** (12 km. NW): This small village is the site of the only Neolithic caves in Macedonia. **Levkádia** (17 km. E.): Levkádia (17 km. E.): A Macedonian *tomb vault* from Roman times, which was excavated in 1954–6; its façade consists of two tiers of columns, the lower being Doric and the upper ones Ionic. The painting on the façade is well-preserved, and depicts warriors with spears and swords, Hermes as leader of souls (Psychopompos), and two judges in the underworld (lower murals); there is a battle of centaurs, above a small cornice, and a *terracotta frieze* with paintings of infantry and cavalry fighting barbarians. S. of the tomb are two ruined Roman buildings, which were once decorated with mosaics, and the remains of a building from the 6C AD. To the left of the turning to Levkádia are two more Macedonian *tombs*: the first consists of a passage, a vestibule and a vaulted tomb chamber; the other, across the road, has some well-preserved *paintings*.

Návpaktos / Naúpaktos / ΝΑΥΠΑΚΤΟΣ
Aetolia / Central Greece   p.294 □ E 8

This is a picturesque little harbour with some 8,000 inhabitants, situated on the N.

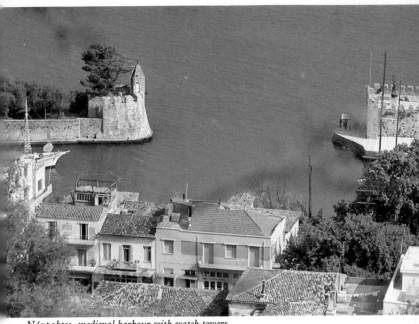

Návpaktos, medieval harbour with watch-towers

shore of the entrance to the Gulf of Corinth. It has an interesting history: it was founded by Dorians in about 1000 BC, and, due to its strategic location, was turned into a fortress controlling access to the gulf from the 5C BC onwards. During the Middle Ages it was controlled by the Venetians (1407–99) under the name of *Lepanto*; it was then occupied by the Turks and recaptured by the Venetians in 1687 and held until 1700. The major naval battle of Lepanto (1571) is named after it, although it took place further W. near the island of Oxiá. The son of Emperor Charles V, Don John of Austria, won a decisive victory for the Christians (Papal forces, Spain, Venice, Genoa) over the Turks, who had launched their fleet from Lepanto (Návpaktos). Cervantes, the author of 'Don Quixote', fought in the battle and lost an arm.

Kastro: A well-preserved Venetian fortress with a splendid view and *ramparts* extending down to the shore.

Also worth seeing: The small medieval *harbour* (with its watch-towers).

Environs: Near the village of **Vélvina** (*c.* 8 km. N., the *Bélbina* of antiquity) are the remains of an ancient *acropolis* with a *walled rampart* and a *ruined temple* on the upper terrace. Nearby are the remains of a Hellenistic temple (which include a portico). Some 30 km. to the E. along the coast road, between the villages of *Marathiás* and *Khánia (Paralía Sérgula)*, are the vestiges of the ancient town of *Glýpha*, with an outer ring of walls (polygonal masonry) and a badly preserved inner wall. There are the remains of a *round tower* and a *cistern* cut into the cliff. The ancient terraced town was situated opposite the small island of Trizonia. On the straits, 9 km. SW, are the ruins of the 14C Venetian *fortress of Antírrion (Kástro Rúmelis)*, which was strengthened by the Turks in the 16C; originally built on the site of a temple of Poseidon.

Návplion/Nauplia/ΝΑΥΠΛΙΟΝ
Argolís/Peloponnese   p.294☐F 9

This is the capital of the nome of Argolís, with a population of 9,280, and is dominated by the 700 ft. high fortress of Palamidi and the 260 ft. cliff of Akronavplía. It has some fine neoclassical houses and some interesting churches.

History: According to legend, the town was founded by Nauplios, the son of Poseidon and Amymone. Nauplios's son, Palamides, is said to have introduced the Greek alphabet.
Traces of ancient civilizations dating back to Neolithic times (3rd millennium) have been found near Akronavplía. In the 7C BC it was an Argive trading centre, and there is a defensive wall dating from the end of the 3C. It was abandoned in Roman times. In the 12C it was fortified by the Byzantines, and in 1210 the fortress was taken by the Franks, who surrendered it to the Venetians in 1389. In 1540 it was occupied by the Turks, but was recaptured by the Venetians under Morosini in 1686. It was known as *Napoli di Romania*. The Venetians managed to hold it until 1715, when the Turks reoccupied it. In 1829 it became the capital of Greece and the seat of Capodistrias, the President, and in 1831 he was murdered in front of the church of Ágios Spyridon by the Mavromichali brothers. In 1833 the first King of Greece, Otho, Prince of Bavaria, entered Nauplion.

Akronavplía: The citadel has a number of fortresses: at the W. corner is the Castel del Greci: originally 12&13C Byzantine, it was built over by the Venetians; the Castel dei Franchi was constructed below the Byzantine castle, and no trace of it remains. The site of the Castel Toro, built in 1473, is now occupied by the old Xenia hotel. In 1706 the Turks built the Castel Toro's Grimani Bastion, which was linked to the Palamidi fortress opposite. Another fortress was built in 1702 near the Byzantine one.

Palamidi: The strenuous climb (857 steps) to this fortress can be avoided by driving via the village of Prónia. Near the church of the Evangelistria was the site of the first Greek national election, which ratified Prince Otho of Bavaria as King of Greece. The *Lion of Bavaria* was carved in the cliff by the sculptor Siegel as a monument to the Bavarian soldiers who died of an outbreak of plague in 1833–4. The Palamidi fortress was built by Governor Sagredo in 1711–14, and surrounded by a wall. It had seven interconnected forts, each with a large cistern, to be able to withstand a long siege.

Isle of Burtzi: A Venetian fortress was built here in the 15C, and an octagonal tower was added later. A 500 yard long underwater barrier runs from Akronavplía to Burtzi and closes the entrance to the harbour.
In the years after the Turkish occupation it served as the residence of the executioner, who was not allowed to live in the city.

Ágios Spyridon: This Venetian church was built in 1702 and contains wall paintings.

Ágios Georgios: This was built in 1619; it served as a mosque during the Turkish occupation and was converted into a Catholic church in 1703.

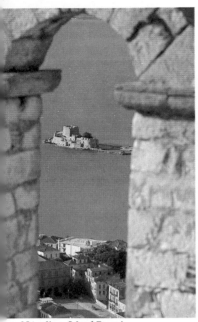

Návplion, Isle of Burtzi

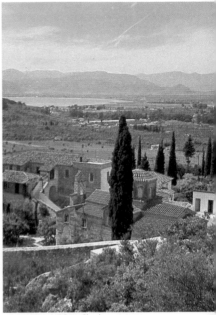

Agia Moni (Návplion), monastery

Metamorfosis tu Sotiros: This was a Turkish mosque which was converted into a Catholic church by King Otho; it has an interesting wooden apse inscribed with the names of the fallen Philhellenes.

Vulcftiko: This is a former mosque situated on Syntagma Square; it is where the first Greek parliament sat.

Museum: This is housed in the arsenal used by the Venetian fleet in 1713, which is on Syntagma Square.

The ground floor has finds from pre-historic times: early Helladic vases from Asíni, Tíryns and Berbáti, and middle Helladic ceramics from Mycene. There are late Helladic bronzes from Midéa (bronze armour); funerary stele from Mycene; remains of wall paintings from Tíryns and Mycene, and terracotta idols.

The first floor houses finds from a tomb in Tíryns, Geometric vases and small ornaments, 5C red and black figure vases and a terracotta bath.

Local History Museum (Odos Vassileos Alexandrou): This houses a fine collection of manuscripts, weapons and jewellery, and also some interesting etchings and photographs of monuments which are no longer standing.

Environs: Agía Moní (4 km. down the road to Epídavros): This is a Byzantine monastery built in 1444 near the *Kanathos Spring*, where Hera bathed once a year and returned to a state of virginity. There are some remains of an aqueduct and some ancient walls. **Asíni** (9 km. SE): Mentioned in the 'Iliad' (II, 560), this was identified by the Swedish Archaeological School as being near the resort of Tolón. The area has been occupied since middle Helladic times (1900–1600), as the tombs and remains of houses on the slopes of Barbouna show. The hill of Asíni is the site of a Hellenistic fortification: the entrance, which is in the NE, has two polygonal towers, between which is a gate with a 6 ft. long sill, leading through to a courtyard which is a platform cut from the hill. On top of the wall are the foundations of a Roman building, and there is a small 16C *church* on the slopes above. **Acropolis of Kasarmi** (14 km. E.): This was built by the Argives in the 5C BC, and has polygonal masonry. Centuries later it was taken by the Franks. There is a round tomb near the acropolis which dates from the 15C BC, and suggests that the settlement must date back to Mycenean times. 2 km. away is the *Acropolis of Kastraki*, which dates from the same period as that at Kasarmi, and also has polygonal masonry. **Ligurió**, 25 km. NE, has the remains of a pyramid-shaped building from the 4C BC near the church of Agia Marina.

Náxos/Naxos (I)/ΝΑΞΟΣ
Cyclades/Aegean Islands   p.300☐L 11

This is the largest of the islands in the Cyclades, with an area of 166 sq. miles and a population of some 17,000. It is covered in vegetation.

History: Naxos is the legendary haunt of the god of wine Dionysos, and seems to have been originally settled in the 3rd millennium, to judge by the numerous Cycladic finds. This is where Theseus, son of the king of Athens, is said to have abandoned his bride Ariadne after their flight from Crete, a myth which was later connected to that of Dionysos. The island was settled by Ionians in about 1000 BC, and the town of Naxos was founded. It was of considerable importance in the 7&6C under the tyrant Lygdamis, when sculpture and crafts flourished; in the 5&4C it joined the Athenian maritime league, and later fell under Egyptian, Macedonian and (from 37 BC) Roman rule. It came to prominence again in 1207 with the establishment of the Frankish-Venetian island Dukedom of Naxos by Marco Sanudi. It fell to the Turks in 1566 (although the aristocracy remained relatively independent), and in 1830 it was reunited with Greece.

Náxos/Naxos (*c.* 5,000 inhabitants): The capital is situated on the W. coast, on the site of the ancient settlement of the same name; all remains of the latter, however, have been covered over by more recent buildings. Near the harbour area is the small island of *Palátia* ('palace island'), which is connected to the mainland by a stone breakwater and which has an ancient marble *temple doorway* from around 530 BC, which is visible from afar; it is 20 ft. high and 12 ft. wide, and is the remnant of an unfinished 6C temple in antis which was built as a monument (524 BC) after the collapse of the tyrant Lygdamis. Only the foundations and some individual fragments, column bases, drums and the doorway composed of three marble blocks, which is a famous feature of Naxos, are still standing. An early Christian *basilica* was built inside the ancient ruins in the 5&6C, but little is left of it. The other island in the harbour area (also with a breakwater) has the remains of a 15C *chapel* which was founded by the Hospitallers. The Grotta quarter has yielded traces of a Mycenean settlement, near the ancient agora (which has been built over). On the peak of the hill above the old quarter of the town with its picturesque flat-roofed houses are the ruins of the Frankish *fortress (kastro)* from 1260, which houses a Catholic nunnery and convent school. There are traces from the Venetian period on the hill, including the partially-collapsed *ducal palace*, with coats-of-arms, the severely damaged *Palazzo Barozzi* and the *Sommaripa Palace* (both 13&14C). Nearby is the 13C Catholic *cathedral* (dedicated to the Mother of God), which is the seat of a Catholic bishop. The *Archaeological Museum* is in the old Collège Français (1637), and houses Cycladic finds (marble idols) and vases.

Environs: NE of the town (*c.* 2 km.) is the former nunnery of *Chrysóstomos*, a castle-like structure with a tower house, which may have originally been a watch-tower. The iconostasis in the church bears two images of the Pantocrator and one of Chrysostom. 8 km. NE, on the coast near the village of *Engarés* is the fortified *Faneromeni monastery* and church (1603). Near the village of **Áno Sangrí** (*c.* 12 km. SE) is a 14C Venetian tower and the monastery of *Ágios Nikolaos*, which has a domed church and 13C wall paintings. Near Khalkí, 16 km. SE, are a number of old *refuge towers* which were built in case of Saracen raids in the 13&14C, and a number of Frankish churches and chapels; the church of *Protothoroni* has 10C frescos in the dome of the Pantocrator with saints, and the cross-in-square church of *Ágios Georgios* (Diasoritis) has some partially damaged 13&14C frescos, including a Last Judgement in the narthex. Near the village of *Moni*, 20 km. E., is the church of the *Panagia Damiotissa* with 12&13C frescos, and nearby, in the direction of Mélanes, are the uncompleted *marble kouroi* of *Fleriό* (7C BC). The nearby ruins of the *Apana Kastro* ('upper castle') are interesting, dating from about 1250: around the ruins of the castle, which was surrounded by three walls with towers, are some ruined houses and chuches. The *Zeus Grotto* (remains of an old cult area) is on the slopes of Mt.Zias (Mt.Zeus), which, at 3, 300 ft., is the highest point in the Cyclades; the area is accessible from *Filóti*, some 19 km. inland, and there is a magnificent view from the peak. Further to the SE is the ancient

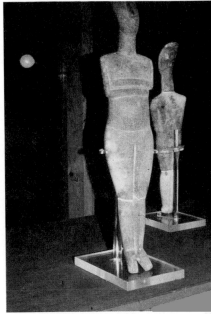

Náxos, Cycladic idol (Arch.Mus.)

marble *Tower of Khimaron*. The village of *Tragaia* contains the church of *Panagia Drosiani*, which has 14C frescos, and the small church of *Ágios Konstantinos* has frescos dating from 1311. Near the village of *Apíranthos*, *c.* 26 km. E., is the church of *Ágios Ioánnis*, which has some fine frescos from 1309. Apíranthos itself has a small *museum* which houses Cycladic finds. The village of *Apóllonas* is on the site of an ancient settlement with a temple of Apollo (N. coast, 48 km.); nearby is the ancient marble quarry of *Ston Apollona*, near which are the 33 ft. long, half-completed marble blocks of an unfinished *Kouros* from the 7C BC. It was probably intended to be a statue of Dionysos, but was abandoned due to lack of material; only the outline has been completed. A statue of Apollo of similar size and by the same school stood in front of the Oikos of the Naxians in

Delos. Above the marble quarry is the ruined medieval fortress of *Kastro Kalogeros* from the 13&14C.

Néa Ankhíalos/ΝΕΑ ΑΓΧΙΑΛΟΣ
Magnisía/Thessaly   p.294□F 6

Founded in 1906 by refugees from Asia Minor, the town now has a population of around 3,000; it occupies the site of the ancient settlement of *Pýrasos*, on the NW shore of the Gulf of Vólos, 20 km. SW of the town of Vólos. It was inhabited in pre-Grecian times (3rd millennium).

Acropolis: The remains of the ancient acropolis are situated on a hill and include an old shrine to Demeter and Kore.

The remains of four **basilicas** from early Christian times have been uncovered near the coast.
Basilica A (5C): This is a ruined church with a nave and two aisles, and two rows of eight columns each. The narthex is to the W., and there are periboloi on three sides and a propylaion leading to the atrium (narthex) on the fourth. Near the church are the remains of an early Christian house with a paved courtyard and bath.
Basilica B (5C): The ruins include a row of cleric's seats on either side of a bishop's throne. There is a courtyard with portico (W. portico 12 ft. wide with column bases exposed) leading to Basilica A; 120 ft. of the E. portico have been uncovered; this used to lead to a cistern under the acropolis of Pýrasos.
Basilica C (4&5C): This was the largest of the basilicas, and was built on the site of a Roman building. It has an atrium with portico and geometrical mosaics of figures and animals. There is a baptistery to the W.
Basilica D (7C): The remains of a church with a nave and two aisles and fragments of some mosaics.

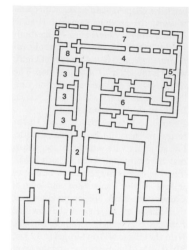

Nekromanteion, Oracle of the Dead at Acheron **1** sacred area **2** dark passage **3** chamber **4** passage in which the sheep was slaughtered **5** S. labyrinth **6** main room with three aisles **7** exterior passage **8** purification chamber

Local Museum *(Musio)*: This contains some interesting architectural fragments, inscriptions and mosaics from ancient Pýrasos and the early Christian basilicas.

Environs: Mikrothívai (5 km. SW): Nearby are the remains of the walls of the ancient settlement of *Phthiotic Thebes*. The *acropolis* had its own *wall* (Cyclopean walls to the E.), with the remains of a 5C *Temple of Athena*, a *stoa* and a *theatre*.

Nekromanteíon/
Oracle of the Dead at Acheron/
NEKPOMANTEION
Préveza/Epirus   p.290□C 6

The Nekromanteíon, some 50 km. S. of Igumenítsa, is situated on the hill of the monastery of St. John, where the rivers Acheron and Kokytos merge and the W.

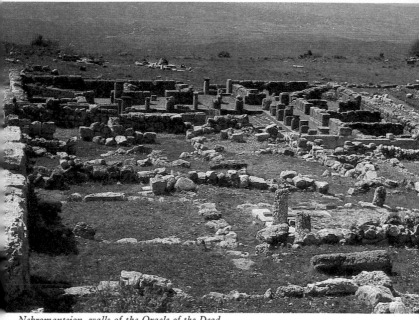

Nekromanteion, walls of the Oracle of the Dead

bank of lake Acherusia, now dry, lay. The Oracle of the Dead is first mentioned by Homer. Excavations have revealed that the ruins we see today are Hellenistic (4C BC) but finds from the 2nd millennium suggest there was a prehistoric settlement of *Kichyros*. The names Kichyros and Persephone, and the cult of Persephone and Hades, are also pre-Hellenic in origin, and their roots reach back into prehistory. The existence of such a place is remarkable in that the common ancient belief was that mountain caves, gorges, and rivers which disappeared underground were entrances to the Underworld. According to ancient belief, the souls of the dead were carried by Hermes as far as the shores of the lake, where they paid an obol to Charon, who rowed them to Hades. The souls of the dead had supernatural abilities, and could tell the futures of those still alive.

Whoever wanted to make contact with the dead had to prepare himself both physically and spiritually. He would be led by a priest to the N. entrance, which had three arched gates. On the left side of the entrance was a bath and two rooms, which were where the visitor slept. He had to eat pork, beans, barley bread and mussels, and drink milk and water, and to undergo a number of magic ceremonies to cleanse himself. The high priest spoke prayers and incomprehensible magic words. Before the petitioner passed down the E. passage, he threw a stone onto a heap to his left, to cast away evil influences. Then he underwent a symbolic purification ceremony, washing his hands in water, and then entered the hall of the E. passage to begin the last phase of preparation. The amount of time he had to spend there is unknown, but the prescribed foods were more precise, the magic ceremonies more significant and the tests more difficult. The absolute isolation, the darkness and the silence all helped to harmonize the mind of the petitioner. When the time eventually came for meeting with the souls of the dead, he went together with the high priest down the E. passage, taking the gifts for sacrifice and libation with him. In the corridor he sacrificed a sheep in a hole in the ground, and then entered a labyrinth, a complex passage designed to suggest to him that he was taking the dark and mysterious path to Hades. The labyrinth had three iron gates, and after the visitor had passed the last one he entered the main room, where he cast aside another stone and poured the libation to the gods of the Underworld on the ground. It was in the main room that the shadows of the dead were said to appear and make contact with the petitioner; the extensive physical and spiritual preparations in the darkened chambers and the firm belief in the reappearance of the dead must have put the petitioner into a state of high psychological tension. The beans and lupins, which have been found during the course of the excavations, must have played an important role in the proceedings: the beans, when eaten, could produce hallucinations. When the priest decided that the petitioner was in a suitable condition, he allowed the shadows of the dead to appear, and the oracle priests tried with all the means at their disposal to remove all possible doubts about the appearance of the dead: Cerberus began to bark, the priests cried to the gods of the Underworld, and the shadows of the dead appeared. The petitioner could then ask questions of them.

Excavations in the main room have revealed a number of iron wheels, a large bronze kettle and winches, all of which presumably formed part of a device for raising and lowering figures, serving to stage an appearance of the dead returning.

The petitioner then had to leave the Nekromanteíon by a different route, so as not to see anything of the tricks. He was led by the priests through the E. passage down a parallel route, and had to spend three further days in a room. After that he left in the direction of the river Kokytos and made his way home. He had to maintain absolute silence, for the punishment of revealing the secrets of the Oracle of the Dead at Acheron was death.

The shrine was put to the flame by the Romans in 167 BC, during their destruction of 70 towns in Epirus and capture of 150,000 prisoners. In the 1C BC the Romans moved into the shrine, and in the 18C the monastery of St. John was built there.

The Oracle of the Dead at Acheron was discovered and explained as a result of the excavations and theories of Professor Dakaris. The actual shrine consists of a square structure, which was separated into a main room and two side rooms by two parallel interior walls. Beneath the main room is an underground room of comparable size cut into the rock, which may have been connected with the original caves of the prehistoric cult; this is the palace of Persephone and Hades, and the buildings, together with the passages and other rooms date from the late 4 or early 3C. Later, around the end of the 3C, an additional complex with a central courtyard was built to the W. of the shrine. It comprises chambers and store-rooms which also served as residential rooms for the priests and the petitioners. The entrance to the courtyard is on the N. side of the shrine.

Environs: Efýra: On the site of the present-day village of Mesopótamos was the ancient town of *Ephyra*, which was also known as *Kíchyros*; it was a Peloponnesian colony during the 4&3C and was eventually taken by the Thesprotes in 343/2 BC. Near to the Oracle of the Dead (660 yards) is Ephyra's acropolis (1300 yards in circumference). **Kassópi** (*c.* 20 km. S.): This was an ancient town which developed out of a Bronze Age settlement, and was a centre for the worship of Aphrodite. It was the political centre of the state of Kassopaia, and minted its own bronze coins which bore an image of Aphrodite and a dove, her symbol. The town was destroyed by the Romans in 167 BC, and at the end of the 1C BC the inhabitants were forced to move to Nikópolis. Kassópi is among the best-preserved ancient towns: the *agora*, which was used for political gatherings, could accomodate 6,000 people, and was bounded on the W. side by two large stoae; there was a small theatre on the E. side, which also served as the odeion, and the *prytaneum*, or katagógion, which was the town's official hostel. There was a cistern in the SE corner, which was used for the production of porphyry, a valuable red dye. The large *theatre* in the NW of the town was built in the 3C BC and had seating for 6,000; it is remarkably similar to the theatre of Dodóni. An underground *chamber tomb* (heroon) has been found in Kassópi, which seems to be a Macedonian tomb dating from Hellenistic times, and is known as the

'Vasilospito', or 'king's residence'. It is carved into the rock at the SW corner of the city centre. **Pandosía:** This was situated on the hill of Kastri, which is the site of the village of the same name; it was once the most significant Elian colony and the capital of the state of Elis in Kassopaia, and had a wall about a mile in circumference incorporating 22 square towers. It was destroyed by the Romans in 167 BC, but they later made it the capital of the Epiriot League. **Zálongo** (*c.* 20 km. SE): A huge stone group of dancing women was carved on the peak of the mountain of Zálongo in 1954 by G.Zogolopoulos. It depicts the women of Souli, who died as heroes in 1802, leaping from the peak to avoid falling into the hands of the Turks.

Neméa/NEMEA
Korinth/Peloponnese   p.294☐F 9

The ancient town of Neméa was situated 5 km. from the present-day village of the same name, which is some 30 km. SW of

Kassópi, prytaneum

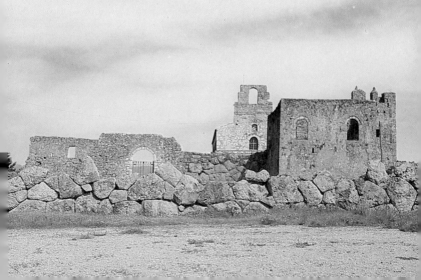

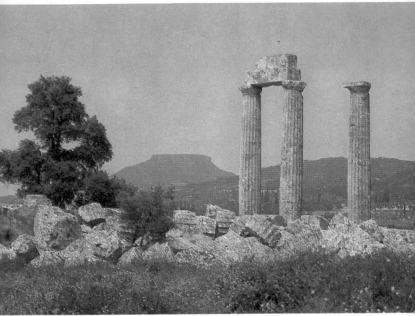

Neméa, the three columns of the Temple of Zeus

Corinth. It is known as the place where Herakles slew the Nemean lion, and as the site of the Nemean Games, which were held every two years in remembrance of the king's young son Opheltes. According to the Seven against Thebes, they passed through Neméa looking for a spring, and Opheltes's nurse showed them one, leaving the child alone for an instant. He was bitten by a snake and died.

Temple of Zeus: Some remnants of the Doric peripteros are still standing from 330–20, and three of the original 6 x 12 columns are still upright. It was built on the site of an older temple, which had a 6 ft. deep adyton instead of an opisthodomos, with steps going down into it. This may have been the shrine to Opheltes.
To the E. of the temple are the remains of an extended altar, and to the S. are the foundations of a building, 282 x 66 ft., and dating from the same period as the temple, which seems to have been a *xenon* (guest residence). An early Christian basilica with a nave and two aisles was built over it in the 5C. To the W. are the ruins of a *palaistra* and a *bath*, and 550 yards E. of the temple are the remains of the stadium.

Archaeological collection: Situated near the ancient baths.

Environs: Phliús (*c.* 3.5 km. NW): The *acropolis* stood to the right of the road which leads to Kutsí. The *agora*, which has been tentatively identified with the foundations of a large (120 x 85 ft.) building with square columns on the inside, was in the area of the *theatre*, from which a section of the stage and a few of the seats survive. **Kleonaí** (*Kleoné, c.* 15 km. E.): This

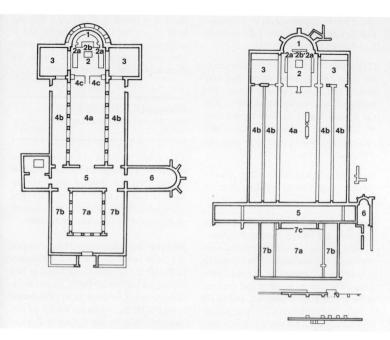

Nikópolis, Basilica A and Basilica B **1** apse **2** sanctuary (**2a** choir stalls, **2b** bishop's throne) **3** transept **4** main church (**4a** nave, **4b** aisles, **4c** ambo) **5** narthex **6** diakonikon **7** atrium (**7a** court, **7b** colonnade, **7c** phiale)

includes the scattered remnants of the ancient walls; to the E. is the *Herakleion*, with the remains of a small temple and two *altars* which were erected to the heroes Kreatos and Eurytos, who were both killed by Hcraklcs. **Titáne** (towards Kastráki-Sikyón from Phliús): Scattered remains of the ancient *acropolis* in the area of the graveyard; according to Pausanias there was an Asklepieion and a Temple to Athena here.

Nikópolis/ΝΙΚΟΠΟΛΙΣ
Préveza/Epirus p.294□C 6

This town was founded by Caesar Augustus after the naval battle of Actium in 31 BC and dedicated to the god Apollo; Augustus arranged for the inhabitants of other Epirot cities, such as Ambrákia, Pan-

dosía, Kassópi and others, to be moved to Nikópolis ('victory city'). Thus it quickly became a trading centre, and its two ports, Kómaros and Bathy, linked east and west. At the time of Diocletian it was the capital of Epirus and had a population of 300,000. At the end of the 1C AD the philosopher Epictetes arrived and founded a celebrated philosophical school; the Apostle Paul also came to preach the Gospel. In AD 375 Nikópolis was destroyed by a huge earthquake, and during the rule of the Emperor Justinian it was given new fortifications, and became the most important city in Epirus and an bishop's seat. From the beginning of the 9C to the mid

11C it was sacked repeatedly by Bulgarians and Saracens, and was eventually destroyed in a Bulgarian raid in 1034.

City walls: These were built under Justinian from bricks, small stones and fragments, and bound by lime mortar. The main gate, with its two round towers, is on the W. side, and to its W. is a small theatre, the *odeion*, known now as the 'skoteinon' (dark). Nearby is a large aqueduct with four cisterns.

Roman theatre (near the village of Smyrtúla): a huge Roman building near the *stadium.*

Early Christian basilicas: Excavations have revealed two important churches. *Basilica A* (*Hagios Demetrios* or the *Dumetios basilica*): This was built in the middle of the 6C and is known for its mosaic pavement. The atrium, narthex and the transepts are covered in mosaics, and in the centre of the left arm is a Christian and geographical map of the world. There is complementary mosaic in the right arm, with the central theme of Paradise.

Basilica B (*Basilica of Alkyson*): this was built at the beginning of the 6C and is larger than basilica A; its reliefs were also covered in mosaics, but all that remains are the heads of two donors or saints.

Nísyros (I)/ΝΙΣΤΡΟΣ
East Aegean Islands (Dodecanese)/Aegean Islands   p.300☐O 11

This island is almost circular and has an area of 16 sq. miles and a population of around 1300. It is situated between the islands of Kos (10 miles S.) and Tilos, and is secluded, fertile and picturesque, with an extinct volcanic crater in its centre.

History: According to mythology, Nísyros is a huge lump of rock whoch Poseidon broke off the neighbouring island of Kos during his battle with the giants and threw into the sea. The giant he hit, Polybotes, is said to be buried under the island (the volcano). Nísyros was settled by Dorians from Kos in around 800 BC, and the island was a member of the Athenian maritime

Nikópolis, the Roman theatre

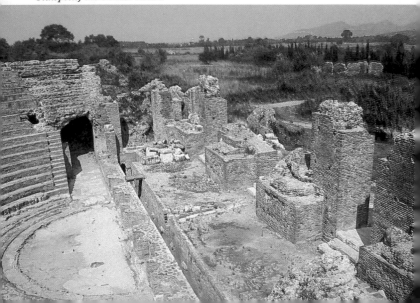

league in 479; it was later ruled by Rhodes. It was captured by the Hospitallers in 1312 and conquered by the Turks in 1533. From 1912 until its return to Greece in 1948 it was under Italian protection.

Mandráki: This is the capital, with some 800 inhabitants; it is also the only port, and is attractively situated on the slopes beneath the fortress, which includes an *acropolis* and a *ruined medieval castle*. The ancient *mole* is now above sea level, and its remains are covered by houses. Beneath the ancient acropolis was the *ancient town of Nísyros*, which was mentioned by Strabo in the 1C AD, and of which there are traces to the SW of the harbour. The *ancient walls* are relatively well-preserved and consist of large blocks of black lava stone up to 12 ft. thick, and a colossal *gate* to the NE with 13 ft. stone slabs and an inscription. Inside the fortress are the remains of a 5&6C early Christian *basilica*. The *ancient graveyard* from the 6C BC has provided some important finds, and is situated outside the fortress near *Ágios Ioánnis*. Most of the finds from Nýsiros are now situated in the Mu-seum at Rhodes. The medieval *kastro* was built by the Hospitallers in the 15C. Also of interest is the *cave church of Panagia Spilianí* ('Madonna in the cave') dating from 1600 and containing a fine iconostasis from 1725. The monastery contains a valuable *library* and an interesting collection of *utensils and votive offerings*. There seems to have been an ancient *sanctuary to Zeus* to the E. by the church of *Agia Triada* ('trinity').

Environs: Near the mountain village of *Emporió*, 8 km. E., which was a refuge for pirates and Turks, are the remains of a 15C *Hospitallers' castle*, and the monastery of *Panagia Kyra*. Near the village of *Páli*, 8 km. NE, are the remnants of an early Christian basilica; the area also has hot sulphur springs. By the village of *Nikiá*, 13 km. SE, is the entrance to the extinct *crater of Stephanos*, which has some interesting mud lakes, fumaroles and small craters. The crater is 2.5 miles across—the island is only 4—and is the result of an eruption in 1522. The 2,460 ft. peak is known as Diabatis and the plateau as Lakkí.

Nikópolis, aqueduct

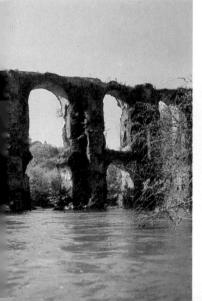

Nikópolis, Alkyson basilica

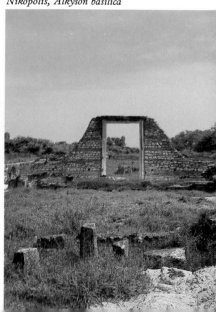

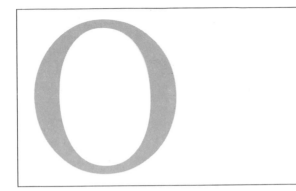

Olympía/Olympia/ΟΛΥΜΠΙΑ
Elis/Pelopponese   p.294☐D 9

Olympia, which together with Delphi, Delos, and the Acropolis in Athens was one of the most important cultural centres in ancient Greece, is situated in the middle of the W. Peloponnese, with its rolling countryside and rich alluvial soil, in the district of Elis. The modern town of *Olympía*, which is close to the excavations, has a population of about 1000 and attracts many foreign tourists.

History: A number of ancient myths surround both the town, which was settled in the second millennium BC, and the Olympic Games, which began in 776 BC and took place every four years thereafter. It seems that Rhea, the earth-goddess, and

Olympia, palaistra

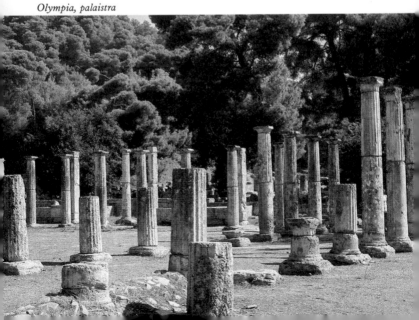

Kronos, the god of the sky, were worshipped here in pre-Hellenic times (the name of Mt.Kronos, 410 ft., which overlooks the site, itself points to this). Kronos and Rhea were believed to be the parents of the principal Greek divinities from Mt.Olympos (Zeus, Hera, Poseidon, Demeter, Hades, and Hestia). Legend relates that Zeus's son Herakles marked out the sacred grove (the Altis) and himself introduced the Olympic Games in honour of his 'Olympian' father (whence the name Olympia). It was also believed that the legendary Pelops, eponym of the Peloponnese ('Peloponnesos' means 'island of Pelops'), ruled either here or in nearby Písa. He won King Oinomaos's daughter in marriage after beating him in a chariot race (the Olympic chariot races were instituted to commemorate this).

In historical times, the rulers of Elis and Písa were responsible for holding the Olympiads or festivals of Zeus. This was originally a regional celebration, but it developed in the 6&5C BC into a panhellenic festival, held every four years, and attended by groups of competitors and envoys from the whole of Greece and its colonies (including Sicily). In their heyday, the games used to last nearly a week. They took place during the period of the first full moon after the summer solstice (round about July), which was also the first week of the Greek New Year, so that they were coincidentally a kind of New Year festival. The four-yearly festivals were used as the basis of ancient chronology: for example, the first Olympiad was held in 776 BC, so Olympiad 1.4 represents 773 BC; Ol. 87.3 = 430; Ol. 111.4 = 333 BC, and so on. The last Olympic Games in ancient times, which were the 291st in the series, were held in AD 385, after which they were abolished, as being 'pagan' practices, by edict of the Emperor Theodosius I.

A truce (ekecheiria) was declared during the festival week, the guarantee of which was largely maintained by Sparta, the most powerful state in the Peloponnese. The number of events gradually increased: middle and long distance races (400 and 5000 metres) were added to the sprint of c. 200 metres (1 stadion = 192 metres) and a race in armour, quoits (pale), boxing (pygme)

Olympia, early Christian church

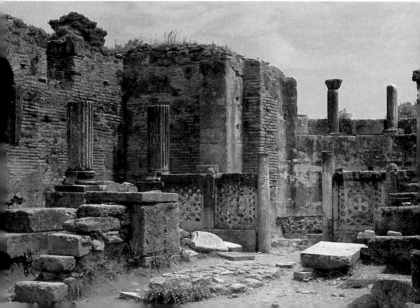

and freestyle wrestling (pantokraton) were also introduced at the same time. The pentathlon was the supreme individual event, comprising running, long-jumping, discus, javelin- and quoit-throwing, but the most significant sport of all was the chariot race (with 2 or 4 horses), in which nobles and princes frequently competed, using victory to further their own ends. The religious festivities (sacrificial processions) took place at night during the full moon (in celebration of Zeus). The victors were crowned by the 'umpires' (Hellenodikes) with olive branches, and a triumphal return was organized in their home town (with victory statues in Olympia and poetic hymns, such as those by Pindar from the 5C BC). The games began to be secula-

rized in the 4C BC and reached a peak of athletic professionalism under the Roman Empire.

During antiquity Olympia was a meeting point for large numbers of spectators and consequently a political flashpoint with diplomatic manoeuvring behind the scenes. In the 6C AD the deserted religious buildings were destroyed by an earthquake and then covered by a layer of mud when the Alpheios (Alfios) and Kladaos (Kladeos) rivers burst their banks. After its rediscovery in the 18C (Chandler, Montfaucon, Winckelmann) the German Ernst Curtius began systematic excavations in 1875, and these are still being continued under the supervision of the German Archaeological Society.

Olympia, sacred precinct with archaeological excavations: 1 present-day entrance **2** gymnasion and field of Mars **3** E. stoa of the gymnasion **4** S. stoa of the gymnasion and Ephebeion **5** palaistra **6** present-day path of the Kladeos river **7** swimmimg bath **8** Greek bath **9** Kladeos hot springs **10** Roman guest house **11** heroon **12** theokoleon (priest's house) **13** Pheidias's workshop with Byzantine church **14** Roman Altis entrance **15** Leoniadion (guest house) **16** S. warm springs **17** bouleuterion (council chamber) **18** south hall **19** Hellenistic Altis wall **20** original Altis entrance with gate and triumphal arch **21** great Temple of Zeus **22** Kallistephanos olive tree **23** temple forecourt with offerings and ramp **24** Shrine of Pelops (Pelopion) **25** Temple of Hera (Heraion) **26** Philippeion **27** prytaneion/hestiarion (altar of Hestia) **28** exedra of Herodes Atticus (nymphaion) **29** metroon **30** treasury terrace with treasuries **31** echo hall **32** SE building (Hellanodikeion) **33** villa of Nero **34** hippodrome **35** stadium entrance **36** ancient stadium **37** S. bank of the stadium **38** Kronion hill **39** ancient Altis walls **40** area flooded by the Alpheios river

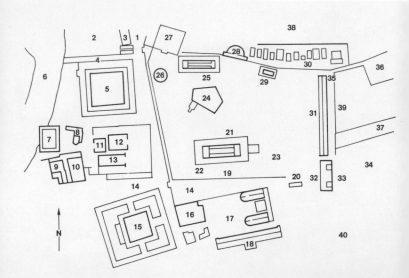

The first Olympic games of the current series was held in Paris's Olympic Stadium, on the suggestion of the French nobleman Pierre de Coubertin. The games, whose location changes regularly, have been much impeded by war (unlike in antiquity). In 1980 the Greek president Karamanlis made the (idealistic) suggestion that the games should return to their original location of Olympia.

Excavation Area: This is situated between the Kladeos river to the W. and the Alfios river to the SE and E; the N. boundary is the Kronos hill. The *sacred shrine* of the Altis is situated in the centre, and has been covered by plane and olive (now pine) trees since ancient times. The *Altis* was dedicated to Zeus, the son of Kronos, and was an approximately square area measuring some 600 x 600 ft. where, as in the oracle of Zeus at Dodona, the father of the gods' presence was felt through the rustling of the trees. Other important religious centres were later sited here, most notably a temple of Zeus and Hera, which was surrounded by a *peribolos* (Altis wall). The *W.*

and *S. walls*, which were extended by the Romans, had a number of gates, some of which are still recognizable among the remains. The Greek (interior) walls are without mortar, and the Roman (exterior) ones are of mortared tufa blocks. In Roman times the procession to the sanctuary entered through the SW gate and left through the NW. The Altis was bordered to the N. by a *retaining wall* on the Kronos hill and to the E. by a stoa ('Echo Hall'). To the E. were the *stadium* And the *hippodrome*, which were later covered by the river Alfios, to the SW was a large *guest house* (Leonidaion), and to the S. an *administrative building*.

Temple of Zeus Temple: The remains of this Doric temple from around 457 BC are still impressive today, especially the foundations; it was built by the architect Libon from Elis. The massive limestone substructure of the peripteros, with its 6 x 13 Doric columns and an area of 210 x 90 ft., has been completely excavated. The restored *shell limestone columns* were some 35 ft. high, and many of the column bases and

Olympia, prehistoric house (c. 1700 BC)

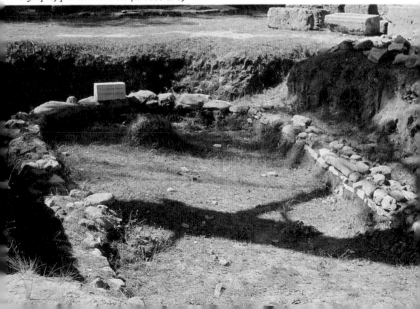

capitals have survived. There was a broad *ramp* leading up to the E. front of the temple. The stylobate of three high steps, rests on a substructure of carefully dressed ashlars. The *interior* is divided into the *pronaos*, *cella* and *opisthodomos*. A bronze door leads from the pronaos into the cella, which is divided into a wide *central aisle* and two narrow *side aisles* by two rows of 7 Doric columns (two-tiered). Dark paving in the centre of the cella point to the original location of the chryselephantine *cult-image*; a *colossal statue of almighty Zeus* by the Athenian sculptor Pheidias, which dated from around 430 BC. It was some 40 ft. high and depicted the god seated with gold hair and clothing, and an ivory face and body. The *wooden throne*, some 30 ft. high, was also richly decorated with gold and ivory. His right hand held a 6ft. Nike (goddess of victory), and his left the sceptre with the eagle of the gods. His feet rested on a gilded stool supported by lions. (Description by Pausanias, 2C AD.) Nothing remains from this statue apart from a few scattered pieces of materials and a clay model: it was taken to Byzantium by The-

odosius II around AD 420, and was destroyed in a fire in 475. It was one of the seven wonders of the ancient world.

The Parian marble *figures* from the pediment, some of which are larger than life size, were discovered almost in one piece, and are now housed in the museum.

Those on the *E. pediment* depict the preparations for the legendary first chariot race of Olympia (once Písa) between King Oinomaos and Pelops, son of Tantalus, to win the king's daughter Hippodameia. Zeus can be seen in the centre. The theme of the *W. pediment* is the battle of the Lapiths against the Centaurs.

Temple forecourt In front of the temple to the E. are the plinths of a number of *sacred statues*, including those of champion charioteers, olympic victors (Olympionikes), a *Nike* (of Paionios), the *nine Trojan heroes*, a statue by Praxiteles to the S. and a Zeus figure (Zeus of Plataia). In the NE were the statues of the women of Elis, the bronze bull of Eretreia, and monuments to Mikythos and Dropion. The *holy olive tree* (kallistephanos), from which the

Olympia, remains of the Leonidaion

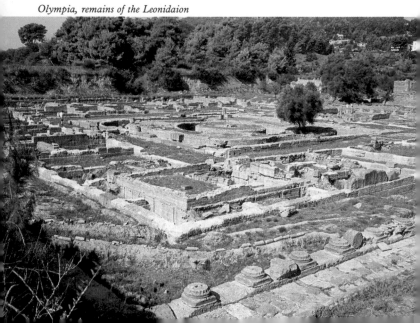

victors' olive branches were taken, stood in the SW by the peribolos. To the SE was the site of the original entrance to the Altis.

Pelops monument (Pelopion): There is an earth mound surrounded by a pentagonal wall in almost the exact centre of the Altis (between the Temples of Zeus and Hera), which is said to be the *tomb* or shrine of Pelops, the son of Tantalus. There are remains of *Mycenean walls* in the E. of the area, which are from the apsidal building, and may come from the high altar of the original religious settlement from the 2nd millenium. The famous *Olympia Altar of Zeus*, which was used for bull sacrifice, may have been to the NE.; Pausanias describes a 25 ft. high urn on the stone pedestal.

Temple of Hera (Heraion): The remains of the oldest temple in the shrine are located to the NW of the Altis; they date back to 600 BC and are constructed on foundations a century older. The austere Doric peripteral temple had 6 x 16 columns (some wooden) and was probably originally dedicated to the divine pair Zeus and Hera. The cella (to the W.) contained the *cult-figure* of a seated Hera, with a standing figure of Zeus wearing a helmet; the statue base has survived. The original oak columns were gradually replaced by stone ones in various styles, especially in Roman times. The columns of the peripteros of plastered limestone have been partially preserved. The temple is roughly 60 x 165 ft. (first Doric peripteros) with a flat saddle roof some 25 ft. high with wooden timbers, unlike the later Doric stone temples. To the E. of the temple is the ruined *Altar of Hera*.

Metroon: In the N. of the Altis, E. of the Temple of Hera, was a small 5&4C peripteral temple with 6 x 11 Doric columns and an area of 35 x 65 ft; dedicated to Rhea, the 'Great Mother' of Zeus and the gods. In Roman times it was consecrated to the cult of Caesar Augustus, whose statue is in the cella.

Treasuries (Thesauroi): The *foundations* of some small *temples in antis*, which were built to house the votive offerings from the various Greek states, are situated on a terrace at the foot of the Kronos hill. These *treasuries* date from the 6&5C and are simple square structures with double-columned porches between the projecting side walls (ante). From W. to E.: the *House of Sikyón* (6C BC), with 20 x 60 ft. foundations and well-preserved shell (metope frieze, front timbers); Houses of *Syrakús, Epidámnos* (Durazzo), *Byzántion* (Byzantium), *Sýbaris* (S. Italy), *Kyréne* (Libya), *Selinús* (Sicily), *Metapóntion* (Lucania), *Mégar* and *Géla* (Sicily).

The *steps* in front of the treasury terrace is from the 4C BC, and has some 16 stone plinths in front of it, which once supported the *Statues of Zanes* (Zancs = Zeus). From the 4–2C, any athlete who broke the Olympic rules, e.g. by accepting bribes, had to pay a fine sufficient to commission a bronze figure of Zeus.

Nymphaion fountain: Between the Temple of Hera and the treasuries, in the N. of the Altis, The rich Athenian Herodes Atticus commissioned a semicircular fountain, with niches for statues of the emperors, in about AD 160. This is the most interesting remnant of the final golden age of Olympia in the 2C AD, and included a 2 mile long water system and 83 spouts (decorated with lions' heads) which supplied the participants with drinking water. There was a marble-clad brick *basin* measuring 90 x 14 ft. and two *round marble buildings* consisting of eight (some have been re-erected) Corinthian columns with *fountains*, one on each side.

Philippeion (Philippion): The *substructure* and *stylobate* of the monument (Heroon) to the family of King Philip II of

Macedon, which takes the form of a round temple and dates from *c.* 338 BC, is situated in the NW corner of the Altis, to the W. of the Temple of Hera. The Ionic peripteros around the cella, whose interior contains 12 Corinthian columns, was commissioned by his son Alexander the Great. The cella housed the five chryselephantine statues of the Macedonian royal family, which were the beginning of their personal cult. During the 114th Olympiad, in 324 BC, Alexander the Great was declared a god.

Prytaneion (Prytanion): In the NW of the Altis, by the entrance and to the W. of the Temple of Hera, the ground-level walls of the *administrative building* (prytaneion) can be identified. The remains date from the 6C BC, when the prytanis (rector) was the local authority whose task was to guard the *eternal flame* (hestia) in the S. of the building. This square (20 x 20 ft.) area was the centre of the building, around which the other (later) rooms and a *colonnaded courtyard* at the rear were built. Many alterations were made in Roman times. The N. section included the *hestiatorion* (dining room), where important guests and Olympic victors were fed and entertained at public expense. To the N. of the prytaneion are the remnants of a Roman cold bath whose *mosaic floor* has been uncovered.

Gymnasion: This was situated outside the Altis to the NW, near the modern entrance, and was used for the track and field events. The ruins we see today date from the 3&2C, with a flat stadium-like area, 720 x 400 ft., which was used as a practice area for running, jumping, discus, and spear-throwing. There were *colonnades* on all four sides, and there are remains of the double-aisled Doric *E. stoa* some 40 ft. wide, and the single-aisled *S. stoa, c.* 18 ft. wide. The W. stoa, which had a retaining wall, was washed away by the river Kladeos.

To the SE are the remains of a three-aisled Corinthian *ornamented door* (propylon), which was built in the 2C BC as the entrance to the Altis.

Palaistra: This was the 3C BC *wrestling and boxing school,* a building some 220 ft. square with an *interior courtyard* (ring area) 130 ft. square and surrounded on all four sides by Doric *colonnades.* Behind the ring were the rooms used by the competitors for washing, oiling and dressing. The foundations are identifiable, and some of the pillars have been restored.

Priests' House (Theopoleion): The 5C BC remains of the foundations of the old priests' house are to be found to the S. of the Palaistra; the original building consisted of six square rooms around an *interior courtyard* (with fountains), but was much rebuilt and extended in Hellenistic and Roman times (it has a Roman peristyled court to the E.). The three theopoloi (theokoloi) acted as high priests for the offering of the sacrifice.

Baths: The area to the W. of the priests' house was used for various forms of bathing from the 5C BC onwards. The old *steam bath* was adjacent to the priests' house, and had a circular *steam room* (tholos) and a columned portico in front of the two rooms. Later, in the 2C BC, it was converted into a Heroon (hero's shrine) with a small altar.

Further to the W. are the remains of the Greek *hip baths* from the 5C BC, with some partially preserved stone *bath tubs.* The SE section had a *hypocaust* heated by ducts of warm air built in around 100 BC. The ancient 5C BC *open air bath* was situated further to the W., and was 80 x 50 ft. in area and 5 ft. deep. It was Greece's first open air bath. Around AD 100 the *Kladeos hot baths* were built to the S., a structure covering 4,300 sq. ft. and including an atrium, impluvium, a 390 sq. ft. room with a mosaic floor, cold bath (frigidarium), steam bath (laconicum), warm bath (caldarium) and dressing-rooms. To the S. of the hot baths are the remains of the foundations of a 2&3C AD Roman *guest house* with a number of rooms and a colonnaded courtyard.

Pheidias's workshop: To the S. of the priests' house, excavations have revealed the foundations of the building used by Pheidias, the sculptor who made the massive *Golden Zeus* statue for the Temple of Zeus in 430 BC. Clay models, remains of tools and ivory fragments have been discovered (including a pot bearing the inscription 'property of Pheidias'). The workshop, which was the same size as the cella of the Temple of Zeus, was later converted into an equipment room (pompeion), and then in the 5C AD into a Byzantine church, of which there are still some remains.

Leonidaion: To the S. of Pheidias's workshop (in the S. of the outside area) are the ruins of the ancient guest house which was built by the architect Leonidas in the 4C BC. It was an almost square structure, *c.* 270 x 270 ft., surrounded by *Ionic colonnades* (138 columns), of which the column capitals and bases are still preserved. It was Olympia's most extensive building: it had an *atrium* in the centre, with an *impluvium*, fountains and lawns, surrounded by a Doric *peristyle* of 44 columns. Behind this were the *guest rooms* for the honoured guests of the Olympiad, and also for the Roman governor.

Bouleuterion: To the S. of the Altis enclosure, by the S. Roman perimeter wall, are the remnants of two parallel *buildings* (100 x 45 ft.) ending in apses and dating from the 6C BC; they were built on a two-layered foundation from regular square limestone blocks with central columns, fragments of which are still identifiable, supporting the timbers. They were probably the site of meetings of the council (boule). The courtyard in between the two buildings was where the Olympic competitors gathered before the statue of Zeus Horkios ('Zeus God of Oaths') to take the

Olympia, mosaic on the S. hall

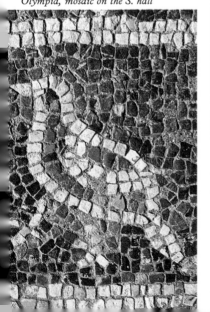

Olympia, Leonidaion

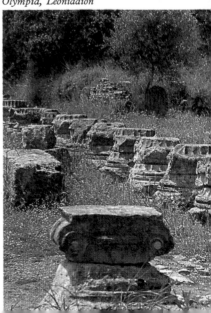

Olympic oath. The *surrounding wall* dates from Hellenistic/Roman times (forecourt with Doric colonnade). It was the site of the old entrance to the shrine of Zeus, on the road from Elis to Olympia. In the 4C BC, the *south stoa* (limestone remains) was built, with a 270 ft. Doric colonnade along its S. front, facing the old festival route. To the W. of the Bouleterion are the remains of *baths* from the 3C AD, when the whole area was completely rebuilt.

Villa of Nero (SE building): To the SE by the Altis wall are the ruins of various brick buildings, including the *Villa of Nero*, which dates from around AD 67 and was built on the site of a 4C BC building with two interior rooms and a three-sided colonnade (SE building). To the E. are the remains of other Roman buildings, including one with an octagonal room, to the SW of which are the remains of an *altar* to Artemis from the 5C BC. The neighbouring *Roman fortress gate*, whose foundations are still standing, was built in the form of a *triumphal arch* in anticipation of visiting emperors.

Echo Hall: The E. end of the Altis is formed by a long 4C BC *colonnade* (stoa), which is known as the 'echo hall' because of its sevenfold echo, or 'stoa poikile' because of its numerous paintings. It is 320 x 40 ft., with 44 Doric columns facing the Altis, in front of which *pedestals* of statues still stand. The entrance to the stadium was N. of the hall, and the S. exit led to the hippodrome.

Stadium: Outside the Altis to the NE, below the Kronos hill, was the original *Olympic running track*, which was 600 ft. long. It was named *stadion* ('place of war') after the battlefield. The original finishing line (terma) was the sacred area in front of the temple; in the 6C BC it was flattened and surrounded with a *south wall* (spectator ring). The stadium and the religious cen-

tre developed together, until in the 4C BC the erection of the echo hall separated the stadium from the sacred precinct. The *new stadium* simply had earth embankments for some 40,000 spectators. The *start* and *finishing lines* can still be made out. 20 runners (with starting holes) started 3 ft. apart. The *umpire's chair* was situated to the S.; it was not until Roman times that it was converted into a stone seat for important guests. The seat of the priestess of Demeter, the only woman permitted to be present, was on the N. side. The 4C BC stadium was excavated and restored to its original condition in 1961-2 by the German Archaeological Society.

There are no remains of the *hippodrome* (horse track), which was situated to the S. of the stadium, as the area was covered by the river Alfios. It seems to have been around 2,300 x 1,000 ft. in area, and the teams had to run around the taraxippos ('horse shocker') stone.

Also worth seeing: A small *memorial* for the founder of the modern Olympic Games, *Pierre de Coubertin* (1862-1932), is situated outside the excavation area on the road to Tripolis, and contains his heart.

Archaeological Museum (Archaiologiko Musio): This is housed in an old building on the edge of the excavations, which was set up by the German archaeologist Dörpfeld, and a new building some 1.5 km. away on the Tripolis road.
Pediment Hall: The hall exactly matches the frontage of the Temple of Olympian Zeus, and there are fragments of the celebrated Parian marble *pediment* of the temple on the wall.
East pediment: This is the masterpiece from the façade of the Zeus temple which depicts the preparations for the legendary first Olympic chariot race between Pelops

Olympia, Praxiteles's Hermes ▷

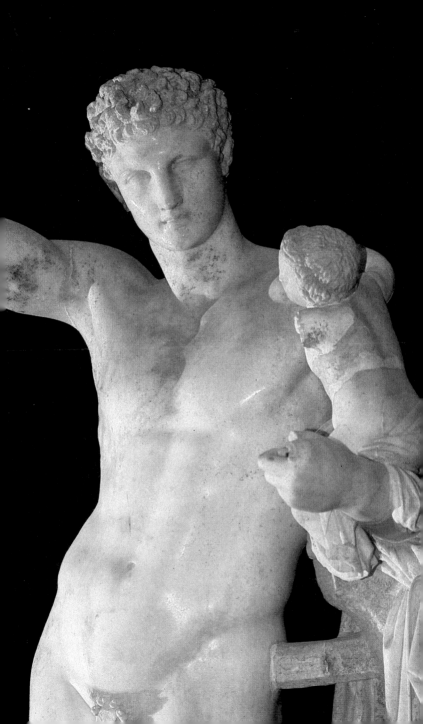

the son of Tantalus and Oinomaos the King of Olympia (formerly Písa); according to the legend, the prize for victory was the king's daughter Hippodameia. 13 suitors had already paid for failed attempts with their lives. The arbiter of the race was Zeus himself, depicted in the centre, looking at Pelops and Hippodameia (to the left). Pelops' four-in-hand (quadriga) is waiting for the starting signal. In the left hand corner of the pediment is a couchant figure symbolizing the river Alpheios. The right side is almost a mirror image, with King Oinomaos and his wife Sterope, with his four-in-hand and the figure of the river Kladeos spectating. According to the legend, Pelops won by skilful control of his chariot and killed the king, whom he then succeeded.

West pediment: This is where the legendary battle of the Thessalian Lapiths against the neighbouring Centaurs is depicted. The battle is said to have started among the guests at the wedding of the Lapith King Perithoos to the daughter of King Adrastos of Argos, Hippodameia. The drunken centaurs (horses with human upper parts) tried to ravish the Lapith women.

In the centre of the pediment is the god Apollo watching over the conflict; on the left is Perithoos's friend, the Athenian hero Theseus, fighting a centaur, and on the right is King Perithoos himself.

In the corners there are men fighting and women looking on.

The connection between the E. and W. pediments seems to be the *struggles for Hippodameia*, the name borne by both the heroines. They are by unknown Olympian masters and date from 470–456.

Metopes from the Temple of Zeus: There were six of these beneath each pediment (3 of the originals are in the Louvre, with copies on display here) and they depicted the 12 Labours of Herakles: 1. the killing of the Nemean lion with a club and the wearing of its pelt; 2. the killing of the nine-headed hydra of Lerna; 3. the hind of Ceryneia; 4. the Erymanthian boar; 5. the Stymphalian birds; 6. the cleaning of the Augean stables; 7. the capture of the Cretan bull; 8. the horses of Diomedes; 9. the girdle of the Amazon; 10. the oxen of Geryon; 11. the golden apples of the

Olympia, arch, remains of the original vaulted stadium entrance

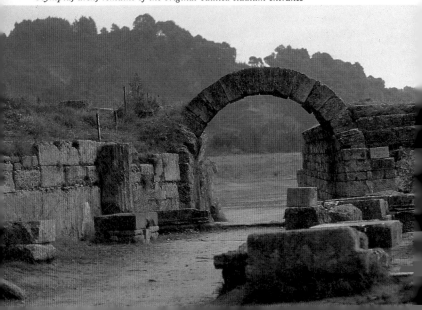

Hesperides; 12. the abduction of Cerberus. The metopes which have survived (in fragmentary form) also date from 470–56, and are displayed in the museum in no particular order.

At the back of the room is the *Nike* (goddess of victory) of Paionios, which dates from 429 BC and once stood in front of the Temple of Zeus.

The new museum includes *small bronzes* from the Geometric and early archaic periods, *terracotta votive offerings*, weapons, tools, pedimental sculptures and various finds from the Altis excavations. The most impressive piece is Praxiteles's gleaming marble *Hermes*, dating from the 4C BC, it is still in good condition and depicts the young Hermes carrying Dionysos to the nymphs to bring up. The child is resting and reaching for a grape which is being offered to him by the Messenger of the Gods. *Room 1:* late Geometric *bronze horse*, Geometric *bronze tripod* (9C BC) with Herakles and Apollo fighting; other *tripod fragments* (griffin-head grip); *helmet* made from a wild boar's tusk; pottery and bronze figurines. *Room 2:* Ge-ometric, archaic *bronzes*; helmets, weapons, shields, greaves (broken as sacrificial offerings); a *head of Hera*, the remnant of a statue of Hera from the 6C BC temple; cornices and acroterion from the *Temple of Hera* and the treasuries. *Room 3:* Pedimental sculptures from the *Treasury of Mégara* and other buildings in the Altis; terracotta figures; bronzes and archaic black figure ceramics. *Room 4:* An interesting *terracotta group*, 'Zeus bearing off Ganymede' (votive offering from 490 BC), and parts of the *Persian booty*. Other rooms contain sculptures from classical, Hellenistic and Roman times, and ceramics from the same period, as well as inscriptions, bronzes and objects pertaining to the ancient Olympiads.

Museum of the Olympic Games: A small museum has been set up in the village of Olympia by the I.O.C. (International Olympic Committee), which provides a survey of the modern Olympic games from 1876 to the present day with a display of medals, photographs and other documents.

Orchomenós, monastery church of the Dormition of the Virgin

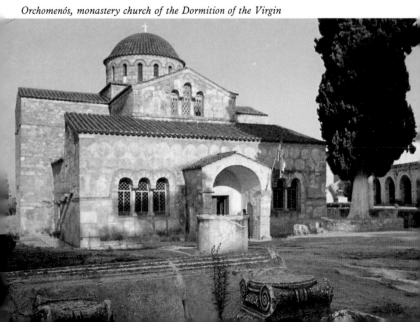

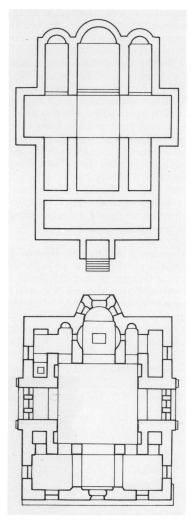

Orchomenós *(above):* **Koimesis tis Theotoku.** This is the only church in Greece which combines elements of a vaulted basilica (a nave, two aisles and vaulted arches) with those of a cross-in-square church (full walls cutting off the nave). *(below):* **Treasury of Minyas,** a Mycenean beehive tomb (tholos) with a dromos and a pyramidal door with a massive slate support. On the E. side is a square tomb chamber connected to the domed building by a passageway.

Environs: Near the *new museum* are the remains of a *Mycenean acropolis* where *chamber tombs* have been excavated, along with Roman and early Christian tombs.

Orchomenós/ΟΡΧΟΜΕΝΟΣ
Boeotia/Central Greece   p.294□G 7/8

Orchomenós is a small town of some 5,000 inhabitants, 13 km. from Levádia, which comprises the two villages of *Petromágula* and *Skripú*. Skripú was built on the site of an early Helladic (2600–1900) town; the remains of the ancient settlement of Orchomenós are situated near the road which leads past Skripú's Byzantine church to Mt.Akontion.

In pre-Grecian times, Orchomenós was inhabited by a Thessalian tribe, the Minyans, who took their name from one of their kings, Minyas. According to mythology, the Argonauts were descended from this king's daughter. Orchomenós and Thebes had a long-standing feud, and when Thebes reached the zenith of its power (364 BC), Orchomenós was taken and destroyed by the Thebans.

Excavation area: Traces of the ancient town date back to early Helladic times. The fortifications surrounding the *acropolis* are still standing (a stone staircase of 88 steps leads up to the W. summit, 1,100 ft. high), and they date partly from the 7C and partly from the 4C BC.

Traces of Bronze Age buildings have been discovered near the graveyard of Skripú, to the W. of the Byzantine church, and the adjacent site contains the most interesting remnant of 14C Mycenean culture, King Minyas' huge *beehive tomb*, which was uncovered by Schliemann in 1880-6. It is known as the *Treasury of Minyas*, and is 46 ft. across, connected by a corridor with a square side chamber, whose 8 ft. ceiling is decorated with spirals and rosettes. According to tradition, King Minyas was buried here. The courtyard outside the domed tomb contains an interesting collection of tomb reliefs, ceramic fragments and inscriptions.

The remains of a *temple of Asklepios* on the lower slope survives from Hellenistic times, when Orchomenós was rebuilt by Philip of Macedon and his son Alexander the Great, following its destruction by the Thebans.

According to Pindar and Theocritus, Orchomenós was known for the worship of the Graces, to whom a *temple* was consecrated on the E. side of the beehive tomb, where the Byzantine church of the Dormition now stands.

The most recent excavation, under the supervision of the Greek archaeologist Spyropulos, uncovered the small but beautiful *Theatre of the Graces* on the W. edge of the acropolis.

Koimesis tis Theotoku: This is Skripú's Byzantine church, which was commissioned by the Byzantine governor of Central Greece, Protospatharios Leon, and built on the foundations of an older (5C) church, as is apparent from inscriptions on the walls dating from 873/4. It was dedicated to the Mother of God and to the apostles Peter and Paul, and was the katholikón (main church) of a Byzantine monastery. Stylistically, it is a cross between an early Christian basilica and the later cross-in-square church which appeared in the 10C. It clearly displays the transitional nature of the Byzantine style.

There is a row of fine Byzantine sculptures along the exterior wall, including two peacocks on the S. side and a monster with a human head on the E. side. The style

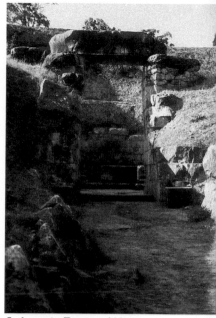

Orchomenós, Treasury of Minyas

shows the Oriental influence dominant at the time.

The old frescos on the interior walls have unfortunately been lost.

Church of St. Nicholas (ton kambion). Not far from Skripú's church is a small, attractive Byzantine chapel dedicated to St.Nicholas, situated in a small valley full of almond trees. It is built in a meadow (kambos), and is consequently known as 'ton kambion' or 'sta kambia'. It is 10C in origin, and is dependent upon the monastery of Hósios Lukás. Inside, it has interesting frescos from the time of its building.

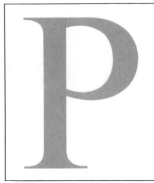

Paianía (Liópesi)/ΠΑΙΑΝΙΑ
Attica/Central Greece   p.296□H 9

This town, which is *c.* 17 km. SE. of Athens on the eastern foothills of Mt.Ymittos (Hymettos), marks the northernmost point of the region of Mesogia, the interior of Attica. The ancient deme of *Paianía*, which was one of the oldest in Attica, though nothing of it has survived, was the birth-place of the famous orator Demosthenes (384–322 BC).

The modern town has several fine churches (Zoodochos Pigi, Ágios Athanasios, Ágios Dimitrios, and Ágios Spyrídon) which contain *frescos* by the school of Georgios Markos (17C). The church of Zoodochos Pigi also contains frescos by the modern icon painter Kontoglu (part of his 'Dodekaeorton', a cycle depicting the twelve great feasts).

Environs: Some 4 km. to the W, on the slopes of Mt.Ymittos, is the interesting cave ('spílaio' in Greek) of *Kutúki* (41,000 sq. ft.), in which there are beautiful stalactites and stalagmites. About 8 km. to the S., on the E. slopes of Mt.Ymittos, (and still in the Mesogia) is the village of **Koropí** which contains the Church of the Transfiguration (Metamorphosis), a Byzantine church with 10C frescos. Other churches contain paintings by the school of Georgios Markos of Argos. In 1949, excavations carried out nearby on the E. slopes of Mt.Ymittos revealed the remains of a **temple**, with a peribolos, which was dedicated to Apollo Parnopios. Some 6 km. to the N, near the village of *Agía Paraskeví*, and situated on the N. slope of Mt. Ymittos, is the monastery of *Ágios Ioánnis (Kynigos)*. It has a Byzantine cross-domed church dating from the 12C with narthex (also domed) dating from the 16&17C. The frescos, which have been whitewashed in part, also date from this latter period.

Palaiokhóra/Paleókhora/ΠΑΛΑΙΟ-ΧΩΡΑ
Chaniá/Crete   p.298□E 14

This is a small but very charming town, with a profusion of flowers and sandy beaches, which lies at the W. end of the S. coast of Crete, at the base of a peninsula which juts out into the sea. Many people still call it *Selínou-Kastelli*, a Greek rendering of its old Venetian name *Castel Selino* which it took from the Venetian *fort* on the promontory opposite. This was built in 1279 and restored by the Ottomans in

1325. Apart from its powerful curtain walls, only some slight ruins of it have survived.

There are nine small frescoed Byzantine churches worth seeing in the environs of Palaiokhora.

Súgia (Syia, Sóugia, Sóuia): This town lies on the S. coast of Crete, some 15 km. to the E. of Palaiokhóra, from where it is best approached by boat. Súgia (which was called Syia in antiquity) was once the port for Elyros. **Lissós:** 10 km. from Palaiokhóra. It is best to make for the ancient Lissós on foot (heading W.) from Súgia. Otherwise it can also be reached directly by boat from either Súgia or Palaiokhóra. Lissós (also called Ágios Kyrikos) dated from the 7 or 6 C BC and was connected with Górtys in antiquity. Up till now, the ruins of a *theatre*, an *aqueduct*, and a *Sanctuary of Asklepios* dating from the 3C BC have been excavated here. The temple revealed a beautiful Roman floor mosaic. **Kántanos/Kándanos** is 20 km. N. of Palaiokhóra and is richly endowed with Byzantine churches. There are 15 small churches from the late Byzantine period in Kántanos itself, and 100 more in the environs, some of which have well preserved and often very beautiful frescos. Especially noteworthy is the *Church of the Archangel Michael* (in Kántanos) whose frescos date from 1328. Nearby is *Anisaraki* whose churches of *Agia Anna, Agia Paraskeví* and *Panagia* contain 15C frescos that have been executed with great beauty. Apart from Anisaraki, it is especially worth visiting *Ágios Georgios. Trakhiniákos* contains the church of *Ágios Ioánnis* in which there is a series of excellent 14C frescos. The churches of *Agia Paraskeví* and *Profítis Ilías* in the same locality boast some interesting frescos which are in good condition. **Teménia** (5 km. SW. of Kántanos) contains the Church of *Christ the Saviour* (Sotiros Christou), which dates from the 13–15C; its bell tower and drum are faced with rough stone which has not been whitewashed (as is generally the practice). The frescos in the niches of the long walls have been well preserved. Some 5 km. to the SE. of Teménia, and about 5 km. NE.

Páros (Páros), the ancient harbour

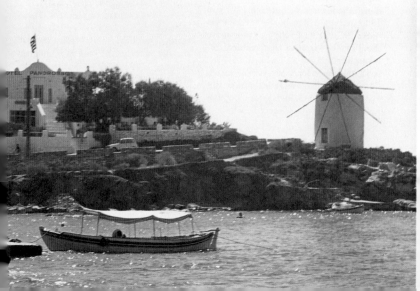

of Súgia, is **Moní**, which contains the small church of Ágios Nikólaos dating from the beginning of the 14C. Its very beautiful fresco of St.Nicholas was painted by Ioánnis Pagoménos around 1315. The same artist painted an extraordinarily animated and indeed vibrant fresco in 1347 in the *Church of the Panagia* near **Skafidia-Prodómi** (some 8 km. to the SW. of Moní) which is also well preserved.

Párga/ΠΑΡΓΑ
Préveza/Epirus   p. 290□C 6

A beehive tomb dating from 1320–1200 BC has been discovered to the E. of Párga. This was the site, in antiquity, of the town of *Toryne*, a colony of Elis. In the Hellenistic period Toryne was moved farther west, and centred on the fortified hill where today the remains of its acropolis can be seen. In the late Byzantine period, Párga was one of the most important towns in Epirus. The modern town was settled in the 14C. During the 15C it was ruled by the Venetians, who also built the fort; but in 1539 it was captured and entirely destroyed by the Turks. Many of the inhabitants abandoned the town then. Between 1797 and 1800, and again from 1807–15, Párga was under French rule. In 1817 it was given to the Turks by virtue of an agreement between England and Ali Pasha; in 1819 the inhabitants abandoned the town and resettled in Corfu. Párga remained under Turkish rule until 1913. Today it is a popular holiday resort, with a lovely beach.

Páros (I)/ΠΑΡΟΣ
Cyclades/Aegean Islands   p.300□K/L 10/11

This is one of the biggest and most beautiful of the Cyclades (75 sq. miles; population *c.* 7,500). It is roughly oval in shape (9 miles long, 6 miles wide) and has been known since antiquity for its dazzling white marble or lychnite.

History: There are some remains on the island indicating that it was settled as early as the 3rd millennium BC. The local marble was already being quarried during the prehistoric Cycladic period (2600-1600 BC), when there were also trading links with Crete and Mycene. After having been colonized by the Ionians around 1000 BC, Paros reached the peak of its prosperity during the 8-6C BC. Colonies were now established in northern Greece, including that of Thásos around 700 BC. It was from Thasos in particular that Paros acquired gold (coins were first minted here around 600 BC). Marble exports also contributed to the island's wealth (as did its schools of sculpture). Thanks to the unfortunate part it had played in the Persian War (when it was forced into an alliance with the Persians), Paros lost its influence after the Greek victory at Salamis in 480 BC. In 477, it was obliged to surrender its precious metals to Athens; and later, in 376 BC, it had to pay exacting tributes to the Athenian maritime league. Paros came under Roman rule during the 1C BC, and during the reign of Constantine (AD 312-27) was referred to as a 'splendid city'. In later centuries, it was frequently laid waste by Arab corsairs (notably in 835 and 965), and then between 1207 and 1389 it formed part of the duchy of Naxos. After that, the island was an independent feudal state until 1537, when it was captured by the Turks. In 1830 it became part of a newly liberated Greece.

Páros (also *Parikiá*): This picturesque town (population *c.* 2,000) is the capital of the island and lies on its W. coast on the ruins of the ancient city of Paros. Some traces of prehistoric and ancient buildings (notably the foundations of a temple) can be found on the *acropolis*, which is also the

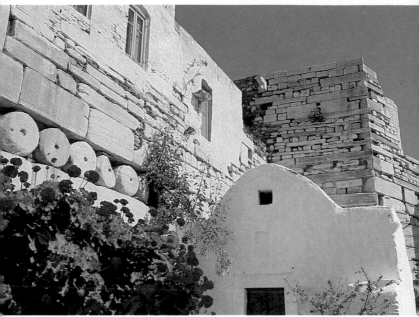

Páros (Páros), house and ancient wall

site of the ruined Venetian *castle (Kastro)* dating from 1260. The castle walls were built partly from blocks of ancient marble, for example the drums of Doric columns. The *Frankish tower*, which has been preserved, also contains numerous pieces of ancient buildings. The old city wall dated from before 489 BC (the ancient city was bigger than the modern one). Near the harbour, above what was the ancient agora, is the interesting *Katapoliani* church ('the church below the town'), which is worth seeing. Its construction took place in three stages during the 5–7C AD. Originally, a small three-aisled *basilica* (now the chapel of *Ágios Nikólaos)* was erected, around AD 400, over a late classical gymnasion. Then around 600 another three-aisled basilica, dedicated to the Mother of God, was attached to it. A baptisterion, or baptismal chapel, was added on to its S. side. Finally,

the large basilica was converted into a cross-domed basilica during the reign of Justinian (527–65). Four great piers support the dome above the crossing; the nave and transept are barrel vaulted. Various fragments from ancient buildings, including columns and architraves, have been incorporated in the church (for example, the fronts of the galleries). The vaults in the main part of the church are composed of stratified layers of red, green, and white stone, which contrast with the white marble galleries. The decoration also consists of marble insets, which include rhombi, rosettes, the Greek cross, etc. The *dome above the altar* rests on four green marble columns in the centre of the choir. The lower *altar table* and the *pedestals of the altar* are ancient (from the drums of Doric columns). There is a small *side altar* to the left with antique decoration depict-

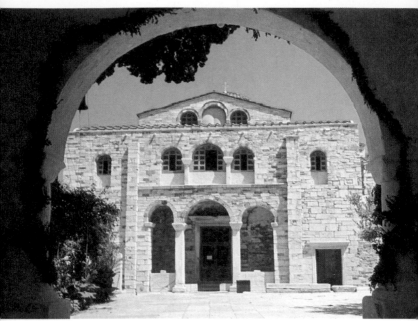

Páros (Páros), Katapoliani church near the harbour

ing bulls' heads and garlands. The *apse* contains gradines (synthronos) for the clergy. By the choir, to the left, is the entrance to the chapel of *Ágios Nikólaos*, which dates from the 5C and is the oldest part of the church. Its *frescos* and the beautiful stone *iconostasis* were executed in the 17C. The somewhat dull early Byzantine design is enlivened by the galleries. The church was severely damaged by earthquakes in the 10&18C; in 1960 it was restored to its original Byzantine form by the Greek architect Orlandos. Legend has it that the first building on the site was founded by St.Helena, the mother of Constantine, around AD 330. There is an annual pilgrimage every 15 August. Not far from the Katapoliani Church is the *Archaeological Museum*. The courtyard contains sarcophagi, tomb reliefs, and fragments of ancient buildings. By the entrance is the *mosaic floor*, depicting the labours of Herakles, from the ancient gymnasion now underneath the oldest part of the Katapoliani Church. The entrance hall contains the *capital* of an Ionic column from the tomb of the poet Arkhilokhos (*c.* 650 BC), who was revered as a hero, together with two inscriptions concerning him, which date from the 3&1C BC. The other rooms contain various examples of Parian sculpture from the archaic and classicl periods, including an early classical marble *statue of Nike* which is almost life-size and an archaic *figure of Demeter*. There are also some *Cycladic idols* and a smll *collection of vases*. It is worth noting the fragment of the famous *Marmor Parium* (of which the other and larger surviving fragment is in the Ashmolean Museum, Oxford). This was a *chronicle inscribed on marble*, composed in 263 BC and covering

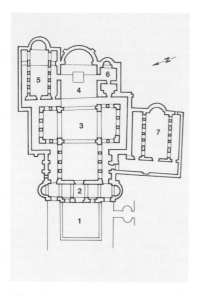

Páros, Katapoliani church 1 atrium **2** narthex **3** old naos, 6C **4** sanctuary **5** chapel of Ágios Nikólaos **6** diakonikon (chapel) **7** baptistery

over 1318 years of Greek history. It begins with the reign of Kekrops, the legendary founder of Athens, and mentions the alleged date of Homer's birth.

Environs: Near *Tris Ekklesiés* (about 1.2 km. to the NE.) are the foundations of a three-aisled early Christian *basilica* dating from the 7C. The tomb of the Parian poet Arkhilokhos (7C BC) is supposed to hve been on this site. There are the remains of a *Sanctuary of Aphrodite* on Mt.Kumados to the N. of the town. Near the sanctuary is the *Delion*, an enclosed sacred precinct containing a *rock altar* and a small *temple* (31 ft. 5 in. x 17 ft. 10 in.), where the three Delian divinities, Leto, Artemis, and Apollo, were worshipped. The remains are very slight, but the view is superb. To the S. of the town, on Mt.Arakas, can be seen the rather scanty remains of a *Sanctuary of Pythian Apollo*, which possessed no

temple; beneath it was a *Sanctuary of Asklepios* dating from the 4C BC, of which there are also only slight traces. 5 km. to the E., at *Márathi*, are the marble quarries where the famous lustrous-white Parian marble was mined from antiquity until the 15C AD. By the entrance to the tunnels (two of which are still passable) there is an ancient *relief* depicting nymphs. Today, the marble is extracted by open-cast mining to the NE. of the monastery of Ágios Minas. Nearby, in the centre of the island, is its highest mountain, Profitis Ilias (2,477 ft.), which offers a splendid view over the Cyclades. Beneath it is the 17C convent of *Christos ton Dason*. It is worth making an excursion to the *Valley of the Butterflies (Petaludes)* nearby. On the E. coast, near *Márpissa* (c. 19 km.), are the ruins of a Venetian *fort* dating from the 15&16C. It is worth seeing the monastery of *Longovárda* (c. 6 km. to the NE.), which was founded by a Lombard monk in the 17C (and is now a school for fresco painting). The church, built in 1657, contains some fine wall paintings. The monastery was restored in the 19C. On the NE. side of the island (some 20 km. from Paros) is the pretty little port of *Náusa/Náussa*, whose harbour (once used for the shipping of marble) contains a *round tower* from its 15C Venetian castle. In the town itself are the *Church of the Transfiguration (Metamurfosis)*, dating from the 16C, which contains an important *collection of icons* (notably from the 16C Cretan-Venetian school, but there are also some Russian ones). Nearby is the small cross-domed church of *Ágios Georgios* whose frescos exemplify folk art. In the western part of the town can be seen the monastery church of *Athanasios* which contains a carved wooden iconostasis of 1695. The monasteries of *Ágios Georgios* (which has a carved iconostasis) and *Ágios Andreas*, both dating from the 17C, are near the town. Exactly 3 km. to the SE of Náusa are the ruins of a Hellenistic round tower called *Palaiópyrgos* (33 ft. in diameter). The small neighbouring island of *Antíparos* (13.5 sq. miles; population *c.* 500) lies to the W. of Paros. It contains some sites, near its main village, *Kastro*, which is in the N. part of the island, where traces of the Cycladic culture were discovered. In the centre of the island, there is a cave with stalactites in which inscriptions by King Otto and Lord Byron can be seen.

Pátmos/Patmos (I)/ΠΑΤΜΟΣ
East Aegean Islands (Dodecanese)/
Aegean Islands   p.296□N 10

Pátmos, the smallest and northernmost island of the Dodecanese (13 sq. miles), is rocky and mountainous, and of volcanic origin (only the N. is fertile). The coastline is oddly shaped, with a narrow isthmus dividing the island at its centre. It is situated to the S. of Ikaría and Samos, roughly on the same latitude as the ancient cities of Dídyma and Miletus in Asia Minor.

History: Pátmos was originally settled by Dorian immigrants, and later by Ionians. It played virtually no part in the history of the ancient world. Under the Romans, it was used, like other Aegean islands, as a place of banishment. Thus it was that St.John the Evangelist was exiled here in AD 95/96 during the reign of the Emperor Domitian (AD 91–96). Legend relates that St.John, who may possibly be identified with the favourite disciple of Jesus, composed his Revelations (or Apocalypse) here. The island was deserted in Byzantine times, until an abbot called Christodulos was given permission by the Emperor Alexios I Komnenos in 1088 to found a monastery, which enjoyed special privileges such as tax exemption and right of freehold. The monastic community was initially exclusively male (as on Mt.Athos) and in its early years lived according to strict rules. Gradually, the monastery was enriched by considerable landed property (off as well as on the island) and valuable donations. Its autonomy was not infringed either by the Venetians, who held the island from 1207–1537, or by the Turks, who

Pátmos (Pátmos), fortified monastery of Ágios Ioánnis

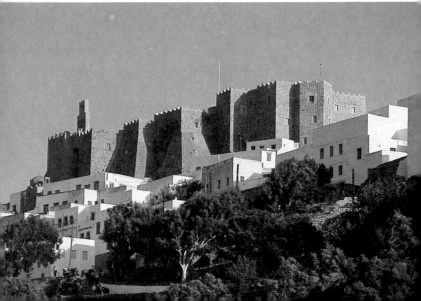

occupied it from 1537, though the latter did exact an annual tribute. Patmos was administered by Italy from 1912 until 1948, when it was handed back to Greece.

Pátmos (population 850): The island's capital (which is also called *Khóra*, meaning 'village') is situated on a hill 426 ft. high, in the S. part of the island. The fortified monastery of *Ágios Ioánnis (Theologos)* towers above it like a castle. Its lower walls date from the 11C and were reinforced in the 15&16C.

The monastery has the appearance of a polygonal castle, with towers and battlements, and was built from the volcanic stone found on the island. The impressive *entrance court*, dating from 1698, is surrounded by high white arcaded walls and leads into the 12C exo-narthex of the church. The pointed arches here are supported by four *ancient columns* (which are not the only ancient fragments to be incorporated in the church). The *frescos*, which depict the *Evangelists* (including St.John) and the *Day of Judgement*, date from the 18&19C; the ornamented wooden doors are older. Between the arches a wooden simantron can be seen. To the right is the chapel of the blessed Christodulos ('slave of Christ'), the monk who founded the monastery. The decoration of his Byzantine sarcophagus, together with a precious reliquary, were part of a Russian endowment of 1796, as also was the furnishing of the three-aisled *church* (katholikon) with lamps, candlesticks, and choir stalls. The ornamented *iconostasis* was executed about 1820. The pavement tiles date from the original foundation and are of ancient origin. To the right of the katholikon is the *Chapel of the Mother of God* (Theotokos), which was added in the 12C. This contains old *frescos* dating from the 12&13C (and rediscovered in 1958) which it is worth seeing: they include the *Mother of God* with the archangels Michael and Gabriel (behind the iconostasis, which dates from 1607); above this are Abraham and the three angels. There are also Byzantine frescos to be seen at the entrance to the 11C *refectory* (trapeza), depicting the *Passion* and the *Church councils*, which date from the 12C and the 14C respectively. It

Pátmos (Pátmos), ancient manuscripts from the monastery library

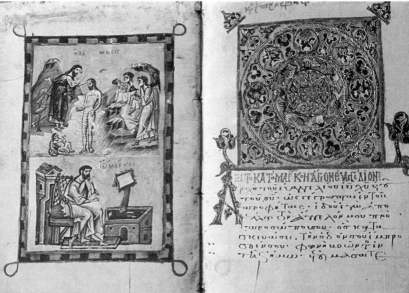

is worth seeing the old *marble tables and benches* which date from the original foundation. Five steps lead up from the refectory to the monks' cells, the treasury, and the library. The richly endowed *treasury*, which is said to be the most important monastic collection in Greece outside Mt.Athos, contains precious Byzantine and post-Byzantine *icons*, including the famous 11C *mosaic icon of St.Nicholas* which is set in a 13&14C silver frame, and the 12C icon showing *St.Theodoros*. There are also precious church vessels, church vestments dating from the 15–18C, the crown of Patriarch Grigórios (who was murdered by the Turks in 1821 in Constantinople), and the tiara of the 11C Emperor Alexios I. The *library* is also famous and houses precious *parchments* and old *codices*, including 33 leaves from the *Codex Porphyrius* which contains parts of St.Mark's Gospel, 247 leaves from the *Book of Job* with 8C illuminations, a MS. written in 941 of the *Discourses of St.Gregory of Nazianzus*, and various old gospels. The *deed of foundation* of the monastery displaying the golden seal (or golden Bull) of the Emperor Alexios I Komnenos and dating from 1088, is outstanding (its scroll is 24 ft. 4 in. long). Christodulos himself laid the foundations of the library, which is now unique, by bringing with him from his previous monastery at Miletus the manuscripts which he had saved from destruction by the Turks. It was above all this library which enabled Patmos to become an intellectual and spiritual centre of the E. Aegean (at times there were over 300 monks living in the monastery). The roof gardens offer a marvellous panoramic view of the whole island and the sea surrounding it. The modern *Khóra* grew up gradually around the foot of the monastery as a protected settlement for the married lay brothers (although at first no women at all had been allowed on Patmos). In the 16&17C its important fleet conferred on it an economic prosperity which is still reflected by the so-called *captains' houses*, imposing buildings several storeys high which appeared in the 16–19C, and by the more than 50 churches and chapels which are scattered through the town.

St. John's Cave (Spilaion Apokalypseos):

Pátmos, view from Khóra across the Bay of Grikou

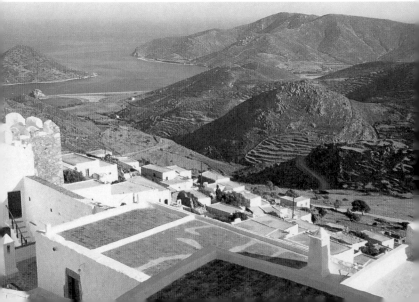

Beyond the town of Patmos in the direction of the port of Skala is the legendary *cave* where in AD 96 St.John is said to have had his visions of the end of the world and to have dictated them to his pupil Prochoros as the *Apocalypse*. A certain spot in the floor of the cave is known as St. John's pillow. The cave, which contains the so-called *Rock of the Trinity*, was converted into a church and furnished with precious decorations and icons and a 17C iconostasis. Apart from St.John's silver-framed 'pillow', one can also see the rock which was his 'desk'. Above this cave-church is the *Convent of the Apocalypse (Moni tis Apokalypseos)*, which was built in the 17C and includes a *Chapel of St. Anne* (the mother of the Virgin Mary) in memory of the Dowager Empress Anna, who was the mother of the founder of the convent. It was here that the famous theological college (and seminary) 'Patmias', was established in 1713: it produced some important theologians who were in touch with the theology and philosophy of the West.

Also worth seeing: In *Khóra* there are the Convent of *Zoodochos Pigi* (in the SW part of the town), which was built in 1607 in the typical style of island architecture, and the *Evangelismu* monastery, dating from 1936, which stands on the slope of Mt.Profitis Ilias (882 ft. high).

Environs: The port of *Skála* (population 1200) lies some 5 km. to the NW. of Khóra in a protected bay which opens to the E. The ancient city of *Patmos* was situated here, on *Kastelli hill*, where some insignificant ruins are preserved of the 4C BC *Acropolis* and some ancient *tombs*. It seems likely that there was an ancient *Sanctuary of Artemis* either here or on the site of the monastery. Some other traces of ancient times, including a *stairway* cut into the rock and leading down to the sea, have been discovered near *Pétra*, also known as

Kallikátsu/Grígos, to the SE of Khóra. The monastery's old farmland was near *Kámpos* (11 km. to the NE), in the fertile northern part of the island. Nearby was the *Monastery of the Panagia*, with its medicinal waters. There were also some slight traces of an ancient settlement (notably some remains of a temple) near here.

Pátra/Pátrai/Pátras/ΠΑΤΡΑΣ
Achaía/Peloponnese   p.294☐E 8

This lively port (population *c.* 112,000), the capital of the nome of Akhaía, is situated in the NW part of the Peloponnese, on the Gulf of Patras. After its destruction by the Turks in 1821, it was rebuilt in neoclassical style. It is now a commercial city, an important traffic junction (at which car ferries from Italy disembark), and the seat of a modern university.

History: A number of different communities or demoi united, around 1100 BC, to found the ancient city, which was called *Pátrai*. Some slight traces of a Mycenean settlement can still be found; however, it did not acquire any importance until the time of the Achaian Confederacy, *c.* 280 BC. Under the Romans (after AD 146), Pátrai became a port of transshipment to Italy. At the same time, the designation of 'Achaia' was extended from the province of that name to the whole of southern Greece (although Homer had described the Greeks in general as 'Achaians'). The Apostle Andrew, who is the city's patron saint, is supposed to have worked here around AD 60 and to have been crucified here. The 8–10C saw a period of Byzantine rule; later, in 1205, the Frankish principality of Achaía was established here. From 1408 until 1430, the city was ruled by the Venetians, and then, from 1460 onwards, by the Turks. Archbishop Germanos proclaimed the Greek War of Liberation from here in 1821. The city itself was liberated in 1828.

Roman Odeon (Agiu Georgiu Street): This is in the lower part of the town (kato polis), near the ancient agora (of which little has remained). It was built in the 1C AD and destroyed in the 3C; the *walls of the skene* were rebuilt fairly recently with doors and niches. There are some mosaic fragments. Excavations conducted nearby have revealed Hellenistic, Roman, and early Christian ruins and tombs, together with some mosaics.

Kastro (Akropolis): The fortress, or *Kastro*, was built in the Byzantine period (in the 9C) on top of the remains of an ancient Sanctuary of Zeus and Artemis. The northern *curtain wall* is Byzantine, as is the rectangular *keep* at the NE. end (at the top of the hill). This is encircled by a bridged moat, and was reinforced by the Palaiologi around 1430 by the addition of ramparts. The later fortifications (notably at the E. and S. ends) date from the Venetian and Turkish periods. The *main gate*, at the E. end, is crowned by a large Turkish tower. The fortress, which has now been converted into a park, offers a superb view over the city and the Gulf of Patras.

Archaeological Museum (Arkhaiologiko Musio): This contains interesting *sculptures* (part of which are fragments) showing scenes from the battle of the giants; a Roman Herakles; a classical statue of a woman; a mosaic depicting wrestling; a relief of Asklepios; a copy of a sculpture of Athena by Pheidias; and various fragments (notably heads and torsoes) of korai. On the first floor there is a *collection of vases* dating from the Mycenean until the Roman periods.

Also worth seeing: The Byzantine church of the *Pantokrator* (near the Kastro) is said to occupy the site of an ancient temple of Zeus. The church of *Ágios Andreas* (which is near the harbour and was built in 1836) houses St. Andrew's skull, which was brought here ceremonially in 1964 from Rome, where it had been kept for 500 years. The famous festival of St. Andrew is held here every 30 November.

Environs: The Venetian-Turkish fortress *Kastro Moria*, also known as the Castle of the Moréa, is situated some 10 km. to the NE near **Ríon** *(Rhíon)*, on the narrow strait (only 2 km. wide at this point) which leads into the Gulf of Corinth, from where the car ferry now crosses to Antírrion. The castle was built in 1400 and reinforced by Sultan Bajezid II in 1499. In the Middle Ages, the whole Peloponnese was called *Morea*, supposedly because of its mulberry trees. On the other side of the strait, on the mainland, is the fortress of **Kastro Rumelis** (Castle of the Rumeli), which dates from the 17C. The region of central Greece was known in medieval times as *Rumeli*, meaning 'country of the Romans'. The Byzantine **Girokomiu Monastery** (2.5 km. to the SW., in beautiful surroundings, and with a splendid view) was founded in the 9C and is one of the oldest in the Peloponnese. The picturesque mountain village of **Khalandrítsa** (22 km. to the SW.) lies beneath the foothills of Mt. Panakhaikon (c. 6,561 ft. high). Nearby there are some Byzantine and Frankish remains dating from the period of the Frankish barony (13C). The town of **Káto Akhaía** (24 km. to the SW., on the Gulf of Patras) is the site of the ancient *Dýme*, which played a part in the Akhaian Confederacy, and, later, of a Roman colony; but there are hardly any ancient remains. Some 13 km. NW from here, near the fishing village of **Áraxos**, can be seen the prehistoric acropolis *Kastro tis Kalurias*, which was already inhabited in Neolithic times. The *enceinte* has Cyclopean walls roughly 15 ft. thick which were restored in classical times; the date of their original construction is unclear. The main entrance, by means of a *gateway* set beneath a *tower*, is to the SE. In front of it are the *remains of an altar* which, according to an inscription dating from the 4 or 2C BC, was dedicated to Artemis and other deities, and shards from 9C BC vases. There is a second entrance, which has been walled in, in the middle of the front.

Pélla/ΠΕΛΛΑ
Pélla/Macedonia   p.290□F 3

Pélla lies on the road between Thessaloníki and Édessa and is the capital of the nome of Pélla. King Arkhelaos of Macedonia transferred his capital here in the 5C BC. Its zenith came during the reigns of Philip II and Alexander the Great. It was here that the tragedian Euripides (4C BC) lived out his last years. Pélla was, until the excavations conducted in Vergína in 1978, the most important archaeological site in northern Greece. However, very little of its ancient riches remains to be seen, since the city was captured and destroyed in 168 BC by the Roman consul Aemilius Paulus after his victory in the battle of Pydna. According to the ancient sources, it took him a whole day to display its plundered treasures during his triumphal procession in Rome.

Before its seizure by the Romans, the treasure was kept on a small island which was near the city and connected to it by a bridge. The appearance of the area has greatly changed since then as a result of the alluvium deposited by the river Axios, so that the city, which in ancient times was on the coast, now lies well inland. Fragments of massive *walls* dating from classical times have been found on the site of what was once this island, to left and right of the road from Thessaloníki.

There are various ancient ruins (including living quarters, an old wall, and a stoa) on the road to Palaiá Pélla (about 130 yards to the left of the road).

Acropolis: There are actually two, one on the site of the ancient Pélla, and the other, which has not yet been excavated, farther to the W.

Pélla, house of the lion hunt

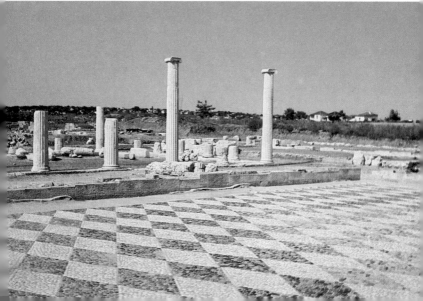

'House of the Lion Hunt': This is the most impressive building in the excavations at Pélla and takes its name from the subject depicted in its floor mosaic. It measures 164 ft. x 328 ft. and has three open courts, a room with a *floor mosaic*, and a central court with a peristyle of six Ionic columns on each side.

Museum *(Arkhaiologiko Musio):* There are various displays worth seeing, notably the remarkable *floor mosaic* from Block I., which is made of natural pebbles of different colours and dates from the Hellenistic period. It depicts a lion hunt (archaeologists believe it represents General Krateros rescuing Alexander during his lion hunt near Susa), a pair of centaurs, a griffin eating a deer, Dionysos riding a leopard, and other hunting scenes. Three other mosaics, depicting the battle of the Amazons, a deer hunt, and Theseus's abduction of Deianeira, are worth seeing. The museum also contains many sculptures, including a marble dog (460 BC), bronze statuettes (notably one of Poseidon, which is a Hellenistic copy), and a small bronze statue of a horseman dating from the 5C BC. The *coin collection* and the many architectural fragments are also interesting.

Environs: On the right-hand side of the road from Pélla to Édessa (2.5 km.) is the *Spring of Alexander the Great*, where he is said to have watered his horse Bukephalos. The *Via Egnatia*, a Roman road, passed by here.

Pentéli/Pentelikón/ΠΕΝΤΕΛΙ
Attica   p.296☐H 8

The Attic plain is separated at its NE end from the Plain of Marathon by Mt.Pentelikon, now called Mt.Penteli (3610 ft. high), which is the site of ancient marble quarries.

History: The slopes of Mt.Pentelikon were inhabited in ancient times by a considerable number of old Attic demoi or village communities which belonged to Athens's sphere of influence. Its rich reserves of the marble which made it famous began to be quarried about 570 BC. The main buildings of classical Athens (notably the acropolis) were built of this ferruginous and finely-grained Pentelic marble, which differed from the white Parian marble in that it acquired, with age, a honey-coloured yellow tint. The quarries were exploited until the Roman period, and some mining is still carried out today in the Valley of Dionysos to the north.

Penteli Monastery (Moni Pentelis): This is worth seeing. It lies beyond *Néa* and *Palaiá Pentéli* (meaning respectively New and Old Penteli), and was built in 1578 on the S. slope (1,378 ft. high) of Mt.Pentelikon. The church, which was restored in 1858, is Byzantine and has *frescos* in the narthex dating from 1233 and depicting parables from the Bible. It contains some fine 17C *paintings* and *icons*, and there is a fine *reliquary* in the sanctuary (which is also decorated with 16C paintings). The *bell tower* and the lovely *cloister* of this once wealthy monastery are more recent. There are still monks living here.

Environs: Nearby there can be seen the ruins of the *marble castle* known as *Kastello Rododafni* or 'castle of the oleanders', which was built in the 19C in neo-gothic style by Kleanthis for the Duchess of Piacenza. **Ancient marble quarries** (45 minutes walk NW. from the monastery; some 2,300 ft. up): These can be reached on foot by an ancient paved way. To the NE of the largest quarry, beneath a rock, is the entrance to a *cave with stalactites* (*speleia* means 'cave') in whose wall a Byzantine double-headed eagle has been carved: this was an early Christian place of worship. The old quarries still contain ancient building blocks, including the *drums of columns*, which had turned out to be flawed and had been abandoned. They can also still show us the ancient techniques of quarrying, by means of which the stone was hewn, polished, and transported down the valley. The *summit of Mt.Penteli* (3,638 ft.) can be reached by a 1 ¼ hours' walk from the quarries. It affords a magnificent view over the whole of Attica. In ancient times, a statue of Athena, the patron goddess of Attica, stood on the peak known as *Brilettos*. Although the S. face of Mt.Penteli has been disfigured by the quarries, the N. slope is covered with pine forests which lend it an idyllic beauty (see Diónysos).

Phaistós/Festós/ΦΑΙΣΤΟΣ
Iráklion/Crete   p.298 ☐ G 14

The ruins of Phaistós occupy a splendid site on a hill 60 km. to the S. of Iráklion, in the middle of Crete. The view stretches across the blooming expanse of the plain of Messára, then passes to the huge massif of Mt.Ida (Psilorítis) in the N., and finally westwards down to the bay in the Gulf of Messara. Even today the ruins of Phaistós have a majestic look about them. Not only their size, but also their clear and harmonious proportions allow us to guess something of the brilliance, the added awareness of being alive, which distinguished the ancient inhabitants of this place.

According to legend, the palace at Phaistós was founded by Rhadamanthys, who was one of the sons of Zeus and Europa. (The other two were Minos and Sarpedon. Minos ruled at Knossós, Sarpedon at Mália, and Rhadamanthys at Phaistós). He is said to have visited the cave of Zeus every nine years and to have brought back with him new laws which he then enforced

throughout his kingdom. The laws of Górtyna were also supposed to have originated from him.

Archaeology and history: The Italian School of Archaeology in Athens has been excavating the ruins of Phaistós since 1900. Its work has established the existence here, just as in Knossós, of two palaces, of which the second, which lasted from about 1650 to 1400 BC, had been built on top of the remains of the first, which had stood there from about 2000 until 1650 BC; however, the two can be more easily distinguished here than in Knossós. In fact, recent excavations have discovered two more palaces on the site, of even greater antiquity. In any event, it is certain that Phaistós was settled in the Neolithic. Several phases of construction can be distinguished in both the Minoan palaces, each of which can still be clearly recognized. The first one must originally have been destroyed in a great fire, then rebuilt, then devastated once again, this time by an earthquake. It was then rebuilt again, only to be destroyed almost entirely by a combination of fire and earthquake around 1650 BC.

The second palace was then built over the ruins of the first, but around 1400 it too was destroyed. Parts of the old palace can still be clearly identified in the W., NW., and SW. areas of the site. Several houses have now been excavated which show that the palace was originally surrounded by a trench.

Phaistós was resettled after 1400, and was still of some importance even in classical Greek times (as is shown by the remains of a Greek *temple of Rhea* to the SW). It was later destroyed by Górtyna.

The palace is smaller than the one at Knossós; but, since it has been left as it was, it is also more impressive, and its peaceful and harmonious proportions are more powerfully affecting. Like all large Minoan palaces, it is arranged around a

Phaistós, lay-out of the palace 1 N. courtyard; the foundation walls are Hellenistic **2** remains of Hellenistic and Roman earthworks **3** steps from the neopalatial period **4** main staircase from the neopalatial period **5** W. courtyard; here, where the theatre was situated, there are traces of building from almost every period from Neolithic onwards **6** neopalatial orthostat wall **7** neopalatial propylon and steps **8** purification bath from neopalatial times **9** protopalatial megaron **10** store rooms from neopalatial period **11** room of the columns (neopalatial) **12** altar **13** conneting corridor (neopalatial) **14** small courtyard (neopalatial) **15** queen's megaron (neopalatial) **16** large columned hall with open courtyard (neopalatial) **17** cult pool **18** king's megaron (neopalatial) **19** protopalatial archive room where the celebrated discus was found **20** sections of buildings from the protopalatial period **21** neopalatial washroom **22** neopalatial workshops **23** E. courtyard, where a metal smelting furnace was discovered **24** private rooms for the royal children (neopalatial) **25** small neopalatial courtyard with porticoes **26** central courtyard, where bull games etc. took place **27** well **28** neopalatial crypt with square pillars **29** neopalatial rest room **30** passage between W. and central courtyards **31** section of wall between the passageway and the row of chambers **32** store rooms **33** passage between the store rooms **34** main entrance from the protopalatial period, where remains of a still older propylaion were found **35** protopalatial chamber **36** protopalatial corridor **37** protopalatial bastion **38** early Palatial corridor **39** large protopalatial chamber **40** ramp which led from the original S. courtyard round the bastion and through a corridor (36) to the upper palace **41** protopalatial orthostat **42** protopalatial bedroom **43** protopalatial store rooms **44** protopalatial room with seats **45** stairs which led through a corridor to protopalatial chamber (44) **46** remains of a pre-Mycenean structure **47** Temple of Rhea from Greek times

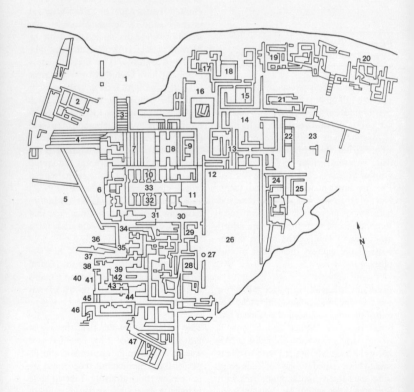

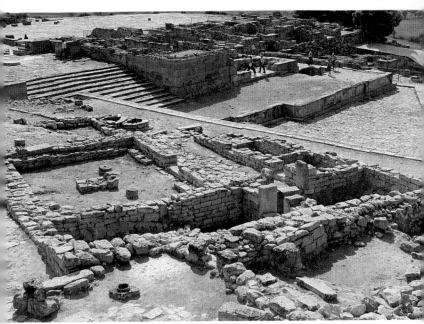

Phaistós, view over the palace area

Phaistós, ancient bath

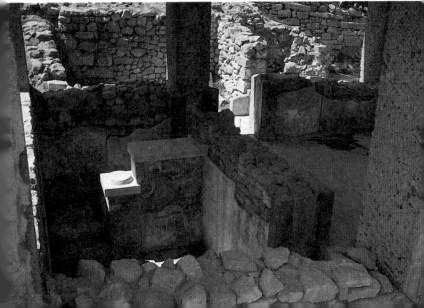

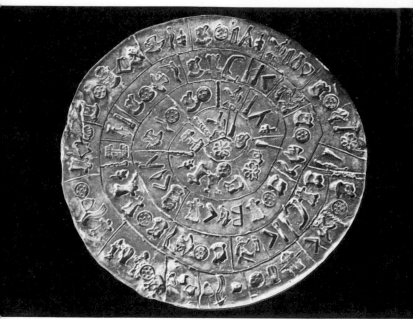

Phaistós, the 'Phaistós discus' (Nat.Mus.Iráklion)

central courtyard. The SE. part long ago collapsed and is now hard to identify because it has been farmed over.

The *royal apartments* are at the N. end. The steep acropolis must even then have offered its inhabitants a stunning view. In front of the excavations there is a tourist pavilion, and one's tour of the site starts from here, beginning at its NW end. The most interesting piece discovered here is the so-called *Phaistós disc*, dating from about 1650 BC, which was found in 1908 in the NE area of the site. This is a disc of fired clay, 16 cm. in diameter. Both sides are covered by hieroglyphs, which are grouped in 61 different sections and can be broken down into 45 separate characters. The technique whereby the characters have been stamped on to the disc with the help of matrices can be regarded as the oldest form of printing in Europe. The hi-

eroglyphs run around the disc, whether from the outside inwards to the centre or vice versa, and comprise clearly recognizable symbols (for example, fish, ram, beetle, house, ship, flower, the sun, the human head) each of which appears several times. They have not yet been deciphered. The disc is now in the Archaeological Museum in Iráklion, together with other finds from Phaistós, such as Linear-A tablets, ritual objects and ceramics (some of which are very old), sacrificial tables, figures of animals, pithoi, jugs, vases, cups, and so on.

Environs: Ágios Ioánnis: Behind this village stands the small 14C church of *Ágios Pavlos*, which one can reach by taking the footpath from Phaistós to Mátala. The church is Byzantine and built of quarry-stone; its harmonious proportions

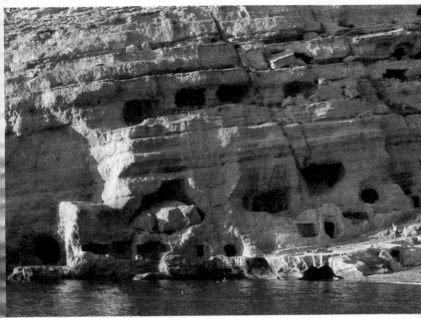

Mátala (Phaistós), cliff caves

make it very beautiful. **Mátala:** 11 km. SW of Phaistós (16 km. by road). This was the ancient Metallon, which was once the port used by Górtyna, and presumably also by Phaistós. According to legend, Zeus assumed the form of a bull to abduct Europa, the daughter of King Agenor of Phoenix, and bring her to these shores. He then changed into an eagle and fathered Minos, Rhadamanthys, and Sarpedon, the future kings of the Minoans. Not only Zeus and Europa seem to have liked the picturesque Bay of Mátala, for it has been inhabited since time immemorial. The bay is lined by high sandstone cliffs containing many *caves* which lie in horizontal rows, with a narrow rock-path running in front of them and connecting the caves in the same row. In this way, the cliffs look like a multi-storeyed block of flats. The caves have always been popular, for many of them are potentially equipped with several rooms and even fireplaces and niches where people could sleep. Indeed, they are said to have been used, from time to time, as living quarters and as burial places.

Phigalía/ΦΙΓΑΛΕΙΑ
Elis/Peloponnese   p.294☐E 10

This town (which is 5 km. to the S. of Bássai) is set in the middle of some impressive mountain country. The view from here stretches as far as the W. coast of the Peloponnese.

Ancient city: Above the modern Phigalía are the remains of the ancient city, including an *agora*, a *Temple of Dionysos Akratophoros*, and the *tomb of the men of*

Oresthasion. The *Sanctuary of Eurynome* was situated on a terrace outside the city walls. (Eurynome was one of the daughters of Tethys and Okeanos).

Environs: A difficult walk of 3 hours leads to the waterfalls of *Aspra Nera* ('white water') and the **Gorge of the Neda**, which is only passable when the river-bed is dry. Near the gorge is the Sacred Precinct of the Black Demeter, who used to be depicted as having a horse's head. Neda was thought to be one of the entrances to the underworld. **Mt.Lykaion** (about 3 hours' climb) is named after Lykaion, son of Pelasgos and Kyllene, who was the mythical king of Arkadia. Legend relates that Zeus once appeared to Lykaion in disguise while he was travelling through Arkadia. Lykaion and his sons, in order to discover whether he was a man or a god, served him the flesh of a child. Zeus punished the whole family, killing all his sons and turning Lykaion himself into a wolf. Pausanias reports that human sacrifices were still being made in his life-time (2C AD) during which everyone present would eat a portion of the flesh. One should visit the *altar* mentioned by Pausanias as well as the *stadium* and *hippodrome*, in which the Lycaean Games were held.

Philippi / ΦΙΛΙΠΠΟΙ
Kavála / Macedonia   p.292☐I 2

The ancient city was originally founded in the 4C BC by the Athenian Kallistratos, who gave it the name of *Krinides*. Its gold mines ensured that it would develop rapidly. In 356 BC it was captured and fortified against the Thracians by King Philip of Macedonia, who renamed it after himself. A century after the fall of the Macedonian state, Philippi was made famous by the battle in which Mark Antony and Octavian defeated Brutus and Cassius, the assassins of Julius Caesar. The victors then converted the old Greek settlement into a Roman colony, putting up their new buildings on the foundations of the old ones, which were now destroyed. In AD 49, St. Paul visited the city, where he taught and

Philippi, basilica B and forum

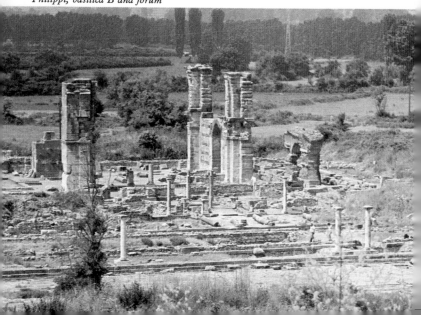

founded the first Christian community in Europe. It was here, too, that, he and Silas were cast into prison. A number of Christian churches were erected later on the sites of ancient buildings.

Forum (left of the main road from Kavála to Dráma): This dates from the reign of the Emperor Marcus Aurelius (161–180) and was the centre of the Roman city. The floor was paved with marble. Access was gained through three archways, and there were porticoes on three sides. The forum also contained two temples at its edges.

The decumanus passed in front of the forum, dividing the city in two and extending on both sides beyond the city into the Via Egnatia. At the W. end of the city stood the Amphipolis Gate, with the Via Egnatia beyond it. 2 km. to the W. of the Amphipolis Gate stood an arch, built at the beginning of the 1C AD, which marked the line of the pomerium (the religious boundary of a Roman city). At the N. end of the forum, next to the decumanus, can be seen the remains of a *tribune* and an *Ionic building*. There are numerous Latin inscriptions on the floor. There are several buildings in the same area, of which the oldest (near the S. stoa of the forum) dates from the Augustan period.

Basilica A: This dates from the end of the 5C and is situated just beyond the NW corner of the forum. It has a nave and two aisles, a transept, and a semicircular apse where the Bishop's throne or synthronon was kept. Another basilica is being excavated to the W. of Basilica A. Its screen and ambo (or pulpit) have been discovered.

Basilica B: This dates from the 6C AD and is situated to the S. of the forum. It consists of a narthex, the main part of the church (comprising a nave and two aisles), a baptisterion, and a diakonikon (which comprises two rooms).

Acropolis: The hill of the acropolis rises to the right of the main road. Its buildings (dating from the 10C AD) were erected on the ruins of those built in the 4C BC by Philip II.

Ancient theatre: At the foot of the acropolis and to the right of the main road is the ancient theatre, dating originally from the 4C BC. It was reconstructed in the Roman period, when it acquired its present shape. In the 3C AD it was used for combats between gladiators and against wild animals. In the present day, it provides the setting for classical dramas which are put on here each August within the framework of the Festival of Philippi-Thásos.

Archaeological Museum (*Archaiologiko Musio*): This is a small museum, set on the right of the main road, which contains many interesting objects discovered in the area.

Also worth seeing: In front of Basilica B there was a **palaistra** dating from the 2C BC. Nearby were a small **amphitheatre** and the **latrines** (which are still well

Philippi, Corinthian capital

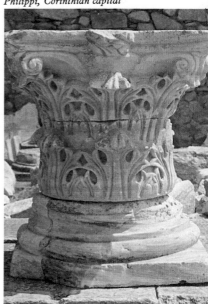

preserved). To the right of the main road there are stairs leading down to a kind of **crypt** (which was once a Roman cistern). Tradition has it that this was the site of St. Paul's prison.

Pílion/Mt.Pélion/ΠΗΛΙΟΝ
Magnisía/Thessaly   p.294☐ G 6

This long mountain range (whose main summit is 5,416 ft. high) occupies the peninsula separating the Gulf of Volós (also called the Pagasitic Gulf) from the Aegean Sea to the E., and extends to the N. as far as Mt.Ossa.

History: Greek myths present Mt.Pélion as the home of the centaurs (wild beasts having the upper part of a human and the lower part of a horse; they were a favourite theme in classical art). The centaurs, who descended from Ixion, King of the Lapiths, and the fairy Nephele (the word means 'cloud'), were the embodiment of brutality and lechery. One exception was

Philippi, theatre, Mars relief

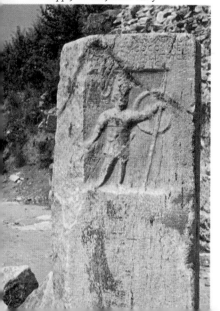

the wise centaur Cheiron (Chiron), who was venerated as having discovered the art of medicine (healing and herbal medicine). Asklepios, the god of medicine, was said to have acquired his knowledge from him. Chiron was also the tutor of Jason and Achilles and the friend of Achilles's father Peleus. This mountainous region enjoyed no great importance in ancient times, and did not do so until the period of Turkish occupation, notably the 18C, when the inaccessible mountain villages banded together to form wider organizations which became a stronghold of the renascent Greek nation. It was essentially these associations, together with their secret 'Greek schools', which gave the post-1821 independence struggle its spiritual force. Their financial support was provided by the local silk producers and weavers, who by the 17&18C had achieved a considerable prosperity; indeed, the residences built at that time for the powerful families of the day still survive in many villages around here. Nowadays, this region, with its lovely scenery and woodlands, is a popular holiday resort for the people of Vólos.

Zagorá (47 km. NE. of Vólos): This is a municipality consisting of four parts, which is situated on a mountain crest 1,640 ft. high (Zagorá means 'mountain pass'). In the 17&18C it became the effective capital of the villages around Mt.Pílion, and indeed, thanks to its 'freedom schools', a centre of Greek culture; its large *library* (Ellinomusio) possesses rare manuscripts which are still extant. It is worth seeing the *houses* built for the eminent families of the day, including the Konstantinidis, Prinkos, Kassavetis, and Papastathis families. Also of interest are the chruch of *Ágios Georgios*, which contains works of popular art, the basilica of *Agia Kyriaki*, which has beautiful panelling, and *Agia Paraskevi*, which has an excellent carved wooden iconostasis. (All three churches are 17C). The town affords a marvellous view over the port of

Khorevtó (5 km.) and the whole Aegean coast. Near the village of *Purí (Puríon)*, 8 km. N. of Zagorá, one can see the remains of an archaic-Doric *temple* and some ancient houses.

Kissós (59 km. NE. of Vólos): This charming mountain village overlooks the NE. coast and offers a superb view over the port of *Ágios Ioánnis* and the Aegean. It contains the beautiful church of *Agia Marina* (dating from 1802) which has frescos painted by Pagonis and also some attractive icons on the wall behind the altar.

Tsangaráda (50 km. E. of Vólos): This mountain village is made up of four parts and situated at a height of 1,640 ft. amidst oak and chestnut forests. Some of its houses are built in the popular style, some are neoclassical. There is a beautiful view down to the sea and the coastal town of Mylopótamos nearby. The village of *Murési* (between Tsangaráda and Kissós) contains some old houses and paved streets, and the 18C churches of Agia Triada and the Panagia.

Miliés (29 km. SE. of Vólos): This lovely inland town was also a stronghold of Greek culture during the Turkish occupation. One can still see some *mansions*, the old library, the old freedom school (now restored), the churches of *Agia Triada* (which has post-Byzantine frescos) and *Ágios Athanasios* (which houses a good library), and finally the church of the *Taxiarchis*, with its fine iconostasis. Nearby, a little to the S., are the remains of the ancient settlement of *Korópe*, which contains the ruins of a temple (with a peribolos built in tufa) and some votive inscriptions which belonged to a sanctuary of Apollo (towards Afétes). The village of *Vysítsa*, which has some fine 19C mansions, is also near here.

Drákia (18 km. E. of Vólos): This mountain village, 1,640 ft. up, may derive its

name from the word for 'dragon', which in modern Greek fairytales resemble the centaurs of ancient myth, and thus ultimately from the centaurs themselves, who were supposed to live nearby. It is worth seeing the *house* of the Triantafyllos family which is richly decorated inside. The small church of *Ágios Georgios* contains frescos by the 19C painter Pagonis. On the village square there is a *memorial* to the resistance fighters who were executed during the German occupation. There is a paved path from here to the village of *Khánia*, which stands at the head of a pass, 3,937 ft. high (it is planned to introduce a cable car). On the road to *Agriá* (which is on the W. coast), near *Anemútsa*, can be seen the Church of the Cross (Stavros), which contains an interesting iconostasis (which has been carved and painted).

Portariá (14 km. NE of Vólos): This is the favourite resort of people from Vólos. It stands 1,970 ft. up and contains several *mansions* (including those of the Sulia and Tsopotu families), the *Sisaki house*, the church of *Ágios Nikólaos* (on the village square), which has niche reliefs in the popular style, the chapel of *Agii Anargyri* (which contains examples of popular art), and a 13C monastery. From here there is a climb through lovely beech forests to the summit of Mt.Pílion (5,417 ft.). The summit offers a magnificent view over the regions of Magnisia and Euboea and Mts.Ossa and Olympos. The wise centaur Chiron was supposed to have lived here in a cave. Beneath this peak, the pass of Khánia (3,940 ft.) links the eastern and western parts of Mt.Pílion. The mountain village of *Makrynítsa* (3 km. NW. of Portariá), which stands 2,625 ft. up, contains old, half-timbered *mansions* with wooden carvings and carved balconies. The *Museum of Popular Art* (Laografiko Musio) is accommodated in the Topali House. It is also worth seeing the old churches of the *Agia Panagia* (dating from 1272), *Ágios*

Ioánnis (on the main square), *Ágios Athanasios, Ágios Georgios* and *Agia Magdalini*. The niches in these churches contain stone reliefs in the popular style. there are also some fine stone reliefs on the *village fountain* in the square and pictures by the painter *Theophilos* (1868–1934).

Áno Vólos (4 km. NE. of Vólos): This is a pretty little medieval town on the slopes of Mt.Pílion which has a lovely view down to the port of Vólos and the Gulf. On Episkopi hill can be seen the old church of *Agii Theodori* which has Byzantine reliefs (depicting St. Michael, the Madonna, and Christ) and some old frescos. The *Kontú house* contains some interesting frescos by Theophilos, who was born and died on Lesbos and achieved world fame as an artist painting in the popular or naive genre.

Towns also worth seeing: On the S. prong of the southern part of the peninsula are the well preserved old villages of **Metókhi** (*c.* 44 km. SE. of Vólos) and **Argalastí** (42 km. SE.), which contains an 18C monastery and has a marvellous view over the Gulf above **Milína** (54 km. to the SE). The charming village of **Trikéri** (Trikérion), on the extreme SW. point of Pílion, can only be reached by ship from Vólos. It contains some well-preserved houses in the style typical of the region, and is famous for the colourful old folk costumes which are worn on feast-days. On the Trikéri promontory is the attractive *Monastery of the Panagia* (where it is possible to stay).

Piraiás/Piraeus/ΠΕΙΡΑΙΑΣ

Attica   p.294□H 9

Piraeus (Piraiás in modern Greek) has today regained its position as the main port of Greece and one of the most important Mediterranean ports. The city has grown as fast as Athens and now embraces some 500,000 inhabitants (the combined populations of Athens and Piraeus come to about 3 million). Both the ancient and the modern port centred on a tongue of land (the peninsula known as Akti) which has three natural harbours on either side of it. The port is about 10 km. from the centre of Athens and can be reached by the underground ('elektriko' in Greek), of which Piraeus is the W. terminus.

History: Apart from some Neolithic remains discovered on the Kastella hill, the known history of Piraeus begins in earnest around 510 BC when the same Kastella hill (*c.* 285 ft.; also known as Munykhia) was fortified. Around 493 BC, Themistokles decided that Piraeus should be the site of Athens's main port (also its naval harbour), and laid out a new city with streets intersecting each other at right angles, according to the design of Hippodamos of Miletus. Defensive walls and moles were constructed. After the victory over the Persians, the 'Long Walls' (some 5 miles long) were built, guaranteeing secure access from Athens by means of a protected corridor (as well as a place of refuge). The southernmost 'leg' (for the long walls were imagined as Athens's legs stretching to the sea) extended as far as the ancient square of Phaleron (Faliron) on Phaleron Bay (where the Kephissos river debouches). The Long Walls were razed by the Spartans during the Peloponnesian war, around 404 BC, but were rebuilt again ten years later by Konon (in 394 BC). Piraeus reached the peak of its ancient prosperity as a port and centre of commerce during the 5&4C BC; but then, during the Hellenistic and Roman periods (notably after it was destroyed by Sulla in 86 BC) it was overshadowed by the free ports of Alexandria, Delos and Rhodes. In the Middle Ages the place was practically deserted, having dwindled to a little fishing village. (The Venetians called it *Porto Leone* after the ancient lion which stood at the entrance to the harbour until they removed it and placed it in front of the Arsenal in Venice). After the country had won its freedom from Turkish rule, Piraeus, like Athens, grew very quickly, so that it was soon repopulated and restored to its old position as the main port of Greece. Today, it is the focus of the operations of all the Greek shipping lines (having replaced the port on the island of Syros in this respect) and the most important industrial city in the country, enjoying administrative autonomy.

Main harbour (Kentriko Limani): This is the biggest and most important harbour, occupying the inner part of the NW bay, which, of the three bays, constitutes the deepest inlet. It was well-known as a commercial port (emporion) in ancient times, when it was called Kantharos (meaning 'goblet' or 'vessel') because of its enclosed appearance. Its N. end (where Karaiskakis Square stands today) was the site of Perikles's large granaries (the makrai stoai) and also the centre of the ancient commercial port. Today, this is the docking area for ships bound for the Cyclades and the islands in the Saronic Gulf. The area near the last dock to the NW. was in ancient times a marsh (which the walls of Themistokles and Konon traversed). Near the modern Lárissa Station (to the W.) there was a temple of Aphrodite Euploia, the goddess of sea journeys (it was built around 394 BC, but no trace of it remains). The small Etionia peninsula to the NW has some slight traces on it of the wall of Konon as well as two round towers which belonged to the Aphrodision Gate; the wall of Themistokles passed 220 yards to the NW. At the NW and SW outlets from the main harbour, there were docks for warships (of which some slight traces are preserved), ship-sheds, in which triremes were kept during the winter and repaired, and some arsenals (of which virtually nothing has survived). The harbour of Kan-

tharos occupies an area of nearly half a square mile and is up to 36 ft. deep.

Zea harbour, or **Pasalimani** (which means 'Pasha's harbour'): Zea harbour (nowadays called Pasalimani) lies to the SW. of the main harbour, on the other side of the Akti peninsula. This natural harbour, almost round in shape, was converted into a proper naval base by Themistokles's addition of strong walls and moles which almost closed it off and could actually do so with the help of chains. It could take up to 200 triremes (warships with three rows of oarsmen and a battering-ram om the bow). During the winter, ships which needed protection were docked and repaired in ship-sheds on the shore. Some remains of these can be seen in the water near the shore, notably in the E. and W. areas of the bay. There were some 196 ship-sheds (known in ancient Greek as neosoikos, which has been corrupted in modern Greek to neosikos, meaning 'dock'); each was about 130 ft. long and 21 ft. wide, and all were connected to each other by rows of columns which supported the roof. To the NW. was the large arsenal (skeuotheke, or skevothiki in modern Greek), built by Philon around 340 BC, where the ships' rigging was kept.

Today Zea harbour is the main yacht marina in Greece, and its inner and outer basins can accommodate and provide supply facilities for about 350 yachts (and also hydrofoils).

Mikrolímano (also called Turkolímano): This is the smallest of the three harbours, situated to the SE of the other two, with the Bay of Fáliron beyond it. It lies at the foot of Munýchia hill and was known as Munýchia harbour in antiquity. Its moles render it almost wholly circular. The remains of some 82 ship-sheds, where triremes could be housed, can still be seen in the water near the shore. Today this picturesque yacht marina is well-known for its numerous fish restaurants. A little farther on, close to the *Bay of Fáliron*, is the *memorial* to General Karaiskakis, one of the heroes of the independence struggle, who was killed here in 1827. The stadium nearby is named after him.

Munychia acropolis (now called *Kastella hill*): *Munýchia hill* (now called *Kastella hill*) rises about 285 ft. above Mikrolimano harbour, offering a magnificent view of Piraeus, Athens, and the coast. This was the oldest part of ancient Piraeus. There was an old sanctuary of Artemis Munychia here. The Attic month corresponding with the modern April was called Munychion after her because it was during that month that the spring festival known as the Artemisia was held. Unfortunately, as throughout Piraeus, virtually no ancient ruins are preserved, since they were built over during the reconstruction in the 19C. The only exception are the remains of strong *fortified walls*, 13 ft. high, which were excavated to the NW. of the church of Ágios Ilias. There was also an ancient *theatre* here, which has been taken over by the modern Veakia open-air theatre.

On the part of the hill overlooking the area between Mikrolimano and the Zea harbour there are some slight remains of a *sanctuary of Asklepios (Asklipíon)*, fragments of whose bas-relief are in the museum.

On the coast there are remains of *baths* which were hollowed out of the rock and are nowadays called the *caves of Zenon (spiláio Zínonos)*. Nearby is the place called *Freattyda*, which is supposed to have been the site of the ancient *Serangeion*, where murderers were tried.

Ancient city: The remains of the ancient town are very largely lost because the modern city has been built on top of them. However, the ancient rectangular street plan designed by Hippodamos was essentially retained by the Bavarian architect Schaubert and the Greek Kleanthis when they rebuilt the city in the 19C. The *Akti* peninsula also had a rectangular street plan, in ancient as in modern times, which was, however, set at an angle to the grid of the rest of the city. There are remains here, in some places, of the *wall of Themistokles*, which traversed this area, protecting the rest of the city from invasion from the sea. To the NW of Zea harbour, near the Archeological Museum in Filellínon Street, there are some slight remains of a Hellenistic *theatre* dating from the 2C BC which was a copy of the Theatre of Dionysos in Athens. On the coast of the Akti peninsula, which has a lovely view of the sea, there are a few traces of the *sea-wall* of Konon (built around 393 BC.

Near the station (to the SE. of the main harbour) there are some remains of the *Asty Gate* (meaning 'city gate') and of the Northern Long Wall which began beyond it.

Archaeological Museum (Arkhaiologiko Musio, 38 Filellínon, near Zea harbour): This contains objects dating from the classical, Hellenistic, and Roman periods, which were discovered in and around Piraeus. These include a number of interesting *tomb reliefs* dating from the 4, 3&2C, notably the *stele* of Chairedemos and Lykeas, warrior of Salamis (dating from around 410 BC. There are also *bronze weapons* fashioned in the 6&5C BC; a *statue* of Aphrodite Euploia; Roman *portraits* and *statues of emperors*; a relief depicting the shield of Athena Parthenos (this is the so-called Piraeus Relief, which dates from the reign of Hadrian and is in neo-Attic style); a *figure of Hermes* which was discovered in 1959 (the bronze statues of Apollo and Artemis which were found at the same time are now in the National Museum in Athens); and black and red figure *ceramics*, dating from the 6&5C BC.

Naval Museum (Navtiko Musio, Freattyda Street, facing Zea harbour): This interesting museum provides a picture of Greek naval history from ancient times until the present day. there are *models* of ancient and modern ships, *busts* of the admirals who played their part in the liberation struggle of 1821, old *uniforms*, and *pictures* of sea-battles. The museum also incorporates part of the wall of Themistokles.

Environs: The Bay of **Fáliron** (*Phaleron* in ancient Greek) was the original and oldest anchorage for Athenian ships until the harbour was constructed at Piraeus. Its sandy bay was a favourite swimming resort for the people of Athens until industrialization began here at the end of the 19C. The beaches are now heavily polluted.

Plataiai/Plataia/ΠΛΑΤΑΙΑΙ
Boeotia/Central Greece   p.294☐G 8

Plataia is situated some 16 km. to the SW. of Thebes. It became famous after the third and most important battle between the Greeks and the Persians, the first in which the Persian army was decisively defeated, had been fought near here. The battle took place on the northern foothills of Mt.Kithairon, near the river Asopos and very close to the modern village of Kókkla, in 479 BC. With the notable exception of Thebes, the Greek cities had united their forces to face the common enemy. Mardonios, the commander of the Persian army (some 300,000 strong), chose as his battleground the area around the river. The Greek forces, totalling some 110,000 men, were divided into three groups, Athenians, Spartans, and Peloponnesians, but came under the overall command of Pausanias, King of Sparta. He at first intended to meet the enemy to the N. of the Asopos valley. For eleven days there were some minor skirmishes. When Pausanias then changed his mind and the Greeks moved to take up

new positions, Mardonios took advantage of this situation to begin his attack. Herodotus has given us a vivid picture of the battle. Once Mardonios had been killed in the fighting by a Spartan soldier, the Persians panicked and fled. The victorious Greeks shared between themselves the booty which the Persians left behind, including Mardonios's sumptuous tent.52 years later, in 427 BC, Plataia was captured, after two years of siege, by the Thebans and Spartans. This restored Thebes to its predominant position in the Boeotian Confederacy.

There are virtually no remains left of the ancient city. The circular *city wall* of ancient Plataia, which had a circumference of some 2.5 miles, can be seen to the E., before one enters the modern village. There are some remains of a sanctuary which was probably dedicated to Hera near the NW area of the wall. No trace is left of the old temple of Demeter.

Póros (I)/ΠΟΡΟΣ
Saronic Islands/Aegean Islands p.294☐G/H 10

Póros (11.6 sq. miles; population 4,300) lies at the S. end of the Saronic Gulf and is today a favourite holiday resort. The strait between Póros and the mainland, which has given the island its name ('poros' means 'ford'), is only 280 yards wide.

History: The island was settled by Mycenean times. (It was known in antiquity as *Kalaúreia (Kalávia)*, which provides the setting for Hölderlin's novel 'Hyperion'). After the 7C BC it became the religious centre of a defensive amphiktyonic alliance of states in the Saronic Gulf. It lost its importance after Athens and Aegina developed their sea power in the 6&5C. Many Albanians settled here in the 17C AD.

Póros (population 4, 000): This town,

which was founded in the late Middle Ages, lies on the strait (which is only 280 yards wide), opposite the town of Galatás on the mainland. Its brilliant white houses have helped to make it a favourite holiday resort. The cruiser 'Averoff', which owes its fame to the events of 1912, during the Balkan Wars, is moored in the bay, beneath the Naval School established in 1856.

Environs: *Monastery of the Panagía* (in Zoodóchos Pigi, which means 'life-receiving spring', 8 km. E.): It is worth seeing the gilded wood iconostasis from Asia Minor. There are some beautiful icons of the Virgin Mary in quasi-Italian style. The courtyard contains the tombs of Admirals Apostolis and Tombasis, who played a part in the struggle for liberation in 1821. *Sanctuary of Poseidon* (in the middle of the island, some 15 km. away): This was the seat of the cult at the centre of the amphiktyonic confederacy of the Saronic Islands. The ruins were discovered in 1894. One can still see the foundation trenches of the old *Temple of Poseidon* (built in the 6C BC. Just to the W. was the starting point of the

Sacred Way (of which only some remains of the foundations are preserved) leading to the ancient city of *Kalaúreia.* It was here, in 322 BC, that Demosthenes took his life while fleeing from the Macedonians.

Pórto Germenó/ΠΟΡΤΟ ΓΕΡΜΕΝΟ
Attica/Central Greece   p.294☐G 8

This small swimming resort and harbour is situated some 71 km. to the NW. of Athens on the Kolpos Alkyonidon or Halkyonic Gulf, the easternmost bay of the Gulf of Corinth.

History: Legend relates that Halkyone (Alkyone) was so grief-stricken after the death at sea of her husband Keyx, the king of Trachis in Thessaly, that the gods took pity and turned them both into kingfishers ('halkuones' in ancient Greek). This peaceful bay and the islands which lie in it (known as the Alkyonides) were then named after them.

Póros (Póros), Poseidon shrine

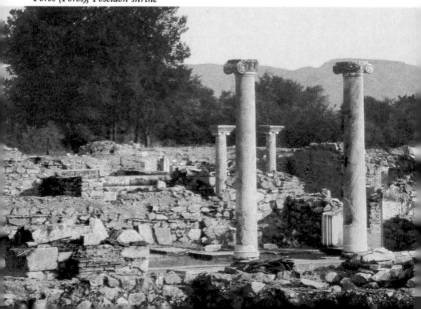

In historical times, this area belonged to Megara's sphere of influence. The ruins of the Megarian fortress of *Aigosthena*, which date from the 4&3C BC, are to be found here.

Aigosthena fortress: This well preserved *acropolis* or fortress is situated just outside the entrance to the town of Pórto Germenó, some 550 yards E. of the shore. It has impressive *walls* and many square *towers* dating from the late 4C BC. Virtually nothing remains of the S. wall, but the N. wall is still in good condition. It incorporates a fine gate 130 yards from the sea; and there is an interesting corner tower (46 ft. high) at the SE. corner. Inside the fortress there are remains of the cells of a Byzantine *monastery*, together with its 12C *church*. By the N. wall, towards the coast, are the foundation walls, which were excavated in 1954, of an early Christian *basilica* dating from the 6C. It measured 82 x 66 ft., and had a nave and four aisles, a main apse, narthex, and baptisterion. A cruciform *church of the Panagia* belonging to the monastery was built over it in the 12C.

Environs: Víllia (*c.* 20 km E., 1,900 ft. above sea-level): This beautiful mountain village is set on the SE. foothills of Mt.Kithairon, which towers to a height of 4,593 ft., and marks the boundary between Boeotia and Attica. According to legend, Oedipus, the son of the king of Thebes, was exposed here as an infant (see Sophokles's play on the subject). There is a beautiful climb up to Elatia peak (4,593 ft.) which affords a magnificent view. *Eleutheraí fortress* (now known as *Elevtheraí, c.* 25 km. E.): There are some impressive remains of the ancient city, which was built here in 345 BC, on the strategically important road between Thebes and Athens. At the entrance to the *Kaza Gorge* can be seen its *ramparts* with their two-storeyed *towers*. The *N. wall*, built of regular square blocks, is up to 10 ft. thick, and has square towers, each of which incorporates a gate on the ground floor and has embrasures in the upper storey. Eleutheraí was the birthplace of the famous sculptor Myron (who lived in the 5C BC) copies of whose *discus thrower* were produced on a considerable scale in Roman times. The

Póros, view over the island's capital

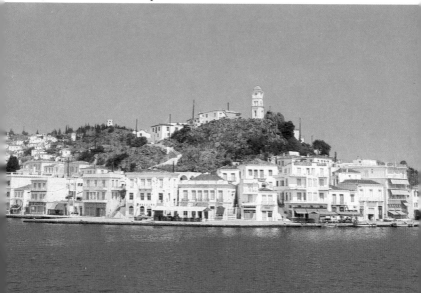

fortress was 330 yards long by 110 yards wide, and possessed had two main towers. There are some traces of an older structure, which was destroyed by the Spartans in 421 BC. This fortress, which guarded the border between Athens and Boeotia, was also known in ancient times as *Pánakton* (today it is also called *Gyftókastro*, meaning 'gypsy fortress'). The remains of two early Christian *basilicas* (each with a nave and two aisles, and dating from the 5&6 BC) were excavated here on the SE slope. On the plain (to the N. of the road) are the remains of a *temple of Dionysos*, built in the 5C BC, which marks the site of the ancient city of Eleutheraí, whose cult of Dionysos made it well known in ancient times. Nearby there are some slight traces of the old Attic deme, or community, of *Oinóe* (now called *Inói*). At the S. end of the village are the ruins (which stand 16 m. high) of an ancient *tower* of regular square stones. There are some few traces of the ancient frontier town of **Erythrai** (also known as *Kriekúki; c.* 30 km. to the NW) at the foot of Mt.Kithairon, near the ancient Boeotian city of Plataia. This town contains the 19C churches of the *Evangelismos* and *Profítis Ilias.*

Pórto Ráfti/ΠΟΡΤΟ ΡΑΦΤΗ
Attica/Central Greece   p.296☐H 9

This small harbour, which lies on the E. coast of Attica, some 35 km. SE of Athens, on a sandy bay with many inlets, has become a popular summer holiday resort. The name of Pórto Ráfti means 'tailor's harbour' and derives from the 10 ft. high Roman marble statue, popularly known as *Ráftis* or 'the tailor', which stands on the island of *Nisí Ráftis*, or 'tailor's island', offshore.

In ancient times the area S. of the bay on Mt.Koroni was the site of the important harbour of *Prásiai*. Its *walls*, incorporat-

ing six gates, and a defensive wall across the isthmus (1,040 yards), are preserved. These fortifications were built by Patroclos, an admiral of the Ptolemies, around 265 BC. The port rose to some importance in the 7&6C from its trade with the Cyclades. It was from here, too, that the Athenian emissaries (theoroi) departed to attend the festival of Apollo on Delos.

Many *Mycenean tombs* have been discovered in this area (near Peirati). Some Late Helladic tombs dating from about 1400 BC were also found near Ágios Spyrídon. On the N. side of the bay there are some slight traces of the ancient deme of *Steireía*. The most important finds from this area are now in the Museum at Vravróna (Braurón).

Potamiés/Potamiá/ΠΟΤΑΜΙΕΣ
Iráklion/Crete   p.298☐H 14

This village is situated to the N. of the Lasíthi plateau, not far from the N. coast of Crete. On a hill just outside the village there is an abandoned monastery, within whose walls is the small cross-domed church of the *Panagia Guverniotissa*, which contains some remarkable 14C frescos (notably the Pantocrator).

Environs: Avdú/Avdhoú: Avdú lies 5 km. to the S. and contains the 14C churches of *Ágios Georgios* and *Ágios Antonios*, which are both frescoed. **Kerá:** 10 km. farther on towards the plateau of Lasíthi, is the pass near Kerá, which is marked by a number of ruined Venetian windmills. Beneath the village lies the Monastery of the *Panagía Kardiótissa*, which was founded in the 18C. The plateau of Lasíthi begins 5 km. farther S. It is famous for its many wind-pumps (there are over 10,000), with their white linen sails, which are used for irrigation and have made it very fertile. It was used from time immemorial as a place of refuge for people fleeing from foreign invaders. **Pigí:** To the SE of Avdú is the village of Pigí, which contains the basilica of *Ágios Pandeleíon.* This consists of a nave and two aisles; it has some beautiful 14C frescos, and was probably built on the foundations of an early Christian basilica. **Psykhró/Psikhró:** This village lies some 20 km. S. of Kerá. From here one can climb the 560 ft. up to the stalactite cave known as *Diktion Antron,* or the *Diktaean Cave,* which was first investigated by archaeologists in 1886, three years after it had been rediscovered by Cretan shepherds. But it was only later that its real importance was recognized, first by Arthur Evans in 1894 and subsequently by David George Hogarth in 1908: this was the cave supposed in very early times to have been Zeus's birthplace. Hogarth, with the support of his many assistants, was the first to work the cave free of all the rock which had collapsed and covered it over the centuries, thus discovering shards of ancient ceramics, some of which can be dated as far back as the 19C BC. He established

that the cave had been a place of pilgrimage from the most ancient times until the birth of Christ, indeed as late as the age of the crusaders. **Karfí/Karphí:** To the SE of Potamiés, between Kerá and Lagú, is Karfí, the site of an ancient settlement in which a post-Minoan sanctuary has been discovered. The small sculptures and cult objects which were found here are now in the Archaeological Museum in Iráklion.

Préveli/ΠΡΕΒΕΛΙ
Réthymnon/Crete   p.298☐F 14

Moní Préveli is situated high above the S. coast of Crete, between Frankokástello and Agía Triáda, near the mouth of the river Megalopotamos. The surrounding countryside is sparse and mountainous, and the wild setting of the place gives it a romantic beauty.

The *monastery* is dedicated to St.John the Evangelist and was built by the Venetians at the beginning of the 17C. Its towers, which contain small windows and are

Kerá (Potamiés), fresco, detail

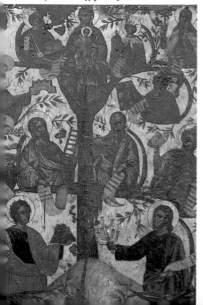

Psykhro (Potamiés), Diktaean Cave

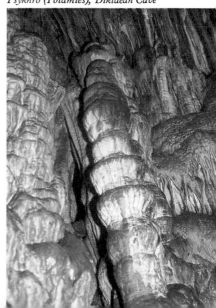

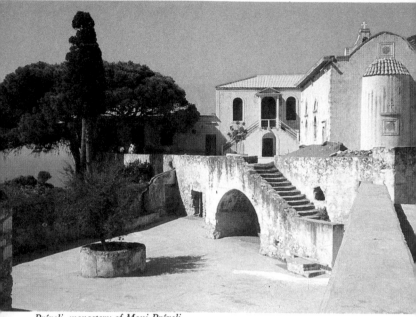

Préveli, monastery of Moni Préveli

mostly pointed, could easily be mistaken at first sight for early Romanesque rather than baroque. Like Moní Gouvernéto, it was used as a sort of fortress during the fight for independence here, thanks to the protection offered by its massive walls. The monastery possesses a *collection of Byzantine church art*, notably some precious icons. The *church* contains the socalled miraculous Cross of Christ, which is decorated with a very beautiful relief depicting the baptism of Christ.

Environs: Káto Préveli: some 4 km. to the NW. of Préveli is the village of **Levkóia.** On the way to Levkóia, set in a gorge, can be seen the little chapel of *Agia Fotini*, whose 14C frescos are well worth seeing. Just before the road enters Levkóia, set on a river bank, are the ruins of the *Káto Préveli Monastery*, which was evidently a

precursor of Moní Préveli. There is a bridge across the river which was built in the 19C as a copy of a Venetian original.

Préveza/ΠΡΕΒΕΖΑ
Préveza/Epirus   p.294 □ C 6

This town is situated at the entrance to the Ambracian Gulf, on the site of the ancient city of Berenike, and just across the strait from Áktion (Actium), where the famous sea-battle was fought in 31 BC. Préveza began to develop after the decline of Nikópolis in the 11C, and came under French, Venetian, and Turkish rule, until in 1700, during the war between Venice and Turkey, it was completely destroyed. A similar disaster befell it again in 1798, during the war between Turkey and

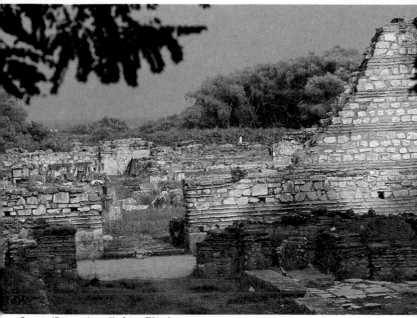

Oropós (Préveza), walls from Elátria

France. It remained under Turkish rule until 1912. Today, Préveza is a small town with a population of about 12,000, which offers many lovely beaches (Ágios Georgios, Panorama, Pantokratoras, and Alonakia), and where many tourists choose to spend their holidays. The ruins of the Venetian fortress provide a beautiful view over the Gulf of Arta.

Environs: Oropós (*c.* 30 km. N.): This village stands on the site of the ancient city of *Elátria*, which was an Elian colony. The remains of the walls which encircled it can still be seen. **Rogí** (*c.* 32 km. NE.): To the W. of the modern village of Néa Kerasús, and situated on the bank of the river Luros (known in antiquity as Kharadros), can be seen the acropolis of the ancient city of *Vukhetion* (which was another colony of Elis). The fortress was built by the Byzan-tines. **Ágios Geórgios** (*c.* 50 km. NE.): It was near this village that the Roman aque-duct supplying water to Nikópolis began. **Asprokháliko** (2 km. NW. of Ágios Ge-órgios): A Palaeolithic cave was discovered to the left of the main road to Ioánnina. The objects found there are displayed in the Museum at Ioánnina, in Room A. These stone implements are the oldest found in Greece and date from 38,000 BC.

Pýlos/ΠΥΛΟΣ

Messenia/Peloponnese   p.298☐D 11

This small town (population *c.* 3000) is situated in a sheltered bay 3 miles long and nearly 2 miles wide. The bay is protected from the sea by the island of Sphakteria. There are narrow channels to the N. and

S. of the island which allow the passage of ships.

History: During the Middle Ages, the town was commonly known as *Navarino*, which is a corruption of 'ton Avarinon', meaning 'of the Avars', and referring to the Slav invasions. The modern Pýlos has little connection with the ancient city of that name, for the latter lies farther to the N. There are no ancient remains at all on the site of the modern town. The *neokastro* at the S. end of the bay was built by the Turks in 1573. From 1686 till 1715, it was held by the Venetians. During the Greek war of liberation, the fort was captured by Greek forces; but when Ibrahim Pasha besieged it in 1825, they were unable to hold out. Ibrahim set up his headquarters there and carried out reprisals throughout Messenia.

The turning point in the Greek struggle for independence was the *naval battle of Navarino*, which was fought in 1827. The Turks had refused an armistice with Greece. France, Great Britain and Russia, who all maintained official relations with Greece, decided on a demonstration of force. The allied fleet was commanded jointly by Admirals de Rigny, Codrington, and von Heyden, and counted 27 ships with 1276 cannon. The Turkish fleet was deployed in the Bay of Navarino and comprised 89 ships with 2438 cannon. When the Turks let off some shots, the allies interpreted this as the opening of hostilities. The battle began at 12 noon and ended next morning with the defeat of the Turks, who had only 29 ships left.

Museum: This contains pieces commemorating the naval battle. There are also some Mycenean ceramics and a few Hellenistic objects.

Bay of Navarino: A motor boat from the harbour will conduct visitors across the bay. In calm water, one can see the wrecks

of the Turkish-Egyptian fleet. In the S. part of the bay is the little *island of Pylos*, which has a memorial to the French sailors who fell at Navarino. The *island of Sfaktiría* is uninhabited. Near the *Panagoula* dock, where a small church stands, is the memorial to the Russian sailors. From here one may climb to a plateau where there are two wells. This is where a Spartan force was besieged by the Athenians in 425 BC, as described by Thucydides. The siege lasted 72 days, after which the Athenians decided to attack. Of the original Spartan force of 420, only 192 survived the battle, and these were forced to surrender. On *Mt. Ilias* there are the remains of an ancient fortress in which the Spartans took refuge. The Sykia channel between Sfaktiría and the Koryphasion promontory is only some 110 yards wide. There are some remains here of a dock dating from the 4C BC. At the top of the hill surmounting the promontory stand the ruins of the *acropolis of Pýlos*, which was occupied by the Avars from the 6–9C AD. The Frankish name for this place was Chastel de Port de Jonc, but after the 16C it was known simply as Palaiokastro.

Some towers, both round and square, and part of the surrounding wall, have been preserved. In the N. and W. areas of the site, the castle has been built over the foundations of the ancient structure, which date from the 4C BC. Beneath the NE corner of the wall is the the the entrance to the *grotto of Nestor*, which has stalactites in the form of animals and animals' hides. According to legend, it was here that Hermes hid the cattle he had stolen from Apollo and later hung their hides. Near Voidokoilia harbour (the name means 'ox's belly'), to the N. of the Koryphasion promontory, there is an extensive Mycenean cemetery. The tholos tomb, known in ancient times as the *tomb of Thrasimedes*, was discovered to contain precious grave furnishings.

In the middle of the bay is the island of Khelonáki (meaning 'small tortoise'), where the memorial to the British sailors who fell in the battle of Navarino can be seen.

Environs: Palace of Nestor (17 km N.): This Mycenean palace is one of the best preserved in Greece. Systematic excavations were begun by archaeologists from the University of Cincinnati in 1939 in the area around Ano Englianós. They had inferred the existence of a palace there from the many tholos tombs in the vicinity. On the very first day they discovered fragments of frescos, Mycenean beakers, and Linear-B tablets.

History: Pýlos was ruled by the Neleids, who took their name from Nestor's father Neleus, who had come here from Thessaly. Nestor, who succeeded his father, fought in the Trojan War with 90 ships and came home ten years later unharmed. Telemachos, Odysseus's son, came to Pýlos when he was enquiring after his father and was regally entertained there before departing to Sparta to see Menelaos.

The palace was built in the 13C BC and destroyed by fire around 1200.

Palace: This consists of a number of buildings. The main building, 164 ft. long by 105 ft. wide, was the king's residence. To the SW there is another, smaller residential block. To the NE there is a long building which may be supposed to have been the palace workshop, in which, judging from the evidence of the objects discovered there, leather and metal goods were repaired. To the NW of the workshop there was another residential block, probably the slaves' living quarters. The palace had two storeys, and had stairways leading to the upper storey, which housed the women's apartments. The roof and the walls were built of wood, as also were the columns and the door frames. The inner walls were plastered and painted.

Main building: The entrance, or propylon, was to the SE. To its left were two small rooms which were the palace archive, and in which some one thousand Linear-B clay tablets were discovered. This script was deciphered in 1952 by M. Ventris and J. Chadwick, who discovered that the language was a predecessor of ancient Greek. The tablets, measuring some 3 in. by 5-10

Nestor's palace (Pýlos)

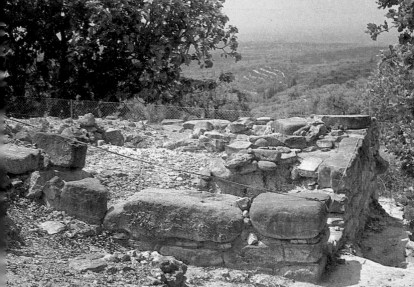

in., represent a sort of inventory of goods, implements, and cups. Some of them give information concerning the names and origins of suppliers.

After passing through the propylon (1,2), one enters a courtyard (3) at the end of which stood a portico (4), with 2 wooden columns supporting its entablature. On the left-hand side of the court there were two rooms (7,8), one a larder, and the other a waiting-room for guests wishing to visit the king. A bench ran around the walls of the waiting-room, which were frescoed. Two jugs of wine (or pithoi) were found in one corner. Hundreds of wine jars were discovered in the larder, where they may still be seen, arranged just as they were found. The portico led into a hall (5) which led into the *throne room* (6), which measured 36 ft. 9 in. x 42 ft. 4 in. In the middle of the throne room there was a large hearth, with a diameter of 13 ft., around which 4 wooden columns were grouped to support the roof. The earthenware tubes which were discovered during the excavations served to let out the smoke above the hearth. To the left of the fireplace there was a sacrificial table. The throne occupied an elevated position in front of the right-hand wall. It was probably made of wood and decorated with inlaid ivory. What has survived of the wall decoration shows a lion and a griffin, as well as a lyre-player sitting on a rock. The stuccoed floor was divided into ornamented squares; the square in front of the throne depicted an octopus. To the right of the throne there is a depression in the floor which was used for libations. The king was thus able to offer the libation from his throne.

To the left of the throne room there were two magazines, which were found mainly to contain vessels. Immediately behind the throne room were two large store-rooms (9,10) where oil was kept. These led into another store-room for oil (11).

To the right of the throne room were five more rooms of varying size. One of these may be assumed to have been another oil magazine, for it was found to contain painted storage jars. The other rooms seem to have been standing empty when the fire overwhelmed the palace. All that has been found there were some remains of burnt ivory in one of the rooms.

Returning to the hall (5), 8 steps on the right-hand side led to the upper storey. There must have been 21 steps altogether. This would mean that the ground floor was 10ft. 8 in. high. On the left-hand side of the hall there are remains of two more staircases. To the right of the courtyard (3) there was a large room which was perhaps the king's private apartment. The courtyard also gives access to a *bath*, which is the only one dating from the Mycenean period to have been preserved on the Greek mainland. It contains a decorated earthenware tub, in front of which there was a step. Set on one side was a platform on which the water jugs stood. To the right of the courtyard there was a large room with a hearth which was the *queen's room*. This contains the remains of frescos showing griffins, lions, and leopards.

SW building: These are actually the ruins of an earlier *palace* which dates from the late Helladic III A (the main palace must date from the late Helladic III B and is thus more recent). The two palaces were separated by a courtyard. A large room with two columns at the entrance and one in the middle led into the *old throne room* (which did not have a hearth). The northernmost room was used for wine storage.

NW building: This was primarily a workshop. One small room in this block may be supposed to have been a small sanctuary; there are the remains of an altar in front of it. Another room, in which many bronze fragments were found, may have been a store-room for raw materials. The middle room comprised the workshop itself. 56 clay tablets were discovered here providing information about repairs of leather and metal goods as well as the supply of both commodities. The large room which stands to the NE. of the site was the wine magazine.

Beehive tombs: About 110 yards to the NE of the palace there is a tholos tomb with a diameter of 30 ft. 8 in. Although this had been plundered, it still contained, when excavated, such precious things as gold rings, amethysts, and gems. There are other tombs scattered around the site, which have also yielded many finds.

Environs: Khóra (*c.* 3 km. NE.): The *museum* contains objects discovered in the Palace of Nestor (including frescos, pottery, and clay tablets) and from the environs (notably gold beakers from a tomb at Peristería near Kyparissia). **Gargaliáni** (*c.* 10 km. NW): This contains an 18C church which is worth visiting.

Pýrgos/ΠΥΡΓΟΣ
Elis/Peloponnese   p.294☐D 9

Pýrgos (population *c.* 20,000) is capital of the nome of Elis and a busy trading centre. It is worth seeing the Alambra theatre and the market, both neoclassical buildings.

Environs (14 km. NW): Near Katákolon are the remains, now under water, of the ancient city of **Pheía**, which was built in the 6C BC. One can still see a Frankish fort which was built on the foundations of the ancient acropolis. Near **Epitálion** (7 km. S.) there are some remains of Greek and Roman buildings. The ruins of the Mycenean town of *Thryoéssa* stand on a hill nearby.

Pýlos, palace 1,2 propylon **3** courtyard **4** portico **5** vestibule **6** throne room **7** banquet hall **8** waiting room **9,10,11** store rooms **12** bath **13** queen's chamber

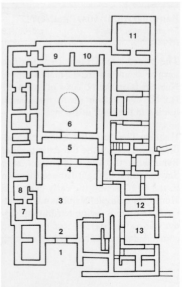

Nestor's palace (Pýlos), megaron

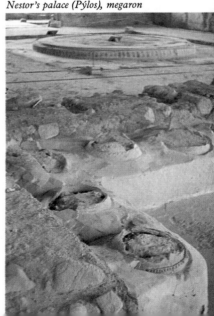

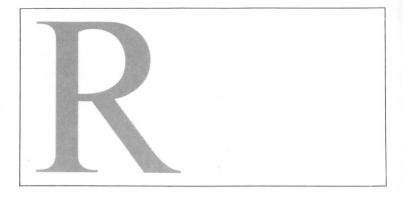

Rafína/ΡΑΦΗΝΑ
Attica/Central Greece   p.296☐H 8/9

This picturesque harbour on the E. coast of Attica, S. of the Bay of Marathon, about 27 km. NE of Athens, is a popular tourist and sea-bathing resort; there is a connection by ferry to S. Euboea and the Cycladic islands of Andros and Tínos.

The area around the old Attic deme of *Araphén* (hence the modern name Rafína) was inhabited as early as the neolithic period (3rd and 2nd centuries BC). There are traces of early fortifications.

Environs: Daú Pentéli (*c.* 5 km. W.): A fine monastery on the E. slopes of Mount Pentelikon. It was founded in the 12–13C, rebuilt as a larger monastery complex in the 16–17C and restored in 1949. The church shows traces of the Byzantine, Armenian-Georgian and Anatolian styles. **Pikérmi** (7 km. SW): Attention was drawn to the village because of interesting palaeontological finds. Fossils of large mammals from the Tertiary and Pliocene periods (*c.* 8 million years old) connected with the fauna of E. Africa were discovered (traces of apes, rhinoceros, giraffes and antelopes among other things). In the bathing resort of **Lútsa** (*c.* 5 km. S.) traces of

the foundations of a Doric *Temple of Peripteros* were found (13 x 6 columns on a stylobate of 62 x 39 ft.) dating from the 4C BC. It is presumed that the temple, which has a cella but no opisthodomos, was dedicated to the goddess Artemis Tauropolos, who was also worhipped in nearby Vravróna (q.v.). The shrine was part of the old Attic deme of *Halaí* ('salt town'), which is known to have stood on this site (Halaí Festival of Dionysos).

Ramnús/Rhamnús/ΡΑΜΝΟΥΣ
Attica/Central Greece   p.296☐H 8

The ruined site of the ancient fortified town of Ramnús with its famous shrine to Nemesis is on the N. coast of Attica, 57 km. NE of Athens in the narrow passage leading to the Gulf of Euboea.

History: The shrine to Nemesis, the goddess of justice, in the old Attic town of Ramnús is the most important after Smyrna and it brought fame to the town in the 6–5C BC. In the early period (in Homer, for example) Nemesis was considered to represent divine retribution: anyone who had undeserved good fortune and committed the sin of hubris (overweening pride) was in danger of punishment. In Ramnús her cult was connected with that of the ancient goddess Themis, who also embodied divine justice and order. Themis, the daughter of the sky (Uranos) and the earth (Gaia), bore with Zeus as father the three Horae (goddesses of the seasons) Eunomía (order), Dike (justice) and Eirene (peace). The ancients (Plato) believed that they were the basis for all human society and every state (polis).

In the 5–4C BC the Nemesis-Themis cult seems to have been pursued with very great enthusiasm by the Athenians in Ramnús, involving a large body of priests, gymnastic agones and torchlit processions; the cult persisted into the era of Imperial Rome.

Excavation site: The shrine of Nemesis is about 500 m. S. of the coastal fortress of Ramnús. The flat temple precinct is an artificial terrace supported by a fine *ashlar wall* in the N. and E. On the terrace are the ruins of two *temples* with entrances from the E. The smaller and older temple (6C BC) was dedicated to the goddess Themis (world order). It was a small undecorated anta building with two columns at the front and polygonal walls of which some traces remain. There is a statue of Themis from this temple in the National Museum in Athens.

Temple of Nemesis: The nearby larger temple (*c.*75 by 39 ft.) was a Doric peripteros with 6 by 12 columns; the lower part of the building with column drums and stumps has survived. The temple, built in 430 BC, has incomplete column fluting. In the *cella*, surrounded by the pronaos in the E. and the opisthodomos in the W. stood a cult statue of Nemesis which was famous in its time; it is the work of the Parian sculptor Agorakritos, a pupil of Phidias. The base of the statue with representations of Helen, the supposed daughter of Nemesis, is now in Room 17 of the National Museum in Athens.

Town fortifications: An old path about 400 m. long leads from the temple precinct, with traces of altars and portico, past monumental *remains of graves* (necropolis) to the town fortifications of Ramnús in the N. The only *gate*, flanked by two square *towers* was in the S., on the land side. The Hellenic marble walls from the 4C BC are well suited to the rocky site and are reinforced by other towers. Inside the walls are some remains of a *theatre* (priest's seat with inscriptions), a rotunda (choregos monument), a public building (gymnasium), garrison buildings, cisterns and some remains of modest houses. The upper terrace (entrance above the theatre) was the original *acropolis* (about 328 by 164 ft.) with irregular masonry from the 6–5C BC. It is almost completely in ruins but the ground plan of the buildings, with remains of barracks, watch towers and cisterns, can still be discerned. The lower town and the *harbour* were at the foot of the SE slope to the sea, at the mouth of a torrent.

Réthymnon/Réthimnon/PEΘTMN-ON
Réthymnon/Crete   p.298☐F 14

The third largest town on Crete is on the N. coast, between Iráklion and Chaniá. This charming, sleepy little town looks entirely southern at first sight. The many minarets and wooden houses have a Turkish look, while buildings like the mosque in the fortress seem almost African. Like the rest of Crete the ancient port has had its share of battles and natural disasters, and signs of both still show. The few remains from the Minoan period are in the archaeological museum in Iráklion.

History: In ancient times the town was called *Rithymna*. The port became important under the Venetians; a town wall was built but has been largely destroyed. In 1571 the town was plundered and sacked by the Turks, but it did not finally fall to them until 1645, when it was chosen as the Pashalik, the capital of Crete.

Town centre: Réthymnon has unusually narrow streets and some astonishingly tall houses. Notable features are the numerous balconies with fine Venetian ironwork or Turkish wood carving, the little doors with Arabian panelling or Venetian wrought-iron locks, and the excellent masonry work on arches, columns and pilasters. By the port there are pretty, bright little houses with wrought-iron balconies and wooden shops. The author Pantelis Prevelakis, famous for his novel 'The Cretan', was born in Réthymnon in 1909.

Fortress: The fortress (Fortezza Frúrio) was built between 1573 and 1587 and shows how deeply the town was once involved with the military might of Venice. The fortress stands high on a rocky spur in the N. and is very much an integral part of the town, yet has an uninterrupted view over the port and the sea; it must have made a very powerful impression when it

was first built. The outer walls have survived along with well shafts and ruins of other installations. A palace and St. Nicholas' Cathedral, built inside the citadel in 1585, have completely disappeared, however, to be replaced by a *mosque* with a gigantic dome on an almost square base; it is boarded up, and no longer in use.

Great Mosque: The 18C so-called Great Mosque in the centre of the town has three domes. The railing and the masonry on the tympanum of the former entrance are particularly attractive. The slender minaret, polygonal in its upper part and with two decorative balconies and fine roof is well worth seeing. The Great Mosque is now used as a *concert hall*.

Small Mosque: The Small Mosque is SE of the Great Mosque near the town park and dates from 1725.

Christian Churches: Between the mosques, often themselves originally Christian places of worship, are several Christian churches, in Réthymnon fre-

Réthymnon, Arimondi fountain

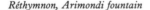

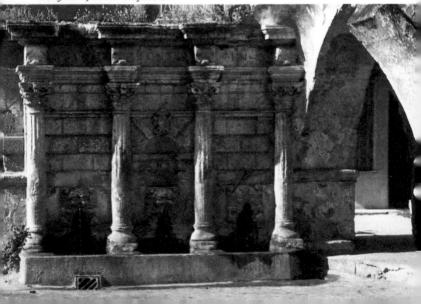

quently dedicated to the Virgin Mary. Many of the churches have frescos.

Venetian Loggia: The delightful early 17C Venetian Loggia was presumably a commercial building, but is now a *museum*, with exhibits from the town and region. The Loggia is by the harbour and has architectural exhibits, bronze and marble sculpture, inscriptions, coins, sarcophagi and small sacred items; most of the exhibits are ancient.

Arimondi well: On the quayside, between the museum and the Great Mosque and a little further N., is a fine 1623 *well*; it has four ancient Corinthian capitals and three fine lion spouts, and was built by Alvise Arimondi, who lived in the fortress palace; the rear wall has survived; the well originally had a roof.

Environs: Phalana: On a hill some 9 km. N. of Réthymnon, just outside the village of Arméni, is Phalanna, a Minoan necropolis also used in the Mycenean period. Most of the rock burial chambers can be reached by steep stairways. The larger chambers, which have unfortunately been robbed, used to contain sarcophagi. **Kirjána:** Kirjána is reached via Plátanes (Plataniés) (E. of Réthymnon) on the path to Arkádi. It has a little church with an icon of Christ by Damaskinos, which was partially destroyed by the Turks. In **Arkádi/Arkádhi:** (23 km. SE of Réthymon) is one of the national shrines of Crete, the monastery of Arkádi, set at almost 1,000 ft. on a rocky plateau. In 1866 peasants of the region took refuge in the monastery with their wives and children during a revolt. The Turks besieged the monastery for two days. When the people inside saw that there was no means of escape, as the enemy was already storming the gates, they decided to blow themselves up. Their motto was 'freedom or death', and on November 8 the abbot himself gave the order to light the fuse on the powder barrel. The terrible explosion killed almost 1,000 Cretans, but also 1,800 Turks. The anniversary of the explosion is a *national holiday* throughout Crete. The 17C monastery buildings were also partially destroyed in

Réthymnon, arcade

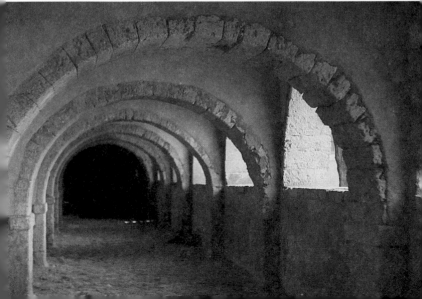

cellent condition. **Apóstoli:** Apóstoli is the next village to Thrónos, and also has a church with fine frescos and the *Monastery Ágios Assomatos*. N. of the village traces of the *ancient Sybritos*, which played a not unimportant role in Roman times, have been revealed. **Amári:** 5 km. S. of Apóstoli is the delightfully sited village of Amári, which has two Byzantine churches: *Agia Anna*, with frescos dating from 1196 and *Ágios Theodoros*, with frescos dating from 1588. **Vyzári:** 6 km. from Amári *ruins* of a Roman village have been revealed; there is a fine mosaic floor (AD 250–300). **Furfurá/Fourfourá/Foufeurás:** Furfurá is 7 km. S. of Vyzári and has the Byzantine churches of *Ágios Georgios* and *Panagia*. **Níthavris:** If you follow the road which eventually reaches the S. coast at Agía Galíni a little further to the S., you reach Níthavris with its Byzantine *Panagia Church*.

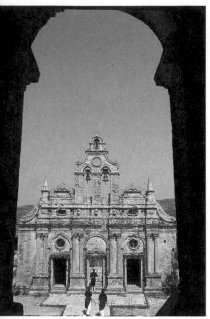

Arkádi (Réthymnon), monastery church

the explosion. The exterior of the rectangular monastery is very plain, but there are interesting features inside: cloisters, finely decorated gates and a little courtyard with an open-air staircase. The *church* of 1587 is particularly notable; it contains numerous icons, some of them valuable, and has a beautifully balanced façade with splendid Renaissance doorways, round and oval windows, twin Corinthian pillars and a bell tower in three sections. The small *monastery museum*, principally devoted to the monastery's battle with the Turks, is also worth seeing. **Thrónos:** E. of Réthymnon a road leads via Prasses to Messára. It runs through charming countryside along the SW slopes of Mount Ida and passes through several enchanting villages, including Thrónos, about 30 km. from Réthymnon; the *Panagia church* was built in 1491, and has numerous frescos in ex-

Ródos/Rhodes (I)/ΡΟΔΟΣ

East Aegean Islands (Dodecanese)/
Aegean Islands   p.300☐P/Q 12/13

The 'rose island' of Rhodes (540 sq. miles, *c.* 63,000 inhabitants) is the fourth largest island in the Aegean after Crete, Euboea and Lesbos. It is considered to be the 'Pearl of the Dodecanese' and in the last two decades has become a tourist paradise. The island is 48 m. long, and up to 22 m. wide. The highest point is Mount Atavyros (3, 986 ft.).

Rhodes has a mild climate, luxuriant vegetation and beautiful buildings.

History: Rhodes was known in mythology as the home of the sun-god Helios. The island was inhabited by the Telchines, legendary metalworkers, as early as the 3C BC. In about 1400 BC Akhaian-Cretan Greeks settled in the three towns of Líndos, Kámeiros and Ialysós and the island was

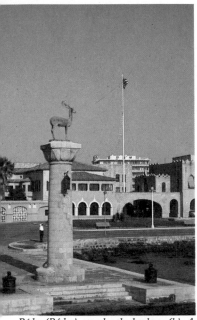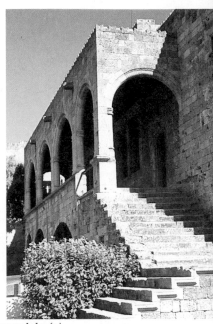

Ródos (Ródos), stag by the harbour (l.), Auvergne lodge (r.)

conquered by advancing Dorians in 1100 BC. During a successful period in the 7&6C BC the Rhodians founded colonies throughout the Mediterranean, and also the so-called 'Hexapolis' ('Union of Six Cities'). From 479 BC they were members of the Attic Sea Alliance. Following the Attic pattern, the Rhodians decided in 408 BC to found a common island capital (Rhodos) on the N. coast. The geometrical design of the town (in grid squares) was intended by Hippodamos of Miletus for a city of 100,000 inhabitants. Rhodes then rose to power and wealth and was able to establish itself as an independent Aegean port. After the unsuccessful siege by Demetrios Poliorketes of Macedon (305 BC) the famous 98 ft. bronze statue known as the *Colossus of Rhodes* was built by the harbour. It was considered to be one of the Seven Wonders of the World. The earth-quake of 227 BC destroyed the Colossus and a large part of the town. In the 2C BC there was a quarrel with Rome over the rival port of Delos and Rhodes was taken by Cassius, the murderer of Julius Caesar, who took many statues back to Rome. From that time it had no economic significance, but was famous for its schools for orators, philosophers and sculptors: Cicero, Cato, Pompey and Caesar were among those who studied in Rhodes. Between AD 500 and 1000 the town was frequently plundered by Goths, Persians and Arabs. The Venetians were granted privileges on the island by Byzantium in 1082, and the Genoese were given similar rights from 1243. It was then occupied and fortified in 1309 by the Knights of St.John; they had been driven out of Jerusalem and made it into a bastion in the struggle of Christianity against Islam. It then flourished again until it was conquered by the Ottoman Sultan Suleiman in 1522. After the Knights of St.John were forced to leave the island for Malta, Rhodes was under Turkish rule for 400 years. It was annexed by Italy in 1912, and returned to Greece in 1948, along with the other islands of the Dodecanese.

Ródos/Rhodes (approx. 30,000 inhab.): The capital, in the NE of the island, was founded in 408 BC and designed on a geometrical plan for a population of 100,000; only a third of the area of the ancient town is now inhabited. The line of the old streets, which had an underground water and sewerage system, can still be seen in places, particularly in the old town. The streets intersect at right angles; they are just over 13 ft. wide and enclose residential blocks of about 500 by 600 yards, with axes running from N. to S. and E. to W. Little survives of the *temple precinct* by the commercial harbour (Elevtheria Gate) except part of a 3C BC *Temple of Aphrodite* and of a *Temple of Dionysos* with halls, and remains of the *ancient city wall* by the port.

The actual *sacred precinct* with ancient *acropolis* is in the SW of the town (Mount Smith), where remains of a *Temple of Zeus and Athene* were revealed by Italian archaeologists. S. of the acropolis three 3C BC *columns* still stand on the foundations of a Dorian *Temple of Apollo* or Helios, from which there is a splendid view. Nearby are the partially restored 2C BC *stadium* and the *odeion*, a terraced building like a theatre but without a stage, with seats for about 800 spectators; it was used as a lecture theatre (auditorium) for the pupils of the philosophy school. Between the odeion and the acropolis are various 2&1C BC *nymph shrines* with niches and statues. S. of the shrines and the old town are remains of ancient *tombs*, of which the most striking is the so-called 'Ptolemy Grave', a Hellenic *rock burial chamber* in the ancient cemetery in the suburb of *Rodíni*, which has a hall with columns and grave niches with barrel vaulting. The three harbours in the NE, the *Mandraki harbour*, the *commercial harbour* and the *Akándia bay* were also part of the ancient town, but next to nothing of them has sur-

Ródos (Ródos), Grand Master's palace

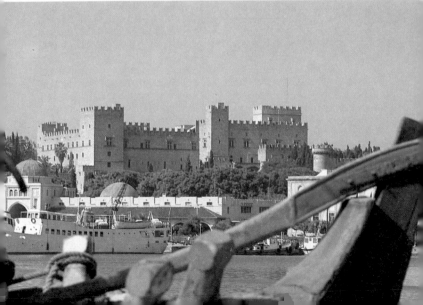

vived. The *Colossus of Rhodes* is said to have stood on the mole of the *Mandráki harbour* on the site of the present St. Nicholas tower and windmill. The remains of the 105 ft. bronze statue of the sun god Helios, destroyed by the earthquake of 227 BC, were sold to a Jewish merchant as late as AD 654.

The medieval *Old Town* of the Knights of the Order of St.John is W. of the commercial harbour. It is surrounded by a thick outer defensive wall, and was divided by another wall into a *knights' quarter (Collachium)* and a *merchants' quarter (Burgus)*. The knights' quarter still retains its medieval appearance and atmosphere. This is where the *inns* of the various national groups (Tongues) of the Order were sited: the 1507 *Inn of Auvergne* with a roofed gallery and external staircase (near Symi Square, with the arms of Guy de Blanchefort over the doorway (1512&13)), the *Inn of Italy* (1519) and the *Inn of France* (1492–1503), the finest and largest building. Over the doorway are the *arms* of the Grand Prior d'Amboise. On the *Street of the Knights* (Odós Ippóton) is the *Inn of Spain* (1437 or 1510, connected to the *Inn of Provence* by an archway.

At the E. end of the Street of the Knights, near the harbour, is the *Inn of England* (*c.*1520). The *Inn of Germany*, the seventh national group or Tongue, by Arsenal Square, has not survived. Opposite the Inn of England is the *Hospital of the Knights*; this large, severe building dating from 1440–89, with an oriel chapel above the gate, reflects the principal concern of the Order: care for the sick and pilgrims. The rooms are arranged around a courtyard in the manner of a caravanserai. The 164 ft. *upper hall* with groin vaulting was used as a hospital. Above the main entrance is a *relief of angels* with a *coat of arms* of the Order. The building now houses the *Archaeological Museum* (see below). The *Street of the Knights* is worth seeing: it is cobbled and follows the line of one of the ancient streets; in the 15C it was the principal street of the Knights' quarter, and it is now the only surviving example of a late Gothic street in the E. Mediterranean. The Knights' Inns have courtyards with arcades and are built of ashlar; they have

Ródos (Ródos), knights' hospital (l.), lions in the museum (r.)

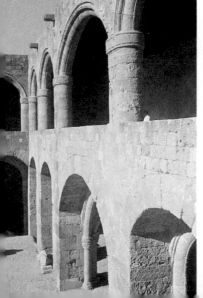
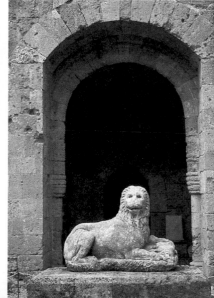

arched entrances to their lower storeys, cornices and battlements in the upper parts, and also turrets, gargoyles and sculpted coats of arms. At the W. end of the Street of the Knights is the *Chapterhouse of St. John,* and opposite this *loggia,* which has largely been restored, and the remains of the nearby Gothic *Church of St.John,* is the *Palace of the Grand Masters.* This monumental building was destroyed by an explosion in 1856 and the Italians restored the façade *c.* 1925 from old engravings, with the intention of its being used as a palace by Mussolini; the interior is somewhat overblown. The old 14C palace was a citadel in its own right within the city walls: by the massive entrance are two towers with battlements, then come the great entrance hall and the marble-paved courtyard with 10 granaries and other storerooms. In the upper storey are several large rooms which served as council chambers. The building now houses a *museum* of Roman and early Christian *mosaics,* especially from Kos. At the centre of the *merchants' quarter* (Turkish quarter from 1523) is *Sokratus Street* which, like the Street of the Knights, follows the line of an ancient street. At the W. end is the fine *Suleiman Mosque,* built shortly after his victory in 1522 by Sultan Suleiman and restored in the 19C. Various Byzantine churches were turned into mosques in the 16C: the 12C *Church of Our Lady* by the harbour became the *Red Mosque.* 14C Byzantine frescos were revealed in the *Ilk Mihrab Mosque* and also in the *Pegial ed Din Mosque,* the former Phanúrios Church of 1335. Also worth seeing are the *Aga Mosque* (Sokratus Street), the *Kavakli Mestshiti Mosque,* the *Demirli Mosque* (former Byzantine Church) the *Tekkeci Mosque* (1765), the *Abdul Celil Mosque* (former 15C church) and the *Dolapli Mestshiti Mosque* (destroyed in 1943), a former Byzantine church on a cruciform ground plan, which has now returned to Christian worship. Near the harbour are the 1531 *Ibrahim Pasha*

Mosque and the fine 1503 *Commercial Court,* which has a staircase and Gothic loggia on the ground floor and a 1507 d'Aubusson coat of arms and a French fleur-de-lys window in the façade. Over the entrance is a 1505 d'Amboise coat of arms. The 15C *Archbishop's Palace* is also worth seeing, along with the 15C ruins of the three-aisled Gothic *fortress church* (St. Mary) and the remains of *St.Katharine's Hospice,* founded in the 14C and restored *c.* 1516. By the mill mole (St.Katharine's Gate) are the Byzantine Church of *Ágios Pantelimon* and the ruins of the 14C *Church of Our Lady.* The most impressive monument from the period of the Knights of St.John is the *city wall:* the Byzantine walls were continually strengthened from the 14C onwards, particularly under Grand Master Pierre d'Aubusson (from 1476). The corner points were heavily fortified with bastions and the individual Tongues were assigned separate sections to defend. In about 1520 the fortified wall was 39 ft. wide and the parapet 13 ft. wide, with artillery emplacements and outer walls. Almost all of the wall has survived; it is over three miles long and used to include 7 gates and numerous bastions. The surviving *gates* are the most interesting feature: near the Palace of the Grand Masters is the *Antonius gate* with its two towers, and beyond it is the impressive 1512 *Ambois Gate* with towers and a drawbridge, coats of arms of Grand Masters and a five-cornered bastion; then comes *St.George's Tower,* in the W. wall, set on a pointed jutting bastion with a munition store, a relief of St.George the dragon killer and coats of arms of Grand Masters. The section from the Amboise Gate to the St.George Tower was assigned to the Germans. The circular *Spanish Tower* is on a polygonal terrace. The Spanish section ran as far as the circular 1441 *St.Mary Bastion,* and it was here that the Turks entered the city in 1522, having stormed the *St.Mary Gate* (Athanasios Gate). The *Kóskinu Gate* complex in the S., which includes the *St. John Bastion*, is also worth seeing. It is decorated with a relief of St. John and the splendid coat of arms of Pierre d'Aubusson. Between the Kóskinu Gate and the *Italian Tower* was the section defended by the Knights of Provence, the homeland of most of the Knights of St. John; there are several wall towers and many coats of arms of the Grand Masters. The *Italian Tower* in the SE was protected by an enormous bulwark 49 ft. in diameter, with arrow slits. On the harbour side is the smaller *St. Katharine's Tower* (by the mill mole) and the *Marine Gate* (Harbour Gate) built in 1478 under Pierre d'Aubusson: it has two fine battlemented towers with machicolations. Above the gateway is a *relief* 'Madonna with Child between Peter and John' and the emblem of France between coats of arms of the Order. In the NE is the *St. Paul Tower*, refurbished *c.* 1477. The nearby *Freedom Gate* (Pyli Elevtherias) was added to the city wall by the Italians. On the tip of the mole is the 1400 *Naillac Tower* (Arab Tower), destroyed by an earthquake in 1863. Outside the Old Town by the Mandráki Harbour is the *administrative quarter* from the period of Italian occupation, in the neo-Gothic Venetian style of the architect del Fausto. The former *Governor's palace* is reminiscent of the Doge's Palace in Venice. The *aquarium* on the N. tip of the island is worth seeing. The *Murat Reis Mosque* (Platía Kunduriotu) with a Turkish cemetery was built on the site of St. Anthony's Church, destroyed in 1480. The *Church of St. John* (now *Evangelismos Church* with its 1925 detached *bell tower* is a copy of the Church of St. John in the Collachium, which has been destroyed.

Archaeological Museum: This is housed in the *Hospital of the Knights* (see above) in the Street of the Knights (Collachium). It contains fine Mycenean finds from the *necropolis of Ialysós*, also a large collection of Minoan, Attic and Rhodian ceramics in the N. wing, and ancient finds from the entire Dodecanese. The famous *kneeling Aphrodite*, a 1C BC marble statuette, is worth seeing, as are the 3C BC life-size marble statue of *Aphrodite 'Thalassia'* and a 2C BC *statue of Aphrodite*. There are also ancient 6C BC *statues of youths* (kuroi) and the fine *funerary stele* 'Krito and Timarista' dating from the classical period (5C BC); the 7C BC Kamiros 'water bowl' (perirrhanterion) is also of interest. Nearby is the *Museum of Folk Art (Laografiko Musion)*, which has a fine collection of furniture, costumes and ceramics from the island. In the *Ionian Bank* (Ioniki Trapeza) by the Freedom gate is an interesting *gallery* of modern Rhodian *folk art*.

Environs: In the charming coastal village of **Rodíni** (5 km. SE) are remains of a Roman *aqueduct* and the famous 3C BC *tombs* (rock burial chambers), wrongly known as 'Ptolemy's Tomb'. In the coastal village of **Trίanta** (10 km. SW) is a fine 18C carved altar wall. The chapel of Ágios Markos in the village of **Paradísi** (17 km. SW) has a Byzantine fresco of St. George. The area of *Petaludes* ('butterflies'), about 26 km. SW, is famous for its countless butterflies.

Ialysós: About 15 km. SW of the capital of the island is the village of Ialysós, which was important in antiquity and inhabited as early as the Mycenean period; it has an Achaian acropolis. In the 10C BC it was settled by the Dorians, who built the fortress on Mount Filerimos (876 ft.). The ancient city fell into decline after the foundation of Rhodes in 408 BC, and by the 1C AD it was no more than a village. At the highest point, in front of the modern church built by the Italians, which has fine cloisters, are the foundations of a 3C BC *Dorian temple of Athene and Zeus Polieus* built on the remains of a temple dating from the 6C BC. In the 6C AD the temple became an *early Christian church* of which the cruciform *baptistery* (16 by 16 ft.) and the semi-underground *Ágios Georgios*

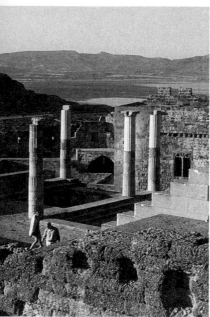

Kámiros (Ródos), baths

chapel with fine 15C *frescos* have survived. On the S. slope is a fine Greek *well house* (limestone with Doric pillars) dating from 300 BC. The *Church of the Panagia* was one of the *monasteries* founded by the Knights of the Order of St.John; it was rebuilt by the Italians. Many *tombs* from the Mycenean period (1400 – 1000 BC) have been excavated on the mound of the fortress of the Knights of St.John; the tombs contained large numbers of burial gifts, including clay vessels and jewellery. Towards the coast can be found the *ancient necropolis* (finds from this site are in the museum in Rhodes).

Kámiros: Roughly 34 km. SW of Rhodes are the ruins of the ancient city of *Kámeiros* (now *Kámiros*), which was excavated by Italian archaeologists in 1929. The town was set on several slopes by the coast and

is a vivid example of the ancient pattern of settlement: founded by the Myceneans, extended by the Dorians and consolidated by the Hellenes. At the lowest point in the NW was the *ancient market place* (agora), next to this an *exédra* and in a hollow on the S. slope was the square *Apollo court* (temenos); this was surrounded by benches and stood in front of a 3C BC *Temple of Apollo*. E. of the agora was an precinct devoted to the cult of heroes with several *altars*. On the paved main road to the S. are Hellenistic *blocks of houses* with side streets and remains of the sewerage system (cf. the ancient residential town on Delos). Some *columns* of the peristyle buildings (ground plans visible) have been set up again. At the S. end of the residential part of the town is a 656 ft. long *Dorian hall* (3–2C BC) with six *columns* which have been set up again. The hall is built over an old *reservoir* (main cistern) and numerous side cisterns. On the S. slope of the town (acropolis) are the foundations of a Dorian *Temple of Athene* dating from the 6–5C BC and extended in the Hellenic period.

Environs: Near the coastal village of *Kastéllos* (13 km. S.) is an impressive *fortress of the Knights of St.John* on a rocky eminence; it dates from 1500 and has d'Amboise and del Caretto coats of arms; there is a view of the smaller island of *Alímnia*. About 26 km. SW of Kámiros is the picturesque mountain village of *Empónas* from which it is possible to climb Mount Atavyros, the highest mountain on the island (3986 ft.); there is an ancient shrine of Zeus on the summit.

Monólithos (*c.* 83 km. SW of Rhodes): This picturesque coastal village on the slopes of Akramytis is near the impressive 15C *fortress of the Knights of St.John*, the most southerly such building, constructed to guard the gulf of Apollakia in the SW of the island. In the S. of the island is the weaving village of *Kattávia* and on the

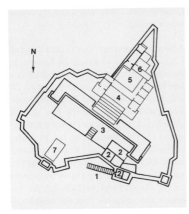

Lindos, acropolis 1 castle steps **2** knights' buildings **3** propylaion **4** upper propylaion **5** colonnaded courtyard **6** colonnaded hall **7** late Roman structure

slopes of Mount Skiadi (2175 ft.) is the former Byzantine monastery of *Skiádi*, which has remains of frescos.

Líndos (56 km. S. of Rhodes): This pretty little village in the middle of the E. coast was important in ancient times for its harbour and its merchant fleet. In the Middles Ages Líndos was a fortified stronghold of the Knights of St. John. *Acropolis of Líndos:* This is set on a 545 ft. cliff by the sea. The Knights of St.John built a mighty fortified wall around the ancient temple precinct under Grand Master Pierre d'Aubusson in 1476–1505. The acropolis is reached from the N. by the steep fortress steps of the Gothic *gate complex.* At the foot of the stairway is an *exedra* hewn into the rock, and next to it on the rock wall an ancient *relief* of a *galley.* The 2C BC relief with stern, lateral rudder and helmsman's seat was the basis for a statue of Hagesandros on the occasion of a victory at sea *c.* 180 BC. The *gate* with Gothic vaults, the *residence of the fortress commandant* (Knights' house) and the partially ruined

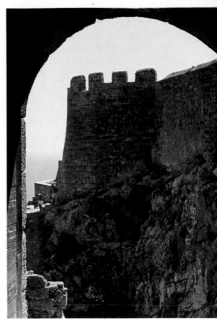

Líndos (Ródos), Hospitaler's fortress

13C *fortress church* of St.John are all that has survived of the fortress of the Knights of St.John. *Ancient temple precinct:* The ruins of a 289 ft. long *c.* 200 BC Dorian *hall with columns* are to be found as propylaea on a terrace in front of the 69 ft. monumental staircase leading to the *upper temple terrace.* Here is the actual Dorian *propylon* with two protruding bastions dating from *c.* 300 BC; it is probably a copy of the Propylaean in Athens. Behind it is a *courtyard with columns* with an *altar* (of which little survives) dating from *c.* 200 BC. In the SE is the *main temple of Athena Lindia* above a *grotto* in the cliff which was the original place of worship. The Doric *temple,* which has been partially restored, is 72 ft. by 26 ft., with four columns on the narrow sides; it was built *c.* 330 BC. The older temple, dating from the 6C BC on the same site was dedicated to the local goddess Líndia and had a wooden votive picture. Along with the Asklepieion of Kos and the city of Pergamon the shrine of Líndos is one of the largest Hellenic architectural sites; it was excavated and restored by Danish and Italian archaeologists. The wonderful view from the temple rock is an impressive feature. On the W. slope of the acropolis hill is the ancient *theatre*, of which some rows of seats and the stage remain. Next to it are the foundations of a Dorian *building with columns* 121 ft. by 101 ft. On Mount Krana opposite the acropolis are some *rock tombs*, some with façades with Doric columns, including the *c.* 200 BC rock tomb of Archokrates. The so-called *tomb of Kleobulos* is near the ancient harbour cape (Ágios Milianós). The circular *tomb* is 29 ft. in diameter and dates from *c.* 100 BC. The present village stands on the site of the ancient town, of which very little remains. The late Byzantine Church of Our Lady

Panagía with icons and 1779 frescos is worth seeing.

Also worth seeing: Near to the village of *Kalythíes*, about 15 km. S. of Rhodes, is the monastery church of *Eleúsa*, which has fine 18C frescos. Near *Kolýmbia*, about 26 km. S. of Rhodes, is the Byzantine monastery of *Tsambiká* and the fine domed church of *Ágios Nikolaos Funtukli* with restored 13–15C *frescos*. The village of *Archángelos*, 32 km. S. of Rhodes, is known for its local *potteries*. Above it towers the *ruined fortress* of the Knights of St.John on nearby Mount Faraklos (1680 ft.); the fortress is also accessible from the neighbouring village of *Malóna* (38 km.). Near the village of *Aláerma* in the middle of the island, about 20 km. NW of Líndos, is the old Byzantine *monastery of Thari*, dating from the 9C. In the domed church are various layers of *wall paintings* from the 11–17C.

Lindos (Ródos), Temple of Athena (l.), tomb of Arkhokrates (r.)

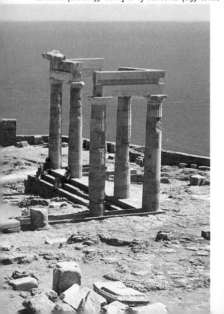
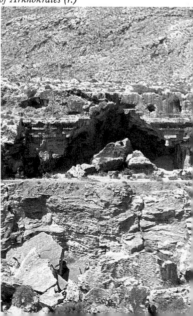

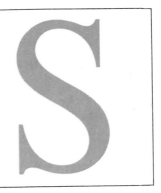

Sagmatá/ΜΟΝΗ ΣΑΓΜΑΤΑ
Boeotia/Central Greece   p.294□G 8

About 9 km. N. of Thebes, near the modern village of Hypaton (Sýrtzi), lies the monastery of Sagmatá. It occupies the summit of Mt.Hypaton, where the ancient temple in the honour of Zeus Hypatos once stood. The present Byzantine main church of the monastery was built from the fragments of this temple in the mid 12C and is dedicated to the Transfiguration of Christ. The church, a 4-columned basilica with a dome, was destroyed by an earthquake in 1914 and rebuilt. Of particular interest is the mosaic pavement. Beautiful Byzantine sculptures adorn the outer walls of the church.

The monastery has a large number of relics, including the *Kara* (head) of St. Clement. The silver reliquaries from post-Byzantine times are of considerable artistic value.

Salamína/Salamís (I)/ΣΑΛΑΜΙΝΑ
Saronic Islands/Aegean Islands   p.294□G/H 9

With an area of 36 sq. miles and some 23,000 inhabitants Salamis is the largest island in the Saronic Gulf. It lies directly opposite the Bay of Eleusis (Elevsína) and is now so to speak a 'suburb' of the port of Piraeus.

History: In the 2nd millennium BC Salamis was probably already a Phoenician base. Homer names the island as the home of the hero Ajax. In historical times it was fought over by the maritime trading cities of Athens and Mégara until it was finally taken for Athens by Solon in 612 BC (securing the port of Piraeus). Salamis became famous through the naval victory of the Greeks here over the numerically superior Persian fleet of Xerxes (480 BC). This important victory for the West is described by the tragedian Aiskhylos in the 'Persae' (472 BC). Salamis later became a Macedonian base (318 BC), until falling to Athens again in 229 BC.

Salamis (c. 18,500 inhabitants): The capital of the island lies at the W. of a two or three mile wide isthmus (E. port of Palúkia). Of interest is the church 17C *Panagia (tu Katharu)* with beautiful frescos (in the crypt) and icons by Markos and Pulakis (Cretan School) on the iconostasis. The church of *Ágios Dimítrios* contains the tomb of the hero of the struggle for liberation Karaiskakis (1821). The *Archaeolog-*

ical Museum has an interesting collection of Mycenean vases, tomb reliefs and stele from classical times bearing inscriptions. *Environs:* The villages of *Kamateró* and *Ampelákia* (*c.* 4 km. SE) were the island's capital and port in classical times. At Kamateró are remains of the *acropolis* (parts of walls) and there are remains of ancient buildings by the harbour mole. Nearby (towards Selínia) is the Byzantine church of *Ágios Ioánnis* with interesting frescos. The village of *Múlki* (or *Aiántio*), about 6 km. SW of the capital, offers traces of its Byzantine heyday: the *Kímisis church* (in the village square) and the *Metamorfosis church* are two interesting cruciform, domed churches from the 12&13C. Nearby are the interesting monastery of *Ágios Nikólaos* (in the SW of the island, about 10 km.) from the 17C with parts of a 12C church and the church of *Ágios Ioánnis* (Kalivítis) from the 15C with a few frescos. The most famous monastery on the island is the *monastery of Faneroméni* (about 7 km. NW) on the NW tip of the island opposite Mégara. It was founded in 1661 and played an important role as a place of refuge from the Turks (1821). The monastery church is a domed building in the form of a Greek cross. Inside are interesting frescos by the Argive painter Georgios Markos and his pupils (1735, Cretan-Italian School), in particular the 'Last Judgement'. Numerous ancient architectural fragments suggest the existence of an ancient sanctuary on this site. The remains of ancient walls on the nearby *Vúdoro (Boúdoron)* are part of the former Athenian fortifications (*c.* 430 BC) opposite the port of Mégara.

Sámos/Samos (I)/ΣAMOΣ
East Aegean Islands/Aegean Islands
p.296☐N 9

This East Aegean island lying just over a mile off the mainland of Asia Minor covers an area of 184 sq. miles and has about 42,000 inhabitants. Wooded and fertile, it has charming scenery.

History: Occupied by Pelasgians since the 3 millennium, it was first occupied by Ionian Greeks around 1000 BC. Its heyday was in the 6&5C BC, when Polykrates rose under an early democratic constitution to become tyrant of Samos (*c.* 532 BC). His raiding fleet was feared, but at his court he was patron to art and science (Herodotus, Anakreon, Ibykos and others). The Samian philosopher Pythagoras (6C BC) emigrated with his school to southern Italy. Massive projects were begun (Heraion, aqueduct). After Polykrates's crucifixion by the Persians (522 BC) the island lost its great importance. A member of the Athenian maritime league, it was nevertheless taken by Perikles after a dispute with Athens (439 BC). In the 4C BC it was ruled alternately by Egypt, Syria and Macedonia. In 190 or 133 BC it became part of the Roman Empire and was a popular holiday island (for Antony and Cleopatra, amongst others). In the 9C AD it became a Byzantine Thema (district). From 1207 it was ruled by Franks, Venetians and Genoese, finally being captured by the Turks in 1475. It took part in the Greek War of Liberation of 1821 and was an independent principality from 1832. Finally annexed to Greece in 1912.

Sámos: The island's capital with some 7,500 inhabitants lies on a deep bay in the N. of the island. It is divided into the harbour quarter and the picturesque Old Town of *Vathý* on the hills. The *Cathedral* (Mitropolis church) has Byzantine icons and in Vathý there are the churches of *Ágios Michael* and *Agia Kara* from the 17C with interesting frescos and wood carvings. The *Archaeological Museum* (by the Xenia Hotel, Public Gardens) contains finds from the ancient town of Samos and the Heraion, including three life-size archaic statues from the Geneleos Group, which were carved around 560 BC by the Samian sculptor Geneleos. Also finds from pre-historic times, a beautiful *tomb stela* from the 4C BC and other *ceramics, ivory idols* and *vases* (small sculptures), numerous *tomb reliefs* and a temple-shaped *sarcophagus.* The *Museum of Ecclesiastical Art (Ekklesiastiko Musion)* in Vathý contains interesting *icons* and old manuscripts from the 13&14C. The *Folklore Museum (Laografiko Musio)* offers a survey of the rich folklore of Samos. The *Picture Gallery* in Vathý displays portraits of Greek freedom-fighters (painted by Lytras) and other documents of the times. The *Library* of Vathý has a valuable collection of old books. The *Palaeontological Museum* contains skeletons of prehistoric animals which lived on the island some 13 million years ago (even rhinos, elephants, giraffes). *Environs:* In the village of *Kamára* on Kap Kótsikas (6 km. E.) lies the interesting monastery of *Zoodochos Pigi* (Mother of God, 1756) with a lovely view of the sea and the coast of Asia Minor. Not far away is the monastery of *Agía Zoni* (16C), also with a beautiful view.

Pythagórion: This picturesque harbour, also called *Tigáni* ('Kettle'), lies about 11 km. SW of Vathý on the S. coast of the island. The town, with a current population of about 1300, lies partly on the site of the *ancient town of Samos.* The present *harbour mole* includes remains of the ancient *Mole of Polykrates* (530 BC). From here the 4 miles of *town walls* (4C BC, with 35 towers and 12 gates) curve around the harbour and hill and are still in good condition. They are built partly of ashlars (E. side), partly of polygonal masonry (W. side) and are up to 14 ft. 9 in. thick. They probably date from the time of the newly-established Samian independence around 322 BC, but they were probably begun under Polykrates. There are few remains of the *ancient town* (mostly built over). The *ancient mar-*

ket (agora) lay near the harbour. The *kastro* (castle) built in 1824 by the hero of the struggle for liberation Lykurgos Logothetis lies SW of the harbour. The ancient castle of the tyrant Polykrates may also have been here, probably on the site of the *Metamorfosis church* (19C), which offers a good view of the Mykale foothills on the Asia Minor coast opposite, where Polykrates was crucified in 522 BC. Many ancient architectural fragments such as Ionic column drums are incorporated in the kastro. Also *remains of houses* from Hellenistic-Roman times with colonnaded courts were excavated here. Ceramic finds indicate that this area was already settled in the 3rd or 2nd millennia. A small *theatre* (not very well-preserved), lies on the slope of the fortified *Kastelli hill* by the monastery of Panagía Spiliani (splendid all-round view). To the W. of the theatre is the entrance of the famous *aqueduct* built by the ancient architect Eupalinos of Mégara. It is a half mile long and a tunnel and was dug by the tyrant Polykrates around 530 BC in order to carry water from a spring to the N. of Mt.Ampelos right through the mountain. Herodotus praised it as one of the wonder's of the world. The *Fountain House* lies NW of the town by the *Agiades* chapel and a pipe (933 yards long) leads to the N. entrance of the tunnel. The tunnel itself (5 ft. 9 in. x 574 ft., plus the water channel) was dug out from the rock from both sides, N. and S. They only just failed to meet in the middle, there is a slight bend. There are buildings at each end of the tunnel. The tunnel is accessible from the S. for about 770 yards but thereafter, beyond a fall, only with a guide. This water supply was carried to the town via further pipes and continued in use until late Roman times. The *Archaeological Museum* contains finds from the nearby Heraion, including a *seated statue* of Aiakes (father of Polykrates), a *Statue of Augustus Caesar,* other *busts of emperors,* archaic and Hellenistic *tomb stele.*

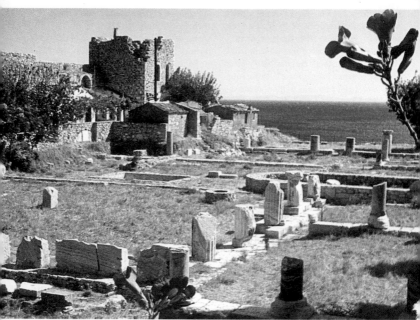

Pythagórion (Sámos), fortress of Lykurgos Logothetis

Environs: The former capital *Khóra* (after the recolonization in the 16C) lies NW of Pythagórion. The town, with a population of 1100, has a few pretty churches: *Agía Paraskeví, Ágios Charalampos* and others. Nearby is the monastery of *Agía Triada* (17C) and the *Stavrós monastery* (1586).

Heraíon: The ruins of the ancient *Sanctuary of Hera* (modern Greek: *Iraon*) lie about 7 km. W. of Pythagórion at the mouth of the river Imbrasos. The place is also called *Kolónna* after the sole surviving upright column. As early as the 3rd or 2nd millennia BC there was a Pelasgian settlement and shrine here, the centre of which was the sacred *Lygos Tree* (osier or chaste shrub). According to myth Hera, the wife of Zeus, was born here, and in antiquity her cult wedding (spring festival) was celebrated here annually. During the 'Hi-

eros Gamos', the cult wedding ceremony, the cult-image (Xoanon) of the goddess was, according to Ionian rite, cleansed and re-dressed by the priestess. Here too stood the first stone *Altar of Hera,* around which the *Sacred Precinct* developed. German excavations (from 1910) revealed that the first *Hekatompedos Temple* from the 8C BC (*c.* 105 x 23 ft., with a later *Peristasis*) was succeeded a second, similar, temple around 670 BC. Next to this were built an *open hall* (230 ft. long) and a *cult-bath* for the image of the goddess. Around 560 BC the architects Rhoikos and Theodoros began building what was then the largest Greek *temple* (335 x 171 ft.). The *cella* was enclosed by a double row of 33 ft. high columns, (8 x 20). Walls and columns were of Poros limestone. The great *Rhoikos temple* was destroyed by fire shortly after its completion. The new building was be-

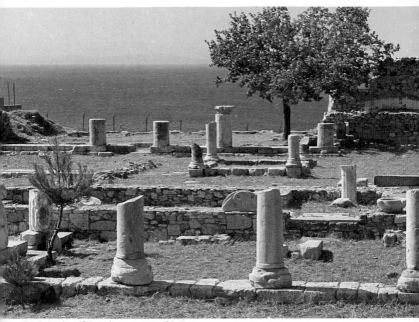

Pythagórion (Sámos), remnants of houses

gun under Polykrates around 530 BC, the foundations being moved about 43 yards in order to create a larger festival square. Parts of the old temple were incorporated and the new temple, which was not completed (death of Polykrates), acquired even larger foundations. The one surviving standing column *(Kolónna)* is from this temple. Various features were added in the 3&2C BC, such as the *marble staircase*. E. of the monumental old temple lay the great tufa *Rhoikos altar* (about 118 ft. x 52 ft. 6 in.), which was rebuilt in Roman times (1C BC). This enclosed the Lygos tree, the stump of which was discovered here in 1963. The remains of the *Sacred Way* with the *Geneleos pedestal* and the *processional route* to the sea are preserved. On the Sacred Way there also stood a small *Statue of Hermes*, a *Temple of Apollo and Artemis* and a smaller *cult-statue temple*. For the visitor

today, orientation is made difficult by the overgrown and sometimes marshy terrain. Nearby lie the remains of an early Christian *basilica* (5C) with a nave and two aisles and a *baptistery*. In the 16C a small cruciform domed basilica, and around 1795 a chapel of *Ágios Nikólaos*, were incorporated.

Other interesting sites on the island: Near the charming mountain village of *Pýrgos* (25 km. W. of Sámos) lies the monastery of *Megáli Panagía* (1586) with well-preserved frescos and a fine iconostasis. Nearby is the monastery of *Tímios Stavros* (Holy Cross) from the 16C with old icons and a carved wooden iconostasis. Near *Vurliótes* (18 km. W. of Samos) is the island's largest church, *Ágios Nikólaos*. The *Panagía church* contains a beautiful old iconostasis. *Karlóvasi* is the second harbour on the N. coast (32 km. W. of Samos) with about 4,500 inhabitants. Of interest are the ruined Venetian *fortress* by the harbour, the three picturesquely arranged little churches around the monastery of *Ágios Ioánnis* and the *Mitrópolis church* (cathedral) with a carved wooden iconostasis and Byzantine icons. Near the harbour lies the 16C walled church of *Agia Pelagia* and the church of the Mother of God, *Theotokos*. Near the harbour village of *Marathókampos* (45 km. W. of Samos) lies the village of *Kallithéa* with old churches, including *Ágios Geórgios* and the 16C *Evangelistria church.*

Samothráki/Samothrace
(I)/ΣΑΜΟΘΡΑΚΗ
North Aegean Islands/Aegean Islands
p.292☐L 3/4

Quiet and isolated, this mountainous island of 68 sq. miles (*c.* 3,800 inhabitants) is well-watered and wooded and rises to a peak of 5,250 ft. (Mt.Fengari). It lies about

Pythagórion (Sámos)

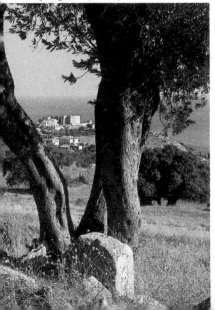

45 miles S. of Thrace (Alexandroúpolis), to which it is linked administratively.

History: The 'Samos of Thrace', as Homer called it, was already populated, before the arrival of the Greeks around 700 BC, by a non-Hellenic Thracian people, who were closely connected to the inhabitants of Troy and the Troad. The mystery cult of the 'Kabeiroi' ('Great Gods'), which reached its height in Hellenistic-Roman times, developed here. In the 6C BC it was an independent island state with its own fleet, territory in Thrace and mint. It joined the Athenian maritime league in the 5C. Later it came under the protectorate of Macedonia (extension of the Sanctuary of the Great Gods) and from 163 BC under Roman supremacy (largely autonomous). The importance of the island as a sacrosanct religious centre in late antiquity (interrupted only by a pirate raid in 84 BC and an earthquake in AD 200) continued until the declaration of Christianity as the state religion in the 4C AD. Following periods of Venetian and Genoese rule (Gattelusi family) the island was captured by the Turks in 1457 and remained in Turkish hands until 1912 (returned to Greece).

Sanctuary of the Great Gods: The ancient town of *Palaiópolis* ('Old City'), which was not abandoned until the 15C, lies in the N. part of the island, about 7 km. from the harbour town of *Kamariótissa*. Not far away from it is the island's principal place of interest, the excavation area of the *Sanctuary of the Great Gods (Kabeiroi).* The particulars of the mystery cult of the Kabeiroi are unclear due to the oath of secrecy of the 'initiated' (Mystes and Epoptes). The pre-Grecian cult entails the work of a goddess of fertility (Axieros) with a male cult partner (Kadmilos). Along with them stand the Chthonic-male Kabeiroi, twins protectors of sailors (Goethe, 'Faust' II), and the pair of underworld gods Axiokersos and Axiokersa (probably later). The incoming Greeks (and later the Romans) equated these demons with their own gods Demeter (Axieros), Castor and Pollux (Polydeuces) as the Kabeiroi, Hermes (Kadmilos) and Hades/Persephone (Axiokersos/Axiokersa). A major difference of this cult from other mystery cults, such as the Eleusinian, was this: Anybody, whether man or woman, adult or child, free-man or slave, Greek or 'Barbarian', could become a member at any time. Admission to the two stages of the Myesis (initiation) and the Epopteia occurred simultaneously through a kind of baptism (catharsis) and confession. Membership emblems were a magnetized iron ring and a headband, Tainia, which protected against danger at sea and the path to the hereafter (perhaps reincarnation). The *cult area* lies on the N. coast, at the confluence of two streams in front of the backdrop of the pine-clad massif. After the discovery of the *Nike of Samothrake* in 1863 excavations were begun (French, Austrian), which were systematically continued by American archaeologists after 1945. *Anaktoron:* In the N. of the excavation area is the *Initiation Building of the Myesis* (1st stage), also described as the *House of the Anaktes* ('Ruling Gods', Kabeiroi). This is a rectangular building of polygonal masonry, 88 ft. 7 in. x 38 ft., with entrances on the W. side, which was built in the 3C BC above an earlier building (probably 6C BC). The 20–26 ft. tall side-walls and supporting pillars of the *main hall* were clad in white stucco. Resting above was the open roof of cross beams. The pavement, rising to the S., was made of crushed loam. In the middle stood a round wooden platform, 10 ft. 8 in. in diameter, and at the sides were benches for the cult dance. In the SE corner was a depression (basin) for libations and catharsis (baptism). The *N. part* of the Anaktoron was somewhat higher up and separated from the main hall by a wooden screen (iconostasis), open at the top, with a stepped door. At the entrance to this inner sanctum (priests' room) stood two bronze statues of the Kabeiroi. Built onto the S. of the Anaktoron was a smaller *Sacred House* (sacristy) with its own entrance (c. 280 BC). In the preparation room, with

Heraion (Sámos), ruins of the Rhoikos temple (l.), altar of Rhoikos (r.)

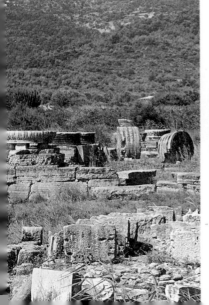

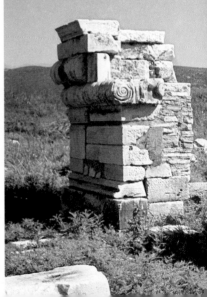

marble benches and loam floor, the white-robed novices waited for the start of the ceremony. Their names were set in the stucco walls on marble tablets. The oldest (pre-Greek) district of the sanctuary lies to the S. of the Anaktoron and is the Double Precinct, divided by remains of walls (from E. to W.) into the *N. and S. court.* Remains of the *Cyclopean walls*, old *altars* and *sacrificial pits* from the 7C BC testify to the origins of the natural sanctuary. It was here that the largest Greek rotunda was founded by the Thracian-Egyptian Queen Arsinoe around 280 BC (foundations preserved). The *Arsinoeion* was a rotunda with *c.* 23 ft. high walls of Thasian marble on an 8 ft. thick limestone base (outer diameter of 66 ft.). On the walls was a 9 ft. 4 in. high pilastered gallery, above which was a Doric entablature and the tiled roof with smoke outlet; above the entrance in the S. was the votive inscription (parts of which are in the museum, together with architectural fragments). The interior, the function of which is unclear, consisted of a simple clay floor, round wooden benches and a sacrificial altar with a smoke outlet in the vaulted wooden ceiling (Corinthian half-columns in the upper gallery). The old ceremonial square was bordered to the S. by the *Temenos* ('Sacred Precinct'). The open paved court, 82 ft. x 32 ft. 10 in., had a *sacrificial hearth* and was used, with its 13 ft. high walls, for mystical cult dances (and Mystery games). An Ionic *Propylon* from 340 BC (39 ft. 4 in. wide, 26 ft. 3 in. high) of Thasian marble forms the entrance in the NE. A fragment of the *propylon frieze* (with cult dancing girls) can be seen in the museum. In the NW of the Temenos is a 26 ft. wide terrace for votive gifts. Adjoining to the S. is the *Sanctuary* (Hieron) of the *Epoptes* (2nd stage of the initiation): This building, 131 ft. x 42 ft. 8 in. and begun around 325 BC, was used as the initiation room of the Epoptes. This structure, unique in Greece at the time, partly anticipates the later early Christian basilica with

nave, two aisles and apse, and was also used for mystery rites (evening meal). The limestone foundations and the lowest layer of marble (Euthynteria) are partly preserved. In 1956 5 columns of the pronaos (double row of 6 Doric marble columns, added on to the N. around 150 BC) were re-erected on a modern foundation. The building was surrounded with Doric entablature (parts in the museum). The N. *pedimental figures* (*c.* 150 BC, now in Vienna) were fully sculpted nature deities; reliefs on the S. pediment. On the roof there were winged *victories* (one of which in the museum). The interior had a coffered wooden ceiling, marble pavement, marble wall benches and a cult hearth in the centre. The inner walls of the unsupported cella, 92 ft. x 36 ft., were painted in the 'First Pompeian Style'. The *apse* (to the S.), separated by a curtain, with a podium was the room of the Hierophants ('priests'). In the middle is a hollow ('crypt') from a later date. Here the remains of earlier cult rooms were excavated (6&5C BC). NW of the Hieron lie the remains of a *Hall, c.* 75 ft. 6 in. x 36 ft., with 8 Doric *limestone columns* on the W. front. This was built around 540 BC for the preservation of votive gifts with a kind of half-timbered walls and wooden timbering with clay bricks. Beneath the stone pavement of 400 BC (originally pebble-stone mosaic) were numerous votive gifts. Adjoining to the S. was a monumental *stepped altar* (*c.* 46 ft. x 56 ft.). The altar court, surrounded by 26 ft. 3 in. high walls with 4 Doric columns on the W. side, was founded around 335 BC by Philip III, half-brother of Alexander the Great (votive inscription preserved). The altar building was later used as a backdrop and ersatz stage for the (poorly preserved) *cult theatre* of 200 BC lying opposite. The stream running between them was covered over with wooden boards (late antique canal). Above the theatre (to the S.) lies the *Nike Fountain* (of Samothrake): In the upper water basin stood the victory goddess, Nike (8 ft.), on a ship's prow; in the lower basin was a representation of a harbour. The votive gifts of the Rhodians (*c.* 190 BC) following a naval victory are now in the Louvre in Paris (copy in the museum). Nearby, to the E. of the theatre, are the foundations of a long *Stoa* from the 3&2C BC, 341 ft. x 46 ft. This hall, with 35 Doric columns on the E. front, was divided into two aisles by 16 Ionic columns and (particularly at the front) intended for votive gifts (gallery). From here there is a good view over the whole sanctuary. N. of the stoa there are remains of various other buildings, including the *House of the Milesian Woman* (founded 3C BC), a small medieval *fortress* (in the 'Ruinenviereck') built from parts of antique buildings. S. of this (opposite the Temenos) the remains of a *Dining House* (for pilgrims) from the 4C BC were uncovered. The actual festival entrance to the cult centre was provided by the *Propylon* on the E. side of the excavation area. This massive *gateway*, the limestone foundation of which survives (along with other architectural fragments), was built around 280 BC by the Egyptian King Ptolemy II (inscription preserved). The propylon with a marble superstructure of 36 ft. x 55 ft. 8 in. had 6 Ionic columns on the E. side and 6 Corinthian on the W. side (Thasian marble). Below it flowed the stream, which swelled when in spate. Also of interest are the remains of the *ancient cemetery* of the propylon with tombs from the 7-2C BC. The *Sacred Way* led from the propylon to the ancient town of Samothrake. The nearby heights provide a view over the ruins of the ancient town with *harbour* and sunken *moles*. The ancient *town walls* survive in part (W. wall). At the harbour are the ruins of an early Christian church.

Archaeological Museum (110 yards from the excavation area): This contains reconstructions and fragments of the cult buildings, parts of the *Temenos frieze*, images of the *Great Gods* and other *statues* (such as the

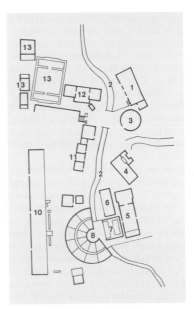

Samothráki, shrine of the great gods 1 anaktoron **2** Cyclopean walls **3** arsinoeion **4** temenos **5** initiation room (2 floors) **6** hall of votive gifts **7** monumental altar **8** theatre **9** Nike niche **10** stoa **11** fortifications **12** house of the Milesian woman **13** guest houses

Nike), *ceramics* and votive gifts from all periods and interesting inscriptions. *Hall A:* Architectural fragments from the *Hall of Votive Gifts* (with votive gifts) and the *Altar Court* (*c.* 330 BC); parts of the entablature from the Hieron and a reconstruction of the acroterion; parts of the entablature from the Arsinoeion (lion's head waterspout, bull's skull); marble stele from the Anaktoron, herald's staff with serpents (Kabeiroi); parts of the roof of the Anaktoron; inscription forbidding entry to the uninitiated; marble altar (4 or 3C BC). *Hall B:* Tieresias and marble sculpture of Persephone from around 450 BC; Ionic column from the Temenos propylon; slabs from the *relief frieze of the Temenos* (*c.* 340 BC) with dancing girls and girl musicians in archaic manner; stele fragments; in the glass display cases there are votive gifts, coins, architectural and sculpture fragments. *Hall C:* Life-size *marble figure of the Nike* from the Hieron (acroterion) from 130 BC; in the glass cases are ceramics (2C BC), vessels from the 6C BC, metal items (votive gifts), oriental-style ceramics, cult ceramics from the 6–4C BC and funerary urns from the necropolis; Athenian black and red figure ceramics, Roman tomb finds, etc.

Environs: About 6 km. SE inland from the harbour of *Kamariótissa* is the present capital, *Samothráki* (or *Khóra*) with some 1500 inhabitants. This was founded in the late Middle Ages by the inhabitants of the old town of Palaiópolis as a place of refuge from pirates and Turks. A Byzantine *castle* overshadows the mountainside houses. Various watch-towers from the Gattelusi period (1431–56) are scattered across the island, including one to the N. of the excavation area. Also of interest is the spa and place of pilgrimage *Thermá* (in the N.) with sulphur springs and a popular festival (9 August). It is also the starting point for the ascent of the island's highest peak, *Mt. Fengári* ('Moon Mountain', 5,249 ft.), ancient *Zerýnthia.*

Sérifos (I)/ΣΕΡΙΦΟΣ
Cyclades/Aegean Islands   p.296☐I 10

This small island (25 sq. miles, about 1300 inhabitants) in the western Cyclades was known in antiquity for its mines (iron, copper, lead). A place of exile under the Romans, historically and administratively it is part of the island of Kea.

Sérifos (also *Khóra,* 'village'): The main town of the island lies 12 km. from the harbour of *Livádi.* Ruins of a Venetian *castle* (13&14C).
Environs: At *Kutalás* (8 km. SW) are the ruins of an ancient *marble tower* (4C BC). About 13 km. N. of Sérifos lies the monastery of *Moni Taxiarchon* from the 16C with frescos from the 18C and rare Byzantine manuscripts. In the neighbouring village of *Panagía* (4 km. N.) stands the

Sérifos, harbour and island capital with ruined Venetian fortress

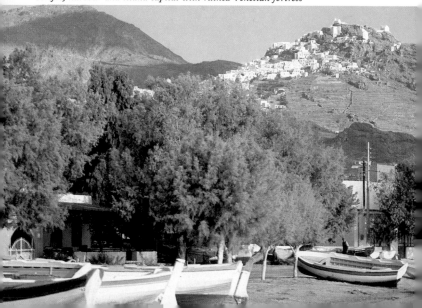

island's oldest church (10C) with the same name.

Serrai/Sérres/ΣΕΡΡΑΙ
Sérrai/Macedonia/N. Greece
p.292☐H 2

Capital (40,000 inhabitants) of the nome of the same name on the border with Bulgaria. Old pre-Hellenistic town, referred to by Homer and Herodotus.

Acropolis: Ruins of a 14C Byzantine fortress on a hill, where the 13C Byzantine church of **Ágios Nikólaos** also stands.

Agii Theodori: Byzantine (restored) metropolis church, an 11C basilica with a nave and two aisles.

Museum *(Arkhaiologiko Musío):* Small archaeological museum with finds from Roman and Byzantine times.

Also worth seeing: The town has three Turkish mosques: *Bezestení, Mosque of Achmed* and *Tzitzirlí.*

Environs: Amfipolis (60 km. SE): Small village on the site of ancient Amphipolis with ruins of walls. Excavations on the site of the ancient *necropolis* (2 km. NW). Remains of a small *Shrine of Clio* were discovered SE of the village. Near the old harbour of Amphipolis are the ruins of a Byzantine *fortress*, which doubtless belonged to the town of *Caesarúpolis,* founded in 837. On the main Thessaloníki-Kavála road, at the mouth of the Strimon by the new bridge, is an enormous Hellenistic *Lion.* Monastery of **Ágios Ióannis Pródromos** (12 km. NW): 13C Byzantine church with the tomb of the Patriarch Genádios II of Constantinople. *Sidirókastron* (24 km. W.): Old Byzantine town. Remnants of a *fortress* survive.

Sífnos (I)/ΣΙΦΝΟΣ
Cyclades/Aegean Islands
p.298☐I/K 11

This island, lying in the S. of the western

Serrai, Agii Theodori

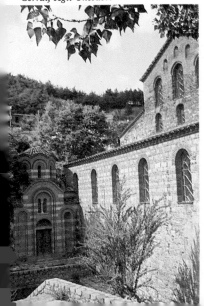

Amfípolis (Serrai), lion

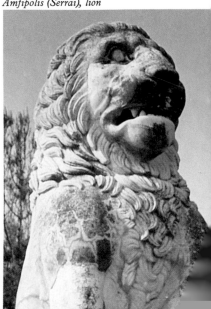

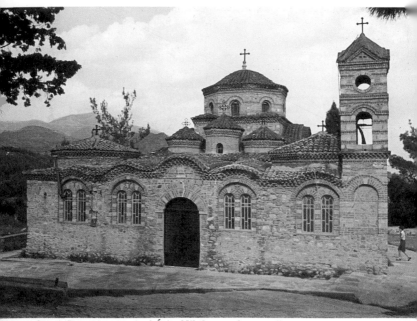

Serrai, Byzantine church of Ágios Nikólaos on the acropolis

string of the Cyclades (26.5 sq. miles, *c.* 2,000 inhabitants), is now known for its pottery.

History: Already inhabited in Cycladic times (*c.* 2000 BC), the island was colonized by Ionians (around 900 BC) and attained prosperity through its silver mines (e.g. the Treasury of the Siphnians at Delphi). It changed hands several times in the Middle Ages. Under Turkish rule it enjoyed relative autonomy.

Apollonía (1,000 inhabitants) The main town lies inland, about 6 km. from the harbour of *Kamáres.* Charming cube-shaped houses. Of interest is the church of *Ágios Sotír* ('Redeemer') with frescos and a beautiful iconostasis (17C).

Environs: The former capital was *Kástro* on the E. coast (about 5 km. E.). With its white houses, little stepped streets and chapels, it is charmingly situated at the foot of the ruined Venetian castle (14C). On the hillside to the NW remains of a marble wall of an *acropolis* from the 4C BC were excavated; also houses from the Geometric period and tombs. The *Panagía (Geraniofora)* church on the hill top stands above the remains of an early archaic *temple* (7C BC). To the W. is the famous *College of the Holy Sepulchre* (17C). In the area of the bay of *Platí-Yialós* (*c.* 6 km. S.) are ruins of ancient houses (at Fidíonas), Cycladic tombs (on the W. shore) and several Hellenistic *watch-towers* (4C BC). In the vicinity of *Exámpela* are various monasteries, including the interesting fortified monastery of *Profítis Ilías* (1145) on the mountain of the same name (2,277 ft.). At Apollonía (3 km. W.) lies the 12C

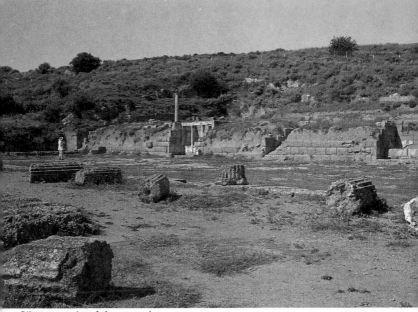

Sikyón, remains of the gymnasion

Mongu Monastery, and about 8 km. N. of Apollonía are ancient mine shafts.

Sikyón/ΣΙΚΞΟΝ
Korinth/Peloponnese   p.294☐F 8/9

This ancient city lies 27 km. NW of Corinth (towards Patras) at the village of Vassilikó.

History: The city enjoyed its heyday in the 7&6C BC under the Orthagoran dynasty, which promoted the arts. The best known rulers included Eupompos, Pausias, Aristokles and Kanachos. The Treasury of the Sikyonians in Delphi testifies to the city's wealth. At the end of the 4C BC the city was captured and destroyed by Demetrios Poliorketes. He had it rebuilt near the present village of Vassilikó, where the acropolis had once stood. The name *Demetrias,* which he gave the town, did not survive, the citizens later naming it Sikyón. In 251 BC Aratos freed the city from tyranny and it became a member of the Achaean League. In AD 23 the city was destroyed by an earthquake.

Museum: This stands on the site of Roman baths (reconstructed) and has a collection of vases, terracotta figures and mosaics from the 4C BC.

Temple: Opposite the museum are foundations of an archaic temple (of Artemis?), which was rebuilt in Hellenistic times.

Bouleuterion: Almost square (133 ft. x 135 ft.) with 16 columns inside, later converted into a bath. Next to it is an elongated

Stoa (348 ft. x 20 ft.) with 17 Doric columns along the front.

Gymnasion (W. of the Bouleuterion): Ruins of the building on two different levels. The upper part with colonnades on three sides was not added until the 3C AD. It was connected to the lower part, dating from Hellenistic times, by a staircase. On both sides of the staircase is a fountain with two columns between antae.

Theatre (to the NW): The lowest rows of seats and the parodoi are in good condition. Further NW is the *stadium* with a well preserved polygonal masonry wall.

Sitía/ΣΗΤΕΙΑ
Lasíthi/Crete   p.298□l 14

Sitía is today a rather isolated, but attractively situated little harbour with 6,200 inhabitants, lying on a north-facing bay at the E. end of the island. The town, which only has a *fort* to testify to its Venetian past and nothing at all from earlier times, played a part in antiquity, being known then as *Eteia*. Under the Venetians *La Sitia*, as it was then called (hence the name of the nome, Lasíthi), one of the four principal towns of Crete. It suffered so much as a result of earthquakes (1303 and 1508), the onslaughts of the Turks (e.g. 1539) and being repeatedly defended by the Eteocretans (e.g. 1341), that it eventually declined to its present insignificance. Leon Kallergis, who was descended from an old aristocratic Cretan family planned a secret uprising against the Venetians in the 14C. He was foiled and executed by being placed in a sack and drowned in the sea—countless new Cretan revolts resulted. Sitía was the birthplace of Vitzentzos Kornáros, whose work 'Erotókritos'—written in Cretan dialect—became a kind of Cretan national epic.

Environs: Toplú/Toploú: Lying in the isolated hills of Kap Síderos, some 20 km. N. of Sitía, surrounded by high, gleaming white walls is Moni Toploú. This seemingly almost impregnable monastery has

Toplú (Sitía), section of the icon by Kornavos (monastery)

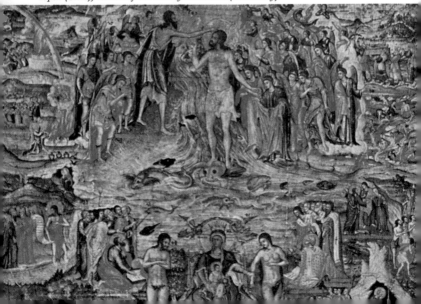

a very warlike name—Toploú being Turkish for 'cannon'. Originally, it is said, the monastery, whose history dates back to the 13C, was armed with a cannon and was a kind of fortress for the bay of Sitía. It suffered from earthquakes and was constantly plagued by Turkish pirates and in 1704 was finally almost totally destroyed. The spacious and extensive complex—all in gleaming white—which we see today was rebuilt from 1718 onwards. The formidable, martial impression of the exterior contrasts with the bright, friendly, often almost frivolous architecture of the *interior* with covered stairways and arches, in which Venetian influence in particular comes to the fore. The small monastery church of *Panagia Akrotiriani* has a saddle-roof with gleaming red tiles. Next to the church entrance hangs a stone plaque with a Greek inscription from the 2C BC. Inside there are numerous *icons*, some new, others dating from the 17&18C. Particularly beautiful is the 'Creation of the World' painted by Ioannis Kornaros in the 18C, with a multitude of tiny Biblical scenes. **Itanos:** 10 km. further N. from

Toploú, on a bay at the tip of the peninsula, 2 km. from Vai, lies ancient Itanos, named 'Erimúpolis' (lonely town) by the locals. In this very isolated spot are *ruins* from Minoan, Greek, Hellenistic, Roman and Byzantine times, as well as remains of an acropolis, a Hellenistic tomb, bases of Roman statues and the remnants of a Byzantine basilica with a nave and two aisles. **Palaiókastro/Paleokastron:** 10 km. S. of Itanos lies Palaiókastro near the NE bay of Crete. Next to it archaeologists discovered the Minoan town of *Heleia*, called Russolákkos by the locals. The extensive excavations, which brought an entire town to the light of day, suggest that Heleia was once one of the largest and most important settlements of the Minoans. Today only a paved road remains clearly identifiable from the settlement. Ceramics, bronzes, stone vessels and painted sarcophagi from the Neopalatial period were also discovered here. On the *Petsofa hill* there once stood a famous Minoan *hill-top sanctuary*. Today there are still remains there of a later sanctuary of Zeus. Around 1450 Heleia appears to have succumbed to

Palaiókastro (Sitía), the Minoan town of Heleia

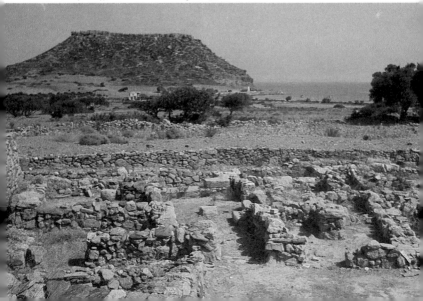

the natural catastrophes that struck the rest of the island. Finds suggest that the town was then rebuilt and became an important Dorian settlement. **Zú/Zou:** On the road to Ierápetra, just beyond the town boundary, are the remains of a *Minoan estate* from around 1600 BC. Some 3 km. further along the road is the village of Zú. To the S. of the village, on the terrace-like side of a hill are the remains of another *Minoan estate* from around 1600 BC. **Akhládia:** Akhládia lies 6 km. from Sitía. A *Mycenean beehive tomb* was uncovered there and about 1 km. from Akhládia are the remains of two Minoan houses. **Praisos:** Praisos lies about 17 km. S. of Setía, spread out over 3 hills by the village of Khandaras and is also known as the Balance of the Eteocretans. It is believed that the Minoans withdrew here, as the stream of incoming mainland Greeks increased, and preserved their language and culture. Excavations threw up finds from Minoan, Mycenean and Hellenistic times. Praisos must have been a town of importance well into Greek times. Inscriptions were found here, dating from 600–300 BC, which were written in Greek characters but in a non-Greek language. Some scholars believe it to be the Eteocretan language. It is certain that Praisos, along with Knossós, Phaistós, Górtyna and Itanos, had developed its own currency around 500 BC. In 1960 the remains of a *Minoan estate* from around 1700 BC were discovered near Praisos. Also near Praisos, at Photula, a *beehive tomb* with a Mycenean terracotta sarcohagus from around 1200 BC was uncovered.

Skiáthos (I)/ΣΚΙΑΘΟΣ
Northern Sporades/Aegean Islands
p.294☐G/H 6

This island (30 sq. miles, 3,900 inhabitants), with charming scenery and lovely pine forests, lies off the Gulf of Vólos (4 km. from the Magnesia peninsula, 10 km. from Euboea). Today it is a popular holiday island (good, sandy beaches).

History: The island, settled by the Ionians around 1000 BC and under the influence of Chalkis (Euboea) in the 9–6C

Palaiókastro (Sitía), remains of houses from Heleia

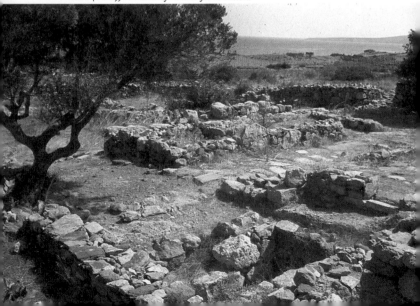

BC, played a negligible role in antiquity. It changed hands during the Middle Ages too (Byzantium and the Venetian Ghisi family) until its capture by the Turks in 1538. Returned to Greece in 1828.

Skiáthos (also *Khóra*): The capital (3,700 inhabitants), only founded in 1829, lies on a beautiful natural harbour in the SE of the island, on the site of the *ancient settlement* of the same name (no remains). Of interest are the churches of *Ágios Nikólaos*, *Mitropolis* and *Panagía* with a bell tower (all 19C). Also note the house of the Greek poet Papadiamantis (1851–1911), now a small museum.
Environs: The medieval capital *Kástro* (inhabited 1300–1830) lies NE of Skiáthos (about 8 km.). The ruins include massive *fortifications* with a *drawbridge*. Of interest is the 17C *Church of Christ* with a carved wooden iconostasis, beautiful Byzantine icons and wall frescos. Nearby (4 km. N. of Skiáthos) is the monastery of *Panagía Evangelístria* (1794) with a carved wooden iconostasis and beautiful frescos from 1822. Also a collection of icons and valu-

able church implements and a library with manuscripts (on the 15 August the rare festival of the 'Laying-Out of the Virgin Mary'). Also worth a visit is the 17C monastery of *Panagía Kunístria* on the W. coast (one-and-a-half hour's walk) and the monastery of *Panagía Kechriá* (NW of Skiáthos) from 1540 (rebuilt in 1738). Both have beautiful Byzantine icons, frescos and iconostases.

Skópelos (I)/ΣΚΟΠΕΛΟΣ
Northern Sporades/Aegean Islands p.294☐H 6

A wedge-shaped island pointing NW (37 sq. miles, about 4,500 inhabitants), with numerous olives and pine-woods, it lies about 6 km. E. of Skiáthos (popular holiday resort).

History: The island, known in antiquity as *Pepárethos,* is supposed to have been settled first by the Minoan Cretan Staphylos, son of the deities Dionysos and Ariadne. Around 800 BC Euboeans from Chalkís

Lutráki (Skópelos), ancient ruins

Skópelos, monastery churches

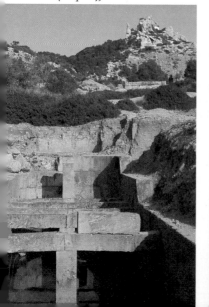

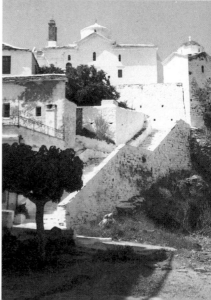

occupied the island, which later became a relatively important member of the Athenian maritime league (479 BC). Subsequently it was ruled by various powers, as it was again in the Middle Ages (Byzantium, Ghisi family, Venetians). Captured by the Turks in 1538, it played an active part in the Greek War of Liberation until being returned to Greece in 1830.

Skópelos (2,500 inhabitants): The island capital is picturesquely situated on the slope of the harbour bay in the NE of the island ('Jewel of the Aegean'). Of interest are its multi-storeyed, tiled *houses* . The town, named 'Skópelos' ('cliff') after its cliff walls, lies on the site of the ancient town of *Pepárethos*. Above the ruined medieval *fortress* are the remains of foundations of an *ancient shrine* (unmarked). By the sea to the E. (at the suburb of Ampelikí)are remains of a *Sanctuary of Asklepios* from the 4C BC, finds preserved in the *Town Hall* (Dimarkhío). Also in the vicinity are remains of Cyclopean (pre-Greek) *walls*. The town has numerous churches and monasteries (on the edge of the town). The churches of *Ágios-Athanásios* (by the Kástro), *Apostles* and *Ágios Nikólaos* (on the cliff) date from the 11&12C with old icons, frescos and carved wooden iconostases. In the town is the church of *St.Michael* with ancient *sarcophagus slabs* on the walls.

Environs: Not far from the town is the interesting *Evangelístria Monastery* from 1712 with a church (four columns), beautiful iconostasis and a valuable Byzantine icon of the *Panagía*. Nearby is the monastery of *Agía Varvára* ('St.Barbara') from 1648 and at the Asklepios Shrine the monastery of *Panagía Livadiótissa* (17C) with a beautiful icon of the Mother-of-God by the Cretan painter Agorastós (1671). Also the monastery of *Pródromos* from 1721 and *Ágii Taxiárches* ('Archangel') with remains of an early Christian church from 672 in the forecourt (old bishop's seat). Preserved

in the *Metamórfosis Monastery* from the 16C are old *documents*. At the village of *Stáfylos* (c. 5 km. SE) an important *Mycenean royal tomb* (1600–1200 BC) with rich *grave goods* (jewellery, implements, swords) was dug up. Further ancient remains were unearthed at *Pánormos* (16 km. SW) and *Glóssa* (25 km. NW) from the ancient towns of *Pánormos* and *Selinús* (now *Lutráki*). Near Glóssa are the ruins of 4 ancient *watch-towers*.

Skýros (I)/ΣΚΥΡΟΣ
Northern Sporades/Aegean Islands
p.296□I/K 6/7

Skýros (80 sq. miles, about 4,000 inhabitants) is the largest island of the Sporades and lies to the E. of Euboea (24 km. E. of Kými). The vegetation is somewhat sparse but the island has beautiful bays for bathing in the W. and is known for its local crafts (furniture, embroidery, pottery, matwork). Popular holiday resort.

History: The young Achilles is supposed to have hidden (dressed as a girl) on this island, which was already inhabited in prehistoric times, until Odysseus persuaded him to take part in the Trojan War. The Athenian King Theseus is supposed to have met his death here (pushed from the acropolis cliff). Kimon had the supposed bones of Theseus taken back to Athens in 470 BC and founded the Theseion. From 469 Skýros was ruled by Athens (settlement of Athenian peasants). Under Byzantium it was a place of exile and for a while (1207–69) held by the Ghisi family. From 1269–1453 it was again a Byzantine possession, then Venetian once more before being taken by the Turks (1538); part of Greece since the War of Liberation of 1821.

Skýros (2,000 inhabitants): The island

capital with its cube-shaped white houses lies on the bay in the NE on the slope below the *ancient acropolis* (fortification walls preserved from the 4C BC). Above it the Venetian fortress (Kastro) was built in the 14&15C (at the entrance a relief with the Lion of St.Mark). In the Kastro is the interesting monastery church of *Ágios Georgios* (1680) with interesting *wall paintings* of Christ. The monastery is said to go back to an old foundation (*c.* 900). Good (seemingly carved) frescos in the two churches of the *Panagía*. In the *Museum of Archaeology and Local Craft (Arkhaiologiko-Laografiko Musíon* in the Town Hall is an interesting collection with proto-Helladic and Mycenean ceramic finds, proto-Geometric vases, sculptures, reliefs and inscriptions (fragments) from Roman to Byzantine times. Also examples of local arts and crafts.

Environs: On the way to *Liniariá* is the destroyed monastery of *Ágios Demetrios* from 1611 (with church). The small harbour of *Liniariá* on the W. coast (11 km. S.) has remains of a medieval *prison fortress* nearby. In the N. of the island, on *Kap Markési,* are remains of a *Temple of Poseidon* (foundations, 75 ft. 6 in. x 45 ft.) with the ruins of a medieval church (apse preserved). In the vicinity are fallen towers and supporting walls from ancient times. Beautiful view from the monastery of *Olympianí* at the foot of *Mt.Olympos* (1,207 ft.). Nearby are Neolithic excavations from the 5th millennium BC (also below the Kastro at Skýros and on Akhíllion Bay). Remains of a Roman *marble bridge* in the S. of the island of *Valáxa* (W. of Skýros).

Spárti/Sparta/ΣΠΑΡΤΗ
Lakonia/Peloponnese   p.298☐F 10

Capital (10,550 inhabitants) of Lakonia, situated in the Eurotas basin. Only a few remains survive from the ancient town.

History: Sparta owes its origins to Dorians who arrived in Lakonia before 1000 BC, subjugated the native population and founded the city by combining five villages. In historical times there were 3 classes of inhabitants. The *Spartiates,* descendants of the Dorians, who occupied Sparta and later also Messenia. Their estates were worked by the enslaved Helots. Resident outside Sparta were the *Perioikoi* ('neighbours'), who were free and autonomous, but had fewer rights than the Spartiates. They were required to give military service, but had no voice in matters of state. The lowest class was formed by the *Helots,* those subjugated by the Dorians. These were slaves of the state with no civil rights. In Sparta there was a dual monarchy. One of the kings was always a member of the Agiade line, the other of the Europontides. These two were primarily responsible for leading the army; administration and politics falling to the *Ephors,* who had the right to indict the kings in the event of a misdemeanor. They were the wardens of the state and were elected every five years. Next to them was the *Gerusia* (Council of Elders), which consisted of the two kings and 28 members elected for life. These formed a kind of state council. The *Apella* (people's assembly) simply had the right vote in matters of law or war.

The life of the Spartiates was regulated by strict rules. Boys were allowed to stay with their families until their 7th year, whereafter they were brought up by the Paidonomos. Manhood was reached at the age of 20, but their rights as citizens were limited (voice in the people's assembly). At the age of 30 they were declared of age. Their daily life was spent in military exercise and at least once a day they took part in the *Syssitien* (communal meals).

The upbringing of the girls was also different to the rest of Greece. They were brought up more liberally, while their physical training was just as strict as that of the boys. They took part in contests and

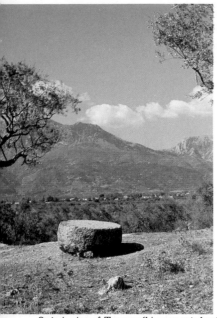 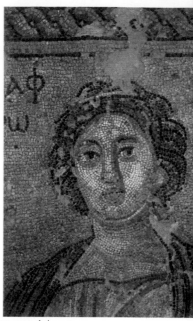

Spárti, view of Taygetos (l.), woman's head, museum (r.)

even competed in the Olympic Games (Kyniska's victory in the quadriga (four-in-hand chariot race) in 396 BC). These strict lifestyles were attributed to Lycurgus, a mythical king of Sparta.

In the 8&7C BC the Spartans expanded in Lakonia and neighbouring Messenia, sub-jugating the population and making them Helots. Around 700 BC the Spartans founded their first colony in Tarentum. They soon held sway over the whole of the Peloponnese apart from Argos. Sparta played an important role in the Persian Wars (Thermopylae, Plataia). The 3rd Messenian War (464–459) led to a grave crisis. In 446/5 Sparta concluded a 30-year peace treaty with Athens, which only lasted 14 years, however (until the Peloponnesian War, 431–404). The Athenian Konon achieved a decisive victory over the Spartans in the naval battle of

Knidos in 394. In 371 the Spartans were defeated at Leuktra, Epameinondas devasted Lakonia and besieged Sparta. The end of Sparta's supremacy was growing near. Epameinondas isolated Sparta by uniting Arkadia (Arkadian League) and fortifying the towns of Megalópolis, Mantineía and Messene. The Spartan monarchy ended with Kleomenes III, who was defeated in the battle of Sellasia in 221. Sparta was forced to join the Akhaian League.

The Romans captured the city in 146. The Perioikoi formed a league and thence-forward called themselves *Eleutherolako-nians*. Sparta flourished to some extent under the Romans. In AD 396 the city was captured by Alaric. In the 9C it was devastated by Slavs and the population moved to the Máni.

After the occupation of Lakonia by the

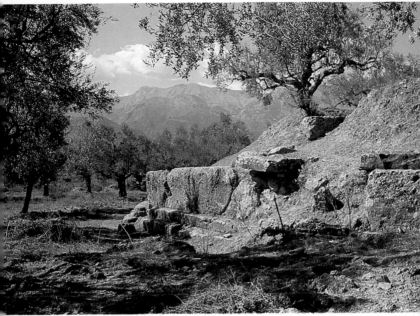

Spárti, SE section of the agora

Byzantines, who gave it the name of *Lakedaimonia,* Sparta was captured by the Franks under Guillaume de Villehardouin.

Acropolis: This was built after the onslaught of the Heruli and the Goths (268 and 386). Near the S. gate are remains of a Roman portico.

On the acropolis hill are remains of two Byzantine churches. One, from the 10C, is dedicated to Ágios Nikon Metanoeite. Next to it is the burial chapel (11C) of the saint. On the N. slope of the acropolis hill is a *cemetery* from the 1&2C AD. In front of it is an old *chamber tomb.*

Theatre (on the SW slope of the acropolis): Hellenistic, only the remains of a few rows of seats and the supporting walls of the cavea from the time of Augustus survive. The theatre was further embellished under Vespasian. W. of the theatre is a *nymphaeum.*

Temple of Athena Chalkioikos: 6C BC, it derives its name *Chalkioikos* from its cladding in bronze plates. In 477 Pausanias fled into the temple and was walled in by the Spartans.

Agora: This lay to the S. of the acropolis. The most important structure in this area was the *Persian Stoa,* built from the proceeds of Persian booty. On the agora stood the statues of Pythian Apollo, Artemis and Leto.

Sanctuary of Leonidas (S. of the acropolis hill): Remains of a building (temple), 41 ft. long and 27 ft. 3 in. wide, from the 5C BC, which can be identified with the *Leonidaion,* where, according to Pausanias, annual competitions were held in honour of Leonidas.

Sanctuary of Artemis Orthia (on the W. bank of the Eurotas): Excavated in 1900 by the British School. Remains of an older and a more recent *altar for burnt offerings*, which can be identified as an earth rampart. Remains of a temple from the start of the 6C. E. of the altars is a Temenos from various epochs.

Remains of a horseshoe-shaped *theatre* from the 3C AD. Here the boys were flogged to test their steadfastness in front of the statue of the goddess. Numerous votive gifts, such as lead figurines, clay masks and plaques with depictions of a sickle (Orthia, goddess of growth) were found.

Museum: This was built in 1875/6 by the Danish architect Th. Hansen, who also built the Academy in Athens. In the entrance hall are stele and inscriptions.

Room I: Pyramidal stele (*c.* 600 BC), adorned on all four sides with reliefs: On two sides are serpents (symbol of the Dioscuri), on the others are the images of two couples (one on each) (Agamemnon-Clytemnestra and Menelaus-Helen?). Bas-relief stele (mid-6C) with an enthroned pair (dead heroes or Chthonic deities): The man with a kantharos, the woman with a pomegranate in her hand.

Room II: Acroterion of a temple (510–480 BC): Bas-relief with three depictions of the Dioscuri.

Room III: Fragment of a capital from the Temple of Apollo Yakinthos at Amyklai (2nd half of the 6C BC); fragment of a statue. Head and torso of a helmeted warrior (so-called Leonidas), found near the Temple of Athena Chalkioikos (495–480 BC); torso of an athlete (?); wings added in Roman times (Eros). *Room IV:* Lead figures of warriors and animals, bronze statuettes from the Sanctuary of Artemis Orthia, Menelaion and Amyklai (end of the 9C to the 4C); clay masks, copies of wooden masks worn at cult dances in honour of Orthia; pithoi with battle and hunting scenes (6C).

Room V: Torsoes, statues and sarcophagus fragments from Hellenistic and Roman times; mosaics with idealized portraits of

Menelaíon (Spárti), temple remains

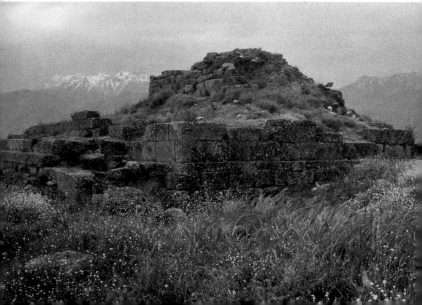

Sappho, Alkibiades (4C AD). Further interesting mosaics in the House of Mouraba depicting Europa astride the bull, Orpheus taming the wild beasts, Achilles between the daughters of Lykomedes, Handing-over of Briseis to Agamemnon, and others.

Environs: Menelaíon (5 km. SE): Excavated by the British School. Remains of a 5C temple — probably a Heroon for Menelaus and Helen, on the site of an older shrine from the 8C BC. **Amýklai** (7 km. S.): On the site of a Mycenean settlement on the hill of Agia Kyriaki are the remains of the Sanctuary of Apollo Amyklaios, who had replaced an earlier vegetation deity. Judging by the finds on the hill the settlement dates back to the Stone Age. A pre-Hellenic deity Hyakinthos was also honoured here. According to legend Hyakinthos was accidentally killed by his friend Apollo while throwing the discus. The flower, which sprang out of the bload-soaked ground, was the first hyacinth. The famous statue of Apollo, nearly 50 ft. tall, was surrounded by stoae. The throne was of chryselephantine and its base

Spárti, museum gardens

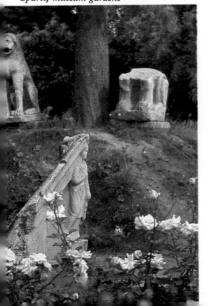

bore reliefs. 1 km. S. of Amýklai was the Shrine of Zeus-Agamemnon and Kassandra-Alexandra (no building remains), a Chthonic shrine (possibly on the site of the church of Agia Paraskevi). To the S. is the Mycenean settlement of *Pháris,* NW of which are the *beehive tombs of Vaphio* from the same time as the Mycenean tombs with rich finds (now in the National Museum in Athens), including two gold cups showing the rounding up of bulls (*c.* 1500 BC). **Sellasía:** (16 km. N.): Famous for the battle in 221 BC, in which the Spartans were defeated by the Macedonian King Antigonos Doson with the help of the Achaean League. Remains of the acropolis (ruins of walls and towers) still to be seen.

Spétses/Spetsai/ΣΠΕΤΣΕΣ
Argolid Gulf   p.294□G 10

This island (8.5 sq. miles, population 3, 500) belonging to the eparchy of Piraeus lies at the eastern mouth of the Argolid Gulf and is a popular holiday resort with the wealthier Greeks.

History: The island, the old name of which was *Pitýusa* ('Pine-land'), played a minor role in antiquity. After Catalan, Genoese and Venetian rule, it was captured by the Turks. In the 16C Albanian settlers arrived. In the 18&19C the island had an important trading fleet, which also took part in the War of Liberation against the Turks (naval victory, 8 September 1822). With the rise of Piraeus as the major shipping centre, the island's economic decline set in and there was considerable depopulation. Following World War 1 Spetsai was for a while the meeting-place of fashionable society.

Spétsai (population 3,200): Attractive harbour with a few interesting captains' houses (18&19C). In the upper town of *Kastélli* (Old Town) lie the remains of the ancient settlement of *Pitýusa* (few traces). Also in Kastélli are 3 interesting churches: The most important is *Agía Triada* ('Holy Trinity', 1793) with a carved wooden iconostasis. Somewhat futher up are the 18C church of the archangels and the church of the *Panagía* (Mother of God) with 18C frescos of the Cretan School (badly damaged by the Turks). *Local Museum* (in the house of Mexis): This houses an interesting naval museum with old models of ships, weapons, uniforms and coins from the time of the War of Liberation (1821). In the suburb of *Agía Marína* is the *Armada Chapel* of 1822 (commemorating the naval victory). Inside is a monumental painting by Kutzis (19C), depicting the battle. In Agía Marína are also the remains of the foundations of two early Christian *basilicas* (5C). Nearby (at Ágii Anárgyri) is the interesting stalactite cave of *Bekíri* (on a wall there are traces of sculptures). At the monastery of *Agii Pantes* ('All-Holy') there is a beautiful view of the straits.

Spili/Spilion/ΣΠΗΛΙΟΝ
Réthymnon/Crete   p.298☐G 14

In the middle of Crete, SE of Réthymnon and NE of Moní Préveli, lies the village of Spili, which is famous in Crete for its good water. There are four interesting late Byzantine churches here: *Ágios Georgios, Ágios Theodoros, Sotíros Christou* and, above all, the small chapel of the *Panagía*, with very well preserved frescos.

Environs: Lampíni/Lambini: Near Spili lies Lampíni with the beautiful domed church of the *Panagía,* the façade of which is particularly fine. During restoration work two layers of frescos, one on top of the other, were brought to light, revealing a *Pantocrator* in the dome.

Mélampes: 20 km. SE of Spili, about 10 km. before Agía Galíni, beautifully situated high above the valleys, is the village of Mélampes with the Byzantine church of *Agía Paraskeví.*

Spiliá/ΣΠΙΛΙΑ
Chaniá/Crete   p.298☐E 13

25 km. W. of Chaniá, S. of the Rodopu peninsula, lies Spiliá. Housed in the main church of the village is a small *icon museum.* Just outside the village is the little church of *Kimisis tis Theotoku,* with very beautiful frescos.

Environs: Episkopí: In addition to the Episkopí at Bizarianó Pediádos there is another Episkopí on Crete, 3 km. S. of Spiliá. In front of the village is the superb round domed church of *Mikhail Archangelos.* Part of the mosaic pavement and, in the narthex, a marble font survive from an early Christian basilica, above which the present church was built around the 7C as a bishop's church—the only such church in Crete. In the 11C the central building was surrounded by a square building. Of the original frescos there remains very little.

Stymfalía/ΣΤΥΜΦΑΛΙΑ
Korinth/Peloponnese   p.294☐F 9

A village lying 62 km. SW of Corinth. Known in mythology as the place where Herakles killed the Stymphalian birds. According to legend the town was founded by Stymphalos, a son of Eleathos.
Extending along the low hill was the acropolis, which bears traces of a *Temple of Athena Polias.* A few remains of three other temples, as well as an aqueduct.

Environs: Pheneós (*c.* 36 km. NW):

Ruins of the ancient town with ruins of an *Asklepieion* and remains of ancient walls.

Súnion/Cape Sunion/ΣΟΥΝΙΟΝ
Attica/Central Greece   p.296☐H 9

Rising 200 ft. out of the sea, at the SE tip of Attica (*c.* 68 km. SE of Athens), is the steep Cape Sunion, on the highest point of which is the famous *Temple of Poseidon* .

History: Even in early antiquity 'Holy Sunion' (Homer, 'Odyssey', III, 278) was an important landmark for ships sailing into the Saronic Gulf (Saronikos Kolpos). Finds of Cycladic idols and Mycenean seals confirm its early settlement (2nd millennium BC). In the 8&7C BC there was probably an early shrine of Apollo without a temple here, from which two 7&6C BC archaic kouroi were discovered (good condition, now in the National Museum in Athens, Room 8). The open sea towards Crete was presumably named the 'Myrtle Sea' (Myrtoon Pelagos) after 'myrtle-wreathed' Apollo (myrtoos). The conversion into a shrine of Poseidon, god of the wild sea and earthquakes, took place in the 6C BC with the building of the first poros-limestone temple, which was destroyed by the Persians around 480 BC.

Temple of Poseidon *(Naos Posidona):* This is one of the few cult buildings of the more feared than worshipped god of the sea. According to myth Poseidon (today: Posidonas), son of Kronos, was granted dominion over the oceans, while his brothers Zeus and Hades were given the realms of heaven and of the dead respectively.

The classical temple, built of the dazzling white local marble, was erected around 444 BC, at the same time as the Parthenon in Athens (perhaps by the architect of the similar Hephaisteion/Thesaion). The

temple stands on a stylobate of three steps, 102 ft. x 44 ft., which is supported on the NW side by a 3 ft. high plinth to compensate for the slope of the ground. Of the Doric peripteros of 6 x 13 columns (34 in all), 9 of the S. and 2 of the N. columns are still standing (or have been re-erected). The *columns,* about 20 ft. high and 3 ft. 3 in. in diameter, have a particularly slender and elegant appearance (more Ionic than Doric) with 16 rather than the usual 20 flutes. The rather coarse local marble, although more easily weathered, has nevertheless retained its whiteness, in contrast to the yellowish Pentelic marble of the acropolis. Between the pronaos to the E. and the opisthomodos to the W. with 2 x 2 columns *in antis* stood the cella (central room for the cult-statue). Parts of the antae and the columns between them survive. Above the *marble architrave* there was probably a sloping wooden roof with marble roof tiles. A carved *frieze* on the pronaos architrave depicted the deeds of Theseus, scenes from the Gigantomachia and the battle between the Lapiths and Centaurs. Fragments of this can be seen at the entrance (other parts are in the National Museum in Athens). On one of the columns Lord Byron, who was particularly fond of Sunion, carved his name, as have many others.

Remainder of the temple precinct: SW of the temple are the remains of foundations of a later portico incorporating parts of columns from the old poros temple of the 6C BC.

In the SE, where the peribolos separates the temple precinct from the cliff edge, the foundations (hewn out of the rock) of an *Altar of Poseidon* are discernible.

The entrance in the N. is formed by poros *propylaia* (5C BC, which were clad in marble and had a portico with 2 columns at the front and the rear. Adjoining (to the E.) was a long *stoa* with 6 central columns (5 bases preserved). In the angle formed are remains of a smaller portico. To the left of the propylaia are parts of the pronaos frieze.

Fortifications: A fortification wall curved around the entire temple precinct to the N. and NE and in parts it is still in good condition. It was laid out during the Peloponnesian War around 409 BC. To the NW are the remains of a *gate,* which led to the artificial ships' berths on the W. coast. A little futher N. on the small bay are remains presumably of *docks* and buildings (granaries). Within this area ancient *streets* have been discovered.

Temple of Athena: About 550 yards NE of the precinct of Poseidon, lying on a low hill on the isthmus connecting the promontory to the mainland, is a *temple precinct* from the 6C BC, dedicated to Athena Sunias. The larger *temple,* 56 ft. x 39 ft., only had colonnades to the E. and S. (peristasis). The *cella* has the foundations of 4 interior columns and is more in the form of a megaron. Against the rear wall is the *base* of the statue of Athena. The

temple was converted around 460 BC (columns arranged 7 x 9). Important fragments from it and some of the capitals are in the National Museum in Athens.

NE of this are the remains of a small *Doric building* (16 ft. x 23 ft.) with a cella, cult statue base and later distyle pronaos. In front of this are sparse remains of an Altar of Athena.

Environs: Opposite the little resort of *Legrená* (4 km. NW) lies the small island of *Patróklu* (or *Gaiduronísi,* 'Donkey Island'). It owes its name to the Ptolemaic general Pátroklos, who attempted, in the 3C BC, to capture the port of Piraeus (Munychia) with his fleet, using the island as his base.

Sými/ΣΥΜΗ

East Aegean Islands (Dodecanese)/
Aegean Islands   p.300□P 11

This little island (22. sq. miles, about 3, 000 inhabitants) lies near the Turkish coast

Ermúpolis (Sýros)

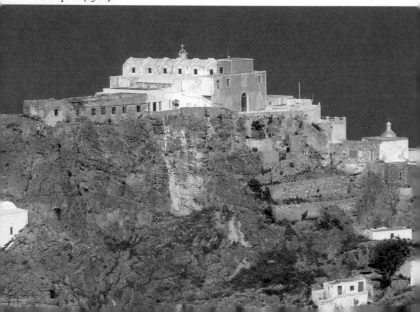

(5–8 miles) between the Knidos peninsula and the island of Rhodes. The now barren limestone island has ben closely connected with Rhodes since antiquity (Hexápolis). Turkish from 1523; between 1912 and 1948, when it was returned to Greece, it was occupied by Italy.

Sými (c. 1,200 inhabitants): The island's capital and beautiful natural harbour lies on the bay in the NE. The pale hillside houses of this town of boatbuilders and sponge-fishermen are overshadowed by the 15C *Castle of the Knights of St. John* (of Rhodes). This stands above the sparse remains of the ancient *acropolis*. Wall paintings survive in the *Panagía church*. The island's archaeological finds are collected in the small *museum (Musíon)*.
Environs: Remains of a Byzantine *basilica* in *Emporió* (3 km. NW). In the S. of the island, on the *Bay of Panormítis* (c. 10 km.) lies the charming monastery of *Ágios Michaél* (pilgrimage place for sailors) with a 12C church and beautiful tower.

Sýros/Syros (I)/ΣΤΡΟΣ
Cyclades/Aegean Islands   p.296☐K 10

With some 23,000 inhabitants, the island is relatively densely populated (33 sq. miles).

History: Syros was occupied by the prehistoric Cycladic culture (c. 2000 BC). The philosopher Pherekydes, teacher of Pythagoras, lived here in the 6C BC. In classical times the island was of little importance (member of the Athenian maritime league). Ruled by Venice in 1207, it soon became part of the Duchy of Náxos (until 1566). Under Turkish rule (from 1566) it acquired important privileges in return for remaining neutral (even in the War of Liberation of 1821).

Ermúpolis (c. 14,000 inhabitants): The 'City of Hermes' was founded as recently as 1822 by refugees from Chíos and Psará. Its heyday was in the 19C (until about 1870) when it was the most important port in Greece, being even more important than Piraeus, and it is still the focal point of the Aegean shipping lines. Various imposing buildings remain from the height of its prosperity: e.g. the *Theatre* (copy of La Scala, Milan), the *Town Hall* of 1876, built by the Bavarian architect Ziller, with a *Museum* (Cycladic finds, idols, grave goods, fragments of sculpture from Hellenistic, Roman and Frankish times). Near the harbour is the orthodox quarter of *Vrontádo* with the cathedral of *Ágios Nikólaos* (19C). The upper town of *Ano-Sýros* (4 km.) was founded by the Venetians in the 13C (Catholic Quarter). There is still the Catholic *diocese* here and the Catholic cathedral of *St. Georg*(converted in 1834). Also the *Capucin monastery* (founded in 1635 by Louis XIII of France), the *Jesuit monastery* (founded by Louis XV in the 18C) and the church of *Ágios Nikólaos* (15C).
Environs: At the village of *Khalandrianí* (12 km. N. of Ano-Sýros) are remains of the *Cycladic settlement (Kastrí*, 'Castle') with a double ring of walls from around 1800 BC. This was once a strongly fortified cave settlement.

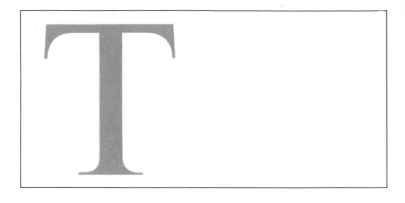

Tanágra/ΤΑΝΑΓΡΑ
Boeotia/Central Greece   p.294□H 8

An old town on a hill in Boeotia (65 km. NW of Athens) on the left bank of the river Asopos, surrounded by a fertile plain. According to mythology, the founder of the ancient town was Poimandros. The famous poetess of antiquity Korrinne was born here.

Archaeological collection: Today's town of Tanágra contains an interesting archaeological collection with finds from the archaic to the Byzantine periods. These include sculptures, ceramics, tombstone reliefs and a large number of inscriptions. The foundations and the mosaic pavement of an early Christian church on the hill of Tanágra are worth seeing.

Témpi/Vale of Tempe/ΤΕΜΠΗ
Lárisa/Thessalia   p.290□F 4/5

The Témpi gorge, down which the river Pinios (Peneios) flows, is some 5 miles long and was eroded by the action of water. It lies 30 km. NE of Lárisa and it divides the massifs of (Kato) Olympos and Ossa. The new stretch of motorway unfortunately detracts somewhat from its charming scenery.

Old myths cling to the valley: it is said that Apollo, after killing the python of Delphi, washed himself in the river. In doing so he glimpsed the beautiful nymph Daphne ('laurel tree') and fell in love with her. When fleeing from the god she transformed herself into a laurel with the aid of her father, the Pinios river. From that time on the laurel bush was regarded as holy by the god Apollo, and missions regularly came to a shrine of Apollo here in order to carry laurel twigs to Delphi.

The narrow valley was the main route from Macedonia in the N. to central Greece in historical times. It was possible, but difficult, to by-pass it by going through other mountain valleys, as Xerxes did in 480 and the Romans in 168 BC.

The so-called *spring of Daphne* is to be found at the narrowest point (road-house). Nearby is a *suspension bridge* (pedestrians). There are ancient traces and *inscriptions* dating from 48 BC near *Lykóstomo*.

On a steep rock nearby there stands the castle of *Kastro tis Oraias* ('castle of the beauty'), wreathed in legend. A famous

Tanágra, two pottery women (Kanellopoulos ▷ museum, Athens)

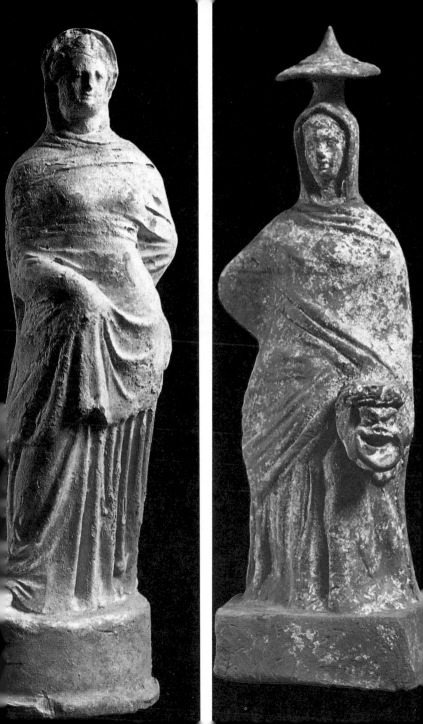

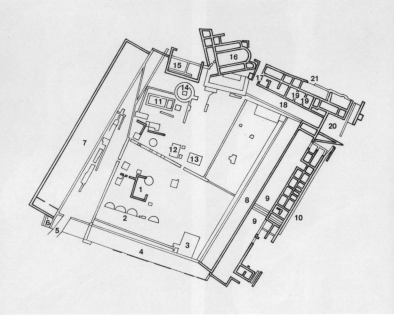

Thasos, ancient agora 1 remains of altar and wall 2 exedrae 3 monumental altar 4 SW stoa 5 entrance 6 W. propylaia 7 NW stoa 8 NE stoa 9 hypostyle gallery 10 ancient street 11 Temenos of Zeus 12 heroon (Caesar) 13 Theagenes altar 14 tholos 15 tufa house 16 basilica 17 passage 18 oblique stoa 19 stores 20 courtyard 21 ancient street

folk song sings of the fate of the 'beautiful mountain girl', who is said to have lived here in the Middle Ages and was abducted by the Turks. At the foot of the rock are the remains of an *ancient fortress*.

At the outlet of the gorge to the NE are the ruins of the ancient fortified town of *Omólion,* and to the SW (towards Lárisa) are the excavations of the ancient town of *Gónnos* (Gónnoi). The archaic settlement (already occupied in prehistoric times) was strongly fortified under the Macedonian king Philip II (4C BC; remains of walls and terraces survive). There are also the founda-

tions of a temple of Athena from the 4C BC, and traces of the agora, as well as the remains of a Byzantine settlement.

Environs: The charming mountain village of **Ampelákia** is on the NW slopes of the Ossa massif (3 km. SW) above the Tempe valley. The restored 17&18C *town houses* still bear witness to the former wealth of the wool spinners and dyers of that time. The *Black House (Mavros),* with its covered wooden terraces and oriels on the top floor and rococo paintings inside, is worth viewing. George Schwarz (Georgios Mavros) was the president of the first spinner's co-operative, with branch offices in London (cotton and silk) and elsewhere. Near Ampelákia (NE) is the church of *Profitis Elias,* with a magnificent view of the Tempe valley. The massive *Ossa* range (up to 6,500 ft.) rises S. of Tempe. According

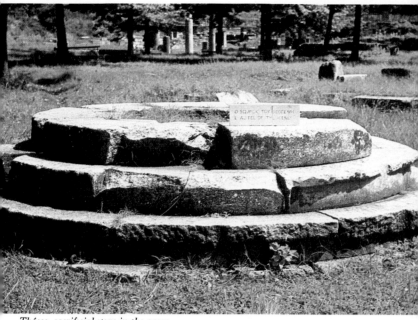

Thásos, sacrificial stove in the agora

to the myth, the giants built this mountain range in order to be on a level with the gods on Mt.Olympos. One of the peaks in the Ossa massif, Kíssavos, can be climbed from Ampelákia (with a guide). On the S. slopes of Ossa is the small town of **Agiá** with the neighbouring ruins of the ancient town of *Melíboia* (today: *Melívia*), reputedly the home of the Homeric hero Philoctetes. The church of *Agii Apostoli,* and the small *town museum* with its local finds, are both worth visiting. The town's heyday was in the 17&18C (silkworm breeding). Just to the E. is the 16C monastery of *Ágios Panteleimon,* with its beautiful *frescos.* It is also possible to climb Kíssavos from Agiá via the mountain village of Anatolí. The *palaiokastro* (a medieval castle) of *Skíti,* and the small fishing village of Agiókampos (on the Aegean coast), are some 5 km. SW of Agiá. Another way of

climbing Ossa is through *Sykúrion* (19 km. NE of Lárisa) and *Spiliá* ('cave'). To the NE of the Ossa massif, by the sea, is the fishing village of **Stómion** ('river mouth') with the nearby 13C monastery of *Ágios Dimítrios* (at an altitude of 4,250 ft.), which was damaged by a fire in 1869 (remains of frescos). Nearby (5 km. SE) is the coastal town of Kókkino Neró with a mineral spring.

Thásos/Thasos (I)/ΘΑΣΟΣ
North Aegean Islands   p.292□I/K 3

Thasos is the northernmost of the Aegean islands, with an area of 154 sq. miles and some 16,000 inhabitants. It is in the SE of the Gulf of Kavála (46 km.) and only 6 km. from the Thracian coast. The island is fertile and has richly varied scenery.

History: The island derives its name from Thasos, the grandson of Poseidon. It was settled in about 680 BC by Ionian colonists from Paros (Cyclades), mainly due to its gold mines and the marble. In 491 BC the island was occupied by the Persians, and the magnificent marble walls were razed. Thásos joined the Athenian maritime league and, in the Peleponnesian War, changed sides several times between Athens and Sparta (431–404 BC). During the Macedonian era (from 340 BC onwards), the island retained a certain degree of independence, which was confirmed by the Romans in 202 BC. It became a diocesan seat in AD 431; from 1204 onwards it was Venetian, and after 1306 it was Genoese (Gattelusi family). It was a Turkish possession from 1466 onwards. It was not until 1912 that the island was united with Greece.

Thásos/Thasos (about 2,000 inhabitants): The main town of this island is also known as *Limín* ('harbour'), and stands in the N. on the site of the ancient capital of the same name. The ancient naval harbour, the agora, the fortifications with the acropolis, and other features, are all worth seeing. The remains of the *ancient naval harbour* (partly under water) are NE of the present ferryboat jetty on the site of today's fishing port. The *ancient agora* is to the S. of the naval harbour and was originally an open square which, in the Hellenistic-Roman period (3C BC–1C AD), was surrounded with *stoai*. The foundations and colonnades have survived. The Doric *NW stoa* on the harbour side was built in the 3C (about 320 ft. long). There were once 35 columns, some of which have been rebuilt. The *SW stoa* comprised 33 columns and extended beside the W. entrance (propylon). It is 250 ft. long and dates from the 1C AD. The *main entrance* (with a monumental altar from the 3C BC) lay in front of it. The *SE stoa* (302 ft. long, 33 Doric columns), dating from the 1C AD with the remains of a *monument of Glaukos* from the 7C BC (Glaukos was a general from Paros and a companion of the poet Arkhilokhos), is on the side of the town facing the mountain. Behind the stoa there is a group of ruined houses along an ancient

Thásos (Thásos), gate in the ancient city wall

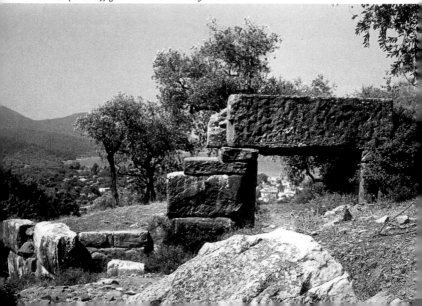

road with underground drainage channels. The *NE stoa* (diagonal stoa) from the 2C BC closes the square. The *bouleuterion* was here (5C BC, altered several times; finally a 4C early Christian *basilica* was built over it). Next to this are an ancient *building* with shops (remains of foundations) and the passage of the *theoroi* (high officials). Inside the agora are the remains of the *temenos of Zeus Agoraios* (Zeus as the patron of the market) dating from the 5&4C BC. The sacred precinct included a *temple in antis* (38 ft. x 20 ft.) and parts of an altar (sacrificial hearth, sacrificial channel).

Ancient town wall and acropolis: A tour of the ancient town walls is well worth while. Dating from *c.* 495 BC (some of them have been razed and rebuilt), they connected the acropolis with the harbour area. These walls consist of a ring of polygonal marble blocks and interesting ancient gates. The *Chariot Gate* linked the ancient commercial harbour with the agora. Some remains of a goddess (Artemis?) on a chariot can be discerned on the relief of the gateway; Hermes is holding the horses. The relief on the *Hermes Gate* also shows the god Hermes (the other figures have been destroyed). To the SW is the *Gate of Zeus and Hera* with a relief of the goddess Hera and the gods' messenger Iris (*c.* 411 BC). The *Silenus Gate* (*c.* 494 BC) displays, on a large relief, a nude Silenus with a kantharos. The gate was later protected by a Hellenistic tower. Nearby is the *Parmenon Gate* (*c.* 492 BC) with an inscription. Only some slight remains of walls survive from the ancient *acropolis*, situated at an altitude of 445 ft. (with a good view). The terraced wall and the foundations of a temple of *Athena Poliuchos* ('ruler of the town') from the 5C BC are SW of the castle hill. Nearby are the remains of a *shrine of Pan* with a rock relief of the god Pan. On the summit are the remains of the late medieval *castle*, which was built by the Genoese Gattelusi family in the 14C. In antiquity there was a shrine to *Apollo Pythios* here (there are still some ancient fragments in the walls of the castle, e.g. a *relief of a meal at a funeral*, 4C BC.).

Archaeological Museum (beside the agora): Rich finds from the excavations carried out

Thásos (Thásos), chariot gate: relief (Artemis and Hermes)

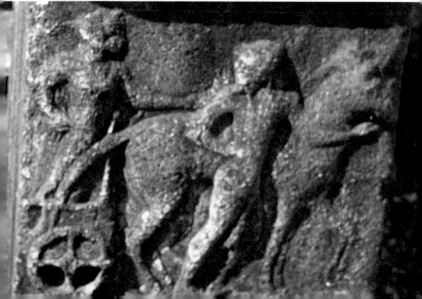

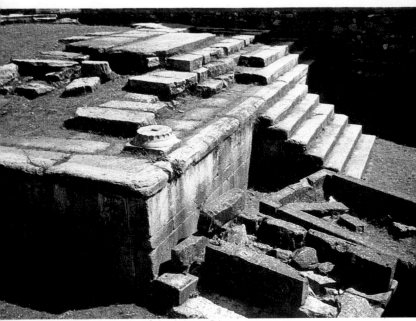

Thásos (Thásos), remains of the shrine to Dionysos

on the island by the French School are on display here, especially from the archaic epoch. The larger-than-life archaic sculpture of the Kriophoros of Thásos (6C BC) is famous: the nude kouros is pressing to his breast a ram which is to be sacrificed. There is also a 5C BC relief (protome) of *Pegasus,* the mythical winged horse. In the same room there are terracottas from the Herakleion (540–525 BC). Aphrodite and Eros on a dolphin (stone sculpture). Works by the well-known Thasian schools of sculptors (from classical to Roman times, including a head of Dionysos from the 3C BC). Finds from the Artemision: ivory lions' heads from Phoenicia (7C BC), broken pieces of archaic korai (terracotta), and other items. Also worth seeing: the scant ruins of the 4C BC *shrine of Poseidon* are to be found by the ancient naval harbour. Nearby is the *shrine to Dionysos* from the

6C (few traces survive). The ancient residential district was in this area. Not far away is the Hellenistic *theatre* (3C BC), whose orchestra was rebuilt under the Empire for gladiator combats (76 ft. in diameter). Above the agora are remnants of the *shrine of Artemis* (7C BC) and of an administrative building *(Theoreion).* There are some more ancient remains SW of the agora: a Roman *odeum* (2C AD) with a Roman road leading to the *arch of the emperor Caracalla* (AD 212–217); *shrine of Herakles (Herakleion),* 6C, mentioned in Herodotus. Only the foundation walls survive of this walled precinct with its altar, hall and temples in antis.

Environs: The ruins of a 6C early Christian basilica are to be found at *Cape Evraiókastro* (about 2 km. NE). The *kastro,* which was founded in 1434 and is situated in the S. of the island near the harbour

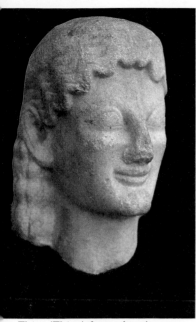

Thásos (Thásos), kouros (mus.)

of *Limenária* in the SW, 42 km. from the capital, was a place of refuge under the Turks. Its role was later taken over by the town of *Theológos* (about 55 km. S.). The N. port of Thasos did not become the capital of the island again until 1912. The remains of an ancient *shrine to the Dioscuri* (7C BC, traces of terrace and colonnades) survive at *Alíki* (about 52 km.). The ruins of two early Christian basilicas (5C) are to be found nearby.

Thermopýles/Thermopylae/ΘΕΡ-ΜΟΠΥΛΕΣ
Phthiótis (Ftiótis)/Central Greece   p.294☐F 7

The Kallídromon massif, which rises to a height of 4,600 ft., comes close to the shore of the Gulf of Maliakós at the so-called

'gates of heat' (Thermopylae), some 15 km. SE of Lamiá. In antiquity, a narrow pass (the pass of Thermopylae), which is 4 miles long, ran between the mountains and the sea and linked central and southern Greece (Attica). It was so narrow at three points (W., centre and E.) that it was only wide enough for one wagon at a time, but it has since been considerably widened by alluvium deposited by the delta of the river Sperchios. The present national road (a motorway) roughly follows the course of the ancient coast and road.

History: Thermopylae, named after the adjacent hot mineral springs, became famous when the Spartan king Leonidas heroically defended it against the vastly superior Persian force led by Xerxes (480 BC). After Leonidas had successfully held out with his Spartans, he was defeated by the treachery of a Thessalian, Ephialtes who led the Persians round to his rear along a mountain path (Anopaia). The Spartans defended their hopeless position to the last man, and they became national heroes. The traitor's name, Ephialtes, has survived to the present day as 'efialtis', the modern Greek for 'nightmare'.
Thermopylae played a strategic role in later times too, in the invasion of the Gauls under Brennus in 279 BC and in the victory of the Romans under Glabrio over the Syrian King Antiochos III in 191 BC (Alaric the Goth also passed through when he invaded Greece in AD 395).

W. pass: The *fortress of Anthele* (today: *Anthili)* stood above the steep W. pass. Nearby was the famous *Shrine of Demeter Anthéle*, itself the seat of an amphiktyonie (confederacy), religiously and politically this was closely connected with that of Delphi.

Central pass: Some remains of the old *Phocian wall* (6C BC), which ran in a zigzag and had a *tower* to the W., still survive here. The modern *Thermopylae monument*

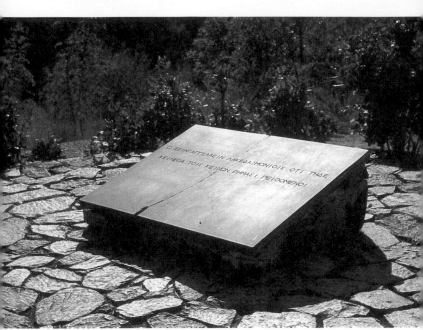

Thermopýles, memorial to Leonidas and his Spartans

(1955), with a statue of Leonidas, stands by the road. It bears the famous epigram of the poet Simonídes (556–468 BC): 'Go, tell the Spartans, thou who passest by, that here obediant to their laws we lie.' The ancient monument (with a statue of a lion) was probably a little further to the E., on the mound of Kolonos, some 35 ft. high (mentioned in Herodotus). This is the 'Spartan hill', where numerous iron and bronze Persian arrowheads have been discovered. There is a model of the ancient battle in the small *museum*. Nearby, at the foot of a steep rock, are the thermal springs of *Therma Lutra*, from which Thermopylae (Lutra Thermopyles) took its name in antiquity. The hot sulphur springs (40 degrees C) are used to treat skin diseases and complaints of the respiratory organs. The modern village of *Thermopýles* is a little further to the E.

E. pass: This was protected by the ancient *fortress of Alpenoi* (today: Alpini), of which slight traces survive. A little to the W. are remains of the wall built by Antiochos in 191 BC, which was intended to prevent the Romans from forcing a way along the mountain pass of Anopaia. Nearby is a hill where Herakles is said to have defeated the Kerkopes ('dragon men'). The town is still called *Drako-Spilia* ('dragon's cave'), probably in memory of this.

Environs: Iráklia (about 5 km. NW): Traces of the ancient harbour of *Trachís* are to be found nearby. The town played a part in the story of Herakles as the 'Herákleia Trachinía'and it features in Sophokles's tragedy 'The Women of Trachís. NW of the Kallidromon massif (about 23 km. S. of Lamía), is the interesting convent (Panagía) of **Damásta Theotókos**, situated at an altitude of 2, 430 ft. The church (katholikón) is 11C and contains frescos (1818 and 1913). The convent was used as a refuge in the War of Liberation (1821). A monument to the hero Athanasios Diakos (1821), who was murdered here by the Turks, stands on the bridge over the Sperchios at **Alamána.** The castle of *Bodonítsa,* which was built by the Frankish family of Pallavicini in 1205 and taken by the Turks in 1410, stands by the mountain village of **Mendenítsa** (some 10 km. SE of Thermopylae). Fragments from an *ancient fortress* (Pharygaí in antiquity) are to be found in the *ring of walls* (inner rampart), which is reinforced by towers. The outer rampart, with the intermediate wall, is better preserved. **Skárfia** (14 km. NE): Nearby are traces of the ancient Lokrian town of *Skárphe.* The site of the ancient capital of Lokris, *Thrónion,* is on a hill nearby.

Thérmos/ΘΕΡΜΟΣ
Aitolia/Central Greece   p.294□E 7

The ruins of what was once the splendid shrine of Thérmos (named after former hot mineral springs), which was the centre of the Aitolian league, are to be found in the high valley NE of Lake Trichonis (35 km. SE of Agrínion). The assembly of the Aitolian league (panaitolikon) was held from 367 BC onwards at this cult site, but finds have also been discovered here from the prehistoric and archaic periods. Philip V of Macedonia devastated it in 218 and 206 BC, destroying some 2000 statues (later rebuilt). Some remains of the *surrounding walls* and of the *rampart* (1110 x 660 ft.), with towers, have survived.

Temple of Apollo *(Apollon Thermios):* The ruins of this building are by the N. wall of the rampart. The unusual N.-S. alignment of the temple (*c.* 625 BC) fol-

lows that of a still older building (10 or 9C BC) with a U-shaped *colonnade.* The large temple was a Doric peripteros (15 x 5 columns, cella 105 x 23 ft.). The original columns were of wood. Some parts of the *pediment frieze* are in the National Museum in Athens (clay frieze). Some traces of a Helladic *shrine* (megaron), with the pronaos, cella and the rear wall of the apse all aligned in the same direction (N.-S.), are to be found in the NW corner. Other surviving features are the remains of a *temple of Artemis,* the foundations of two *stoai* and other buildings (shops, hence the by-name *Palaio-Bazari:* 'old bazaar').

Museum: Some fragments of the shrine are displayed here, including a *sphinx acroterion* with a well-preserved head and wings, *roof terracottas,* some with good paintwork, clay vessels (fragments), and important shard finds.

Environs: Near the village of **Agía Sofía** (*c.* 5 km. NW) is the church of *Ágios Nikólaos,* which incorporates some ancient fragments from Thérmos (column drums, pilasters with capitals, etc.). Nearby there are also the remains of a *basilica* and a small *Turkish bath* (Hamam). The remains of Hellenistic *watch-towers* are to be found on the slopes of the Panaitolikón massif.

Thespiaí/ΘΕΣΠΙΑΙ
Boeotia/Central Greece   p.294□G 8

The name of this ancient town (about 19 km. W. of Thebes) is derived from Thespis, its mythological founder. Eros, the god of love, was worshipped in Thespiaí from remote antiquity onwards. His original cult image was a rough stone. Hetaire Phryni, a native of the town, later dedicated a famous statue made by her lover Praxiteles to the god of love. Subsequently, Nero had the statue brought to

Rome. A festival (Erotidia) was held every four years in honour of Eros.

Temple of the Muses: A temple was dedicated to the Muses in Thespiaí and there was another such temple in the adjoining village of Askri. Some remains of the foundations can be seen to the S. of the present village of Thespiaí, within the later Byzantine fortifications.

Church of St. Kharálambos: A pilgrimage church from the Turkish period.

Thessaloníki/Saloniki/
ΘΕΣΣΑΛΟΝΙΚΗ
Thessaloníki/Macedonia   p.292□ G 3

This is the second largest city in Greece and the main town of Macedonia. It lies on the Gulf of Thermaikós, which derives its name from the old town of *Thérmi* (a few km. E. of Thessaloníki).

History: The historian Strabo reports that King Kássandros of Macedonia united 26 small settlements in 316/15 BC and founded the present city of Thessaloníki, which was named after his wife Thessalonike (step-sister of Alexander the Great). The city developed rapidly, owing to its favourable coastal position. After the battle of Pýdna (168 BC) and the conquest of Macedonia by the Romans, Thessaloníki became the main city of the Roman province of Macedonia. The city was particularly important because it was on the main route from Italy to Constantinople, the Via Egnatia. It was at the same time a cultural and economic centre. Cicero, the great Roman orator, lived in exile here in 58 BC. The Apostle Paul spent the winter of 49/50 in the city, preaching and founding a church. Galerius, the successor of Diocletian, made Thessaloníki his residence in the period of the Roman tetrarchy. Emperor Theodosios (AD 390) fortified the city and turned it into a military base to counter the Goths. Under Justinian, it was the second most important city of the Byzantine Empire and a major economic centre. The Saracens took

Thessaloníki, Byzantine city walls

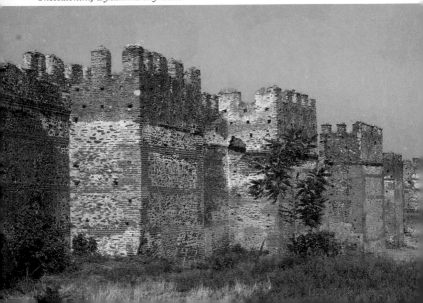

Thessaloníki in 904 after a siege lasting three days and 22,000 Greeks were enslaved. In 1185 the city was captured and laid waste by the Normans. After the Fourth Crusade, Thessaloníki became the capital of a Frankish kingdom (1204–23) ruled by Boniface of Montferrat. It was recaptured by the Greeks in 1223. The Despots of Epirus ruled it from 1224 to 1242, and in 1246 the city was recovered by the Byzantine Empire. The Turks controlled it for three years from 1391, and then the city became Byzantine again (1402). It fell to Venice and Genoa in 1423. The Turks under Sultan Murad II conquered Thessaloníki in 1430. The Greek inhabitants were either killed or sent into slavery. 20,000 Jews who had been expelled from Spain moved to Thessaloníki. From the mid 16C onwards they were the driving force behind the new economic upsurge. It was not until the 18C that Greeks gradually began to return.

Thessaloníki took part in the Greek War of Liberation from the very outset. However, the insurrections were bloodily put down by the Turks, who continued to rule until 1912. The Greek king George I was murdered in Thessaloníki in 1913. The Allied powers landed an expeditionary army in Thessaloníki during World War 1 and a government of 'National Defence' was formed here by Venizelos. The city, especially its picturesque centre, was completely destroyed in a great fire in August 1917. In World War 2, Thessaloníki was occupied for four years by the Axis powers (1941–44).

Today the city is an important Balkan economic centre. It has a modern university, two conservatories, a State-run theatre, a symphony orchestra, a teacher's college, and an ecumenical centre for the study of theology in accordance with the texts of the Church Fathers (the first such institute in the world).

City wall: This began at the White Tower and ran northwards through the present university campus to the *acropolis,* whence it continued westwards, turning southwards at the site of the present Platía Metaxa (Vardari), where it ended by the sea. The protective ring around the town

Thessaloníki, palace of the Roman emperor Galerius

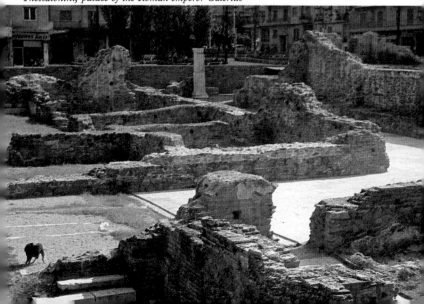

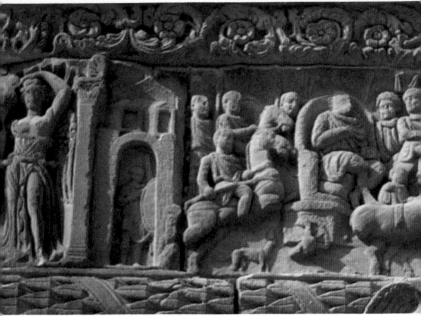

Thessaloníki, bas relief on the Arch of Galerius depicting an imperial triumph

was closed by a wall leading from this southern point to the White Tower. The N. section with a round tower (see Acropolis), and also some remnants outside the university (beside Panepistimiu Street) and in the Platía Metaxa, are all that survives today. The wall originally had seven towers, of which only two survive: one is the White Tower, and the other, as already mentioned, is to the N. Archaeologists are not certain whether the city wall dates from the Hellenistic or from an earlier period. The final fortifications were built under Emperor Theodosios I (379–95). The 27 ft. to 34 ft. high walls formed a trapezium and ran for between 4 and 5 miles.

White Tower (at the end of Vasileos Konstantinu Street in a park on the shore): This 100 ft. high tower is 15C, but stands on older foundations. In the 18C it was a

janissaries' prison, and was known as the 'tower of blood'.

Arch of Galerius: This triumphal arch was built in AD 303 on the occasion of the victories of the Roman emperor Galerius over the Persians in Mesopotamia and Armenia. It stood at the intersection of two important Roman roads. The four zones of bas-reliefs set on top of one another depict the battles and the triumph of Galerius. The famous scene of sacrifice on the right-hand side above the altar shows Diocletian on the left and Galerius on the right. Underneath there is a scene from the campaign waged by Galerius against the Persians. It shows elephants and native animals in the foreground of an Oriental town. The arch connected the present *Rotónda* (Ágios Geórgios, probably originally a mausoleum) to the *palace* and the

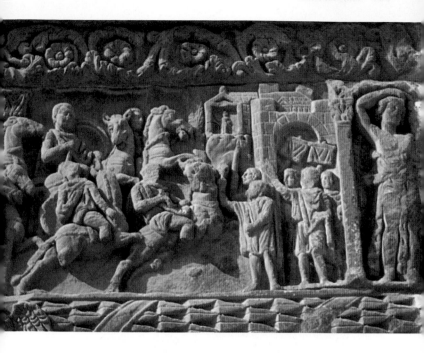

hippodrome. The sculptors of the triumphal arch were probably Greeks, as can be seen from the Greek inscriptions.

Rotónda (Ágios Geórgios): A round building erected in 306. Some years later it was transformed into the Christian church of Ágios Geórgios, with some slight alterations being made. The Turks converted the church into a museum in 1791. A minaret which still survives was erected beside the building. Since 1912 the building has once again been used as a church, and at present it is a museum and a university church.

The *mosaics* and the *wall paintings* in the Rotónda are famous. In the *dome* are 8 realistic panels of saints praying. The traces of some more mosaics (12 figures) have been discoverd above these panels, and below the keystone the remains of a large Christ have been found. All that survives of this latter is the halo and the cross of a sceptre. The faces of three of the original four angels can still be made out in the vault. Two of the eight niches have retained their mosaic decoration, with plant and geometric motifs. In the niche to the left of the entrance there is an *ambo*, various Roman and Byzantine reliefs, architectural fragments, and an *apse*. A mosaic panel on a gold background (St.Andrew) can be seen to the left of the apse. In the 10C this apse was decorated with frescos of which traces have survived. *Sarcophagi* and *tombstones* from the Roman and Byzantine periods, and also two *monuments*, are to be found in the park by the church.

Ancient palace: This was to the S. of the Arch of Galerius, opposite the Rotonda, on the site of the present Plateía Navarínou

(Navarínu Square). Remnants of an octagonal building, which was probably converted into a church under Justinian, have been discovered here. To the NE of these foundations there was an open *hall* with four rooms at its side. The walls of this structure survive up to a height of 3 ft. The floor to the SE of these rooms has mosaics with geometric ornaments which survive in good condition.

Ágios Panteleimon (near the Arch of Galerius): The church was built in the

Thessaloníki, Ágios Dimitrios **1** portal **2** staircase leading to the crypt (now a museum) **3** chapel of St.Euthymius, decorated with frescos **4** aisles **5** main apse **6** pillar with a mosaic of St.Demetrius with a dignitary, and a fragment of the miracle of St.Demetrius **7** mosaic of St.Sergius **8** mosaic of St.Demetrius between two dignitaries **9** painting: St.Lukas Styriotos **10** fresco: the capture of Thessaloníki by the barbarians **11** fresco: St.Demetrius at prayer **12** fresco: the monk S.Joasaph and St.Gregorios Palamas **13** monk being pursued by a monster **14** narthex **15** nave **16** hexagonal marble pedestal marks the site of St.Demetrius's ciborium **17** illuminated calendar for the years 1474–93, listing the feast days in the Orthodox calendar **18** traces of a mosaic and a 15C Florentine sarcophagus **19** mosaic fragment: St.Demetrius with angels **20** 13C tomb of St.Demetrius, with 14C frescos

13C. Its dome rests on four arches. There is a second, smaller dome over the narthex. The *wall paintings* include: a well-preserved Virgin Mary in the *prothesis*, and Church Fathers in the *diakonikón*.

Agía Sofía (at the intersection of Agía Sofia Street and Ermou Street): This church was built between 690 and 730 on the site of what was probably a 4C secular building. The church has a transitional form half-way between the basilica with a nave and two aisles on the one hand, and the Greek cross form with a dome on the other. The side wings, the rows of columns which delimit the aisles, and the galleries above the aisles, are basilican. The square ground plan, the dome supported on a broad arch, and the tunnel vault, are all indicative of the cruciform lay-out. In the NE corner there are remains of an *apse*, a *chapel* with a synthronon, the *bishop's throne*, and the *reliquary chamber*. The church was much damaged by a fire in 1890. The Turks restored it as a mosque in 1907–10. There are some splendid, unusual capitals inside. They have acanthus

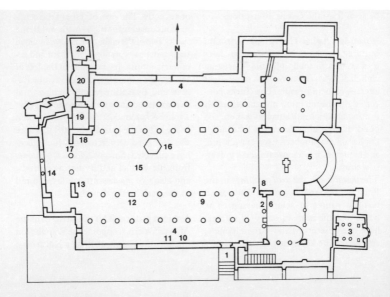

leaf decorations and probably originate from an earlier building (5C). In the dome of the apse there is the beautiful, captivatingly simple 9C mosaic of the Virgin and Child on a gold background. In the place where the infant Christ is depicted, it is still possible to make out an earlier mosaic with a cross which may date from a century earlier. The monogram of Emperor Constantine VI, that of the Empress Irene, and the name of the bishop Theophilos, are to be seen in the apse. On the curve of the arch in front of the apse there is a large golden cross on a silver ground, and in the dome of the apse is a Virgin and Child in dark garments on a gold ground. The mosaics in the large, main dome depict the Ascension (the Pantocrator on the Heavenly Throne, two angels below Christ, the twelve Apostles, and the Mother of God praying between two angels). It is notable that Christ and the Mother of God are wearing a halo, while the Apostles are not.

Ágios Ioánnis: An early Christian church, which was linked to catacombs, is to be found underground below the square not far from the S. side of the Agía Sofía church.

Panagía Akhiropiitos or **Agía Parasekevi** (N. of Agía Sofía): One of the first early Christian churches. It is thought to have been built after the third ecumenical synod (431). It is a basilica with a nave, two aisles, and a wooden ceiling. The church was named after a miraculous icon of the Panagia Achiropiitos (that is: 'not made by human hand'). The dimensions of the nave are 120 ft. x 51 ft. and it is divided from the aisles by twelve marble columns on each side (Corinthian capitals on the lower order, Ionic on the upper one). Remains of old *mosaics* survive under the arcades of the galleries. The *frescos* on an outside wall of the nave date from the 13C and depict the forty martyrs. The church was partly built on the site of a Roman villa, from which a fragment of the *mosaic floor* can be seen at the end of the left transept. A further *chapel* was recently discovered by the right aisle near the former main entrance.

Thessaloníki, Panagia Khalkeón (l.), Rotónda (Ágios Geórgios) (r.)

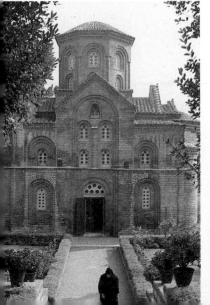 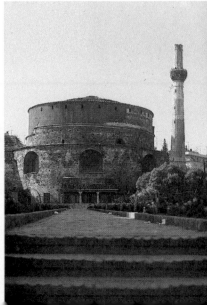

Panagía Khalkeon (on the Plateía Dikastirion): The church is in the form of a cross with equal arms, with a two-domed narthex projecting in front. These domes were probably added later (late 11C). The name of Panagía Khalkeon means 'Mother of God of coppersmiths'. The church is also known as the Theotokos church. According to an inscription, it dates from the year 1028 (or 1044). *Frescos* from the period of its building survive in the narthex *(Last Judgement)* and in the dome *(Ascension)*. The frescos above the W. portal date from the 14C. Christophoros, the founder, lies buried in a niche on the N. side.

Some further frescos are to be seen on the walls in the sanctuary, to the right and left of the apse *(Last Supper)*. On the dome: *Nativity, Adoration of the Magi, Crucifixion* and numerous Saints. Above the W. entrance is an inscription naming the founder of the church as Christophoros, who hoped that the Mother of God might pardon his sins and those of his wife.

Forum (Archaia Agorá): The Roman agora, which was discovered in 1966, is on the Plateía Dikastiríon, behind the Panagía Khalkeon and about 550 yards to the left of it. The complex dates from the 4C AD. On all four sides there were double colonnades on a krepis of three steps. Some of the columns have been found on the E. side. A *mosaic floor* also survives there in good condition. On the S. side are a double underground *stoa* (cryptoporticus) and some other rooms. An important early Christian *wall painting* survives in one of these.

Odeion (Odíon): The foundations of a small odeion or theatre dating from the period of the Roman tetrarchy (AD 300) were discovered on the E. side of the forum in 1961–2. The **cavea** (Koilon) is in a poor state (only seven kerkides). The odeion was also used for animal fights.

Ágios Dimítrios (in Agíou Dimitríou Street, some 550 yards N. of the forum): The church is a large basilica with a nave and four aisles and was built above a 4C *crypt* and extensive Roman baths. Remains

Thessaloníki, basilica of Ágios Dimitrios

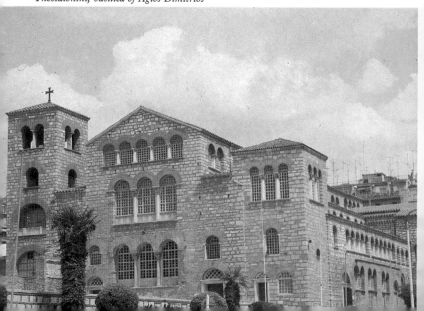

of these have been uncovered beneath the apse of the church. St. Demetrios (Ágios Dimitrios), the patron saint of Thessaloníki, is said to have been incarcerated in this crypt and to have died a martyr's death under Diocletian in 303. The church was used as a mosque from 1493 to 1912 and was rebuilt in 1926–48 after the fire of 1917, with all the surviving parts being incorporated in the work. Several mosaics and remains of frescos may be seen inside: in front of the narthex is a fresco of a monk, a painted calendar with a calculation of the Easter days for the years 1474–93, and the remains of the 7C mosaic of *Demetrios with angels*. The most important mosaics in the church are to be found in front of the main apse: *St. Demetrios with two children* (7C), *Madonna with a Saint* (11&12C); *St. Sergius* (8C) on the pillar to the left of the choir; *St. Demetrios with two founders* (7C) and *St. Demetrios with a cleric* (7C) on the pillar to the right of the choir. In the S. side aisle are: *St. Lukas Styriotos,* the *monk Joásaph, St. Gregorius Palamas* (12C), and another mosaic above the door to the narthex. There are two more 11 or 12C frescos on the side wall: *St. Demetrios praying* and the *conquest of Thessaloníki by the barbarians*. At the end of the right aisle, two staircases lead to the so-called *tomb of St. Demetrios,* a small 13C chapel with beautiful frescos (early-14C), which were uncovered in 1917 (after the fire). The items to be seen include remains of the thermal springs, the dungeon of St. Demetrios, the fountain from which miraculous oil flowed, tombs, and mosaic fragments.

Agii Apostoli (on the Plateía Lachanagoras): Cruciform church with 14C dome. A monogram of the patriarch Niphon (1312–15), who was probably the founder of the church. The façade is richly decorated with patterned brickwork, particularly on the wall of the E. side (geometric motifs, meanders etc.). Inside there are mosaics and wall paintings dating from the period of the Palaiologi. The *Pantocrator and the Prophets* are depicted in the dome, and on the pendentives are the *four Evangelists*. The *Nativity and Baptism of Christ* are in the S. vault, and in the W. vault the *Transfiguration* and the *Baiophoros*. The

Thessaloníki, 14C Agii Apostoli

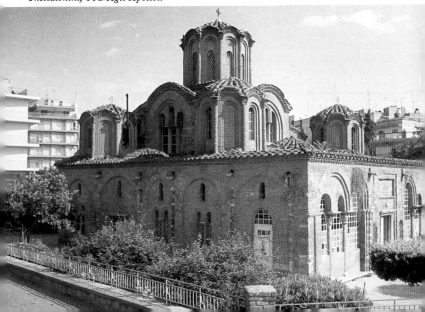

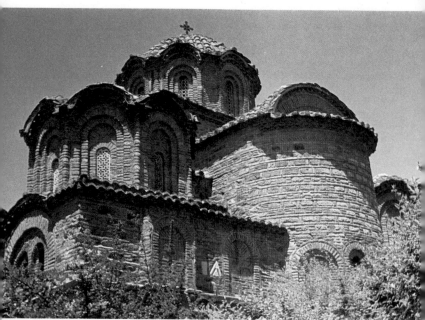

Thessaloníki, church of Agia Aikaterini

Crucifixion and *Resurrection of Christ* are in the N. vault. The *Dormition* is depicted on the W. wall above the entrance. The mosaics of *St. Ypapanti* and the *Annunciation* have survived. The first of these is influenced by the art of painting, while the second is rooted in 11&12C mosaic art. The wall paintings mainly depict scenes from the life of the Mother of God. Her family tree is in the E. corner of the S. aisle. The E. corner of the N. aisle is a chapel to *Ágios Ioánnis Prodromos*; decorated with scenes from his life.

Agía Aikateríni (in the upper city, behind the present Dioikitirion): A cruciform church with one central dome and four smaller domes at its four corners. It was built in the late 13C. Inside are remains of wall paintings (contemporary with the building of the church) depicting saints and scenes from the Gospels. The church was transformed into a mosque under the Turks.

Prophitis Ilias (N. of Ágios Dimítrios): A cruciform church with a dome and a clover-leaf plan. The church was built in the 14C and may have been the katholikon of the Nea Moni monastery, which was built in the 14C by the monk Makarios Khoumnos. The ceramic decoration of the church façade is a beautiful piece of work. The church was converted into a mosque during the period of Turkish rule. The wall paintings of the narthex were whitewashed at that time.

Ágios Nikólaos Orphanos (in the upper city, in Herodotou Street): The church consists of a central area surrounded by an aisle, and dates from the early 14C. From the 17C onwards it was part of the monastery of Vlatadon. The church and some remains of the *propylon* survive from the small monastery existing at that time. Its columns bear beautiful capitals whose colours have survived in good condition to the present day and the original *templon* has survived almost in its entirety. The church is of interest for its *paintings*. Nearly all the surfaces inside are covered with them. These too are early 14C, and their subjects are arranged in zones. Saints are depicted in the lower zone, and in the upper zone are subjects from nine iconographical cycles: calendar of twelve festivals, Passion and Resurrection of Christ, life of St. Nicholas, etc.

Osios David (at the end of Agias Sofias Street): This church dates from the late 5 or 6C. The very well-preserved early Christian *mosaic* in the apse is worth seeing and depicts the vision of the prophet Ezekiel. Christ is in the middle, and the four symbols of the Evangelists are at the corners. The prophet Ezekiel may be seen on the bank of the river Chorar at the bottom right, and on the left is the prophet Habakkuk.

Agii Taxiarches (between Akropoleos Street and Dionisiou Street): This church was probably built in the 14C. The inside of the church was decorated with paintings: Ascension, Crucifixion.

Moní Vlattadon or **Vlattadon Monastery** (to the right of Vlattadon Street): The church was built in 1320 – 50 by the brothers Vlattai or Vlattádes, monks from Crete. It includes the 14C *church of Christ's Transfiguration* and the *chapel of St. Peter and St. Paul* (to the right of the choir), with frescos from the 14C which are a typical examples of the Macedonian school of painting. The Vlattadon monastery is the only one of the twenty monasteries of Thessaloníki to have survived to the pres-

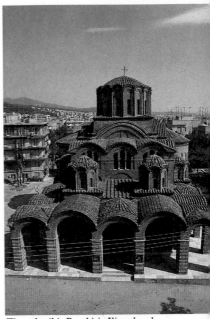

Thessaloníki, Prophitis-Ilias church

ent day. Its library has a collection of valuable manuscripts. There is a fine view of the city and the sea from the garden.

Acropolis (also **Kastro**): The citadel is part of the city wall and occupies the highest point of the city. The oldest section of the fortifications dates fom the 4C AD and was built during the Byzantine and Turkish period on the site of the Hellenistic acropolis. The rampart dating from the 4C (period of Theodosius, 379 –95) was built in the Byzantine period and later altered. Note the following gates and towers: the 14C *tower of Manuel Palaiologos* with a verse inscription containing the founder's and builder's names; *Palaiologos tower*; *tower of Andronikos II Palaiologos* dating from the 14C, with an inscription; *gate of Anna Palaiologou* with an inscription dating from 1355. Behind the city wall is the *acropolis*. It was known as the *Heptapýrgion* ('castle of the seven towers') or, in Turkish, *Yedi-Kule*. It cannot be visited today because it is used as a State prison. Some remains of the middle tower, the broadest of the seven, are visible and according to an inscription it was built in 1431.

Archaeological Museum *(Arkhaiologiko Musío):* This museum (opened 1963) stands in the Plateia Khanth at the beginning of Leophoros Stratou Street. It contains finds from the whole of northern Greece: prehistoric vases from Macedonia and Thrace, finds from the Geometric period (tombs, vases, copper jewellery, iron weapons), statues from the archaic and classical periods (finds from the old town of *Thermai),* a collection of vases, jewellery, weapons, household effects and tools from the town of Olynthos, and also finds from tombs from *Dervéni* (NE of Thessaloníki on the main road from Thessaloníki to Kavála), copper and silver vessels, pots, weapons, gold and alabaster jewellery. A number of sculptures from the Roman period, and a collection of sarcophagi and pavement mosaics which were found in Thessaloníki, are also displayed. Most of the finds from *Vergína* are on display in a hall to the right of the entrance: two gold larnaces (one of the king, the other of the queen), with the star of the Macedonian dynasty on the lid. Two diadems (one gold, the other silver). Two gilded bronze greaves. Silver quivers (gilded) showing scenes of the capture of a town. Golden wreath with leaves and flowers. Three golden discs with the star of the Macedonian dynasty. Iron armour plate (the only one from ancient times), decorated with golden strips and lions' heads in relief. Iron helmet. Iron sword, decorated with gold. Golden wreath, with life-sized leaves and fruits. Numerous objects of silver or bronze (skyphos, jug, situla, kyathos, lebes, lykhnoukhos etc.). Five small heads of

ivory (members of the family of King Philip II). All these finds are dated 350–325 BC. Among the other finds in the museum, the following are of particular interest: two large *kraters* of gilded bronze from Dervéni (4C BC); one is particularly beautiful, depicting Dionysos and Ariadne at a Bacchanalia.

Works from the archaic period (fragments of an Ionic temple from Thessaloníki) up to the 4C AD, are to be seen in the *sculpture rooms: kouros* from Rítini (6C BC), *kouros* from Thrace (6C BC), *tomb stela of Theognetos* from Kassándra, *head of a goddess* (Roman copy of an original by Pheidias), *head of Serapis* (Roman copy of the work by Briaxis, 4C BC), small painted *terracotta statue of Aphrodite* (Roman copy after a work by Kallimachos, 5C BC).

Mosaics: Mosaic floor depicting Dionysos and Ariadne, Zeus and Ganymede, Apollo and Daphne, and dating from the 3C AD. *Ceramics:* Jugs and vessels from Servia Kozanis, vessels and jewellery from Axiokhori and Ágios Mámas, craftsmen's tools and vessels from Armenokhori, Perivolaki and Molyvopyrgos — all from the prehistoric period.

Smaller objects: Large and small vases and amphorae (especially from Olynthos), black-figure krater from Chalkidiki (all from the 6C BC, bowl with lid (4C BC), and black-figure kraters from various sites (6C BC). Finally there are kraters and vases from Olynthos (4C BC). From the Neolithic: a pale green vase from a Hellenistic tomb from Neápolis (Thessaloníki) showing a hunting scene, and other items. *Roman sculptures:* A statue of Augustus (from Thessaloníki), the torso of a statue of Claudius (from Thessaloníki), the head of Vespasian, a woman's head (from Edessa), and a fine tombstone relief with two portraits (from Thessaloníki), a headless statue, possibly of the emperor Hadrian (found in Thessaloníki), the statue of a woman from Thessaloníki, the bronze head of a man, the muse Thalia, the muse Erato, and a Roman copy of the *Great Herkulan Woman.*

Also note a 4C BC Greek *papyrus*, the oldest in the Greek language, and two fine gold and enamel Byzantine *bracelets*.

Also worth seeing: Folklore museum *(Ethnologiko-Laografiko Musio,* Vasilissis Olgas Street): splendidly colourful national costumes, silver and gold jewellery, wood and metal. **Early Christian tombs with wall paintings:** These date from the late 3C or early 4C to the early 5C. They are variously decorated with plant motifs, false marble, figures, and scenes from the Gospels. The tombs are outside the city wall: in the W. (old main railway station, Panagía Phaneroméni, Neápolis), in the E. (from the Archaeological Museum to Heptapyrgion), and in the area of Agía Triada Street. Some of the wall paintings are on display in the Archaeological Museum. **Gregoriou Palama** (at the intersection of Agía Sofia Street and Mitropoleos Street): A crypt was discovered in the cellar during the repairs to this church after the earthquake which struck Thessaloníki in

1978. This crypt is historically important and dates from the Turkish period.

Environs: Moní Agías Anastasías (60 km. from Thessaloníki on the road to Basilika): An old Byzantine monastery built by the Empress Theano. **Prehistoric settlement** (near Thessaloníki airport): A Neolithic settlement; numerous finds are exhibited in the Archaeological Museum in Thessaloníki.

Thíra/Santorini (I)/ΘHPA
Cyclades/Aegean Islands   p.300☐L 12

The southernmost island of the Cyclades (about 6,500 inhabitants), it has an extremely interesting geological history. The original surface area of the island was almost halved (now 29 sq. miles) by an enormous volcanic eruption in about the middle of the 2nd millennium BC, and what had been a circular island became sickle-shaped (with a number of associated islands). The sea flowed into the crater,

Thessaloníki, Ágios Nikólaos Orphanos

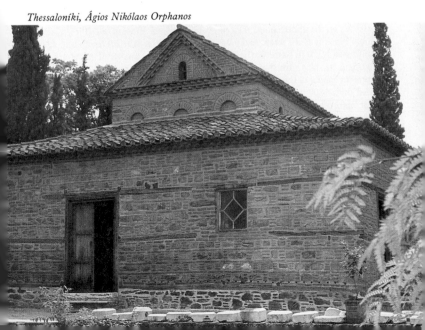

which is up to 1,280 ft. deep. The Kaiméni islands are the result of later volcanic eruptions (the last earthquake was in 1956); and they still emit sulphurous fumes.

History: The most recent excavations show that the island was occupied by the beginning of the 2nd millennium and that it maintained very close contacts with Minoan Crete. It remained uninhabited for centuries after the volcanic eruption in *c.* 1600 BC. The first new settlers, in *c.* 1000 BC, were Dorians from Lakonia, who founded the ancient Thíra (Théra) in the SE. It was from here that the North African colony of Kyréne (Cyrenaika) was founded in *c.* 630 BC. Thíra joined the Athenian maritime league in 430 BC. The island was a naval base and garrison under the Ptolemies; it was later joined to the Roman province of Asia. In the Middle Ages, Thíra was ruled by Venice and the Duchy of Naxos. It was captured by the Turks in 1537. In the Middle Ages Thíra was named *Santorin* by the Venetians (after Santa Irene, the island's patron saint).

Thíra (also *Firá*): This, the most picturesque capital (about 1,500 inhabitants), is in the W., on the upper rim of the crater. From here there is a steep, rocky descent of up to 1,120 ft. to the harbour of *Skála* (there are steps with sharp bends). The present capital of the island was not founded until 1809, when the medieval town of *Skáros* (3 km. N., with a Venetian *ruined castle* dating from 1206) had to be abandoned owing to a landslide of rock. The *Archaeological Museum* of Thíra has a rich collection of Cycladic idols, Minoan ceramics from Akrotíri dating from the 2nd millennium, Mycenean, Geometric and archaic ceramics from various places on the island, and also tomb stele, vases and sculptures from Hellenistic-Roman times, as well as a notable collection of ancient inscriptions and other items.
Environs: The inaccessible ancient town

of *Théra (Thíra)* is in the SE of the island (some 16 km. from the capital) on the rocky ridge of *Mesavuno* (1,150 ft.) between the villages of *Perissa* and *Kamári*. The ancient harbour was also at Kamári. The area of the old town, with *rock tombs* (Byzantine town wall) and the chapel of *Ágios Stefanos* (on the foundations of a 5C early Christian basilica), begins at the Sellada pass in the NW. Below the town is the *Evangeslismós chapel*, near the Hellenistic *Heroon;* from here the way turns sharply to the ancient *agora* (about 360 ft. long and 65–100 ft. wide). This is the site of the *Stoa Basilike* ('royal portico'), a rectangular hall with twelve columns dating from the 1C BC (some remains survive). In the rear are some houses and alleyways from the Hellenistic residential quarter. The remains of a small *temple of Dionysos* are nearby. Above the agora, at the highest point (1,210 ft.), are the *gymnasion* and the Ptolemaic *Governor's Palace*. SE of the agora are the Ptolemaic *theatre* (rebuilt in the 1C AD), and opposite is a house with a peristyled courtyard. Next to it are the *rock shrine* to Isis, Serapis and Anubis, and also the remains of the temple of *Apollon Pythios* (later a church). In the NW is the temenos of *Artemidoros* (Ptolemaic admiral) with *rock reliefs* (including a lion). Houses and remains of *baths* are to be found SE of the theatre. The main shrine is in the SE of the area, with the 6C BC Temple of *Apollon Karneios* (remains of cella and pronaos, with no peristasis). Adjoining this is the *festival terrace* with a supporting wall (6C BC), where cult festivals were held (gymnopaidiai). Names dating from the 7C have been scratched in early Greek script (from right to left) on the adjacent limestone rocks. Further, erotic, inscriptions are to be found by the *grotto* of Hermes and Herakles (Ephebic cult). The shrine ends in the *Gymnasion of the Epheboi* (2C BC), a rectangular courtyard with buildings on both sides of a round building. The sections in the SE of the ruined

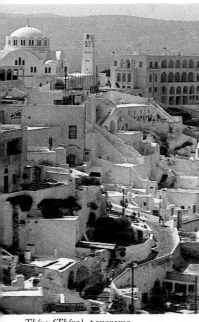

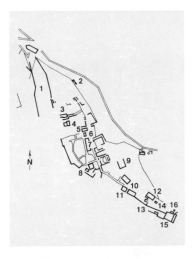

Santorini, the ancient Théra 1 Byzantine walls
2 Artemidor temenos **3** garrison **4** gymnasion **5**
Dionysus shrine **6** agora **7** stoa basilica **8** Temple
of Apollo **9** baths **10** houses **11** cistern **12** Temple
of Apollo Karneios **13** rock inscriptions **14** temple
terrace **15** gymnasion of the Epheboi **16** grotto of
Herakles with rock inscriptions

Thíra (Thíra), panorama

town date predominantly from the archaic-Doric period (7&6 BC), while most of the remains of buildings in the NW are from Hellenistic-Ptolemaic times (275–146 BC) when an Egyptian admiral (Nauarch) governed the island. The German archaeologist Hiller von Gaertringen played a major part in the excavations (1895–1903). The village of *Périssa* (15 km. SE), with the impressive 19C church of *Ágios Stavros,* lies below the ancient ruined town. The architecturally interesting five-domed church stands on the ruins of a Byzantine basilica *(Agía Irini).* Nearby are the remains of a *Heroon* from the 1C, with inscriptions recording title to land from the 3&4C. A small Doric *temple* from the 3C BC has survived in its entirety. Built of white marble ashlars, with an ancient marble ceiling and a beautiful door frame, it stands by the village of *Emporió* (12 km.

SE). The temple was dedicated to Thea Basileia ('goddess queen') and is today the chapel of *Ágios Nikólaos.* There are a few remains of the medieval Venetian *fortress* at Emporió. Until 1800, the capital of the island was the village of *Pýrgos* (about 8 km. S.), with the remains of the 13C Venetian fortress of *Kastelli.* The small Byzantine castle church of *Theotokaki* (10C) has some fine frescos and inscriptions. Close by is the interesting monastery of *Profítis Ilías* ('prophet Elijah'), dating from 1712, on the mountain of the same name. The mountain itself is the highest in the island and offers a good all-round view. The monastery contains rare relics and a small *museum* (in the sacristy) with post-Byzantine icons, carved crosses, ecclesiastical utensils, garments, and manuscripts. Nearby there is also the 11C church of *Panagía Episkopí* (1.5 km. E. of

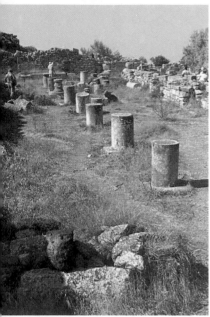

Thíra (Thíra), stoa basilica

Pýrgos); worth seeing for its frescos and icons (11&12C).

Akrotíri (15 km. SW): Since 1967 the remains of a *Cycladic-Minoan settlement* have been uncovered below a 3 ft. thick layer of pumice stone near this small town with its 13C Venetian *walls*. The settlement referred to comprises houses rising several storeys and dating from the period before the volcanic eruption in *c*. 1500 BC. The inner walls were, in similar fashion to the Cretan palaces, frescoed with landscapes, animals and people (swallows, antelopes, apes, and also ladies, boys, etc.). Here we also find the first example of a Cretan-Mycenean room (about 7 ft. 2 in. x 8 ft. 6 in.) painted throughout and surviving in an undamaged condition (the so-called *breakfast room*). There was once probably a Minoan military base here. It is prin-

cipally the everyday objects that have been found here (clay vessels, mortars, oil lamps, etc.) and these offer an insight into life at the time. Most of the ceramic finds have remained in situ (small *museum* at the excavation site), whereas most of the frescos have been removed to the National Museum in Athens. Prof. Marinatos, who was in charge of the excavation work, was killed here in 1974 by a collapsing wall.

Ía (11 km. NW of Thíra): A picturesque harbour in the N. of the island (steep cliff), with the remains of a 13C Venetian *kastro*. Nearby (by the village of *Finikiás* and *Cape Kolúmbos*) there are a few remains of ancient settlements and *tombs* (necropoles). Lying offshore to the W., is the island of *Thirasía* (accessible by boat): there are some ancient remains in the N. and inscriptions; the *Panagía Kímisis* monastery (on Cape Trypití) and the cave village of *Potamós*. Boat trips can be made from the harbour of Thíra to the geologically interesting offshore volcanic islands of *Kaiménes*, with their craters and sulphur vapours.

Thísvi/Thisbe/ΘΙΣΒΗ
Boeotia/Central Greece   p.294□G 8

Near to Thísvi (about 30 km. SW of Thebes), there the remains of walls of polygonal masonry from an ancient fortress. There are a number of tombs, (probably early Christian) on the hills around Thísvi. Nearby is the beautiful monastery of *Makariótissa*, which is originally said to have been Byzantine.

Environs: The post-Byzantine monastery of *Hósios Seraphim Dombó* is near Khóstia (to the W.), on a bay of the N. shore of the Gulf of Corinth. In accordance with the founder's wishes, women are not allowed to enter the monastery church.

Thívai/Thebes/ΘHBAI
Boeotia/Central Greece   p.294☐G 8

Thebes (about 16,000 inhabitants) is the centre of southern Boeotia.

History: According to the myth, Thebes was founded by Kadmos, who came from Phoenicia, and as a result its inhabitants were also known as Kadmeoi in antiquity. In his search for his sister Europa, who had been abducted by Zeus in the guise of a bull, Kadmos came to Delphi to consult the oracle. There he was advised to give up the search for his sister and to follow the cow which was to meet him on the way. He was to found a town in the first place where the cow knelt down. This happened on the site of what was later to become Thebes. After killing a dragon which was sacred to Ares, Kadmos sowed its teeth (dragon's teeth). The first inhabitants of Thebes sprouted from these teeth. It is said that they are the origin of the Labdakids, who ruled Thebes and included Oedipus and his father Laius.

In the Mycenean period and in historical times, Thebes was known as *Eptápylos* ('seven-gated') owing to the seven gates in the old town wall. Sophokles wrote: 'Only in the seven-gated town of Thebes does a human woman give birth to a god.' No other town became as famous as Thebes, either in mythology or in the historical period. The town was the scene of bloody battles and tragic events which provided Aischylos and Sophokles with subjects for their tragedies.

In the historical period, Thebes was one of the thirteen major towns of the Boeotian Confederacy. The continual battles between Athens and Thebes stemmed from the difference between their political systems. Democracy ruled in Athens, and oligarchy in Thebes.

The first war between the two towns broke out in 510 BC, the Thebans being

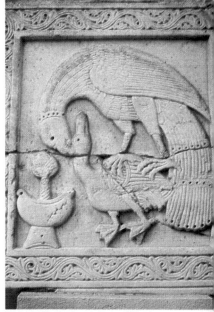

Thívai, Byzantine sculpture (Mus.)

defeated. Thebes was allied to the Persians from the start and, in 490 BC (battle of Marathon), Thebes did not fight on the side of Athens against Darius. The Thebans adopted the same friendly attitude towards the Persians during the battle of Plataia in 479 BC. After the Athenian victory, the Thebans lost their primacy in the Boeotian Confederacy for 23 years.

In the Pelopennesian War, the Thebans fought on the Spartan side against the Athenians. There was later an alliance between Athens and Thebes against Sparta. During the war against the Spartans, two Theban heroes, Epameinondas and Pelopidas, became famous for their bravery and brilliant generalship. Pelopidas defeated the Spartans at Tegyra (374 BC). Three years later, Epameinondas gained the famous victory at Leuktra (371 BC). Thebes lost its power with the death of these two heroes. The end of Theban hegemony came with the conquest of Thebes by Philip II of Macedonia and his son Alexander the Great. In 335 BC, the latter completely destroyed the rebellious city—the only house which was spared was the one which had belonged to Pindar, the famous Theban poet. Thebes developed into an important economic and cultural centre in the Christian-Byzantine period. Tradition has it that the spread of Christianity in this town is associated with Luke the Evangelist, to whom the cemetery church in Thebes was dedicated. According to another tradition, the first bishop of this town was Rufos, mentioned by Paul the Apostle in his Epistle to the Romans (16, xiii). The ruins of numerous early Christian churches, and interesting early Christian sculptures (today they are in the Museum of Thebes), demonstrate the importance of Thebes at that time. To the N. of the large Kastelli (castle) of Thebes there is a smaller hill, *Mikro Kastelli*. On the S. side of this there is a *catacomb* from the time when Christians were persecuted. A head of Christ, painted black, is to be seen on a wall; this is a rare example of early Christian art.

At the time of Justinian, and from the 8C AD until the Frankish conquest in 1204, Thebes was one of the most important manufacturing and trading centres of Byzantine Greece. Magnificent silks and carpets were woven here. The town reached its economic and cultural zenith in the 10C and 14C. There were also some 2,000 Jews living here at that time who were engaged in silk production. In addition, there were Venetians, Genoese and Pisans who enjoyed special trading privileges under a favourable treaty concluded with the then emperor Alexios. Thebes was the capital of central Greece in Byzantine times, owing to its great economic and cultural importance, and the Byzantine Strategos (governor) resided here.

In the mid 12C Thebes was captured and pillaged by the Normans of Sicily. In addition to their rich booty, the conquerors also took with them to Sicily many beautiful Theban women and skilled silk weavers, in order to develop the industry in Sicily.

In 1205 Thebes fell under the influence of Duke Othon de la Roche, who made Thebes the capital of his duchy. French domination ended in 1311 when Thebes was taken by the Catalans, who were in turn expelled in 1388 by the Florentines led by Nerio Acciaiuoli. These were followed by the Turks. The last Florentine ruler, an Acciaiuoli, was killed by the order of Muhamed II, the Turkish conqueror. Thebes was not freed from Turkish rule until 1829.

Chapel of St. Gregory the Theologian: This small Byzantine chapel stands near the cathedral of Thebes and, according to an inscription dating from AD 872, was built by Kandidates Basileios, the Byzantine governor.

Agía Photini: An interesting Byzantine

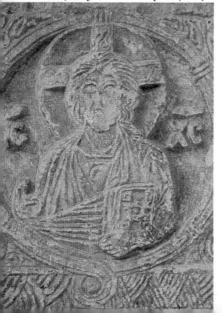

Thívai, early Christian sculpture (Mus.)

church dating from the 10C and situated about 1 km. SE of Thebes.

Palace of Kadmos: The remains of this building are in the centre of the town.

Museum: This, one of the most important museums in Greece, stands at the end of Pindaru Street at the N. entrance to the town. Interesting finds from the prehistoric to the Roman period are on display. In addition, beautiful early Christian and Byzantine sculptures, and also a mosaic floor, are to be seen in a room outside the entrance to the museum. In the garden of the museum there are a large number of tomb reliefs and important inscriptions which were found in Thebes and its environs.

The museum consists of four rooms: the first two of these contain sculptures from the Geometric and archaic periods. One interesting exhibit is the *kouros of Ptoion*. Painted tomb stele from Thebes and Tanágra are to be seen in the third room. In the last room there are painted Mycenean sarcophagi and ceramics.

The museum also displays some interesting finds from the most recent excavations carried out in the grounds of the palace of Kadmos. They include some cylindrical seals bearing cuneiform script from the 14C BC which seem to confirm the myth that Kadmos brought the first written characters from Phoenicia.

The last remaining wall of the famous Frankish palace, built by Nicholas II, Saint Omer, Duke of Thebes, stands on the N. side of the garden. This palace was later destroyed by the Catalans.

Customs: There is an interesting festival, the *Vlákhikos Ghamos*, which is held every year on Shrove Monday and attracts many visitors.

Environs: Inófyta (Staniátes): This village, some 31 km. from Thebes, takes its name from the large vineyards which were once to be found in the vicinity. In 456 BC there was a famous battle here in which the Athenians won a great victory over the Thebans.

The low *Mt. Fikion*, also known as *Sphin-*

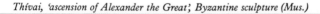

Thívai, 'ascension of Alexander the Great', Byzantine sculpture (Mus.)

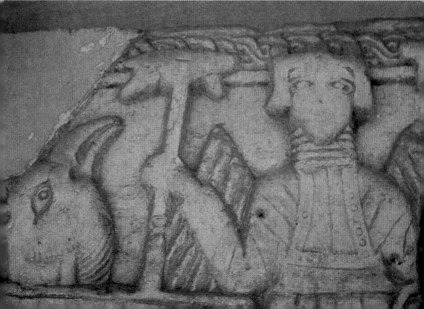

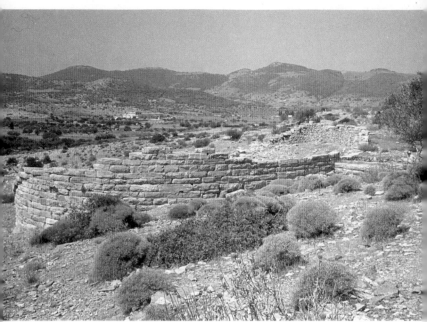

Thorikós, remains of the 4C BC theatre

gion, stands to the NW of Thebes, not far from the town. Today the railway station of the village of Vája is nearby. The mythical Sphinx is said to have lived on the mountain in antiquity.

Thorikós/Thorikón/ΘΟΡΙΚΟΣ
Attica/Central Greece   p.296☐H 9

The ruins of the port of Thorikós, the main town of an ancient Attic deme, are on the SE coast of Attica, some 4 km. N. of the present harbour of Lavrion (58 km. SE of Athens).

History: The site was occupied, prior to the arrival of the Greeks, in the Neolithic, and has numerous finds from the Mycenean period (beehive tombs). According to the myth, king Kephalos ruled here. Disguised as a stranger, he discovered his wife Prokris being unfaithful. When he was out hunting, she followed him, having herself now become jealous, and he killed her, thinking her to be a wild beast. In historical and classical times, the town was the capital, and from 412 BC onwards also the fortress, of the region of Laúrion (see entry), with its silver mines. It had an important harbour through which timber was brought from Euboea and ore traded with Athens, the Cyclades and Crete.

Excavation site: Traces of dense human settlement from the Neolithic (from 2900 BC onwards) until the Hellenistic period have been found on the saddle-shaped mountain of *Velaturi.* Three Mycenean *beehive tombs* have been discovered on the slope leading up to the peak (in the E.).

The oldest of these (16C BC) is some 30 ft. long and 11 ft. wide (oval ground plan), and part of the dome survives. A smaller Mycenean *chamber tomb* (cut into the rock, *c.* 1200 BC), and another oval beehive tomb which was later the site of an archaic cult of hero-worship (shard finds from the 7–5C BC), have also been found. Some remains of a *Mycenean wall* and of a building dating from the same period (2000–1800 BC) and standing above a group of pre-Mycenean dwellings have been discovered on the peak. On the S. slope are a necropolis (*c.* 1800 BC) and archaic finds from tombs. *Ancient fortified town:* The upper town was on the mountain slopes and was surrounded by a *circular wall* over a mile long (some remains, with a square tower, survive in the SW). The 4C *theatre* was inside the S. rampart, on the slopes of Velaturi. The *cavea*, which is roughly oval and measures 177 x 69 ft., had some 5,000 seats arranged in two tiers (the upper tier was not added until later). The lower tier is divided up by two stairways, with the *seats of honour* between them in the lowest row. The *orchestra* is not backed by a stage building, but only by a terrace wall. At the W. edge of the orchestra there is a small temple in antis to *Diónysos* measuring about 30 x 21 ft. a relic of early dramatic performances held in honour of the god Dionysos (Dionysia). The associated *Diónysos altar* was located opposite, to the E. of the orchestra. The temple and altar date from the 5C BC. In the E. section of the cavea are two *rock chambers* which were probably related to the cult of Dionysos. There was a cistern to the N. *Ancient residential quarter:* From 1963 onwards Belgian archaeologists have uncovered extensive parts of the town, with well-preserved *houses* from the archaic and classical periods in the vicinity of the theatre. Some remains of *workshops* (ergasteria) and *ore-washing plants* from the 5&4C are to be found some 220 yards NW of the theatre. These are square buildings with

washing plants for the silver ore which was ground in a mortar. On the peninsula of Ágios Nikólaos are some remains of the ancient *harbour castle.* To the SW of the theatre are some remnants of a *Temple of Demeter Kore* from the 5C BC (Ionic peripteros).

Tílos (I)/ΤΗΛΟΣ
East Aegean islands (Dodecanese)/
Aegean Islands   p.300□O 12

This quiet and barren island with an area of 24 sq. miles (400 inhabitants) is a link in the chain of islands Nísyros—Tílos—Khálki and lies half-way between Kos and Rhodes.

History: In *c.* 1000 BC the island was settled by the Dorians and had close relations with Rhodes (in the 7&6C). It then became a member of the Athenian maritime league (479 BC). In the 4&3C it was relatively independent and had its own coins, and from 42 BC onwards it was under Roman rule. From 1310 onwards the island was ruled by the Knights of St. John of Rhodes until it was taken by the Turks in 1522. After a period of Italian administration (1912–48) it was returned to Greece.

Megálo Khorió ('large village'): This, the main village of the island (only 175 inhabitants), has stood on the N. bay of the island since antiquity. The rectangular ancient *village wall* (parts of which survive) surrounded the residential area, the ancient graveyard and the *acropolis.* The remains of the latter are on the hill of *Ágios Stefanos* NW of the village: ancient *gateway, marble steps* and *sections of wall.* There was probably also a *Temple of Zeus and Athena* here (traces survive). *Ágios Stefanos, a castle of the Knights of St. John* (14&15C), was later built here (remains of cisterns and of a church with 16C frescos). The *ancient graveyard* with tombs, stone slabs and inscriptions is below the kastro (to the S.) and is still used today. Most of the finds were taken to the museum of Rhodes (jewellery, grave objects). *Remains of the ancient village wall* are to be seen by the church of the archangel *Michael* (in the village).

Environs: The abandoned medieval village of *Mikró Khorió* ('small village') is picturesquely set in the hills some 8 km. to the SE. Nearby is the harbour of *Livádia* (*c.* 11 km. SE), with a population of about 175 people. It was inhabited in antiquity (few traces). The ruins of the 15C fortress of *Kastro Mesaria* are N. of Livádia. There is another ruined fortress near *Agriosykiá* (with a beautiful view of the sea). The monastery of *Ágios Panteleímon*, with a fine view, is worth a visit. It stands on a rock in an idyllic spot some 10 km. to the SE, and is surrounded by old walls and a tower. The church (1703) has some fine *frescos* (by Gregorios from Sými) dating from 1776. There are also some 20 Byzantine churches scattered around the island, with frescos from the 13–16C.

Tínos/Ténos (I)/ΤΗΝΟΣ
Cyclades/Aegean Islands   p.296☐K/L 9/10

The island of Tínos (75 sq. miles, *c.* 10,000 inhabitants) is between Andros and Mykonos in the E. string of the Cyclades. It is the most famous Greek Orthodox place of pilgrimage (the pilgrimage takes place on 15 August, the date of the Dormition).

History: It was an early Euboean-Ionian settlement dating from *c.* 1000 BC (like Andros) and it was the centre of a Poseidon cult in the Cyclades (Poseidon the serpent-slayer), but was otherwise unimportant politically. Andrea Ghizzi conquered the island for Venice in AD 1207, and it remained under Venetian rule for 500 years. Almost all the inhabitants became Catholic at that time (today about a quarter of them still are). The Catholic Tiniots were subjugated by the Turks in 1714, and remained neutral in the War of Liberation in 1821. Refugees arriving from Asia Minor strengthened the Orthodox element

Tínos (Tínos), remains of the Venetian hill fortress of Exóburgo

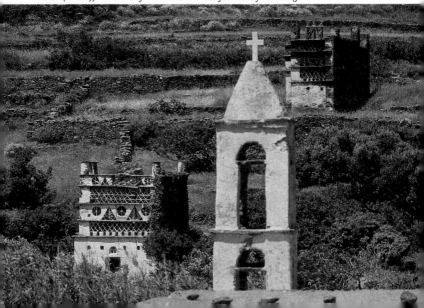

once again until Tínos, following the discovery of a miraculous icon (1822), became what it is today, a kind of Orthodox Lourdes.

Tínos (about 3,400 inhabitants): This, the main town of the island, has buildings of dazzling whiteness and owes its importance to the pilgrimage church of *Panagia Evangelistira* ('Annunciation'), standing on rising ground with a wide processional route. This church was built in 1823 on the spot where the miraculous *icon of the Mother of God* was discovered (on the foundations of an ancient temple). In the substructure is the site of the discovery. Here there is a fountain with holy water, a font and votive gifts. The inside of the church is rich in jewellery, gilded items, ornaments and votive gifts (of little artistic importance). The miraculous icon is also here. The courtyard (portico) and entrance are worth seeing, with marble paving and a mosaic floor. The *Archaeological Museum* (processional route) houses a collection of vases, reliefs, and other finds, mainly from the nearby *Shrine of Poseidon*.
Environs: The *Shrine of Poseidon and Amphitrite* (3 km. NW) near *Kiónia:* Some remains of a Doric *peripteral temple* (6 x 8 columns; 69 x 53 ft.), a monumental *altar* (some 36 ft. square), and a *well*, have survived from the ancient-Hellenistic pilgrimage site (founded in the late 4C BC). By the shore there was a stoa (560 ft. x 50 ft.) for the pilgrims and a sacred way leading to the shrine, and to the N. there was a tripartite eating-house (hestiatorion). The sacred precinct was built in two phases (4 – 2C BC), and was destroyed and rebuilt several times (Roman baths in the 2C AD). Excavations by the French School of Athens (work was resumed in 1973) led to a considerable increase in knowledge. *Exóburgo* (or *Bórgo*), the medieval capital, with the ruins of a Venetian hill-top fortress (1,750 ft.), is in the interior of the island (about 10 km.); fine panoramic view. An-

cient sections of wall (8C BC) were discovered nearby, to the S. and W. of the Exóburgo hill. There are also: remains of buildings and, further E., traces of the shrine (8C BC, rebuilt in the 5C) of a goddess (Amphitrite?). Venetian houses and wells are still to be found in the neighbouring village of *Lutrá. Xinára* (12 km.) is the seat of the Catholic bishop. The convent of *Kekhroyúnion* (9 km. N.) is not far away. It was founded in the 9C and in its katholikon are some old icons, and also a small library of manuscripts, as well as the cell of the nun Pelagia who discovered the miraculous icon of Tínos. There are ancient tombs near the village of *Kardianí* (15 km. NW). In the fishing village of *Istérnia* (25 km. NW) there is an interesting church whose domes are faced with ceramics. There are old dovecotes on the road there.

Tíryns/ΤΙΡΥΝΣ
Argolís/Peloponnese   p.294 ☐ F 9

The castle of Tíryns stands on a rock only 85 ft. above the fertile plain of Argolís. According to the myth it was built by Proitos with the aid of the Cyclops. Akrisios, the brother of Proitos, ruled over the neighbouring town of Árgos, and his grandson Perseus was the founder of nearby Mycenc. Tíryns must therefore have been built two generations before Mycene. The excavation finds confirm the tradition which has come down to us. Herakles, the son of Zeus and Alkmene, was born here. He was obliged to enter the service of King Eurystheus, his cousin, and perform his twelve Labours. At the time of the Trojan War, Tíryns, together with Árgos, was part of the kingdom of Diomedes. The town was devastated by fire in Mycenean times and was later recolonized.
Excavation was begun by Schliemann in 1876, and in 1884 he continued them in conjunction with Dörpfeld.

Acropolis: Excavation work in the area of the acropolis is still being carried out today. The work has shown that the area was settled as long ago as 2500 BC. The present castle was not erected until shortly after 1400 BC, when the walls of the *upper castle,* were built. There was an earlier fortress here from the middle Helladic period onwards and a palace (stucco remains survive) from the late Helladic period. In *c.* 1300, the E. and S. walls were strengthened, the E. entrance was altered, and the *central castle* to the N. was incorporated in the structure.

Some 100 years later, the *lower castle* was added, the S. wall was reinforced, and the propylon and the ramp were enlarged. The lower castle has not yet been completely excavated.

The entrance to the castle was on the E. side. A wide ramp (15 ft.) led up to the *main entrance* in the outer wall. This opened into the space between the inner and outer walls, with the lower castle lying to the right and the way to the palace to the left. The arrangement and decoration of the outer gateway (propylon) are similar to those of the Lion Gate at Mycene. The threshold and the lower half of the gate posts survive, the latter having large bolt-holes to enable the gate to be barred.

There follows a second gate. This formed the earlier entrance to the castle but it was incorporated in the later phases, and after this there is a *forecourt,* with a colonnade on its left (E.) side. Some of the stone bases on which wooden columns rested survive. A modern staircase leads to the E. *gallery,* which ran inside the wall and is 100 ft. long, 5 ft. 7 in. wide, and 13 ft. high. The gallery had a corbelled vault and to its E. there opened six rooms of equal size.

On the W. side of the forecourt is the *Great Propylaia,* consisting of two porches with columns. A door led northwards from the inner one to a corridor and the queen's megaron. The propylaia led to the *outer palace courtyard.* In similar fashion to the forecourt, a stone gallery flanked by five rooms ran along its S. side. To the W. of this there was an outside tower. The staircase leading to this gallery was built in an L-shape and is still in good condition. On

Tíryns, watch hut

Tíryns, altar on the acropolis

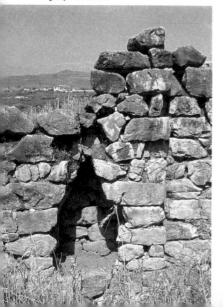

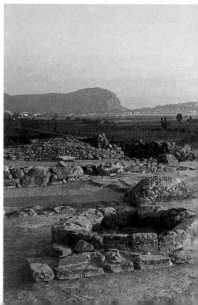

the N. side of the outer courtyard were two smaller rooms and another *propylaia* which resembled the first one but was smaller. It opened into a *large inner courtyard* (58 ft. 3 in. x 66 ft. 5 in.) surrounded by columns on three sides. There is a sacrificial altar to the right of the propylaia.

Opposite the altar was the entrance to the *great megaron*, or throne room, with a portico (31 ft. 8 in. x 15 ft. 9 in.) which was connected by three doors to the prodomos (31 ft. 10 in. x 15 ft. 5 in.). In the left-hand (W.) section of the prodomos was a door giving access to the W. chambers.

A door led from the prodomos into the domos (32 ft. x 38 ft. 9 in.), in the middle of which there was a round hearth, 10 ft. 10 in. in diameter, and outside which there were four wooden columns which supported the roof. The throne was against the E. wall. The floor had a layer of stucco and was painted.

The *royal chambers* adjoined the W. side of the megaron. The floor of the bath consisted of a faced limestone slab weighing some 20 tons.

A corridor led from the W. chambers to the *small megaron*. This has an outer courtyard with a row of columns on its E. side. The megaron (16 ft. 6 in. x 19 ft. 6 in.) had a portico which opened into the corridor through two doors. The domos (18 ft. 6 in. x 24 ft. 11 in.) had a decorated floor. There was a four-cornered fireplace in the middle, and to the right of this the throne stood on a slight elevation. To the right (E.) of the megaron there was a complex which itself resembled a megaron, and also a staircase which led to the second floor.

The small megaron and the rooms adjoining in the E. were not assigned to the queen or to the heir as has often been assumed, but originate from an older phase of construction dating from the period before the complex was extended to the west.

In the NW corner of the large megaron, some stairs descend to a paved path leading to a square tower, whence a staircase

(65 steps survive) led to the W. entrance which had a postern gate 4 ft. 10 in. wide. The central castle to the N. of the palace was separated from the lower castle by a wall. The castle had two more entrances in the N. and NW. Two passages in the NW wall descended within it to cisterns. Late Mycenean buildings have been discovered in the lower castle.

Environs: About 1 km. to the E., at the foot of Mt.Profitis Ilias, there is a **beehive tomb** which has survived unscathed. There was an oil press here in Roman times.

Tríkala/Tríkkala/ΤΡΙΚΑΛΑ
Tríkala/Thessaly   p.290□E 5

This charming little town (35,000 inhabitants) in the NW of the Thessalian plain is an agricultural centre for cereals, rice, cotton and tobacco.

History: This town was occupied from pre-Greek times onwards (middle of the 3rd millennium BC), and bore the name of *Tríka (Tríkka)* in antiquity. Legend has it that the home of Asklepios, the god of medicine, was here, and Tríka was his fief. He was said to be the son of the god Apollo and of the faithless Thessalian Koronis. Kheiron (Khiron), the famous centaur, brought up the orphan and taught him the art of healing.

The *Shrine of Asklepios* (hardly any traces survive) in Tríka was known far and wide and was the oldest shrine in antiquity. Hippocrates of Kos worked here for a time, and died in this area (Lárisa).

In the Middle Ages, Tríkala, which has long been known for its horse breeding, was the seat of Serbian prince (Tsar Dushan, 14C) and later of a Turkish Pasha.

Acropolis: The ruins of the Byzantine-

Serbian fortress *Kastro* are on the acropolis hill (today: Profítis Ilías) above the ancient remains, of which little survives. There is a fine panoramic view. Some remains of a Hellenistic *retaining wall* (probably from the Shrine of Asklepios) have been discovered by the church of *Ágios Nikólaos* nearby.

Also worth seeing: The picturesque Turkish *bazaar* with its narrow alleyways. The Turkish *mosque* (Tsamí) dating from 1550, with a beautiful dome and minaret. The battlemented *clock tower*. The churches of Ágios Ioánnis, Ágios Stefanos and Agii Anargyri date from the Byzantine period. The most important finds discovered in the environs (mosaics, stele, amphorae, coins, etc.) are in the *Archaeological Museum* (Musio). In the *church museum* (in the Mitrópolis church) there is a 10C manuscript Gospel belonging to Emperor Constantine Porphyrogennitos, and also ecclesiastical vessels.

Environs: The *remains of walls* (with towers and gates) of the ancient town of

Tegéa (Trípolis), temple ruins

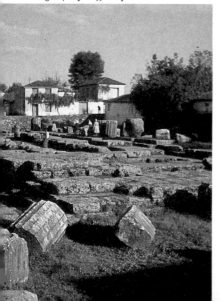

Pélinna *(Pelinnaion),* situated near the town of *Taxiárchai,* are some 20 km. E. of Tríkala. There are also the remains of the Byzantine settlement of **Palaió Gardíki,** containing the medieval ruined church of *Agía Paraskevi* (fine view of the plain of Tríkala). **Neokhóri** (24 km. E.): Pretty old churches and the interesting *Orfanú monastery,* with wall paintings and the nearby towers of a Venetian *castle.* The remnants of an ancient *necropolis* (belonging to the town of *Peirasíai*) are near the village of **Vlochós** (some 37 km. E.). In the vicinity are the ruins of the Frankish *Kastro Petrino* ('stone castle'), built on some ancient remains (Phákion), and also the ruins of *Kastro Kortíki* (ancient Limnaíon). The remains of the ancient fortress of *Gomphoi* (destroyed in 48 BC), and traces of the ancient Thessalian town of *Oikhalía,* are to be found between the villages of **Pýli** (18 km. SW) and **Musáki** (21 km. SW). The 16C *Ágios Vissárion* monastery, with numerous cells and a beautiful 18C carved wooden *iconostasis* (templon), is near to Pýli. Fine *ecclesiastical vessels* and old *manuscripts* are to be seen in the *monastery museum.* The neighbouring monastery of *Agía Gura* (17C) is also worth a visit. The neighbouring village of **Dúsiko** has the tomb of St. Vissárion (the patron saint of Tríkala) and a *ruined 14C fortress.* At the entrance to the narrow pass of **Stena Portas** (about 21 km. SW), which leads to the heights of the southern Pindos massif, is the church of *Panagía Portas,* which is worth seeing. It was founded in 1283 by Johannes Dukas, the son of the Despot of Epirus. The church has some fine *mosaics* from that time, and also 15C *wall paintings.* This architecturally interesting building has a domeless, cruciform naos (one nave, two aisles and a tunnel vault), and a domed 14C narthex. The *templon* (marble choir screen) with its beautiful decorated columns dates from *c.* 1283. The Pindos road leads towards Árta via the charming mountain villages of *Eláti* (32 km. W.) and

Petrúlion (48 km. W., at an altitude of 3, 600 ft.).

Trípolis/ΤΡΙΠΟΛΙΣ
Arkadia/Peloponnese   p.294☐F 10

This important commercial town (20,000 inhabitants) is the capital of Arkadia and is the key to communications within the Peloponnese. During the Frankish period, Trípolis had an important fortress and was known as *Dropolitsá*. The town was taken by the Venetians in 1688. A century later it fell into the hands of the Turks. At the time of the Greek struggle for liberation in 1821, Trípolis was besieged by the Greeks under the leadership of Kolokotronis, and after three months the town was finally captured.

Environs: Tegéa (9 km. SE): Ancient town with the *Temple of Athena Alea*, where Orestes and the Spartan king Pausanias took refuge. The cult of Athena Alea was introduced by King Aleos in the 9C

BC. According to the legend, Herakles violated Auge, the daughter of Aleos, near a fountain here. In *c.* 550 BC, after protracted battles, Tegéa was obliged to recognize the hegemony of Sparta and conclude a treaty. After the defeat of Sparta at Leuktra in 371 BC, Tegéa entered the Arkadian League. The town was conquered by Antigonos Doson in 222, by Lykurgus of Sparta in 218, and then by Makhanidas in 210. Alaric destroyed the town in the 4C AD. Tegéa was the seat of a Frankish barony until 1296, and the town was then taken by the Byzantines. The archaic temple dating from the 6C burned down in 395 BC. Skopas from Paros undertook the decoration of the new temple which was built in *c.* 340 BC. The pedimental figures and the statues of Asklepios and Hygieia are by him. The W. pediment showed the battle between Achilles and Telephos in the plain of Kaikos, while the E. pediment depicted the hunt for the Kalydonian boar, with Meleager and Atalanta. In the E., the metopes depicted Herakles fighting Kepheus and his sons, and in the W. they were

Mantineia (Trípolis), two rows of theatre seats

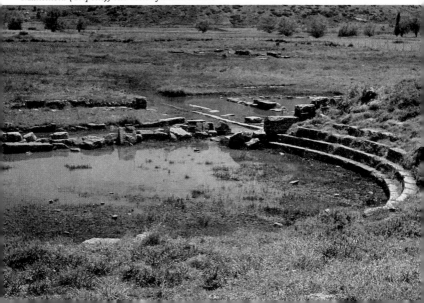

devoted to the Telephos myth. The temple housed the ivory statue of Athena by Endoios, and the skin of the Kalydonian boar. These items were in the archaic temple. In 31BC, after the battle of Actium, Augustus had the ivory statue brought to Rome. The temple was a Doric peripteros, with six columns in the front and 14 at the sides, and a height of 31 ft. The overall height up to the acroteria of the pediment was 51 ft. 6 in. The walls of the cella were articulated by Ionic half-columns with Corinthian capitals. In the N. was an ancient fountain (where Herakles did violence to Auge). Near the temple is the *museum* with fragments of sculptures (torso of the nymph Agno of Skopas) from the temple, and Geometric ceramics and bronzes. The site of the ancient Phylaktis, with the remains of a shrine of Athena Polias and a shrine of Demeter and Kore, is to be found at **Ágios Sóstis** (5 km. SE). At **Palaiá Episkopi** (7 km. SE) there are the remains of a Roman *theatre* (on the site of a 4C theatre) with parallel walls which were once part of a stage. The *agora* was to the W. of Palaiá Episkopí. In front of the modern church in the park there stood a single-aisled, 5C early Christian basilica, with a *mosaic* depicting sea creatures, the four rivers of Paradise (Gikhon, Pison, Tigris and Euphrates), and personifications of the months. In the Middle Ages the town was known as *Nikli* and a fortress was begun in 1248. **Pallántion** (8 km. S.): In antiquity this was the seat of king Evandros who—so the legend has it—founded a colony on the Palatine hill in Rome before the Trojan War. The remains of a megaron, a 5C temple and of two 6C BC buildings are to be found here. To the S. of the acropolis are the remains of a *temple* (late-6C BC) dedicated to Poseidon and Athena Soteira. **Aséa** (11 km. SW): This town was settled from Neolithic times until the middle Helladic period (2000–1600 BC). The ancient acropolis was used again in the Hellenistic period. Remains of Ne-

olithic dwellings. **Mantineía** (*Mantinía*, 16 km. N.): It was near the narrows of Skopi that the battle between the Spartans led by king Agis and Árgos, Elis and Mantineía, the allies of Athens, was fought in 418 BC and ended in a victory for the Spartans. The second battle of Mantineía was fought between Thebes and the Spartans in 362. The Thebans were victorious in this battle; but Epameinondas, their general, fell. Some remains of the wall surrounding the ancient town may be seen. Two rows of seats survive of the *theatre*. To the SW is the *Bouleuterion,* and further S. is the *agora,* with a few remains of buildings. Numerous finds from the Hellenistic period. **Orchomenós** (30 km. N.): Known in Homeric times, it was built by the son of the Lykadon, the King of the Arkadians. Some remains of the *Shrine of Artemis Mesopolitis* (three column bases), of another, 6C Doric *temple* (dedicated to Apollo, Aphrodite or Athena), and of the *agora,* can be seen in the lower town. There is a small *archaeological collection* in the community centre of the village of Levídi (about 8 km. towards Trípolis).

Troizén/Trizín/TPOIZHN
Argolís/Peloponnese   p.294☐G 10

---

75 km. SE of Nauplia, the village probably occupies the site of the ancient Troizén. Legend has it that Theseus was born here.

History: Troizén was on the side of Athens during the Persian wars. Having fallen out with Árgos, the town later went over to Sparta. The Spartans occupied the town in 275 and 224 BC. In the 9C it was known as *Damalá*. In 1325 Troizén belonged to the Genoese family of Zaccaria, and from 1363 onwards to the Despotate of Mystra.

Town wall: Remains of the wall of the ancient town, which continues as far as the acropolis, are to be found W. of the present village of Damalá. A tower from the 3C BC survives. The *agora* mentioned by Pausanias, with a Roman *bath*, extended N. of the tower. An inscription (*c.* 250 BC) found by the Sotira church details Themistokles's plans for the Athenian women and children to take refuge here from the advancing Persians. There was a *shrine to Artemis Sotira* in the agora.

Shrine of Hippolytos: This stands on a terraced piece of ground about 1 km. from the tower. Hippolytos, who was desired by his stepmother Phaidra, lost his life when a team of horses took fright. Phaidra committed suicide, and Hippolytos was brought back to life by Asklepios. The shrine was built in the late 4C BC and was destroyed by a volcanic eruption in *c.* 250 BC. It consisted of a peripteros with 11 x 6 columns and a narrow opisthodomos.

Church of Episkopi: Standing on the site of a building from the 9C AD, this was erected in the 11C and enlarged in the 12C (a basilica with a nave and two aisles, 31 ft. 3 in. x 70 ft. 3 in.). The S. wall, which dates from the first phase of construction, survives to a height of 11 ft. 9 in. The *stadion* once occupied the site where the church now stands.

Asklepieion: Some remains of this have survived near the Episkopi church. It is a square building (102 x 102 ft.) from the 3rd millennium BC, with a peristyle having 5 x 4 Doric columns. To the S. of the building is a room with two doors. There are some rooms (possibly baths) W. of the peristyle. The building housed the sick who hoped to be cured by the god Asklepios.

Shrine of Aphrodite Akraia: Some remains of the Doric temple in antis, mid-6C BC are to be found on the E. slope.

Environs: Ermióni (about 35 km. SW):

A seaside resort opposite the island of Hydra. An early Christian basilica (6C) with adjoining rooms which served as a baptistery and as accommodation. **Pórto-Khéli** (*c.* 52 km. SW): This is probably the ancient *Halieis*, which was founded by refugees from Tíryns. It has traces of settlements from the Neolithic (4000–2700) and early Helladic period II (2500–2100), and it was also occupied in archaic times, as can be seen from the finds. The acropolis, where there was a shrine to Hera, stood on the rising ground. Remains of a rectangular building (bouleuterion?) survive, and on the slope there was a workshop where Tyrian purple was processed. The foundations of a temple of Apollo and of some houses are under water. **Frankhti cave:** (near Pórto-Khéli, 490 ft. deep) The cave has yielded finds from the Palaeolithic period III and the Mesolithic period. Large quantities of stag bones were found in the older layer of deposits (Mesolithic), and in a later layer the bones of large fish, the food of the inhabitants at that time, were discovered. The human skeletons which have been found are of a race that was small in stature. They date from *c.* 8000 BC.

Týlisos/Tílissos/ΤΥΛΙΣΟΣ
Iráklion/Crete   p.298☐G 14

Týlisos is a fairly large village in the foothills of Ida, 14 km. SW of Iráklion. Between 1902 and 1913, three *villas* dating from *c.* 1800 BC were discovered in the immediate vicinity. Some finds suggest that older houses, probably dating from 2000 BC, stood here before the villas.

Environs: Sklavókampos: 19 km. from Iráklion, along the road from Iráklion to Axos (after the turn-off to Týlisos) on the left-hand side of the road, are the ruins of a large *Minoan villa* which was uncovered by Prof. Marinatos in 1939–41. The building had originally been erected with an upper storey in *c.* 1500 BC. The entrance area, reception room, magazines, private rooms, inner courtyard, and a colonnaded hall, are still readily identifiable.

Týlisos, villas (after J.Hassidakis): **A** the remains of the central villa have been designated as House A: **1** entrance **2** vestibule **3** room with central column **4** and **5** rooms with pillars, store rooms in which pithoi have been found **6** room with no roof **7** staircase to upper storey **8, 9** columns linked by a corridor **10,11,12** magazines **13** staircase **14** air well **15** megaron, with some original paving **16,17,18** nearby rooms where copper vessels and tablets with inscriptions were found **19** corridor

B House B. Only fragments of this villa have been found: **1** entrance **2** possible housekeeper's lodge **3** staircase **4** probably a courtyard

C House C: **1** entrance **2** vestibule **3** housekeeper's lodge **4** corridor **5** staircase to upper floor **6** room where frescos were found (now housed in the Archaeological Museum, Iráklion) **7, 8, 9** rooms with original flooring **10** store room **11** private chamber **12** hall with pillars **13** stairs **14** megaron **15** air well **16** cistern

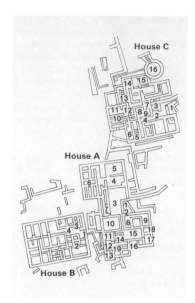

Týlisos, House C, drain

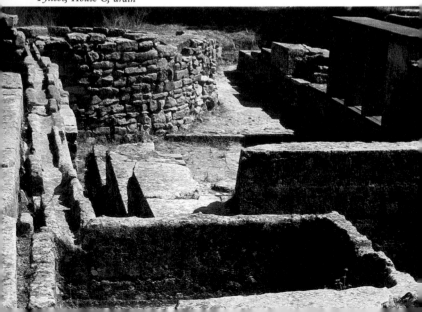

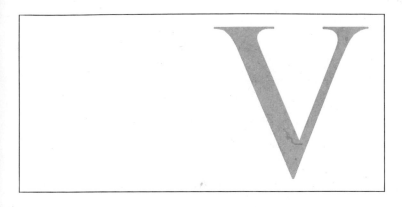

Vathý/Váthi/ΒΑΘΥ
Chania/Crete   p.298□E 14

The village of Vathý, also known as
Kounéni, is about 8 km. from the W. coast
of Crete and has two very fine churches.

Ágios Georgios: This little chapel dates
from 1284 and is thus one of the oldest late
Byzantine churches in Greece. The frescos
in the interior are particularly exuberant
in their colouring; note especially the *Pantokrator* in the apse.

Church of the Archangel Michael:
This little 13 or 14C barrel-vaulted church
has very fine and lavish frescos. The depiction of Christ's Baptism is reminiscent in
some of its detail of the forerunners of the
early Italian Renaissance such as Cimabue
and even Giotto. The balance of compo-
sition is particularly striking (see for example the 'Trumpets of Jericho'.

Environs: Chrysokalitissa: The towering Moni Chrysokalítissa is 10 km. SW of
Vathý near the W. coast; it is set on a hill
between rocky bays in dense woodland.
The architecture of this lonely nunnery
shows the influence of Venice. **Slavop-
úla/Sklavopoúla:** A footpath leads from

Moni Chrisokalítissa to the lonely village
of Sklavopúla, about 8 km. away to the SE;
there is also a wider road from Palaiochóra
(12 km.). There are four late Byzantine
churches in Sklavopúla: *Ágios Athanasios*
with some well-preserved frescos; *Sotiros
Christu* with fine frescos dating from 1422:
the Pantokrator is particularly good; *Ágios
Georgios*, dating from 1290–1, which has
barrel vaulting and interesting and well-
preserved frescos, clearly the work of
several different painters; *Panagia*, dating
from 1518, is a chapel with a single aisle
standing among olive trees; it has some
well-preserved frescos.

Velestínon/ΒΕΛΕΣΤΙΝΟΝ
Magnisiá/Thessaly   p.290□F 6

This little town (*c.* 3,000 inhab.) is an
agricultural centre and railway junction;
it lies at the S. extremity of the plain of
Thessaly, 18 km. N. of Vólos).

History: Velestínon is on the site of the an-
cient *Pheraí (Pherai)*. According to myth
King Admetos of Pheraí was married to
Alkestis, the daughter of King Pelías of
Iolkás (legend of the Argonauts). When he
was dying, his young wife offered to go to

the Underworld in his stead (vicarious death), but she was rescued from Death (Thanatos) by the hero Herakles.

Like many places in the area (e.g. Sésklo, Dimíni) Pheraí was inhabited in pre-Hellenic times. Its most important period was the 4C BC, when it had hegemony over Thessaly; it was later conquered by the Macedonians and the Romans.

Excavations: Little remains of the 4C BC *town walls*. On the edge of the town are remains of the foundations of a 4C *temple* dedicated to Zeus Thaulios, built over a 6C BC shrine (archaic-geometric bronzes have been discovered). Near the ancient *Hypéreia spring* (by the Church of Ágios Charálampos) are remains of the polygonal walls of a shrine to Herakles.

Also worth seeing: SE of the village is the monument to Rigas Feraios, the famous poet of the Freedom Movement, who was born here; he was murdered by the Turks in 1798.

Environs: About 12 km. N. is *Lake Boíbe* (now *Vívi*), well-known in ancient times but now almost dry. According to geologists it is the remains of an enormous Tertiary inland sea which covered the whole of Thessaly. On its W. edge are roughly 8 km. of *cyclopean walls*, which are presumed to have enclosed the largest *Mycenean fortress* in the whole of Greece (assumed to have been called Kerkínion, or Boíbe).

Vergína/ΒΕΡΓΙΝΑ
Imathía/Macedonia   p.290☐F 3

A little village on the archaeological site of the same name, known for the *grave of Vergina*; formerly archaeologists believed that the ancient Aigaí, first capital of the Macedonian state, was the town of Édessa, but excavations by Prof. Manolis An-

dronikos of the Aristotle University in Thessaloníki have now proved that Vergína was the site of Aigaí.

Prince's Palace: The first and largest palace in N. Greece, probably dating from the time of Antigonos Gonatas (278–240 BC). Archaeologists presume that it was the summer residence of the royal family.

Grave of Vergina: This mid-3C BC Macedonian tomb is a few yards below the palace. The fine marble doors, the door posts, a marble throne and the remains of a table can still be seen; the tomb is built of limestone.

Tomb of Philip II: This was the earliest of the three excavated tombs and was discovered under an artificial mound. In the outer room (prothalamos) was a golden shrine containing the ashes of Cleopatra, Philip's second wife, wrapped in a cloth interwoven with golden threads. Inside the grave chamber were: a second golden shrine, metalwork, five small ivory busts of the royal family, some ancient armour,

Véria, bases and stele in the museum court

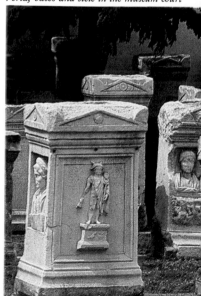

a helmet, a sword, boots, a crown and a diadem; these objects are now in the museum in Thessaloníki. The façade of the tomb is decorated with frescos.

The two neighbouring tombs were probably built for members of the royal family; all the tombs date from 350–325 BC.

Prehistoric necropolis: Over 80 small burial mounds with early Iron Age graves (10–9C BC).

Véria/ΒΕΠΟΙΑ
Imathía/Macedonia   p.290☐F 3

The town has 30,000 inhabitants, was known from 500 BC as *Bérroia* and is part of Macedonia. In 168 BC (Battle of Pydna) it became the capital of a Roman republic; Pompey wintered here in 49–8 BC.

Town fortifications (2 km. outside the town, at the fork of the Thessaloníki and Náussa roads): Behind a town gate excavated in 1960 there are remains of two towers on the right of the road. The round one is Hellenic and the square one dates from the time of the Gothic invasion. There are remains of the ancient *town wall* and of an old Turkish *mosque* near the main square.

Ágios Christos (Makariotis Street): A 14C church with fine frescos.

Profitis Ilias (Chiu Street): The church has an iconostasis and a fine icon.

Archaeological Museum (*Archaiologiko Musio*): The museum houses numerous finds from prehistoric, ancient, Hellenic and Roman times, most of them from the surrounding area.

Also worth seeing: *Ágios Nikolaos, Ágios Stephanos, Ágios Georgios, Agia Paraskevi, Agia Photoni:* all these churches are decorated with frescos and icons.
Rostrum of St.Paul (Vima Apostolu Pavlu): The Apostle Paul visited the town in 56 –7 and preached here.
Archontika (noblemen's houses): Typically

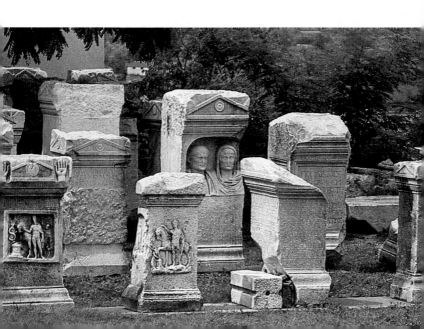

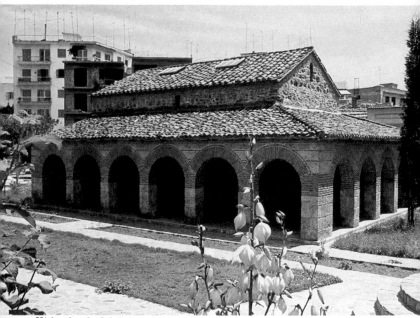

Véria, church of Agia Paraskevi

Balkan 18C houses, as found in Kastoriá and Siátista.

Environs: Alexándria (24 km. NE): A little town near to which is the archaeological site of *Nissos* with post-Roman remains. **Nikomídia** (18 km. NE): Prehistoric settlement. **Panagia Sumelá:** Historic monastery on Mt.Vermion (*c.*3 km. NW): An icon of Our Lady ascribed to St.Luke is worshipped in the church; there is a pilgrimage on the 15 August.

Vólos/ΒΟΛΟΣ
Magnisía/Thessaly   p.294□G 6

This lively trading and industrial town is in a bay of the Gulf of Pagasitikos at the foot of the wooded Mount Pilion (Pelion).

It is the capital of the nome of Magnisía and has an important harbour exporting grain, olive oil, cotton, tobacco and other produce of Thessaly. There are also ferry connections to the N. islands of the Sporades (Skiathos, Skópelos).

History: The modern town, whose name perhaps derives from *Mólos* ('mole'), has few sights because of the severe earthquake of 1955; most of the buildings date from that time or later. Its ancient name of *Iolkós* (excavations in the N. of the town) is surrounded by numerous myths: the first ancestor of the Iaones, Jason, is said to have set out from here in the mid 2C BC in the first Greek ship (with 50 oarsmen) to what was later Ionia in Asia Minor. In his ship 'Argo' with his companions Herakles, Orpheus, Nauplios, Amphiaraos, Castor, Polydeukes etc. he brought the Golden

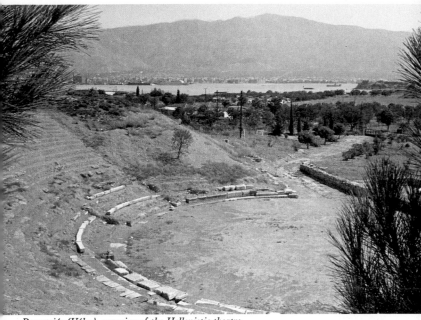

Demetriás (Vólos), remains of the Hellenistic theatre

Fleece, (an allegory of the blazing morning sun), from Kolchís (Aía) on the Black Sea, assisted by the king's daughter and sorceress Medea. This tangled legend points to the fundamental importance of the area for the development and settlement of the Greek tribes (Ionian and Aeolian) in prehistoric times, but since the classical era the role of Iolkós has dwindled into insignificance.

Excavations of Iolkós: The tumulus (magula) containing the excavations is in the N. part of the town on the road to Lárissa. Greek archaeologists discovered remains of two consecutive *Mycenean palaces* (unfortunately houses have been built on parts of the site); the older of the two could date back to the period of the Jason legend, under King Pelias, *c.* 1400 BC. The second building was destroyed by fire

c. 1200. Fragments of a *stucco floor* in the N. suggest an even older palace dating from the 15C BC (Mycenean clay fragments). The site was inhabited even in the early Bronze Age (*c.* 2500 BC.

Also worth seeing: The present town consists of two parts, the New Town on the coast (promenade) by the destroyed Turkish *port kastro* (bazaar), and the Old Town (*Áno Vólos*, which extends to a height of 2,600 ft. on the slopes of Mount Pilion (Goritsa quarter).

Archaeological Museum (*Archaiologiko Musio*): The museum is in the SE part of the town in the direction of Miléa (Athanasaki) and contains a number of fine exhibits. The collection of over 200 painted Hellenic *grave steles* from the nearby ancient harbour town of Demetriás

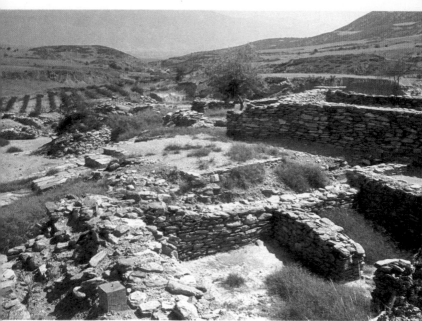

Sésklo (Vólos), remains of walls and houses

is well worth seeing; there are also ancient grave steles from Phalanna near Lárissa (3C BC to the end of the Roman period). Among the fragments of sculpture are a fine head of Asklepios (Hellenic), a torso of Aphrodite from Skópelos, a headless statue of a youth etc. There are also prehistoric clay fragments, idols, ceramics, vessels and neolithic tools from the tumuli in the neighbouring villages of Sésklo, Dimíni, Rachmáni and Mycenean Iolkós, and also bronzes from the geometric and ancient periods from the Temple of Zeus in Pheraí).

Environs: Roughly 4 km. to the SW are remainsof the ancient port of **Pagasaí** (now *Pagasaí*), which was inhabited even in prehistoric times; the town gave its name to the gulf (Gulf of Pagasitikos). It was the harbour of Iolkós (Vólos) and the presumed departure point of the Argonauts. Later it was the port of the town of *Pheraí* (c. 14 km. NW) and reached the height of its power in the 4C BC; there are remains of walls in the N. and W. Pagasai declined as a result of the establishment of the new port of **Demetriás** (c. 6 km. NW of Vólos) c. 293 BC by the Macedonian General Demetrios Poliorketes ('Conqueror of Towns'). There is a massive *defensive wall* about 8 km. long, 13 ft. high and 7 ft. thick and also remains of roughly 80 fortified towers, some of which are in good condition. The main tower is in the SW, and in the SE are remains of the agora and the *temple* of Athene Iolkia and three harbour basins in the N., W. and S. 20 years ago ruins of a Hellenic *theatre* with good acoustics were excavated. Bronze Age discoveries have also been made nearby (2500 BC), along with traces of Mycenean buildings.

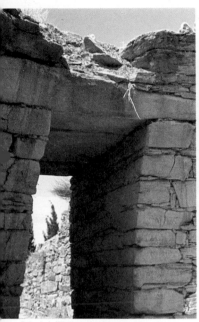

Dimini (Vólos), beehive tomb

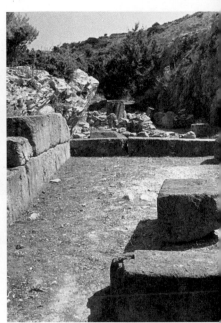

Vravróna, Iphigenia grotto

In the villages of **Dimíni** (6 km. W.) and **Sésklo** (*c.* 16 km. W.) important excavations were undertaken which led to discoveries about the settlement of Thessaly before the Indo-Germanic-Greek immigration. This so-called Dimíniki or Sésklo culture (*c.* 4000–2000 BC) is also known as the Pelasgian culture after the legendary original inhabitants of Greece. The excavations revealed villages with *clay brick houses* on shallow mounds (magula), some of which are protected by multiple *ring walls* (in Dimíni up to six) and narrow *gates*. The principal houses (megarons) of these arable farmers and cattle breeders consisted of an outer courtyard or hall and a main living room with a walled hearth (hestia) surrounded by wooden posts (columns). The influence of these pre-Hellenic megaron buildings can be traced to later Greek architecture in places like

Mycenae, Tíryns and Pýlos. At the edge of the village are remains of a Bronze Age *beehive tomb*. The numerous finds (ceramic fragments, tools and implements) are now housed in the museum in Vólos.

Vravróna/Braurón/ΒΡΑΥΡΩΝ
Attica/Central Greece   p.296□H 9

On the E. coast of Attica, about 38 km. N. of Athens, are remains of the ancient *Artemis Shrine of Braurón*, now known as Vravróna or Vraóna.

History: According to myth Artemis, the daughter of Zeus and Leto and the twin sister of Apollo, the god of light, was born on the island of Delos. She was worshipped as the goddess of (chaste) nature and vir-

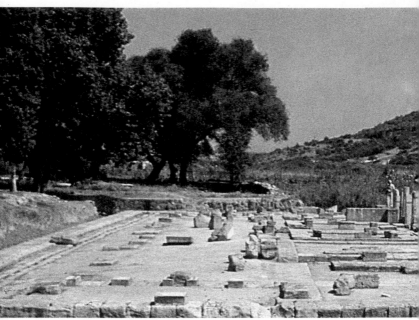

Vravróna, N. stoa, cells of the she-bears

ginity (Parthenía, Lat. Virginitas); the hind and the she-bear were sacred to her. Because Agamemnon had killed a hind at Aulis (Temple of Artemis) he had to sacrifice his daughter Iphigenia. Artemis replaced her with a hind, however, and took her away to serve as her priest in distant Tauris, in the modern Crimea. There she is said to have freed her brother Orestes and brought him back to Braurón along with the cult idol of Artemis Tauropolos (see Goethe's and Euripides' versions of 'Iphigenia'). From the 8C BC Braurón was the most famous shrine of Artemis in the whole of Attica, reaching the peak of its importance in the 5&4C BC. Every five years the Spring festival of the Braurónia was celebrated in Artemis' month of Munichion (March/April); the whole of Attica, and Athens in particular, was involved: virgins dressed as 'bear-girls'

performed the dance of the bears, and were dedicated to Artemis.

Excavation site (Shrine of Artemis): Recent excavations by Greek archaeologists (since 1948) have revealed the *shrine*, which was set on the NE slope of a fortress mound (remains of a prehistoric settlement and of Mycenean fortifications); many of the finds are in the museum.

Temple of Artemis (Artemision): N. of the chapel of Ágios Georgios (15C, with restored 15&16C frescos) are the foundations of a small 5C BC Doric *Temple of Artemis* (33 by 66 ft.). The former prostylos building with pronaos, three-aisled cella and adyton was built over an older temple (remains of walls) dating from the 6C BC which had been destroyed by the Persians. Along the N. side of the temple was a

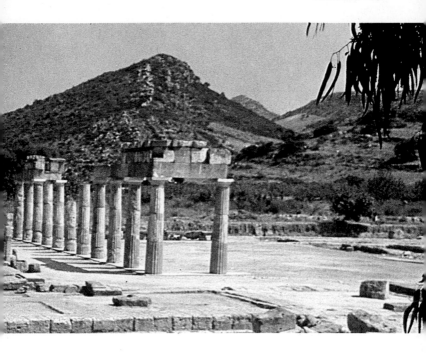

temenos wall leading E. which marked the N. limit of the temple precinct. In the SW are remains of terraces and terrace walls. *Grotto of Iphigenia:* What is probably the oldest part of the shrine is about 30 yards SW of the temple by a cleft in the rock on the mountainside. It is assumed that the tomb of Iphigenia, priestess of Artemis and daughter of Agamemnon, was in this tufa cave, which has now collapsed. The grotto cult has been proved to have existed here since the 8C BC. After the collapse of the grotto entrance (vault) a small *shrine* with two chambers was erected nearby over older rooms with an entrance in the NW. The so-called *sacred house* (remains of the foundations) in the SE of the cave was the residence of the priestess of Artemis and part of the old place of worship. Nearby, on the E. slope of the prehistoric *acropolis*, neolithic clay fragments

have been found and also traces of a *habitation* of the middle or late Helladic era. *Court complex ('Court of the Bears'):* In about 430 BC the temple precinct was enlarged to the N. by the addition of a large court complex (*c.* 79 by 89 ft.). It was framed by a horseshoe-shaped arrangement of *columned halls* in the W., N. and E. The fluted Doric *columns* of the *N. hall* (stoa of the she-bears) and part of the *architrave* have been reconstructed. Three rooms in the W. and six in the N., each 20 by 20 ft. and with places for couches, show the outline of the *rooms of the bear-maidens*, which are behind the halls on the N. and W. sides. Each one had 11 couches (klinai). Behind the N. walk was a long narrow *stoa* for sacred gifts (statue bases for kuroi and korai have survived). Between the *sacred hall* and the *cell buildings* (N.walk) there is an *entrance* (propylon) on each side leading to the temple precinct. The W. propylon led to a bridge over the brook Erasinos, which burst its banks in the 3C and destroyed the N. walk. A second, later *entrance* can be seen in the W. walk.

Museum *(Archaiologiko Musio):* This little museum houses interesting finds from the shrine and the surrounding area, but the more important items are in the National Museum in Athens. In the *foyer* are models of the Artemision and the funerary stele of a youth from Pórto Ráfti (4C BC); there are other steles in the *museum courtyard*, which has a fine view of the bay. *Room 1:* Votive gifts, jewellery, small 7C BC statues of Artemis and vessels from the 8–4C BC. *Room 2:* Numerous sculptures from the shrine of Artemis, above all bear-maidens (arktoi) and representations of children (5&4C BC), also votive reliefs (4C BC) with Artemis motifs.
Room 3: Fine *relief* of seated Zeus, Leto, Apollo and Artemis (4C BC), terracotta, votive reliefs, Artemis statues and a classical *circular altar*. *Room 4:* Prehistoric and Mycenean finds from Braurón and the sur-rounding area (Anávyssos, Peráti), and geometric ceramics.
Room 5: Fragment of a marble sphinx from Pórto Ráfti (6C BC), tomb (naiskos) from Merénda, (4C BC; in the showcases protogeometric (9C BC), geometric (8C BC) and archaic (6C BC) vases found in Merénda.

Environs: Just over 500 yards away from the Shrine of Artemis are the striking remains of a large 6C **early Christian basilica** of the so-called 'Hellenic type', which was common at the time: it has a rather broad nave to which a little chapel was added later; the nave is separated from the aisles by two rows each of 7 greenish Euboean marble columns (two have been reconstructed). Originally only the nave had an apse; later a chapel was added in the S. aisle and a side apse in the N. aisle. The sanctuary (bema) with a bench for the clergy is prolonged into the nave by two *antae*. The *reliquary* (enkainion) has survived the destruction of the basilica in the 7C. The three-door narthex in the W. has a *purification well* and remains of 7C *tombs*;

Vravróna, rooms of the bears, with couches

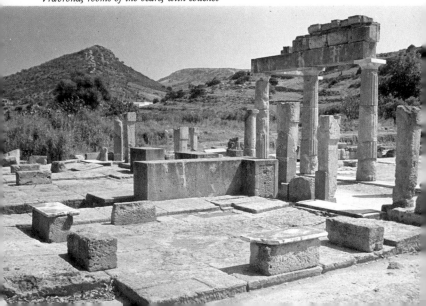

it leads to the two-door *exo-narthex*, which is in the form of a portico with 6 columns, of which 5 have been reconstructed; beyond this is the forecourt. To the N. are a *chapel* (sacristy) and a *pilgrims' lodging*. At the S. end of the narthex/exo-narthex are various side rooms and a round stove. Also, above the ante-room, is the circular *baptistery* with a *font* let into the floor. To the S. by the church complex is a little porticoed building which was also use to accommodate pilgrims.

Vuliagméni/ΒΟΥΛΙΑΓΜΕΝΗ
Attica/Central Greece   p.296☐H 9

This well-developed harbour resort is on the *Apollo Coast* (Akti Apóllona) in the SW of Attica on a peninsula with a number of attractive bays; it is about 25 km. SE of Athens.

The foundations of a 6C BC *Temple of Apollo* (Apollon Zosterios) and various auxiliary buildings for priests and pilgrims have been excavated on the isthmus (also known as laimos 'neck') of the peninsula, near the luxury resort of Astéra. The remains of the ancient temple gave the entire coast its name.

Near the coast in the steep foothills of the Ymittós range is an emerald-green freshwater lake, the Limni Vuliagmensis. The lake is fed by mountain springs containing chlorine and sulphur; the water temperature is *c.* 20 degrees C. and the lake has been developed as a *thermal spa*.

Environs: The Old Attic deme of **Anagyrús** has an interesting 7–5C BC *necropolis*; the site is in the village of *Vári* (7 km. NE), which is reached via the resort of *Várkisar* (5 km. NE). Inscriptions suggest that Hephaistos, Athene and the Dioscuri were worshipped here, but very little remains of their cult sites. N. of Vári (about an hour on foot) in the foothills of the Ymittós

mountains is a fine *Pan grotto* or nymphs' grotto (Spílaio Nymfón). According to inscriptions in the two chambers of this limestone cavern it was used for the worship of Apollo, Pan and the Nymphs. In the larger of the two caves, next to a primitive altar to Apollo, are a relief by the sculptor Archimedos, the image of a seated goddess and a lion's head. At the back of the cave is a spring with more sacred reliefs and inscriptions. Between the resorts of **Vúla** (*c.* 5 km. NW) and **Glyfáda** (8 km. NW), popular with the Athenians for their cool summer weather, the remains of the ancient deme of *Aixoné* (Aixoní) have been discovered. In the *Shrine of Demeter* at the foot of Mount Ymittós the famous fertility festival of Thesmophória was celebrated annually after the autumn sowing. Only women and girls were allowed to take part in the festival, which was the counterpart to Eleusis; it is described by Aristophanes in his play 'Thesmophoriazusae' (*c.* 411 BC). In the garden of the *Villa Kannelopulos* are the remains of the ancient Aixoné *theatre*. The famous ancient historian Thucydides (455–396 BC) was also born here. On the N. edge of Glyfáda, between the road and the beach by the Antonopulos café are the ruins of an *early Christian basilica*, which is said to have been built on this site in memory of the Apostle Paul's first landing. Excavations have shown that the area around Glyfáda was already inhabited in the neolithic period (beehive graves of 2300–1500 BC). Near the neighbouring Athenian suburbs of **Ágios Kosmás** (*c.* 10 km. NW) and Palaió Fáliron (Old Fáliron, *c.* 12 km. NE) traces of the early Helladic and Mycenean periods have been discovered. S. of Vuliagméni the coast road leads to the resort of Anávyssos (*c.* 25 km. SE), where sparse remains of the *coastal fortress of Anaphlystos* have been found near *Néa Fókaia*; it was built to defend the Attic mining area of Lávrion (Laúreion) to the SE, and sea traffic to Piraeus (see Lávrion).

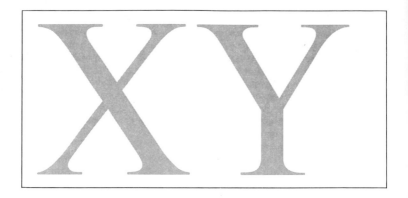

Xánthi/XANΘH

Xánthi/Thrace   p.292☐K 2

Capital of the nome of Xánthi (35,000 inhab. including a Turkish minority). It is a picturesque town, with numerous large houses.

Mitropolis Church: A fine collection of Byzantine sacred pictures, icons, crosses and coins.

Folk Museum (Archaiologiko kai Laografiko Musio): Folk costume and folk art.

Environs: Ábdira (26 km. SE): Ionian colony, the home town of Leucippus and Democritus, the founder of Atomism (5C BC). The area is known for its excavations: remains of walls from the Hellenic period have been discovered. **Moni Agiu Nikoláu:** Historic monastery on an island in Lake Vistonis, connected to the mainland by a bridge.

Ýdra/Hydra (I)/ΥΔΡΑ

Argo-Saronic Islands/Aegean Islands
          p.294☐G/H 10

This island, a long bare rocky ridge in the S. of the Gulf of Saranikós, is *c.* 34 sq. miles in area, 25 miles long, up to 3 miles wide and has *c.* 2,500 inhabitants; it has become a popular holiday resort.

History: The island of Hydra (ancient name *Hydréa*) was of little importance in ancient times, and few finds have been made. In about 1580 the island was resettled by Albanian refugees from Mystrás. They were fishermen and sailors and also, because of the poverty of the island, notorious pirates.

Ýdra/Hydra (2, 300 inhab.): Before the War of Liberation in 1821 the principal town on the island still had 15,000 inhabitants, 38 churches and a splendid merchant fleet. The merchants' houses above the harbour date from this period (early 19C): the houses of *Vulgaris, Tombasis, Vuduris, Miaulis* and above all *Kunduriotis* (museum documenting the 1821 War of Liberation). By the quay is the *Panagia* church: cloisters of the former 17C monastery and 1808 marble bell tower. In the suburb of *Kaló Pigádi* are 17C houses and some tiny chapels. Nearby is the 15C monastery of *Profítis Ilias* on the mountain of the same name (1,640 ft.). On the E. tip of the island is the 16C *Monastery of Zurwas*, from which there is a very fine view.

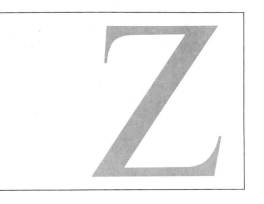

Zagorochória / ΖΑΓΟΡΟΧΟΡΙΑ
Ioánnina / Epirus   p.290☐C 4/5

N. of Ioánnina and between the mountain ranges of Tymfí and Mitsikeli is the region of Zagóri, which consists of 44 villages known as Zagorochória. It is divided into Anatolikón (E.) Zagóri with 8, Kentrikón (central) Zagóri with 26 and Dytikón (W.) Zagóri with 10 villages.

The buildings in this region have interesting features such as wall paintings, carved wooden ceilings, spiral staircases etc.

History: The cyclopean walls in the villages of Skamnélion, Asprángeli and the old cemetery in Vitsa, and many other finds point to the fact that the Zagóri region was settled at the same time as the rest of Epirus. Zagóri was destroyed by the Romans in 167 BC when they conquered 70

Zagorochória, old bridge

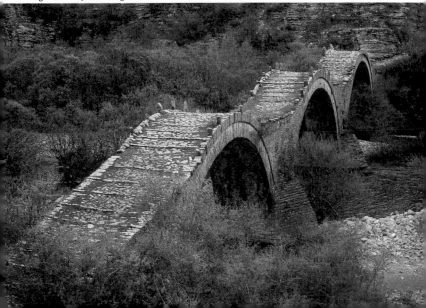

towns in Epirus and took 150,000 of their citizens back to Rome. Some place names indicate Slavic immigration and the word Zagóri itself is Slavic in origin: it means 'the region behind the mountain'. In the Turkish period Sinan Pasha granted the Zagorochória a number of privileges. A federation (koinón) was established, with a representative based in Ioánnina. He was responsible to the Turks for the whole region and was elected for a year by a representative from each village. He was charged with the collection of taxes levied by the Turks, and addressed himself to any problems which arose in the villages. This system of self-administration lasted until 1868, and the Zagóri region remained under Turkish rule until 1913.

Vitsa (37 km. N. of Ioánnina): The *Church of Ágios Nikolaos* has fine 17C wall paintings.

Grevenition (44 km. N. of Ioánnina): The 672 *Votsas Monastery* has 17C wall paintings.

Asprángeli (Zagorochória), fountain

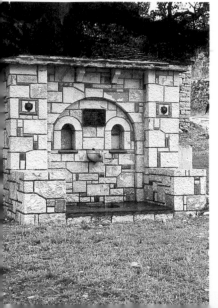

Monodéndrion (40 km. NW of Ioánnina): The *Church of Ágios Minas* has wall paintings and a very fine 1619 iconostasis. The 1414 *Monastery of Agia Paraskevi* is on the left side of the Vikos gorge.

Negádes (48 km. N. of Ioánnina): The *Church of Ágios Georgios* has wall paintings and a carved wooden templon.

Tsepélovon (51 km. N. of Ioánnina): *Church of Ágios Nikolaos* and *Church of Kato Panagia*; the *Monastery of Prodrómu Rogovu* has wall paintings and a carved wooden templon.

Vrysochórion (82 km. N. of Ioánnina): The *Monastery of Agia Triada* has a fine carved wooden templon and an underground church.

Zákynthos/Zakynthos (I)/ΧΑΚΥΝΘΟΣ

Ionian Islands   p.294☐C 9

This beautiful S. Ionian island has had the same name since the time of Homer. It is 157 sq. miles in area and has *c.* 30,000 inhabitants. The Venetians called it *Zante* and coined the flattering saying 'Zante— fior di Levante' ('Zante — the flower of Levant').

History: In Homer 'wooded Zakynthos' was part of the Achaian island empire of Odysseus. The E. Panic colony of Saguntum is said to have been founded from here even before the Trojan War (*c.* 1200 BC). In 455 BC the Spartans made a vain attempt to conquer it. Later Zakynthos became a Roman naval base and subsequently the prize of many conquerors (Vandals, Saracens, Normans, Venetians); the Turks alone never set foot on the island. From 1485–1797 it was under Venetian rule, and from 1815 until it became part of Greece in 1864 it was part of the English Island Protectorate. After the Turks conquered Crete in the 16C numerous Cretan painters fled to Zakynthos, and thus the island became a centre of Graeco-Italian painting, producing a mixture of Byzantine icon painting and the style of the Venetian Renaissance. Three important poets were born on Zakynthos: Dionysios Solomos (1798–1857), the author of the Greek national anthem ('Ode to Freeedom'); Andreas Kalvos (1792–1867), the author of patriotic hymns and the bilingual (Italian/Greek) poet Ugo Foscolo (1778–1827), one of the co-founders of Italian Romanticism.

Zákynthos/Zakynthos (10,000 inhab.): The principal town on the island, on the E. coast opposite the Peloponnesian mainland. It is dominated by the ruins of a 15&16C Venetian *fortress*, almost the only building to survive the devastating earthquake of 1953, which destroyed most of the 60 or so churches on the island. The following churches were restored or rebuilt:

Zákynthos (Zákynthos), church façade

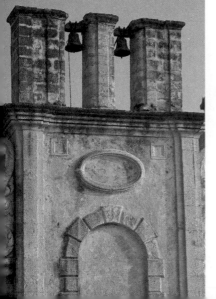

the *Faneromeni* (Revelation) church of 1650, the *Kyria ton Angelon* (Lady of the Angels) church of 1687 and the 17C church of the patron saint of the island *Dionysios*, whose feasts are celebrated with great splendour on 24.8 and 17.12. The pretty church of *Ágios Nikólaos* by the harbour is also worth seeing. In the *museum* (in Solomu Square) are numerous 16–19C icons and also 17&18C wall paintings by Damaskinos, Tsanis, Kallergis and Doxaras. There are splendid carved figures from other churches on the island, and also Hellenic and Byzantine sculptures and rare manuscripts.

Environs: In the interior of the island is the village of *Machairádo* (10.5 km. SW), with a fine icon and iconostasis in the church of *Agia Mavra*. At the summit of Mount Skopos (10 km. SE) is the *Monastery of Panagia Skopiotissa*, which has fine 6C icons. On the W. coast are the monasteries of *Ágios Georgios* (about 25 km.) and *Anafonitria*, the home of St. Dionysios.

Zarós/ΖΑΡΟΣ
Iráklion/Crete   p.298☐G 14

This little town *c.* 12 km. NW of Górtys in the foothills of Mount Ida became prosperous because it had an excellent water supply: it used to supply Górtys by means of a massive aqueduct, part of the brick wall of which has survived in the town.

Vrontisi: On a hill 2 km. NW of Zarós is the Moni Vrontisi monastery, a complex dating from the first half of the 17C and showing Venetian influence. The well with figures of Adam and Eve is particularly striking. Five icons by Damaskinos, formerly in the monastery, are now in the *Agia Ekaterini Church* in Iráklion. There are 14C frescos in the monastery church.

Valsamónero: It is a 50 minute walk from Vrontisi to Valsamónero; it can also be reached by car from the village of Vorizia. The monastery dates from 1332–1431. All that now remains is the two-aisled church of *Ágios Fanoúrios* (Phanourious), with a wide roof, bell gable, arch, and finely decorated portals, windows and rosette. The interior has *late Byzantine frescos* dating from *c.* 1400 which are among the finest on Crete. Those in the N.—oldest—aisle represent the life of Our Lady, in the S. aisle the life of St.John the Baptist and in the W. part, a kind of porch, the life of Ágios Fanoúrios. The key of the church may be obtained in Vrontisi or Vorízia.

Environs: Kamarés: The village of Kamarés, some 6 km. N. of Valsamónero (it can be reached via Vorízia), is the starting-point for a walk to the *Kamarés Cave*; al-

low about 4 hours. The cave is at 4,987 ft. on the S. slope of Mount Ida. English archaeologists discovered objects from the middle Minoan epoch here; the multi-coloured vases are now in the Iráklion Museum. Another four-hour walk leads to the *Idaean Cave*, at a height of 5,249 ft. In 1884 the archaeologist Ernst Fabricius discovered a cult site here, the *Idaion Antron*, which existed from the 11&9C BC and survived until the Roman period. Remains of a sacrificial altar and small bronze statues were found. The Idaean cave, like the Diktaean, was dedicated to Zeus. According to legend he grew up here and was suckled by the goat Amaltheia, and the cave was clearly used for the worship of Zeus for centuries. The *Psiloritis* can be reached on foot in five hours, but only with a guide, from either the Kamarés Cave or the Idaean cave. At 8,087 ft. it is the highest mountain on Crete and was revered in ancient times as 'Ida', the divine mountain.

Valsamónero (Zarós), monastery gate and bell tower

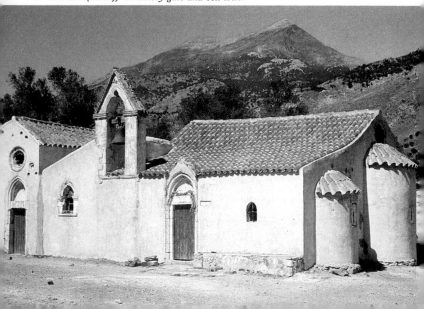

List of minor towns and places of interest (including alternative forms of names in the headings). The entry in which they appear is indicated by the → symbol

Pánormos→ Kálymnos
Pánormos→ Melidóni
Pánormos→ Skópelos
Paradísi→ Ródos
Paraléa Tyroú→ Ástros
Paramythiá→ Igumenítsa
Paravóla→ Agrínion
Parikiá→ Páros
Parthéni→ Léros
Passavá (fortress)→ Máni
Pátras→ Pátra
Patróklu (island)→ Súnion
Paxí→ Kérkyra
Páxos→ Kérkyra
Pelasgía→ Almyrós
Pelikáta→ Itháki
Pélinna→ Tríkala
Pélion, Mount→ Pílion
Pentelikón→ Pentéli
Pérama (caves)→ Ioánnina
Peráti→ Pórto Ráfti
Perdíki→ Ikaría
Périssa→ Thíra
Peristeriá→ Kalamáta
Peristeriá→ Kyparissía
Petalúdes→ Ródos
Pétra→ Lésvos
Pétra→ Pátmos
Petrálona→ Chalkidike
Petrúlion→ Tríkala
Phalanna→ Réthymnon
Phalásarna→ Kastelli Kissámu
Phaleron→ Piraiás
Pharis→ Spárti
Phársala→ Fársala
Pharsalos→ Fársala
Pheía→ Pýrgos
Pheneós→ Stymfalía
Pherai→ Velestínon
Phliús→ Neméa
Phódele→ Iráklion
Photike→ Igumenítsa
Phylé→ Akharnai
Phýrra→ Lésvos
Phýskeis→ Ámfissa
Pigí→ Melidóni
Pigí→ Potamiés
Pijí→ Potamiés
Pikérmi→ Rafína
Pipéri (island)→ Alónnisos
Piraeus→ Piraiás
Pláka→ Límnos
Platamón→ Kateríni
Platanistó→ Évia
Plátanos→ Górtyna
Plátanos→ Léros
Plathý→ Marathónas
Plátsa→ Máni
Platýstomo→ Lamía
Pleurón→ Mesolóngi(on)
Plofútis→ Léros
Póli→ Kásos
Poliókhni→ Límnos
Pólis→ Itháki
Politiká→ Évia
Polýgros→ Chalkidike
Polýkhnitos→ Lésvos
Polyrrhéneia→ Kastélli Kissámu
Polyrrínia→ Kastélli Kissámu
Póros→ Levkás
Portariá→ Pílion
Portítsa→ Kardítsa
Porto-Khéli→ Troizén
Potamiá→ Potamiés
Potamós→ Kýthira
Pothiá→ Kálymnos

Potídaia→ Chalkidike
Praísos→ Sitía
Prásiai→ Pórto Ráfti
Préspes→ Flórina
Préssos→ Sitía
Prokópion→ Évia
Prosotsáni→ Dráma
Prusós (monastery)→ Karpenísion
Psachná→ Évia
Psará (island)→ Chíos
Psathúra (island)→ Alónnisos
Pseira (island)→ Móchlos
Psikhró→ Potamiés
Psíra (island)→ Móchlos
Pteleós→ Almyrós
Ptóon→ Kopaís
Purí→ Pílion
Púrko→ Kýthira
Pýdna→ Kateríni
Pýli→ Tríkala
Pylíon→ Kos
Pyrgíon→ Chíos
Pýrgos→ Ámfissa
Pýrgos→ Sámos
Pýrgos→ Thíra
Pýrgos-Dirú→ Máni
Pythagórion→ Sámos

Rakhóna→ Almyrós
Repanídi→ Límnos
Réthimnon→ Réthymnon
Rhamnús→ Ramnús
Rhíon→ Pátra
Rhizenía→ Górtyna
Rhodes→ Ródos
Rína→ Kálymnos
Rínia (island)→ Dílos
Ríon→ Pátra
Risómylos→ Aigion
Róda→ Kérkyra
Rodíni→ Ródos
Rodokhórion→ Náusa
Rogí→ Préveza

Salamís→ Salamína
Saloniki→ Thessaloníki
Sámi→ Kefallinía
Samikón→ Lutrá Kaiáfa
Samothraie→ Samothráki
Santorin→ Thíra
Sariá (island)→ Kárpathos
Sáros (island)→ Kárpathos
Savathianón→ Iráklion
Selinús→ Skópelos
Sellasía→ Spárti
Sérres→ Sérrai
Sérvia→ Kozáni
Sésklo→ Vólos
Siátista→ Kozáni
Sidirókastron→ Sérrai
Sigríon→ Lésvos
Síkinos (island)→ Íos
Skafidia-Prodrómi→ Palaiokhóra
Skála→ Kefallinía
Skála→ Pátmos
Skála→ Thíra
Skála Eresú→ Lésvos
Skála Oropú→ Amphiáreion
Skamnélion→ Zagorochória
Skandálion→ Límnos
Skántzura (island)→ Alónnisos
Skárfia→ Thermopýles
Skáros→ Thíra
Skíti→ Témpi
Sklaverokhóri Pediádos→ Bizarianó
  Pediádos

Sklavókampos→ Týlisos
Sklavopoúla→ Vathý
Sklavopúla→ Vathý
Skotússa→ Fársala
Skripú→ Orchomenós
Sofádes→ Kardítsa
Soughia→ Palaiokhóra
Soújia→ Palaiokhóra
Sparta→ Spárti
Spércheia→ Karpenísion
Spétsai→ Spétses
Spílaion→ Grevená
Spilion→ Spili
Spinalónga→ Ágios Nikólaos
Stáfylos→ Skópelos
Stágira→ Chalkidike
Stavrós→ Itháki
Stená Pórtas→ Tríkala
Stení→ Évia
Stómion→ Témpi
Strátos→ Agrínion
Stúpa→ Máni
Stylída→ Lamía
Stýra→ Évia
Styx→ Kalávryta
Suflí→ Alexandrúpolis
Súgia→ Palaiokhóra
Syia→ Palaiokhóra

Taxiárchai→ Tríkala
Tegéa→ Trípolis
Télendos (island)→ Kálymnos
Teménia→ Palaiokhóra
Ténos→ Tínos
Thaumákoi→ Fársala
Thebes→ Thívai
Theológos→ Thásos
Théra→ Thíra
Thérma→ Ikaría
Thermá→ Samothráki
Thermá Lutrá→ Thermopýles
Thermopylae→ Thermopýles
Thermí→ Lésvos
Thirasía (island)→ Thíra
Thisbe→ Thísvi
Thorikón→ Thorikós
Thrónos→ Réthymnon
Thryóessa→ Pýrgos
Thuría→ Kalamáta
Tilissos→ Týlisos
Titáne→ Neméa
Tithoréa→ Amfíklia
Toploú→ Sitía
Toplú→ Sitía
Tolophón→ Itéa
Tragaia→ Náxos
Trakhniniakos→ Palaiokhóra
Triánta→ Ródos
Trikéri→ Pílion
Trizín→ Troizén
Trypití→ Mílos
Tsangaráda→ Pílion
Tsaritsáni→ Elassóna
Tsepélovon→ Zagorochória
Tsépi→ Marathónas
Turliani (monastery)→ Mýkonos
Tymfristós→ Karpenísion
Týrvanos→ Lárisa

Válaxa (island)→ Skýros
ValLey of the Muses→ Askri
Valsamónero (monastery)→ Zarós
Vámvaka→ Máni
Vári→ Vuliagméni
Vasilikí→ Gúrnia

Glossary

Abacus: Square slab above the echinus of a capital and supporting the entablature.

Abaton: or **Adyton:** The sanctuary in a temple, within the cella and closed to all but priests.

Acanthus: Leaf ornament on a Corinthian capital, modelled on the leaves of a Mediterranean plant.

Acropolis: The hill-top citadel of a Greek polis.

Acroterion: A plinth at the top or end of a pediment for statues or ornaments; by extension, the ornaments it bears.

Aegis: Wonder-working cloak or shield of the Goddess Athena, decorated with the head of the Gorgon Medusa.

Agones: Public festivals involving competitions, usually athletic, a pervasive feature of Greek life. The Olympic Games or the Dionysia of Athens are probably the best-known examples.

Agora: The market place, assembly area and political centre of a Greek polis or city state.

Aisle: Division of a church or other building running parallel to the long axis and divided from other such divisions by an arcade or arcades of columns or pillars.

Ambo: A reading desk found by the choir screen in early Christian and Byzantine churches. The predecessor of the pulpit.

Amphiktyonie: League of Greek city-states, centred on a shrine, for example Delphi.

Amphiprostyle: A form of temple with porticoes at either end but not along the sides.

Amphora: Large two-handled vessel for wine and oil, etc.

Ante: A pilaster placed at the end of a projection of the cella wall of a temple.

Antis, in: An early form of temple in which the columns at the front are between antae.

Apse: Semicircular projection behind the choir or sanctuary.

Aqueduct: Ancient water channel, often borne by a series of arches. development of the Greek Hydrogogeíon.

Arcade: A series of arches borne by columns or pillars.

Arch forms: See diagram.

Archaic period: Period of Greek architecture and sculpture in the 7&6C BC.

Architrave: Lowest section of the entablature, resting on the capitals of the columns.

Archon: High official in a Greek polis.

Ashlar: Squared masonry.

Basilica: Originally the royal hall (Stoá Basiliké) with a double colonnade and used as a court or for trade. From the 4C on it became a form of church with a nave and two or four aisles, a pitch-roof over the nave and lower lean-to roofs over the side aisles.

Base: Pedestal for statues or for Ionic and Corinthian columns.

Bay: Division of space by columns, pillars or arches; the distance between the axes of two columns in a temple.

Bema: The raised sanctuary in Byzantine churches.

Bomos: Square or rectangular ancient sacrificial altar.

Bothros: Sacrificial channel by ancient sacrificial altars.

Bouleuterion: City council chamber.

Capital: Uppermost part of a column, supporting the entablature or arch. See diagram for various forms.

Caryatid: Carved female acting as a column and supporting the entablature.

Cathedra: Decorated bishop's throne in the Byzantine church.

Cavea: The scallop-shaped auditorium of a Greek or Roman theatre.

Cella: The main internal room in an ancient temple, containing the cult-image.

Cenotaph: Monument to a person buried elsewhere.

Chiton: Tunic.

Choir: Normally at the E. end of a church, containing the altar. In the Middle Ages the choir was often partitioned from the body of the church by a choir screen or, in Byzantine churches, an iconostatis.

Choregos: A rich citizen who met the expenses of producing dithyramb, tragedy and comedy.

Chthonic Deities: The Earth Gods, Demeter, Persephone, Gaia and Pluto.

Classical: High point of Greek (Athenian) culture and art (c. 480-330 BC).

Clepsydra: Ancient fountain house, water clock.

Cloister: Courtyard on one side of a church, surrounded by arcaded and vaulted walks.

Coffer: Square panel framed by the beams of a ceiling.

Column: Wooden or stone upright with a round cross section. For the accepted orders of columns see the entries for Composite, Corinthian, Doric and Ionic orders.

Composite order: Roman combination of elements from the Corinthian and Ionic orders.

Conch: Semicircular apse with a half dome.

Corinthian order: Base and shaft similar to Ionic order, goblet-shaped capital, with a double row of acanthus leaves.

1.Round arch 2.Basket arch 3.Lancet arch 4.Ogee arch

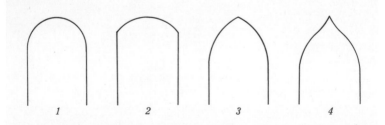

1   *2*   *3*   *4*

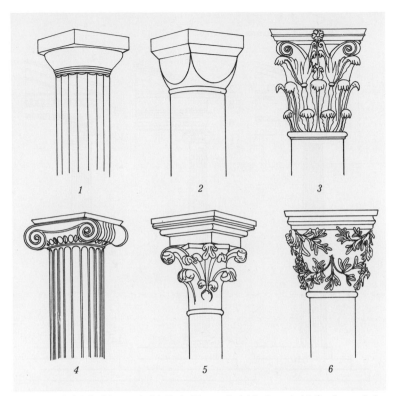

1.Doric capital 2.Cushion capital 3.Corinthian capital 4.Ionic capital 5.Crocket capital 6.Foliate capital

Crepidoma: The three steps forming the base of a temple.
Crossing: The intersection of the nave and transepts.
Crypt: Lower church, usually beneath the apse. Often an old burial place over which a church has subsequently been built.
Curvature: Slight rise in or arching of the horizontal parts of a building.
Cycladic culture: Island culture of the Cyclades (3rd millennium BC).
Cyclopean walls: Massive walls built of irregular blocks, named after the Cyclops.

Deme: Village, the smallest political division of the state.
Diakonikón: The right (south) side apse of a Byzantine church.
Diázoma: Passage between the rows of seats of the cavea.

Dimíni Culture: Greek continental culture from the first half of the 3rd millennium BC, named after the excavations at Dimíni, near Vólos, Thessaly.
Dipteros: A double colonnade around a temple.
Dipylon: Ancient double gateway.
Doric order: Column without a base, a maximum of 20 flutes separated by arrises; capital with echinus and abacus; entablature with triglyphs and metopes.
Dromos: Entrance or passage into Mycenean beehive tombs.

Echinus: Moulded section of a Doric capital.
Entasis: The slight swelling of the lower third of a Doric column.
Ephebos: Youth.
Epiphany: Manifestation of a god or

Christ; a feast to celebrate this.
Epistyle: Entabulature directly supported by the capitals of the columns.
Epitaph: Memorial tablet or stone in the wall or on a pillar, often above the tomb of the deceased.
Eschara: Ancient altar for burnt offerings.
Eso-narthex: Inner narthex of a Byzantine church.
Euthynteria: Lowest step of the crepidoma.
Exedra: Normally a semicircular assembly room with benches. In Byzantine churches it takes the form of a domed apse.

Fluting: Vertical grooves on the shaft of a column.
Frieze: decorative strip above a temple architrave. In the Doric or-

552

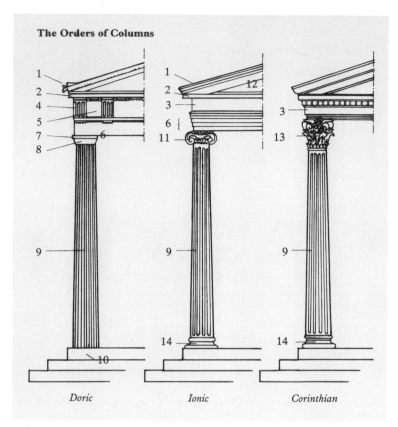

The Orders of Columns

Doric   Ionic   Corinthian

1. Sima 2. Geison 3. Frieze 4. Triglyph 5. Metope 6. Architrave (Epistyle) 7. Abacus 8. Echinus 9. Shaft 10. Stylobate 11. Volute 12. Tympanum 13. Acanthus 14. Base

der it comprises metopes and triglyphs; in the Ionic it may be plain or sculpted continuously.

Geison: Cornice of the roof of a temple.

Geometric style: Early phase of the archaic (c. 950-700 BC), so-called because of the geometric ornamentation on the vases of the period.

Gigantomachia: Battle of the Olympian Gods and the Giants, a favourite theme of Greek sculpture.

Gymnasion: A sports ground, often with colonnades and other buildings (changing and wash rooms) surrounding it.

Hekatompedon: From the Greek meaning 100 feet. Ancient temple 100 feet long.

Helladic Culture: Mainland Greek culture from around 2600 to 1200 BC; Early Helladic up till 2000, middle Helladic until 1600 and Late Helladic/Mycenean up until about 1150 BC.

Hellenism: Greek art and culture at the time of Alexander the Great (from about 300 BC).

Heraion: Shrine of Hera, on Samos, for example.

Herm: Four-sided pillar normally decorated with a head of Hermes. Herms stood along streets and in squares.

Heroon: Shrine of a hero (demigod such as Herakles).

Hierophantes: Mystery priest in antiquity, at Eleusis and Samothrake, for example.

Hippodamus's plan: Ancient town lay-out with a regular grid of streets. Hippodamus was a town planner from Miletus in the 5C BC.

Hippodrome: Elliptical horse racing track, at Olympia, for example.

Hoplite: Armoured foot soldier. The heart of a Greek army.

Hydria: Large water vessel.

Hypocaust: Under-floor heating in ancient baths.

Hyposkenion: Lower part of the stage.

Iconostasis: Screen decorated with icons dividing the sanctuary and the naos of a Byzantine church.

Illumination: Small, hand painted-picture in old manuscripts.

Impluvium: Open, inner courtyard in Hellenistic and Roman houses containing a cistern.

Ionic order: Column with sub-divided base, shaft with 20 flutes separated by fillets; typically, the Ionic capital has two volutes.

Kanephoroi: Maidens bearing baskets

Kantharos: Drinking vessel with handles and high foot.

Katholikón: Main church and nave of a Byzantine monastery.

Kore: Statue of a maiden.

Kouros: Statue of a youth or young God, Apollo for example.

Krater: Two-handled vessel for wine and water.

Kylix: Two-handled, shallow drinking vessel.

Lékythos: Oil flask with a narrow neck.

Leskhe: Assembly room.

Logeion: Centre, front of the stage

Loggia: An open gallery, often on an upper storey.

Meander: Right-angled pattern forming a frieze, named after the winding river Meandros near Miletus in Asia Minor.

Mausoleum: Large monument, often in the form of a house or temple, named after the tomb of King Mausolos.

Megaron: Main room of a Mycenean palace, possibly the model for the ground plan of the Greek temple.

Metope: Rectangular relief between two triglyphs on the frieze of a Doric temple.

Metróon: Shrine of the mother goddess Cybele.

Minoan culture: Pre-Greek Cretan culture, c. 2600-1100 BC, named after King Minos of Crete.

Monopteros: Small, usually round temple with no cella and a single row of columns.

Mycenean culture: Early Greek or late Helladic mainland culture, named after the excavation site of Mycene, Peloponnese (c. 1600-1150 BC).

Naiskos: Small temple.

Naos: Interior of a temple (see cella); Byzantine church and the main area inside it.

Narthex: Vestibule of a Byzantine church; usually divided into an exonarthex (outer vestibule) and esonarthex (inner vestibule).

Nave: The central, larger side to the W. of the crossing in a normally oriented church, separated from the side aisles by arcades; by extension the whole W. arm of the church.

Necropolis: Burial ground.

Nymphaion: Shrine dedicated to nymphs; richly decorated grotto with well.

Obelisk: Free-standing pillar with a square ground section and a tapering point.

Octagon: Eight-sided building.

Odeion: Normally round (roofed) structure for musical performances.

Oikos: Cult-room in a sanctuary.

Opisthodomos: Enclosed, rear hall in a Greek temple (behind the cella), containing votive offerings or used as a treasury. The opposite of the pronaos.

Orchestra: Area in front of the stage house used for the dances of the chorus. Later used by the musicians.

Order: One of the standard forms of column and entablature developed in antiquity.

Orthostatic: Ancient substructure with upright stone slabs.

Palaiastra: Normally square, colonnaded courtyard for wrestling and other sports.

Palladion: Cult- and protective image of the Goddess Pallas Athena.

Panagía: The All Holy, Mother of God and common name for churches, icons dedicated to the Virgin.

Pantocrator: The image of Christ the Lord in the domes of Byzantine churches.

Paraskenion: Sides of the stage.

Parodos: Side entrance to the orchestra.

Peplos: Long female outer garment (frequently on statues of women).

Peribolos: Sacred precinct or the wall surrounding it.

Peripteros: Temple with a circuit of columns. See also dipteros.

Peristasis: Outer colonnade in a peripteral temple.

Peristyle: Colonnade of the inner colonnaded courtyard of a house.

Pillar: Upright pier with a rectangular or polygonal cross section.

Pilaster: Engaged pillar.

Pinax: Painted wooden, clay or stone tablet.

Pithos: Large pottery storage jar.

Polygonal wall: Wall built of polyg-

1. Barrel vault 2. Tunnel vault split into bays by transverse arches 3. Sail vault 4. Groin vault 5. Domical vault 6. Stellar vault 7. Coffered vault 8. Mirror vault

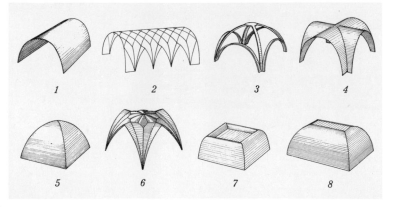

onal, as opposed to squared, stones.

Poros: Tufa, limestone, used as the basic building stone in many Greek temples; hence poros as opposed to marble temples.

Portico: Colonnade, similar to the stoa.

Prohedria: Seat or gallery of honour for the judges in a theatre or stadium.

Pronaos: Vestibule of a temple, opposite of the opisthodomos.

Propylaia: Monumental entrance to a temple precinct. The Propylaia of the Acropolis, Athens served as the model for later buildings.

Propylon: Gateway.

Proskenion: Front of the stage in a theatre.

Prostasis: Projecting portico.

Prostylos: Temple with colonnaded portico at the front.

Prothesis: Left (normally N.) side apse of a Byzantine church, as opposed to the diakonikon.

Protome: Heads of men or animals decorating buildings or vessels.

Prytaneion: Form of town hall. Court, official seat of the magistrates.

Pylon: Entrance to Greek temples and palaces.

Pyrgos: Tower, fortification, bastion.

Pyxis: Shrine.

Quadriga: Four-in-hand chariot

Refectory: Dining hall in a monastery; Trapeza in Greek.

Relief: Sculpture which is not in the round but attached to its background; the degree to which it projects determining whether it is classed as alto- mezzo- or bas-relief.

Reliquary: Structure of some form containing a relic of a saint.

Sekos: Longitudinal wall of the cella in a temple.

Sésklo culture: Mainland pre-Greek culture and art (c. 3,500-2,900 BC), named after the finds at Sésklo near Vólos in Thessaly.

Sima: Moulded eaves, often decorated with water-spouts in the form of lions' heads along the flanks of the temple.

Skene: Stage house behind the orchestra, originally used as a changing room and to support the scenery.

Stela: Upright funerary slab or column, bearing inscriptions and reliefs.

Stereobate: Stone base of a temple.

Stoa: Hall with one side in the form of a colonnade; similar to portico.

Stylobate: Top step of the substruc-

ture supporting the columns of a temple.

Temenos: Sacred precinct, as at Delphi, enclosed by a peribolos.

Terma: Stone finishing line in a stadium.

Terracotta: Fired, unglazed pottery.

Thesauros: Store room, treasury, at Delphi or Olympia for example.

Tholos: Round building or temple (Delphi); vaulted and domed in the Byzantine church.

Tunnel vault: Continuous, normally semicircular, vault.

Triglyph: Stone slab with three grooves above the architrave of a Doric temple and separating the metopes.

Tripod: Three-legged kettle, dedicated as a votive offering.

Triumphal arch: Decorated arch.

Tympanum: Panel at the top of an arch or on a pediment decorated with reliefs.

Volute: Coiled ornament, found on Ionic capitals.

Xoanon: Carved wooden cult-image.

Xystos: Roofed colonnade in a gymnasion.